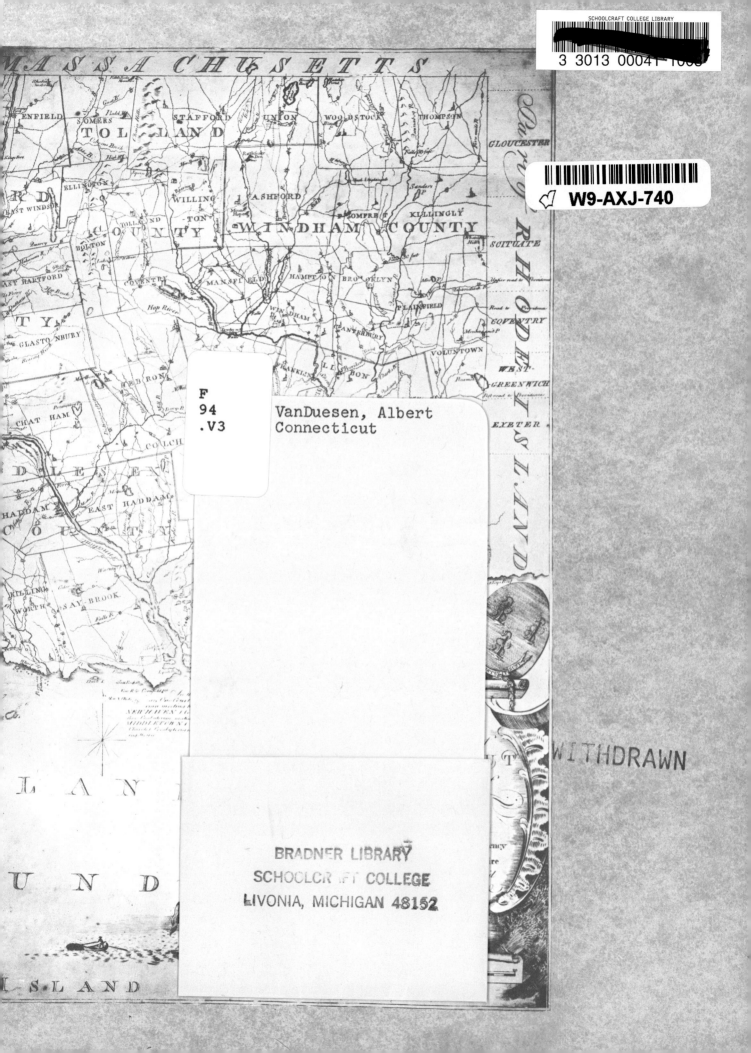

CONNECTICUT

CONNECTICUT

Albert E. Van Dusen

ASSOCIATE PROFESSOR OF HISTORY

UNIVERSITY OF CONNECTICUT

AND

STATE HISTORIAN

RANDOM HOUSE   NEW YORK

LIBRARY OF CONGRESS CATALOG CARD NUMBER: 61-6263

LITHOGRAPHED IN CONNECTICUT BY CONNECTICUT PRINTERS, INC.

MANUFACTURED IN THE UNITED STATES OF AMERICA

DESIGNED BY ANDOR BRAUN

To Wilda

Thanks are due for permission to quote material from the publications and writings of the following:

The Bobbs-Merrill Co., Inc., *The Western Reserve*, by Harlan Hatcher, 1949.

Carrington Publishing Co., New Haven *Journal-Courier*, February 5 and 7, 1919.

The Catholic University of America Press, *A Political History of Connecticut During the Civil War*, by Brother J. Robert Lane, 1941.

Harper & Brothers, *Traitorous Hero*, by Willard Wallace, 1954.

The Hartford *Courant*.

The Hartford *Times*.

Houghton Mifflin Co., *Diary of Gideon Welles*, 1911.

The Honorable Richard C. Lee, Mayor of New Haven (Correspondence).

J. B. Lippincott Company, *My Experiences in the World War*, by John J. Pershing, 1931.

Little, Brown & Company, *Triumph of Freedom*, by John C. Miller, 1948.

The Macmillan Company, *The Yankee Exodus*, by Stewart Holbrook, 1950.

Rowland W. Mitchell, Jr. (Dissertation).

The New England Quarterly, "On Some Early Aspects of Connecticut History," by Charles M. Andrews, xvii (March 1944), 22–24.

New London County Historical Society, *Connecticut's Naval Office at New London During the War of the American Revolution*, by Ernest E. Rogers, 1933.

The New York Times, May 28, 1944; October 22, 1948; October 16, 1958.

Vermont Historical Society, "John Clarke's Journal (1824–1842)," ed. Arthur Wallace Peach, *Proceedings*, x (Dec. 1942), 188.

Yale University Library (Historical MSS Room Collections).

Yale University Press, *Connecticut Yankee*, by Wilbur L. Cross, 1943; *The American Rebellion*, ed. William B. Willcox, 1954.

CONTENTS

CONNECTICUT

Preface

THE real origin of this history dates back to college years at Wesleyan shortly before World War II. The late Professor George M. Dutcher, an eminent scholar and inspiring teacher, first keenly stimulated my curiosity about Connecticut's history. A Wesleyan Honors College research project under his supervision provided a first step toward a University of Pennsylvania doctoral dissertation dealing with certain aspects of Connecticut's Revolutionary period. A few years later, in 1952, the State Library Committee through former Chief Justice William Maltbie asked me to be state historian and to prepare a one-volume history of Connecticut. This task sounded so exciting and challenging as to be irresistible. There had been no survey of Connecticut's history for many years and the time seemed propitious for a new attempt.

Since Connecticut is one of the oldest and most historic of American states, most people assume that there are numerous modern and scholarly studies of the towns, counties, leaders, and major periods of its history. Unfortunately there are relatively few modern scholarly books dealing with these aspects of the state's development. Although some state histories can be satisfactorily written from monographs and other secondary sources, I had to spend much time examining primary source materials. Where reliable secondary materials were available, of course they were employed. For very recent periods newspapers, of necessity, have generally provided the major source of information.

In any project as ambitious as a history of a colony and state extending over 325 years, one is able to cover only a minute fraction of the recorded history. Hence it has been necessary to be highly selective. Except for Chapters 18 and 19, the basic approach has been chronological. Because political history offers a more definite chronological framework, that approach has dominated. Yet a serious attempt has been made to indicate some of the major social, economic, religious, military, and cultural aspects of Connecticut's evolution from tiny Puritan agricultural village to cosmopolitan industrial state. Within the space limits prescribed it has been impossible to deal with numerous topics of significance. It is also obviously true that no two students of Connecticut's long and complex history would choose exactly the same subjects to discuss or would apportion the total space in the same manner.

The following features of Connecticut's history seem to be particularly significant and have received emphasis:

1] Connecticut's vigorous variety of Puritanism.

2] The remarkable degree of political independence of the colony.

3] The great military and supply contributions during the Revolution.

4] The population's tremendous expansive power, especially westward, during the nineteenth century, and consequent strong influence of Connecticut institutions in many of the new states.

3

5] The unusual number and importance of inventors who helped revolutionize manufacturing.

6] Unusually heavy provision of men and materiel to the Union cause in 1861–65.

7] Rapid industrial expansion of the late nineteenth and early twentieth centuries, and accompanying labor legislation.

8] The revolution in the composition of the population since the Civil War, and some of the major effects.

9] The huge volume of war contracts making Connecticut an "arsenal of democracy" in World Wars I and II.

10] The long era of Republican political dominance from 1858 to 1928, and the trend toward the Democrats from 1930 to the present.

11] The vigorous economy of the post-World War II period.

Since most subjects necessarily are treated briefly, the footnotes should be of special value to those seeking further information on a particular topic or wishing a starting point for their own researches. Space limitations have required the elimination of nearly all explanatory footnotes. The number of footnotes has been limited to one per paragraph (and some paragraphs have none) in order not to distract readers having no interest in them. Those planning research in Connecticut's history will certainly want to consult the official state archives, located at the State Library in Hartford. That library, the Connecticut Historical Society, and the Yale University Library are the three richest sources of manuscript and printed materials dealing with Connecticut's history.

The author is under deep obligation to many people who have made suggestions and helped in many other ways. In working for the State Library Committee I have found its members uniformly helpful and sympathetic in their consideration of all problems of mutual interest. In the early years of the project Judge Maltbie, serving as liaison for the committee, gave freely of his time and great wisdom. After Maltbie's retirement from the committee the late Chief Justice Edward J. Daly likewise gave wise counsel and strong backing in working out arrangements with the publisher and in other problems. His successor, Chief Justice

Raymond E. Baldwin, has been a tower of strength. Somehow amidst his incredibly busy schedule he has found substantial amounts of time to handle various practical problems, and more important, to discuss at length and answer questions about his three eventful terms as governor. Former Governors John Lodge and Abraham Ribicoff favored the project, and Governor John N. Dempsey has sincerely supported it.

At the Connecticut State Library, where the largest amount of research has been done, willing co-operation by the staff has always been the rule. In the earlier stages of the work (1953–56) the state librarian, James Brewster, did everything possible to expedite the project. His successor, Robert C. Sale, has assisted the project in many important ways. He made available to us extra help from his staff to aid in the final drive for completion. I am especially grateful to him and to those who helped so much in this. Since 1953 the following present or past staff members have cheerfully given special aid to my wife and myself countless times: George W. Adams, Margery S. Blake, Jean T. Blume, Doris E. Cook, Frances Davenport, Minnie De Nezzo, Wesley G. Dennen, Lovina Goodale, Marjorie Case Hartman, Virginia A. Knox, Nellie P. McCue, Isabelle Maclean, Arline G. Maver, Donald Poulin, Rockwell H. Potter, Jr., Ruth Powers, Cecile M. Reynolds, Marjorie Swain, and Hilma L. Talcott.

At the Connecticut Historical Society the staff has always been extremely helpful. The Director, Thompson R. Harlow, has been exceedingly generous with his time in advising upon many phases of the project and has made every facility of the society available to us. His counsel and encouragement have been invaluable. Staff members Frances Hoxie, Phyllis Kihn, Marjorie Waterman, and Assistant Director William L. Warren have helped in ways too numerous to recount.

In New Haven numerous staff members at the Yale University Library, especially Mrs. Zara Powers (retired) and Alexander Vietor, curator of maps, have helped on many occasions. Ralph Thomas and Rollin Osterweis of the New Haven Colony Historical Society gave excellent suggestions on New Haven's role in Connecticut's history.

In work at the Massachusetts Historical Society, the John Carter Brown Library, the Library of

Congress, the New York Public Library, New York Historical Society, and Duke University Library, I always found a genuine spirit of helpfulness. At the Wilbur Cross Library of the University of Connecticut, Roberta Smith, reference librarian, gave valued assistance upon numerous occasions. Dwight C. Lyman of the New London County Historical Society has been of great help. Williams Haynes, Stonington author, has generously shared his wide knowledge of and enthusiasm for Connecticut's history. Edouard A. Stackpole, Curator of Mystic Seaport, gave valuable assistance on maritime matters, including whaling.

Dr. Leonard W. Labaree of Yale University read eight chapters and provided a number of valuable suggestions for improvement. Mrs. Marjorie Case Hartman, formerly head of Local History and Genealogy at Connecticut State Library, read most of the first twelve chapters and made many helpful observations.

For Connecticut's political history in the late nineteenth and early twentieth centuries I am under deep obligation to Frederick Heath, Middlebury College, and Samuel McSeveney, Los Angeles State College. Edward B. Holloway of Milford provided some excellent bibliographical "leads."

The administration and Board of Trustees of the University of Connecticut substantially aided the early stages of this project by the grant of a sabbatical leave during the 1955–56 school year for research and writing. Each of the successive heads of the History Department, Edmund A. Moore (to 1958), André Schenker (acting, 1958–60), and Robert W. Lougee (1960–   ), gave sympathetic understanding and assistance.

Research and/or typing help has been given under state subvention for varying periods by Mildred Bosworth, Alline Burton, Dorothy Dean, and Virginia Stallman. For brief periods Diane Cascio, Kendall Richardson, Violet Schroeder, and Daniel Showan ably carried out specific research assignments. For the "stretch" drive in the late summer and fall of 1960, Ruth Sweeney cheerfully and efficiently typed for long hours, preparing the final draft to meet insistent deadlines. To all those anonymous friends who have helped in any manner I also wish to express my heartfelt appreciation.

Most important of all has been the devoted and skillful work of my wife, who has served uncomplainingly and often for cruelly long hours as a full-fledged research associate since late in 1955. She did much basic research, especially on some of the more complex topics. She also made innumerable textual improvements, carried out the lengthy and onerous preparation of the footnotes for publication, and performed a seemingly endless number of other tasks. To her I have dedicated this book.

Albert E. Van Dusen

Storrs, Connecticut
February 17, 1961

Chelmsford Cathedral. The tower, south porch, and chancel date from fifteenth century and would have been familiar to Hooker.

Backgrounds in England and Massachusetts Bay

A Vigorous and Expanding England — Growing Persecution of the English Puritans —
Thomas Hooker's Career Through Cambridge — Hooker Wins Fame and Persecution —
Hooker Flees to Holland — A Fresh Start in Massachusetts Bay — A "Strong Bent"
Toward Connecticut

A Vigorous and Expanding England

THE roots of Connecticut lie deep within the mother country, England. The men who in the 1630's pushed through the magnificent virgin forests from Massachusetts or sailed tiny vessels up the Connecticut River were born and bred Englishmen — a fact of which they were intensely proud. To understand these pioneers and their dreams, one must know the tight little island and the vigorous civilization which nurtured them.

Despite occasional setbacks the level of civilization in England had climbed steadily during the late Middle Ages. Isolated from the Continent by the English Channel, its culture and institutions developed in ways quite distinctive from those of the Continent. Not until the ending of the bloody Wars of the Roses in 1485, however, was England able to move rapidly toward real national unity and strength. Under the shrewd, tough, and efficient rule of the first Tudor King, Henry VII (1485–1509), and of his more famous son, Henry VIII (1509–47), England became a nation in the modern sense of the word. The turbulent nobles co-operated or were crushed, law and order increasingly prevailed, national finances were re-organized, towns grew, commerce expanded, and Englishmen began to feel a growing pride in their country and its rulers.[1]

England, sooner or later, felt every important current which swept the Continent. The Reformation proved no exception, and it finally shook England to its very foundations. Conditions were ripe for a revolt against the Roman Catholic leadership, and the explosion came under Henry VIII in the 1530's. Undoubtedly the growing nationalism added to the appeal of a break from Rome. Much popular sentiment of an antipapal and anticlerical nature existed in England upon which Henry could easily capitalize. Henry's marital difficulties precipitated the open rupture which finally resulted in England's departure from the Roman Catholic Church and the creation of the Church of England with the king as its head. In ritual, in hierarchy, and in most points of creed the new Church of England closely resembled the Catholic Church.[2]

Under Edward VI, Henry's boy successor, Protestantism was pushed by the king's counselors, but Queen Mary (1553–58) effected a quick return to Catholicism and ordered persecution of the more prominent Protestant leaders. With her death and the accession of Elizabeth in 1558, the religious course of England once again was set upon a definite, though conservative, Protestant course.[3]

During the long reign of Elizabeth (1558–1603) England reached new heights of culture, prosperity, and power. Elizabeth seemed to combine the financial acumen of her grandfather, Henry VII, with the instinctive understanding of the masses displayed by her father, Henry VIII. Although she did not initiate most of the glories of her reign, she made them possible.[4]

The bitter diplomatic, colonial, and commercial rivalry of Spain and England reached a climax with the invasion of England by the Spanish Armada in 1588. The smaller English fleet, under Sir Francis Drake, scored an overwhelming victory and ended the Spanish threat. This complete triumph occurred in a period of burgeoning English nationalism and patriotism and nourished English ambitions to build an overseas empire. As Spain's power declined England's steadily increased.[5]

The continuing economic development at home and sincere encouragement of Elizabeth's government provided a sound basis for this expansion overseas. Before her reign England had been too poor to finance colonization and too weak to block Spain. The revolutionary shift of the world's main trade routes from the Mediterranean to the Atlantic opened glittering possibilities for England's future expansion. It meant that Spain, France, and England, the great Atlantic powers, would fight it out for world-wide naval and commercial leadership. When Spain completely failed to topple England from the list of aspirants, England's eventual primacy was made more likely. Fortunately for England, also, France became too absorbed in attempts at land expansion in Europe to push overseas colonization vigorously.[6]

Following Spain's lead in American explorations, Henry VII in 1497 dispatched John Cabot to America, where he explored much of the northeastern coast and gave England the claim to that area which included the future Connecticut. For many decades afterward English interests in America consisted chiefly in raiding the Spanish Main, often with fabulous success under such Elizabethan sea dogs as Drake and Hawkins. Meanwhile Frobisher, Davis, and others vainly sought a northwest passage to the east. These glamorous exploits were actually of less immediate significance than the steady but unspectacular build-up of English trade in such regions as the Baltic and the Mediterranean. Many regulated trading companies were chartered, especially during Elizabeth's reign, to exploit the trade of a specific area. After 1600, joint-stock companies became more common and proved well suited to spreading the high risks of investment in faraway areas. Fortunately, too, England at last was beginning to have sizable amounts of surplus capital available for overseas enterprises.[7]

At home among England's population, which by the early 1600's had passed four million, major economic and social changes were occurring. The medieval economic and political system had largely disappeared. The feudal manor and its inevitable concomitant — serfs tied to the land — had gradually been replaced by independent landholding yeomen, by tenant farmers, and by day laborers. Agriculture remained the occupation of a large majority of Englishmen, and the methods employed continued to be highly inefficient. Gradually the increasing prosperity of the urban centers of northern Europe affected English agriculture strongly. The urban demand for good woolen cloth shot upward and this greatly encouraged sheep raising — an occupation highly favored by English climate and terrain. For sheep raising to be efficient, however, thousands of small farms and fields needed to be consolidated and enclosed as larger areas. For practically all other types of agriculture, too, larger land units proved more profitable. So the enclosure movement became an extremely important development, spread over several centuries. By the early 1600's the process already had driven thousands of yeomen, rural tenants, and day laborers from the land and had transformed many of them into unemployed and dispirited vagrants. Many eventually found work in the growing cities.[8]

English industry continued to operate principally under the "domestic" system, which meant that the capitalist "put out" his raw materials for manufacture within private cottages. This was especially true in the cloth industry — the one industry which produced an important surplus for sale abroad. The remainder of England's industry was geared almost exclusively to the domestic market. The iron industry still largely fed itself upon England's great forests, although the use of coal was increasing in various types of manufacturing.[9]

In the eastern counties, such as Norfolk, Suffolk, and Essex, from which the heaviest migration to New England occurred, the cloth industry was particularly well developed. As early as 1301 Colchester, Essex, claimed sixteen weavers and eighteen clothiers and tailors. The enclosure movement had proceeded very rapidly in this part of England, and before 1600 most of the land was already divided into enclosed farms and sheep pastures. The raising of sheep and the manufacture of cloth in the eastern counties received added impetus from the arrival of large numbers of experienced Flemish workers who were especially skilled in weaving. Large fortunes were made, as evidenced by the magnificent fifteenth- and sixteenth-century churches which still grace such eastern towns as Hingham, Lavenham, and Norwich.[10]

Although agriculture predominated in the eastern counties, as in other parts of England, the economic life of the area was remarkably diversified. Potash making, cheese making, shipbuilding, and fishing — each occupied large numbers. Towns such as Colchester, Ipswich, Maldon, and Harwich carried on a brisk trade with the Continent and developed a hardy crop of mariners. This varied economic background would prove most valuable to the pioneers who faced the problem of earning a living in the New England wilds.[11]

The practice of government regulation of economic activity was transported to the American colonies. Under the Tudor and early Stuart rulers the English people were accustomed to a large degree of governmental intervention. Colonization, moreover, was a risky and expensive business which required a large amount of capital and the blessings of the government. The economic philosophy of the period, known later as *mercantilism*, exhibited clearly the reliance upon considerable governmental economic control. This system aimed primarily at economic self-sufficiency, and it involved careful regulation of imports and ex-

ports in order to establish a favorable balance of trade. Home industries were encouraged, and the government chartered companies to help dispose of surplus manufactures abroad. Colonies were considered highly desirable as cheap sources of raw materials and good outlets for English manufactures. Finally, a build-up of the English merchant marine was deemed essential to keep the profits of the carrying trade in English hands.[12]

The colonists carried to New England certain important concepts and attitudes. The spirit of individualism, strong in England, was clearly marked in these pioneers. Closely allied to this was a decided feeling for individual liberty — both of body and of mind. The well-established English court system, trial by jury, and the body of legal precedents which constituted the common law provided a cherished model for the New England colonies. In the courts the average Englishman found protection against injustices perpetrated by the king, his agents, or his fellow men. He also regarded Parliament as an instrument to protect individual rights. Loyalty to nation and to sovereign characterized the average Englishman, and this feeling long survived the separation by three thousand miles of ocean.[13]

In social class structure the English background also played an important role. In common with other European countries England had strongly marked class lines. The upper class, particularly in the form of the country gentleman, completely dominated English political life, though a growing mercantile middle class was beginning to assume importance. Although few of this upper class migrated to New England, some country gentry, like John Winthrop, Sr., did come in the early waves. In any event, the traditions of the upper class were brought to America and generally adopted by the new aristocracy which developed there.[14]

Growing Persecution of the English Puritans

UNDER Queen Elizabeth, a religious compromise calling for moderate Protestantism, known as the Elizabethan Settlement, was put into effect. It re-established, approximately, the conservative Anglican Church existing at Henry VIII's death. The doctrine of the National Church was defined in the thirty-nine articles enacted by Parliament in 1571. The queen, a shrewd politician, knew that a middle-of-the-road religious position was the only practicable one. If she moved to radical Protestantism, her Catholic subjects might throw their support to Mary Queen of Scots, and also receive aid from Catholic Continental powers, such as France. On the other hand, the Protestant reformers would be estranged if she traveled much closer to Catholicism. So Elizabeth had to walk a tightrope, to follow a *via media*. Many Protestant reformers had fled England during the severe persecutions under Queen Mary, and had studied abroad under leading reformers in Geneva, Zurich, Frankfurt, and elsewhere. They surged back to Elizabethan England, eager to lead their country along the reform route. Although these reformers became well known under Elizabeth, one must go back at least to William Tyndale, translator of the New Testament and martyr (died, 1536) under Henry VIII, to find an important early exponent of English religious dissent. Tyndale based his faith upon the Bible and individual interpretation of it. Admittedly, he did not advocate a radical break from Catholicism, as did John Calvin, the real father of Puritanism.[15]

It was under Elizabeth in the late 1560's that the term "Puritan" began to be widely employed. In many ways the Puritan outlook coincided with growing religious tendencies of England, so that the Puritans became a powerful force by the 1570's and 1580's. Gradually they developed into three distinct groups: 1] the Presbyterians, who followed Calvin's injunctions on church government; 2] the Brownists or Separatists, later known as Independents or Congregationalists, who advocated independence in policies for each individual church; and 3] the largest group, who advocated remaining within the Church of England and reforming it, often called simply Puritans, or "reformers." To the individual Puritan the heart of his religion developed through an experience of *conversion* which he believed separated him from the generality of men and endowed him with the benefits and responsibilities of the elect. This conversion involved a "rebirth" in which the individual truly felt the wrath and redemptive love of God. A fervent sermon often caused this experience. All Puritan groups held in common, too, ideals of strict piety in everyday life and a burning desire to create a godly, righteous nation. As one authority expressed it: "The mainspring of the Puritan's mechanism was his moral consciousness." Every action was moral, and every moment and every word required an accounting.[16]

By the 1570's and 1580's the Puritans became so powerful that they won the strong enmity of the queen. A substantial number of keen clerics and laymen were attracted to Puritanism by its promise of thoroughgoing reform of the English Church, which involved stripping it of most of the accretions of centuries and returning to the simplicity of the apostolic age. The Puritans desired that ministers, elders, and all other officers should be elected popularly by congregations and synods. Elizabeth would have none of it, since it involved a radical change in the National Church and a significant reduction of royal authority. As early as the 1560's the Court of High Commission moved vigorously against dissenters. In 1567 one congregation was discovered in Plumber's Hall, London, and promptly prosecuted. Twenty-seven of them spent a year in Bridewell Prison, and others languished there for longer terms. This London group adhered to principles basically Congregationalist.[17]

In 1583 the queen saw to it that a strict and efficient disciplinarian, Whitgift, was elevated to Archbishop of Canterbury. He pleased Elizabeth by displaying great firmness against the growing Puritan numbers and influence. Even important members of Elizabeth's Council (Leicester, Burghley, and Walsingham) strongly sympathized with the Puritan cause and resented Whitgift's tough measures to obtain conformity. In 1585–86 the Puritans organized a thorough survey of their districts to show the need for reform and turned up an impressive number of clergy whom they listed in such categories as "drunkard and ale house haunter," "gamester," "unable to preach," "pot companion," "incontinent," "common barrater," and "common swearer." In Essex the survey of 335 benefices revealed 173 ignorant and unpreaching ministers, 61 pluralists, 10 nonresidents of single benefices, and 12 "preachers of scandalous life." It is not surprising that nonconformity in England reached its highest level in Essex. It found many strong adherents, too, in such counties as nearby Norfolk, Suffolk, and Cambridge, as well as Lincoln, Oxford, Northampton, Rutland, and Kent.[18]

Despite great efforts, the Puritans lost ground in the last fifteen years or so of Elizabeth's reign. Very energetic action by the government uncovered and destroyed the backbone of organization in about twenty counties, so that the Puritan movement temporarily lost its aggressiveness. In Elizabeth's last years they definitely were on the defensive against heavy governmental attack.[19]

With the accession of James I of Scotland in 1603 Puritan hopes of favorable treatment soared, but were promptly dashed at the Hampton Court Conference of October 1603. Puritan clergy soon faced the grim alternatives of strict adherence to all prescribed ceremonies or immediate loss of their positions. Nearly all Puritan demands for reform of the Church were peremptorily rejected. About three hundred Puritan ministers lost their livings, but the majority conformed outwardly, if unenthusiastically. Some who could not endure the rigorous outward conformity emigrated to Holland and a few Separatists, in 1620, founded Plymouth, Massachusetts.[20]

Charles I's reign made life for ardent Puritans virtually intolerable. In the religious sphere, as in others, Charles possessed a genius for earning quick and deep enmity from many of his subjects. Add to a rigorous Anglican religious policy arbitrary taxation, flouting of Parliament, and economic depression, and one can see why the situation of the late 1620's set many Englishmen to thinking of a fresh start in the New World. For ardent Puritans the growing religious persecution by Charles and his minions outranked all other factors as a basic reason for migration. Among the men who considered starting life anew across the broad Atlantic were several future leaders of Connecticut, especially Thomas Hooker.[21]

Thomas Hooker's Career Through Cambridge

THOMAS HOOKER, "the father of Connecticut," probably was born in the hamlet of Marefield, county of Leicester, England, on or about July 7, 1586. At the time, Marefield boasted only a half-dozen or so houses. Almost nothing is known of his parents or of his youth beyond the bare account given by Cotton Mather. Hooker's parents apparently possessed at least modest means, for Mather declares that they were "neither unable, nor unwilling to bestow upon him a liberal education; whereto the early and lively sparkles of wit observed in him, did very much encourage them." Mather notes, too, that young Hooker's qualities of mind and character convinced his friends that he was "born to be *considerable*."[22]

Where and from whom young Hooker received his elementary schooling is unknown, but his secondary education apparently occurred at Market Bosworth, in the grammar school founded in 1586 by a wealthy Londoner, Sir Wolstan Dixie. Market Bosworth, a small market town, was located about twenty-five miles west of Marefield.[23]

In March 1604 Hooker entered Queen's College, Cambridge, as a sizar, or scholarship student. Later he transferred to Emmanuel College, from which he received his B.A. in 1608 and M.A. in 1611. Cambridge University, at the beginning of the seventeenth century, was not inhospitable to Puritanism; and many of the faculty and students, fresh from contact with Continental religious reformers, had returned to Cambridge full of fervor for dissenting beliefs and practices.[24]

Emmanuel ranked clearly as the most Puritan of all Cambridge's colleges. It was established in 1584 under a charter granted to Sir Walter Mildmay, Elizabeth's Chancellor of the Exchequer. Although a Puritan at heart, Mildmay managed throughout his career to retain high popularity and strong influence with Elizabeth. At Emmanuel the Puritan faith found outward manifestation in simple but evangelical chapel services, without surplice or prayer-book ritual, and with students seated around a table to receive communion. By 1617, near the close of Hooker's Emmanuel career, the college numbered over two hundred undergraduates, the second largest among Cambridge's colleges.[25]

Early in the college's history, Queen Elizabeth, hearing a rumor that it was a center of Puritanism, spoke one day to Mildmay: "Sir Walter, I hear you have erected a puritan foundation." "No, madam," he replied, "far be it from me to countenance any thing contrary to your established laws, but I have set an acorn, which when it becomes an oak, God alone knows what will be the fruit thereof." Little did he or anyone dream that one of the fruits would be the Puritan colony of Connecticut![26]

Hooker found life at Emmanuel and in the Cambridge community highly stimulating. Among those students he came to know well was John Cotton, destined to be the foremost divine of Massachusetts Bay. William Ames, the Puritan theologian who influenced Hooker deeply, resided at Cambridge during part of Hooker's career there. After Hooker took his Master's degree in 1611, he remained for further study until about 1618. From 1609 to 1618 he held a fellowship under the Wolstan Dixie Foundation, and served as dean in 1616–17.[27]

During the later years at Emmanuel, Hooker underwent an agonizing soul-searching experience which, for a long period, almost prostrated him. Eventually he experienced a conversion and decided to enter the ministry. The last few years at Emmanuel were chiefly occupied with theological studies and laying the foundations of his own philosophical and theological beliefs, which provided a solid basis for his powerful sermons of later years. The philosophical and religious works of a writer named Alexander Richardson seem to have given Hooker the groundwork for his thinking. Then and in later years he derived great inspiration from the writings and personality of William Ames. Hooker declared that *"If a scholar* was but well studied in Dr. *Ames* his *Medulla Theologiae,* and *Casus Conscientiae,* so as to understand them thoroughly, they would make him (supposing him versed in the scriptures,) a *good divine,* though he had no more books in the world."[28]

Hooker Wins Fame and Persecution

HOOKER's whereabouts and activities for about two years after his departure from Cambridge are undocumented matters of conjecture. Very possibly he engaged in some preaching and studying in London and its vicinity. It is probable that his pronounced Puritan views rendered it difficult to obtain the Bishop of London's approval for a suitable rectorship.[29]

Hooker's first recorded charge, covering approximately 1620–26, was a humble one — the rectorship of St. George's Church, Esher, Surrey, a small village about sixteen miles southwest of London. He did not require the consent of the bishop for this place, as it was bestowed directly by a patron, Francis Drake. For Hooker the most important event at Esher was romantic — he fell in love with Susannah Garbrand, Mrs. Drake's maid. They were married April 3, 1621, and for some time continued to live at the Drakes' home.[30]

In the meantime Hooker's preaching talents were becoming known rather widely, especially since he preached frequently in and around London. Apparently he ardently desired to go to Colchester to be near his friend John Rogers of Dedham, whom he considered *"The prince of all the preachers in England,"* but the arrangements fell through. In or about 1626 he received a call to become lecturer at the Church of St. Mary in Chelmsford, Essex. Hooker accepted the position, which offered greater opportunities for service to a far larger parish. Chelmsford itself, a busy town about thirty miles northeast of London, offered a sharp contrast to the quiet village of Esher. He apparently assumed his duties early in 1626.[31]

A lecturer in an Anglican church usually preached on Sunday afternoons and market days. Thus he could provide more, and often better, preaching than would ordinarily be done by the regular vicar. In many cases these lectureships were endowed by prosperous Puritans. The masses seem to have welcomed the lecturers, but the system quickly roused the acute dislike of William Laud and his adherents, who attempted to restrict them. King James I, in 1622, and Charles I, four years later, issued proclamations forbidding the discussion of almost all the vital subjects (for example, predestination, nature of God's grace), which lecturers frequently presented.[32]

Hooker's reputation as a powerful preacher spread rapidly and he attracted large congregations, including some persons of high social rank, such as the Earl of Warwick. Mather discloses how an irreligious man and his companions decided to visit Hooker's lecture in order to mock him and create a disturbance. The ringleader had not been long at the lecture "before the *quick and*

Emmanuel College, Cambridge University. From a painting c. 1670 in the Master's Lodge.

powerful word of God, in the mouth of his faithful *Hooker*, pierced the soul of him; he came out with an awakened and a distressed soul, and by the further blessing of God upon Mr. *Hooker's* ministry, he arrived unto a true *conversion*." Later he followed Hooker to America.[33]

Another time, when Hooker preached at Leicester, a town burgess who had long opposed Hooker hired fiddlers to play so loudly outside the church as to drown out the preacher. Hooker's voice boomed forth so powerfully and eloquently, however, that it overcame the screeching musicians. The burgess himself was so moved by Hooker's message that he underwent a conversion, begged the preacher's forgiveness, and became an ardent Puritan![34]

Upon another occasion, when preaching at Chelmsford before a huge congregation on a national day of fasting, he bluntly prayed to God that He would enlighten the king and set him upon a pious course. Royal judges heard the stinging rebuke to His Majesty, but Hooker was not persecuted for this bold criticism. Mather asserts that Hooker's preaching produced "a great reformation" in conduct among the masses of the people in the Chelmsford area.[35]

Serious trouble for Hooker developed rather quickly when he came under the close surveillance of William Laud, Bishop of London, who had conducted a thorough and unrelenting campaign against Puritan principles and preaching since his elevation to the bishopric in 1628. Such influential preaching as Hooker's, occurring so close to London, could not fail to disturb a man of Laud's High Church outlook and stanch determination. Early in 1629 he obtained from Charles I certain additional orders which severely restricted lecturers' activities. Armed with these royal orders, Laud proceeded methodically to silence all important nonconformist preachers.³⁶

In 1629 the storm broke over Hooker's head. Definite intimations appeared in a letter written on May 20 by Samuel Collins, vicar of Braintree

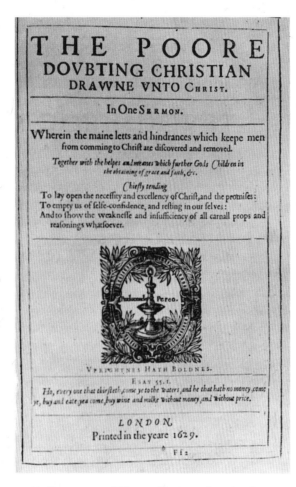

Earliest sermon of Thomas Hooker to be printed.

(near Chelmsford), to Dr. Duck, Laud's Chancellor. This letter reveals vividly the deep impact of Hooker's work as well as the nature of the opposition to him:

Since my return from London I have spoken with Mr. Hooker, but I have small hope of prevailing with him. All the favor he desires is that my Lord of London would not bring him into the High Commission Court, but permit him quietly to depart out of the diocese. . . . All men's eares are now filled with ye obstreprous clamours of his followers against my Lord . . . as a man endeavouring to suppress good preaching and advance Popery. All would be here very calme and quiet if he might quietly depart. . . . If he be suspended . . . its the resolution of his friends and himself to settle his

abode in Essex, and maintenance is promised him in plentifull manner for the fruition of his private conference, which hath already more impeached the peace of our church than his publique ministry. His genius will still haunte all the pulpits in ye country, where any of his scholers may be admitted to preach. . . . There be divers young ministers about us . . . that . . . spend their time . . . in conference with him . . . and return home . . . and preach . . . what he hath brewed. . . . Our peoples pallats grow so out of tast, yt noe food contents them but of Mr. Hooker's dressing. I have lived in Essex to see many changes, and have seene the people idolizing many new ministers and lecturers, but this man surpasses them all for learning and some other considerable partes and . . . gains more and far greater followers than all before him. . . . if my Lord . . . tender his owne future peace . . . let him connive at Mr. Hooker's departure.

About a fortnight later Collins wrote that Hooker's case was attracting great attention and even drowned out the "greate question of Tonnage and Poundage." All of the nearby counties buzzed with discussion of the case. Hooker was cited to appear before Laud and bond of fifty pounds was taken for his later appearance.³⁷

Hooker was pointedly warned against continuance of his Puritan practices and his preaching upon forbidden topics, but he persisted in his chosen course. On November 3, 1629, the Reverend John Browning, rector of Rawreth, Essex, wrote Laud that Hooker was continuing his former practices and that the obedient clergy should be defended against such men. He foresaw serious disturbances in suppressing Hooker, and offered his assistance in quieting the Chelmsford people after his removal.³⁸

Many of the Essex clergy strongly supported Hooker in his battle against the strict forms prescribed by Laud. On November 10, forty-nine of them signed a petition to Laud declaring that they knew Hooker to be "for doctryne, orthodox, and life and conversation honest, and for his disposition peaceable." Hence they asked cessation of all proceedings against him. Unluckily for Hooker, a week later forty-one Essex clergy begged Laud to enforce all regulations against nonconformists. The exact date of Hooker's departure does not appear in St. Mary's records, but he departed quietly, probably late in 1629.³⁹

Hooker did not go far — only to Little Baddow, a

hamlet about four miles east of Chelmsford, where he set up a small school in a house called "Cuckoos Farm." Doubtless many of his followers informally visited Hooker and found further inspiration and counsel from his words. As his usher or assistant, Hooker secured John Eliot, later to become famous as a missionary to the New England Indians. It is very possible that the close association with Hooker led Eliot to make his shift from teaching to the ministry.[40]

Hooker Flees to Holland

WHILE at Little Baddow, Hooker apparently could not resist the temptation to do some preaching, and doubtless this activity caused the High Court of Commission, at Laud's instigation, again to stretch out its tentacles for Hooker. He decided that he would not receive fair treatment and ought to move to Holland, where many nonconformists already had migrated. The Earl of Warwick provided a safe sanctuary for Hooker's family, while Hooker fled just ahead of government agents, boarded ship, and reached Holland safely.[41]

In common with many of the other English exiles in Holland, Hooker, in general, did not enjoy the experience. He went first to Amsterdam, where he was considered as a possible colleague of John Paget in the English Church. Paget, a conservative and cranky old man, severely cross-examined Hooker, who clearly enunciated his Congregational creed. The local church-governing body, the Classis, to Paget's joy, ruled that no man with such beliefs should be chosen pastor. Recognizing the situation as hopeless, Hooker soon pushed on to Delft, where he served two years as an assistant to the pastor of the Scottish Presbyterian Church, the Reverend John Forbes.[42]

Hooker's final move in Holland took him to Rotterdam, where he became a colleague of Ames and Hugh Peter. Ames died in 1632 and Hooker wrote a lengthy preface for Ames's final work, *A Fresh Suit against human ceremonies*. Hooker's great admiration for Ames was reciprocated, and Ames said that "*though he had been acquainted with many scholars of divers nations, yet he never met with Mr. Hooker's equal, either for preaching or for disputing.*" The Dutch years were diffi-

cult ones for Hooker, but there is no doubt that the associations with Ames, Peter, and the others, and the difficult experiences contributed much to his general maturation and preparation for a role of leadership in New England.[43]

A Fresh Start in Massachusetts Bay

OVER a period of many months Hooker's interest in going to America slowly increased. As long as Laud and his principles dominated the English Church there could be no future for Hooker in his native land. In Holland, too, he saw little prospect of any large opportunities for leadership in the Puritan cause. America, then, seemed to be the logical outlet, especially since the Massachusetts Bay Company had well-developed plans. Some of the Puritans sought to obtain Cotton and Hooker as their joint religious leaders, but they soon realized that "a couple of such great men might be more servicable asunder than together." For some time leaders of the Massachusetts Bay Company had been urging Hooker to go to New England.[44]

In 1632 a band of Essex County people, especially from around Earls Colne, a village about eighteen miles northeast of Chelmsford, immigrated to Massachusetts and settled temporarily near Boston. Since many of them had been faithful followers of Hooker at Chelmsford and clung to hopes that Hooker would come as their minister, they were called "Mr. Hooker's Company."[45]

By 1633 Hooker had decided to cast his lot with those in Massachusetts Bay, so he quietly returned to England to arrange his affairs before sailing. Mather quaintly describes Hooker's close escape from arrest:

Returning into *England* in order to a further voyage, he [Mr. Hooker] was quickly scented by the pursevants [officers]; who at length got so far up with him, as to knock at the door of that very chamber, where he was now discoursing with Mr. *Stone;* who was now become his designed companion and assistent for the *New-English* enterprize. Mr. *Stone* was at that instant smoking of *tobacco;* for which Mr. *Hooker* had been reproving him, as being then used by few persons of sobriety; being also of a sudden and pleasant wit, he stept unto the door, with his pipe in his mouth, and such an air of speech and look, as gave him some credit with the officer. The officer demanded,

Seventeenth-century ship of type which carried many colonists to America. Drawn by Gordon Grant.

Whether Mr. Hooker *were not there?* Mr. *Stone* replied with a braving sort of confidence, *What* Hooker? *Do you mean* Hooker *that lived once at* Chelmsford! The officer answered, *Yes, he!* Mr. *Stone* immediately, with a diversion like that which once helped *Athanasius*, made this true answer, *If it be he you look for, I saw him about an hour ago, at such an house in the town; you had best hasten thither after him.* The officer took this for a sufficient account, and went his way; but Mr. *Hooker,* upon this intimation, concealed himself more carefully and securely, till he went on board, at the *Downs,* in the year 1633, the ship which brought him, and Mr. *Cotton,* and Mr. *Stone* to *New-England:* where none but Mr. *Stone* was owned for a preacher, at their first coming aboard; the other two delaying to take their turns in the publick worship of the ship, till they were got so far into the main ocean, that they might with safety, discover who they were.[46]

Samuel Stone, Hooker's intended assistant, was born in Hertford, Hertfordshire, England, in 1602, the son of John Stone, a freeholder. After a preparation at Hale's Grammar School in his home town, he matriculated at Emmanuel College in 1620, and earned the B.A. in 1623, the M.A. in 1627. While holding a lectureship at Towcester,

he received the fateful invitation to journey to New England and become Hooker's assistant. Stone happily accepted.[47]

The eight weeks' voyage to Boston on the ship *Griffin* was marked by daily preaching. Little wonder, with the abundance of preaching talent aboard! Cotton, Hooker, and Stone all loved to preach, and they had many appreciative listeners among the two hundred passengers, including John Haynes, later to be governor of Connecticut.[48]

On September 4, 1633, Hooker and the others first set foot upon American soil at Boston. Undoubtedly a warm welcome was accorded all of the passengers. Hooker and Stone soon proceeded to nearby Newtown (Cambridge), where their congregation eagerly awaited them. On October 11, 1633, Hooker and Stone were ordained as pastor and teacher, respectively. This meant that Hooker would concentrate upon preaching, exhortation, and practical applications of faith; and Stone, upon explanation and inculcation of doctrine.[49]

16

The arrival of the triumvirate of Cotton, Hooker, and Stone made the "poor people in the wilderness" say that "the God of heaven had supplied them, with . . . their three great necessities; *Cotton* for their *clothing, Hooker* for their *fishing,* and *Stone* for their *building.*"[50]

Shortly after their arrival in the New World, Cotton wrote to a friend in England and explained why he and Hooker had decided to come to America. In the first place, the door had been shut to their English ministry. Cotton observed that "If we may and ought to follow God's calling three hundred miles, why not three thousand?" In the second place, they both felt that the Lord had called them to the ministry in Massachusetts. Finally, they had come to "enjoy the liberty, not of some ordinances of God, but of all, and all in purity." In other words, they came to worship in their own way. Unfortunately no letter of Hooker's exists which explains clearly his reasons for migration, but it seems safe to assume that Cotton understood Hooker's motives and accurately represented them.[51]

By arriving in 1633 Hooker escaped most of the rigors of pioneering. William Wood, a contemporary, described Newtown as "one of the neatest and best compacted Townes in New England, having many faire structures, with many handsome contrived streets. The inhabitants most of them are very rich, and well stored with Cattell of all sorts."[52]

Although Hooker had no Boswell to chronicle his activities in detail, he seems to have worked happily with his Newtown flock and to have been involved in most of the major affairs of the colony. Upon one occasion in 1634 he joined with Cotton and Thomas Welde to admonish his friend John Eliot, teacher of the Roxbury Church. Eliot had dared to criticize the magistrates' methods in concluding a peace with the Pequots.[53]

Hooker's influential standing among the oligarchical leadership of the colony was demonstrated when he was selected to refute Roger Williams at the famous trial in October 1635. Williams, with his persistent opposition to the ruling clique over such matters as the charter, the special oath required of freemen, his desire for a free church, and his separatist opinions, had roused deep en-

mities. Each man hit hard at the other. Hooker argued skillfully and seems to have convinced everybody except Williams that he was in error! In any case, public sentiment was such that Williams was sentenced to banishment.[54]

A "Strong Bent" Toward Connecticut

HOOKER and his people did not remain satisfied in Newtown very long. Just eight months after Hooker's arrival they asked the colonial Court for permission either to have more land or to move away, and noted that they suffered from "want of land." To show that they meant business they sent out a few men to look over land in Agawam and Merrimac and spread word of their intended departure. In June, Winthrop reported that six Newtowners had gone "to discover Connecticut River, intending to remove their town thither."[55]

When the Court met in September 1634, Newtown's petition comprised the chief business. They advanced three reasons for departing: 1] lack of adequate land for their cattle, for maintenance of ministers, and for new settlers; 2] the fertility and expansiveness of Connecticut and danger of its seizure by the Dutch or others; 3] "the strong bent of their spirits to remove thither." In opposition, reasons were advanced which boiled down to fear that such an emigration would weaken the colony and lure away future settlers. The discussion waxed hot. In the midst of the debate Elder Goodwin of Newtown irreverently addressed one of the assistants, for which he was reproved, and he humbly acknowledged his error. When the vote was cast, the deputies favored the move by a margin of fifteen to ten, but only a minority of assistants favored the removal. Perhaps to allow the disputants to cool down, a day of humiliation was proclaimed, and Cotton preached. The Newtown group then agreed to accept additional land offered by Boston as the condition of staying.[56]

What really had caused such a speedy disenchantment of the Newtown leaders with Massachusetts Bay? John Winthrop, Sr., the historian of early Massachusetts, tended to gloss over any fundamental differences. Yet some must have existed to cause Hooker and most of his congregation to seek such an early departure from Massa-

*Thomas Hooker (1583–1646) as he is imagined
to have appeared.*

chusetts. Perhaps the historian Hubbard analyzed the situation accurately when he declared: "Two such eminent stars, such as were Mr. Cotton and Mr. Hooker, both of the first magnitude, though of differing influence, could not well continue in one and the same orb." Certainly Hooker disagreed with Cotton upon various religious matters, including that of admission to the churches, and a lengthy controversy ensued which undoubtedly made departure seem attractive to Hooker. Already among the people of Dorchester, Roxbury, Watertown, and his own Newtown, Hooker had gained many enthusiastic followers, many of whom migrated to Connecticut under his banner.[57]

Religious differences did not move the majority of migrants to Connecticut, for they planned to establish a colony with substantially the same church and creed as found in Massachusetts. Economic motivation, instead, dominated most of the Connecticut-bound, who were powerfully drawn by the glowing reports of a fertile valley and a navigable river. Later they reported as the official reason for departure that "vpon experience they found that place [Boston area] would be too streight [cramped] for soe great a number if they should continue all there long together." Thus land hunger, joined with personal dissatisfactions of leaders such as Hooker, John Haynes, and Roger Ludlow, proved decisive in sparking the migration to Connecticut.[58]

In 1635 the Massachusetts General Court officially gave permission to the dissatisfied settlers to leave, provided they continued under Massachusetts rule. No real enthusiasm marked the Massachusetts action, which was performed in a spirit of resignation to the inevitable. The entire battle illustrates well the fear with which the rulers of older settlements usually regarded the growth of the western frontier. The attractions of the Connecticut River Valley proved irresistible, however, not only to many in Massachusetts Bay but also to various other groups of Englishmen and to some Dutchmen as well. As a result, a race to establish domination in the fertile valley soon developed.[59]

Settlement of the Connecticut River Valley

Connecticut River Valley Attracts Dutch and English Settlers — Founding of Three River Towns — Saybrook and Agawam Settled — The Natural Setting — Geologic Change Affects Connecticut's Topography — Connecticut Indians — Sixteen Indian Tribes — The Pequots Take to the Warpath — River Towns Accept Pequot Challenge — The Pequots Meet Their Doom — Evolving a Framework of Government — The Fundamental Orders — Springfield Lost, Saybrook and Other Towns Gained

Connecticut River Valley Attracts Dutch and English Settlers

THE Connecticut River entered the pages of modern history in 1614, when the Dutch mariner Adriaen Block first explored it in a small boat, the *Restless*, only forty-four and a half feet in overall length. He sailed at least to the present northern line of the city of Hartford, and perhaps proceeded to the falls at Enfield. Block named the stream the Fresh River or Fresh Water.[1]

Luckily for the later English interests, the Dutch failed to follow up Block's discoveries by energetic colonizing. For the next decade and more, Dutch fur traders carried on with the Indians a trade which may have reached the large total of 10,000 beaver skins annually. In the 1620's the Dutch leaders at New Amsterdam laid plans for several fortified settlements on the River. Accordingly, they acquired a strategic piece of land at the mouth of the River and named it Kievit's Hoeck. In 1627 they sent Captain Isaac de Rasière to Plymouth with friendly proposals for a joint commercial venture in Connecticut. The Plymouth leaders were quite suspicious, however, and it

proved impossible to reach any sort of agreement. Finally, on June 8, 1633, Jacob Van Curler purchased from the Pequots, owners by conquest, a small tract of land now within the city of Hartford. Quickly erecting a small fort, the Dutch mounted two cannon upon it, called the place the House of Good Hope and encouraged nearby Indians to trade freely there. Thus by 1633 the Dutch had acquired two toe holds upon the shores of the Connecticut River.[2]

As it turned out, the Dutch barely edged out the English for primacy of settlement in the general Hartford area. For several years English colonists in Plymouth and Massachusetts Bay had felt a growing curiosity about the land in the Connecticut River Valley. Local Connecticut Indians, fearful of the bellicose Pequots, visited Plymouth and Boston in 1631 and described in glowing terms the attractions of the valley. Stimulated by these reports, energetic Edward Winslow of Plymouth in 1632 made an exploratory tour up the Connecticut River to see what possibilities existed for fur trade and colonization. Very probably he landed and selected the actual spot for the settlement which soon afterward became Windsor.[3]

Founding of Three River Towns

THE Dutch proposals and Winslow's expedition seem to have stimulated Plymouth to further action. The colony sent out a bark under aggressive William Holmes. On board he carried several Indians, original proprietors of this area. When he arrived opposite the Dutch fort at Hartford, the Dutch peremptorily ordered him to halt while they inquired as to his intentions. Holmes crisply replied that he held a Plymouth commission with orders to proceed upriver to trade. The Dutch threatened to open fire with their two cannon, but Holmes pushed on unmolested. On September 26, 1633, the Plymouth contingent reached the spot purchased from the Indians earlier and quickly erected the house frame which they had carried from Plymouth. Around this building they rapidly constructed a stockade, or palisado, against possible attack by hostile Indians or the Dutch. Thus Windsor was founded.[4]

The Dutch soon retaliated with an expedition of seventy men against the tiny settlement, but found the defenders so determined that they returned to Hartford without firing a shot. A vigorous written protest was served upon Holmes by the directors of the West India Company, but to no avail. In a later move to cut off the fur supply of the English, the Dutch attempted to establish a new settlement above the English one, but a sudden smallpox epidemic broke out among the Indians and wrecked their scheme.[5]

The same year, John Oldham, a restless adventurer from Dorchester, traveled overland with a few companions to look at the country in the lower Connecticut River and to trade with the Indians. Receiving a cordial reception from an Indian sachem who presented him with a beaver skin, Oldham noted that Indian hemp of good quality grew naturally in the river meadows and he purchased some of it. He reported, too, that Connecticut contained many desirable sites for settlements.[6]

In the settlement of Connecticut, the early comers — both Dutch and English — soon lost control of the situation as they became inundated by a wave of new settlers. The restlessness apparent in Newtown, Dorchester, and Watertown in 1634 broke out even more vigorously the next year. Although Hooker's Newtown flock had spearheaded the agitation of 1634 for removal, Dorchester and Watertown led the migration to Connecticut. The people of Dorchester had come to Massachusetts from southwestern England, chiefly from Devon and nearby counties. This region had more early contact with North America than any other in England, beginning with Cabot's voyage from Bristol in 1497 up through the numerous fishing and fur-trading trips of the 1620's. The chief organizer of the carefully chosen Dorchester band had been the Reverend John White of Dorchester, Devon. As spiritual leaders, the Reverend John Maverick of Devon and the Reverend John Warham of Exeter were selected. For lay leadership, two members of the government of the Massachusetts Bay Company came forward — Edward Rossiter and Roger Ludlow. The remainder of the company included a nice balance of solid country gentry of means, military figures, especially Captain John Mason, and a large number of vigorous young men. This hand-picked company, numbering about 140, almost entirely composed of intensely religious persons, assembled at Plymouth, where they held a solemn day of fasting and prayer at New Hospital in the city. In the morning White preached a farewell sermon, and in the afternoon the people formally elected Maverick and Warham as their ministers. Soon afterward they boarded their ship, *Mary and John*. Captain Roger Clap, a passenger, records that they "came, by the good Hand of the Lord, through the Deeps comfortably; having Preaching or Expounding of the Word of God *every Day* for *Ten Weeks* together, by our Ministers." On May 30, 1630, they landed at Nantasket, the first of the Massachusetts Bay Company's fleet of seventeen ships to arrive in New England. Shortly afterward they settled at Dorchester, which had land well suited to cattle.[7]

Much discussion preceded the move from Dorchester. In September 1634 Roger Ludlow led the fight against migration, and some lively debate ensued. By early 1635 Ludlow had changed sides and vigorously championed the move. He and others seem to have become increasingly dissatisfied with the Bay Colony's leadership, and saw at-

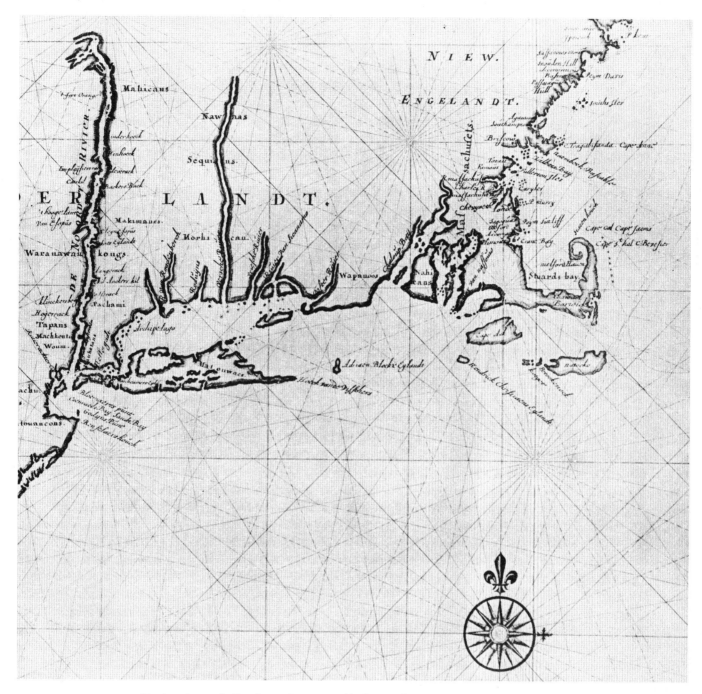

Portion of an early Dutch map (c. 1625–30) reflecting the voyage of Adriaen Block up the Connecticut River.

tractive possibilities in the Connecticut Valley. The migration began in the summer of 1635, when a handful of Dorchester citizens settled at Windsor close to the Plymouth group. In November, sixty more men, women, and children, with their livestock, arrived at Windsor. Unfortunately they scarcely had prepared temporary shelter when an early and rigorous winter descended upon them. Many provisions sent by boat failed to arrive. In

mid-November the River had frozen over, and by the end of November provisions began to fail. A few, in desperation, fled by land back to Massachusetts and all but one of these managed, with the aid of friendly Indians, to reach their destination. Starvation faced the remainder of the new settlers, and as a last resort seventy men, women, and children went down to the mouth of the River to meet a provisions ship. Not finding this relief,

Adriaen Block's Restless *passes Hartford in 1614.*

they boarded another ship, the *Rebecca,* which temporarily was frozen in the river ice. Rain came, providentially freeing the ship, and the half-starved and frozen pioneers returned to Boston. Those few who stuck it out at Windsor suffered extremely. Only by hunting and timely aid from Indians did they survive the winter, but many of their cattle perished. Those who withstood the horrors of the 1635–36 winter had little to fear from the future.[8]

In the spring of 1636 Warham and the other settlers arrived. As a result of these moves, nearly one-half the Dorchester population had come to Connecticut, including a majority of the more influential landowners and leaders.[9]

The new settlers, displaying no regard whatever for the Plymouth title to the Windsor area, went ahead with settlement on the high ground west and above the Connecticut River. They trespassed to the extent of actually taking part of the land specifically purchased from the Indians by Plymouth, an action engendering much bitterness. In July 1635 Jonathan Brewster, resident agent of Plymouth, wrote to his employers that the Bay settlers were flocking in and were covetously eying the Plymouth land. He promised to do what

he could "to withstand them," as it seemed to him a poor reward for all of the trouble, expense, and dangers involved in Plymouth's pioneering. Indeed it was, but the fundamental fact remained that the Bay Colony possessed much greater resources of men and wealth, and almost inevitably would obtain control of the River settlements. Unfortunately a prolonged dispute ensued and finally, in 1637, Plymouth sold most of its land to the Dorchester group. The problem was legally settled, but ill will lingered for many years.[10]

In the meantime another of the River towns, Wethersfield, had been started. It is very possible that Oldham visited the site of future Wethersfield during his 1633 exploratory trip. In any event, he came with eight or nine companions to Pyquag (Indian name for Wethersfield) in the fall of 1634 and erected temporary houses to pass the winter. Highly restless and adventurous, Oldham does not seem to have tarried long at Pyquag. Others of a more stable nature followed from Watertown the next spring, including two ministers, Richard Denton and John Sherman, and Wethersfield became firmly established. Altogether about thirty Watertown families migrated in 1635–36, and they were soon joined by settlers from other places, including some directly from England. Whereas Windsor and Hartford were settled by large church groups coming as *units,* Wethersfield was founded by *individuals* whose official connection with Massachusetts was tenuous.[11]

The last and most famous of the migrations to the valley from the Bay Colony occurred in June 1636, when Hooker's company finally departed from Newtown. Here is Cotton Mather's classic account of their journey:

Accordingly in the month of *June,* 1636, they removed an hundred miles to the westward, with a purpose to settle upon the delightful banks of *Connecticut River:* and there were about an hundred persons in the first company that made this removal; who not being able to walk above ten miles a day, took up near a fortnight in the journey; having no pillows to take their nightly rest upon, but such as their father *Jacob* found in the way to *Padan-Aram.* Here Mr. *Hooker* was the chief instrument of beginning another colony . . .

The Hooker party brought, too, 160 head of cattle, as well as goats and swine. Mrs. Hooker was carried the entire way on a litter.[12]

The Newtown contingent did not come to a deserted area, since the Dutch remained; and they found also an advance party of Newtowners who had come the previous winter and undergone its terrible privations. These settlers were to be the "northsiders" in the future town of Hartford.[13]

One of the chief factors which had delayed Hooker's Newtown emigration was the uncertain matter of legal rights to settlement in Connecticut. Strictly speaking, all of the settlers in 1634 and 1635 had been squatters. The best existing legal title to Connecticut land was the Warwick Patent. On March 19, 1631/32, Robert, Earl of Warwick, transferred to certain gentlemen a large amount of land in New England, including what became Connecticut. This patent simply conveyed certain lands, but did not bestow any governmental powers or create a corporation. Three years later, in 1635, six of the grantees reached an agreement with John Winthrop, Jr., to establish a colony in Connecticut, of which Winthrop would be governor. William Fiennes, Viscount Say and Sele, Robert Greville, Lord Brooke, and Richard Saltonstall took leading parts in these negotiations. They provided generously for Winthrop by voting £2,000 plus men and ammunition to establish a

fort and houses at the mouth of the Connecticut River. Winthrop promptly embarked for Massachusetts, where he sought information about the seemingly illegal settlements already made in the land covered by the Warwick Patent. He stated bluntly that all in Connecticut or going there should put themselves under the Warwick grantees, and emphasized that this area lay outside Massachusetts' jurisdiction. To Hooker and others this constituted a major problem. From October 1635 to March 1636 numerous conferences took place in an effort to reach a satisfactory solution. It was to their mutual interest, since the grantees desired settlers and the colonizers badly needed a secure legal title. Finally an ingenious compromise was hammered out whereby Hooker and associates recognized as legal the claims of the Warwick grantees and acknowledged Winthrop as governor. In turn Winthrop and his fellow agents approved the proposed settlements. Since the agents lacked authority to permit formation of an independent government, both groups accepted the Massachusetts General Court as a sort of go-between.[14]

On March 3, 1635/36, the General Court issued a commission giving to eight men, already in Connecticut or about to go, wide authority to carry on judicial duties, issue decrees, and even wage war. They could call inhabitants of the towns together to act as a general court to carry out the authority granted. Here in simple form one finds a logical antecedent to Connecticut's Fundamen-

Hartford's first meeting house (built 1635).

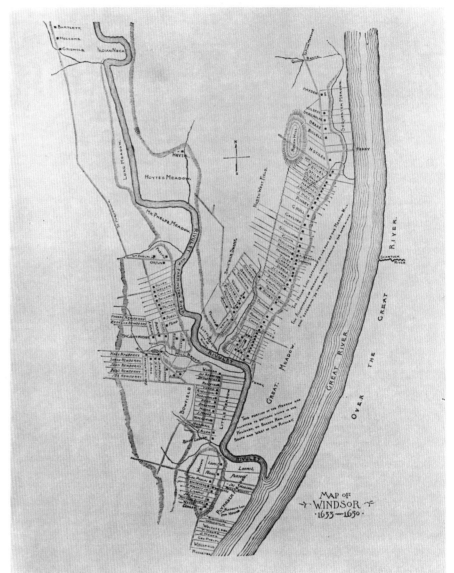

Map of Windsor, 1633–50.

tal Orders. Under this document five of the eight commissioners — Roger Ludlow, William Phelps, John Steel, William Westwood, and Andrew Ward — met in Newtown, issued a few orders, gave the oath to constables for the three towns, and approved the dismissal of seven Watertown men who promised to erect a church of their own in Wethersfield.[15]

Saybrook and Agawam Settled

As a result of the initial spurt of colonization in the 1630's, the roster of settlements upon the Connecticut was expanded to take in Saybrook and Springfield (Agawam). Saybrook differed from the other settlements in that it started principally as a fort. In November 1635 the younger Winthrop sent about twenty men to take possession of the River's mouth and to erect some houses. On November 24, 1635, the party tore down the Dutch arms at Kievit's Hoeck and began their own settlement. The next March the military engineer, Lion Gardiner, arrived to supervise construction of a fort and to take command of it. In April Winthrop himself finally arrived, although he did not stay long. Until 1644 Saybrook was considered a separate colony.[16]

Springfield was founded by William Pynchon, one of the eight men appointed by the Bay Colony to govern Connecticut. In 1636 Pynchon and a few others came in two shallops to Springfield, where they constructed a trading house, at

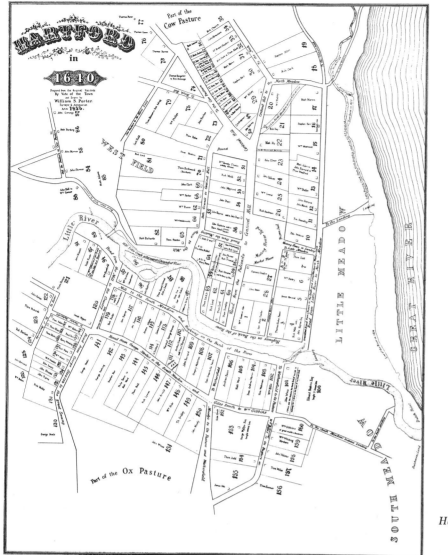

Hartford in 1640.

first on the west bank, later on the opposite side. For a few years Springfield was considered and considered itself a part of Connecticut, but in time serious differences arose which caused Springfield to throw in its lot with Massachusetts.[17]

The Natural Setting

IF one excludes from view the impressive symbols of modern civilization — superhighways, telephone and electric lines, power and gasoline stations, radio and TV towers, skyscrapers, automobiles, and so on — Connecticut, in its natural setting, today very closely resembles the picturesque land which so strongly attracted the English pioneers of the 1630's. Then, as now, it was an attractive land of hills, forests, rocks, ravines, and numerous lakes and rivers. Connecticut, without its vast western land claims, ranked among the mainland colonies as larger only than Delaware and Rhode Island. It contained about 5,000 square miles — not a large area even in an age of primitive transportation. When the boundaries finally were settled, the northern line, with Massachusetts, ran about 87 miles; the eastern, with Rhode Island, about 50; that on Long Island Sound, nearly 100; and the western, with New York, about 75.[18]

Within these tight limits the colonists discovered a remarkably varied terrain. Along the coast they saw a narrow, flat coastal plain. Access to the interior was easiest by the major river valleys —

the Thames in the east, the Connecticut in the central part, and the Housatonic in the west. Of these rivers the Connecticut was the largest, navigable for the greatest distance, and it led to the widest and most fertile valley — the central valley of Connecticut. Actually, below Middletown the River leaves the broad valley, which continues southwesterly toward New Haven. The deep, rich, alluvial soil of the central valley, ranging from fine loam to stiff clay, has afforded excellent crops through more than three hundred years of cultivation by white men. The first settlers displayed good judgment, for some of the very best valley land was found in the Hartford area. Travelers at the end of the colonial period commented upon the fertile and prosperous appearance of the central valley. This valley actually is only ten to twenty miles wide, and within it are found many hills, including some impressive traprock summits such as Mount Higby, Beseck Mountain, and the Hanging Hills of Meriden, which range up to about 1,000 feet in height.[19]

To complete the broad topographic picture, the colonists found along each side of Connecticut a long, low, north-south range of hills, known now as the Eastern and Western Highlands. These areas gradually rise as one goes northward, reaching about 1,300 feet in Union in northeastern Connecticut and 2,380 feet on Mount Frissell in Salisbury at the northwest corner. This loftiest area in the northwest is part of the Taconic range of mountains. While the highlands provided fine scenery, they afforded only rocky and thin soils, which rapidly became thinner from erosion caused by natural run-off plus cultivation.[20]

As in other colonies of eastern North America, Connecticut was clothed largely with magnificent virgin forest, broken occasionally by Indian clearings. The natural woods included ash, basswood, beech, birch, buttonwood, chestnut, elm, hickory, maple, oak, pepperidge, poplar, sassafras, sycamore, walnut, whitewood, wild cherry; and among the coniferous (soft wood) trees, balsam, cedar, hemlock, and pine. The oak, pine, and whitewood ranked especially high in economic value. From the tall whitewood trees, for example, the settlers made fine boards and clapboards for their houses. Many of the great forest areas were nearly clear of

underbrush and small trees, as the Indians often burned over the country to capture deer and other game.[21]

The fauna of Connecticut was quite varied. Deer, bear, moose, fox, raccoon, mink, otter, wildcat, and wolf abounded. To make it even more of a hunter's paradise, turkey, heron, partridge, quail, and pigeon throve in vast numbers. Of the predatory animals the wolf constituted the principal threat and was gradually exterminated as settlements grew.[22]

To add to its attractions, the country provided a great quantity of waterfowl and fish. Ducks, wild geese, broadbills, teal, sheldrakes, and wigeons crammed the rivers, lakes, and bays. On the shores one could find clams, lobsters, oysters, and shellfish in abundance. Most of the rivers teemed with fish; the Connecticut River, especially, was an angler's dream with its large variety, including excellent salmon.[23]

The rivers of Connecticut provided not only fish and vital transportation but also water power. Every important stream in Connecticut, thanks especially to glacial action, had its fall line within the colony, so that gristmills sprang up in all sections. For the later settlers the Housatonic and tributaries, such as the Naugatuck, offered an unusual number of excellent mill sites because of numerous waterfalls.[24]

In geological terms, Connecticut has a drowned coast, so that an irregular coastline with good harbors exists. New London offered the finest harbor, but many other good sites attracted the early settlers. In fact, for the small sailing craft of the seventeenth century, often under fifty tons, harbors which have no commercial importance today offered very satisfactory facilities.[25]

In July 1680 the colony, as part of a reply to queries from the English Committee for Trade and Foreign Plantations, included information about its harbors. Speaking of New London, they noted that "Ships of great burthen may com up to the town and lye secure in any winds." Amplifying this information later, they spoke of "New London or Pequot River, wher a ship of 500 tunn may go up to the Towne, and com so near the shore that they may toss a biskit ashoare: and vessels of about 30 tunn may pass up about 12 miles above

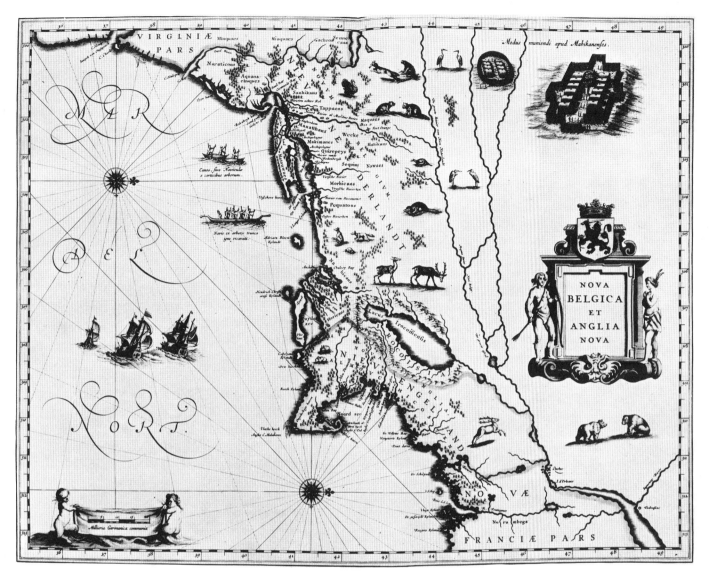

William Blaeu *map of New*
Netherlands and New England
(c. 1635).

Along the Connecticut River.

N. London, to or neer a town called Norwich." On the Connecticut River itself the entrance had only ten to twelve feet at high water, and vessels of sixty to eighty tons could navigate the sixty miles to Hartford, but were stopped by falls six miles farther up at Enfield. Ships up to three hundred tons used New Haven and Fairfield, while small vessels of thirty or forty tons could put in easily at Guilford, Milford, Norwalk, Stratford, and Stamford. Altogether, the seventeenth-century colonizers found a very favorable situation for making settlements upon Connecticut's shores and rivers and for carrying on trading and fishing from these ports.[26]

Geologic Change Affects Connecticut's Topography

THE irregular surface of Connecticut represents the results of hundreds of millions of years of geologic change. All of the land once was covered by great seas. Later, near the end of the Archeozoic era, perhaps more than one billion years ago, marine deposits were folded and formed lofty mountains. Plant life of simple form — algae — existed and has left fossil records in the shales and slates of late Archeozoic and early Proterozoic times. By the mid-Paleozoic era, perhaps 400,000,-000 years ago, as the land again rose, great earth-

Cathedral Pines in Cornwall. "White, yellow and pitch pine . . . grew plenteously in many places."

quakes shook all of New England. Most of the Connecticut rocks date from the Paleozoic era, though the superficial surface features which catch the eye reflect changes of the later Mesozoic and Cenozoic eras. In late Paleozoic times gigantic snow- and ice-covered peaks of truly Alpine proportions towered over the landscape, and from the huge peaks avalanches frequently fell, shattering the silence. These lofty mountains covered the eastern and western portions of Connecticut. When the Mesozoic era, or Age of Reptiles, arrived (about 200,000,000 years ago) mountain growth ceased and the mountains began to be worn down slowly. Debris from the mountains was carried down to the flatter central area. By the end of the period the great mountains had disappeared and the surface resembled a rolling peneplain covered by sluggish, meandering streams. Ponds and lakes slowly appeared, and the Triassic sandstones took shape under the combined interaction of river, lake, and wind-blown deposits. The great central lowland was mostly shaped during the Triassic period of the mid-Mesozoic Age.[27]

As the Cenozoic era, or Age of Mammals (the past 60,000,000 years or so) commenced, Connecticut was affected by the Tertiary uplift. In this movement the land surface was elevated in the form of a fairly even incline, of which the highest portion was found in the northwestern corner. This action gave a new lease on life to the rivers, which began a fresh cycle of erosion, cutting into the hard crystalline rocks and creating deeper entrenched meanders. The less resistant sandstones of central Connecticut were worn down most rapidly. River terraces developed, and modern Hartford is located upon one.[28]

One last natural agent remained to complete the etching out of Connecticut's topography — glaciation. The climate grew bitterly cold as great sheets of ice hundreds of feet thick moved southward and covered all of Connecticut, probably including the highest summits. Several times this great sea of ice moved over the land. The enormous weight of the ice carried along soil and stones and bedrock. Probably much of Connecticut's topsoil was deposited in Long Island Sound, but quantities of soil and boulders from Massachusetts, and even from Vermont and New Hampshire, in turn were left here. After thousands of years the climate gradually warmed up and the ice sheet slowly melted. Powerful as the glaciers were, they exerted only secondary effects upon our topography. The main valleys and highlands far predate the glaciers. The glaciers moved soil haphazardly about, smoothed contours of hills, and scratched, gouged, and polished the rocks, forming striae. In Connecticut the glacier seems to have become stagnant, and the decaying mass of ice slowly melted. As it dissolved, loose material, known as glacial till or drift, was deposited in small hills or drumlins, very common in northeastern Connecticut townships such as Woodstock, Pomfret, Putnam, Ashford, and Mansfield. Small serpentine ridges, clay beds, and sand plains

Housatonic River gorge.

were also created by slowly melting glaciers. In some cases the courses of rivers were radically changed by large dams of glacial debris. The Farmington River, for instance, which once had flowed into the Sound at New Haven, was forced to cut a new route northward through an old gap at Tariffville, and then eastward to the Connecticut River at Windsor. The glacial movements, by disrupting drainage patterns, also helped create many of the more than 1,000 lakes and 400 swamps in Connecticut. The glacier, for example, scoured out a rock basin 108 feet deep — whose bottom is 82 feet below sea level — now called Lake Saltonstall. Many of the small ponds, such as Job Pond near Portland, have their origin in kettle holes — depressions formed as the ice melted. The glacial age scarred Connecticut superficially and carried away much fine topsoil, but it enriched the land scenically and economically with hundreds of lovely lakes and ponds, beautiful waterfalls, undulating ridges and elongated drumlins, picturesque boulders, sand plains, and fine harbors.[29]

When one considers the rocks of Connecticut as a whole, he notes that the Western Highlands, mostly Paleozoic, are composed primarily of various types of gneiss — a metamorphic rock formed by heavy pressure, heat, and water into a more compact crystalline condition. Some areas of granite and marble exist also. The highest areas of Connecticut, especially around Bear Mountain, are made up of Salisbury schist — another very hard, metamorphic rock. Across the central valley one runs primarily into later sedimentary Triassic rocks, mostly softer sandstones; but igneous lava traprock areas, such as the Hanging Hills of Meriden and Mount Higby, are interspersed. Farther east one again enters a land predominantly of gneiss, with small areas of schist at Bolton and the Moosup-East Killingly region and a larger area in Ashford, Willington, Stafford, and Union. There is no question that Connecticut offers an interesting variety of rocks and a diversified landscape.[30]

Connecticut Indians

THE Indians contributed much to Connecticut's history and lore, including the name "Connecticut" itself. In the Algonkin language *Quinnetukut*

and variants such as *Quinetucquet, Quenticutt,* and *Quaneh-ta-cut* meant "on the long tidal-river," a fitting name for the region. "Connecticut" represents the English colonists' written approximation of the sound of the Indian name.[31]

Within the present boundaries of Connecticut lived one of the densest concentrations of Indians in North America — though scanty in comparison even with the white population at the end of the colonial period. Perhaps as many as 6,000 or 7,000 Indians inhabited Connecticut in the 1630's, though any figure given can be only a rough estimate. The Indians clustered the thickest along the coastal areas, where fishing provided an easier and more certain subsistence than did hunting; but in such locations the population was surprisingly thin. The Quinnipiacs, who held the choice coastal area from modern Milford to Madison, including New Haven, in 1638 informed Davenport that they had 47 men in all — which meant perhaps 250 persons in the entire tribe. The Pequots, fiercest of the Connecticut Indians, could muster only about 500 to 600 warriors. Few as the Indians were, however, they comprised a formidable obstacle to the handful of English pioneers in the 1630's.[32]

All of the Connecticut Indians belonged to the loose Algonkin confederation. The Algonkin tribes possessed no unity, but quarreled and fought viciously with one another, which tendency gave the whites a splendid opportunity, not neglected, to play one tribe against another. Apparently their languages contained enough basic similarities so that the members of different tribes could understand each other. J. Hammond Trumbull claimed that the following distinct Algonkin dialects were spoken in Connecticut and bordering areas: *1*] Pequot-Mohegan; *2*] Niantic and Narraganset (in Rhode Island also); *3*] Nipmuck (into Massachusetts); and *4*] Quinipi (Quinnipiac).[33]

Connecticut Indians lived largely by hunting and fishing. Armed with bow and arrow, the Indian braves ranged the great forests in search of deer, moose, bear, raccoon, rabbits, and squirrels. In addition they sought, for furs only, wolves, foxes, and wildcats. The woods teemed with pigeon, partridge, quail, and turkey, while the rivers and ponds provided ducks, geese, and cranes in

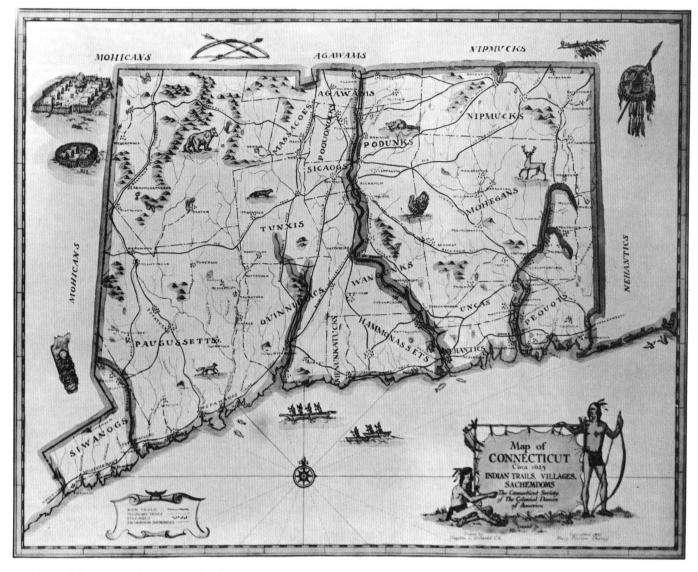

Map of Indian trails, villages, and tribes (c. 1625).

abundance. The Indians trapped beaver and otter, chiefly for their warm skins. They usually hunted alone, but occasionally a large number banded together for a grand hunt, in which huge quantities of game would be taken.[34]

In contrast to the twentieth century, when angling for relatively scarce fish is often a difficult sport, the Indians of the seventeenth century found fish everywhere and in vast quantities. The Indians used varied methods of catching their fish — rude hooks, nets, spears, basketry traps, pounds, and weirs. For some of the larger fish, such as sturgeon, they employed nets made of wild hemp. So numerous were the fish that even the

small children would wade into shallow streams and spear them with crude sticks. As might be expected, the Indians employed canoes in much of their fishing.[35]

The Connecticut Indians, in common with others, displayed no great love for agriculture, but they did make some clearings and engage in it upon a limited scale. Using crude sticks or hoes of wood, bone, or stone for digging, they raised maize, pumpkin, squash, beans, sweet potatoes, and tobacco. Corn ranked as the principal food and was eaten boiled on the ear, roasted, or even popped. Much corn was made into cornmeal and hominy. For winter's food they stored both dried

32

corn and fish in large pits. When the tilled land around the village became depleted the Indians simply moved their village to a new site.[36]

Sixteen Indian Tribes

THE fiercest of the sixteen local tribes were the Pequots, whose name, according to Roger Williams, meant "destroyers of men." Having migrated not long before from the Hudson River region, they pushed southward, cutting the Nehantics (Niantics) in two, and settled along the coast in the Groton-Stonington-Mystic area. Because of their location and belligerent disposition,

against them. The Podunks lived along the Connecticut from Warehouse Point to Hockanum, Manchester, Glastonbury, Vernon, and Bolton, and they had an important summer village at South Windsor.[39]

Farther south lived the Mohegans, a tribe of the same stock as the Pequots. Their separate identity became established by the 1630's, when the bitter Uncas, spurned as leader of the Pequots, split the tribe and moved away to the northwest with his followers. Uncas was a confirmed troublemaker who allied himself with the colonists but kept both whites and Indians constantly in turmoil until his death about 1683. The Mohegans developed into

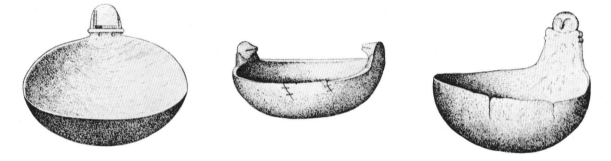

Mohegan and Niantic wooden bowls.

a serious collision with the whites could be expected. Luckily the three River towns were located far enough away from the Pequots so that settlement proceeded there without immediate interruption.[37]

Other tribes in eastern Connecticut included the Western Nehantics (Niantics), centered about Lyme and Waterford, and the Nipmucks, who spread down from central Massachusetts into Union, Woodstock, Thompson, Putnam, Somers, Stafford, and parts of adjoining towns to the south. Apparently the Nipmucks, rather peaceable by nature, were often dominated by the tribes around them.[38]

Moving into central Connecticut one met the Podunk tribe, whose village Block visited in 1614. Later, in 1631, it was Wahginnacut, a Podunk chief, who paid a visit to Plymouth and Boston and described in glowing terms the beautiful Connecticut Valley and its trading opportunities. The Podunk desire for English settlers stemmed from hatred of the Pequots and desire for protection

a major power among the Indians of southern New England.[40]

At Hartford the earliest settlers found the local Saukiogs, ruled by Sequassen. In 1636 he sold to the English what later became Hartford and West Hartford. Sequassen engaged in fierce battles with the Pequots and Mohegans and suffered severe defeats. As a result, the Saukiogs remained quite friendly with the colonists and lived near Hartford until about 1730. Sequassen himself became infuriated by the English co-operation with Uncas and supposedly hired an assassin at Waranoco (Westfield, Massachusetts) to slay Governor John Haynes, Governor Edward Hopkins, and William Whiting. He planned to blame it all upon Uncas and the Mohegans. In any event, the plot failed, Sequassen fled, and the Mohegans brought him back to Hartford; but nothing could be proved, so Sequassen soon was freed. From what is known of Uncas' treacherous nature, he may very well have been behind the entire plot.[41]

South of the Podunks and Saukiogs lived the

Wangunks. In the 1630's this tribe's sachem, Sequin, father of Sequassen, lived at Pyquag (Wethersfield). The Wangunks and the Dutch enjoyed trading together in the years after Block's voyage. Later the Wangunks moved their government seat to Middletown. Their sway extended from Wethersfield and Middletown as far east as

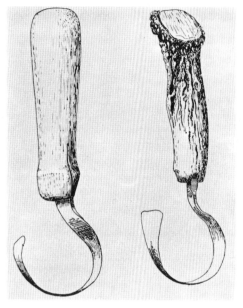

Mohegan knives.

East Hampton, south to Haddam, and west to Berlin and Meriden.⁴²

In the central portion of Connecticut, besides the Podunks and Saukiogs, there lived the Poquonocks around Windsor, Bloomfield, and East Granby, and the Tunxis tribe, centered in the Farmington-New Britain-Berlin area. Throughout the colonial period the Tunxis tribe always maintained friendly relations with the whites and made a large land cession in 1640.⁴³

Farther north dwelled the Agawams, who spilled over from Massachusetts into Suffield, Hartland, Enfield, and Granby. Near them were found the Massacoes, centered at Weatogue and covering much of present Canton, Simsbury, and parts of Granby, East Granby, and Barkhamsted.⁴⁴

Along the Sound, running west from the Connecticut River, were located at least five distinct tribes: 1] the Hammonassets, around Saybrook and Clinton; 2] the Menunketucks, in Guilford

and Madison; 3] the Quinnipiacs, in the New Haven area; 4] the Paugussetts, in the Bridgeport-Stratford-Waterbury region; and 5] the Siwanogs, primarily a New York tribe, who extended into the Greenwich-Stamford coastal section and inland to New Canaan, Wilton, and Ridgefield. Not one of these five tribes seems to have been powerful, nor did any cause the white settlers serious trouble.⁴⁵

In the seventeenth century most of western and northwestern Connecticut was uninhabited except by occasional fierce Mohawk hunting parties from New York, who effectively kept out other Indians. Only much later, when the Mohawks had learned the power of the English settlers, did they cease attacks upon the Connecticut Indians and permit a westward movement by them. Gradually the remnants of several tribes pushed westward to New Milford and Kent and organized a new tribe called the Scatacooks. For most of the first century of the colonization period, however, the future Litchfield County remained uninhabited.⁴⁶

The Connecticut Indians fell not only under the political shadow of the Mohawks and the Iroquois confederacy in general but also under their cultural influence. The architecture, basketry, ceramics, costumes, decorative designs, embroidery, and implements all show the strong impact of Iroquois models.⁴⁷

Except for the Pequots, the Indians of Connecticut generally co-operated with the white settlers, sold land to them, and lived peacefully close to them. A partial explanation of this behavior lay in their great fear of the Mohawks to the west, which made the Connecticut Indians extremely anxious to have English friendship — their only hope for security.⁴⁸

The Pequots Take to the Warpath

THE hostility of the powerful Pequots threatened the very life of the infant River colony before it was even firmly established. The Dutch earlier thought that they had obtained a solid agreement with the Pequots for trade which should be open to all Indians. Quarrels developed, however, and some Indians engaged in trade with the Dutch were slain by the Pequots. The irate Dutch, in attempting to punish the Pequots, succeeded accidentally in killing Wopigwooit, Pequot chieftain. Immediately the Pequots wanted revenge upon any whites available. In 1633 a small band of English traders, under Captain John Stone of Virginia, who had stopped to trade and hunt around the mouth of the Connecticut, was wiped out by the Pequots in a violent encounter. After the bloody affray the Pequots became uneasy over their situation. They feared their traditional enemies, the Narragansets, as well as possible English retaliation, and they still desired future trade with the English. The next year, therefore, they sent no less than two sets of peace emissaries to Boston bearing generous presents and large promises. Finally an agreement was achieved under which the Pequots promised to deliver up those guilty of the slaughter of Stone's party and to allow the English to make settlements in Connecticut. In return, the English promised to carry on a friendly trade with the Pequots. Governor Winthrop noted that the agreement was put in writing and "the two ambassadors set to their marks — one a bow with an arrow in it, and the other a hand."[49]

After a peaceful year in 1635 the Pequots struck again in 1636. The colorful John Oldham, who had been in and out of the good graces of Plymouth and Bay Colony rulers, in 1636 went on a trading expedition to Long Island Sound. While he was close to Block Island, Indians swarmed over his boat and brutally murdered him. John Gallop, cruising in the area, noted with alarm that the deck of Oldham's vessel was full of Indians. Boldly attacking them, Gallop and his four assistants routed the Indians, boarded the boat, and found Oldham's mangled body. The slaying caused a sensation in Boston, and loud cries for revenge went up.[50]

After thorough investigation it was established that Block Island Indians had perpetrated the deed, but the Pequots had given the murderers refuge. As a result, a special expedition of ninety men under Captain John Endecott was dispatched to Block Island, where they failed to capture any Indians but destroyed much property. They proceeded next to the fort at Saybrook, where Lion Gardiner begged them not to attack the Pequots. As he bluntly explained: "you come hith[e]r to

raise thes wasps about my eares, and then you will take wing and flee away." Unconvinced, the expedition pressed on, failed to engage the Pequots in a battle, and again resorted to wholesale destruction of canoes, crops, and wigwams. This unwise pillaging won the undying hatred of the Pequots and paved the way for a serious war.[51]

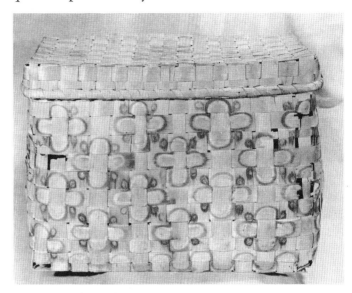

Mohegan decorated basket.

The Pequots apparently hoped to exterminate all of the colonists in Connecticut, and they instituted an almost continuous siege of the English Saybrook fort. A small white column which attempted to sally forth and burn a nearby marsh was nearly taken and barely regained the fort after the loss of several men. Sometimes the Indians, staying just out of range, "would imitate the dying Groans and Invocations of the poor Captive English." Amidst the grave dangers surrounding Saybrook, Lion Gardiner's son, David, was born on April 29, 1636 — the first recorded birth of a white child in Connecticut.[52]

The Pequot threat was greatly enhanced by their plans for a strong alliance with the Narragansets. The Bay authorities informed Roger Williams of this ominous development and asked his aid in preventing it. Williams, who had been banished by the Bay authorities, nevertheless unhesitatingly went alone in a canoe through stormy seas to the Narraganset Indians, where he spent three days in delicate and dangerous negotiations. A rival delegation was on hand:

. . . the bloody Pequod ambassadors, whose hands and arms, methought, wreaked with the blood of my countrymen, murdered and massacred by them on Connecticut river, and from whom I could not but nightly look for their bloody knives at my own throat also.

Certainly Williams, on this occasion, displayed superb courage, and may well have decisively influenced the Narragansets not to conclude a Pequot alliance.[53]

The Oldham murder, the close siege of Saybrook, and the wooing of the Narragansets had

Among those who gazed helplessly at the mocking Indians was the chaplain, John Higginson. Realizing the critical nature of the Indian threat, he penned a lengthy letter to John Winthrop in which he urged strong action against the Pequots.[55]

River Towns Accept Pequot Challenge

ON May 1, 1637, the General Court at Hartford decided that the time had come for strong action

Massacre at Wethersfield, Connecticut, April 23, 1637. Drawing by Jared B. Standish.

clearly presented ample evidence of the implacable hostility of the Pequots. Soon they provided a fourth and decisive illustration. In April 1637 a large party of Pequots paddled their canoes up the Connecticut to an observation point near Wethersfield. They observed a small party working in the adjacent meadows along the River, completely unaware of the large raiding party. The Indians struck suddenly; a short and violent struggle followed; at least six men and three women were slain and two young women were carried away. The Pequots vanished as rapidly as they had come. Passing the Saybrook fort, they raised poles upon which they had stretched the victims' clothes as sails.[54]

and it ordered an offensive war against the Pequots. Ninety men were to be raised, of which Hartford should contribute forty-two, Windsor thirty, and Wethersfield eighteen. They appointed Captain John Mason to command the expedition. Thoughtfully they provided one hogshead of good beer and, if there were only "3 or 4 gallons of stronge water," then they would add "2 gallons of sacke." Each town was assigned its quota of corn, butter, salt, beans, pork, and so on. Every soldier was expected to carry one pound of powder, four pounds of shot, and twenty bullets. On June 2, thirty additional men were ordered out, and on June 26, ten more.[56]

At this juncture there came an embarrassing of-

36

fer of help — from Uncas, chief of the Mohegans. After his withdrawal from his native Pequots he had been eagerly awaiting an opportunity to overthrow Sassacus, Pequot chieftain. A man of outstanding physique and grandiose ambitions, Uncas hoped not only to regain control of the Pequots but also later to oust Miantonomo, chief of the Narragansets. Co-operation with the English appeared to offer the best chance of achieving these ends, so he offered Mason himself and eighty Mohegan warriors. Despite strong advice to reject the offer, Mason accepted it.[57]

As might be expected, it was an uneasy alliance. About May 15 the expedition left Hartford. The two groups proceeded slowly downstream, but the Indians chafed at the delays when the white boats stuck on shallow spots. Finally Uncas asked permission for his warriors to go ahead on foot to Saybrook, and despite misgivings, permission was granted. The Indians arrived there first and were received skeptically by Gardiner, who determined to test their fidelity. He reported that six Pequots had passed in canoes the previous night. ". . . you say you will help Maior Mason but I will first see it, therfore send you now 20 men . . . ," he ordered Uncas. Gardiner continued: ". . . fetch them [the Pequots] now dead or aliue and then you shall goe with Maior Mason els not." The Mohegans set out in pursuit and, according to Gardiner, killed four Pequots and brought in one captive. Captain Underhill of the garrison carried word of their reassuring performance upriver to Mason's party.[58]

Upon his arrival Underhill discovered that Mason's party had been engaged in agonizing discussion as to whether the Indians could be trusted. At that very moment Samuel Stone, the chaplain, was praying that the Mohegans could be trusted. Immediately afterward Underhill delivered his good news.[59]

Upon arrival at Saybrook an informal council of war was held. The two Wethersfield girls had been rescued by the Dutch and reported that the Pequots were well armed and were keeping a sharp lookout for the colonists. Mason detached twenty of the least fit of his men and sent them home. They were replaced by nineteen Massachusetts men under Captain Underhill from the garrison. In the meantime Hooker had written Governor Winthrop that the expedition was under way, although he doubted that the River towns could muster sufficient strength. He closed with the urgent plea: "I hope you see a necessity to hasten execution, and not to do this work of the Lords revenge slackly."[60]

Captain Mason has described the factors which received primary consideration in the Saybrook discussions: 1] the continuous watch kept upon the River by the Pequots; 2] their superior numbers and guns; 3] if a landing were tried on the Mystic River, the only suitable spot nearer than Narragansett Bay, the Pequots "might much impede our Landing, and possibly dishearten our Men"; 4] "By Narragansett we should come upon their Backs, and possibly might surprize them unawares, at worst we should be on firm Land as well as they." Despite the strategic advantages to the approach from Narragansett Bay, the men at first refused. They knew their orders to attack directly and realized too that the new plan was highly dangerous. It required friendly co-operation from Miantonomo and his Narragansets, and the utmost secrecy, to stand any chance of success. Again the chaplain was asked to seek divine guidance and he spent a night alone in prayer. The next morning Stone told Mason that he felt certain that divine approval for the new plan was manifested. The men trusted Stone implicitly and speedy agreement was reached.[61]

The little fleet sailed slowly past the entrance to the Pequot harbor where the Pequots awaited their landing expectantly and confidently. The English boats continued onward, however, amidst the insults of the Indians, who concluded that the white men were afraid to land. The Pequots, in a mood of celebration, began making plans for further attacks upon the River settlements.[62]

Upon reaching Narraganset country, Mason and his men found a warm welcome. Miantonomo, while blessing their venture, warned grimly of the ferocity of the Pequots. The next day the little expedition marched twenty miles to the Nehantic fort whose Indians behaved suspiciously and refused admission to the fort. Seeing this, Mason gave strict orders that a guard be placed around the fort and that no Indian be allowed to enter or leave, in order to prevent a leakage of information to the Pequots. The entire force camped there, and not a single Nehantic tried to stir from the fort.[63]

The next morning a pleasant surprise greeted Mason. A band of Narragansets appeared, eager to join in the march against the Pequots and full of boasts as to their destructive prowess. The march resumed on a very hot day. When the army approached the Pequot River, the enthusiasm of the Narragansets dropped off remarkably and they began to fall behind. Learning that the Pequots had two forts, Mason decided to attack the nearer one. His men pitched camp and silently passed a clear moonlit night. In the distance the guards could hear the Pequots singing "until Midnight, with great Insulting and Rejoycing." After a short rest the men were roused and the little army marched about two miles. Mason then called for some of the Indians to come up and asked where the fort was. *"On the Top of that Hill,"* they replied. He inquired as to where the other Indians were. *"Behind, exceedingly affraid."* Mason ordered them not to flee but to watch and see whether or not the English fought.[64]

The men were assembled and then divided into two groups. Underhill and his men were to enter one gate; Mason led his detachment toward the other one. The Pequot fort at Mystic was enclosed by a wall of logs standing on end and inside, grouped upon each side of a middle lane, were many huts with roofs of straw mats. The two narrow entrances to the fort were blocked by brush and branches.[65]

Not a sound was heard from the fort as Mason and his men crept toward the northeast entrance. As they got within about five yards, a dog barked, and an Indian cried *"Owanux,"* meaning *"Englishmen."* Quickly they rushed the main entrance and Mason, surging in over the brush pile, called to his men to follow. Lieutenant Robert Seely pulled the brush aside and the others entered.[66]

Mason saw no Indians and ran into a wigwam. Immediately he was surrounded by the occupants. At the crucial moment one of the soldiers, probably William Heydon, entered the wigwam and disconcerted the Indians enough so that Mason escaped. Reorganizing his efforts, Mason led a march down the main lane. As the Indians fled

they perceived that Underhill's men were advancing from the other end. Wild, disorganized fighting followed as the Indians scattered and dodged about. A few tried to escape over the wall, but were driven back by Mason's guard outside. Although the Indians were dazed, they still outnumbered Mason's force. Snatching a firebrand from a wigwam, Mason tossed it into the roof mat. It caught and a stiff wind quickly spread the flames throughout the fort. Mason and his men escaped and drew the net outside tighter as the holocaust quickly consumed the fort and most of its inhabitants. Nearly all of those who managed to get outside, including women and children, were slain either by the whites or by their Indian allies. Within an hour the fierce fire had subsided. The doughty Mason summed up the astonishing turn of events:

They were taken in their own Snare, and we through Mercy escaped. And thus in *little more than one Hour's space* was their impregnable *Fort* with themselves utterly Destroyed, to the Number of *six* or *seven Hundred,* as some of themselves confessed. There were only *seven* taken *Captive* & about *seven escaped.*

In the affair Mason saw the workings of a benign Providence: "Thus did the LORD judge among the Heathen, filling the Place with dead Bodies!" The modern reader is more likely to react to this coldblooded slaughter of the Indians with chilled horror.[67]

There was little time, however, to celebrate the victory, as their provisions and ammunition were nearly exhausted and chieftain Sassacus and his warriors of the other fort were aroused and advancing. The Narragansets had deserted, but Uncas and his Mohegans stayed. About twenty fit men were required to carry and attend a few badly wounded soldiers, which left Mason only about forty white effectives. Their boats were at an unknown distance, and time of arrival was uncertain.[68]

While they were considering the critical situation they suddenly saw in the distance their vessels entering the harbor. Joy, however, immediately changed to alarm as the Pequots, at least three hundred strong, approached. Mason boldly led a small squadron of men against them to test their disposition. The Pequots backed off. En-

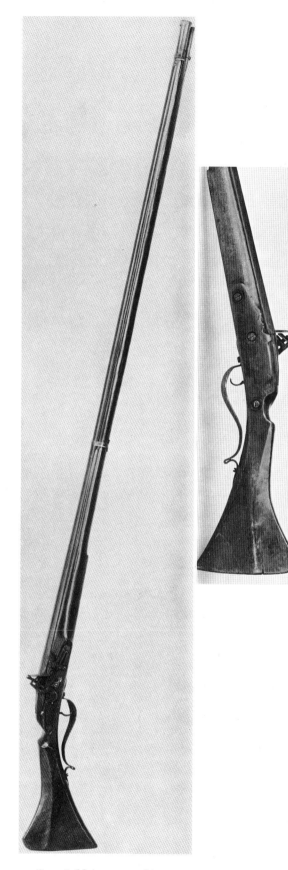

couraged, Mason's force then began the march to their boats. Meanwhile the Pequots discovered that their fort was leveled and, shouting imprecations, rushed after the English. The rear guard fired upon them and checked their advance. The Indians continued a worrisome harassing action until Mason's men reached a point two miles from the harbor, when the Indians departed. Marching on to the landing, Mason greeted Captain Daniel Patrick, who had brought forty men from Massachusetts. The first and decisive phase of the Pequot War had ended.[69]

Since there was not space enough on the boats for all of his force, Mason, with twenty men, marched back along the shore and reached the Connecticut River at sunset, to be greeted by a salute of guns from Saybrook Fort. The next day his forces were reunited at Saybrook and feted by Gardiner.[70]

The Pequots Meet Their Doom

THE surviving Pequots meanwhile turned against Sassacus and blamed him for their terrible defeat. Some even wished to kill the chief, but cooler heads prevailed. Three courses were considered: 1] an attack of revenge against the Narragansets; 2] the same against the English; or 3] flight westward. Sassacus preferred to fight. Those in favor of fleeing prevailed, and the survivors — men, women, and children — began a panicky trek westward toward the Hudson.[71]

Mason's forces returned home and were acclaimed. A fortnight later news arrived that several Massachusetts ships had brought 120 men, under Captain Israel Stoughton, for an offensive against the Pequots. The General Court, meeting at Hartford on June 26, 1637, voted that John Haynes and Roger Ludlow consult at Mystic Harbor with the Massachusetts leaders about any further offensive. A quick agreement was concluded there to pursue the Pequots by a joint land and water expedition.[72]

In the meantime the Pequots had traveled very slowly because of their children and the necessity of obtaining food by hunting and digging for clams. The pursuing forces gained rapidly. A captured Pequot serving as a scout reported that

One of oldest guns used in Connecticut. Made in Scotland (c. 1600–20) (owned by Ben F. Hubbell).

his tribesmen were close at hand and frightened. The pursuers stepped up their pace until they reached a hilltop from which they could see the Pequots on the farther side of a swamp in Fairfield. Seeing the whites descending the hill, the Indians took cover in the swamp.[73]

At this point a council of war was called and various courses of action were proposed. While some preferred to surround the swamp and push into it, this would inevitably cause the death of many women and children. Thomas Stanton, who knew the Indian language, volunteered to enter the swamp and parley with the Pequots. Many thought it too dangerous a mission, but he insisted upon going. His companions waited anxiously, fearing the worst. An hour or so later, as it was growing dark, he came out of the swamp leading two hundred Pequots — old men, women, and children.[74]

During the night Mason and Patrick moved their men so as to surround the Indian warriors as effectively as possible. About half an hour before dawn the Indians, with loud shouts and shrieks, attempted several times to break through Patrick's men, but were repulsed each time. Mason, in alarm, moved his men toward Patrick's and encountered the Pequots. The next Indian attack rolled back against Patrick's side and this time about 60 or 70 knifed their way through and escaped. All of the remainder, except for a few killed, were captured, which added 180 to the group of prisoners. The fleeing remnant found no refuge and the heads of many were sent to Hartford and Windsor by other Indians. As a special token of friendship to the colonists, the Mohawks forwarded to them the head of Sassacus.[75]

In desperation the few surviving Pequots offered to become subjects of the whites if their lives were spared. They were called to Hartford, together with Uncas and Miantonomo. Inquiry revealed that 180 to 200 Pequots still lived. Eighty were allotted to Uncas, the same number to Miantonomo, and twenty to Ninigret, a Nehantic chief. The Pequots promised to renounce forever their name and their country. Unfortunately some of them broke the agreement and settled in their old haunts. For the third time Mason set out to fight the Pequots. This time, however, there was no real

fighting, as the Pequots clearly lacked the heart for it. They no longer possessed either the numbers or the spirit to challenge the colonists. Mason, in characteristic phraseology and pleading a religious justification, closed his history of the war: *"Thus the LORD was pleased to smite our Enemies in the hinder Parts, and to give us their Land for an Inheritance."*[76]

The defeat and decimation of the Pequots ended the major Indian threat to Connecticut's orderly expansion. Had the Pequots struck more quickly and effectively, it is possible that all settlements on the River might have been destroyed or abandoned. Connecticut possessed its first military hero in resolute Captain John Mason, who provided highly intelligent as well as daring field leadership. Never again would Connecticut families know such great terror from the Indians.

Evolving a Framework of Government

CONNECTICUT's rudimentary government, providing for rule by eight men, lasted only about one year. This group, called "the magistrates," consisted of Roger Ludlow, William Phelps, William Pynchon, Henry Smith, John Steel, William Swaine, Andrew Ward, and William Westwood. They did not attempt to select a governor, since John Winthrop, Jr., had been acknowledged as head of the territory.[77]

Interestingly enough, the founding fathers of Connecticut quickly decided to drop the town names transplanted from Massachusetts. Newtown was changed to Hartford, apparently derived from Hertford, the home town in England of Samuel Stone, lecturer in Hooker's church. Watertown became Wethersfield, the name of a town in Essex County, England, undoubtedly very familiar to some of the settlers from that area. Finally, Dorchester assumed the name of Windsor, after the town on the Thames near London, where a royal palace was located.[78]

On May 1, 1637, as a method of providing wider representation in the time of the Pequot crisis, the General Court was convened for the first time. Under the new scheme the people of the towns met to elect representatives or "committees" who would join with the magistrates in a "General

Court" at Hartford. This body, in its epochal session on May 1, consisted of six magistrates and nine "committees," or representatives. Hooker claims that after the local elections the representatives met in Hartford and, by some unknown method, chose the magistrates. This implied that it would be possible for the elected representatives to change the personnel of the magistrates.[79]

In 1637 and 1638 the three towns co-operated under this simple form of government. They dealt with such matters as terminating the Pequot War and paying off the soldiers. Every "common souldier" was to receive 1s. 3d. per day, "the Sergants 20d, pr day, the Leiftenant 20s. pr weeke, the Captn 40s. pr weeke." A sum of £620 to meet Pequot War expenses was ordered raised from the three towns and Springfield, on a quota basis, payable in money, wampum, or in good beaver.[80]

Even in the simple life of the infant towns some measure of economic regulation was found essential. A shortage of Indian corn threatened early in 1638. The General Court felt that if each man were free to deal with the Indians, in the existing seller's market the Indians would greatly elevate prices. To prevent this, private trading was strictly forbidden under penalty of five shillings per bushel thus bought. At the next session, on March 8, 1637/38, William Pynchon of Springfield was given a monopoly of such purchases on condition that he deliver adequate supplies to Hartford at fixed prices. Likewise, the beaver trade was limited to a few responsible persons — William Pynchon of Springfield, Roger Ludlow and George Hull of Windsor, William Whiting and Thomas Staunton of Hartford, and George Hubbard and Richard Lawes of Wethersfield. All interlopers risked a penalty of five shillings per pound of beaver traded.[81]

The bitter Pequot War impressed Connecticut's leaders with the necessity for better military preparedness. As a result, in March 1637/38 the General Court made Captain Mason "publique military officer of the plantačons of Conecticot" with an annual salary of forty pounds. All able-bodied males above sixteen, with a few exceptions, were ordered to bear arms and receive ten days of military training annually. Also, a powder magazine was ordered set up at each of the four towns.[82]

The steady growth of the towns and the increasing complexity of their common problems by 1638 led to a desire for a more definite and formal statement of fundamental law. The need, also, for some kind of loose union with Massachusetts Bay and Plymouth was realized, though this required longer to achieve.[83]

On May 31, 1638, Hooker delivered a memorable sermon of which, fortunately, brief notes were preserved by an auditor. The heart of the sermon is found in these words:

1] That the choice of public magistrates belongs unto the people, by God's own allowance.

2] The privilege of election, which belongs to the people, therefore must not be exercised according to their humors, but according to the blessed will and law of God.

3] They who have power to appoint officers and magistrates, it is in their power, also, to set the bounds and limitations of the power and place unto which they call them.

Hooker supported his doctrine by asserting that the foundation of authority lay in "the free consent of the people," and that given a free choice, the people would be more disposed to give willing and loyal obedience to their rulers.[84]

There can be no doubt that Hooker's sermon strongly influenced those who later that year labored over the new frame of government. No information is available as to who worked upon it, when, and what procedures were employed. The conciseness, brevity, and clear organization of the final document bear the hallmarks of a skilled lawyer, which indicates strongly that the chief author was the only trained lawyer in the colony — Roger Ludlow of Windsor, educated at Balliol College, Oxford, and at the Inner Temple, London. The circumstances of adoption are uncertain, as authorities differ. Trumbull declares that all the free planters met at Hartford on January 14, 1638/39, deliberated, and adopted the Fundamental Orders. Dutcher, citing the *Colonial Records* for December 1, 1645 — ". . . the generall Orders formerly made by this Court . . ." — concludes they were adopted by the General Court. Whether a special meeting of freemen or an unrecorded meeting of the General Court adopted them, or some other method was employed, still remains a mystery. In any event, it is highly probable that a small committee, dominated by Ludlow, actually hammered out the document.[85]

The Fundamental Orders

THE Fundamental Orders consisted of a preamble and eleven "orders." The preamble states that the towns of Windsor, Hartford, and Wethersfield join together so that "there should be an Orderly and decent Gouerment established according to God to Order and dispose of the affayres of the people." This civil covenant corresponded to the religious covenant adopted by individual churches.[86]

The frame of government called for a General Court to meet in April and September. At the April session a governor and six magistrates were to be chosen on an annual basis. No person could serve as governor more than once in two years. The governor must belong to "some approued congregation" and have experience as a magistrate. To avoid hasty, ill-considered choices, the names of nominees were presented at a previous General Court by the deputies from the towns. Each town could nominate two persons and the Court could add as many more as it wished.[87]

The three towns were to elect four deputies apiece and any future towns could send whatever number the Court thought suitable. No religious qualification for voting was stipulated. The deputies had complete power to speak for their town, but the towns were ordered to abide by all laws which the Court passed. The supremacy of the General Court over the towns thus was explicitly stated.[88]

The governor was required to convene the General Court, but it could be dissolved only upon its own consent. The magistrates, with the governor and deputy governor, made up a special court to administer justice. Fear of too powerful magistrates — gained from the Massachusetts experience and Hooker's opposition thereto — clearly appeared in several provisions. One stated that if the governor or majority of magistrates failed to call the Court in regular or special session as prescribed, then the freemen could take the initiative

in calling a meeting of the General Court. Another section provided for advance meetings of the deputies only, to set up an agenda for the full session of the General Court. Actually no such preliminary session was ever held.[89]

Taken as a whole, the Fundamental Orders provided only a sketchy outline of a government — far less detailed than the New Haven Fundamentals of 1639 and 1643. While the General Court clearly secured the supreme power, no definite division of political, judicial, executive, and administrative authority was delineated. In the General Court no rules of procedure were stated, nor was a speaker provided. Of interest, too, was the utter lack of any reference to the king or to the English Government. Impressive claims have been made for the Fundamental Orders — as the first written constitution in the world, as the beginnings of American democracy, and as the prototype for the Federal Constitution, among others.[90]

Whether or not the Fundamental Orders merit classification as a constitution is uncertain. Leading scholars have differed sharply in their interpretation. Charles M. Andrews took a negative stand. He noted that the word "fundamental" was commonly employed by New England Puritans simply to mean a general law. He felt that the architects of the Fundamental Orders did not intend them to be an organic law. In fact, they were so little considered inviolate that they were frequently added to, and eight times altered, in the period to 1660. On the opposite side one finds scholars such as George M. Dutcher and William M. Maltbie. Dutcher asserts that the Fundamental Orders "with some amendment, served the settlers as their constitution until they received the charter from Charles II in 1662." Judge Maltbie believes that in the eyes of the Connecticut leaders and people of the 1639–62 era the Fundamental Orders were considered a constitution and were observed as such. Regardless of the interpretation preferred by the modern student, there is no doubt that the Fundamental Orders clearly expressed the democratic principle of government based upon popular will — the concept so ably enunciated in Hooker's 1638 sermon. Some provisions copied Massachusetts' legislation of the previous few years, but the document as a whole definitely reflects a more liberal outlook. As one writer has well expressed it, the Fundamental Orders were the child of the General Court of Connecticut, and the grandchild of the General Court of Massachusetts.[91]

Springfield Lost, Saybrook and Other Towns Gained

THROUGH a series of events Springfield soon withdrew from political association with the River towns. In the beginning, two of its founders, William Pynchon and Henry Smith, were included in the famous Massachusetts Commission of 1636. Located only about twenty-four miles upstream from Hartford, Springfield quite conceivably could have remained part of Connecticut if serious misunderstandings had been avoided. In March 1637/38 the General Court gave Pynchon the monopoly of Indian trade up the river in return for supplying Indian corn, an arrangement which he apparently neither asked for nor desired.[92]

On April 5, 1638, at a General Court which Pynchon himself attended, a complaint was made that he had not been as careful in promoting the corn trade as he ought to have been. Undoubtedly Pynchon defended himself, but a fine of forty bushels of Indian corn was levied against him. Probably he was furious, as he never again attended the General Court.[93]

Other issues arose to drive a deeper wedge between Springfield and the lower River towns. Hooker and Pynchon did not seem to get along very well. The former strongly objected to Massachusetts' claims to Springfield and deeply resented Pynchon's willingness even to consider them. Very possibly doctrinal differences separated the two leaders. The economic interests of the two areas differed, also, as Springfield concentrated upon fur trade, the lower towns upon agriculture. In any event, Springfield ceased to participate in Connecticut's General Court and soon completely withdrew. In 1641 Massachusetts offered tempting bait by appointing Pynchon as a magistrate and judge for Springfield. When the New England Confederation was organized in 1643, Springfield entered as a part of Massachusetts.[94]

Sad as was this loss for Connecticut, it was soon balanced by the addition of new settlements. Movement out of the River valley progressed slowly because of the densely wooded hills on both sides. On January 16, 1639/40, the Court empowered six men to survey the Tunxis River area with a view to settlement. Soon afterward a small group of settlers pushed the ten miles westward over the hills from Hartford and made their settlement along the Tunxis River. On December 1, 1645, the Court voted "that the Plantation cauled Tunxis shalbe cauled Farmington . . ." and set its boundaries.[95]

The Pequot War accidentally speeded up Connecticut's expansion along the coast. Roger Ludlow and others who participated in the Pequot swamp fight in July 1637 were highly impressed by the land which they saw in the area. Two years later Ludlow returned and purchased land from the local Indians and began a settlement. He ran afoul of the General Court and was haled before them on October 10, 1639, because "offence hath beene taken att some of his pr[o]ceedings in his late jorney to Pequannocke, and the parts thereabouts." Ludlow had been authorized to purchase land and settle at Pequonnocke (western part of Stratford), but the lands at Uncoa (Fairfield) had appeared equally alluring. Ludlow justified his conduct by claiming that he had saved this additional land for Connecticut from the Dutch and New Haven Colony. After rebuking him mildly, the Court ordered a committee to view the new settlement and recommend a solution. To complicate the situation, Ludlow's expansionist activities had produced ill will in New Haven, which considered him a poacher upon their land, and had caused protests from the Milford settlers, under the Reverend Peter Prudden, with whom the committee was to confer. Upon receiving the special committee's report, the Court, in January 1639/40, saw fit to confirm Ludlow's actions and settlement at Fairfield. Apparently he lost little if any prestige from the incident, for he was re-elected a magistrate on April 9, 1640. He continued to serve as magistrate as long as he lived in Connecticut. A stormy petrel, Ludlow felt keen dissatisfaction over the failure of Connecticut and New Haven to back Fairfield against a threatened

Dutch attack. This may well have been the culminating factor in a series of disagreements and an unpleasant court case which led to the departure of one of Connecticut's most influential pioneers. In 1654 he returned to England, where he accepted an important post at Dublin under Cromwell's government. He left behind him many monuments — drafting of the Fundamental Orders, the legal code of 1650, years of service on the General Court and as Connecticut commissioner to the New England Confederation, and founding of the new towns of Fairfield and Stratford.[96]

The Saybrook settlement meanwhile had failed to realize the dreams of its founders. Because of changing conditions in England and the Puritan ascension to power in the 1640's, the Puritan "men of quality" who had planned to settle in Saybrook remained in England. It is true that two of them, Lord Say and Sele and Lord Brooke, found themselves memorialized in the name "Saybrook." The settlement, however, stayed largely a military fort, from which minor trading took place. Only George Fenwick, of the gentlemen who signed Winthrop's commission of 1635, actually settled in Saybrook. He acted as head from 1639 to 1644.[97]

Gradually, as it became obvious that Saybrook never would be the retreat planned for upper-class Puritan gentlemen, the River towns developed an interest in absorbing it. As already seen, Saybrook Fort had co-operated in the Pequot War. In August 1639 the General Court sent Deputy Governor Ludlow, Thomas Hooker, and Thomas Wells to discuss with Fenwick details of the proposed confederation of Connecticut with Massachusetts. They found Fenwick cordial and receptive to the idea of co-operation, but he requested that any decisions upon boundaries be delayed. The General Court acquiesced. That October, by no accident, Fenwick was nominated as candidate for magistrate, although he does not appear to have been elected.[98]

In the early 1640's Saybrook grew slowly and lost its primarily military nature of earlier years. In 1643 Connecticut asked Fenwick to join with it, if he could do so without loss of the privileges he held. In September 1643 Fenwick, together with Edward Hopkins, attended the first meeting of the New England Confederation. The next January he was nominated for Connecticut magistrate and, in April, elected.[99]

As a logical denouement, the next year, 1644, brought the transfer of Saybrook to Connecticut's jurisdiction. In October the General Court appointed a distinguished committee of six, including Governor Hopkins, Deputy Governor Haynes, and Captain Mason, to negotiate with Fenwick. Two months later the famous agreement was effected which made Saybrook, for all practical purposes, an integral part of Connecticut. Fenwick conveyed the fort and the land, but not the jurisdiction, to the perpetual use of Connecticut. He promised also "if it come into his power" to turn over all the lands from Narragansett Bay to Saybrook. In return, Connecticut agreed to give Fenwick, for ten years, specified duties on all corn, "Biskett," livestock, and furs transported downstream past the fort, and the personal use of a house, wharf, and adjoining land. The agreement constituted a bill of sale of land, made on the assumption that Fenwick represented all the grantees and associates. Probably the consent of these persons was needed to make the document legally valid. Fenwick proceeded to England, probably in 1645, held important positions under Cromwell, and remained there until his death in 1657; but there seems to be no indication that he ever obtained the approval of the other living grantees, or a renewal of the original Warwick Patent. Perhaps once he resumed a busy governmental career in England he simply lost interest in Saybrook and Connecticut. However that may be, Saybrook, from December 1644 on, was considered a Connecticut town with all normal responsibilities and privileges, and it grew rapidly and prospered. Connecticut had acquired a strategic town which assured practical control of the Connecticut River.[100]

A highly strategic location on Connecticut's coast, the mouth of the Thames River, with its magnificent harbor, exerted an early appeal to the colonials. In February 1640/41 the General Court authorized a survey of the "Pequot Country and disposeing of the Tymber there, as also to settle Inhabitants in those p[a]rts." The next year the Court bestowed 500 acres "about Pequoyt Country" upon Captain John Mason and an equal grant to the soldiers who served with him. The Court in April 1642 made provision for general distribution of 10,000 acres in the area, but it remained for John Winthrop, Jr., to launch the first actual settlement. In Massachusetts, interest in the Thames River area had reached a high pitch, largely as a result of glowing reports by Captain Israel Stoughton, who had camped there during the Pequot War. In 1644 Winthrop procured a grant from Massachusetts "at or near Pequott." He looked over the ground around the mouth of the Thames River in 1645 and probably made a start at settlement that year; but most of the permanent settlers apparently did not arrive until the next year. According to John Winthrop, Sr.:

A plantation was this year [1646] begun at Pequod river by Mr. John Winthrop, junr., Mr. Thomas Peter, a minister, (brother to Mr. Peter of Salem,) and this court power was given to them two for ordering and governing the plantation till further order, etc., although it was uncertain whether it would fall within our jurisdiction or not, because they of Connecticut challenged it by virtue of a patent from the king . . . for it mattered not much to which jurisdiction it did belong, seeing the confederation made all as one; but it was of great concernment to have it planted, to be a curb to the Indians, etc.

Three months later Winthrop noted that some of the families which had gone to "Pequod" lived in Indian wigwams while their new homes were being constructed. The younger Winthrop, always a model of diplomacy and circumspection, did not allow the disputed jurisdiction over his new settlement to upset him. Soon the Confederation took up the question and ruled in favor of Connecticut, and the next year (1647) reaffirmed this decision. Massachusetts did not seriously challenge the vote, nor did Winthrop. Connecticut rolled out the welcome mat for Winthrop and his followers in May 1648 by commissioning Winthrop as "Magistrate at Pequoyt." Three years later, in 1651, he was elected an assistant in the Court (a member of the small aristocratic upper chamber of the legislature), a clear sign that Connecticut considered him one of its leaders.[101]

Meanwhile, in 1650, a number of families migrated from Gloucester, as a covenanted church, with their minister, Richard Blinman, and joined with some in the infant town to form its first church. In 1657/58 the town's name officially became "New London." Blessed by Connecticut's finest harbor and a favorable agricultural hinterland, New London grew rapidly into one of Connecticut's principal towns.[102]

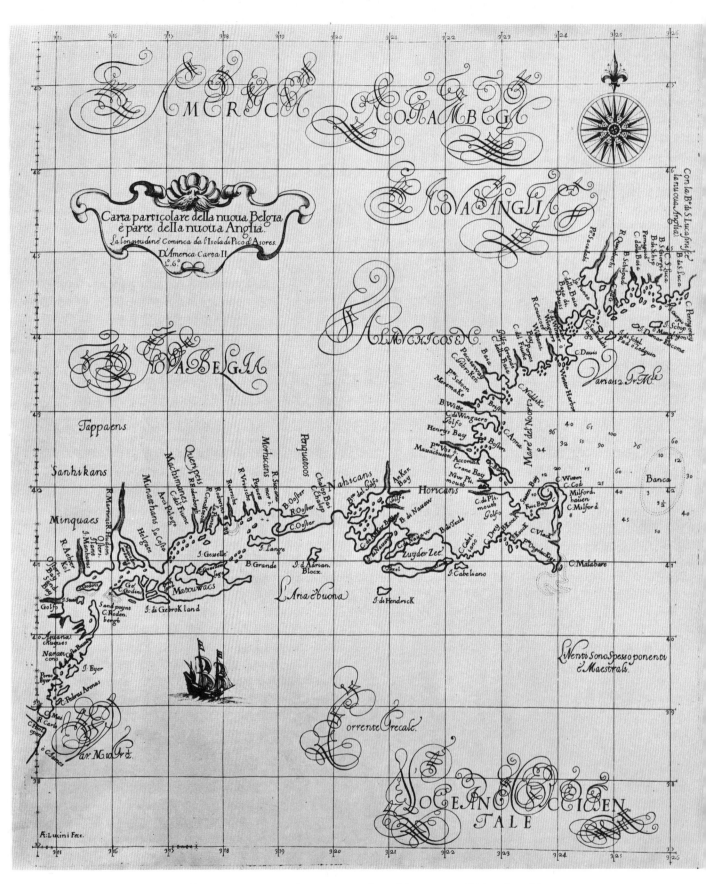

Dudley map of 1646. First known map with word "Connecticut" (Conokteook).

CHAPTER 3

Founding of New Haven and Developments of the 1640's in the Connecticut Area

English Background of New Haven — Preparations in England and Massachusetts Bay — Setting Up the "Bible State" — Milford and Guilford, Children of New Haven — Branford, Stamford, and Southold Complete the New Haven Family — Intercolonial Co-operation — The New England Confederation — Drunkenness, Profanity, and Other Vices — Strict Familial Standards — Economic Aspects of Life — Hooker and His Influence

English Background of New Haven

TO find the spiritual roots of the New Haven Colony one must go back to St. Stephen's Church, Coleman Street, London, where the parishioners in 1624 elected as their new vicar a promising young clergyman, John Davenport.[1]

Born at Coventry in 1597, Davenport attended the local grammar school, where he studied under an enthusiastic classicist, Dr. Philemon Holland, who imbued him with a genuine love of the classics. In 1613, at the tender age of sixteen, he entered Merton College, Oxford, as a batteler, or scholarship student. Some misunderstanding soon arose with the warden of the college and he transferred his allegiance to Magdalen Hall, but too slender financial resources compelled him to leave before graduation. Almost immediately, although only eighteen years old, he secured a position as a preacher in a chapel attached to Hilton Castle, near Durham, where apparently he remained from late 1615 to the spring of 1616.[2]

Davenport next went to the London area, where his activities for three years are uncertain, although he probably engaged in preaching. In 1619 he was chosen lecturer and curate of St. Lawrence

Jewry Church, located next to the Guildhall in the heart of London. Here he quickly built a solid reputation as an excellent preacher, and after five years he received the call to the adjacent parish of St. Stephen's.[3]

His career there nearly ended before it began, because of a charge of Puritanism made against him, which caused the Bishop of London to refuse his approval until the royal pleasure was learned. Davenport declared forcefully that he was not a Puritan — apparently a sincere and accurate reflection of his position then. Intercession on his behalf by powerful friends, especially Sir Edward Conway, resulted in the certification of his acceptability by the Bishop of London. Although distressed by certain conditions within the Church of England, he still genuinely desired to work within it for reform.[4]

His parish had 1,400 communicants, many of them partners in the prosperous livery companies and trading houses of the neighborhood, although some were from the numerous craftsmen, shopkeepers, and poor people who filled the lesser residences. Davenport stayed extremely busy, both with his parish duties and with varied community affairs, but he found time to complete the interrupted work at Oxford and in June 1625 received the Bachelor of Divinity degree. His popularity was enhanced by the courageous way in which he visited and comforted his parishioners during the very dangerous plague of 1625.[5]

After Laud's accession to the bishopric of London in 1628, Davenport's path became steadily rougher. As Laud increased his efforts to obtain conformity in every minute detail, Davenport's outlook began to change. It is not surprising that he began to take a lively interest in the affairs of the Massachusetts Bay Company while it still was in England. In January 1630/31 he became involved in a bitter quarrel with his curate, Timothy Hood, over the reading of the litany, the wearing of the surplice, and other points. Hood, a lazy and unsatisfactory assistant who had been dismissed, tried to revenge himself by bringing charges of Puritan practices against Davenport. The latter presented a strong and apparently successful rebuttal to Laud, in which he explained that his church was very crowded, so that variations from prescribed ritual were inevitable.[6]

During the next two years, 1632–33, several events deeply disturbed Davenport, whose opposition to Puritanism as a result slowly but surely eroded away. Laud succeeded in crushing a very influential Puritan company called the feoffees, which had been active raising revenues and purchasing church livings or positions in which Puritan ministers were placed. In 1633 the feoffees, in which Davenport had become active, were ordered dissolved and the king secured control of their church positions. As a result, Davenport's confidence in the possibility of reforming the Church was nearly destroyed, and further events of the year dissolved any lingering hopes.[7]

That same year John Cotton, fleeing from Boston, Lincolnshire, and Thomas Hooker, also in deep trouble, conferred with Davenport in London and sought to win him over to the Puritan migration to America. Deeply moved, perhaps even converted to their views, Davenport still refused to sail with them.[8]

The final blow to his hopes for a fruitful career in England came in August 1633 when George Abbot, Archbishop of Canterbury and brother of a parishioner of Davenport's, died. Charles I promptly appointed William Laud to the exalted position. The next day Davenport, fearing the worst, fled from London and probably very soon afterward resigned his post at St. Stephen's. There can be little doubt that he had become converted to a vigorous type of Puritanism and was ready to leave England. More than the illiberal leadership of the Church and the combined influence of Hooker and Cotton were involved, as Davenport apparently had close contacts with a group of Congregationalists under John Lothropp of Southwark. In addition, he was familiar with the writings of Ames, Richard Hooker, and others. About mid-November 1633, disguised in a gray suit, hiding under a large beard, and posing as a merchant named Stone, Davenport crossed the Channel.[9]

Like Hooker, he found Holland unpleasant. For a time he preached for the ailing and irascible John Paget, but incompatibility caused him soon to withdraw. Later he served as assistant to Hugh Peter at Rotterdam, and when Peter departed he headed that church. In the meantime Cotton had written highly optimistic letters to him about conditions in New England.[10]

Preparations in England and Massachusetts Bay

DAVENPORT, adopting a new disguise, returned to England, where he found his former flock at St. Stephen's in distressing condition and political and religious warfare tearing England asunder. He decided that New England offered the best hope for Puritans, and providentially his trusted friend Theophilus Eaton appeared on the scene. Son of a clergyman, Eaton while in school at Coventry had become acquainted with the younger Davenport. Eschewing the ministry and disappointing his father, Eaton sought his fortune in the mercantile world of London. Beginning as an apprentice but endowed with great business acumen, he soon established his own firm and engaged in the Baltic trade. At one time he served as deputy governor of the wealthy East-Land Company, and acted as commercial agent of Charles I at Copenhagen, Denmark. He had been one of the original patentees of the Massachusetts Bay Company. Rich in ability, influence, and coin of the realm, Eaton was an ideal man to handle the

*The Reverend John Davenport
(1597–1669/70).*

myriad problems involved in organizing an expedition to America.[11]

Working smoothly in harness together, Eaton and Davenport marshaled their followers, many of them well-to-do and all stanch Puritans. The Eaton and Davenport families, including some relatives and a solid group of St. Stephen's parishioners, comprised the nucleus to which was added about a score of families from the neighborhood. They chartered a nearly new ship, the two-hundred-and-fifty-ton *Hector* of London, and members of the company, for the most part, invested their entire fortunes in the venture. Although economic factors were not overlooked, there can be no doubt that religious considerations ranked

highest as the driving force behind the migration. Puritans of the strictest and most doctrinaire type, the Davenport-Eaton Company devoutly desired to establish a "Bible State" in New England.[12]

After long, arduous preparations and vexatious delays, the *Hector*, and apparently a second ship, sailed in May for New England. In his *Journal*, under date of June 26, 1637, Governor Winthrop recorded: "There arrived two ships from London, the *Hector*, and the [blank]. In these came Mr. Davenport and another minister, and Mr. Eaton and Mr. Hopkins, two merchants of London, men of fair estate and of great esteem for religion, and wisdom in outward affairs."[13]

Davenport's intimate friends John Cotton and

49

Hugh Peter greeted him very warmly, Eaton found many old associates of the Bay Company, and the others soon located old neighbors from London and elsewhere. The Davenport-Eaton group had left England with the definite expectation of settling within the Massachusetts Bay Company's territory. Various sites were offered in Charlestown, Newbury, or in any unoccupied place; but none really satisfied the group, dominated by London merchants, who sought especially a good harbor.[14]

As time passed they began to look beyond the immediate Massachusetts Bay settlements for a possible location. As a result of the Pequot War, enthusiastic reports were circulating concerning Quinnipiac (New Haven). Captain Israel Stoughton had given the governor and Council a glowing account of the land, its easy access, and the need of possessing it before it was taken by "an ill neighbour," meaning the Dutch; while Captain Underhill also reported very favorably of "Queenapiok." On August 31, 1637, Eaton and others left to look over the Quinnipiac site, which made such a highly favorable impression that a few men apparently stayed to hold the area over the winter.[15]

Doubtless Eaton reported back to his associates that they had found their Promised Land. The Massachusetts situation discouraged them, especially the explosive Anne Hutchinson affair, in which Davenport himself, in company with Cotton, had played a leading role in trying unsuccessfully to force Anne Hutchinson to recant. She held religious beliefs contrary to those of the Puritan leaders. This and other evidences of dissension heightened the desire to set up an entirely separate colony.[16]

Since their company was small, Davenport and Eaton invited volunteers from among the Bay populace; and they found eager takers, including the Reverend Peter Prudden, a graduate of Emmanuel College, Cambridge, and some Puritan families from Hertfordshire — a group which had arrived at Boston only five weeks after the *Hector*. John Cotton himself contemplated joining the emigration, but finally decided to remain. On March 12, 1637/38, Davenport and Eaton informed Bay authorities of their intentions to depart, and on March 30 they sailed for their new home.[17]

Setting Up the "Bible State"

ON April 24, 1638, in the freshness and promise of early spring, the hardy Puritans disembarked and began the long-anticipated task of establishing a solid foothold upon the shore of New Haven Bay. The next day being the Sabbath, the company gathered under a huge oak tree to hear their pastor, John Davenport, preach on a text from Matthew: "Then was Jesus led up of the spirit into the wilderness to be tempted of the devil." In the afternoon Peter Prudden held forth on "The voice of one crying in the wilderness, Prepare ye the way of the Lord, make his paths straight."[18]

Some of the first year was devoted to putting up temporary shelters, often in cellars or pits — a far cry from the pretentious homes, resembling the better ones of Coleman Street in London, which they were to build later. Luckily the Indians of the area were friendly, weak, and very willing to cede large tracts of land. By treaties of November and December 1638 and May 1645, Davenport and Eaton acquired a sizable area that stretched along the coast and inland as far as the future Wallingford, Cheshire, and parts of Bethany, Orange, Prospect, Meriden, and Woodbridge. In the initial agreement of November 24, 1638, with the local sachem, Momaugin, the Indians sold all of their lands in Quinnipiac, reserving hunting and fishing rights, in return for "twelve coates of English trucking cloath, twelve alcumy spoones, twelve hatchetts, twelve hoes, two dozen of knives, twelve porengers & foure cases of French knives and sizers." In the 1645 agreement the Indians asked for and received a reservation of about 1,200 acres in the future East Haven-Morris Cove section. By and large, the New Haven Colony treated the Indians much more fairly than was customary at that period, and amicable relations prevailed through the years. The Indians, incidentally, were highly impressed by Davenport's devotion to books and dubbed him "*So big study man.*"[19]

In the summer of 1638, under the supervision of a surveyor, John Brockett, the town plot was laid out in nine squares, of which the central one was reserved for a market place and became the famous New Haven Green, still a beauty spot of green amidst a rushing modern city. The other

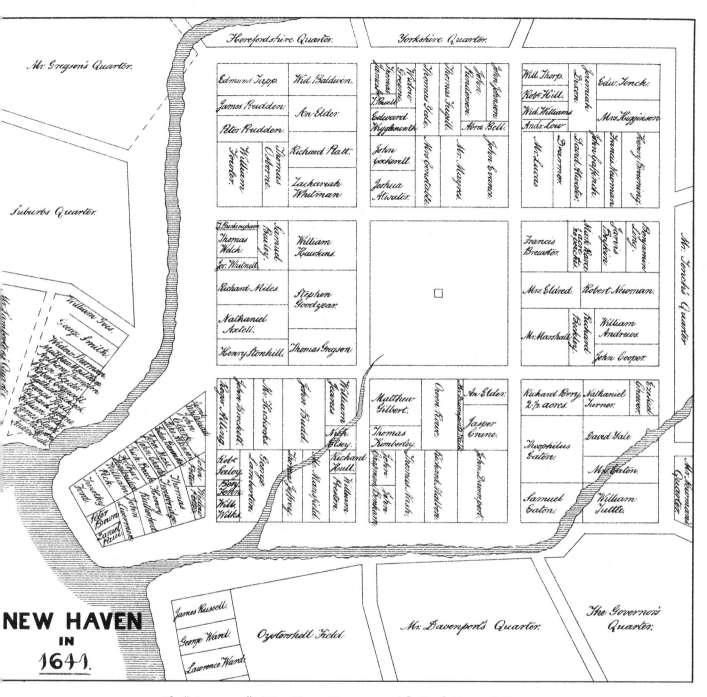

The "nine squares" of New Haven. From a copy of the Brockett map of 1641.

eight squares proved inadequate to house the entire company, so that two "suburbs" were added.[20]

During the early months of settlement the colony apparently functioned under a provisional government, based upon a business agreement made in England, and some type of plantation covenant set up either in Massachusetts or in New Haven. Since a large investment was involved, the hard-headed London businessmen must have insisted upon definite, formal articles of organization.[21]

Much inward soul searching and vigorous outward discussion preceded the momentous meeting of June 1639 to organize their church. After voting that the Scriptures provided "a perfect rule" for the government of men, they decided to choose twelve men who in turn would select seven as the founders of the permanent church and state.

These seven pillars were: Davenport, Eaton, Jeremy Dixon, Thomas Fugill, Mathew Gilbert, Robert Newman, and John Ponderson. When each of these men gave his own personal profession of faith, Davenport's was so long and eloquent that John Cotton sent it to England to be printed with one of his sermons. It reveals how slight were any doctrinal differences between the Church of England and the Puritan leaders, though of course large differences existed over matters of church government and services. In August 1639 the church covenant was drawn up and the church organized around the seven leaders. The new covenant served as a model for other churches on the Sound and was even proudly sent to England by John Cotton.[22]

This June meeting voted "that church members onely shall be free burgesses, and thatt they onely shall chuse magistrates & officers among themselues to haue the power of transacting all the publique ciuill affayres of this Plantatio[n], of makeing and repealing lawes, devideing of inheritances, decideing of differences thatt may arise and doeing all things or businesses of like nature." Thus were laid the foundations of a theocracy, or church state, in which a strictly limited church membership controlled the political franchise. The leaders of church and state would be largely the same and would possess an almost identical outlook. There is little doubt that their model, prepared by Cotton for Massachusetts Bay, was the code of laws called "Moses his judicials."[23]

On October 25, 1639, the "seven pillars" convened as the civil court and launched New Haven's new civil government. They admitted nine members of approved churches as burgesses, which meant sixteen voters in all. Davenport read two passages of Scripture which described a proper magistrate, after which they elected Eaton "a member of this church, a man well known and approved by the court as fittly quallified for thatt office according to the said descriptio[n]."[24]

The first piece of business for the new government proved to be unpleasant in nature. Nepaupuck, an Indian, was accused of murdering at least one English settler. Indian witnesses acknowledged that he was guilty, so upon such conclusive evidence the court adjudged him guilty.

The next day he was decapitated and his head displayed in the market place as a grim warning.[25]

Late in November the court ordered construction of a meeting house fifty feet square. The edifice was expected to cost £500, to be raised by a tax of 30s. per £100 assessment, payable in three installments.[26]

The highly restricted nature of the settlement was reflected clearly in another action of the same session:

Itt is ordered thatt Mr. Eaton, Mr. Davenport, Robt Newman, Mathew Gilbert, Captaine Turner and Thomas Fugill shall from hence forward have the disposeing of all the house lotts yett vndisposed of about this towne, to such persons as they shall judge meete for the good of the plantatio[n], and thatt none shall come to dwell as planters here w[i]thout their consent and allowance, whether they come in by purchase or otherwise.

The "Bible State" held high the barriers against those of other faiths and of ill reputation![27]

Despite every effort, however, unseemly behavior did occur, especially among servants, as the official records attest:

William Bromfield, Mr. Malbons man, was sett in the stocks for prophaining the Lords day and stealing wine from his Ma[ste]r w[hi]ch he drunk and gave to others.

John Jenner accused for being drunke w[i]th strong waters was acquitted, itt appearing to be of infirmyty & occasioned by the extremyty of the colde.

Edward Woodcliff for slaundering his Ma[ste]rs wife was whipped seveerly and sent out of the plantatio[n], being a pestilent fellow, and a corrupter of others.

Thomas Moulenor the elder, and Robert Campio[n] were fined 5s apeece for affronting the court.[28]

Mindful of the infant colony's safety, the court ordered that every man bearing arms should furnish himself with a musket, a sword, and appurtenances, powder and bullets, and have them ready for inspection by Captain Turner at a set date. A guard was organized in June 1640, and on September 1 the town appointed Captain Turner "to have the comaund and ordering of all martiall affayres of this plantatiō[n]," and those on duty were instructed to come to Sunday meeting "compleatly armed, and all others also are to bring their swords, no man exempted save Mr. Eaton, o[u]r pastor, Mr. James, Mr. Samuell Eaton and the 2 deacons." At the same session occurred the simple declaration: "This towne now named Newhaven." The reason for the choice is unknown, but its adoption in a sense marks the end of the initial period of establishing a solid foothold.[29]

The theocratic state was so solidly undergirded with worldly goods that by 1643, with about eight hundred population, it boasted of no less than ten persons having estates of £1,000 or more. Headed

ford, Milford, Branford, Stamford, and Southold on Long Island. An important group within the original New Haven settlers was that headed by the Reverend Peter Prudden, a powerful preacher in Hertfordshire, England, who succeeded in bringing fifteen families from his parishioners to Massachusetts. Being in close accord with the beliefs of Davenport, he persuaded his people to cast

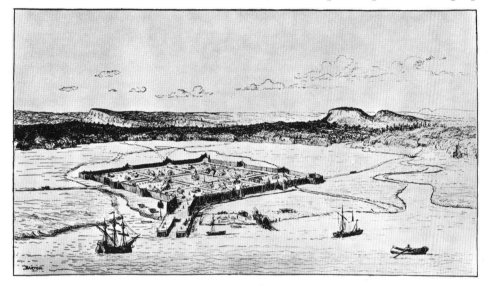

Early New Haven surrounded by a palisade.

by Eaton with £3,000, the list included, among others, Davenport, Francis Brewster, Stephen Goodyear, William Hawkins, and George Lamberton. In the range of £400–£900, a substantial estate, one finds no less than twenty-seven more persons. Landholdings ranged from around 20 acres to the 963 held by Eaton. Among the poorer class, those with an estate of £10–£50, a typical holding — including lands in the "first division," the "neck," "meadow," and the "second division" — ran around 40 acres; while those of medium wealth, say £100–£499, held about 90 acres; and those of means, with £500 or more, averaged approximately 280 acres apiece. Although a small colony, New Haven probably ranked as the wealthiest English group settling in America in the seventeenth century.[30]

Milford and Guilford, Children of New Haven

NEW HAVEN proved to be a prolific mother of new colonies, with no less than five offspring: Guil-

their lot with those going to New Haven. The Prudden group was given a separate allotment of land, located in the northwest corner of the nine central squares in New Haven, where they lived and worked in smooth harness with the Davenport-Eaton circle; but they never forgot the dream of their own separate settlement. In the summer of 1638 Prudden preached at Wethersfield, where he won an enthusiastic following, some of whom wished to launch a new colony under his direction.[31]

The combination of Wethersfield sentiment with that among Prudden's group in New Haven led quickly to establishment of a new settlement. In February 1638/39, five men consummated with Ansantawae, a sachem of the Paugusset Indians, the purchase of a tract of land around the mouth of the Wepawaug River, ten miles west of New Haven. This particular area had been suggested by Sergeant Thomas Tibbals, who, as he marched across it during the pursuit of the Pequots in 1637, noted its fine promise.[32]

53

In the fall of 1639 Prudden and his flock, including a small Wethersfield contingent, marched the ten miles westward from New Haven to settle Weatogue, quickly renamed Milford. Altogether over fifty planters were involved in the initial migration. The town promptly organized itself upon the model of New Haven and even selected its "seven pillars." Within a very few years, how-

or heal all contentions." Milford's smooth and rapid progress upon all fronts attested Prudden's wise and diplomatic leadership.[34]

Milford remained an independent colony for several years, but gradually sentiment grew for joining the New Haven Colony. When Milford applied for membership, New Haven rejected the application, because Milford had enfranchised

The old stone house built for Henry Whitfield at Guilford (c. 1639).

ever, it ceased to insist upon church membership as a prerequisite for political activity. By four later purchases from the Indians in the 1655–61 period, Milford rounded out its boundaries. In the early years the economic life of the little theocracy revolved about farming, but before long a thriving coastal trade developed, in which Alexander Bryan played the leading role.[33]

Prudden remained the dominant religious and intellectual force in Milford's life until his death in 1656. Cotton Mather spoke highly of his career at Milford, "where he lived many years an example of piety, gravity, and *boiling zeal*, against the growing evils of the times." Among his good points, he "was noted for a singular faculty to sweeten, compose and qualify *exasperated spirits*, and stop

six nonmembers of the church. Eventually a compromise was effected whereby Milford promised for the future to admit only church members as freemen, and in October 1643 it joined the New Haven Colony.[35]

Guilford, a second offshoot of New Haven, stemmed from the great energies of Henry Whitfield. The son of a prominent English lawyer, young Whitfield, showing leanings toward the ministry, was educated at Winchester and New colleges, Oxford, and then took a church at Ockley, Surrey. He became friendly with several leading nonconformists, including Hooker, Davenport, and Cotton, and was converted to their viewpoint by Cotton. Deciding to make a new start in America, Whitfield collected a company of followers from his native Surrey and adjoining Kent counties. In May 1639 they embarked in the first ship to sail directly from England to New Haven.[36]

Late in September 1639, soon after arrival, they concluded the purchase of land at Menunkatuck from Shaumpishuh, sister of Momaugin. Whitfield's company, almost exclusively husbandmen, was attracted to Menunkatuck because in topography and fertile soil it closely resembled their native counties. In the early years of Guilford the settlers, mostly humble country-bred farmers, devoted themselves almost exclusively to farming.[37]

The Whitfield Company at least equaled, if it did not surpass, New Haven in the rigorousness of its theocracy, and it created the most restricted political franchise in New England. In 1643 they carefully elected seven men — Whitfield, John Higginson, Samuel Desborough, William Leete, Jacob Sheafe, John Mepham, and John Hoadley — to exercise control over admission of new members. In 1643 the settlers adopted Guilford as the official name of the town, undoubtedly after Guildford, Surrey. Whitfield himself seems to have been by far the richest settler, even though he had sacrificed much of his estate to migrate with his flock, whom Mather refers to as "a multitude of poor people . . . who could not live without his ministry."[38]

Since Whitfield and his wife at the time of their arrival had eight or nine children (and eventually ten), it is not surprising that they rushed the erection of a handsome house, begun in 1639 or 1640, still known as the "Old Stone House." Located in an attractive spot, this stone structure, extensively restored, still stands and is often called the oldest stone house in the United States. Undoubtedly by far the finest residence of early Guilford, it was the scene of the first worship services in the infant settlement.[39]

Branford, Stamford, and Southold Complete the New Haven Family

ANOTHER of New Haven's children was Branford, located a few miles to the eastward, known originally as Totoket, and also purchased from the Indians. In 1640 New Haven bestowed it upon Samuel Eaton, a clergyman and brother of Theophilus Eaton. The former went back to England for the purpose of recruiting settlers, but for various reasons never returned. Four years later New Haven invited a group of planters from Wethersfield, headed by William Swaine, to settle at Totoket under promise to join New Haven and operate under the fundamental agreement. The Wethersfield contingent was small, perhaps only a dozen or so families, but it formed the nucleus. It is probable, too, that a few scattered settlers already were established in Totoket prior to the arrival of Swaine's party.[40]

As pastor the Totoket people called the Reverend Abraham Pierson, who came from Southampton, Long Island. A Yorkshireman and a graduate of Trinity College, Cambridge, he had first landed in Boston. Migrating to Southampton with a group from Lynn, Massachusetts, he welcomed the chance to take the church at Totoket.[41]

The settlement, considered a part of the New Haven Colony, functioned religiously and politically in close accord with its parent. In 1653 Totoket became Branford, apparently named for Brentford, Middlesex, a suburb of London.[42]

Acting for New Haven in 1640, Captain Nathaniel Turner purchased from Indians a tract of land forty miles westward called Rippowams, later renamed Stamford. It just happened that Wethersfield was then in the throes of internal dissension, so that one faction, under the Reverend Richard Denton, was very much attracted by an offer from Davenport (who earlier had tried to mediate the Wethersfield dispute) to settle in Stamford. After agreeing to recognize New Haven's authority and to copy its theocratic system, the Denton group, a majority of the Wethersfield church numbering over thirty families, quickly moved to Stamford. Mather referred to Denton as "a *little man*, yet he had a great *soul;* his well-accomplished mind, in his lesser *body,* was *an Iliad in a nut-shell.*" A restless soul, Denton ministered to the Stamford parish only four years and in 1644 moved to Hempstead, Long Island.[43]

The last of the New Haven entourage was Southold, on the eastern end of Long Island, facing the Sound and New Haven. In 1640 ambitious New Haven purchased the land from an agent of the Earl of Stirling, who had received all of Long

Island from the Council for New England. The original band of settlers under the Reverend John Youngs came from Salem, Massachusetts. The Indian name for the area, *Yennicock,* soon was replaced by "Southold," Youngs's home in Suffolk, England. In 1643 Southold too was joined to the New Haven Colony, but probably because of distance, acted more independently than the other towns.[44]

During the process of expansion from 1638 to 1643 New Haven had remained literally a *town* with a town government only. The formation of the New England Confederation in 1643 forced New Haven and its outlying fledglings to organize tightly together if they wanted the vital protection offered by the Confederation. So Guilford and Milford, still nominally independent, were absorbed. The New Haven Colony, or New Haven Jurisdiction as they often called it, by 1644 thus consisted of New Haven, Branford, Guilford, Milford, Southold, and Stamford.[45]

The organization of the new colony took place at a General Court meeting on October 27, 1643, when a Fundamental Order was adopted as a frame of government. As might be expected, only members of approved churches were permitted a voice in the government. Each October the General Court, composed of two deputies from each town, was to elect a governor, deputy governor, treasurer, secretary, and marshal. To the surprise of no one they elected Theophilus Eaton as the first governor. A special court of magistrates was established to handle the more important legal cases, while the individual town courts continued to function. None of the courts provided trial by jury — unlike those of all other New England colonies. Thus a powerful theocracy upon John Cotton's model came into existence.[46]

Intercolonial Co-operation

As the New England colonies expanded and became firmly established, common problems, such as uncertain boundaries, Dutch and French rivalries, the Indian danger, and relationships with the mother country, emphasized the need for intercolonial co-operation. A series of specific disputes highlighted the lack of an organization to settle intercolonial differences. As already seen, a bitter verbal battle had developed between the rival groups from Plymouth and Massachusetts Bay who claimed the same lands at Windsor. Other disputes included that between Massachusetts and Plymouth over their boundary, which, after much agitation, was peacefully resolved in 1640. The heated debate between Massachusetts and Connecticut as to which should control Springfield also produced much ill feeling. Eventually Springfield cast its lot with Massachusetts, but its economic life inevitably remained closely tied to the lower Connecticut River settlements.[47]

Relations between the Dutch and English colonials mirrored the hostility of the mother countries. Both sides claimed the large areas lying between them, and the presence of the Dutch fort at Hartford remained a special source of irritation to Connecticut.[48]

The Puritan colonies, with their similar religious institutions and political and social organizations, shared a feeling of common aspiration and mission. Just before the Synod of 1637 in Newtown, Massachusetts, the first proposal for some type of confederation of these colonies was advanced. Since Plymouth was not represented, the matter was briefly discussed and dropped.[49]

The next year, stimulated perhaps by bad relations between the Bay and Connecticut, the Massachusetts Council advanced a plan under which each colony should provide two or more commissioners empowered to decide upon articles of union. Winthrop ascribed their differences principally to Connecticut's "shyness of coming under our government," but admitted that there were other issues too. He criticized Connecticut sharply for choosing as its political leaders men lacking adequate learning and for allowing its ministers to assume a leading role in the "managing of state business." In the summer a Connecticut delegation consisting of John Haynes, William Pynchon, and John Steel carried a reply to the Massachusetts General Court in which several revisions to the Massachusetts plan were offered. Some warm discussion ensued and counterproposals were made which were referred back to Connecticut.[50]

Soon afterward, in August 1638, Winthrop,

claiming that he wrote only in a friendly spirit, exacerbated relations by a very sharp letter to Hooker, in which he charged Connecticut with encouraging the Narragansets to nonco-operation with Massachusetts, altering the proposed articles unfairly, and following an overbearing policy toward Springfield.[51]

Apparently the letter created a profound impression, as Hooker penned a lengthy reply protesting vigorously against the widespread vilification of Connecticut prevalent in Massachusetts. He claimed that those interested in migrating to Connecticut were told that "their upland will bear no corn, their meadows nothing but weeds, and the people are almost all starved." Even in England, he asserted, deliberate efforts were fostered to frighten passengers from sailing for Connecticut. Hooker asked bluntly, "Do these things argue brotherly love?" and he denied the three charges leveled by Winthrop. Hooker adopted a particularly unyielding position on Springfield, which he felt clearly owed allegiance to Connecticut. The result of these differences was a temporary impasse.[52]

Powerful underlying forces, however, were pushing all the colonies toward some kind of union. The Indian menace, featured by rumors of a projected Indian alliance under Miantonomo against all English settlers, alarmed Connecticut. Expansionist tendencies of all the colonies heightened the acerbity of boundary disputes, while the shadow of Dutch and French encroachments was deepening. Moreover, England, in the throes of civil war, could not be counted upon for assistance or interference.[53]

In 1642 negotiations among Massachusetts, Plymouth, and Connecticut entered an active phase. Some Connecticut proposals were discussed by the Massachusetts General Court, referred to a committee for additional study, and their revisions returned to Connecticut. In May 1643 commissioners from four colonies convened at Boston to seek agreement upon articles of union.[54]

The New England Confederation

AFTER further discussion, the representatives of Massachusetts, Plymouth, Connecticut, and New Haven drew up the articles for "the United Colonies of New England," or the New England Confederation. The purpose of this union was to "enter into a firm and perpetual league of friendship and amity, for offence and defence, mutual advice and succor upon all just occasions, both for preserving and propagating the truth and liberties of the gospel, and for their own mutual safety and welfare."[55]

Under the articles each colony was guaranteed its independence and territory. Rhode Island, Maine, and New Hampshire pointedly were excluded, probably chiefly because of their lack of an orthodox Puritan outlook and Massachusetts' desire to annex these areas. Each colony in the Confederation was expected to contribute money for the common defense in proportion to the adult male population, and was entitled to send two commissioners to an annual meeting at which matters concerning war and peace, boundary disputes, fugitives from justice, Indian affairs, and other common problems would be decided. Six votes were required to pass a resolution — which meant that the three smaller colonies, theoretically, could override Massachusetts. John Winthrop and Thomas Dudley signed for Massachusetts, Edward Winslow and William Collier for Plymouth, George Fenwick and Edward Hopkins for Connecticut, and Theophilus Eaton and Thomas Gregson for New Haven.[56]

Although a significant pioneering effort at intercolonial co-operation, the Confederation proved almost impotent in times of trouble, since it possessed no power either to discipline an obdurate colony or to apply pressure to individuals, and resembled only a joint committee. Despite its internal weaknesses, however, the Confederation provided valuable experience in learning to work together, and it helped prevent the smaller colonies from being totally dominated by Massachusetts.[57]

At the beginning of its history the Confederation faced a serious Indian problem. A quarrel developed in 1643 between Uncas, Mohegan chief, and another chief, Sequasson. Governor Haynes and the Court made efforts to end the dispute, but to no avail. Uncas engineered a sudden attack upon Sequasson, killed seven or eight of his men, and took much booty. The repercussions were swift. Miantonomo, an ally of Sequasson, asking permission of the English to seek revenge against the Mohegans and receiving sanction, led about 1,000 warriors against Uncas, who could muster less than half as many. Despite the odds, Uncas and his men triumphed and even captured Miantonomo. Uncas received a letter from Rhode Island's Samuel Gorton, a friend of Miantonomo, which threatened dire retribution if he harmed his captive. Uncas took his prisoner to Hartford, where he was placed in white custody, and the matter of his fate was referred to the Boston meeting of the commissioners, who ruled that it was not safe to release him or proper to execute him. At this unsatisfactory junction "five of the most judicious elders" of the Bay, asked to render a decision, all recommended death for Miantonomo. The four charges given as the basis for so harsh a sentence, as recorded by Winthrop, seem quite inadequate when matched against Miantonomo's proven record of valuable service to the English upon important occasions, as in the Pequot War. Yet, without the pretense of a legal trial, the unfortunate Miantonomo was turned over to Uncas, who took him away and executed him — a serious stain upon the annals of the four colonies.[58]

For slightly more than two decades the Confederation functioned actively, with much of their time occupied by strained relations with the Dutch. Time was working for the more numerous English colonists, whose settlements were gradually hemming in the Dutch. The little Dutch post at Good Hope, virtually encircled by the Hartford settlers, proved to be a constant source of bickering. In answer to a letter of complaint from the Confederation, referring to alleged misconduct by the Dutch garrison, Governor Kieft replied that "when we heare the inhabitants of Hartford complayninge of vs, we seeme to heare Esops wolfe complayninge of the lamb." On September 19, 1650, at Hartford, the Dutch and Connecticut reached an agreement. It provided only a truce, however, and in 1653 Governor Stuyvesant sent two long letters to the commissioners at Boston, in which he cited scores of serious English depredations upon the Dutch of the House of Hope. In 1654, at the end of the first Anglo-Dutch War, the General Court simply ordered the entire Dutch settlement sequestered, which action terminated the Dutch colonial effort in Connecticut.[59]

The acquisition of the House of Hope came as the logical result of a serious Dutch scare the previous year which threatened to wreck the Confederation. Persistent rumors spread over Connecticut that the Dutch and Indians were planning to massacre all of the Connecticut colonists on Long Island and the mainland, and caused a severe panic. Several sessions of the Confederation commissioners in April, May, and September 1653 found the six representatives of Connecticut, New Haven, and Plymouth lined up solidly in favor of war against the Dutch, but Massachusetts adamantly opposed it. Under Confederation regulations such a majority was decisive, and Connecticut and New Haven leaders, engaging in a heated correspondence with the Bay authorities, pointed out with vigor the duty of the Bay to yield. Undoubtedly New Haven, which already had collided with the Dutch on the Delaware and elsewhere, especially desired the complete elimination of Dutch hegemony in North America. Massachusetts stuck by its position, however, and the end of the Anglo-Dutch War in 1654 caused the fear of Dutch-Indian attack to subside. Massachusetts' unyielding stand had severely strained the Confederation, but it doubtless saved New England from a needless war.[60]

Drunkenness, Profanity, and Other Vices

ALTHOUGH a majority of the colonists who settled the River towns and New Haven were of an excellent type, the records of both colonies attest the failure of some to meet the exacting moral standards expected of good Puritans. This situation is amply reflected in the Connecticut act of April 1640, which speaks for itself:

Forasmuch as many stubborne & refractory Persons are often taken w[i]thin these libertyes, and no meet place yet pr[e]pared for the detayneing & keepeing of such to their due & deserued punishment, It is therefore Ordered that there shall be a house of Correction built, of 24 foote long & 16 or 18 foote broad, w[i]th a Celler, ether of wood or stonne . . .[61]

In an age of heavy drinking it is scarcely surprising that drunkenness occurred occasionally. On August 1, 1639, one finds this action of Connecticut's Court:

These following were censured & fined for vnseasonable and imoderate drinking att the pinnace.

Thomas Cornewell, 30s.	Samuel Kittwell, 10s.
Jno. Latimer, 15s.	Thomas Vpson, 20s.
Mathew Beckwith, 10s.	

In 1643 the Court passed an order requiring a license for sale of wine and "strong water." A few years later it took notice of "that great abuse w[hi]ch is creepeing in by excess in Wyne and strong waters" to impose a limit of a half-hour's stay for drinking in any tavern. The keeper of the inn was saddled with the responsibility of not serving too much, however large the appetite of his customers![62]

As a port town New Haven naturally experienced difficulties with inebriated persons. In the summer of 1648 an instance occurred of a wild evening drinking party at the house of Robert Bassett, who "confesed he had not seene the like since he came." After hearing details of the carousing, the Court levied fines upon Bassett and some of his hilarious comrades. In an earlier case of 1640, Thomas Fran[c]kland, "for drinking strong liquors to excess and entertaining disorderly p[er]sons into his cellar to drinking meetings," was whipped and fined twenty shillings, deprived of his cellar and lot, and permitted to remain in New Haven only upon his good behavior. Both towns obviously considered drunkenness a very serious offense, but in neither place do the records indicate any widespread lack of sobriety.[63]

Other offenses which drew the wrath of the authorities were profanity and failure to observe proper respect toward the constituted authority.

Ed: Veare of Wethersfyeld is fined Xs. for cursing & swereing, and also he is to sitt in the stocks at Wethersfyeld, two howers the next Trayneing day.

In New Haven a citizen who reproved Bamfeild Bell for singing "profane songs" was called by Bell "one of the holy brethren that will lye for advantadge." After hearing witnesses, the Court ordered a severe whipping for Bell. Richard Gildersleeve in 1640 was tried for uttering "p[e]rnitious speeches" against the state and fined forty shillings by the Court at Hartford. An interesting case involving disrespect toward the church leaders occurred in 1648:

The Courte adiudgeth Peter Bussaker, for his fillthy and prophane expressions (viz. that hee hoped to meete some of the members of the Church in hell ere long, and hee did not question but hee should,) to bee cõmitted to prison, there to bee kept in safe custody till the sermon, and then to stand in the time thereof in the pillory, and after sermon to bee seuerely whipt.[64]

The servant and apprentice class seem to have caused both colonies much concern. In June 1644 the River towns, observing that many servants and apprentices ran away from their masters before their terms of service expired, ordered that after such escapees were apprehended they should serve three times the usual term. Serious lack of respect toward master or mistress apparently was not unknown:

Susan Coles, for her rebellious cariedge toward her mistris, is to be sent to the howse of correction and be keept to hard labour & course dyet, to be brought forth the next lecture day to be publiquely corrected, and so to be corrected weekly vntill Order be giuen to the contrary.

Even in the home of Thomas Hooker some improper behavior was detected: "Walter Gray, for his misdemeanor in laboring to inueagle the affections of Mr. Hoockers mayde, is to be publiquely corrected the next lecture day." One can imagine the gossip sparked by this flirtation![65]

Strict Familial Standards

IN matters of familial relationship, courtship, and marriage, the Puritans adopted a strict attitude in Connecticut as in Massachusetts. Both in the River towns and in New Haven bachelors were considered as objects of suspicion whose movements were regulated. As early as February 1636/37 Connecticut legislated that no single young man could keep house alone, nor could he stay with any family except by permission of the inhabitants of the town concerned. New Haven likewise required bachelors to live in families where the master would supervise them and report upon their activities and conversation![66]

Then, as in later times, some persons rushed into marriage and repented at leisure. In 1640 the Court noted that some were entangling themselves "by rashe & inconsiderat Contracts" for marriage to the great grief of themselves and their friends. To obviate this the Court ordered that at least eight days' public notice be given of intent to marry before a contract was entered into and that eight more days elapse before the actual ceremony. Young people under age were forbidden to enter a marriage contract or even to encourage a suitor without the knowledge and consent of parents or guardians; nor were third parties to intermeddle! The foreword to this law stated clearly the Puritan belief that the prosperity and well-being of their state depended upon families which abided by "the rules of God." Although specific positive evidence of happy family life in this early period is almost impossible to uncover, the very small number of divorces is quite suggestive.[67]

Consciousness of social class had been strong in old England and was carried over to New England. The influence of frontier conditions and the greater opportunities open to all comers tended to blur class lines and feelings, but it did not destroy them, as is illustrated in a Connecticut act of 1641 which ordered the town constables to note every person who dressed beyond his social station and to warn him to appear before the Court.[68]

Economic Aspects of Life

IN a newly settled land full of economic opportunities but lacking adequate manpower to exploit them, various economic problems arose very quickly. The shortage of all kinds of labor, skilled and unskilled, inevitably forced wages up beyond accustomed levels in England. In an attempt to meet this situation, Connecticut in June 1641 enacted a sweeping bill fixing wages of all carpenters, plowrights, wheelwrights, masons, joiners, smiths, and coopers at 20*d.* for eleven hours of work in the period March 10–October 10, and 18*d.* for nine hours of work in the remainder of the year. All other artisans and "cheife laborers" were permitted 18*d.* in summer and 14*d.* in winter. Prices for boards and for farm work with oxen and horses also were specifically established.[69]

In New Haven, which earlier became more of a trading center, the Court in 1640 decreed that "comodityes well bought in England for ready mony, shall nott be solde here above 3*d* in the shilling for proffitt and adventure above what they cost w[i]th charges." For wholesale transactions, a markup of one-eighth only was permitted. Commodities brought from other mainland colonies were to be priced according to the risk, which implied a lower profit margin. New Haven approved a price control act far more comprehensive than that of Connecticut, which set maximum wages and prices for the principal types of skilled labor, agricultural labor, seamen, sawing, felling timber, carpentry, fencing, boards and planks of various sorts, and lime.[70]

In 1641 New Haven enacted even more detailed legislation. Skilled artisans were permitted two shillings daily in summer and twenty pence in winter — slightly higher than the Connecticut rates. Because of the shortage of money, the law provided that all goods bought and sold and all wages should be paid for "either in corne . . . or in worke . . . or in cattell of any sort . . . or in good march[en]table bever." In Connecticut, taxes were accepted in the form of Indian corn.[71]

In both colonies, because of lack of staples desired by England, a shortage of money developed from the steady drain to pay for manufactured goods of the mother country. In 1640/41 Connecticut tried to remedy the lack by legislating that each family should procure and plant at least one spoonful of English hemp seed. The second year every family with a plow team was to sow a minimum of one rood of hemp or flax.[72]

The same year the Court

. . . doe find a great expence yerely to be laid out to fetch in supply frō[m] other p[a]rts in such comodityes as are of necessary vse, and not knowing how this Comonwelth can be long supported vnlesse some staple Comodity be raysed amongst o[u]rselues w[hi]ch may in some sort . . . defray the chardge, — haue therefore thought . . . that all incouridgement be giuen for the full imployment of men & cattle . . . for English grayne . . .

Those who volunteered to raise "English grain" (wheat) were to be granted a hundred acres of plowing ground and twenty acres of meadow.[73]

Apparently many farmers concentrated upon grain raising, but with discouraging results. In 1644 the Court noted complaints from Massachusetts and Plymouth that grains from Connecticut were flooding their markets. Meanwhile prices had dipped to low levels. The Court decided to channel all sales out of Connecticut through the hands of Edward Hopkins and William Whiting, who would pay the owners four shillings per bushel for wheat and three shillings for rye. Who-

hemp. The fine virgin forests afforded timber for homes, tar and pitch for boats, and some desperately needed export items — pipe and hogshead staves and headings. Other exports included corn (the principal one), beaver skins, biscuit, bread, and livestock, mostly to nearby coastal areas, such as Boston, New Amsterdam, Long Island, and far-

Early Connecticut painted one-drawer blanket chest (owned by Mrs. Frank Cogan).

ever tried to export these products independently was to forfeit one-half the grain involved.[74]

All of these efforts reflect the large economic difficulties inherent in the rocky, hilly land of Connecticut, where the basis of life had to be agriculture. The typical Connecticut settler raised corn, wheat, rye, and other grains, and bred horses, cattle, swine, and sheep (which at first were imported, mostly from England). Oxen were chiefly used for plowing, and they originally were imported from England, Ireland, and Holland. The cattle provided the settlers with food, hides, transportation, and plowing. The average villager had a garden near the house in which he raised vegetables and small quantities of tobacco, flax, and

ther south; but the grand total of such trade in the 1640's was quite small.[75]

Both Connecticut and New Haven tried to encourage the local exchange of goods. In 1643 Connecticut granted authority for a weekly market in Hartford, on Wednesdays, for all kinds of commodities, cattle, and merchandise. The next year New Haven decreed that there should be two annual markets, in May and September respectively.[76]

In both colonies extremes of wealth and poverty seem to have been quite rare, but the presence of a few wealthy men undoubtedly helped to get each colony launched. John Haynes spent several thousand pounds of his personal fortune in helping to establish the River colony, and at his death left a large "Mansion House" around which were "Outhouses, Barns, Stables, Orchards & Gardens." George Wyllys possessed one of the finest residences in New England, while Richard Lord owned an estate worth about £3,000.[77]

Edward Hopkins ranked among the wealthiest inhabitants of early Hartford. A prosperous London merchant, he had emigrated with Davenport and Eaton, but soon moved to Hartford, where he spread his investments among the fur trade, retailing, fishing, and milling. In September 1640, while governor, he was granted a monopoly of trade up the Connecticut River at Waranoco for a seven-year period, and he also managed a scheme of importing raw cotton for several Connecticut towns. Hopkins and Haynes, both pillars of Hooker's church, regularly alternated as governor and deputy governor — a reflection of the close connection between great wealth, religious orthodoxy, and political power. According to Cotton Mather, Hopkins contributed large sums to the indigent, and he climaxed his benefactions by willing a large sum for schools in Hartford, New Haven, and elsewhere. The career of Hopkins, prior to his final return to England for service under Cromwell, exemplifies the attractive economic opportunities available in Connecticut to the affluent and enterprising capitalist.[78]

Hooker and His Influence

IN the early summer of 1647 "an epidemical sickness" swept through parts of New England. Winthrop reports that it seized the victims "like a cold, and a light fever with it." Few died —

not above forty or fifty in the Massachusetts, and near as many at Connecticut. But that which made the stroke more sensible and grievous, both to them and to all the country, was the death of that faithful servant of the Lord, Mr. Thomas Hooker . . . who, for piety, prudence, wisdom, zeal, learning, and what else might make him serviceable in the place and time he lived in, might be compared with men of greatest note; and he shall need no other praise: the fruits of his labors in both Englands shall preserve an honorable and happy remembrance of him forever.

Thus Winthrop paid graceful and sincere tribute to his friend.[79]

There is no doubt that Thomas Hooker towers over all other men in influence upon early Connecticut. A very modest man, he left a rich legacy, though one keenly debated by later historians. In a broad sense, all of Hooker's previous life had been a preparation for those eleven crowning years at Hartford, 1636–47, when at last he could play the dominant role in shaping the kind of Puritan state which he had envisioned in old England.

In Hooker's last decade he continued to maintain close contact with Boston, and in 1637 he returned to serve on the council summoned for Anne Hutchinson's trial. Two years later he, with Haynes, spent a month at Boston, mostly discussing confederation possibilities. In September 1643 he attended the Cambridge Synod, and two years later he again walked the familiar streets of Cambridge during a church council. There his famous book, *A Survey of the Summe of Church-Discipline*, prepared at the request of the church, was approved and ordered sent to England for printing. In 1643 Hooker, Cotton, and Davenport were invited to attend the Westminster Assembly in England, but after mature consideration they decided that they could not achieve enough to be worth the time and effort required.[80]

In view of Hooker's unquestioned pre-eminence in Connecticut, it is strange how few references to him one finds in the records. Probably this stems partly from his remarkable ability to win people's co-operation and affection; during his entire ministry at Hartford only one person was censured and one excommunicated. When the congregation became thoroughly agitated over some question, Hooker would have the matter tabled. Before the next meeting he "would ordinarily by private conferences, gain over such as were unsatisfied." In the admission of new members Hooker insisted that the elders conduct the required examination. Before major matters were presented to his church he frequently went to his leading elders and carefully explained such proposals. With such careful groundwork and a genuine regard for the feelings of his parishioners, it is scarcely surprising that peace and brotherly love pervaded Hartford's First Church — a condition in sharp contrast to the situation a few years after his death.[81]

Hooker's broad philosophy was well reflected in the Fundamental Orders and his sermon which sparked them, his heated correspondence with Winthrop, and his *Survey*. This last work was prepared unwillingly but deliberately as an answer to a vigorous anti-New England Presbyterian tract by Samuel Rutherford. Hooker's manuscript was sent upon New Haven's famous ghost ship,

living elsewhere, he never had an opportunity to revise them. In the preface to *A Survey* Hooker frankly admitted, moreover, that he lacked a graceful literary style:

As it is beyond my skill, so I professe it is beyond my care to please the nicenesse of mens palates, with any quaintnesse of language. They who covet more sauce than meat, they must provide cooks to their minde.

The Reverend Thomas Hooker's house.

which was lost with all hands and cargo. Again Hooker bent to the task of composition, but death intervened before he finished. Friends saw to it that the unfinished manuscript was forwarded to London, where it finally appeared in print in 1648. In his *Survey* Hooker gave what has been called "the supreme exposition of the Congregational church polity."[82]

Hooker's fame as an author has never been great, perhaps largely because of the circumstances surrounding the publication of nearly all his works. Most of them seem to be collections of sermons and lectures prepared only for oral delivery, and some apparently were printed without Hooker's knowledge, merely from notes taken by some auditor. Since his books were all published in England either posthumously or while he was

In his sermons and treatises one finds no deep theological works but rather the down-to-earth, blunt, and well-organized meditations of an active pastor.[83]

Although Hooker often has been grouped with Cotton and Davenport in the great triumvirate of early Puritan theocrats, he definitely is the most liberal of the group. Giving to individual members of the church more voice than the Massachusetts or New Haven leaders considered desirable, Hooker placed greater emphasis upon the individual congregation and less upon the synod. He showed more concern than most theocrats with the New Testament and with man as a reasonable creature rather than as a miserable sinner. Hooker was a genuine theocrat, however, and an ardent Puritan within a puritanical system. Yet he worked purposefully and successfully to give the people of Connecticut a more democratic church and state than existed in the Bay Colony. As his famous 1638 sermon attests, the covenant of Hooker was based upon "the free consent of the people." Men were free to join with one another in the fellowship of the faith, and were held together in a basically voluntary relationship. Hooker believed, too, that the church covenant resembled "*all other bodies politick.*"[84]

Although Hooker enunciated a doctrine of congregational control over the elders, he reserved great power for the minister over the church members, who "must give way while he delivers the mind of Christ out of the Gospel, and acts all the affairs of his Kingdome, according to his rule; and as it suits with his mind."[85]

In the modern sense of the word Hooker was not a democrat, but he opened the door, perhaps unwittingly, so that Connecticut could progress in that direction. Hooker's ecclesiastical democracy was confined to the "Saints," and his political democracy to the pious and respectable. Unlike Winthrop and Cotton, he held out hope that in time all men could achieve full religious and civil rights. By stressing that authority emanated from *below* and should not be imposed from *above*, he was anticipating the doctrine of popular sovereignty. In comparison with Roger Williams, Hooker seems quite conservative and orthodox, but for his time and place he must be classified as a "liberal." In view of his great contributions as a preacher and minister, a theologian, a pioneer colonizer, and shaper of the Fundamental Orders, Hooker deserves to be ranked among the foremost figures of seventeenth-century America.[86]

CHAPTER 4

From the Code of 1650 to the Charter of 1662 and Absorption of New Haven

Mr. Ludlow's Code — Mission to London — A Remarkable Charter — New Haven and the Regicides — New Haven versus Connecticut — New Haven Surrenders

Mr. Ludlow's Code

ALTHOUGH Connecticut's people believed in a rule of law and the General Court began passing laws as early as April 1636, the colony was slow in codifying its laws, perhaps because no urgent need was felt. Although in December 1642 the Court listed a dozen "Capitall Lawes," or laws carrying the death penalty — among them the practice of witchcraft — it was not until four years later that the Court asked Roger Ludlow to draw up a code of laws for the colony. For several years, however, he was too busy to concentrate upon this task. In Massachusetts, meanwhile, demands for a legal code resulted in the drawing up of the General Laws and Liberties of 1647, published the next year, which apparently proved to be a very useful guide to Ludlow.[1]

In May 1650 Connecticut adopted the codification prepared by Ludlow, often called "Mr. Ludlow's code" or "the code of 1650." This Puritan code began with a ringing statement advocating the rule of law and the protection of individual rights:

. . . no mans life shall bee taken away, no mans honor or good name shall bee stained, no mans person shall

be arrested, restrained, banished, dismembered nor any way punnished; no man shall bee deprived of his wife or children, no mans goods or estate shall bee taken away from him, nor any wayes indamaged, vnder colour of Law . . . vnless it bee by the vertue or equity of some express Law of the Country warranting the same, established by a Generall Courte, and sufficiently published, or in case of the defect of a Law in any perticular case, by the word of God.[2]

The provisions of the code reflect many of the pressing problems of the times, including defense and Indians. The section entitled "Military Affaires" declared that all persons above sixteen years, except magistrates and church officers, should bear arms, and every man above sixteen should possess a good musket and ammunition. Each soldier should train six times yearly and be subject to a grand review twice annually. The soldiers could choose military officers, whom the Court would confirm.[3]

In a lengthy section dealing with Indians, the chief of every tribe was made responsible for actions and damage committed by any Indian of the tribe. Noting that the Indians were growing "bold and insolent" and freely entering white homes, strict measures were enunciated against their handling arms or causing damage. No Connecticut citizen or foreigner could sell arms to Indians, trade with them except in their boats, or own houses or live among them. At least twice yearly an attempt was to be made to instruct the Indians in the Christian religion. Ludlow inserted also the 1646 declaration of the Confederation, which incorporated a severe policy toward Indian offenders. The magistrate of any town where an Indian committed an offense was given full jurisdiction over him, and if he fled, his tribe was held liable to heavy punishments.[4]

For the proper upbringing of children every parent should teach his children enough that they could "read the Inglish tounge" and the "Capitall Lawes." At least once weekly the father must catechize his children "in the grounds and principles of religion." Nor was this all, for every child was to receive training either in husbandry or in another honest calling. A selectman who discovered the master of a family to be still willfully negligent after one warning could find a more proper master until a boy reached twenty-one and a girl eighteen. This harsh provision seems to have served chiefly as a threat rather than as a basis for actual punishment. The Puritan emphasis upon education is proverbial:

It being one chiefe project of that old deluder Sathan, to keepe men from the knowledge of the Scriptures . . . and that Learning may not bee buried in the Graue of o[u]r Forefathers . . . It is therfore ordered . . . that euery Towneshipp within this Jurissdiction, after the Lord hath increased them to the number of fifty houshoulders, shall then forthwith appoint one within theire Towne to teach all such children as shall resorte to him, to write and read . . .

Either the parents or the inhabitants of the town would pay the teacher's salary. When a town reached a hundred families, it should establish a "Grammer Schoole" providing preparation for the college at Cambridge.[5]

The code contained significant sections upon judicial procedures and constables. A grand jury of twelve or fourteen men was to act as often as required "to make presentment of the breaches of any Lawes or orders or any other misdemeanors." In civil suits involving less than forty shillings the case was tried by the magistrates. For other cases the magistrates would impanel a jury of six or twelve, and agreement of four or eight jurymen

respectively was adequate for a decision. If the jury failed to reach a decision, a special verdict could be drawn by a majority of the magistrates, with appeal to the General Court possible. As for the constable, he was to pursue diligently all "Hue

A Colonial hornbook, used in instruction of small children.

and Cryes, after Murthers, Malefactors, Peacebreakers, Theeues, Robbers, Burglarers and other Capitall offendors . . . ," as well as Sabbath-breakers, inebriates, vagrants, and disorderly persons. Each town was to choose its constable annually, and all citizens were required to assist him when help was requested.[6]

The forefathers found the adequate regulation of innkeepers one of their most difficult problems.

As early as June 1644 the Court had ordered that each town should open "an Ordinary," or inn, for care of travelers, and the code continued this obligation of towns. Although ordinaries were essential, yet excessive drinking occurred there:

And euery person found drunken, viz: so that hee bee thereby . . . dissabled in the vse of his vnderstanding, appearing in his speech or gesture, in any of the saide howses or elsewhere, shall forfeitt ten shillings; and for excessiue drinking, three shillings, foure pence; and for continnuing aboue halfe an houre tipling, two shillings six pence; and for tipling at vnseasonable times, or after nine a clock at night, fiue shillings . . . and for want of payment, such shall bee imprisoned vntill they pay, or bee set in the stocks, one houre or more, in some open place, as the weather will permitt, not exceeding three hours at one time . . .[7]

The code contained a section upon "Idlenes" which stated that the constables should apprehend idlers and remand them to the magistrate. In similar vein,

Vppon complaint of great disorder by the Vse of the Game called Shuffle Board, in howses of Common Interteinement, whereby much precious time is spent vnfruitfully and much waste of Wyne and Beare occasioned . . .

the game of shuffleboard was prohibited. Likewise, profanity was a legal offense punishable by a fine or a period of one to three hours in the stocks.[8]

In the category of what the present generation calls "blue laws" one finds a few examples in Connecticut's code. Attendance at Sunday worship service(s) and at special services upon fast and thanksgiving days was required, and unexcused absence called for a fine of five shillings.[9]

In addition to requiring church attendance, the code dealt vigorously with any who interrupted the preacher or challenged him. Censure awaited the first-time offender; and one who for a second time broke forth into similar "contemptuous carriages" could be fined five pounds. If the latter was unwilling to pay the fine he could be placed on a stool four feet high on lecture day, "with a paper fixed on his breast written with Capital Letters, AN OPEN AND OBSTINATE CONTEMNER OF GODS HOLY ORDINANCES."[10]

The maintenance of the ministers of the Puritan Church was made an obligation upon every taxpayer, whatever his own personal religious beliefs.

In October 1644 the Court had adopted the recommendations of the Confederation commissioners for ministerial support, and these were incorporated into the code. This provision was not impractical as long as the settlers were so largely homogeneous in religious outlook, but it held the seeds of future trouble when large nonconformist elements appeared.[11]

New Haven Colony similarly, in 1655, formally approved the collection of laws which were submitted by the governor as "most necessary to continew as lawes here." Rigorous Puritanism was even more pronounced in New Haven's code than in Connecticut's. It provided, for instance, that proud and presumptuous profanation of the Sabbath by "unlawful sport" and the like, as a sin against the known command of God, was punishable by death. As in Connecticut, every inhabitant was required to support the clergy of the official church. The Puritans had not come to Connecticut for religious toleration but to worship God exactly as *they* thought proper. For the strict Anglican conformity espoused by Archbishop Laud they substituted an almost equally inflexible Puritan theocracy which in many aspects appears excessively harsh to most Americans of today.[12]

Mission to London

AFTER living happily under the Fundamental Orders and Ludlow's code, in 1660 Connecticut suddenly awoke to a grave threat when disturbing "intelligence" arrived from England — Charles II had been officially restored to the throne. The rule of Cromwell and the Puritans had created a sense of security in Connecticut, but now that complacency was shattered by the realization that Connecticut was operating without any firm legal basis whatever. The Warwick Patent, Indian land grants, and the Fundamental Orders certainly possessed no authority in the eyes of the English Government. Strong fears existed that the new government in England, unfriendly to Puritans in general, would assume absolute control over all of the Puritan colonies.[13]

Connecticut's leaders decided that their best hope lay in petitioning for a legal charter from Charles II. Governor Winthrop therefore lost little time in calling an unofficial meeting on February 14, 1660/61, to talk over the foreboding situation and agree tentatively upon a course of action. On March 14, 1660/61, the legislators resolved:

... it is our duty and very necessary to make a speedy address to his Sacred Maiesty, our Soveraigne Lord Charles the Second ... to acknowledge our loyalty & allegiance to his highnes, hereby declareing and professing ourselues, all the Inhabitants of this Colony, to be his Highnes loyall and faythfull subjects. And doe further conclude it necessary that we should humbly petition his Maiesty for grace and fauour, and for ye continuance and confirmation of such prividges and liberties as are necessary for the comfortable and peaceable settlement of this Colony.

In May the Court chose as a committee to complete the preparations Governor John Winthrop, Jr., Deputy Governor John Mason, and seven others. Besides preparing a petition to the king they composed letters to such "noble p[e]rsonages" as might appear helpful. In June these documents, plus detailed instructions for the agent, were laid before the Court and approved.[14]

To go to England and carry on the delicate mission the Court chose the finest possible representative — Governor John Winthrop, Jr. The eldest son of Massachusetts' famous leader, he was born February 12, 1605/6, at Groton, the Winthrop family's manor in Suffolk. Receiving his grammar school education at Bury St. Edmunds, he entered Trinity College, Dublin, but apparently he did not graduate. For a short time he studied law at the Inner Temple, London, but soon found that law held no fascination. There followed a brief period of military experience and of travel as far as Constantinople. In 1631 he emulated his father in coming to Massachusetts, where he received a very warm reception. Within three years he was chosen magistrate and later frequently re-elected. Although one of the founders of Ipswich, he soon moved to Salem. Early interested in various industrial schemes, especially iron manufacturing, he journeyed to England in 1641 and returned with not only financial backing but also a group of skilled workers. He took a prominent part in iron enterprises at Saugus, Massachusetts, and New Haven Colony. In 1646 he initiated the settlement at Pequot, soon renamed New London.[15]

Thenceforth he devoted most of his time to Con-

necticut's interests. Despite heavy public responsibilities he actively practiced medicine for years, as evidenced by his voluminous medical notes now kept at the Massachusetts Historical Society. In 1648 New London elected him a magistrate, though he still held a Massachusetts office. Soon afterward he moved to New Haven, which wanted him to direct the local iron works. In 1651 Connecticut chose him as an assistant, and in 1657 elected him governor. So great was Winthrop's popularity that in 1660 the Court voted to eliminate the provision of the Fundamental Orders restricting a governor's tenure to only one year in any two. Thenceforth Winthrop enjoyed an uninterrupted tenure, with re-election yearly until his death in 1676.[16]

In choosing Winthrop to make the fateful trip overseas, Connecticut had selected the man by far the best equipped in experience, knowledge, and personality for achieving the goal. When Winthrop embarked from New Amsterdam on July 23, 1661, he carried with him the petition and address to the king and several letters, as well as elaborate personal instructions.[17]

Arriving at London in September, Winthrop took up residence with William Whiting on Coleman Street, next door to Davenport's former church. Procuring a charter was a tedious and complicated business, and Winthrop found that the Puritan colonies in America had many enemies, including Samuel Maverick, close friend of the Earl of Clarendon, the Lord Chancellor. Maverick had recommended that both Connecticut and New Haven be "reduced under his Ma[jes]ties obedience."[18]

Fortunately Connecticut and Winthrop possessed powerful friends who included Lord Say and Sele, recently Lord Privy Seal; Lord Brooke, also a grantee under the Warwick Patent; and the Earl of Manchester, then Lord Chamberlain of the Household. Being widely known, Winthrop doubtless used his many months in England to good advantage socially as well as officially. While there he was proposed and admitted as a member of the Royal Society — an honor accorded to very few Americans.[19]

When he learned that his petition was not in approved form, Winthrop proceeded to have another drawn up. Lord Say and Sele, though ill, gave Winthrop valuable introductions and spoke in his behalf to Clarendon. Early in 1662 Winthrop

sary steps and on May 10, 1662, as a writ of privy seal, was enrolled and the same day received the great seal.[20]

John Winthrop, Jr. (1606–76).

presented his final petition to Sir Edward Nicholas, one of the chief secretaries of state, who referred it to the Attorney General. Upon receipt of a favorable opinion, the secretary, acting in accord with instructions of the king in council, had a warrant issued under the royal sign manual empowering the Attorney General to draw up the charter, apparently with Winthrop's own version as a guide. The charter then went through all neces-

Winthrop, not being ready to leave England immediately, apparently entrusted the precious charter to two Massachusetts agents, Simon Bradstreet and the Reverend John Norton, who were on the point of sailing. They arrived in Boston on September 3, 1662, and probably on the next day handed it over to the Connecticut delegates, Samuel Wyllys and John Talcott, at the current meeting of the Confederation. Unquestionably

Wyllys and Talcott brought the document back to Hartford and turned it over to Secretary John Allyn.[21]

A Remarkable Charter

CONNECTICUT's charter of 1662 was truly an amazing document which gave to the people of Connecticut not only a clear legal basis for their colony but also, and most important, a very high degree of self-government. The moderate religious policies of the colony, resulting in no serious complaints against it at London, had made Winthrop's task much easier.[22]

King Charles II, in this charter, made of John Winthrop, Jr., and others a body corporate called the "Governour and Company of the English Colony of Conecticut in New England in America." The members of the company were the freemen of the colony, and the company could lease, grant, alienate, bargain, sell, and dispose of property as other corporations could do. The document provided for a governor, deputy governor, and twelve assistants, to be chosen annually in May by the freemen. For the first year the charter specifically named the governor — Winthrop; the deputy governor — Mason; and the twelve assistants. Twice a year the assembly, with not more than two members elected by each of the towns from among the freemen, was to meet and act upon the business of the corporation. The freemen of Connecticut, enjoying all the "liberties and Immunities" of natural-born Englishmen, were required to take the oath of supremacy. Full judicial powers were granted to the legislature or to the governor or deputy and any six assistants. The lawmaking powers resided in the legislature, but it must enact none "contrary to the lawes and Statutes of this our Realme of England."[23]

The land tenure granted to the freemen of Connecticut was that of the Manor of East Greenwich — the freest of any in England. In return, the Crown was to receive one-fifth of all gold and silver ore mined — an utterly chimerical hope, as it turned out! Other important provisions authorized the erection of courts, the free carrying on of trade, the raising of troops whenever necessary for defense and safety, the execution of all laws passed and published under the common seal of Connecticut, and the enjoyment of fishing rights on the coasts and adjoining seas.[24]

The charter established Narragansett Bay as the eastern boundary, the Massachusetts line on the north, Long Island Sound and the ocean on the south. On the west, Connecticut was to run all the way to the "South Sea," meaning the Pacific Ocean. This grant was so generous that it produced protracted boundary disputes with Rhode Island, Massachusetts, New York, and Pennsylvania.[25]

Winthrop could take justifiable pride in Connecticut's charter of 1662, as the essentials of the Fundamental Orders were perpetuated and most of his and Connecticut's suggestions were embodied, although the colony failed to obtain exemption from English customs duties. To all intents and purposes the freemen could run their government in the accustomed pattern, with so little English control as scarcely to be noticed. Circumstances undoubtedly favored Winthrop's mission, but his diplomacy still merits the highest accolades.[26]

New Haven and the Regicides

THE news of Charles II's accession likewise deeply alarmed New Haven, which had greatly enjoyed the Puritan rule in England, during which a number of its most eminent leaders — including Richard Malbon, Francis Newman, and David Yale — had returned to England.[27]

An event related to the Restoration caused much excitement in New Haven. Two of the men who had signed the death warrant of Charles I, Colonels William Goffe and Edward Whalley, fled to Boston. Word reached Boston that warrants were out for their arrest, so they fled, arriving at Davenport's home on March 7, 1660/61. Royal agents, hearing that the regicides were there, quickly followed. The agents demanded aid of Deputy Governor William Leete, who cleverly delayed them while giving others an opportunity to spread the news to New Haven. A Sabbath intervened, and when the royal agents finally reached New Haven they were frustrated at every turn. In the meantime, thanks to the great hue and

Charter granted to Connecticut by Charles II in 1662.

cry raised over the agents, Whalley and Goffe had fled to a mill two miles north of the town. After a fruitless search the officers went on to New Amsterdam in hopes that their victims could be found there.[28]

When the storm had blown over temporarily, Whalley and Goffe were taken by Richard Sperry to a spot high on West Rock. Here in the famous "Judges Cave," where several huge slabs of traprock provided protection against wind and rain, the regicides stayed for nearly a month. Their devoted friend Sperry daily brought them food from his house nearly a mile away. For the next three years or so the regicides lived at various places in the colony, but chiefly at Micah Tomkins' home in Milford. In 1664 four royal commissioners

arrived in Boston with instructions, among others, to apprehend the regicides. Whalley and Goffe returned to their cave, but soon fled to Hadley, Massachusetts, where the local minister concealed them.[29]

A third regicide, Colonel John Dixwell, later boldly moved from Hadley to New Haven, adopted the pseudonym James Davids, and became a highly respected member of the community. He married twice, in 1673 and in 1677, was admitted to the First Church, and after his death on March 18, 1688/89, was honorably buried in the Green behind the church. New Haven's involvement in the concealment of two regicides was strongly suspected and reprobated by English authorities and caused some resentment.[30]

A

HISTORY

OF THREE OF THE

JUDGES

OF

KING CHARLES I.

MAJOR-GENERAL WHALLEY, MAJOR-GENE-
RAL GOFFE, and COLONEL DIXWELL:

WHO, AT THE RESTORATION, 1660, FLED TO AMERICA;
AND WERE SECRETED AND CONCEALED, IN
MASSACHUSETTS AND CONNECTICUT,
FOR NEAR THIRTY YEARS.

WITH AN ACCOUNT OF

Mr. THEOPHILUS WHALE, of Narragansett,
Supposed to have been also one of the Judges.

BY *PRESIDENT STILES.*

They wandered about—being destitute, afflicted, tormented—they wander-
ed in deserts, and in mountains, and in dens and caves of the earth.
—Of whom the world was not worthy.——
Be not forgetful to entertain strangers : for thereby some have entertained
Angels unawares.   Heb. xi. and xiii.

HARTFORD: PRINTED BY ELISHA BABCOCK.

1794.

EZRA STILES   S.T.D. LL.D.

Prefident of Yale College.

Adventures of the regicides have remained of interest to later generations.

New Haven versus Connecticut

NEW HAVEN's internal position meanwhile was precarious and growing weaker, and Eaton's death in 1658 removed the most enterprising leader. Some of the outlying towns, restive under her iron rule, were openly threatening secession. As a result of the failure of the Delaware venture, the loss of the "Great Shippe," and growing expenditures, the colony felt too poor to send its own agent to England to plead for a charter. So, turning first to Massachusetts, the colony asked her to present New Haven's case. Nothing came of this, so Gov-

ernor Leete in desperation begged Winthrop to speak also for New Haven and try to obtain a single charter which would legalize the claims of both colonies, including land "beyond Delaware" for New Haven — undoubtedly a naïve request. In any case, Winthrop had already sailed, and may never have seen Leete's letter. Winthrop's instructions, moreover, clearly called for a charter which would include all of the New Haven colony.[31]

When news of Connecticut's charter reached New Haven, consternation prevailed among the leaders. To make matters much worse, several of the outlying towns, Southold, Stamford, and

72

Greenwich, flocked to Connecticut's standard; and Guilford threatened to bolt. Just Milford and Branford stayed loyal, and Milford only to 1664.[32]

In October 1662 a committee from Connecticut's General Court appeared at New Haven, thrust a copy of the charter under the unhappy eyes of New Haven's magistrates, and asked that the union be effected immediately. This precipitated a two-year struggle between the two Puritan colonies.[33]

New Haven offered stubborn resistance, with Davenport and Nicholas Street spearheading the forces against union. The possibility of an address to Charles II was broached but not followed up. Meanwhile Connecticut's assembly in March 1662 /63 appointed a special committee to carry on further negotiations. Large promises were made, including noninterference with the New Haven churches; a proportionate number of assistants; acceptance of New Haven freemen as freemen in Connecticut; and representation by two deputies from each town in New Haven's jurisdiction; but all to no avail.[34]

After Winthrop's return to Connecticut, further negotiations went on, again with little success. New Haven feared union as the complete triumph of the less orthodox political and religious practices of Connecticut, an eventuality so dreadful to some that they seriously considered settling in New Netherlands. Stuyvesant and the West India Company encouraged such plans, and they might have worked out had not serious boundary disputes with Connecticut delayed matters and the English capture of New Amsterdam in 1664 ended them.[35]

At the beginning of 1664 New Haven's Court asked John Davenport and Nicholas Street to prepare a paper outlining New Haven's grievances. This was done in "Newhavens Case Stated," a hard-hitting attack upon Connecticut's "unjust pretences & Encroachments." Connecticut replied that it acted upon the basis of a definite charter and, in addition, had made generous promises. As for appeals by New Haven to England and English friends, there was no more force in those than "in a dreame of rich reuenues to an awakeing poore man."[36]

In April 1664 a special royal commission, created to examine conditions in New England, concerned itself with such matters as reducing the Dutch claims to Long Island and nearby land, apprehending the regicides, and checking upon enforcement of the Navigation Acts. Equipped with four vessels and 450 men, the commissioners, after the fall of New Amsterdam, turned their attention to New England's internal conditions. Obviously the deep-seated differences between Connecticut and New Haven could be used by the commissioners as a lever for recommending punitive action against both. Massachusetts, at this juncture, strongly advised Connecticut to reach an agreement with New Haven before all of the New England charters were nullified. Connecticut promptly dispatched John Whiting, associate pastor of Hartford's church, and Thomas Bull to New Haven with news of the Bay's practical advice, the activities of the commissioners, and another request that New Haven accept the union.[37]

New Haven Surrenders

SINCE the seceding towns no longer were paying taxes, New Haven's treasury was nearly empty and its situation almost hopeless. Inclusion in Connecticut, though unpalatable, began to appear preferable to being swallowed up in the Duke of York's Anglican colony, which had been granted boundaries extending from the Connecticut to the Delaware River. A Confederation commissioners' meeting at Hartford in September urged final settlement of the dispute, and Connecticut protested the presence of the two New Haven commissioners. A meeting of New Haven's Court a few days later revealed a serious weakening of opposition to union, but it broke up without any decision. In October Connecticut appointed magistrates from New Haven for service under Connecticut. In November Milford showed that the end was near by voting to join Connecticut.[38]

At the end of the month a vote of three of the royal commissioners gave Long Island to New York and fixed Connecticut's western and southern bounds at Mamaroneck River and Long Island Sound respectively, which meant recognition of New York and Connecticut claims to *all* of the New Haven Colony. On December 13, 1664, at a

General Court of New Haven, the freemen reluctantly voted to submit to Connecticut, and a few weeks later the town of New Haven also yielded.[39]

The merging of New Haven into Connecticut then went ahead rapidly. In April 1665 the General Assembly at Hartford placed eight of the leading men of the former New Haven Colony in nomination for assistants in Connecticut, and in May four were chosen — William Leete, William Jones, Benjamin Fenn, and Jasper Crane. In late May and August 1665 the General Assembly actions and laws of Connecticut were read to town meetings of the former New Haven Colony towns. Absorption of New Haven had been achieved![40]

A few die-hards of the New Haven Colony preferred emigration to rule by Connecticut. After complicated negotiations with the proprietors of New Jersey, some inhabitants of Branford, Guilford, Milford, and New Haven, under the spiritual leadership of Abraham Pierson of Branford, migrated in 1666 to the Passaic River in New Jersey and founded Milford, later called Newark. By 1673 the new "Bible State" was firmly settled and numbered eighty-six families.[41]

For John Davenport, too, the cause of Christ in New Haven seemed miserably lost, and he welcomed an invitation in September 1667 from Boston's First Church. Unfortunately a vociferous minority there opposed Davenport because of his age and theology. The New Haven church, wanting to keep him and spare him the factional strife in Boston, refused to dismiss him. Finally, in November 1668, under dubious and unclear circumstances, Davenport accepted a call to the Boston church. Since his coming precipitated a secession of the vocal minority, he knew little peace of mind in Boston and died there soon afterward in March 1669/70 — a sad ending for the energetic and far-seeing spiritual commander and cofounder of New Haven.[42]

It is possible that with good luck the New Haven Colony might have existed longer; but the long-range outlook could only have been very discouraging. Commercially it had done poorly, since it possessed no great river or hinterland. Moreover, the advances of Connecticut and New York blocked all hopes of future territorial expansion. The ultraconservative policies concerning church membership and political rights had created enough dissatisfaction so that many envied Connecticut's more liberal attitudes. The key to New Haven's collapse, however, clearly lay in her lack of a charter, which left her finally unable to resist her confident neighbor, Connecticut.[43]

New Haven's defeat was inevitable and, in the long run, for the best. Only by joining the two colonies together could there be created one with large enough dimensions to exercise real influence in intercolonial and, later, in national affairs. It is regrettable, however, that Connecticut, sincere and solid as were its beliefs and legal position, adopted such a bullying approach in pushing the matter of union. New Haven brought both its rich heritage and a galaxy of able leaders to Connecticut. In 1676 its own William Leete (last governor of New Haven) was elected governor of Connecticut — a position he held until his death in 1683. Furthermore, New Haven served as one of Connecticut's two capital cities until 1875, when Hartford became sole capital.[44]

CHAPTER 5

King Philip's War and Andros' Challenge to the Charter

Intimations of Indian Trouble — Connecticut Enters King Philip's War — Campaign Against the Narragansets — A Period of Discouragement — The Indians Are Finally Crushed — A Threat from New York — Report on Connecticut in 1680 — Ominous Moves Toward Centralization — Andros Pays a Visit and the Charter Disappears — The Overthrow of Andros

Intimations of Indian Trouble

IN the three decades after the crushing of the Pequots the New England Indians still could muster a formidable force of warriors, but the colonists, allied with Uncas and his Mohegans, tended to relax. The Narragansets, feeling that the death of Miantonomo was an enormous miscarriage of justice, no longer attached any confidence to the white man's courts. Further enraged by the white alliance with Uncas, the Narragansets smoldered for years, awaiting an opportunity for revenge.[1]

As a result of the 1638 agreement dividing up the remnants of the Pequots, Uncas obtained temporary control of the northern part of the Pequot territory and almost doubled the size of his tribe. In 1666, two white men were appointed as overseers to advise the Indian governors and protect the rights of the Indians. The next step came in the establishment of reservations, one comprising 2,000 acres in New London, set off in 1667, the other in North Stonington, in 1683. Earlier, in 1659, the Assembly had created the Golden Hill reservation for the Poquonock Indians. Thus the Connecticut Indians became abjectly dependent upon the white settlers.[2]

Some sustained missionary effort occurred in New England, especially by John Eliot in Massachusetts; but in Connecticut there was less missionary activity. Around 1661 Abraham Pierson of Branford started preaching to nearby Indians, but he apparently enjoyed very little success before his departure to New Jersey. In 1671 the Reverend James Fitch of Norwich began work among the Mohegans, and by great efforts won a few converts. Some funds of the Society for Propagating the Gospel in New England, founded in England, were used in the Connecticut missionary efforts. Of the 4,000 or so Christian Indians in New England by 1675, however, only a handful lived in Connecticut.[3]

Uneasiness and suspicions pervaded not only the Narragansets but also most of the other large tribes as well. In 1662 the venerable Massasoit, sachem of the Wampanoags and great friend of the infant Plymouth Colony, passed away. The Wampanoags, seeing their former extensive sovereignty being steadily whittled away, grew increasingly hostile. Plymouth, adopting an overbearing attitude in the face of the growing opposition, and treating Philip, second son of Massasoit and current sachem of the Wampanoags, with

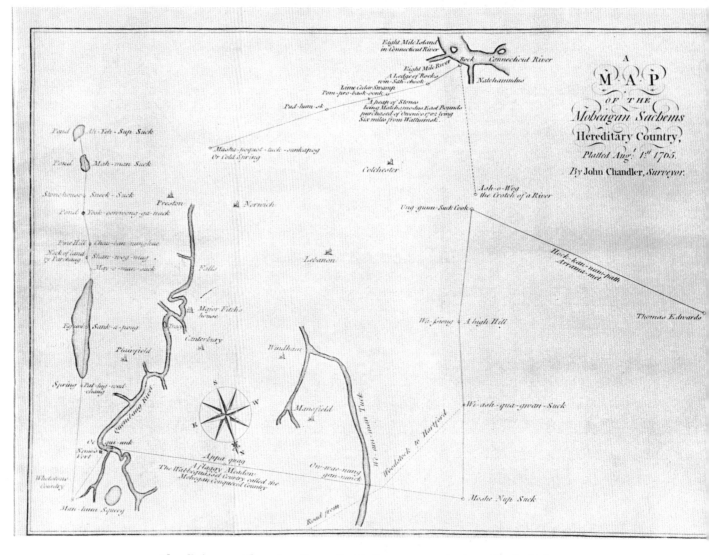

Chandler's map of the eastern Connecticut Indian country — dominated by the Mohegans.

marked disrespect and severity, attempted to disarm completely this tribe, who had become accustomed to owning muskets and opposed giving them up.[4]

On the surface, the Indian threat at the beginning of 1675 did not appear grave. The whites, numbering perhaps 80,000 in New England, could assemble about 16,000 men of military age. The Indians, including those in Maine, probably could put in the field only about 3,500 warriors. The Narragansets, located in western Rhode Island and eastern Connecticut, commanded perhaps 1,000; the Nipmucks and allied tribes, of central Massachusetts and the northeastern fringes of Connecticut, could muster about 1,000. The Massachusetts and Pawtucket tribes together approximately equaled the Nipmucks; while the Wampanoags and their kindred, of Plymouth and eastern Rhode Island, totaled about 500 braves.[5]

Connecticut's Assembly in November 1673 passed an act revealing widespread carelessness about preparedness and ordering a "muster-master" to oversee a program aimed at remedying arms deficiencies of the militia. The martial spirit of the early days had become greatly vitiated at the very time when the many new, isolated frontier settlements offered tempting targets to the still bellicose Indians. Land acquired aggressively by the white men, often by methods which seemed unjust to the Indians, formed a major cause of increasing interracial antagonisms.[6]

Connecticut Enters King Philip's War

AFTER serious war scares in 1667, 1669, and 1671, King Philip's War erupted in June 1675 at Swan-

76

sea, Massachusetts, where several whites were killed. At first it was a local conflict between the Wampanoags, under their chief, Philip, for whom the war was named, and Plymouth and Boston. Apparently it was sparked by the conviction and hanging of three Indians for the murder of a Christian Indian. Large forces were raised by the colonists, who found it impossible to maneuver the Indians into a large-scale battle. Meanwhile, attempts through an armed demonstration to ensure the neutrality of the Narragansets failed dismally and served merely to unite the Indians all over New England in a loose alliance against the colonists. Philip, of the Wampanoags, and Canonchet, of the Narragansets, played leading roles in welding together this dangerous conspiracy.[7]

Despite long contact with Indians, the New England settlers generally refused to adopt Indian tactics for fighting. When Captain Benjamin Church inquired of Indian allies how they held such a great advantage over the whites in the woods,

They told him, that the Indians gained great advantage of the English by two things; [they] always took care in their marches and fights, not to come too thick together; but the English always kept in a heap together; [so] that it was as easy to hit them, as to hit a house. The other was, that if at any time they discovered a company of English soldiers in the woods, they knew that there were all, for the English never scattered, but the Indians always divided and scattered.[8]

In the early stages of the war, with only the Wampanoags in open opposition, Connecticut, although more cautious and conciliatory than Massachusetts, began to take measures for defense. (Rhode Island, incidentally, remained essentially neutral throughout the war.) The first alarms in Connecticut were sounded by Stonington and New London, which caused the governor and assistants on July 1, 1675, to order thirty dragoons and ten troopers raised and sent to those towns. The same day a letter, with information about the Indian attacks and advice to check up on defenses, was dispatched from Hartford to New Haven and nearby towns. A few days later Captain Thomas Bull was selected to assume command of the defense of the southeastern area. Captain Wait Winthrop soon invaded the Narra-

ganset country and joined Captain Samuel Hutchinson of Massachusetts in forcing a short-lived treaty upon the Narragansets. At a special session on July 9 the Assembly set up a special council, under the governor, to take care of all emergencies which might arise between meetings of the Assembly.[9]

Luckily Connecticut was not in immediate danger because of her location — distant from the fighting area — and because of the firm Mohegan alliance. Uncas, though aged, still greeted with enthusiasm the opportunity to strike again at his old enemies, the Narragansets. The authorities in Connecticut gladly accepted Mohegan aid upon most expeditions and thus escaped the ambushes which wiped out so many Massachusetts militia.[10]

In the summer ominous signs of a spreading Indian alliance appeared. A party of marauding Nipmucks attacked Mendon, Massachusetts, in mid-July, and followed this with a fearful assault upon a garrison house at Brookfield which failed but left the town mostly in ruins. Once the Nipmucks went on the warpath, the conflict inevitably spread through central Massachusetts to the Connecticut River Valley. Connecticut's northern frontier lay dangerously exposed and Hartford cooperated closely henceforth with Springfield, as well as with Boston and Plymouth.[11]

News of the Nipmuck attack upon Brookfield and a plea for help from Major John Pynchon of Springfield caused an emergency meeting of the governor and his War Council "about 1 in the morning" on August 5, 1675. Forty men, under Lieutenant Thomas Watts, were ordered to march to Springfield and place themselves at Major Pynchon's disposal. The next day the Council called for a hundred dragoons in Hartford County, sixty in New Haven County, and seventy in Fairfield County, "to be in readiness upon an hower's warning for a march." Several bands of Mohegans and Pequots, including some under Joshua, a son of Uncas, marched into Massachusetts.[12]

By late summer of 1675 rumors spread of unrest among the Connecticut River Indians. Hearing of the disaffection of the Nonatuck Indians near Northampton, the colonists determined to disarm them by a surprise attack. The venture failed, however, as the Nonatuck warriors escaped into a swamp near Mount Wequomps, from which they greeted their pursuers with a hot volley.[13]

Since the valley offered a convenient invasion route from Massachusetts into Connecticut, the Connecticut Council rightly regarded the war as of greatly increased gravity. Late in August they appointed Major Robert Treat as commander of Connecticut troops, a post which he held for the remainder of the war. Treat scarcely had begun his march northward when word of Indians skulking close to Hartford brought his troops back. Meanwhile the Pocumtuck Indians struck Deerfield, were repulsed, and vented their wrath by burning all buildings beyond the range of rifle fire and driving off the cattle.[14]

Connecticut took immediate steps to establish night watches in all towns, to use armed companies for doing work in the fields, and to patrol the main roads. Meanwhile, on the valley frontier, a surprise Pocumtuck attack occurred at Northfield, some men were shot down, and the survivors, plus women and children, took refuge in the stockade. Treat's forces rushed to the rescue, found the shocked survivors too worn out for further resistance, and supervised the abandonment of the town. As the summer of 1675 drew to a close the Indians held the upper hand — a fact made even clearer by another massacre near Deerfield, caused by carelessness. This resulted in evacuation of Deerfield.[15]

Just two days earlier, on September 16, the Confederation had voted to call out 1,000 men, including those in service, of which Connecticut's share was 315. In spite of this action, the unimpressed Indians continued their depredations, and on October 5 they struck Springfield, destroying thirty houses. Meanwhile wild rumors swept over Connecticut. Indians were spotted at Glastonbury, while the Reverend Thomas Fitch of Norwich reported that Philip's Narragansets planned an invasion of the colony. Governor Andros of New York caused great consternation by writing that 5,000 or 6,000 Indians would soon move into western Connecticut and attack Hartford. Again special security measures were taken, and Treat was recalled with 60 men. Later, when no invasion eventuated, this force returned to the northern frontier.[16]

Campaign Against the Narragansets

ALTHOUGH the war had spread considerably, the Narragansets still had maintained an uneasy neutrality. When they refused to deliver up refugees of the warring Wampanoags, the Confederation early in November considered declaring war against the Narragansets. At first, Connecticut representative Governor Winthrop tried to counter the belligerency of Massachusetts and Plymouth; but finally, after further discussion, he supported the war declaration and the calling up of 1,000 additional men to serve under Major Josiah Winslow of Plymouth.[17]

In Connecticut preparations for the showdown with the Narragansets went ahead rapidly, with Major Robert Treat being named to lead Connecticut's five companies of men, numbering 315. Wages were set, a commissary appointed, 300 bushels of wheat ordered reserved, and no provisions were permitted to be exported out of New London County for two months.[18]

On December 18 the troops of the three colonies, including 300 whites and 150 Indians from Connecticut, rendezvoused at Pettaquamscut in Rhode Island. After a night in bitter cold, the combined army set out for their objective, a fortified winter village of the Narragansets on a hillock in the middle of a cedar swamp. Almost impregnable, except when the swamp was frozen, the unusually strong stockade was reinforced with a hedge and inner embankment of rocks and clay. Outside, a number of blockhouses and flankers commanded every approach.[19]

Avoiding an ambush, thanks probably to the Mohegan and Pequot scouts, the army approached the fort soon after midday on December 19. Some of the Massachusetts men in the front column quickly detected the one weak point in the defenses — an unfinished section of stockade protected only by a large tree and a nearby blockhouse. Immediately they charged across the frozen swamp. Part of the Narragansets, armed with rifles, aimed murderous volleys at the whites, who fell in large numbers. After this failure Major Samuel Appleton rallied the remainder of the Massachusetts men, who cleared out the nearby flanker. Meanwhile the Connecticut troops, labor-

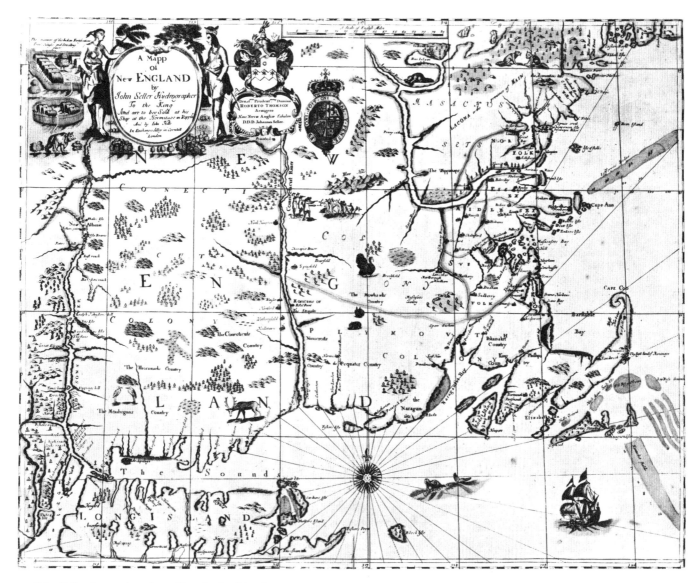

John Sellers' map of southern New England in 1675.

ing under a blistering fire, pushed resolutely through the breach in the palisade, despite the loss of Captain John Gallop, Captain Samuel Marshall, and Lieutenant Nathaniel Seely, and the mortal wounding of Captain John Mason. Behind them came the Plymouth contingent, and vicious hand-to-hand fighting broke out among the wigwams. Possibly by accident, but more likely by deliberate design, the wigwams caught fire and waves of flames soon engulfed the fort. As in the Pequot encampment forty years earlier, a fearful massacre of Indians followed, including many women and children. The Narragansets were badly beaten, but some warriors escaped. The victorious whites, having suffered about 20 per-

cent casualties, then debated what to do as darkness approached and a snowstorm sprang up. Finally the decision was made to retreat to Wickford.[20]

The eighteen-mile march back through deep snow was a nightmare of suffering and exhaustion. About two the next morning, after twenty-two of the grievously wounded had expired, the main body stumbled into Richard Smith's plantation at Wickford. Connecticut's casualties in the affair were high — out of the three hundred Connecticut men in action about forty were killed and as many more wounded. The little army was so battered and morale so low that Major Treat felt it essential to return his forces to Connecticut.[21]

While the heavy losses suffered by the Narragansets in the "great swamp fight" seriously weakened the tribe, they rendered the surviving warriors desperate partners in the widespread Indian alliance. Peace negotiations were carried on, but neither side trusted the other and each hurried preparations for the spring campaigns. The Confederation called for a thousand additional men to fight the Indians.[22]

A Period of Discouragement

IN Connecticut the severe casualties and great hardships of the previous campaign caused discouragement and slowness in recruiting men for the new offensive planned. The governor and Council adopted a lenient attitude "towards raw souldyers, vnacquainted w[i]th marshall discipline" in order to spur enlistments. Many Connecticut men felt disinclined to march forty or fifty miles into the wilderness to fight Indians when others were skulking about only fifteen miles away.[23]

Late in January about 1,400 men from the three colonies made a five-day raid upon the Indians which accomplished little beyond burning wigwams, driving the Narraganset warriors deeper into the wilderness, and creating some very hungry pursuers! Philip, meanwhile, moved his winter quarters to Schaghticoke, near Albany, New York, where he carried on dangerous intrigues with the Mohawks and the French, as well as with Dutch traders. The New England authorities, and especially Governor Winthrop and the War Council, engaged in a prolonged correspondence with Governor Andros of New York over the Indian activities in his area.[24]

During the late winter and early spring the Indians redoubled their attacks all along the frontier. This came as the logical outcome of the first wartime meeting of Philip and Canonchet with the Pocumtuck and Nipmuck chiefs and others, held March 9, 1675/76, near Northfield. Apparently the Indians decided to seek a decisive victory, while their women and children cultivated crops and fished unmolested in the fertile and abandoned Connecticut Valley between Deerfield and Northfield.[25]

For a time the Indian plans seemed to be progressing smoothly. Raiding parties struck successfully against many towns, including Lancaster, Concord, Northampton, Springfield, Groton, Medford, Marlborough, and Weymouth. The towns on Narragansett Bay mostly were abandoned, and few settlers remained even in Providence, though Roger Williams' great reputation with Indians won him personal immunity from attack. One band of Indians even gave Connecticut a direct taste of invasion by slaying Henry Denslow in Pine Meadow (now Windsor Locks), looting the empty houses in Simsbury on March 26, and then firing them.[26]

In April sorrow enveloped the colony when Governor Winthrop, who had gone to Boston as one of Connecticut's commissioners to a Confederation meeting, fell ill and died suddenly on April 5, 1676. He was interred in the same tomb with his father. Thus ended the career of one of Connecticut's most beloved and talented colonial leaders.[27]

The Indians Are Finally Crushed

THUS far 1676 had brought an almost unchecked series of Indian triumphs; but the tide of battle suddenly began to change in April of that year with the unexpected capture of Canonchet. The chief was taken near Pawtucket River by a group of Connecticut volunteers under Captains George Denison, James Avery, and John Stanton, aided by Indian allies. They offered Canonchet his life if he would persuade his tribe to cease fighting, but he haughtily refused and requested that Oneko, son of Uncas, put him to death. The sentence of death was prescribed, and Pequots, Mohegans, and Niantics joined in cruelly executing him. So perished the audacious, if arrogant, leader of the Narragansets, whose loss irreparably injured the Indian cause.[28]

Although serious Indian depredations continued through the spring, their power was waning; while the whites, making more use of friendly Indians, fell into fewer ambushes. At Norwich, Major John Talcott collected a force of about 240 whites and 200 Indians, which went into the Nipmuck country on a largely fruitless chase called by Talcott's men the "long and hungry march." More profitable was the expedition in June, made with Massachusetts forces, during which they swept the valley near and above Hadley and ended the large-scale Indian raids in the Connecticut Valley. This was followed by a general offensive into the Narraganset country, during which Talcott's little army enjoyed great success, ruthlessly clearing

Indian ally shot him dead. Full of pride and bitter resentment against the English, who were steadily breaking up cherished Indian traditions, Philip may have started the war in the conviction that it was the last chance of saving his tribe. The uprising had soon become too broad for Philip to control, and he acted only as one leader among many

Buttolph-Williams House, Wethersfield (1680).

large areas of Indians and slaying or capturing over 200 of them.[29]

The weakening Indian resistance to this raid and others made by Massachusetts revealed clearly by the spring of 1676 the near collapse of the whole Indian alliance, precipitated by failure of their food supply. The Indian will to fight had weakened so greatly that a Massachusetts and Plymouth offer of pardon to Indians who voluntarily surrendered brought in over three hundred during July.[30]

In the meantime the search went on for King Philip, the symbol of Indian treachery to most New England colonists. Soldiers of Captain Benjamin Church, guided by an Indian informer, finally caught up with the fugitive Philip in a swamp near Mount Hope, Rhode Island, where an

Indian leaders, and never as a real commander in chief. To many whites, including authors Hubbard and Mather, he symbolized the Devil himself. In any event, Philip fought with courage and dignity until the end came.[31]

Late in July Connecticut troops under Major Talcott began their final campaign against remnants of the enemy. Picking up the trail of about 250 desperate Indians fleeing westward, the Connecticut men caught them on the evening of August 15 at their camp on the banks of the Housatonic near Great Barrington. An Indian managed to shout an alarm before Talcott's men closed in. In the ensuing attempt to encircle the Indians some 35 were killed and 20 were captured, while the remainder escaped to the Hudson. Thus ended Connecticut's fighting in King Philip's War, though scattered fighting continued elsewhere.[32]

The disposition of the Indian prisoners and those who voluntarily submitted posed a serious problem for the Assembly, which decided that Indians surrendering by the next January should not be sold as slaves but should be placed in service for ten years, after which they should dwell peaceably in their respective towns. James Fitch, of Norwich, who had worked ably as chaplain and in keeping the friendly Indians loyal, warned against trusting Uncas with care of Indian prisoners, and worked closely with the governor and Council in resettling the Indians under English supervision. Indian constables were appointed to publish orders, serve warrants, and collect the new annual tribute of five shillings per head. All Indian youngsters were put out as apprentices for ten years. By terms of a new agreement in 1681 Uncas turned over his lands to be divided into farms and agreed to accept the advice of the legislature upon all major matters, including war and peace. In turn Governor Leete pledged perpetual friendship, equal justice, and sufficient lands for the Indians. If not a highly lenient postwar settlement, it was far more humane than Plymouth's policy of selling many captives into slavery.[33]

Although Connecticut suffered far less than Massachusetts Bay and Plymouth, the war still cost heavily in human and financial terms. For long periods an average of one-seventh of the militia were on active service, in addition to many volunteers. Taxes soared from a levy of one penny on the pound in May 1674 to a peak of eighteen pence in October 1676. Aside from the Simsbury burning, all towns escaped unscathed; and the Indians within the colony actively aided the whites, so that not a single Connecticut party was ambushed. Only in the great "Swamp Fight" did Connecticut troops suffer heavy casualties. For New England, as a whole, it was very fortunate that the Indian power was decisively broken before the beginning of the French-English intercolonial wars.[34]

A Threat from New York

KING PHILIP'S WAR constituted a spectacular threat to Connecticut's safety, but less dramatic and far more serious dangers to the colony's way of life began to take shape in the 1670's and emerged in the 1680's.

This growing danger revolved about the stern figure of Major Edmund Andros, an English soldier and aristocrat who in 1674 was appointed governor of New York by the Duke of York. Scarcely had he taken office when he dispatched a strong letter to Governor Winthrop warning him that Connecticut must cease encouraging the Long Islanders, who were in a state of near rebellion against the duke's government. Unfortunately for Connecticut, the Duke of York in 1674 obtained a new patent from Charles II confirming him in possession of "all the Land from the west side of Conecticut River, to the East side of Delaware Bay." On May 1, 1675, Andros wrote a letter demanding that all land west of the Connecticut River be surrendered to him quickly. Secretary John Allyn, answering for the Connecticut Assembly, stanchly asserted Connecticut's rights under its charter of 1662. Andros' claims came as a great shock, for in 1667 special commissioners, to settle the New York–Connecticut line, had run it from Mamaroneck Bay northward on a line twenty miles east of the Hudson River. The Duke of York simply ignored this settlement which Connecticut had accepted.[35]

On July 8, 1675, Andros suddenly appeared before Saybrook with several armed sloops. The townspeople, recovering from their shock, turned out the militia and manned the fort. Reinforcements quickly arrived in the form of militia under Captain Thomas Bull. The Assembly quickly drew up a statement strongly protesting Andros' apparent invasion and announcing their intention to resist openly any attempt by him to exercise authority in Connecticut. On July 11 Andros, drawing his sloops up before the fort, raised the king's flag on board and demanded that the fort and town surrender. Captain Bull responded by raising the English flag and arraying his men for action. On the morning of July 12 Andros obtained permission to come ashore to confer with Bull and town leaders. Upon Assembly instructions Bull negotiated warily with Andros. Apparently the governor succeeded only in having his commission and the royal patent read. Seeing that a sanguinary engagement probably would ensue if he attacked, Andros discreetly sailed away.[36]

Connecticut's legislators were disturbed enough by Andros' expedition to prepare a "Narrative" of Connecticut's early history and of relations with Andros, culminating in a strong request that Andros not be allowed to make further demands or forays. Governor Winthrop or James Richards, whoever could leave first, was requested to present the "Narrative" and copies of the Andros-Connecticut correspondence to the English Government. There is no record, however, of any further action.[37]

Report on Connecticut in 1680

OVER four decades had passed since the founding of the three River towns when, in 1680, the governor and Council received a letter from the English Committee for Trade and Foreign Plantations asking for information on twenty-seven questions and requesting a "speedy and particuler Answer." The official answers provide much significant data upon Connecticut's institutions and economy.[38]

The governor and Council stated that the militia numbered 2,507, which suggests a total population of about 12,500 persons. They estimated that the Connecticut Indians could muster "500 fighting men," but added that the Indians no longer provided any valuable furs.

In regard to commerce: "Our cheif Trade, for procuring of cloathing, is by sending what provisions we rays to Boston, where we buy goods with it, to cloath vs." Altogether the colony had about twenty "petty" merchants. "Some Trade, only to Boston som to Boston & the Indies, other to Boston & New York, others to Boston, the Indias & Newfoundland." Few foreign merchants brought goods to Connecticut.

The surplus products of the colony and its pattern of trade in 1680 are well described:

The Comodities of the country are wheat peas Ry Barly Indian corn, & porck beif woole Hemp flax Cyder, parry & Tarr deal Boards pipe Staves horses . . . the most is Transported to Boston & there Bartered for Cloathing. Some Small Quantities directly sent to Barbadoes Jamaicoh & other Caribia Island, & there Barterd for Suger Cotton Wool & rumme, & Some Money, & now & then rarely Some vessells are laden w[i]th Staves pease porck & Flower to Maderah & fyall & there Barter their Comodities for wine; we have no need of virginia Trade most people planting so much Tabacco as they Spend o[u]r wheat having

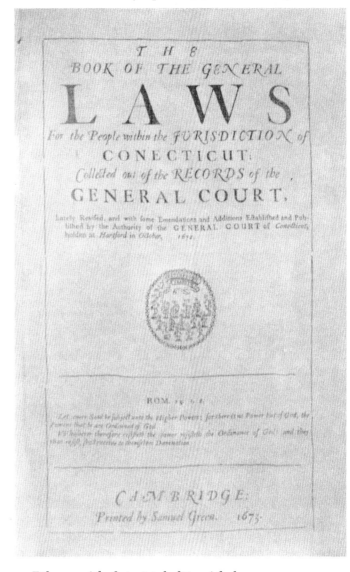

Title page of the first printed edition of the laws of Connecticut.

been much blasted & o[u]r pease spoyld with wormes for sundry years past abates o[u]r tra[de]

Of the twenty-six towns officially established, the colony's leaders named Hartford, New London, New Haven, and Fairfield as largest in size and in volume of trade. They considered the colony well endowed with oak, pine, and spruce for shipbuilding, but listed only twenty-seven Connecticut vessels of all types, ranging from eight to

The Leffingwell Inn (oldest parts dating to 1675) at Norwich. Recently moved out of way of Connecticut Turnpike approach and restored by the Society of the Founders of Norwich.

ninety tons. Lack of monied men with capital to expand industry and trade was cited as a leading problem.

In religion, they indicated that the great majority of the populace were Congregationalists, but there were "some moderate Presbeterians" and a handful of "7-day, men" and "Quakers." In the twenty-one established churches preaching was conducted twice on Sundays and occasionally on Lecture days; and the law required heads of families to instruct and catechize children and servants. The ministers were supported by taxes paid by each town, with salaries ranging from fifty to a hundred pounds annually.

Immigration apparently was very slight — in some years none or only a family or two; while three or four Negroes were imported yearly from Barbados. Even so, the population was increasing steadily, thanks to a very high birth rate. The number of men in the militia, sixteen to sixty years of age, had jumped from 2,050 to 2,507 in eight years — an increase of over 20 percent.

Concerning poor relief, the governor pointed out that each town cared for its own poor, but that few needed it, since labor was scarce and wages high. Day laborers received 2*s.* or 2*s.* 6*d.* a day; but provisions were cheap — Indian corn, 2*s.* 6*d.*

per bushel; peas, 3*s.* per bushel; and beef, 2½*d.* per pound.

Appended to the official reply was a letter signed by Governor Leete which stressed the poverty of the people of Connecticut, whose last Indian war had cost not less than £30,000. In a largely agricultural colony, crops had been poor in recent years, and prices of imported goods had risen. If New London and other places could be made free ports for ten to twenty years, "it would be a great means to move men of estates to trade, and Setle there." From the official information provided the English, one obtains a picture of a small colony practicing mostly a subsistence agriculture, with economic diversification checked by a serious lack of capital.

Ominous Moves Toward Centralization

IN the 1670's imperial policies at London were beginning to veer in a more authoritarian direction, which boded no good for Connecticut. The Revenue Act of 1673, the creation of the Lords of Trade in 1675, and the making of New Hampshire a royal colony in 1679 clearly foreshadowed trouble for New England.

English concern over the northern colonies was

84

natural, for they were not producing staples marketable in England. As a result, these colonies sought other outlets and began to develop home manufactures, and their efforts in both directions increased their competition with the English. Some English leaders felt that if all of these colonies could be united under one powerful royal government, the production of hemp and naval stores and opening up of mineral resources could be pushed, and would give the colonies valuable raw materials to send the mother country in return for her manufactured goods.[39]

Another important consideration in English eyes was the need for stronger colonial government, to meet the growing French threat in America. France had replaced Holland as England's great international competitor; and the Dominion of Canada, France's absolutist government in America, suggested the need for a similar Dominion of New England. In English eyes, defense problems, which the individualistic New England colonies did not fully comprehend, rendered integration vital. English officials thought, too, that a centralized administration might break up the widespread violation of the mercantilistic Navigation Acts. Edward Randolph, as special agent of the Lords of Trade, made an intensive study of conditions in New England. He reported a complete disregard in Massachusetts of the English acts of trade, and as a result, Massachusetts' charter was annulled in 1684.[40]

Since Connecticut also was charged with violations, three writs of *quo warranto* were issued against her, among other colonies, on July 17, 1685,

Interior scene at Leffingwell Inn.

and April 21 and October 23, 1686. These writs paved the way for vacating the charters and instituting direct royal control.[41]

Apparently Charles II had planned to add Connecticut and Rhode Island to the New England consolidation; but his brother and successor, James II, more absolutist in general, and holder of New York, greatly preferred joining Connecticut

against Connecticut was accompanied by six articles of high misdemeanor. Using the 1673 printed edition of Connecticut laws as his source, Randolph charged the colony with making laws contrary to those of England, enforcing a Connecticut oath of fidelity, ignoring the oath of supremacy and allegiance, denying freedom of worship to Anglicans, and several less serious charges.[44]

The Hempsted House in New London (dating to 1678).

with New York to give that colony a good agricultural basis. Even some western Connecticut groups favored union with the New York group of colonies.[42]

Connecticut's fear of losing its charter had been apparent in October 1679, when a boundary dispute with Rhode Island had exacerbated feelings in both colonies. The Assembly wrote the king beseeching him to continue Connecticut "in the full Injoyment of all the Limits mentioned in o[u]r sayd charter." When Charles II died in 1685 Connecticut addressed the new king, James II, and after painstakingly extending condolences and humbly expressing affection, begged the new sovereign to permit "the continuance of the liberties & properties Granted to us by o[u]r Late Soveraigne Charles the Second of blessed Memorie."[43]

The issuance of the first *quo warranto* writ

In May 1686 Randolph returned to New England, and on the twenty-seventh he wrote to Governor Treat and Council and informed them that he had two *quo warrantos* against the colony whereby "his Ma[jes]tie intends to bring all New England under one Governem[en]t and nothing is now remaineing on yo[u]r part but to think of an humble submission and a dutifull resignation of your charter." Luckily both of these writs became void because they were not served soon enough, but Connecticut's position remained precarious. In June 1686 James II commissioned Edmund Andros as governor of the Dominion of New England.[45]

Worried by delivery of the first two writs, the Assembly voted to have the colony's agent again petition the king for preservation of the colony's charter. Also, they pointed out that it would be harmful to divide the colony, and if it had to be disposed of, they preferred to be together under another government and in full possession of property.[46]

All was to little avail, however, as a third writ was served upon Governor Treat at Hartford on December 28, 1686, informing him that Connecticut's charter was to be surrendered. About a month later Governor Treat wrote on behalf of the Assembly to the Earl of Sunderland, Secretary of State, as follows:

May it please your honour, we are his Majesty's loyal subjects, and we are heartily desirous that we may continue in the same station that we are in, if it may consist with his princely wisdom to continue us so: But, if his Majesty's royal purposes be otherwise to dispose of us, we shall, as in duty bound, submit to his royal commands; and, if it be to conjoin us with the other colonies and provinces, under Sir Edmund Andros, his Majesty's present governor, it will be more pleasing than to be joined with any other province.

Unfortunately the English interpreted this as a complete willingness to surrender the charter, and in June 1687 instructions were drawn up under which Andros was to take over the government of Connecticut, with Governor Treat and Secretary Allyn becoming members of Andros' council.[47]

Andros himself made further attempts through letters in February 1686/87 to obtain a clear-cut submission. Connecticut adroitly answered that it could not do anything until replies were received to several letters sent to the king. When Andros sent his secretary in June the Connecticut leaders again squirmed out of open submission by referring to the delayed royal reply. At a special Assembly session on June 15 Governor Treat read a communication from agent William Whiting at London and asked whether an additional agent should be sent to plead the colony's cause. Considering this too expensive, the solons voted to request Whiting to carry on with "whatsoever shall be needfull to be don." Then a peculiar incident occurred:

Sundry of the Court desireing that the Patent or Charter might be brought into the Court, the Secretary sent for it, and informed the Governo[u]r and Court that he had the Charter, and shewed it to the Court; and the Governor bid him put it into the box againe and lay it on the table, and leave the key in the box, which he did forthwith.

Evidently some of the legislators feared that the charter already had been surrendered to Andros![48]

Andros Pays a Visit and the Charter Disappears

THE summer passed uneventfully, but on October 22, 1687, Andros wrote to Governor Treat and announced his intention of visiting Hartford to assume the reins of government. On October 26 he set out from Boston in regal style with a retinue of seventy-five men. Learning of Andros' expedition, Governor Treat hastily called together those members of the Assembly who were in or near Hartford. When Andros crossed the Connecticut River at Wethersfield, the troop of horse of Hartford County, under Captain Samuel Talcott, greeted him and escorted the party to Hartford, where several militia companies, the governor, and the assistants officially welcomed him. It is highly doubtful that Andros was given the affectionate treatment described in Gershom Bulkeley's *Will and Doom*, our fullest extant account of Andros' Connecticut visit.[49]

The next morning Andros and his party accompanied the governor and Assembly to the public meeting house. Then Governor Treat escorted Andros to the governor's chair, where Andros ordered read his commission as governor and the king's orders for annexation, and at this time he probably demanded the surrender of the charter itself. Governor Treat launched into a long and dramatic speech depicting the many privations and dangers experienced in establishing and expanding the colony. Since late October days were short, candles were lighted. Then followed one of the most dramatic episodes in Connecticut's history:

The important affair was debated and kept in suspence, until the evening, when the charter was brought and laid upon the table, where the assembly were sitting. By this time, great numbers of people were assembled, and men sufficiently bold to enterprise whatever might be necessary or expedient. The lights were instantly extinguished, and one Captain Wadsworth, of Hartford, in the most silent and secret manner, carried off the charter, and secreted it in a large hollow tree, fronting the house of the Hon. Samuel Wyllys, then one of the magistrates of the colony. The people appeared all peaceable and orderly. The can-

Sir Edmund Andros.

dles were officiously re-lighted; but the patent was gone, and no discovery could be made of it, or of the person who had conveyed it away.[50]

This story of secreting the charter in the great Charter Oak tree soon grew into one of Connecticut's cherished traditions. Whether or not the charter ever was actually put there, even for a few hours, is a matter of conjecture. It does seem fairly certain, though, that the charter actually was spirited away under cover of darkness. Twenty-eight years later, in 1715, the colony voted twenty shillings to Wadsworth for "securing the Duplicate Charter of this Colony in a very troublesome sea-

son when our constitution was struck at, and in safely keeping and preserving the same ever since unto this day."[51]

Despite the charter's mysterious disappearance, both Andros and Connecticut leaders felt that Connecticut had been absorbed into Andros' dominion. The official Connecticut record of the event reads as follows:

His Excelency Sr Edmond Andross Kn[igh]t, Capt. Generall & Gov[erno]r of his Ma[jes]ties Teritorie & Dominion in New England, by order from his Ma[jes]tie James the second, King of England, Scotland, France & Ireland, the 31 of October, 1687, took into his hands the Goverment of this colony of Conecticott, it being by his Ma[jes]tie annexed to the Massachusets & other colonys under his Excelencies Goverment. FINIS[52]

Andros added Governor Treat and John Allyn to his council. The following day Andros' council proceeded to name justices of the peace and sheriffs, and taxes already levied were confirmed. Andros then left Hartford, "saw the justices of the peace in their respective counties and sheriffs sworn, commissionated military officers in each town and custom officers in the several sea ports." He undoubtedly felt vexed at his failure to obtain the charter, or a positive vote of submission by the Assembly, which merely had recorded, not approved, what had happened.[53]

The Overthrow of Andros

ALTHOUGH Governor Andros ostentatiously professed his undying friendship toward Connecticut, he quickly adopted an autocratic pattern of rule by such measures as restricting freedom of the press and requiring advance filing of bonds with sureties for all intended marriages. To finance his administration Andros instituted exorbitant fees of various kinds, such as one of fifty shillings for probate of a will. Those involved in settlement of estates were required to transact their business at Boston — a long and expensive journey. Andros' most upsetting action came in his declaration that land titles of the colonists under the old charter were invalid and all Indian deeds denoted no more than "the scratch of a bear's paw."[54]

Andros continued his despotic policies, and even received official encouragement in 1688, when New York, which he had formerly governed and then lost, was added to his realm. The main weight of his exactions fell upon Massachusetts and Plymouth, but Connecticut generally disliked his arbitrary rule. It is very probable that Andros' administration would have encountered serious opposition, if not open revolt, even without a revolution in England.[55]

In the mother country, meanwhile, a constitutional crisis had developed. James II as king soon had revealed himself as an arbitrary despot who demanded a thoroughly subservient Parliament. An avowed Catholic himself, he appointed many Catholics to important governmental offices. When he ordered all Anglican clergy to read a Declaration of Indulgence, the clergy largely ignored the order. James struck back hard by ordering seven bishops tried on the charge of publishing a seditious libel. Public opinion overwhelmingly favored the bishops, who, despite royal pressure, were acquitted. When a son was born to James, it meant a Catholic heir to the throne. Leaders of the two parties, the Whigs and Tories, united in an appeal to William, ruler of the Netherlands, and his wife Mary, daughter of James II by his first wife, both Protestants, to assume the English throne. James quickly fled to France and the "Glorious" or "Bloodless" Revolution of 1688–89 thus was quickly consummated. William and Mary came in as the new sovereigns, but with clearly limited powers. Parliament had made a king and could unmake him if he attempted to rule arbitrarily. A bill of rights was enacted, as well as other popular safeguards.[56]

The news of revolution in old England precipitated a quick revolution in New England. On April 18, 1689, armed crowds at Boston seized Randolph and others, but Andros escaped to the nearby fort on Castle Island. When later he came into Boston to parley with popular leaders he was promptly arrested.[57]

In Connecticut, news of the Glorious Revolution in England and its counterpart in Boston caused great excitement. During the previous fall and winter some Connecticut leaders, led by James Fitch of Norwich, evidently had been canvassing methods of overthrowing the Andros regime in the colony. Bulkeley's *Will and Doom*, a pro-Andros version of Andros' overthrow, refers to the suspicious coincidence by which John Winthrop of New London, son of Governor John Winthrop, Jr., and a member of Andros' council, arrived at Boston "the very day that Sir Edmund was apprehended; his siding with the transaction, taking advice there, and busy promoting of the Revolution here after he came back." According to Bulkeley, a session of the Assembly was called in highly irregular fashion, and on May 8, 1689, the day before the session, many of the legislators met informally in Hartford to discuss what ought to be done.[58]

On May 9, 1689, ". . . it was voted by the Free-men that they would re-establish the Goverment as it was before and at the time when Sr Edmond Androsse tooke the Goverment, and so to have it proceed as it did before that time according to charter." Governor Robert Treat and Deputy Gov-ernor James Bishop again assumed their places. The old assistants were reinstated, with Samuel Wyllys and John Winthrop being added. All of the old laws were once more declared to be in force, and a full slate of justices of the peace was chosen.[59]

The Charter Oak tree. From painting by Charles D'Wolf Brownell.

CHAPTER 6

Boundary Disputes and Intercolonial Wars, 1690-1764

The Charter: A Pandora's Box — Connecticut versus Rhode Island — Massachusetts Tries to Reduce Connecticut — New York Tries to Reduce Connecticut — Connecticut Enters King William's War — Further Indecisive Fighting — Connecticut's Role in Queen Anne's War — Connecticut Fights in King George's War — Connecticut in the French and Indian War

---

The Charter: A Pandora's Box

WHEN John Winthrop, Jr., obtained the generous charter of 1662 from King Charles II, he undoubtedly felt jubilant. Yet the charter contained the seeds of sharp future discord with each of Connecticut's neighbors in its description of the colony as "bounded on the East by Norrogancett Riuer comonly called Norrogancett Bay where the said Riuer falleth into the Sea, and on the North by the Lyne of the Massachusetts Plantation and on the South by the Sea, and in longitude as the Lyne of the Massachusetts Colony runinge from East to West that is to say, from the said Narrogancett Bay on the East to the South Sea on the West parte with the Islands therevnto adjoyneinge."[1]

Connecticut versus Rhode Island

WHILE Winthrop was in London, Dr. John Clarke also was there, working for a new Rhode Island charter. After Winthrop had secured the Connecticut charter the two men met and reached a tentative agreement upon the common Rhode Island–Connecticut boundary. The territory under discussion included that obtained from the Narraganset Indians, extending from Narragansett Bay to the Pawcatuck River, which earlier had been the object of a three-cornered dispute among Rhode Island, Massachusetts, and Connecticut. The New England Confederacy in 1658 had ruled that the Mystic River was the proper boundary between Connecticut and Massachusetts. After receiving the 1662 charter, Connecticut considered the 1658 decision invalid; and Rhode Island meanwhile doggedly asserted its claim to much of Massachusetts' claim.[2]

The Winthrop-Clarke agreement placed the boundary at the Pawcatuck River, so that Winthrop waived all lands east of the river. The Rhode Island charter carefully drew the boundary at the Pawcatuck River, conceived as the "Narragansett River" specified in Connecticut's charter. Just when the boundary question seemed nicely settled the Connecticut legislature, declaring Winthrop lacked authority, repudiated the Winthrop-Clarke agreement.[3]

Connecticut, claiming all land to Narragansett Bay, renamed the town of Narragansett as Wickford. Though the townspeople accepted the change, Rhode Island, calling this legalized robbery, demanded a new survey. Meanwhile, in 1665, royal commissioners arrived with plenary powers to adjust all important intercolonial disputes. After listening to Rhode Island and Connecticut spokesmen, they ruled that all of the dis-

authorities swooped down and broke it up. The next few years brought insincere and abortive diplomatic moves on both sides.[5]

After the end of King Philip's War, Connecticut finally decided to dispatch an agent, William Harris, to petition the king. Harris fell into the

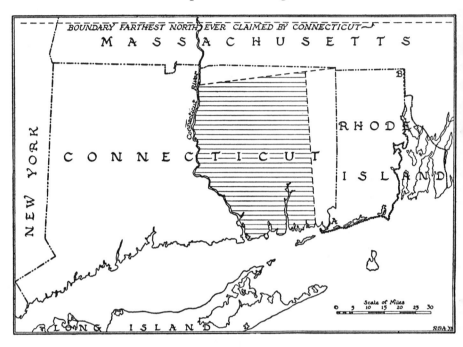

Connecticut–Rhode Island boundary dispute.

puted land should belong to the king, under the name of the "King's Province." Eventually Rhode Island was given temporary control of the area up to the Pawcatuck River, but Connecticut declined to accept these actions as final in the hope that the king and Council would fail to confirm them. For five years unpleasant relations existed while the people of Wickford and Southertown (Stonington) begged Connecticut for protection from Rhode Island. Finally, in 1670, the two colonies appointed three commissioners apiece who convened in New London on June 14–15, 1670, and discussed their differences so stormily that nothing was achieved. Rhode Island threatened an appeal to the king if Connecticut tried to advance its authority beyond the Pawcatuck.[4]

Despite the Rhode Island Assembly's expressed hope of solving their differences, serious border incidents flared up. Rhode Island's deputy governor and seven magistrates set up a court within the disputed land east of the Pawcatuck River; and soon afterward, in May 1671, Connecticut

hands of Algerian pirates, was freed, and finally reached London, only to die there soon after his arrival. Connecticut then wrote a letter to London in defense of its case, a step copied by Rhode Island.[6]

The next year, 1680, brought open conflict in which Rhode Island arrested Stephen Richardson, a Connecticut constable exercising his duties at Westerly. When Rhode Island adamantly rejected Connecticut's demand to free him, the latter retaliated by seizing Joseph Clarke, of Westerly, a Rhode Island partisan. In 1683 Charles II, noting the bitter quarrel, appointed commissioners to settle it. The royal board granted all of the Narragansett country to Connecticut, but the decision never was put into effect because the Privy Council failed to take any action.[7]

While Andros was royal governor of New England he studied the boundary dispute and ruled in favor of Rhode Island; but after the collapse of his rule the protracted battle resumed in full fury. After another appeal the English Attorney General, in October 1696, decided in favor of Connecticut. Once again, however, the Privy Council neglected to confirm the decision. In 1699 the Board of Trade asked the Earl of Bellomont, governor of New York, to serve as friendly intermediary, and in September he met at Newport with representatives of both sides. Later he disgustedly wrote London that he had spent "a whole morning upon hearing their Claims and pretensions, — advance of any definitive ruling of the Privy Council. Apparently favorably impressed by their novel attitude, the Privy Council decided that annexation to New Hampshire was impracticable and requested new recommendations. In January 1725/26 the Board proposed a line approximately that of the 1703 agreement, which the Privy Council accepted. A survey in 1728 implemented this decision. After a few final verbal brickbats the two

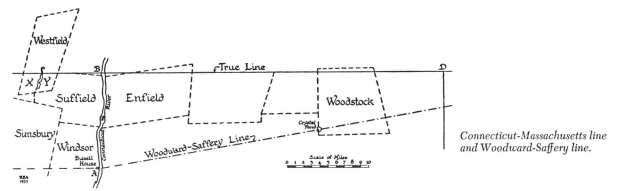

Connecticut-Massachusetts line and Woodward-Saffery line.

all which was manag'd with great heat on both sides, and brought to no Conclusion." Bellomont then told both colonies to send agents to London for a conclusive settlement. Meanwhile a Rhode Island sheriff and four assistants attempted to seize property in Stonington for nonpayment of taxes to Rhode Island. After the sheriff vainly snapped his pistol at Connecticut officers, he and his assistants were arrested and fined by a Connecticut court.[8]

After the dispute had been referred again to England, both contestants had premonitions of mutual disaster — that the Board of Trade would recommend revocation of their charters. Whereupon in a 1703 conference they agreed upon the boundary as the Pawcatuck River from the Sound to the Ashaway River, and then due north to the Massachusetts line. When it came to the actual survey in 1714, however, they interpreted the line differently. Noting that the dispute had dragged on for sixty years, the Board of Trade in the 1720's recommended that both colonies surrender their charters and be annexed to New Hampshire.[9]

Horrified by this proposal, the two colonies, suddenly becoming models of good conduct, fell over themselves in haste to promise acceptance in

colonies in 1742 officially accepted the boundary. This reasonable solution eliminated Connecticut's extreme claims, which would have virtually destroyed Rhode Island. In 1840, and later, a few minor adjustments were made.[10]

Massachusetts Tries to Reduce Connecticut

IN the boundary struggle with Massachusetts, Connecticut found itself in the opposite role — that of a David struggling with a Goliath. The dispute revolved about the location of Connecticut's northern boundary. The Massachusetts charter stated that its southern boundary should run due west from a line three miles south of the southernmost part of the Charles River. In 1642 Massachusetts hired Nathaniel Woodward and Solomon Saffery to survey the southern boundary. After starting the line from what seemed to be the proper point, they decided that it was too much work to run it foot by foot all the way, so they sailed around Cape Cod and up the Connecticut River to a point which they reckoned to be on the same degree of latitude as their starting point! Actually this point was eight miles too far south, and it meant that their line, as it ran eastward, cut

93

an unjustified segment out of Connecticut, eight miles broad at the widest point and four miles at the narrowest point.[11]

After voicing a protest at a Confederation meeting in 1649, Connecticut decided to run its own survey, which John Butcher and William Whiting completed on August 20, 1695. Their report, largely correcting the error of Woodward and Saffery, proved unacceptable to Massachusetts. Meanwhile Connecticut people pushed into lands in Enfield and Suffield and established homes. More altercations ensued until finally, in 1702, the two colonies agreed upon a new joint survey, which returned to Connecticut seven of the eight miles lost earlier. In the end, however, Massachusetts reneged on the agreement. While threats, and even minor raids, took place, each announced the intention of appealing to England; and in 1708 each sent strongly worded memorials to London.[12]

Since strong sentiment existed in England for the revocation of all private colonial charters, it dawned upon the disputants that it would be wise to settle their own boundary before England took drastic steps. In 1713, therefore, the colonies achieved a significant agreement whereby Connecticut allowed Massachusetts jurisdiction over its old border towns, though they were south of the new boundary. In compensation, Massachusetts ceded its neighbor equivalent land on the frontier in western Massachusetts and New Hampshire, and yielded disputed land about Windsor. In 1716 Connecticut sold the northern lands for £683 and donated the money to struggling Yale College. The next year joint commissioners peacefully ran the line from the Connecticut River to the New York line.[13]

This agreement overlooked one vital matter — the desires of those living in Enfield, Suffield, and Woodstock. Influenced especially by higher taxes in Massachusetts, they quickly launched separatist movements. In 1724 Enfield and Suffield unsuccessfully petitioned Connecticut's General Assembly for admission to the colony. In 1747 Woodstock, Suffield, Enfield, and Somers, asking for incorporation in Connecticut, noted their location within Connecticut's boundary line (by the 1662 charter) and stressed that the 1713 agreement had been consummated without their consent.[14]

The 1747 petition found more sympathy among new leaders in Connecticut. After appointing a special committee, the Assembly tried to reopen negotiations with Massachusetts, but the latter, seeing only possible losses from such talks, refused. Connecticut, meanwhile, advanced reasons for annexing the unhappy towns: lack of royal confirmation for the 1713 agreement, and a written opinion of New York's Attorney General stating that no towns south of the Connecticut–Massachusetts boundary could legally be ceded to Massachusetts.[15]

In 1749 Connecticut voted to acquire Enfield, Somers, Suffield, and Woodstock; appointed commissioners to meet those of Massachusetts; and threatened an appeal to Britain. Woodstock, meanwhile, promptly elected two deputies for the October 1749 Assembly session. As a result of these actions, relations between the disputing colonies once again reached a crisis. Although the matter was submitted to Britain, outbreak of the Seven Years' War soon afterward completely extinguished British interest. Massachusetts long fumed and finally passed a resolve in 1768 claiming the four towns and their taxes. Connecticut, however, blithely continued to govern the towns and by 1800 no longer was challenged.[16]

After 1800 three other minor boundary questions were amicably settled. The claims of Southwick, Massachusetts, to portions of Granby and Suffield were compromised by award of a small segment of Granby — the only deviation in the otherwise straight northern boundary from the Connecticut River westward. Likewise, minor adjustments in Enfield and at the junction of Union and Woodstock were peacefully arranged. In May 1827 Connecticut officially accepted these changes and peace at last reigned along the entire line.[17]

New York Tries to Reduce Connecticut

IN 1664 Charles II unwittingly precipitated a major boundary quarrel between New York and Connecticut when he granted to his brother, James, Duke of York, Long Island and "all the land from the west side of Connecticut River to the East side of Delaware Bay." This grant would squeeze Connecticut into a narrow corridor.[18]

Realizing the gravity of the situation, Connecticut in 1664 sent representatives to New York who, after congratulating the New Yorkers upon their conquest of the Dutch, defended the 1662 charter boundaries. Under a compromise agreement in 1664, New York took Long Island, and the Mamaroneck River was designated as the starting point on the mainland. From there the line ran north-northwest to the Massachusetts line, which meant that it crossed the Hudson at Peekskill, hit the projected Massachusetts line more than twenty-five miles west of the Hudson, and gave Connecticut far more land than under the 1650 agreement with the Dutch.[19]

Unluckily for Connecticut, the 1664 agreement never was royally confirmed, and in 1674 the Duke of York obtained a new royal patent again placing his eastern line at the Connecticut River. In May 1675 Governor Andros demanded that Connecticut surrender all land west of the Connecticut River. In reply Connecticut uncompromisingly declared its intention to keep the land granted by the charter and further secured by the 1664 accord.[20]

In July 1675 Andros appeared at Saybrook, but the presence of two companies of militia under Captain Thomas Bull deterred him from overt aggression. In November 1683, after Thomas Dongan became New York's governor, the two colonies agreed upon a line which, in general, ran twenty miles from and parallel to the Hudson. Near the Sound, however, a rectangle of 61,440 acres was assigned to Connecticut, including towns long under Connecticut's aegis. In turn Connecticut surrendered a narrow strip of land from North Wilton to the Massachusetts line, called the "Oblong."[21]

A casualty in this agreement was Rye, considered part of Connecticut since 1665. The people of Rye, however, clearly preferring the lower taxes and greater local autonomy of Connecticut, revolted in 1697 and joined Connecticut, as did nearby Bedford. Open fighting nearly occurred in Rye when Benjamin Collier, sheriff of Westchester, New York, arriving to supervise the election of a member of the New York Assembly, was confronted by fifty mounted and armed troopers from Stamford, determined to uphold Connecticut's claim. Nobody was shot, and New York later offered to pardon the recalcitrant citizens of Rye and nearby Bedford in return for allegiance and taxes.[22]

In 1700 the king confirmed the agreement of 1683, which ended resistance in Rye and Bedford

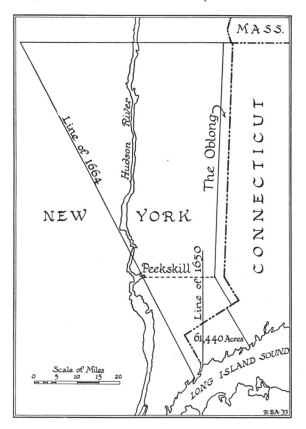

Connecticut–New York boundary dispute.

and discouraged Connecticut. Years of tedious bickering followed, which mostly persuaded New Yorkers that New Englanders were "sharp traders." Conversely, the more democratic Connecticut government distrusted the autocratic New York government. Even so, an agreement was reached at Greenwich in 1725 — virtually the same as that of 1683. A new joint survey, interrupted by an argument and finally completed in 1731, amazingly enough was accepted by both sides.[23]

In 1855 the two states decided that the 1731 line should be resurveyed, since the old boundary markers had disappeared and people living close to the line paid no taxes to either state. After a prolonged dispute, not ironed out until 1880, Connecticut accepted the 1731 line in return for an extension of its southern boundary into the Sound and a clarification of its further course through the Sound. In 1881 both states and Congress ratified the agreement, and *all* of Connecticut's boundaries finally were clearly defined and accepted by all parties concerned. Although still a small colony, Connecticut, through a lengthy battle, had escaped being reduced to a tiny remnant between the Connecticut and Mystic Rivers.[24]

Connecticut Enters King William's War

AS a result of the Glorious Revolution of 1688–89 in England, James II was deposed, and William III from the Netherlands and his wife, Mary Stuart, ascended the English throne. William III quickly led England into the alliance which he earlier had formed against Louis XIV of France and his territorial ambitions. In America, where French and English rivalry in such areas as Newfoundland, Acadia, Maine, and the Illinois country had become acute, the conflict was called King William's War.[25]

Under the energetic Canadian governor, Count Frontenac, the French quickly organized raiding parties, which struck viciously at isolated frontier posts in Maine, New Hampshire, and New York. The town of Schenectady was destroyed in February 1689/90, sixty inhabitants slain, and many captured. These attacks spread panic throughout the northern English colonies.[26]

Connecticut, alarmed at the ominous situation, held a special Assembly session in September 1689 at which the legislators decided to raise 200 volunteers, including local Indians, for assistance on the Massachusetts frontier. When the Assembly met in October, it voted to send sixty men and four officers to Albany, another threatened area. In response to frantic pleas from upper New York, the Assembly, on April 11, 1690, authorized recruitment of 130 whites and 80 Indians, who should "be with all speed raysed and sent to Albany," and it also established a "Councill of War" under the governor to handle emergencies arising between legislative sessions.[27]

Because of the spreading French and Indian raids, delegates from Massachusetts Bay, Plym-

outh, Connecticut (Nathaniel Gold and William Pitkin), and New York convened in New York on May 1, 1690, to plan a military offensive. Massachusetts already had launched an expedition against Port Royal, Acadia, under the energetic direction of William Phips, which surprised the French and easily captured Port Royal. Turning its attention meanwhile toward a land invasion of Canada, the congress set quotas as follows: New York, 400; Massachusetts Bay, 260; Plymouth, 60; Connecticut, 135; and Maryland, "By Promise," 200; for a total of 1,055. Only New York and Connecticut, however, were willing to provide their quotas; and they hoped for substantial Indian reinforcements. Only Connecticut's share was actually realized; while New York managed to get 150 soldiers to Albany. The Indians, learning of a smallpox outbreak in Albany, declared "that the Great God had stopt their way," and only a handful of them appeared.[28]

The choice of a commander precipitated a sharp debate, since Jacob Leisler, New York's governor, preferred his friend Jacob Milborne, who was *persona non grata* to Connecticut. In a letter to Leisler, Secretary John Allyn of Connecticut frankly opposed this choice and suggested as an alternative Fitz-John Winthrop, eldest son of John Winthrop, Jr., who as a young man had served creditably in the English Civil War, under General Monk, and in King Philip's War. Winthrop was accepted.[29]

From the start affairs went badly, as smallpox made serious inroads and rotten pork poisoned half of the Connecticut soldiers. Upon assuming command Winthrop sadly reported: ". . . all things confused and in noe readiness or posture for martching the forces towards Canada, yet everyone disorderly projecting something about it." On July 30, 1690, he ordered the smallpox-ridden army to commence its advance northward toward its distant objective, Quebec. By August 4 Winthrop noted that the pork "was scarce eatable" and the bread supply nearly exhausted. On August 7 the army camped at Wood Creek, from which their commander speeded a frantic call for provisions. They lacked canoes, and owing to the season, they found that bark would not peel and no more canoes could be constructed.[30]

In view of the plainly hopeless situation Winthrop on August 15 ordered a general retreat, except for a small detachment sent on a raid toward La Prairie de Madeleine, opposite Montreal. The main body, meanwhile, returned sick and dispirited to Greenbush, opposite Albany, on August 20. So ended in complete failure the first attempt to invade Canada by way of the Hudson-Champlain Valley.[31]

When Winthrop appeared Leisler promptly ordered his arrest on grounds of neglect and cowardice. An enraged Connecticut filed a strong protest with Leisler, who, badly harassed by internal opposition, immediately freed Winthrop. In October, after hearing Winthrop's account of his leadership, the Connecticut Assembly strongly defended him and voted him forty pounds as a testimonial.[32]

Further Indecisive Fighting

ALTHOUGH the war continued until 1697, it consisted more of rumored raids than actual attacks. Connecticut spent much of her energy in struggling with the governors of Massachusetts and New York for control of her own militia. In 1692, when William Phips became royal governor of Massachusetts, his commission bestowed upon him command of the Connecticut and Rhode Island militia as well as his own. Suddenly, in May 1693, Connecticut refused to acknowledge Phips's claims. Phips was stripped of authority over Connecticut's militia, and command was transferred to Governor Benjamin Fletcher of New York. Apparently a referendum was held in Connecticut on the wisdom of addressing the king and queen concerning continuance of all charter rights, including militia command, and a total of 2,182 persons recorded themselves in favor of such an address. A special legislative session on September 1, 1693, chose Fitz-John Winthrop as agent, drew up instructions, and levied a special tax of a penny on the pound "to defray the charg of ye Colony in sending an agent to England to defend our priuilidges."[33]

In October 1693 Fletcher, accompanied by advisers, proceeded to Connecticut to execute his commission. Experiencing a frigid reception, he delivered a virtual ultimatum, demanding "a speedy Replye in Two Words Yes or No." His aide, Colonel Nicholas Bayard, added warnings that Fletcher would not leave Connecticut until his authority was recognized.[34]

The Assembly, protesting that no express royal orders had come to surrender control of the militia, firmly refused, though they offered six hundred pounds toward the expense of the Albany garrison, or fifty men, whichever Fletcher preferred. Not mollified in the slightest, Fletcher replied that he wanted complete submission. Tradition has it that he ordered his commission read to the Hartford trainbands, which were parading nearby. Captain Joseph Wadsworth, the senior officer, supposedly in a sudden flash of inspiration, shouted loudly, "Beat the drums." When the pandemonium subsided, Fletcher's aide, Bayard, again tried to read the commission, only to be drowned out by another roll of drums. Observing the menacing atmosphere of Hartford, Fletcher thought it discreet to speed his departure.[35]

In April 1694 London made a decision which constituted a partial victory for Connecticut. It noted that the charter explicitly gave command of the militia to the governor, but with provision, in times of crises, for appointment of a chief commander over the militia of several colonies, which decision Winthrop promised to respect. Fletcher was informed that he could call out 120 men from Connecticut, in war periods only, and Connecticut, with English sanction, thus grimly retained management of its militia.[36]

Massachusetts' long northern frontier meanwhile made that colony highly vulnerable to attack by roaming bands of French and Indians, which alarmed Connecticut as the Connecticut River Valley offered a back door into the colony. In the winter of 1690–91 the War Council answered a plea for help from Deerfield by sending some Connecticut militia, while pleas for aid from Colonel John Pynchon of Springfield usually received promises of help. On the other hand, Connecticut eyed suspiciously requests for aid on Massachusetts' northeastern borders in the Maine country.[37]

In 1697 the war officially was terminated by the Treaty of Ryswick, which reflected clearly the virtual stalemate on both sides of the Atlantic by providing that the rivals return to the *status quo ante bellum*. Though Connecticut lost only a few soldiers, the conflict probably cost the colony at least £ 12,000. Hence it is not surprising that the people greeted news of the peace with great joy and that the Assembly voted a day of public thanksgiving "to give thanks to God for all his goodnesse, in speciall the restoration of peace to the English nation."[38]

Connecticut's Role in Queen Anne's War

THE Treaty of Ryswick proved to be little more than a truce, as a serious dispute over the succession to the Spanish throne in 1702 once more brought England into the field against France — a struggle known in America as Queen Anne's War. In the new conflict Connecticut's concern remained the same — protection against the French and Indian invaders from the north. This menace seemed greater because the Iroquois, disappointed by the English efforts in the previous war, in 1701 had made a peace agreement with Canada. To make the situation worse, most of the white inhabitants in upper New York, recalling the collapse of fur trade in the previous war, refused to fight the French, with whom they had developed a lively trade. This forced New Englanders to carry the brunt of the war in the north.[39]

Governor Joseph Dudley of Massachusetts was granted broad command powers over the militia of Connecticut and Rhode Island. Recognizing the strong antipathy of Connecticut's leaders toward him, he proceeded very diplomatically in applying for aid against enemy marauders who practiced local "hit-and-run" raids. In August 1703, on the appeal of Captain Samuel Partridge of Hadley, Massachusetts, Hartford County sent fifty to sixty men who vainly scouted the Deerfield area for enemy forces. Two months later Connecticut established a war council which could send troops to the frontiers.[40]

Warnings of a projected attack from the north reached Deerfield, Massachusetts, in 1703, and the frightened inhabitants crowded inside the old village stockade. Connecticut troops rushed up temporarily, but no enemy appeared. As the winter brought deep snows and biting cold Deer-

field's inhabitants relaxed in warm homes. Only the Reverend John Williams, Deerfield's minister, experienced premonitions of impending disaster.[41]

February 28, 1703/4, arrived, a biting, sharp winter's day. The deep snow had drifted against the stockade so that a man could easily climb over it, yet because the cold was so intense the sentries in the watch towers abandoned their posts. Meanwhile a force of French and Indians, under Hertel de Rouville, swarmed into the village about two hours before dawn on February 29 and commenced a ruthless slaughter and pillage. Parson Williams seized his pistol and aimed at the nearest Indian. The pistol failed to fire, and the Indians quickly seized and bound him. When the butchery ended, about fifty lay dead, and over a hundred half-frozen captives were started on a fearful march to Canada.[42]

The horror of the attack galvanized the Assembly into an emergency session on March 15. It immediately enacted a whole series of laws aimed at real preparedness, including encouragement for voluntary service on Massachusetts' northeastern frontier, and concluded by calling out sixty men for service in Hampshire County.[43]

In May inhabitants of the frontier towns — Simsbury, Waterbury, Woodbury, Danbury, Colchester, Windham, Mansfield, and Plainfield — were forbidden by the Assembly to leave without first securing its approval. The legislature also called for four hundred volunteers; and throughout the summer the colony kept many men on garrison duty in Hampshire County — a safeguard against Deerfield-type massacres.[44]

In 1707 serious warfare resumed with an expedition against Port Royal, the chief French Acadian base. In April Governor Dudley requested that Connecticut provide substantial forces. After careful consideration, the Assembly politely declined and reminded him of previous large contributions to Hampshire County. As a result, Connecticut escaped one of the worst debacles of America's colonial warfare. Despite overwhelming superiority in men and equipment, the Massachusetts army was repulsed by a very inferior French force. When Dudley solicited aid from Connecticut for the second attempt, another refusal ensued.

This invasion ended in as disgraceful failure as the first.[45]

In 1709 the British Government approved a plan, similar to that of 1690, for a two-pronged land and sea attack upon Quebec, in which Connecticut's quota was set at 350 men and was loyally pledged. By late May, 400 British regulars,

New England transports. Ably led by Colonel Francis Nicholson, a royal appointee, the invaders displayed such overwhelming strength as to induce French surrender without a battle. With the fall of Port Royal on October 2, 1710, Acadia became a British colony.[47]

In 1711, with crack British veterans from Marl-

LEFT: *Counterfeit paper money — raised from four to forty shillings.* RIGHT: *Note on reverse side of counterfeit money: Mrs. Elizabeth Allyn reimbursed by colony from fine paid by the counterfeiter.*

Connecticut and New York troops, and some Indians and ship carpenters advanced to Wood Creek, where they learned that because of a setback in the European theater Britain could not send the troops promised earlier. It seemed necessary, therefore, to abandon the entire plan; and again Connecticut and other colonies had spent substantial sums in vain.[46]

A new expedition in 1710 brought together approximately 400 British troops and 1,500 colonials. Of the latter Massachusetts raised 900; Connecticut, 300, under Colonel William Whiting; and Rhode Island and New Hampshire together, about 300. Connecticut furnished five of the twenty-four

borough's army available, the British Government projected another land-sea expedition against Canada. After a conference of governors at New London on June 21, 1711, Connecticut voted to raise its share of three hundred men and also composed a letter to the queen pledging vigorous cooperation.[48]

The sea expedition met a sudden end. At a spot where the Gulf of St. Lawrence was about seventy miles wide, ten British ships ran aground, through some miracle of sheer incompetence, with a loss of over seven hundred men and officers. Though the fleet still carried forces strong enough to overwhelm Quebec, the demoralized leaders thought only of retreat! The naval debacle in turn caused abandonment of the land expedition. The Treaty of Utrecht in 1713 registered limited British gains in the northern area, such as Acadia.[49]

Heavy wartime expenditures forced Connecticut into its initial printing of paper money in June 1709 — an emission of £8,000 of "bills of credit." Later printings raised the total by May 1713 to £34,000, of which £20,000 were still outstanding when peace arrived. Much more important than

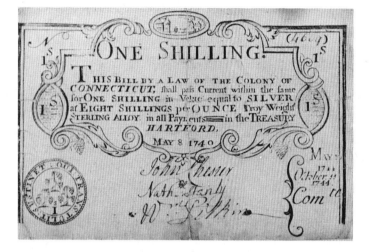

Example of paper money issued during King George's War.

this debt was the colony's escape with slight manpower casualties.[50]

Connecticut Fights in King George's War

SPECIFIC British grievances against Spain and rampant jingoism led in 1739 to declaration of war against Spain — a struggle known as the War of Jenkins' Ear, in honor of a British captain who advertised that a Spanish pirate had brutally cut off his ear. Britain decided to strike a staggering blow against Spanish America through the capture of Cartagena and other key ports. Connecticut loyally raised enough volunteers to fill three transports. Disease, woeful mismanagement, and stubborn Spanish resistance resulted in complete failure of the Cartagena siege as well as later attacks upon Cuban points, and only a pitiful remnant of Connecticut's contingent ever saw their homes again.[51]

The Spanish-British struggle gradually ex-

panded into a general European conflict known as the War of the Austrian Succession and, in America, as King George's War. France had constructed a powerful fortress at Louisbourg on Cape Breton Island which posed a serious threat to British colonial fishing and trading, and even to New England's very existence. Energetic and persuasive Governor William Shirley of Massachusetts, pushing a daring plan for an attack upon Louisbourg, won pledges of support from neighboring colonies. Connecticut promised five hundred well-equipped men under command of Deputy Governor Roger Wolcott.[52]

On March 24, 1744/45, the principal part of an imposing fleet, totaling nearly a hundred vessels carrying 4,000 men, sailed from Boston under command of William Pepperell of Maine. Later seven transports, escorted by Connecticut's sloop *Defence*, carried the small Connecticut army to the rendezvous at Canso in Nova Scotia. At Shirley's suggestion, the Rhode Island sloop *Tartar* joined this fleet as further protection — a fortunate decision as it turned out. Off the Cape Sable shore a powerful French frigate, the *Renommée*, Captain Kersaint, approached the Connecticut fleet. Captain Fones of the *Tartar* skillfully led the *Renommée* away from the eight Connecticut vessels, which then slipped safely into Canso harbor.[53]

Early in May 1745 Pepperell's army opened siege operations against the French citadel. After resisting valiantly through seven weeks of relentless bombardment, the French commander, Du Chambon, on June 17, 1745, capitulated. Wolcott's diary boasted:

This action will appear to be such a conquest as we seldom meet with in history, if we consider the smallness of the army, how ill they were provided, with their other circumstances, together with the strength of the fortifications they overcame.

For once, even the British officers were favorably impressed by the colonials! The following October the Assembly prepared a letter to the king which forcefully described the colony's heavy contributions to the capture of Louisbourg, and humbly requested substantial monetary relief.[54]

News of an imminent French invasion of New England effectively broke up Shirley's ambitious project for taking Quebec by forcing concentration of all available troops for the defense of Boston. The French threat proved a false alarm, and the Treaty of Aix-la-Chapelle in 1748 provided

miding of the public debt, including the issue from 1740 to 1746 of £166,000 in paper bills, which depreciated sharply. Pleas to Britain for reimbursement of extraordinary war expenses even-

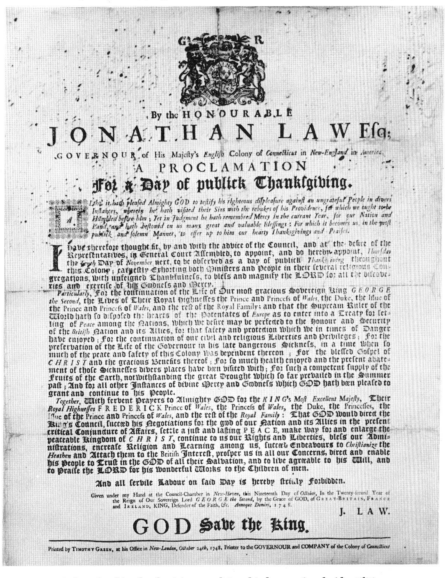

A day of public thanksgiving proclaimed in honor of end of hostilities in 1748.

that all conquered territories on both sides, including Louisbourg, be returned to former holders. Louisbourg's restoration to the French rankled deeply in the hearts of New Englanders, who felt that their brilliant exploit in capturing the fortress, as well as their future trade and safety, had been callously ignored by British diplomats.[55]

Connecticut therefore could show little for the war except heavy losses of men and a steep pyra-

tually brought the colony over £28,000. Despite the currency weakness, economic conditions in the 1740's improved somewhat, largely from the stimulus of supply contracts for the troops.[56]

Connecticut in the French and Indian War

IN the 1750's French–British rivalry in America hit a new peak of intensity. Bitter trade competition in the Ohio Valley exploded into open conflict, marked by forays and by the surrender of Washington at Fort Necessity in 1754.[57]

The same year serious deterioration of British relations with their Indian allies, especially the Iroquois, led the Board of Trade to call a general colonial congress at Albany to devise measures for wooing back their lukewarm allies. In drawing up instructions for the Connecticut delegates — William Pitkin, Roger Wolcott, and Elisha Williams — the Assembly displayed a narrow-minded, provincial attitude in warning against expensive commitments and stating that no agreements reached in Albany would be binding without Assembly approval. After taking steps to improve the Indian situation, the congress discussed and, despite Connecticut opposition, adopted a federal scheme of organization fathered by Benjamin Franklin, known as the Albany Plan of Union. When the plan was considered in October, the Assembly resoundingly rejected it as too grandiose, unsuited to defending the frontiers, highly injurious to British interests, and detrimental to colonial "liberties and privileges." The legislature voted to send the resolution and explanations to the colony's London agent; but there was little cause to worry, as other colonies and the British, too, roundly rejected the plan.[58]

In 1755 British authorities in Nova Scotia, deeply alarmed by the open disloyalty of the large French population, took the drastic step of deporting over 6,000 Acadians to many American colonies, including Connecticut. On January 21, 1756, the very day that the ship *Elizabeth,* from Annapolis Royal, docked at New London with 277 exiles, the Assembly passed a humanely conceived act which called for distribution of an expected 397 Acadians. This distribution was to be in family groups on a quota basis among fifty towns, with the infirm and sick cared for at the colony's expense. Actually about 700 Acadians were landed at New London, and they seem to have received reasonably kind treatment, although the colony refused to aid financially their return trip to Canada. The Acadians of course dreamed of a return to their homeland, and in 1767 some 240 of them departed for Canada.[59]

Connecticut soon discovered that the French

and Indian War was becoming the largest struggle yet. The colony, assigned a quota of 1,000 soldiers for an expedition against Crown Point, organized two regiments under General Phineas Lyman, who, due to Connecticut's large contingent, was elevated to second-in-command under Sir William Johnson of New York. Part of the force, including colony troops under Colonel William Whiting, was ambushed near Lake George, with heavy casualties; but Whiting rallied the survivors and led them back to safety. Soon afterward French Commander Von Dieskau hurled his army against Johnson's in the second of three clashes, known collectively as the Battle of Lake George. According to Francis Parkman's accounts, "Johnson received a flesh-wound in the thigh . . . Lyman took command; and it is a marvel that he escaped alive, for he was four hours in the heat of the fire, directing and animating the men." Although the French regulars fought courageously against makeshift defenses of the colonials' camp, they were repulsed and that evening, in a separate engagement, routed by fresh New Hampshire and New York troops. Later the colonials erected near the lake a fort called William Henry; but the year ended with the French at Crown Point undisturbed.[60]

In accord with ambitious objectives for 1756, Connecticut called out 2,500 men, organized into four regiments, and later authorized 800 more. Such efforts, shared by other colonies, achieved nothing, as Oswego fell to the French. The next year, 1757, when Connecticut furnished 1,400 men, poor leadership helped produce further demoralizing setbacks, especially the repulse of an expedition against Louisbourg and investment of Fort William Henry. News of the critical situation at besieged Fort William Henry precipitated a turnout of about 5,000 Connecticut militia for relief of the beleaguered garrison. Unfortunately the fort had fallen, and Connecticut troops met half-naked escapees from a brutal Indian massacre of some prisoners. Since Montcalm's French and Indian army had burned the fort and quickly withdrawn northward, the Connecticut soldiery could only return home.[61]

Dissatisfaction with the war's conduct produced a new British ministry, dominated by the energetic

William Pitt, who reorganized the entire British effort in America. The colonies responded promptly to increased calls for volunteers, with Connecticut voting to call up four regiments totaling 5,000 men, to serve under Major General Phineas Lyman. Each volunteer was promised a bounty of four pounds and this monthly pay scale:

	£	s.	d.
Regimental Colonel	15	0	0
Lieutenant Colonel	10	15	0
Major	9	1	4
Company Captain	6	0	0
Captain Lieutenant	6	0	0
Lieutenant	4	0	0
Ensign	3	10	0
Chaplain of a regiment	10	0	0
Sergeant	2	0	0
Corporal	1	18	0
Clerk	2	0	0
Drum Major for a regiment	2	0	0
Drummer	1	18	0
Surgeon	8	0	0
Surgeon's Mate	4	0	0
Private	1	16	0
Quartermaster	3	5	0
Adjutant	2	8	0

For "tent and table" a colonel received £45, a lieutenant colonel £18, and a major £12.[62]

With Pitt's masterful direction, the year 1758 brought a dramatic turn. General Jeffrey Amherst, given a large army of regulars and colonials and supported by Admiral Edward Boscawen's fleet, pressed a siege of Louisbourg, which culminated in the surrender of the great fortress on July 26, 1758. The same year Fort Duquesne (renamed Fort Pitt) and Fort Frontenac also fell to British troops.[63]

In the central campaign, involving an invasion of Canada by way of Fort Ticonderoga and Crown Point, little was achieved. During a skirmish in deep woods near the head of Lake George, George Augustus Lord Howe, one of Britain's finest soldiers, was killed. Connecticut troops, under Phineas Lyman, in turn fell upon the French and exacted heavy casualties. The superior army of Abercromby unwisely made a frontal attack against Montcalm's army, entrenched on a ridge near Fort Ticonderoga, and the French repulsed

them with staggering losses. Many of the troops, including Lyman's Connecticut line, desired to dig in, but demoralized Abercromby ordered a prompt retreat to the site of Fort William Henry. Little wonder that the Provincials dubbed their commander "Mrs. Nabbycromby"! General Lyman's pessimistic forebodings — ". . . I really fear I must again bare ye Mortification of returning to my friends without a Conquest over ye enemy" — had proven only too accurate.[64]

Undaunted by Abercromby's dismal performance, Pitt pushed ahead with plans for a climactic victory in 1759. Considering a request for 5,000 men, the legislature decided that 3,600 men represented the practical limit. Three months later, under pressure from Abercromby's successor, General Amherst, it voted to supply 1,000 additional soldiers.[65]

Success crowned British arms in 1759 as Fort Niagara fell to Sir William Johnson's forces; while General Amherst, with many of Lyman's Connecticut troops in his army, using heavy guns, blasted Fort Ticonderoga to rubble. Realizing their hopeless position, the French rear guard on July 26 spiked the guns, blew up the powder magazine, stove in the casks of wine and brandy, and slipped away to the north. Meanwhile General James Wolfe broke the back of French resistance in the memorable battle on the Plains of Abraham, as a result of which Quebec capitulated on September 17, 1759.[66]

The American struggle culminated in 1760 with an expedition against Montreal, in which Connecticut troops participated. Amherst's invading army was blocked by two armed enemy vessels at Oswegatchie, where Connecticut's Lieutenant Colonel Israel Putnam headed a force of 1,000 men, stripped to the waist, who swarmed over the two ships and quickly compelled their surrender. Putnam also spearheaded the seizure of a nearby island fort. Early in September Amherst's forces, arriving before Montreal, were joined by other British troops, which gave them an overwhelming superiority. On September 8, 1760, the French surrendered. The Treaty of Paris of 1763 confirmed the sweeping British triumph in America by stripping France of everything except a few islands.[67]

For Connecticut the conflict had involved greater forces, heavier losses, and far larger expenditures than any of the previous intercolonial wars. From 1755 through March 1764 the colony issued £346,500 in bills of credit, reduced by heavy taxation to a manageable £82,000 early in 1764. Although about one-fifth of the able-bodied men had served from 1757 to the war's end and were removed from productive labor, the colony's paper money remained at face value. Actually the war years brought strong prosperity, buoyed up by large army contracts for beef, pork, flour, wheat, and other items. Parliamentary grants in the 1757–63 period amounted to nearly £250,000 sterling — enough so that the colony levied no taxes from 1766 through 1769. Overall, Connecticut's war record stood high, perhaps highest among the continental colonies.[68]

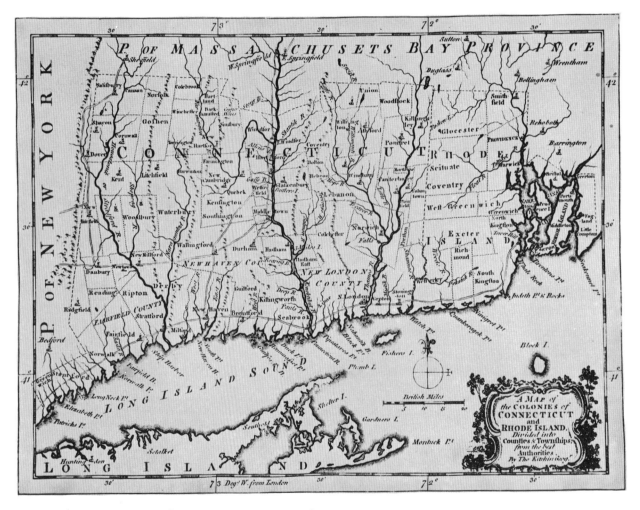

The Thomas Kitchin map of Connecticut in 1758.

CHAPTER 7

Social, Economic, and Religious Patterns
in the Eighteenth Century

A Fast-Growing Population — Family Life — Witches Frighten the People — Farmers, the Backbone of Connecticut — A Land of Small Manufactures — Shrewd Yankee Merchants — The Established Church Dominates — The Great Awakening Shakes the Establishment — Rise of the Anglican Church — Colonial Newspapers and Presses

A Fast-Growing Population

CONNECTICUT's population, estimated at only 800 in 1636 and 2,000 in 1640, grew at an astonishing rate. By the time of King Philip's War it numbered about 12,000; in 1701 perhaps 30,000; and by the census of 1774 it had jumped to 197,842, making Connecticut one of the most densely settled American colonies.[1]

In 1774 the thickly populated area ran along the coast, with tongues spreading northward from Stratford up the Housatonic and Naugatuck rivers to Waterbury, from New Haven northeast to the Connecticut River Valley at Middletown and thence upriver to the Massachusetts line, and from New London northward up the Thames River to Norwich. All but one of the twelve most populous towns were located within this belt:

TOWNS RANKED BY POPULATION AND BY TAX LISTS

Towns Listed in Order of Rank by Population, 1774	Population			1774 Tax List (in £)	Rank by Taxes
	1756 Census	1774 Census	Increase (percent)		
New Haven	5085	8295	63	72,395	1
Norwich	5540	7327	32	68,649	2
Farmington	3707	6069	64	67,519	3
New London	3171	5888	86	36,424	12
Stratford	3658	5555	52	52,000	5
Stonington	3518	5412	54	37,839	11
Woodbury	2911	5313	83	60,600	4
Hartford	3027	5031	66	49,036	8
Wallingford	3713	4915	32	51,051	6
Middletown	5664	4878	−14	43,153	10
Fairfield	4455	4863	9	51,005	7
Norwalk	3050	4388	44	44,076	9

Unlike many colonies, Connecticut lacked any one town so large in population and wealth as clearly to dominate the area.[2]

Litchfield County, Connecticut's last frontier, had largely filled up by 1774, so that recently settled towns such as Canaan, Goshen, Harwinton, New Hartford, Salisbury, and Sharon already ex-

RAN away on the 10th of April laſt paſt from Daniel Cook, of Long-Iſland, a Negro Woman, about 20 years old, ſpeaks good Engliſh, born on Long-Iſland, about midding ſtature, ſhe is a likely wench, had a large pack of cloaths, ſtrip'd ſhort gown, and ſeveral callico gowns; has chang'd her dreſs for man's cloaths, and was ſeen to have a blue broadcloth coat, and the remainder of her cloaths appears to be man's, as ſhe had about 3 or 4 pounds in money——had rings in her ears.

Whoever will take upſaid Negro, and ſecure her in any of his Majeſty's goals, ſo that I can receive ſaid negro, ſhall have a reward of FOUR DOLLARS, and all neceſſary charge paid by me,
DANIEL COOK.
New-London, May 14. 1770.

Typical advertisement for a runaway slave.

ceeded the 1,000 mark. Indeed, Connecticut in 1774 ranked about in the middle of the thirteen colonies in population, and contained approximately 7 to 8 percent of the total population.[3]

The Indians, though slowly dying out in Connecticut, numbered 1,363 in 1774 and lived peacefully on reservations. Stonington, with 237, claimed the largest number; New London, Groton, Lyme, Kent, and Norwich followed in that order.[4]

A more numerous minority group, the 5,101 Negroes, comprised about one-fortieth of the populace in 1774. They were centered especially in the towns of Stratford (319), New London (316), Fairfield (315), New Haven (262), Norwich (234), and

Stonington (219). From the earliest days slaves were held by prominent leaders, including Edward Hopkins, George Wyllys, John Davenport, and Theophilus Eaton, although the average slaveholder owned only one or two.[5]

Despite a harsh slave code evolved over the 1690–1730 period, the observations of Mrs. Sarah Kemble Knight of Boston in the winter of 1704–5 reveal an informal and friendly relationship:

And they Generally lived very well and comfortably in their famelies. But too Indulgent (especially ye farmers) to their slaves: sufering too great familiarity from them, permitting ym to sit at Table and eat with them, (as they say to save time,) and into the dish goes the black hoof as freely as the white hand. They told me that there was a farmer . . . who had some difference wth his slave, concerning something the master had promised him and did not punctualy perform; wch caused some hard words between them; But at length they put the matter to Arbitration and Bound themselves to stand to the award of such as they named — wch done, the Arbitrators Having heard the Allegations of both parties, Order the master to pay 40s to black face, and acknowledge his fault. And so the matter ended: the poor master very honestly standing to the award.

In Connecticut's prevailing agricultural economy of small farms, the slaves' tasks consisted chiefly of simple household chores or field labor at the master's side; but some doubtless assisted their masters in diverse occupations such as lumbering, fishing, whaling, trading, and manufacturing. Occasionally a master, for monetary or humane motives, freed a slave.[6]

Among the few non-English immigrants were a scattering of Dutch, French Huguenots, Acadians, and others. The astute contemporary Jedidiah Morse stated accurately that "The inhabitants are almost entirely of English descent."[7]

Family Life

FAMILY life in rapidly growing Connecticut found its roots in the family institutions of the sixteenth and seventeenth centuries in England, especially among the Puritans. When the English came to New England they migrated usually as family groups, and they founded a stable, monogamous, family-type civilization. The law of April 1640, aiming to prevent rash, overhasty marriages,

The David Judson house (1723) at Stratford — a typical house of its period.

Kitchen-dining room at Stonecrop Farm, Stonington. Home built in 1750 by Paul Wheeler. Above 7'6" fireplace is rare trimmer arch. Home now owned by author Williams Haynes — great-great-great-grandson of Wheeler.

Careful craftsmanship seen in day bed attributed to Eliphalet Chapin.

required publication of intention to marry, as well as recording by magistrates of all marriages which they performed.[8]

The conditions of pioneer life in a country lacking adequate population resulted in few obstacles being placed in the way of early marriage, though Connecticut did require young people under age to obtain consent from parents or guardians before giving "entertaynment to any motion or sute in way of mariedge." Then, as now, parents took a lively interest in courtship, and undoubtedly some tried to arrange favorable matches. A lack of privacy in courtship led to the institution of bundling.

Connecticut sunflower chest made about 1700.

It arose among the lower classes where the young people despaired of courting on winter nights before assorted relatives in the one warm room of the house. They were permitted to lie together, fully dressed, in a bed, usually with a board between them. From contemporary accounts one judges that the custom never was universally approved; and, as wealth increased and homes became larger and better heated, bundling gradually disappeared.[9]

When Mrs. Knight crossed Connecticut in 1704 she commented upon marriage customs:

They generally marry very young: the males oftener as I am told under twentie than above; they generally make public wedings, and have a way something singular (as they say) in some of them, *viz.* Just before Joyning hands the Bridegroom quitts the place, who is soon followed by the Bridesmen, and as it were, dragg'd back to duty . . .

For many decades New England Puritans considered marriage a *civil* rather than a religious ceremony, to be performed by a civil magistrate. Gradually Connecticut people introduced more color and ritual into their weddings, and in 1694 they first authorized clergy to perform marriages.[10]

Occasionally a man and woman insisted upon living together without benefit of magistrate or clergyman. New London tradition delightfully describes such a case. The local minister, the Reverend Gurdon Saltonstall, confronted by such a notorious couple, addressed them thus: "'Do you really, John, take this your servant-maid, bought with your money, for your wife?' 'Do you, Mary, take this man so much older than yourself for your husband?' and receiving from both an affirmative answer, he exclaimed: 'Then I pronounce you, according to the laws of this colony, man and wife.'"[11]

Parental authority was clearly recognized and exerted, often with the rod; and daily prayer and reading of Scripture were practiced. Under the 1650 code parents were required at least once weekly to "catechise theire children and servants in the grounds and principles of religion." Certainly the average child heard the Bible read so often that he knew it well and probably was deeply influenced by it.[12]

Families usually were so large that parents desperately needed substantial help from the older children. One writer describes the busy regime of an eighteenth-century Connecticut farm boy as follows:

He was taught that time was a talent to be always improved; that industry was a cardinal virtue, and laziness the worst form of original sin. Hence he must rise early, and make himself useful before he went to school; must be diligent there in study, and be promptly home to do *"chores"* at evening. His whole time out of school must be filled up by some service, —

farthing, kite-flying, dancing round Maypole, hop-skip-and-jump, cricket, swimming, leap-frog, shooting, and hop-scotch. Children's toys, though rare, were sold in colonial New England, and a few dolls and other items have survived.[14]

Large families were the rule, with eight to twelve children not uncommon. Many young wives had six or seven children in rapid succession, and then, worn out, died from disease or in child-

LEFT: *A book studied by generations of New England children.* RIGHT: *Excerpt from* The New England Primer.

such as bringing in fuel for the day, cutting potatoes for the sheep, feeding the swine, watering the horses, picking the berries, gathering the vegetables, spooling the yarn, and running all errands. He was expected never to be reluctant, and not often tired.

Chopping wood occupied many hours, while hunting and fishing provided pleasant interludes. In many families it was common to bind out several sons as apprentices to learn trades. Girls early mastered spinning of flax, combing of wool, care of infants, sewing, cooking, and eventually all of the major skills useful to them later as housewives.[13]

Although children worked too much and played too little, they apparently enjoyed many games similar to those of today. A quaint book of the Revolutionary era lists and illustrates crudely many popular children's games, called chuck-

birth. The second wife usually bore fewer children and enjoyed more help from older children. Despite a high death rate from children's diseases, one finds some remarkable records of fecundity, such as that of Mary Loomis (1680–1768) of Windsor, who married John Buell of Lebanon in 1696 and left this posterity:[15]

	Children	Grandchildren	Great-grandchildren	Great-great-grandchildren	Total
Survived her:	10	75	232	19	336
Predeceased her:	3	26	42	3	74
	13	101	274	22	410

Although Connecticut seems to have followed a more liberal divorce policy than some colonies, few divorces occurred. The first recorded was granted in May 1655 to Goody Beckwith of Fairfield, whose husband had deserted her. A law of October 1677 established as grounds for divorce adultery, fraudulent contract, willful desertion for three years, or seven years "providentiall absence." Although desertion was the reason cited in most cases, a divorce was granted to Mary Larkum of Enfield in 1753 because of her hus-

Desk attributed to Benjamin Burnham of Colchester (owned by Edward R. Bulkeley).

band's "insupportable exercises of his cruelty" and his threats to kill her.[16]

Although Puritans tended to repress public expression of familial affection, their private letters often reveal ardent affection. One finds General Gold Selleck Silliman writing his father-in-law in 1776:

I am now at Home happy & blessed as a Mortal can be, in the Dear and endearing Company, and delightfull Society of a tender, affectionate, and dearly Beloved Wife, dutiful and affectionate Children all now at Home with us.

It seems quite apparent that Connecticut colonial family life, despite rigorous living conditions, usually brought enduring values and joys.[17]

Witches Frighten the People

IN seventeenth-century Europe, belief in witchcraft was widespread, perhaps partly because Biblical injunctions and teachings of the Church made it seem a deadly sin whose extirpation required drastic penalties. As might be expected, the early settlers of New England brought along this superstition, which manifested itself prominently at Salem, Massachusetts, in 1692.[18]

Early affected by this delusion, Connecticut passed a 1642 law which provided the death penalty for any witch. The *Diary* of Matthew Grant of Windsor says that on May 26, 1647, Alse Young was hanged; which, if true, makes this the first execution for witchcraft in New England. Cotton Mather's *Magnalia* records a Hartford trial the next year in which Mary Johnson was found guilty, "And she dyd in a frame extreamly to the satisfaction of them that were spectators of it." In December 1648 the Court's indictment of Mary Johnson noted "that by her owne confession shee is guilty of familliarity with the Deuill." In the next fifty years at least thirty-three additional persons were charged with or suspected of the heinous crime! Contrary to a widespread belief, however, no witch ever was burned in Connecticut.[19]

Among the most distressing cases was that of "Goodwife" Knap of Fairfield, who was "suspicioned," even though known hitherto as a simple woman of good repute. She courageously resisted repeated brutal attempts to wring a confession from her. When a special committee, visiting her on the very day of condemnation, tried mercilessly to force her to divulge other witches, she adamantly refused and pointedly warned one of them to "take heed the devile have not you." Only when on the scaffold about to be hanged did the terrified woman in confidence tell Roger Ludlow the name of a witch.[20]

In 1662 the last witches were sentenced to death in Connecticut, although the delusion enjoyed one last outbreak around Fairfield in 1692. The most famous of five cases there involved Mercy Disborough, who was charged with bewitching property, such as a canoe, pig, horse, calf, cow, oxen, and the bodies of several neighbors. To test her innocence the court ordered her bound and cast into the water, where she defiantly floated buoyantly. Soon afterward several clergymen drew up a lengthy statement for the Assembly denouncing the methods used in the trial. Mercy Disborough apparently was pardoned, and a swift reaction set in against this mass hysteria, so that no significant cases occurred after 1697. Witches ceased to cast their wicked spells in Connecticut![21]

Farmers, the Backbone of Connecticut

THROUGHOUT the colonial period farmers constituted by far the largest class in Connecticut, and even professional men and artisans normally engaged in part-time farming. In pioneer days the settlers discovered that maize, or Indian corn, provided a dependable food, so they cultivated it as their principal crop. It was planted in small hills three or four feet apart, and in early days fish were used as fertilizer. An old rhyme described the fate of the corn kernels:

> One for the bug,
> One for the crow,
> One to rot,
> And two to grow.

By the late colonial period, yields of twenty to twenty-five bushels per acre were obtained upon moderately good soil. Other popular crops were rye, oats, barley, flax, and hemp; but attempts to expand wheat production were early stymied by black stem rust and other pests.[22]

Many farmers raised substantial amounts of vegetables, especially beans, peas, squash, turnips, and pumpkins, while Wethersfield developed a profitable specialty of onions. Apples ranked as the favorite fruit, though they were often better appreciated when transformed into cider and "apple-jack," or brandy. In the earliest settlement many kinds of fruits grew wild, including blueberries, cherries, cranberries, currants, dewberries, grapes, mulberries, plums, raspberries, and whortleberries.[23]

Among Connecticut's oldest crops was tobacco, which probably was grown by Windsor colonists as early as 1640. The settlers first cultivated the same leaf — often called *poke* or *ottomauch* — raised by valley Indians. Since this leaf possessed a bitter taste, growers later gladly substituted a West Indian variety. By 1700 valley growers already were exporting tobacco leaf, and a detailed act in 1753, regulating inspection of export tobacco, revealed its continuing importance. After 1750, because of Virginia competition and the war, tobacco production declined.[24]

Thanks to the pioneering efforts of Ezra Stiles in New Haven and Nathaniel Aspinwall in Mansfield, silk culture became established by the 1760's. Many farmers, in Mansfield especially, began to raise mulberry trees; and that town led Connecti-

An early specialty of Wethersfield.

cut in silkworm culture and manufacture until the 1840's, when a blight hit the mulberry trees.[25]

Around 1750 a major agricultural change began — a gradual shift away from soil tillage to grazing. Growing markets in other mainland colonies and in the West Indies stimulated farmers to put heavy emphasis upon cattle, horses, mules, sheep, and hogs. Cattle from New York and Vermont were driven to Connecticut for fattening up through a winter, spring, and summer, for sale in the fall. The 1762 reply to the Board of Trade declared that "our staple may be said to consist in pork and beef." The increasing use of timothy, red clover, and the other English grasses materially aided in the production of fatter livestock. The important by-products of these efforts, butter and cheese, were exported, especially from Windham and Litchfield counties, to the south and to the West Indies.[26]

In common with most colonial American farmers, those of Connecticut practiced inefficient methods. With labor scarce, land plentiful, and markets limited, inevitably they carried on *extensive* farming — the application of small amounts of labor to large land areas, with little use of fertilizers. Often seed was poor and tools were clumsy, though the eighteenth century saw gradual introduction of labor-saving tools, such as harrows with wooden pegs, rakes, scythes, forks, and flails. Oxen remained the farmer's chief reliance, although use of horses was increasing.[27]

Timothy Dwight ably summarized agricultural techniques:

The husbandry of New-England is far inferiour to that of Great-Britain. . . . The principal defects in our husbandry, so far as I am able to judge, are a deficiency in the quantity of labour, necessary to prepare the ground for seed; insufficient manuring; the want of a good rotation of crops; and slovenliness in cleaning the ground. The soil is not sufficiently pulverized; nor sufficiently manured. We are generally ignorant of what crops will best succeed each other; and our fields are covered with a rank growth of weeds.[28]

At least one Connecticut agricultural reformer, Jared Eliot (1685–1763), a clergyman, strove energetically to improve agricultural practices as he outlined steps for restoring worn-out land, advocated draining bogs, and urged hemp growing to provide a suitable staple which Britain could use. Even with legislative encouragement, hemp never became a staple, though production did increase.[29]

Connecticut's typical colonial family engaged in subsistence farming, kept some livestock, raised its own food, wool, and flax, made its clothing, and tried hard to be self-sufficient.

A Land of Small Manufactures

WHILE farming dominated, manufacturing was assuming major importance by the early eight-eenth century. In the self-sufficient agricultural economy the average family made much of its own clothing, as well as household and farming utensils and tools.[30]

In the small agricultural village the gristmill usually represented the first manufacturing enterprise, as in Wethersfield, where a dam was built across Mill Brook in 1637 to provide power for Leonard Chester's mill. The early inexpensive

Advertisement from New London Gazette, *June 15, 1770.*

undershot mills, built upon small streams, were designed for small-scale grinding of family grain. Legislation in March 1662/63 established the miller's toll at one-twelfth part of each bushel of corn, and one-sixteenth of other grains. As population grew, larger mills, often of the overshot type, were constructed upon bigger streams. Likewise sawmills appeared early, as indicated in a General Court grant of 1653 to John Winthrop.[31]

The colonists, familiar with the very profitable English cloth manufacture, in February 1640/41 passed a law to encourage the making of woolen cloth, and followed it with orders for each family to grow hemp and flax. In May 1686 the Assembly observed that "Mr. Francis Thrasher [was] improveing himselfe in cloath workeing" and had spent "considerable to fit himselfe to promoate the trade of makeing cloath and searge," as a reward for which he and his servant were exempted from militia and highway duties. Fulling mills for finishing cloth appeared at East Hartford in 1686, at Stamford in 1700, and at Guilford in 1707.[32]

Since clothmaking failed to expand rapidly, the Assembly in 1734 thought it expedient to pass "An Act for the Encouragement of raising Hemp, mak-

Salisbury, and two years later Thomas Lamb set up the first forge at Lime Rock. Before the Revolution blast furnaces were established in Lakeville, Kent, Canaan, and Roxbury, so that the iron industry was well established.[34]

Connecticut's clock industry dates back to 1638, when Thomas Nash of New Haven made what was probably the first American clock. Little more was heard of clockmaking until 1726, when Ebenezer Parmele put a tower clock in Guilford's

LEFT: *Silver open salt by Samuel Parmelee of Guilford.* RIGHT: *Silver cann by Timothy Bontecou, Jr., of New Haven (owned by Philip Hammerslough).*

ing Canvas or Duck, and also for making Fine Linen." In 1766 Christopher Leffingwell inaugurated a stocking-weaving business in Norwich, and between 1773 and 1780 four fulling mills with clothiers' shops and dyehouses began operation. On the whole, however, the colonial American market for cloth remained too limited to stimulate large-scale production.[33]

In iron manufacturing, Connecticut made a start in the 1650's at East Haven — a project in which John Winthrop, Jr., evinced strong interest — and at New London. Since the only good iron deposits were located in Salisbury, Sharon, and Kent, it was inevitable that later the chief iron furnaces would be located in that region. About 1732 the first iron mine was opened at Ore Hill in

meeting house. Connecticut craftsmen, such as Benjamin Cheney of East Hartford, pioneered in making wooden clocks, while at Windsor in the 1742–60 period Seth Young(s) created clocks of rare quality. In 1773 Thomas Harland came from England to Norwich, and for thirty-four years turned out excellent clocks and watches. One of his apprentices, Daniel Burnap, established his own shop at East Windsor about 1780 and became Connecticut's finest clockmaker. Altogether, several score clockmakers were active in the colony from 1725 to 1783, and many of their graceful creations still adorn Connecticut homes and museums.[35]

Shipbuilding began in early colonial times and reached a rather high level in the eighteenth century under the stimulus of growing trade. New London, Norwich, New Haven, Guilford, Branford, Stratford, Fairfield, Saybrook, Middletown, Essex, Middle Haddam, Glastonbury, Rocky Hill, Wethersfield, and Hartford all claimed busy ship-

farmer purchased numerous commodities from the local storekeeper, often on credit, and usually paid for them then or later by bartering such items as corn, rye, oats, cheese, tallow, lard, flaxseed, hoops, staves, horses, mules, cattle, sheep, vegetables, ap-

Colonial topsail schooner — a typical vessel of eighteenth-century Connecticut. Drawn by Gordon Grant.

builders. From the records of vessels registered at New Haven in 1766–67, showing a tonnage range of 15 to 120, it is obvious that vessels even then were small and usually intended for coastal and river trade, but Connecticut ranked as one of the leaders in the quantity built.[36]

Shrewd Yankee Merchants

FROM the earliest days Connecticut Yankees possessed powerful trading instincts. The average

ples, and cider. The local merchant concluded small trades with hundreds of farmers in order to accumulate sufficient products which he in turn could trade profitably with larger merchants.[37]

The typical village or country storekeeper carried a wide variety of items, including a small stock often described as "European" and "West Indian" goods, including molasses, rum, spices, indigo, sugar, many kinds of cloth, dress goods, crockery, glassware, powder, shot, guns, bar iron, and wines. The country shopkeeper in turn carried his produce, or "country pay," to the merchant of a larger coastal or river town, where he exchanged it for the supply of "European" and "West Indian" goods needed to supply his regular customers. The town merchant forwarded the goods received from the country shopkeepers and from his own local customers to a major port, such as Boston or New York, where he procured English manufactures from the importing, or "sedentary," mer-

alty of confiscation for selling without a license. In 1770 the Assembly forbade any peddlers, other than those already licensed, to operate, but exempted persons selling deerskins, beaver furs, and other produce or Connecticut manufactures. "Outside" peddlers were the real target.[40]

Among the famous Connecticut figures who engaged in storekeeping were Benedict Arnold and Roger Sherman. Sherman and his brother kept a

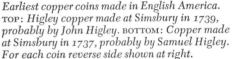

Earliest copper coins made in English America.
TOP: *Higley copper made at Simsbury in 1739, probably by John Higley.* BOTTOM: *Copper made at Simsbury in 1737, probably by Samuel Higley. For each coin reverse side shown at right.*

chant. Because of the chronic dire shortage of coin, a large proportion of trade was conducted on a credit basis, which gradually replaced the earlier crude direct barter.[38]

Advertisements in newspapers and available account books reveal very little specialization into *wholesale* and *retail* classes. Occasionally in his advertising a merchant emphasized one type of merchandise — as in Hartford, where Enos Doolittle advertised clocks; William Ellery, liquors and chinaware; and Thomas Hilldrup, watches.[39]

Ironically the famed peddlers were often unpopular, as local merchants felt that these itinerants frequently sold inferior articles at inflated prices. Hence in 1765 the Assembly voted to raise the peddler's license fee from five pounds (set in 1757) to twenty pounds, and to maintain the pen-

store in New Milford, where they experienced the normal joys and vicissitudes of a local merchant's life. Roger Sherman's ire was particularly roused by the fluctuating and depreciating paper money of Rhode Island and New Hampshire which some customers eagerly forced upon him. This situation impelled him in 1752 to prepare a pamphlet inveighing against unreliable currencies and recommending Assembly action to outlaw their use.[41]

Despite increasing competition, colonial Boston remained the commercial hub of New England to which small coasters plied. Many Connecticut merchants chafed at their great dependence upon Boston importers who stocked the European goods which Connecticut merchants could not buy directly. Small Connecticut coasters loaded up with such items as horses, corn, barley, pork, beef, rye, flax, cider, peas, boards, and pipe staves, which they sold in Boston. In return, they carried back a variety of "European" goods — cloths and finished clothing, glass, powder shot, pepper, silks, tea, and wines. In 1773 more ships entered Boston from Connecticut than from any other colony.[42]

A traveler visiting Connecticut around 1760 aptly likened it "to a cask of good liquor, tapped at both ends, at one of which Boston draws, and New York at the other, till little is left in it but lees and settlings." From New London, New Haven, and ports farther west an increasing commerce was carried on with New York, which was gaining heavily on Boston.[43]

Connecticut merchants also engaged in considerable trade with Rhode Island, especially with Newport and Providence. Much produce flowed from eastern Connecticut towns into Providence, where James and Moses Brown, among others, bought heavily. Jonathan Trumbull, of Lebanon, was a typical inland merchant who traded extensively with Newport, where hard money was obtainable.[44]

In overseas trade Connecticut found only one route highly profitable — that to the West Indies. Attempts to establish large direct trade with Britain or the Continent failed dismally because Connecticut produced very little that either area wanted. The colony's beef, pork, flour, horses, mules, cattle, swine, sheep, poultry, cheese, lumber, and onions were eagerly purchased by West Indian merchants and planters, who returned molasses, sugar, salt, tropical fruits, and coveted bills of exchange. Customs officials at New Haven and New London agreed that the West Indian trade was their principal one. Connecticut merchants usually traded *directly* with the West Indies rather than make that area one stop in the triangular routes so popular elsewhere. The British Leeward and Windward Islands, especially Antigua, Barbados, and Grenada; French Guadeloupe and Martinique; Spanish Hispaniola; Dutch St. Eustatius; and outlying British Jamaica attracted many Connecticut vessels. Just before the Revolution, Nathaniel Shaw of New London, whose ships touched at almost every Caribbean port, typified the enterprising mercantile leadership in the colony.[45]

The Established Church Dominates

IN the seventeenth century, Connecticut leaders clung tenaciously to their Congregational Church, and as a standard they adopted the Cambridge Platform of 1648, drawn up at a synod in Cambridge, Massachusetts. This platform dealt with the necessity of individual spiritual regeneration, the roles of minister, teacher, and elder, the financial support of the Church, the interrelationship of congregations, especially through synods, and the proper sphere of magistrates.[46]

Within a few years a major issue, known as the Half-Way Covenant, rose to agitate New England Congregationalists. This measure called for the Church to baptize the children of baptized parents who had never professed a conversion or fully united with the Church but desired baptism for their children. Though it implied a definite relaxing of standards, with an inferior class of church membership, leading clergymen, including Samuel Stone of Hartford and John Warham of Windsor, supported the measure. Following introduction of the Half-Way Covenant before the General Assembly in August 1657, a decade of heated debate ensued. Finally in May 1669 the Assembly voted a compromise which approved the former practices but permitted toleration to those who wanted liberal steps, such as the Half-Way Covenant. Under this act the serious discord in the First Church of Hartford was settled by the more conservative group, which at first strongly opposed the Half-Way Covenant, departing to form the Second Church of Hartford. Eventually they, too, accepted the covenant, which won widespread but not universal acceptance in Connecticut.[47]

By about 1700 the autocratic behavior of ministers often precipitated serious quarrels with congregations. As a result of the ensuing disorder, many conservatives saw a need for some powerful body to oversee the churches and act as a court of religious appeal in major disputes. The Massachusetts "Proposals of 1705," which aimed at establishment of powerful ministerial associations there, struck a responsive chord among Connecticut's conservatives and especially the Yale College trustees. In 1708 Gurdon Saltonstall, the highly respected minister of New London, was elevated to the governor's seat and promptly urged decisive action. The Assembly ordered ministers and lay representatives of the churches to convene at Saybrook to work out a new form of church discipline.[48]

Meeting in September 1708, twelve ministers and four laymen drew up the famous Saybrook Platform aiming at a uniform and strict church government. It consisted of a "Confession of Faith," the "Heads of Agreement," and the "Fifteen Articles." The first reaffirmed a confession adopted at Boston in 1680, and the second repeated the articles passed in London in 1691 by English Congregationalists and Presbyterians. The novel part of the Saybrook document was the "Fifteen Articles," which provided for powerful "Associations" of pastors and elders, and "Consociations," or unions of churches. Licensing ministers, disciplining churches and pastors, and arbitrating disputes constituted some of their leading responsibilities. The platform signified a shrewd compromise between Congregationalism and Presbyterianism but leaned toward Presbyterianism. In October 1708 the Assembly gave the Saybrook Platform its hearty approval. The new system brought to Connecticut a long period of religious peace, but it also produced a cold formalism and growing indifference.[49]

Despite vigorous attempts to maintain religious uniformity, Connecticut early acquired a few dissenters — Quakers, Anglicans, Baptists, Rogerenes. New Haven enacted very severe laws against Quakers, which provided for swift deportation, and upon return, imprisonment, whipping, and branding. Humphrey Norton, a Quaker who opposed the Southold minister, was severely whipped, branded on the hand with the letter *H* for heretic, fined, and banished. Connecticut, listing much milder penalties, ordered the departure of Quakers within two weeks, though several reported lenient treatment. In 1675 Connecticut enacted a law temporarily freeing Quakers from fines for nonattendance at public worship. Conditions apparently remained unsatisfactory, however, as influential English Quakers petitioned Queen Anne. On October 11, 1705, with advice of her Privy Council, she annulled the Connecticut law

of 1657 against "Heretics, Infidels and Quakers." Scattered Quakers continued to live in the colony until the Revolution, when organized societies began to be formed.[50]

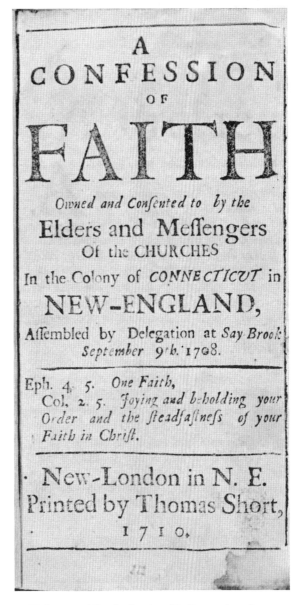

Title page of first book printed in Connecticut. It contained the Saybrook Platform.

The Great Awakening Shakes the Establishment

FOR about three decades after adoption of the Saybrook Platform, indifference to religion steadily increased in New England. In Northampton, Massachusetts, the dynamic minister Jonathan Edwards in December 1734 opened a spectacular revival directed against the prevalent laxness. His crusade won many conversions but affected only a few Connecticut towns. More of New England was turned toward a great religious revival by the English clergyman George Whitefield. Late in October 1740 he toured Connecticut, delivering sermons at Suffield, East Windsor, Hartford, Wethersfield, Middletown, Wallingford, New Haven, Milford, Stratford, Fairfield, Norwalk, and Stamford. A man of fine physique, booming voice, and high dramatic ability, his religious eloquence swept his listeners off their feet. In Hartford he preached "to a vast Concourse of people," and at New Haven the Assembly members joined the throng listening to him. Many conservative preachers shared the hostile sentiments of the Reverend Daniel Wadsworth of Hartford's First Church. Many years later, when he made a return trip through the colony, hearers attested his stirring evangelism. When he preached at Sharon,

An immense Congr[e]gation from this and the neighboring towns attended, and filled the meeting house to overflowing. His text was the words of our Saviour to Nichodemus "Marvel not that I said unto thee, ye must be born again"— Having announced his text he proceeded to discourse upon the doctrine of the new birth and he spake in words of fire — The most astonishing power and eloquence poured from his lips. It is impossible at this day to conceive of the effect which this sermon produced upon those who heard it. My informant . . . spake of the effort as *wonderful* beyond all comparison and *effective* beyond all precedent.[51]

Among the most influential disciples of Whitefield in Connecticut were Eleazer Wheelock (later founder of Dartmouth), Jedidiah Mills of Ripton (Shelton), Benjamin Pomeroy of Hebron, and Joseph Bellamy of Bethlehem. In June 1741 Joshua Hempstead of New London wrote that "there hath been the wonderfull work of God made Evident in the powerfull Convictions Conversion of Divers persons in an Extreordinary manner which began at the preaching of Mr. Mills." The revival spread through the colony in 1740, 1741, and 1742 like an overwhelming flood. Entire towns suspended business and gave themselves up to the religious services, which, according to Benjamin Trumbull, an eye-witness, produced amazing emotional effects.[52]

There existed a fringe of religious extremists represented best by James Davenport, who left his church at Southold, Long Island, to range over Connecticut as an itinerant preacher. An "enthusiast" and "exhorter," he converted many, but earned the violent opposition of others such as Joshua Hempstead, who called his services "Scarcely worth the hearing" and "all Meer Confused medley."[53]

The Great Awakening not only raised public interest in religion to heights not seen since the founding days but also produced a deep split within the Congregational Church between the "Old Lights" and the "New Lights," or "Separates." The New Lights strongly favored the Awakening and often formed "Separate" churches which denied the authority of the Saybrook Platform. They showed greatest strength in the counties of New London, Windham, and eastern Fairfield, but mustered supporters everywhere.[54]

The old order, firmly controlling the Assembly and the ministerial associations, struck back hard. A Hartford County Association meeting in August 1741 questioned "those screachings, cryings out, faintings and convulsions, which sometimes attend the terrifying Language of some preachers" and other activities and teachings of the itinerant enthusiasts. Much sterner action followed at the May 1742 Assembly, which prohibited even ordained ministers from preaching outside their parish without specific invitation, under threat of crushing penalties; confined an association's power of licensing candidates to its own territory; and outlawed any preaching by itinerants, under penalty of deportation from the colony. In October other loopholes were closed by legislation forbidding setting up unlicensed schools or teaching in them; also the ministry was closed to all but graduates of Yale, Harvard or approved foreign universities. The 1745 New Haven Association meeting declared that "Numbers of illiterate Exhorters swarm about as Locusts from the Bottomless Pit: — We think upon the *whole*, that Religion is now in a far worse State than it was in 1740."[55]

In May 1742 the Assembly tried James Davenport and Benjamin Pomeroy as dangerous itinerants. The trial at Hartford almost produced a riot when Davenport addressed a mob from the meeting house steps, and the two prisoners had to be guarded by forty militia, probably to prevent their followers from freeing them. Davenport was found guilty as a mentally disturbed person, marched between files of militia to the river, and deported forthwith to Long Island! Eventually, in 1744, Eleazer Wheelock and Solomon Williams persuaded Davenport to return to the conservative position.[56]

the Established ministers and churches. Religious toleration was increasing slowly in Connecticut when the American Revolution came to an end.[58]

Rise of the Anglican Church

DESPITE intense persecution, the Anglican Church established a firm foothold well before the

Episcopal Church (1771) in Brooklyn, erected by Godfrey Malbone.

The bitter internal bickering among Congregationalists stimulated by the Great Awakening caused many to leave that church and join the Baptists or the Anglicans. The intense persecution induced by the movement eventually led to a general demand for more religious tolerance, as reflected in the 1750 revision of Connecticut's law code which intentionally omitted all religious persecution acts.[57]

In 1770 the Assembly exempted Protestant dissenters who attended their own worship from the penalties for nonattendance at the Established Church. Gradually both Baptists and Separatists gained in public esteem, and in May 1777 the Separatists finally were exempted from support of

Revolution. The Anglican missionary organization, the Society for the Propagation of the Gospel in Foreign Parts, or S.P.G., through its missionaries led this penetration. In 1706 the Reverend George Muirson, S.P.G. missionary at Rye, traveled from Greenwich to Stratford, where in 1707 he apparently preached with deep effect, since the Reverend John Reed, Congregational minister in Stratford, was converted to Anglicanism. In the 1720's Yale's rector, Timothy Cutler, and others, including the Reverend Samuel Johnson of West Haven, were converted. Shortly afterward they went to England for ordination.[59]

On Johnson's return he found that followers in Stratford had built the first Anglican Church in

Connecticut's history. He conducted the first service there on Christmas Day, 1724. The next year a few Anglicans in Fairfield built the second church. In February 1726/27 Johnson reported to the S.P.G. that many parishioners had been imprisoned for failure to pay taxes for support of the Established (Congregational) Church. By 1734 Anglican congregations existed also at New London, Newtown, and Redding. The colorful and dedicated missionary John Beach left the Congregational Church in 1732, and soon afterward he took over the Newtown Anglican parish. He served his parish virtually a half century until his death in 1782 and was one of the few Anglican clergymen who appear to have conducted services during the Revolution.[60]

The revival of religious fervor during the Great Awakening roughly coincided with and helped trigger creation of new Anglican parishes in such towns as Hebron, North Groton (Ledyard), West Haven, Norwalk, Derby, Wallingford, Waterbury, Ripton (Huntington), Stamford, Stratford, Woodbury, New Milford, Norwich, Simsbury, Litchfield, Guilford, and North Guilford. Between 1753 and 1771 additional parishes were formed at Roxbury, Sharon, Cornwall, North Fairfield (Weston), Danbury, Watertown, Milford, and Brooklyn. While Anglicanism continued its steady growth, despite constant harassment by the colony, it proved impossible to secure enough missionaries to serve all parishes fully. The S.P.G. missionaries strongly urged that a bishop be consecrated in the mother country to head the American Anglicans, but nothing was done, much to the joy of the Puritan clergy, who greatly feared an Anglican episcopate in America. In 1766 Samuel Johnson could very properly remind the Archbishop of Canterbury that Anglicans constituted His Majesty's "best friends" here. In 1774 Ezra Stiles estimated that Connecticut Anglicans numbered 2,200 families strong in loyalty to the Crown.[61]

Colonial Newspapers and Presses

CONNECTICUT's first printing press was that of Thomas Short, established at New London in 1709. His earliest known imprint presented the newly adopted Saybrook Platform. In 1755 the first newspaper appeared — the *Connecticut Gazette*, published at New Haven by James Parker. Parker remained in New York, however, and left actual supervision to printer John Holt.[62]

Since the paper began during the French and Indian War, it emphasized military news. Making a Connecticut colonial paper a financial success was very difficult. In a place like New Haven, five hundred subscribers at an annual eight or nine shillings apiece probably represented maximum patronage. Advertising would bring an irregular income. Since mailing newspapers depended upon the whims of postriders, who demanded fees to carry them, the publisher could expect very few distant subscribers.[63]

Before the Revolution most presses and type came from Britain, and good ink was scarce. Much physical strength was required to operate the simple presses, and every sheet required a separate impression for each side. Standing at the printer's side, an apprentice applied the ink with a deerskin ball filled with wool and fastened to a stick. The editor's major problem was the almost casual and haphazard manner in which he secured news. Travelers, friends' letters, and news cribbed from domestic and foreign papers provided a large but uncertain source. The weekly posts from Boston and New York were very useful but often late. Then, as now, publishers fed readers a diet rich in crime and catastrophe. While a publisher rarely editorialized openly, he might try to mold opinion by accepting certain contributions and rejecting others. As time passed, most editors accepted more advertising, until many typical four-page issues contained from one to two pages of it. The printer also published occasional books, funeral and election sermons, official proclamations, and possibly an almanac, sold books, acted as a stationer, and occasionally as bookbinder.[64]

In 1758 Connecticut's second paper appeared — the *New-London Summary*, Timothy Green publisher. After this paper expired late in 1763, another Timothy Green, a nephew, took over the printery and launched the *New-London Gazette*, which enjoyed a long life. This paper took a strong stand against the Stamp Act and other regulatory measures preceding the Revolution.[65]

The next paper, and the most important his-

April 12. 1755.

NEW-HAVEN,

Connecticut

With the Freſheſt Advices

Wm Hanton

NUMB. 1.

THE

Gazette,

Foreign and Domeſtick.

The PRINTER to the PUBLICK:

AT the Deſire of ſeveral Gentlemen in this Colony, as well as the Inclination of the Printer, this Paper is publiſhed here: And as in Great-Britain the Liberty of the Preſs is looked on as one of the grand Bulwarks of the Privileges of the Nation; ſo it is preſumed, that in a Land poſſeſs'd by the Offspring of a People, who bravely fought the howling Wilderneſs with all its ſavage Terrors, rather than become the ſervile Slaves of bigotted Tyrants, ſurely the Liberty of the Preſs will never be leſs eſteemed; but rather, be always zealouſly preſerved inviolate: Therefore, if the Gentlemen of Taſte, or Sons of Learning, in this Colony, ſhall at any Time think fit to favour the Printer with the Amuſements of their leiſure Hours, in what may be thought beneficial or uſeful, either to promote Induſtry or Commerce; or to paint Virtue in its moſt beautiful Colours, in order to allure Mankind to the Love of it; or to dreſs Vice in all its Deformity, and by illuſtrating the bad Effects conſequent to the Practice thereof, make Men flee it; ſuch ſhall always be received with Joy: Alſo due Deference will be ſhewn to Pieces wrote in the juſt Defence of the publick Liberty, provided they appear free from private Pique and perſonal Scurrility: And ſuch Writers are caution'd againſt any Thing that has a Tendency undeſervedly to foment or occaſion Diſturbance in the Peace and good Order of the Colony; for ſuch will meet no kind Reception here; but if at any Time the Printer ſhould happen inadvertently to give ſuch Things a Place, which he is determined never wittingly to do, he hopes the moſt candid Conſtruction will be put on his Actions; for he thinks, 'tis better to be alarmed falſly twice, than by one fatal Security ſuffer a real Harm. The Preſs has always been an Enemy to Tyrants; and juſt ſo far as Tyranny prevails in any Part of the World, ſo far the Liberty of the Preſs is ſuppreſſed: --- In the deſpotick and ſlaviſh Governments of the Turks, no printing is allow'd: Thoſe who love ſuch, had beſt go thither! --- Where the bigotted Prieſthood and Inquiſition prevails, printing is but little encourag'd, and the unenlightened People of Rome or Spain, ſcarce can be ſaid to be one Step above the Turks: --- In France 'tis little better; tho' there the volatile Humour of the People keeps them from ſinking under their great Load of Chains, whilſt he who dares to murmur, ſoon finds Reward in the Baſtille: All thoſe who love a bounded Preſs, to Rome, to Spain, or France may go! --- Even in our Mother-Country, the Tools of Tyrants, and baſe-born Sons of Power, have often ſtrided large to bring the Populace to Slavery; and there, 'tis like, would long e'er now effected it, had not the immortal WILLIAM, that Foe to every Thing perfidious, like our Fore-fathers of this Climate, boldly dared to oppoſe the baſe Deſigns of thoſe, who, guided by the ambitious Views of Lewis, were Enemies to every Britiſh Good, and ventured his ALL, to perfect that, ſo truly called, the GLORIOUS REVOLUTION. --- Here 'tis hoped better Thoughts may guide us: He that does no Harm, cannot be hurt by printing; he that is not guilty, deſires the Sun may ſee his Actions; he that is a Chriſtian indeed, fears no reviling; and he that is a Foe to the Liberty of the Preſs, is a Foe to his Country.

The Utility of a publick News-Paper in an Engliſh Country, is now ſo univerſally acknowledged, as ſcarcely to admit of Diſpute: That the beſt Things are liable to Abuſe, is not denied; yet that can be no juſt Reaſon againſt the Uſe of them; for as all Men cannot be of one Mind, ſo very few, if any, are competent Judges, or able to determine, when a real Good becomes a real Evil; That the latter may never be the Caſe of this Paper, ſhall be the continued Endeavour of its Publiſher. And as it cannot be expected, that publick Intelligences can ſo eaſily, readily, and in ſuch Abundance, be come at here, as in capital Cities, ſo it is earneſtly requeſted of every intelligent Gentleman, who would befriend it, in the ſeveral Towns where this Paper may come, that when any Occurrence worthy of Note happens near them, that they would be ſo good as to communicate it to the Printer, with all convenient Speed; of which due Notice ſhall be taken, with Thanks. The Continuance of publiſhing will depend on the Encouragement it meets with: And ſuch Gentlemen as incline to take it, are deſired ſpeedily to ſignify the ſame, that a proper Judgment may be formed what Number to print; if they pleaſe, alſo to inform the Printer, what Method they may think beſt to have it conveyed to them. All poſſible Care ſhall be taken to give Satisfaction, and that it may anſwer the neceſſary End of conveying true Intelligence, both foreign and domeſtick; for which Purpoſe an extenſive Correſpondence is and will be ſettled. And if by any Means Mankind may be made wiſer and better, and the Printer enabled to ſupport his Undertaking, he will think his Labour not ill beſtowed.

Some Articles of Foreign Affairs in a new Paper, may ſeem to want an Explanation at firſt; tho' it is preſumed, that moſt of the Gentlemen who may read this, are not altogether unacquainted with them: -- The Noiſe made in France between their Parliaments and Clergy, has been the Subject of many Articles in late Papers, and not yet over; tho' ſome Politicians imagine it is only a Fineſſe of that wily Nation to lull and amuſe the Engliſh, while they privately augment their Forces, and invade our American Territories: The laſt is a Truth we can't be Strangers to at this Time.----The young Prince of Heſſe Caſſel, who married the Princeſs Mary of England, has lately renounced the Proteſtant Religion, and embraced Popery, to the Surprize and Grief of his Father, Wife and Country; and this Matter is now the Subject of much Diſcourſe in Europe.---- The Earl of Albemarle, late Engliſh Ambaſſador to France, and Father to the Hon. Commodore Kepple, died ſuddenly at Paris, the 22d December laſt, but a few Days after his Son had ſailed to convoy the Forces lately arrived at Virginia. ----- This may ſerve to explain ſome Affairs, whilſt moſt others will doubtleſs be able to ſpeak for themſelves. The Price will be Seven Shillings and Six Pence *Lawful Money,* per Annum, or an Equivalent in the Currency of the Colony, to be paid Quarterly.

Title page of first issue of Connecticut's first newspaper, The Connecticut Gazette.

torically, appeared in Hartford as the *Connecticut Courant*, whose prospectus was published October 29, 1764. Thomas Green, editor, had learned his trade under Holt at New Haven, and had edited the *Connecticut Gazette* for four years. When Green decided to return to New Haven in 1767, he entrusted the running of a prosperous *Courant* to his assistant and partner, Ebenezer Watson. The *Courant* quickly assumed a militantly anti-British line. As in other contemporary papers, one found little local news, since that could usually be learned quicker at church or tavern, from neighbors or the postrider. Watson was so plagued by inadequate paper supply that in 1775 he joined with Austin Ledyard in starting a paper mill east of the Connecticut River. The *Courant* is con-

sidered the oldest American newspaper in continuous publication in the same city.[66]

Prior to the Revolution two other papers were started: 1] *Connecticut Journal; and New-Haven Post-Boy*, at New Haven, under Thomas Green (*Courant* founder), and 2] *Norwich Packet, and the Connecticut, Massachusetts, New-Hampshire, and Rhode-Island Weekly Advertiser*, under Alexander and James Robertson and John Trumbull. The Robertsons were conservative Scotsmen, whose neutralism in the tense pre-Revolutionary period incurred such strong criticism that they departed for New York. Although all subscription lists remained small, it seems certain that colonial Connecticut newspapers exerted a large influence, especially as promoters of revolution.[67]

The Background of the Revolution

Eighteenth-Century Political Patterns — Relations with the British Government — The Stamp Act Produces Political Turmoil — The Townshend Acts and Internal Politics, 1767–70 — The Susquehannah Question: A Political Powder Keg — Deteriorating Relations with Britain — Moving Toward The Brink

---

Eighteenth-Century Political Patterns

DURING the century before the American Revolution, Connecticut enjoyed more self-government than any other mainland British colony except Rhode Island. At the local level the towns were authorized by the colonial government to make all necessary "Orders, Rules, and Constitutions." Hence they conducted their affairs almost without check, as the voters annually elected a host of officials such as selectmen, treasurers, listers, constables, packers of meat, sealers of dry measures and weights, fence viewers, horse branders, pound and key keepers, tithing men, and grand jurors, as well as two deputies to the Assembly's House of Representatives.[1]

The colonial government, operating under the charter of 1662, acted almost like an independent republic by keeping contacts with royal authority to a minimum. The bicameral General Assembly clearly dominated political affairs. Of its two branches, the Council and the House of Representatives, the latter exercised more power. Under the charter the Assembly wielded almost unlimited authority, including making and repealing laws, levying taxes, distributing lands, setting up

courts and defining their powers, granting pardons, and dissolving itself at session's end. The legislature clearly dominated both the judiciary, which it appointed, and the governor, though the latter could send advisory messages to the solons and preside over the Council. Only in periods of crisis did an able governor, such as John Winthrop, Jr., or Jonathan Trumbull, have the opportunity to display decisive personal leadership.[2]

The method of electing deputies and Council members was somewhat complicated. In April and September each town elected its two deputies for the May and October Assembly sessions. In September each voter wrote on a ballot twenty men whom he considered as worthy nominees for the Council election, and in October the Assembly declared the twenty who received the highest colony-wide totals as candidates for the Council. The following April the electorate voted on these twenty, of whom the twelve obtaining the highest vote constituted the Council for the ensuing year. At the April election the voters also cast separate written ballots for governor, deputy governor, secretary, and treasurer.[3]

Colonial Connecticut never was a democracy, because its leaders strongly opposed such a system. Nurtured in the Calvinistic concept of man as evil, they abhorred rule by the masses and advocated rule by the "elect." Rigorous religious and property requirements were established in the early years, and in 1702 property requirements were adopted which prevailed until the Revolution. They required that for a man to vote in a town or county election he must be an admitted inhabitant of legal age, a householder, a man "of sober Conversation," and possessor of a freehold estate rated at fifty shillings a year. Such admitted inhabitants participated in town affairs and voted for local officials. Under the 1662 charter, however, only freemen could elect members of the Assembly or be elected to that body. In 1702 the requirements for freemen were established as a forty-shillings-a-year freehold estate or forty-pound personal estate, and a certificate from the town selectmen attesting "quiet and peaceable behaviour, and civil Conversation." Finally, the candidate must take the freemen's oath before an assistant or justice of the peace. In 1766 Ezra Stiles estimated that only one-ninth of the populace qualified as freemen.[4]

Until 1765 Connecticut, lacking distinct parties or deeply divisive issues, enjoyed remarkable political stability under control of a small group of families. A governor could count upon annual re-election until death, and during the entire 1659–1784 period the colony had only eleven governors. George Wyllys served as secretary of the colony (and state) for sixty-one years, 1735–96; he succeeded his father, Hezekiah, who had held the post for twenty-three years, and was followed by his son, Samuel, for fourteen years.[5]

Even before the Stamp Act violently upset the colony's equilibrium, religious divisions, stimulated by the Great Awakening and the growing strength of Anglicanism, were beginning to embroil political life. The Anglican missionaries, numbering fourteen by 1760, generally opposed the charter, sought a bishop, and taught loyalty to the Crown.[6]

Since Connecticut was filling up rapidly and a mania for land speculation was growing, eyes inevitably turned westward to lands beyond the Hudson. In July 1753 the Susquehannah Company was organized at Windham by Eliphalet Dyer,

Jedidiah Elderkin, and other prominent figures. The next year it secured from some Indian chiefs a dubious deed to a large tract of land along the Susquehanna River, amounting to about one-third of Pennsylvania. The project almost immediately precipitated vigorous protests from Pennsylvania and from Sir William Johnson, British representative to the Iroquois, who foresaw serious Indian reprisals. Meanwhile, in May 1755, the Connecticut legislature, adding a pious explanation that settlement would benefit British relations with Indians, tentatively approved the venture. Governor Roger Wolcott supported the Susquehannah scheme, while Deputy Governor Thomas Fitch opposed it — a foreshadowing of the deep political split which the Company eventually produced. In the next several years the issue became hotter as the Company pushed plans for colonization despite Governor Fitch's proclamation of 1762 warning against such action. At William Johnson's urging, the Board of Trade considered the problem, and on January 27, 1763, the British Secretary of State wrote to Fitch informing him that no Connecticut settlements could be made until the royal pleasure was known — a warning which was heeded.[7]

Relations with the British Government

IN the century after the granting of the 1662 charter the colony's leaders steered the ship of state past many political shoals. The imperial authorities viewed the charter with suspicion, and frequent attempts were made to put Connecticut under stricter supervision. The colony's strategy, usually defensive, ran the gamut from extreme subserviency to stalwart exposition of basic principles. The Board of Trade commented upon the Connecticut people that "they think themselves by their charters little dependent on the Crown, and seldom pay obedience to royal orders."[8]

Periodically British authorities charged Connecticut with carrying on unauthorized activities such as enacting capital laws, trying robbery and murder cases, inflicting the death penalty, failing to co-operate with other colonies in wartime, denying authority of vice-admiralty courts in illicit trade, and passing laws contrary to those of

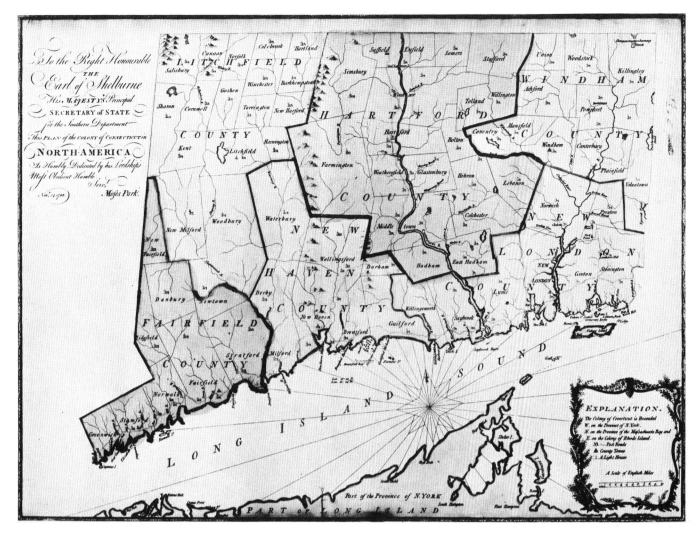

Moses Park's 1766 map of Connecticut.

Britain. The Board of Trade and Privy Council repeatedly urged Parliament to pass an act revoking all corporate and proprietary charters and making all colonies royal. Luckily for Connecticut it had a series of able agents in London — Fitz-John Winthrop (1693–98), Henry Ashurst (1698–1710), Jeremiah Dummer (1710–30), and Francis Wilks (1730–42) — each of whom fought successfully against attempts to destroy the charter.[9]

In 1704 Connecticut almost had a royal governor placed over it by the queen's authority in council. In 1701 and 1706 bills were presented to return to the Crown the government of all American colonies; but the first failed to pass either house, and the House of Lords rejected the second. While Dummer was agent the Crown urged that the colonies voluntarily surrender their charters — a suggestion forcefully rejected by Connecticut.

Probably Connecticut was saved chiefly by the bitter party rivalries of English politics, in which the growing Whig party vigorously opposed Tory attempts to seize the New England charters.[10]

Though most colonies were compelled to submit their laws to the king in council for confirmation or disallowance, Connecticut's charter did not require this. Later, in 1696, the Board of Trade was given power to examine acts of all colonies. It soon demanded to see Connecticut's laws, but only after long delay did it finally receive some of them. The colony displayed more celerity in replying to occasional official queries about its government, geography, population, trade, industry, and the like; but even here the replies revealed a close-mouthed quality.[11]

The colony ran afoul of English interference in one fundamental law — that dealing with disposal

125

of intestate estates. Instead of following English common-law practice under which the eldest son inherited the entire estate, Connecticut soon fell into step with Massachusetts and Plymouth by assigning equal shares to all children except the oldest son, who received a double share. In October 1699 the Assembly made the custom of earlier decades into law by ordering probate courts to distribute intestate property as follows: one-third of the personal estate to the wife forever, plus her dower right; the remainder equally to the children except the eldest son, who was to have a double portion. Governor Talcott explained the deviation from English primogeniture as essential to keep the younger sons within the relatively undeveloped colony.[12]

The Connecticut law finally was directly challenged in the case of *Winthrop v. Lechmere,* when John Winthrop (grandson of Governor John Winthrop, Jr.), denying the validity of the intestacy law, claimed the entire estate of his intestate father, who had died in 1717. After losing his case in the colony court, he carried his appeal to London. His efforts caused the Connecticut intestacy law to be disallowed on February 15, 1727/28, as contrary to the laws of Britain. If not challenged, this decision could have caused chaos in the legal system and agricultural economy of Connecticut. Strenuous protests by colonial agents and a sympathetic consideration by Francis Fane, legal adviser of the Board of Trade, aided Connecticut's cause. In 1730 the board made a careful report which recommended confirmation of all lands already settled, but noted the need for some restrictions and a bill stating precisely the colony's imperial relationship. Parliament, however, failed to take action, and Connecticut continued, albeit uneasily, upon its accustomed course.[13]

The only comprehensive review ever made of the colony's laws was one conducted in 1732–41 by the lawyer Fane for the Board of Trade. In nine careful reports he dealt with 387 acts and 3 resolutions, of which he found 75 objectionable enough to deserve disallowance. Some of these were too severe, others too loose or inexact, but only 7 were clearly at variance with British law. Fane obviously believed that the civil and judicial authorities held too much unchecked power, as in

the ability of a court to inflict a punishment at its own discretion. Many offenses, such as defamation, lascivious carriage, profane speaking, and heresy, were defined so loosely as to permit injustices, but no definite action was taken upon Fane's scholarly reports.[14]

The Stamp Act Produces Political Turmoil

UPON the accession of George III to the throne of Britain in 1760 Connecticut loyally pledged him its "Faith and Constant Obedience, with all Hearty and humble Affection." Enthusiasm for monarch and Britain soon slackened, however, after the Sugar Act was passed in 1764. Providing for much sharper enforcement of the acts of trade, this act alarmed the merchants especially. The legislature ordered three leading New London merchants — Gurdon Saltonstall, Nathaniel Shaw, and Thomas Mumford — to formulate Connecticut's protests and forward them to the colony's agent.[15]

The successful conclusion of the French and Indian War in 1760 was quickly followed by a serious economic depression, prevailing from the Carolinas to New Hampshire, in which the farmers found markets tight and land values declining. In 1765 Connecticut taxpayers fell £80,000 behind in payments, and because of the recent flood of bankruptcy cases the Assembly enacted a lengthy measure for more equitable settlement of such cases.[16]

The mother country, badly needing new revenues after an expensive war, chose this time to inflict upon her colonies a new levy — the stamp tax. The previous year the Connecticut agent had warned of the impending action, and in October 1764 the Assembly approved a protest entitled: "Reasons why the British colonies, in America, should not be charged with internal taxes, by authority of Parliament; humbly offered, for consideration, in behalf of the colony of Connecticut." This forthright protest stressed two arguments: 1] British subjects could rightfully be taxed only by laws which they had approved; and 2] the Stamp Act, or any other internal tax, violated charter rights. In London, Richard Jackson, Connecticut's agent, and Jared Ingersoll, there on private business, co-operated with agents of other colonies in opposing the proposed act. Later, when passage seemed inevitable, Ingersoll prevailed upon his close friend Thomas Whately of the Treasury Office to make the bill more palatable to Americans by exempting several items from taxation and lowering rates upon others.[17]

Final passage produced a sharp split in Connecticut public opinion. Conservatives like Governor Fitch and Jared Ingersoll felt that Parliament was supreme and Connecticut must obey the law. Ingersoll himself accepted appointment as Stamp Distributor for Connecticut. On the opposing side there arose a group calling themselves the Sons of Liberty, dedicated to securing repeal of the act. In Connecticut, as elsewhere, gentlemen of the upper class largely controlled the new organization, but they sought and found support among the lower classes who could provide the "muscle" needed to intimidate Stamp Act advocates. During the winter of 1765–66 the Sons of Liberty encouraged holding of local meetings which passed resolutions condemning the act. In eastern Connecticut, a hotbed of radicalism since Great Awakening days, men such as Israel Putnam of Pomfret, Hugh Ledlie of Windham, and John Durkee of Norwich spearheaded the growing drive against the act. At Windham these "Radicals" compelled Nathaniel Wales, the local stamp agent, to resign in extreme haste. In Wallingford, on January 13, 1766, the Sons proclaimed "That we will oppose the same [Stamp Act] to the last extremity, even to take the field."[18]

Meanwhile Jared Ingersoll, who already had earned much hostility among New Lights and Susquehannah Company promoters, found himself the object of bitter attacks from opponents of the Stamp Act. Hearing that these partisans planned to visit him and force his resignation as Stamp Distributor, he gave Governor Fitch a statement on September 17, 1765, informing him of the rumored attack and indicating that he, Ingersoll, would resign if necessary to avoid serious trouble. The next day Ingersoll decided to ride toward Hartford and try to uncover additional details of the "intended attack." On the second day of his journey, while approaching Wethersfield, he encountered a party of 400 to

500 persons, who soon were joined by 30 more. A little farther along the way Ingersoll met a grim-visaged group of 500 additional men on horseback, all carrying white staves. The entire mob escorted Ingersoll into Wethersfield, where a heated discussion occurred. Ingersoll found the

False news of repeal of Stamp Act.

assemblage so threatening that he agreed to resign as Stamp Distributor, gave three cheers for "Liberty and Property," and threw his hat into the air. At the mob's insistence he accompanied them to Hartford, where he again announced his resignation. Obviously impressed by this incident, the legislature voted to send Eliphalet Dyer, William Samuel Johnson, and David Rowland to the Stamp Act Congress. They also resolved that the governor issue a proclamation urging all officials to "prevent and suppress all riots, tumults and unlawful assemblies."[19]

The new October Assembly, containing a higher proportion of Radicals, promptly approved the petitions drawn up at the Stamp Act Congress. Not

BY THE HONORABLE

WILLIAM PITKIN, Esq;

Governor of his Majesty's English Colony of CONNECTICUT, in NEW-ENGLAND, in AMERICA.

A PROCLAMATION.

GREAT and manifold have been the Displays of GOD's Power, and very conspicuous the Exertions of his kind Providence, towards the Fathers of this Country, whose Hearts he inclined, and whose Ways he directed to find out a Dwelling in the Wilds of America; rich and innumerable the Tokens of his Beneficence to them and their Posterity, in their Preservation and Protection, amidst Variety of Perrils and Hardships to which they were exposed and subjected; and in the Grant and Security of great and invaluable Privileges, Immunities and Blessings which have been handed down, and at this Day happily enjoyed by us. And when of late we were involved in great Difficulties and Distresses in Regard to some of the most important Interests of this and the other British Colonies and Plantations in America; then, our most gracious GOD, the Almighty Governor, did interpose, and raise up wise, able and faithful Friends and Advocates to sollicit, and disposed the Heart of our gracious King, and the Parliament of Great-Britain, to shew their Clemency and Indulgence to the People of America, in the Beneficial Repeal of the late Act of Parliament, so affecting and grievous to them; and thereby doth give a happy Prospect of the Restoration of Peace and Tranquility. Which signal Expressions of Divine Goodness, demand from us, the most sincere Returns of Gratitude, Thanksgiving and public Praises to the bountiful Author of all Good.

Therefore,

Have thought fit, by and with the Advice of theCouncil, and at theDesire of the Representatives in General Court assembled, to appoint, and do hereby appoint Thursday, the Twenty-fixth Day of this Instant, June, to be religiously observed as a Day of public THANKSGIVING throughout this Colony; earnestly exhorting all his Majesty's Subjects, Ministers and People, in their several religious Assemblies, with Joy and Gladness of Heart, to magnify the Lord, and with devout and thankful Minds, to glorify his holy Name, for his Goodness herein wonderfully manifested.

Also, to offer up Supplications to Almighty GOD, for Our Sovereign Lord, King GEORGE the Third, for our gracious Queen CHARLOTTE, their Royal Highnesses, GEORGE Prince of Wales the Princess Dowager of Wales, and all the Royal Family. That GOD would preside in, and direct the King's Councils; over-rule the present Situation of public Affairs, for the Continuation of Liberty and Peace in our Nation and Land; graciously continue to this Colony our most valuable Liberties and Privileges, Civil and Sacred; dispose us to a wise and thankful Improvement of them; give us Favour in the Sight of our most gracious King; bless our Agency at the British Court; promote Harmony and Concord between Great-Britain and her Colonies; heal all unhappy Divisions; grant divine Wisdom, Council and Faithfulness to all in civil and sacred Employment; prevent Animosities and Faction; cause Justice, Righteousness, and Peace to flourish; and bestow upon us Abundance of his Goodness and Mercy.

And all servile Labour is forbidden on said Day.

Given under my Hand at the Council Chamber in Hartford, the twelfth Day of June, in the sixth Year of the Reign of Our Sovereign Lord GEORGE the Third, of Great-Britain, France and Ireland, KING, Defender of the Faith, &c. and in the Year of our Lord, 1766.

WM. PITKIN.

GOD SAVE THE KING.

Printed by THOMAS GREEN, at the Heart and Crown, opposite the State-House, in HARTFORD.

True news of repeal of Stamp Act.

content with this, the legislators adopted a lengthy set of resolutions directed to the British Government which while pledging continuing loyalty to Britain sharply condemned the act as an unconstitutional violation of their fundamental liberties.[20]

Under the Stamp Act, which became effective November 1765, the governor was required to take an oath to execute it faithfully. Despite heavy pressure from Radical friends, Fitch, placing loyalty to Britain first, reluctantly supported it. When informed of his decision the Council was thrown into an uproar, and only four agreed to support his action. Angered by this step, the Radicals stepped up their campaign against the act and against Fitch. In many towns the Sons virtually took control of town meetings. In New London and Milford mobs seized and burned stamped paper. Amidst the growing din, moderates like Roger Sherman and Ezra Stiles scarcely could make themselves heard, while Radicals plotted the overthrow of Fitch and all other Stamp Act supporters. In March 1766, at a colony-wide meeting in Hartford, the Sons of Liberty agreed upon their candidates for governor and Upper House and advocated intercolonial action. As a result of overwhelming strength in New London and Windham counties, the Radicals produced a political revolution by ousting Fitch and his four supporters and electing William Pitkin governor.[21]

Meanwhile British merchants, badly hurt by declining trade with America, fanned popular and Parliamentary opposition to the Stamp Act. After a lengthy and bitterly fought debate, Parliament repealed the act in February 1766. When the happy news reached Connecticut it caused ringing of church bells, shooting of small arms and cannon, composition of a letter of thanks to the king, official proclamation of a day of thanksgiving, and, interestingly enough, pledges by some towns of renewed loyalty to Britain.[22]

The Townshend Acts and Internal Politics, 1767–70

THE next British attempt to tax the colonials, the Townshend Acts of 1767, placing a small tax on imports of paper, glass, painters' colors, lead, and tea, stirred the colony less deeply than the Stamp Act. Gradually, however, spurred by the eastern Radicals, the merchants of the colony joined in the nonimportation agreements set up by the Massachusetts, New York, and Pennsylvania merchants. Imports of British goods slumped sharply, and merchants who ignored the agreements received unfavorable press notices. Attempts were made to encourage home manufactures. However, the collapse of nonimportation in New York in 1770 quickly ended the boycott elsewhere, including Connecticut. In 1770, meanwhile, Parliament repealed all duties except that on tea.[23]

The domestic political struggles in Connecticut continued full blast in the late 1760's, featured by conservative efforts to restore Fitch. In 1766–67 a sharp "paper war" preceded the May 1767 elections, in which Pitkin received 4,777 votes to 3,484 for Fitch. After the death of Governor Pitkin in 1769 a bitter special election in the Assembly saw Deputy Governor Jonathan Trumbull elevated to the governor's chair. Fitch nearly obtained Trumbull's former position, but finally was edged out by Matthew Griswold.[24]

The campaign of 1770 provided an unusually vitriolic spectacle as the Conservatives tried desperately to unseat Trumbull and terminate eastern Radical control. During the campaign a clever anti-Trumbull ballad was sung by some Conservatives:

> Now Will [Pitkin] is dead and his Purser [Trumbull] broke,
>   I know not who'll come next, Sir;
> The Seamen call for old Pitch again, —
>   Affairs are sore perplexed, Sir.
> But the Gunners and some midshippers
>   Are making an insurrection,
> And would rather the ship should founder quite
>   Than be saved by Pitch's inspection.
>   CHORUS
> But this is what I will maintain,
>   In spite of Gunners and all, Sir, —
> If Pitch can save the Ship once more,
>   'Tis best he overhaul her![25]

Despite Conservative gains in 1770, Trumbull won by a 4,700 to 4,266 margin over Fitch, with 805 scattered votes for others. Trumbull lacked the majority required by law, but the Assembly re-elected him. Again the split on imperial and local issues fell neatly along geographical lines, with Fitch's strength largely confined to western Connecticut and to towns along the Connecticut River — a foreshadowing of the future Patriot-Tory division.[26]

The Susquehannah Question: A Political Powder Keg

IN the early 1770's the colony was diverted from its disagreements with London by an explosion of the Susquehannah Company issue. The underlying conditions of intense land hunger and very high birth rate persisted, so that the contrast between expensive, crowded, and often exhausted Connecticut land with vast areas and cheap fertile Susquehannah lands convinced many poor farmers that migration westward afforded the best hope for the future. The prominent and speculating proprietors, moreover, from 1769 on received powerful encouragement from Governor Trumbull. Upon receipt of an opinion from Britain in 1773 which did not deny Connecticut's title, Governor Trumbull openly favored settlement of the western lands. Responding to this lead, the Assembly appointed a committee to seek an agreement with Pennsylvania which would open the way for peaceful settlement, but the effort failed completely.[27]

The next January the Assembly, officially extending its jurisdiction over the Susquehanna country, established a township called Westmoreland. On January 27, 1774, Governor Trumbull issued a proclamation forbidding future settlement in Westmoreland without prior approval of the Assembly. These actions raised an avalanche of Conservative opposition, based upon two important factors: 1] strong fears that the western claims would endanger the charter; and 2] the dominant role of the hated "eastern Radicals" in the Susquehannah Company.[28]

Jared Ingersoll used the newspapers to launch the counterattack, in which he predicted "absolute ruin" if Connecticut pushed its western claims. In New Haven and many Fairfield County towns public sentiment appeared opposed to the Susquehannah claims. On March 30, 1774, in Middletown, the Conservatives staged a convention which attracted representatives from twenty-three towns. In a petition designed for circulation throughout the colony the convention reiterated its belief that the charter was jeopardized and called upon the next Assembly to revoke its recent Susquehannah decisions and prevent the company's proprietors from voting on questions involving their personal interests. Some delegates went further by preparing a slate of Conservative candidates for governor, deputy governor, and Council.[29]

Before and after the convention the Radicals worked energetically for the Susquehannah scheme. Silas Deane, an enthusiastic expansionist, vigorously denounced the opponents as "ignorant partisans and incendiaries," while Roger Sherman described them as greedy landowners who did not want ordinary people to own land. Benjamin Trumbull defended Connecticut's titles and envisaged enormous public and private gains flowing from the venture — so much so that land sales might pay all future government expenses. As Radical spokesmen stepped up their campaign the Conservatives responded in kind, so that tension reached a new peak just before the May 1774 elections. When the votes were counted the Radicals scored a clean sweep. They immediately pressed a request to the Privy Council for a definitive settlement of the jurisdictional dispute with Pennsylvania.[30]

Deteriorating Relations with Britain

PUBLIC interest soon veered away from the Susquehannah problem to a much greater one — that of deteriorating relations with Britain. Passage of the Tea Act of 1773 had attracted little attention in Connecticut except among a few merchants who stood to lose heavily. The colony was deeply stirred, however, by news of the great tea party in Boston's harbor; and the Conservatives, such as William Samuel Johnson, especially feared the retaliation which Parliament might inflict. In Lyme the Sons of Liberty showed their patriotism by burning tea brought in by a peddler.[31]

The election sermon of May 1774, preached by the Reverend Samuel Lockwood of Andover, represented an adroit effort to walk the tightrope between Radicals and Conservatives. While lauding the British constitution as the best in existence, he noted that it required that the rights of subjects, as well as Crown, be "mutually acknowledged, and fully enjoyed." He closed with a strong plea to his eminent audience to "Fear GOD, honour the king, and *pray for all in authority* over us; *that we may lead a quiet and peaceable life, in all godliness and honesty.*"[32]

When news arrived of passage of the tough Coercive Acts of 1774, which rigorously repressed Massachusetts and closed the port of Boston, most Connecticut leaders were deeply shocked. If Parliament, by simple legislative fiat, could virtually destroy a colonial charter, Connecticut's future likewise appeared extremely bleak. During the spring and summer of 1774 various town meetings adopted resolutions of sympathy for Boston, roundly denounced the Coercive Acts, called for an intercolonial congress, and established committees of correspondence. On June 6, 1774, a Norwich town meeting voted to defend American liberties to the limit and to co-operate with other colonies in all reasonable measures adopted by congress in its opposition to the Coercive Acts. At the same well-attended meeting the town established a committee of correspondence consisting of five prominent citizens. In Farmington, townspeople erected a liberty pole, tarred, feathered, and burned an effigy of Tory Governor Hutchinson of Massachusetts, consigned a copy of the Coercive Acts to the flames, and damned the royal ministers as "pimps and parasites."[33]

In May 1774 the Lower House voted a lengthy set of resolutions, "to renew their claim to the rights, privileges and immunities of Freeborn Englishmen" as based upon "the laws of nature" and charter of Charles II. In October the Upper House concurred in spreading the resolves upon the official record. Meanwhile, in July, the colonial committee of correspondence, upon the Assembly's authority, chose delegates to the First Continental Congress, of whom Silas Deane, Eliphalet Dyer, and Roger Sherman, all fervent Radicals, or Whigs, actually served.[34]

In September eastern Radicals met at Norwich and openly recommended that all militiamen in New London and Windham counties be alerted for possible military emergency. On September 15 delegates from towns in Hartford, New London, Windham, and Litchfield counties convened at Hartford, where they agreed upon the necessity of a nonimportation plan.[35]

Moving Toward the Brink

ONE of the most dramatic Connecticut reactions was the so-called "Mansfield Declaration of Independence," passed at a Mansfield town meeting

First Church of Christ,
Congregational at Farmington
(built 1771).

131

on October 10, 1774. Upon careful examination it becomes apparent that this resolution is forceful but falls far short of an outright declaration of independence. The town adopted four resolves:

1] That his Majesty George the Third & his rightful Successors are entitled to our Allegiance . . . So long as the Crown maintains Inviolate the Stipulated rights of the People . . .

Sign for General Wolfe Tavern in Brooklyn. Proprietor was Israel Putnam.

2] That we will defend with our Lives and Fortunes, our natural & Constitutional Rights . . .

3] That in all our Efforts to maintain Liberty, we will injure no one's Property, nor restrain, terrify or Afflict any mans Person . . . unless the Same be necessary in the Common Cause, & can be vindicated by undoubted Reason — & as Union & Uniformity of Conduct is necessary, we rely on the Wisdom of the Continental Congress . . . to Recommend Such measures as may be reasonably adopted . . .

4] That in this Time of difficulty and Danger it is necessary that a Correspondance should be maintained between the Several Towns in this and the other Governments, & that this Town might be Supplied with a Comittee to Correspond as above . . .

Thus it is obvious that a typical town in eastern Connecticut had proceeded far down the road toward independence.[36]

Many moderate Whigs, such as Simeon Deane, Titus Hosmer, and Samuel B. Webb, began to oppose the tendency of extreme Whigs to take the law into their hands. Trumbull and Griswold likewise denounced acts of violence. New Hartford and East Windsor discouraged lawless deeds. Strong-arm methods were employed increasingly, however, as in the case of Jonathan Peters, a Tory, who was ridden on a rail by Hartford Whigs as they shouted, "a Tory a Tory a Cursed Damd Churchman." In Boston, General Gage, hearing of the growing revolutionary temper of Connecticut, forwarded the ominous information to London.[37]

The October 1774 Assembly session vividly reflected the heightening tension. Governor Trumbull, claiming "a darker and more dismal cloud never hung over both Countries," advised preparedness and urged the legislators to live up to their duty of preserving "the invaluable blessings of Freedom contained and secured in and by our Civil Constitution." Apparently highly receptive, his auditors promptly ordered extra training for the militia and a build-up of supplies of powder, ball, and flints.[38]

The First Continental Congress met meanwhile at Philadelphia, drew up a petition outlining basic rights and grievances, and recommended cessation of trade with Britain under a plan called the Continental Association. In late 1774 and early 1775 many towns and several counties held meetings to approve Congress' proceedings and set up committees to implement the Association.[39]

Only in a few places in Fairfield and Litchfield counties, such as Ridgefield and Newtown, were the Tories able to muster substantial opposition forces against the sweeping revolutionary spirit. Connecticut indeed lay on the verge of civil war, as the March 1775 special session made crystal clear. Trumbull called for forthright steps against the Tories, and the Assembly promptly complied by investigating militia officers suspected of Toryism and sending a committee to survey the Tory centers, Newtown and Ridgefield. Connecticut had progressed so far along the path to open revolt against the mother country that only a spark was needed to ignite a war.[40]

CHAPTER 9

Connecticut Fights for Independence, 1775-83

Connecticut Mobilizes — Connecticut Inspires the Seizure of Fort Ticonderoga — Further Preparations and Operations in 1775 — Safekeeping of Prisoners — Military Activities in the Winter of 1775–76 — The Great Step: To Independence — The Patriots Harass the Tories — The Assembly and Press Attack the Tories — Significance of the Tories — The First British Raid: Danbury, April 1777 — War Brings Shortages — Forging the Sinews of War — Connecticut Fights in the Continental Army — Reluctant Soldiers — Military Developments on Many Fronts — Connecticut's State Navy — Connecticut Privateers Strike Heavy Blows — Connecticut: "The Provisions State" — Appalling Supply Deficiencies Intermixed with Successes — "The Financial Merry-Go-Round" — Interstate Wartime Trade — The Caribbean and European Trade — The Perplexities and Pains of Economic Regulation — The Profitable Illicit Trade — Tryon Returns to Haunt Connecticut — A Vicious Blow Against New London and Groton — Troubled Times in Westmoreland — A "Conservative" Revolution — The Heavy Load of a Wartime Governor — Glad Tidings of Peace

---

Connecticut Mobilizes

WEDNESDAY, April 19, 1775, arrived and brought "the shot heard round the world." At ten that morning Israel Bissell, postrider, set out from Watertown, Massachusetts, with a letter giving some particulars of the Lexington engagement and stating that the bearer "is charged to alarm the Country quite to *Connecticut*." Bissell rode hard, so hard that his horse fell dead in Worcester! The next morning, with a fresh mount, he resumed the journey, and by four o'clock Thursday afternoon he had spread the word to Norwich, and by seven, to New London. Through the second night he rode, reaching Lyme at one in the morning, Saybrook at four, Guilford at ten, Branford at noon, and New Haven in the evening. By four o'clock Saturday afternoon Fairfield knew the electrifying

news, and soon afterward every corner of Connecticut was informed.[1]

To the more impetuous Radicals the news demanded immediate action. Colonel Israel Putnam was plowing on his farm in Pomfret when Bissell suddenly appeared with the momentous news. According to his son, old "Put" departed in such haste that he did not even unyoke his team. Apparently he first warned the militia officers of the nearby towns and then raced to Cambridge, which, tradition says, he reached at sunrise the next morning.[2]

In town after town, militiamen organized and marched off to Boston. Archival records of the "Lexington Alarm" rolls list some 3,600 men from nearly fifty towns who flocked to Boston. One of the earliest Connecticut companies to reach Cambridge was the recently formed Second Company of Governor's Foot Guards, under Captain Benedict Arnold. This was a triumph, for they had experienced much difficulty in gaining wholehearted support from New Haven officials. Arnold's first request for powder was ignored by the selectmen. He then drew up the brilliantly clad Guardsmen, whose uniforms were copied from the Coldstream Guards, for drill on the Green. After an appropriate interval, Arnold sent an officer to the town fathers to receive the powder-house keys. He forwarded, too, the crisp injunction that if the keys were not forthcoming within five minutes, his men would break into the supply house and help themselves. Arnold soon had the keys and his men their powder![3]

Connecticut's militia in their first military duty of the war spent an average of about eleven days away from home and suffered no casualties. Much grimmer work lay ahead. Even the costs of the "alarm" — £7,824 6s. 6½d. — soon paled into utter insignificance in comparison with later military expenses.[4]

On April 26 the Assembly met in special session. Governor Trumbull spoke to the lawmakers and urged upon them "Firmness, Steadiness, Deliberation, & Unanimity in the most important Affair that ever came under Consideration within these Walls."[5]

The legislators moved rapidly on a wide front. An embargo was laid upon the export of provisions, including "wheat, rye, indian corn, pork, beef, live cattle, pease and beans, bread flour, and every kind of meal, except necessary stores for vessels bound to sea." One-fourth of the militia were directed to organize and equip themselves for "the special defence and safety of this Colony." They appointed Major General David Wooster and Brigadier Generals Joseph Spencer and Israel Putnam to head these special troops. For Commissary General the legislators chose Joseph Trumbull, who thus began his notable but tragically brief career in that field. Appropriately enough, the first item which the legislature asked Trumbull to purchase was "one hogshead of New England rum."[6]

The Assembly made a start upon other important matters as well. It voted to print £50,000 in paper money and laid a special seven-pence tax. Overseers of powder were appointed and the cannon at New London ordered prepared for use. Routine military appointments were listed. Three merchants were granted permission to export certain items to the West Indies despite the Embargo Act. Religion was not forgotten, as "Considering the dark and gloomy aspect of Divine Providence over this Colony and land . . . it be recommended to all the ministers of the gospel . . . that they earnestly endeavour to dissuade their several congregations from all excess, and all diversions which may be improper in the present day of distress; and that both they and their people cry mightily to God . . . ," to the end of preserving their liberties.[7]

Although the General Assembly actively prepared for war, it took a step seemingly in the opposite direction by sending William Samuel Johnson and Colonel Erastus Wolcott, both Conservatives, on a special mission to General Gage with a letter from Governor Trumbull.[8]

Trumbull's letter reflected the mixed state of mind of the legislature. It affirmed the great alarm in Connecticut over the series of events from passage of the Coercive Acts to the open bloodshed of April 19. Trumbull asked bluntly: "Is there no alternative but absolute submission, or the desolations of war?" He requested that the General explain his actions. Speaking more hopefully, Trumbull declared: "it is to be hoped that the temperate wisdom of the Empire might even yet find expedients to restore peace, that so all parts of the empire may enjoy their particular rights, honours and immunities."[9]

The embassy caused embarrassment among Massachusetts and Connecticut Whigs. General Joseph Spencer, fresh from Boston, informed Connecticut leaders that the embassy "has Disaffected the People of Massechusetts & likewise our own on ye Spot." Governor Trumbull quickly assured Joseph Warren that Connecticut would "act in unison and concert with our sister Colonies." Undoubtedly many legislators agreed with Jonathan Trumbull, Jr., that the mission would put Gage in bad light and would simultaneously give Connecticut Whigs valuable time for further preparations. Probably the only legislators genuinely happy about the mission were the few Tories and the more numerous moderates still found in the

INTERESTING INTELLIGENCE.

Norwich, April 22, 1775, 10 o'Clock, P. M.

Potior visa est Periculosa Libertas quieto servitio. SALUST.

Yesterday Morning, the following was brought by an Express, to Col. Jedidiah Huntington, of this Town, Dated at Pomfret on Monday the 20th Inst. 3 o'Clock, P. M.

SIR,

I AM this Moment informed, by an Express from Woodstock, taken from the Mouth of the Express that arrived there, 2 o'Clock this Afternoon, that the Contest between the first Brigade that marched to Concord, was still continuing this Morning, at the Town of Lexington, to which said Brigade had retreated. That another Brigade, said to be the second, mentioned in the Letter of this morning, had landed with a Quantity of Artillery, at the Place where the first Troops did; the Provincials were determined to prevent the two Brigades from joining their Strength, if possible, and remain still in the greatest need of Succours.

N. B. The Regulars, when at Concord, burnt the Court-House, took two Pieces of Cannon, which they rendered Useless, and began to take up Concord Bridge, on which Capt. ------, who with many, on both Sides, were killed, then made an Attack upon the King's Troops, on which they retreated to Lexington.

In haste, I am, Sir,
Your humble Servant,
EBENEZER WILLIAMS.

To Col. OBADIAH JOHNSON, Canterbury.

P. S. Mr. McFarling, of Plainfield, Merchant, has just now returned from Boston, by Way of Providence, who conversed with an Express from Lexington, who farther informs, that about 4000 of our People had surrounded the first Brigade above-mentioned, who were on a Hill in Lexington; that the Action continued, and that there were about 50 of our People killed and 150 of the Regulars, as near as they could determine, when the Express came away.

NORWICH, April 22.

This Evening, a little after 7 o'Clock, Mr. David Nevins, who Yesterday Forenoon, went Express from this Town, to obtain Intelligence, returned from Providence, with the following important Advices.

ON Tuesday Evening last, Advice was received here from Boston----that a Detachment of the King's Troops had fired upon and killed a Number of the Inhabitants of Lexington, about Twelve Miles from Boston; in Consequence of which an Engagement had happened.

Upon receiving this alarming Intelligence, the Inhabitants of Providence immediately assembled the Officers of the Independant Companies and Militia, with a Number of Gentlemen of the Town, had a Meeting, and two Expresses were dispatched for Lexington to obtain authentic Accounts while others were sent to different parts of this Colony and Connecticut.

The Expresses that went to Lexington returned Yesterday Morning, and relate in Substance the following.

" On Tuesday Night, the 18th Instant, about 1300 Troops very privately embarked at Charlestown-Ferry, in Boats, and after Landing at Cambridge, proceeded towards Concord, in order, as is supposed, to destroy the Province Magazine.

" At Lexington, early next Morning, they came up with a small Number of Men, who were performing the Manual Exercise, and after accosting them in Language the most prophane and insulting, ordered them to lay down their Arms and disperse, which they at first refused to do, but on being threatened they began to disperse, and were immediately fired upon and 8 of them killed.

" The Troops afterwards proceeded to Concord, where they destroyed about 60 Barrels of Flour, and some Gun-carriages; after which they began to retreat, when about 300 Americans coming up, a Skirmish ensued.

" At Lexington the troops received a Reinforcement of 1000 Men and Two Field-pieces, notwithstanding which, the Americans continued to push them closely, and pursued them about 12 Miles, to Bunker's-Hill, in Charlestown, when Night coming on the firing ceased. Our People not thinking it prudent to attack them in so advantageous a Situation without Artillery.

" The Troops immediately intrenched on the Hill, and the Americans, after placing a strong Guard to observe their Motions, marched to Cambridge, at which, and other Places, large Bodies of Americans have since assembled.

" On Thursday the 20th Instant, about four o'Clock in the Afternoon, the Troops suddenly decamped, embarked on board Boats at Charlestown, and returned te Boston. That of the King's Troops, One Lieutenant, and about 70 Privates were killed, a considerable Number wounded, and about 30 taken Prisoners, among whom are Two Captains: That on the Part of the Americans, about 30 were killed, and 3 or 4 taken Prisoners; not a single wounded Man found alive. The Troops having, with a Barbarity heretofore unpractised by British Soldiers, destroyed all they met with: That at Lexington they burnt Four dwelling and Two Out Houses, an aged Man whom they found sick in his Bed, was run through with a Bayonet; and Two aged and infirm Persons were shot in another House: That although the Americans were continually reinforced by small Parties, not more than 300 were at any Time engaged: That they behaved with the greatest Intrepidity; and had they been joined by the main Body which assembled at Concord, while waiting to receive the Troops on another Road, (which it was expected they would take) it is believed the whole Corps would have been cut off."

After the Troops had returned into Boston, 1500 of the Americans marched to Marshfield, in Order to engage what Troops they should find there.

This Morning two Gentlemen, Members of Rhode-Island Assembly, at Providence, informed Mr. Nevins, That on their Way from the Eastward, they heard a heavy and continued Firing, which they imagined was another Engagement, between the Americans and King's Troops at Marshfield; and added, that they perceived in that Quarter, a Line of Fire, about Half a Mile in Length, which had much the Appearance of Building burning.

Printed by ROBERTSONS and TRUMBULL.

Important Advices!

NORWICH, April 24.
MONDAY MORNING, One o'Clock.
About Nine o'Clock last Evening the following Letters were brought here by an Express from Woodstock.

WOODSTOCK, April 23.
SUNDAY MORNING.

GENTLEMEN,

THE Accounts I have yet received from the Army are confused, and no great Certainty is yet to be had of the particular State and Circumstances of our Forces, or those of the Enemy. Thus much, however, may be depended upon; That the British Forces are retreated to Boston:------That the Seige of the Town and Castle is determined upon:----That the Number slain of the British Troops far exceeded that of the Provincials: The Proportion, as near as I can collect, is about Five or Six to One.

Among their Slain are some Officers; the Commander of the first Brigade is supposed to be among the Dead: The Ravages and barbarous Cruelty of our Enemies is almost unparallelled among the Savage Nations.----Old Men, Women, and Children have not escaped their brutal Rage, but in some Instances have been cut in Pieces in a most inhuman Manner.

A Son of the infamous Mandamus Counsellor, Col. Murray, went out with the first Brigade, as their Guide, is among the Slain.

More Men will doubtless be wanted; I therefore wish them to be detached and in Readiness as soon as possible, but not to march till further Orders.

The Troops from Lyme are not yet arrived here, but I hope they will join us this Day.----I wish our Provisions to be ---- readiness as soon as possible, and sent on, unless Accounts are received that ---- sent on, turn.

On meeting the Express from Boston, I beg of you to forward Provisions forthwith, with a further Reinforcement from our Regiment to be ready.

SAMUEL PARSONS.

To the Committee of New-London and Lyme.

CAMBRIDGE, Saturday Morning, April 22.

GENTLEMEN,

I HAVE waited on the general and the several Committees, and they all agree that the Men must come down to this Place, for we know not when we shall be attacked in this confused State. The Troops in Boston are in Motion, and preparing to make an Attack some where; but we have no News from Boston unless by some few of the Inhabitants, that run the Risk of their Lives by getting out of the Town by Stealth, for Boston is shut up!----There is no coming in or going out any other Way!----The People of the Town are all Prisoners, and what their Fate will be, GOD only knows; for the Troops have behaved in a very cruel and barbarous Manner; going into Houses and killing sick People, that were not able to go one Step, putting the Muzzle of the Gun into their Mouths and blowing their Heads in Pieces. Some Children had their Brains beat out!----several Houses and Barns burned!----and, for Miles together, not a House nor Shop but had their Windows broke, and hundreds of Shot in them!----There were about 40 of our People killed; but rather more of the Troops, and 70 or 80 of the Latter are taken Prisoners.---Enough of that, for this confused State!----Pray let the Men be properly inlisted and officered; let there be Teams to bring Provision, and a farther Supply sent immediately after them. Take Care they be sent in good Order.

ISRAEL PUTNAM.

A true Copy. HEZEKIAH BISSEL.

Printed by ROBERTSONS and TRUMBULL.

Extra issued by Norwich Packet *telling of start of the Revolution.*

body. Although Gage made a very prompt and conciliatory answer, the General Assembly had already adjourned, apparently with no real interest in his reply.[10]

Connecticut Inspires the Seizure of Fort Ticonderoga

BEFORE the General Assembly met on May 11, 1775, for the regular session, a Connecticut-inspired expedition had won a signal success in the north. It had originated in a chance meeting between Benedict Arnold, en route to Cambridge, and Samuel H. Parsons, returning to Connecticut to recruit men. Parsons mentioned to Arnold that the American army in Massachusetts lay nearly defenseless for lack of cannon. Arnold immediately spoke of the cannon at Fort Ticonderoga and the dilapidated condition of the fortifications there.[11]

Arriving in Hartford, Parsons talked with certain Whig leaders, including Silas Deane and Samuel Wyllys. This self-constituted Patriot group decided to raise money, supplies, and men, and send them forward without waiting the few days until the legislature convened. Heman Allen, who happened to be in Hartford, was sent with a commission to his brother Ethan to organize a force of his Green Mountain Boys and join those coming from the south in seizing Ticonderoga. The Hartford people also raised three hundred pounds and dispatched Bernard Romans and Noah Phelps as recruiting agents. Meanwhile Captain Edward Mott, who had come to Hartford to recruit for Cambridge service, was persuaded to become supreme commander of the expedition. Captain Mott and seventeen others left for the north on April 29. At Pittsfield, Mott conferred with innkeeper James Easton (formerly of Litchfield County, Connecticut) and Major John Brown, a Yale graduate, who, a short while before, had been in Canada for the Boston Committee of Correspondence. They helped Mott to raise a few trusted men, and the entire body soon moved on to Vermont. At Castleton they met Ethan Allen. Mott, as holder of the money, was elected president of their council of war, and since the majority of men were Green Mountain Boys, Allen was chosen leader of the assault force. He proceeded

that night to Hard's Cove, where men and boats were to assemble for the attack across Lake Champlain the night of May 9–10.[12]

Just as events seemed to be moving smoothly forward, serious complications developed. A very dignified gentleman appeared, clad in brilliant scarlet uniform, and dramatically announced that he was assuming command by authority of the Massachusetts Committee of Safety. It was Colonel Benedict Arnold! Despite Arnold's spirited insistence, the council of war adamantly refused to accede. Arnold rode on to find Allen, certain that he could mount a more efficient attack than that irresponsible frontiersman. Early the next morning Arnold caught up with Allen. It is unfortunate that their interview has not been preserved, for it must have been full of fiercely dogmatic assertions and rich expletives! Certainly it was a very tense moment. The expedition was posed for its take-off and daylight approached. Its commander must be decided! Allen supposedly asked his friend Amos Callender, "What shall I do with this damned rascal? Shall I put him under guard?" Many of Allen's men violently protested serving under any but their leader. After further altercation, Allen suddenly proposed a compromise under which Arnold would march beside him at the front of the column but would give no commands. Both men realized that if they argued much longer daylight would prevent any attack whatever, so they accepted the compromise.[13]

The attack itself went off well, though less than half the men could find room in the two decrepit boats available. They landed silently near the fort about three in the morning. Allen promptly assembled the men and gave them words of encouragement and challenge. He called their venture a desperate attempt which none but the bravest of men would dare undertake. Then he led them forward silently under the towering walls of the dark fortress. As his men quickly climbed through the tumble-down entrance of the south wall, one single sentry spotted them, snapped his musket, but it misfired. He turned and fled, giving the alarm, but it was much too late! Allen and his men soon were swarming over the place. When a British officer asked by what authority he demanded their surrender, Allen claimed he replied:

"In the name of the great Jehovah and the Continental Congress." From what is known of Allen, he probably said something much more vivid, if not unprintable! Be that as it may, the mission was a complete and bloodless success. The invaders soon discovered loot of far more immediate interest than the precious cannon. Captain Delaplace's private cellar yielded ninety gallons of high-grade stock, and the garrison's rum supply provided an even greater magnet! Despite such distractions, the cannon were dragged to Washington's army and used profitably in the siege of Boston. Later, Connecticut, at Allen's urging, compensated Captain Delaplace to the amount of £18 11s. 9d. for rum, "appropriated for the use of the Garrison."[14]

Crown Point, fifteen miles farther up the lake, was even more weakly held, and it fell without a shot to a flying column led by Seth Warner, a Connecticut son who had migrated to Bennington in 1763. More cannon were seized and also taken to the Boston area.[15]

Further Preparations and Operations in 1775

SOON after the regular May 1775 session of the Assembly opened, news of the exploits at Fort Ticonderoga and Crown Point arrived to cheer every heart. Indeed this probably was literally true, as the May 1775 elections had weeded out almost every Tory. Governor Trumbull, seeing a solidly Whig legislature, expressed great satisfaction at the results.[16]

Even before the lawmaking commenced, one could feel the strong temper of the times in the blazingly patriotic Election Day sermon of the Reverend Joseph Perry of South Windsor. He accused England of seeking to establish an "*absolute despotism,* and as the certain consequence, *cruel tyranny,* and the *total slavery* of all America." He called America's cause that "of *religion,* of *liberty,* of our country, and consequently the cause of GOD!" No legislator could doubt the position of this Puritan divine![17]

The Assembly plunged eagerly into further preparations for war. They copied Massachusetts' Congress in adopting the official articles of war, but prefixed these by an eloquent statement of the constitutional grounds for resistance. This summary stressed the Intolerable Acts, and their desire only "to preserve their antient constitution." They extended the embargo, voted the issuance of more paper money (£50,000) to meet growing military expenditures, and ordered large amounts of military supplies and wagons. An act to encourage "Manufacturing Fire-Arms and Military Stores" was passed, and three military officers of Tory inclinations were "broke and cashiered."[18]

Following a precedent of earlier war periods, the legislators created an emergency standing committee, the Council of Safety, to deal with the day-to-day emergencies which might arise when the legislature was not in session. The personnel read like a *Who's Who* of Connecticut: Governor Trumbull, Deputy Governor Griswold, Eliphalet Dyer, Jabez, Samuel, and Benjamin Huntington, William Williams, Nathaniel Wales, Jr., Jedidiah Elderkin, and Joshua West. Later in the war the personnel changed in part, but the Council remained a small body of eminent men, who put in untold hours of work at about 1,200 meetings, mostly held in the "War Office" at Lebanon, the former retail store of Governor Trumbull.[19]

Connecticut soldiers played a prominent part in the operations around Boston. After it was decided to fortify Bunker Hill, Putnam and Prescott took their men instead to Breed's Hill, nearer Boston but more exposed and farther from possible retreat, where the Battle of Bunker Hill actually was fought. In that bloody engagement it remains uncertain who, if anybody, clearly exercised overall command of the New England army, although Putnam and Prescott appear to have the best claims. Out of the battle came an undying piece of American historical lore, Putnam's famous order: "Men, you are all marksmen — don't one of you fire until you see the white [sic] of their eyes." As the British attacked, Putnam strove desperately to reinforce the American lines. Meanwhile Captain Thomas Knowlton's Connecticut men, with Stark's of New Hampshire, manned a rail fence on the flank, close to the Mystic River. Finally, after suffering staggering casualties, the British carried the field, but the New Englanders had performed surprisingly well.[20]

Ensign Amos Wadsworth, militiaman of Farmington, writing frankly to his brother a few days before the battle, expressed simply but honestly thoughts which epitomized the feelings of stanch Patriot soldiers:

I hope I may Conduct with all that Deliberation, Prudence, Fortitude & Courage which becomes every officer & Soldier — I shall not be fond of exposing my life where there is no prospect of advantage to my Self and my Country; but if I must loose my life in the defence of my Country, the Sacrifice will be but small, in proportion to the loss of the Liberties & privileges both Civil & religious, of this extensive Continent — Better to die a freeman, than to live a slave.[21]

Some of Connecticut's citizen-soldiers, however, like those of other states, unaccustomed to the needed discipline of military life, often acted irresponsibly. John Trumbull, one of the governor's sons who served in the Boston campaign, revealed the unhappy state of affairs:

. . . but our Own Soldiers begin to grumble & grow Mutinous, about their Pay — many of them insist on being paid at 4 Weeks to a month — Some Regiments have nearly mutinied — & I'm sorry to say that the Connecticutt Regiments appear the most disaffected of any.[22]

The summer of 1775 was marked by an important special legislative session. Its first act was to order the raising of 1,400 additional men, to serve five months for "the special defence and safety of this Colony." Not since the critical days of the French and Indian War had it been necessary to raise such a large body of men. Another £50,000 were ordered printed to cover mounting military costs. To this session the Massachusetts Assembly forwarded word that several towns in eastern Massachusetts were experiencing serious shortages of provisions, and urged that they be permitted to import provisions from Connecticut. The Assembly bestowed upon the governor power to grant licenses when circumstances justified such a course. Under the precedent laid in this act, hundreds of petitions to export embargoed articles were handled during the war.[23]

Early in the summer a case of injured pride nearly caused a crisis in the military high command. The Continental Congress had made Israel Putnam a Major General, whereas Joseph Spencer, an older man of higher rank in the militia, was given the lower rank of Brigadier General. Spencer threatened to leave the service, whereupon Governor Trumbull sent Samuel Huntington and William Williams to talk with him and try to "reconcile him chearfully to pursue the service." Apparently they worked on him in the morning, and that afternoon the governor and five more Council of Safety members joined in holding a lengthy conference with Spencer until he promised to return immediately to duty at Boston.[24]

Because of the reputed strong Whig sentiments of Connecticut and its seemingly safe location, Congress and other states soon asked permission to incarcerate dangerous Tory or British prisoners in Connecticut. As early as September 4, 1775, the Council of Safety considered a Massachusetts request to relieve its crowded "goals" (jails) by sending prisoners to Connecticut. The Council agreed to take a few, but suggested that Massachusetts apply also to Rhode Island and New Hampshire. In May 1775, with regard to British prisoners of war from Ticonderoga, the Assembly resolved that a special committee "take care of and provide for said officers and soldiers with their families at present, and see that they be treated with humanity, kindness and respect." They were largely taken care of in Hartford.[25]

Safekeeping of Prisoners

AFTER the successful attack upon St. Johns by Arnold and, later, the advance of General Richard Montgomery, many more British troops fell prisoner. These were distributed in such Connecticut inland towns as Farmington, Litchfield, Canaan, Salisbury, Sharon, Simsbury, Hartford, Middletown, Wethersfield, and Windham. Ordinarily these prisoners were not jailed, but simply confined loosely within the town limits on their parole not to try to escape. Occasionally trouble ensued, as at Farmington, when authorities reported their prisoners "turbulent and disorderly" and ready to escape unless tightly imprisoned.[26]

Connecticut was entrusted with two particularly notorious prisoners — Dr. Benjamin Church of Boston, and William Franklin of New Jersey, Tory son of Benjamin Franklin. Church arrived at Lebanon on November 21, 1775, escorted by a captain, sergeant, and seven men attesting his notoriety. They brought orders from Congress that he be "close confined in some secure goal in the

Colony of Connecticut, without the use of pen, ink and paper." General Washington added a note requesting careful compliance. The Council of Safety committed Church to the jail at Norwich and recommended to the county authorities the erection of a strong fence around that jail. Church remained as a prisoner in Norwich until May 27, 1776, when he was transferred out of the state.[27]

Former Governor Franklin came, if anything, even more forcefully recommended! Called by the New Jersey Convention "a virulent enemy to this country," he was turned over to the Continental Congress which in turn sent him in July 1776 to Governor Trumbull for safe care. He went first to Wallingford, but later at Franklin's request the Council bestowed upon Middletown the doubtful privilege of boarding him, and simultaneously classified Middletown as "out-of-bounds" to all prisoners residing at Hartford and Wethersfield. Nor did the Council underestimate Franklin's trouble-making proclivities. He became a center of Loyalist propaganda and even distributed the proclamations and protection promises of the Howe brothers! The rumor spread that some members of the Assembly had accepted the protection documents. Middletown Whigs soon had enough of Franklin and they appointed a committee of Captain Samuel Russell, Comfort Sage, and Seth Wetmore, Jr., to petition Governor Trumbull to "remove Said Governor Franklin . . . for Safety of this Town & State." Meanwhile news of Franklin's machinations had come to the ears of Congress, which decided upon strong countermeasures. A resolve of April 22, 1777, requested Trumbull to order Franklin into close confinement, without access to any person or writing material. Twice Franklin wrote Governor Trumbull about permission to return home. In the second letter he remonstrated "in terms more sharp than decent" against Trumbull's failure to answer the first letter. It is scarcely surprising that the Council rejected his rude request. Eight days later the Council of Safety studied the Congressional resolve and voted to remove Franklin to Litchfield. Doubtless Middletown leaders breathed a gigantic sigh of relief! Apparently Franklin caused less trouble at Litchfield, though extra expenses were incurred by the special guard maintained for his benefit.[28]

Military Activities in the Winter of 1775–76

THE militiamen of Connecticut, like those of other states, displayed an alarming tendency to drift home in dull periods of inaction. Early in December 1775 General Washington sent a rather heated letter heartily condemning the desertion of a number of Putnam's regiment and asking that they be disciplined. Since their term of enlistment had nearly expired and the Assembly was to meet soon, the Council decided to lay the issue before the Assembly and pending the meeting sent Washington a tactful letter breathing ardent patriotism.[29]

In March 1776 the British evacuation of Boston occurred after a long siege in which Connecticut troops — under David Wooster, Joseph Spencer, and Israel Putnam — had played an important role. Colonel Rufus Putnam earlier had suggested to Washington that, since the ground was frozen, the breastworks at Dorchester Heights should be erected above ground by use of chandeliers, or heavy timber frames. His plan was adopted and worked out excellently in erecting the new fortifications which forced Howe to evacuate his army from Boston.[30]

The same month Washington, fearing an immediate British descent upon New York, vigorously entreated Connecticut to rush 2,000 men to New York until he could march his army down there. In immediate response the Council voted to send two regiments of 900 men each. Whether the full number actually went is quite doubtful. Certainly the action of the May 1776 Assembly in raising the penalty for failure to march upon orders from two pounds to ten pounds suggests that many had been guilty and a more expensive deterrent was badly needed to correct this situation.[31]

At the May session the legislators again were preoccupied with military preparations. One-third or one-fourth of each militia regiment was ordered held in readiness for active duty as "minute men." In addition, there should be raised by voluntary enlistment one regiment for a year's service wherever needed in or outside the colony. Finally, they voted to organize two regiments for the special defense of the colony.[32]

The Great Step: To Independence

THE Assembly closed with a ringing declaration in favor of extreme preparedness and righteousness. The situation was indeed terrifying with the . . . United Colonies, being threatned with the whole force of Great Britain united with all such foreign mercenaries as they are able to engage to assist the execution of their causeless vengeance on these devoted Colonies, and to burn and destroy our seaport towns, and to spread rapine, murder and destruction through the whole: in this situation our utmost efforts cannot be too much, and it is the duty of every individual to contribute all in his power to serve and defend our most important cause.

This powerful statement plainly suggests the feeling of Connecticut's leaders that the colony was almost inextricably involved in the struggle and scarcely could withdraw even if such a maneuver were desired.[33]

That the die was cast became more apparent at the special session of June 14–21, 1776. The legislators opened with drastic action against Tories through a sweeping act providing for seizure of property of any "person or persons who have or shall join the ministerial army . . . or have aided . . . the present ministerial measures." In answer to Congressional demand, two battalions were to be recruited by voluntary enlistment for service in the north and seven for New York — all to serve until December.[34]

By all odds the most significant action of the Assembly came in its bold resolve "That the Delegates of this Colony in General Congress be and they are hereby instructed to propose to that respectable body, to declare the United American Colonies Free and Independent States, absolved from all allegiance to the King of Great Britain." Thus, after fourteen months of hostilities, Connecticut officially proclaimed openly for independence. The legislators carefully prefaced this declaration with a statement of causes. Connecticut's able representatives in Congress thus possessed clear instructions.[35]

On June 18 Governor Trumbull issued a proclamation in which he eloquently described the Patriots' grievances and principles. He noted that over 7,000 men had been summoned by the current Assembly. Trumbull asserted: "Affairs are hastening fast to a Crisis, and the approaching Campaign will, in all Probability, determine forever the Fate of *America*." The proclamation ended with customary expressions of religious belief and need for righteousness and repentance.[36]

Because of strong hostility in the middle colonies, especially Pennsylvania, to an open break with Britain, a vote upon Richard Henry Lee's famous resolution of June 7, 1776, for independence was postponed to July 2. On that date Connecticut's eminent quartet — Samuel Huntington, Roger Sherman, William Williams, and Oliver Wolcott — enthusiastically supported the resolution and later affixed their signatures to the Declaration of Independence.[37]

The Patriots Harass the Tories

THE Declaration of Independence forced most Americans to take a definite stand for or against the American cause. It would soon be almost impossible to straddle the fence or to be a genuine "neutralist," yet for many the decision was a difficult and painful one. Religion, politics, social class, and economic interests played their parts, though in differing degrees, as Connecticut citizens pondered the fateful question: Loyalty to George III and empire or to the Continental Congress and a free America?

The Patriot-Tory struggle in Connecticut developed logically from the old Whig-Conservative political struggle of the 1765–74 period. As already seen, the Conservatives were badly beaten in their attempts to gain control of the colony in 1774. Soon afterward Thomas Fitch, Conservative leader, died, leaving no successor. William Samuel Johnson came closest to providing Conservative leadership, but he was too pacifistic and intellectual to provide the militant leadership required to galvanize Tory sentiment.[38]

For many months Patriots had harried and persecuted the Tories, mostly through local committees and mobs. In Farmington two hundred Whigs called upon the Reverend James Nichols, charged with Loyalist sentiments, and after prolonged conversation, persuaded him to confess his sins and renounce his unpopular beliefs.[39]

The notorious Tory parson of Hebron, Samuel

140

John Trumbull's painting of the Declaration of Independence.

Peters, who wrote a spirited if unreliable history of Connecticut, was severely manhandled by Whig mobs. Later, while at a meeting of Anglican clergy in New Haven, he learned that bands in Farmington and Windham had sworn to kill him. Peters promptly fled to Boston and soon afterward sailed to England.[40]

Jared Ingersoll, a moderate Tory of New Haven, was threatened with dire retribution by some of the eastern Radicals unless he left the colony within ten days. Ingersoll was not easily frightened, however, and informed Trumbull of this unlawful threat. Despite all charges, for the time being he continued to live quietly at his home.[41]

The actions of the First Continental Congress of 1774, especially creation of the Continental Association, precipitated the first definite official expression of opinion by Connecticut towns. In the more radical east there was no doubt as to the wholehearted support. Colchester, New London, and Norwich, among others, passed resolutions specifically supporting the Continental Association. Usually a committee was appointed to make certain that citizens obeyed the Association.[42]

In western Connecticut, especially in Fairfield County, conservative patterns of thinking were much stronger, and open Toryism often reared its head. On January 30, 1775, in a crowded meeting, Ridgefield voted to repudiate the Continental Congress and pledged anew the town's allegiance to the king and his government. Asserting that the Assembly's powers were limited, they denounced the local committees of inspection which made life miserable for loyal British subjects and vigorously condemned Congress. Newtown expressed similar sentiments.[43]

The same winter a large group of Tories from Litchfield and Fairfield counties met and stanchly declared their unyielding loyalty to king and empire. New Milford, Danbury, Redding, and Newtown were well represented at these meetings.[44]

The bold moves of the Tories stimulated vigor-

141

ous Whig countermoves in 1775. In the special Assembly session of March, Trumbull noted not only the grave external threats facing the colony but also the internal enemies, those Tories who "with a depraved, Malignant, aviricious and haughty mind" aimed to wreck the "happy Constitution & Liberties of these English Colonies." He asked for "manly" action against them. The Assembly ordered investigation of charges that "the towns of Ridgefield and Newtown have . . . published certain resolutions injurious to the rights of this Colony, in direct opposition to the reported resolves of this House, and of dangerous tendency."[45]

Public opinion hardened considerably against Tories after the commencement of open fighting in Massachusetts. In May 1774 New Haven set up its Committee of Correspondence, and named ultraconservative Joshua Chandler as chairman. He adopted a vigorous Tory position in 1775, but by November public feeling forced his arrest and confinement at home. Chandler's close friend Jared Ingersoll later found it prudent to move to Philadelphia, where he lived until 1777. Eventually, after arrest and imprisonment in the south, Ingersoll returned to New Haven and found the atmosphere not unbearable. By 1780 he reconciled himself to the American cause and worked quietly but effectively for it until his death in August 1781.[46]

Scattered incidents occurred in various parts of the state in 1775 which indicated the deepening strains of divided loyalties. In Waterbury, as a Whig expressed it, "their hath happened a Terrible Rumpus." It grew out of the actions of Josiah Nicholls, who deserted from General Wooster's regiment, apparently at his father's instigation. Later the son re-enlisted at Saybrook, took his bounty, and promptly deserted again. Officers pursued him to Waterbury, and a scuffle ensued with the father, Captain Lemuel Nicholls, who was subdued and bound. The Tories in the neighborhood rallied and freed Captain Nicholls, who immediately disappeared. The Whigs, sending to Southington for reinforcements, finally located Captain Nicholls hiding "on his Belly . . . in a Bunch of Alders" and brought him before the local justice, who bound him over to the County Court. The Tories, numbering eighty to one hundred

men, milled around well into the night but finally disbanded peacefully.[47]

Most of the competition took the form, however, of a long, harassing verbal engagement in which local committees summoned suspected Tories before them to answer charges of all sorts, such as buying tea, proclaiming loyalty to the king, or failing to observe a Continental fasting day. Ashbel Humphrey of Goshen felt the heavy hand of a local committee which instituted a trade boycott and verbally castigated him. In fear and despair he hid out in the woods, and as a last resort fled to the British lines in September 1780. In New Milford a Tory was forced to walk twenty miles to Litchfield with his own goose and there received a generous coating of tar and feathers. In this parlous state he was compelled "to kneel down, and thank them for their lenity."[48]

Anglican clergymen, stanchly Loyalist, fared badly at Whig hands. The Reverend Richard Mansfield of Derby wrote Samuel Peters that violent persecution raged in western Connecticut, where people were dragged "before ignorant, dirty, domineering Committees of Inspection imprisoning some & tarring & feathering others." Fearing for his life, Mansfield fled to Long Island.[49]

The Assembly and Press Attack the Tories

THE aggressive behavior of the towns was not matched by the legislature even as late as October 1775. Although it ordered two Woodbury Tories to appear at the next session, it failed to enact any stringent anti-Tory laws. Meanwhile rumors spread that Tories controlled several western towns, including Newtown, Danbury, Redding, Ridgefield, and Woodbury. Late in November a small "army" of Patriots under Colonel Ichabod Lewis spent two days in Newtown trying to force the Continental Association down the gagging throats of the Reverend Mr. Beach, Tory rector, the unhappy selectmen, and other well-known Tories. Eventually the leading Tories posted bond for good behavior, while the Whigs stripped all Tories of arms. This process was repeated in the nearby towns. At Woodbury resisting Tories soon found themselves marching to the Litchfield jail under enthusiastic Whig escort! As a direct result of this sweep, the Whigs overturned Tory rule in Ridgefield, and in December 1775 the town belatedly approved the Continental Association.[50]

In December 1775 the Assembly passed its first law against Tories, a comprehensive measure prohibiting a wide variety of deeds: providing the British army with provisions or military stores, enlisting or soliciting enlistments in that army, taking up arms against the "United Colonies," and piloting an enemy vessel. If convicted, a person would "forfeit all his estate" and suffer imprisonment up to three years. Even writing or speaking against laws of Congress or of the Assembly became a crime causing ineligibility for all civil and military offices. Finally, town officers and inspection committees could examine any suspected person and disarm him. Thus the anomalous situation was created whereby in Connecticut, still a British colony, it was illegal to be loyal to Britain! Under this act by late summer over fourscore Tories in Newtown were under charges and liable to loss of political privileges. "Denounce, disarm and disfranchise" — that, in short, was the deliberate program of Whigs to eliminate the Tory threat in Connecticut.[51]

The following June the stricter act already referred to, which permitted seizure and confiscation of *personal* property, as well as real estate of Loyalists, was passed. This law and the Declaration of Independence meant the virtual end of tolerance for them.[52]

In October 1776 the Assembly clamped down even further upon Tories. The successful British campaign in New York and the encouragement it gave to adherents in western Connecticut undoubtedly heightened the desire of state leaders to strike a decisive blow against their internal enemies. Since Newtown's two representatives were suspect, one was quietly unseated as "inimical to the American States" and the other voluntarily (?) gave up his place. This Assembly then made treasonable acts punishable by death. The Constitution of 1662 remained in effect, but any reference to the king and allegiance to Britain was deleted. In addition, every freeman and political candidate had to take a special "oath of fidelity" to Connecticut.[53]

Perhaps the best revelation of the deepening hatred of Tories can be found in the appointment of a special committee to visit the western towns and hail before them all inimical persons "when the ordinary mode of prosecution will not be adequate to the mischief apprehended." If the committee found a person dangerous it could send him to a place of detention for as long as the governor and Council of Safety thought fit. This act meant a major suspension of certain civil rights as a wartime emergency measure.[54]

Patriot newspaper editors lost little time in employing publicity against suspected Tories. On April 8, 1776, Ebenezer Watson, *Courant* editor, listing on page 1 "All Persons inimical to the Country," started his roll of iniquity with Stephen Sears of Sharon, Ebenezer Orvis of Farmington, and Jonathan Hill of Alford, Massachusetts. Gradually the list grew.[55]

An anonymous contributor to New London's newspaper in March 1777 summarized in sarcastic fashion the crimes of Tories:

For the Connecticut Gazette.

Now the Rogue is caught, or shrewd Marks of Toryism.

1. Finding Fault with, and refusing to adhere to the Regulations of the Grand American Congress.

2. Voting against Measures evidently blended with the Safety of the Country.

3. Ordering or suffering one's Servants and hired Men, with Teams, Farming Utensils, &c. to pursue the Business of the Field on Continental Fasts.

4. Cuddling with Tories in order to gain Votes; and unwearied Attempts to baffle the Measures of the Committees of Inspection, and to destroy the Influence of those zealously engaged in pleading the Cause of Liberty.

> When these four Lineaments are found,
> Stampt on one Face, however Grave;
> I'll safely sware upon good Ground,
> They indicate a Fool, or Knave.

. . . .

N.B. To bolster up such a wrongheaded Fellow in his Wickedness, Absurdity or Nonsense, injures the Cause of Liberty, and contradicts the Common Sense of America.　　　　A Friend to Justice.[56]

Significance of the Tories

IT is impossible to say exactly how many and what proportion of Connecticut's population was Tory, but the most reliable evidence available suggests that 2,000 to 2,500 Connecticut men took that position at the outset of the war. In 1774 the census counted 38,807 men in the twenty to seventy age bracket. On this basis about 6 percent of the adult males were Tories. Even if this estimate is low, Connecticut still had a smaller percentage than most of the states.[57]

Connecticut's Tories caused consternation and fear out of proportion to their numbers because of their heavy concentration in Fairfield County. President Stiles of Yale estimated that one-quarter of the citizens west of Stratford River remained loyal, which meant 1,500 Tories out of 6,000 adult men. General Selleck Silliman of Fairfield, whose war letters contain valuable information about conditions in Fairfield County, described one session of the Superior Court, held in Fairfield, at which thirty Tories were on trial. He thought two would "swing for it" and that the trials would "have a salutary Effect." He also reported that by 1777 a thousand Loyalists had departed to join the British, with more left than in all the remainder of the state. About one-third of the county's families were Anglicans, and most Anglicans seem to have remained loyal to the mother country. In New Haven, according to Dr. Stiles, about one-seventh of the families were Anglican, and in Litchfield County, one out of twenty-two. Altogether perhaps five hundred to a thousand Tories were located outside of Fairfield County, principally in adjoining New Haven and Litchfield counties, with the majority undoubtedly Anglicans.[58]

In May 1777 the Assembly, no longer fearing state Tories and feeling generous, offered pardons to all who "from ill advice . . . inadvertence and mistaken apprehensions, have absconded and put themselves under the protection of the enemies . . . and would probably return to their duty had they assurance of protection &c." At least a few took advantage of this offer. In May 1778, however, the legislature moved in the opposite direction when it passed a severe act for confiscation of all real and personal estate of those voluntarily joining the enemy. Court records attest the heavy impact of this bill. Until late 1778 Tory *personal* property was usually ordered *sold* for the state and *real* property *leased*. Beginning with the November 1778 session of the Fairfield County Court, *all* Tory property usually fell under the Patriot ax.[59]

The court records show that Fairfield County contained most of the Tories. In the 1777–82 period Fairfield County Court tried approximately *seven* times as many Loyalist cases as its nearest competitor, New Haven County. Norwalk had by far the largest number of cases, followed in order by Stamford, Fairfield, Ridgefield, Newtown, Danbury, Greenwich and Stratford (tied), Redding, Derby, New Haven, and Waterbury. In Litchfield County a few Tories from New Milford, Litchfield, Woodbury, Salisbury, and Washington lost their estates. In the eastern counties cases were exceedingly rare.[60]

Most Tories received only short jail sentences. William Silliman drew up "The Black Roll, May 25th, 1776 of Tories now Confined in Prison," which contained thirty-seven names of persons from Redding, Stamford, Newtown, and Norwalk. Samuel Tuttle of New Haven, tried in August 1777 for breaking the law for high treason, was found guilty, sentenced to one month's imprisonment and fined ten pounds and costs.[61]

Of all Connecticut's Tories only one suffered the death penalty, Moses Dunbar of Wallingford. Born in 1746, he was brought up to be a farmer. At an early age he married Phebe Jerome of Farmington, who died twelve years later. Through the influence of the Reverend James Scovill, an Anglican missionary at Waterbury, they joined the Church of England. As the breach with Britain grew wider, Dunbar became increasingly unable to reconcile himself "to the necessity or lawfulness of taking up arms against Great Britain." Since he spoke his mind freely, he was attacked by a mob which threatened his life and forced him to sign a patriotic declaration. Later a local committee of inspection called him and, after a hearing, ordered him imprisoned. After fourteen days in jail, he was freed. Fleeing to Long Island, he accepted a captain's commission for service in Colonel Edward Fanning's Loyalist regiment. He made the mistake, however, of returning to be married again and was seized. His case went to the Superior Court, where he was tried for treason under the act of October 1776 "for enlisting men for General Howe, and for having a captain's commission for that purpose." Found guilty and sentenced to hang, he escaped from Hartford jail, only to be recaptured. On March 19, 1777, before a "prodigious Concourse" of people, he was hanged. Dunbar went to his death bravely and, as he expressed it, in a "state of peace with God and my own conscience." There was no doubt of Dunbar's guilt, but it is probable, too, that state authorities wished to make an example of him.[62]

In common with other states, Connecticut lost many able citizens among Tories who fled permanently from the state. Some were wealthy men, like Abiather Camp, Amos Botsford, and Joshua Chandler of New Haven. As one examines the Loyalist claims filed with the British Government it quickly becomes apparent that people from all walks of life were represented, including such occupations as farmer, lawyer, merchant, pilot, waggoner, carpenter, shoemaker, weaver, surgeon, clergyman, gristmill operator, shipowner, and a hatter. The majority possessed modest means, judging by the smallness of their claims — more often under £700 than over. More than sixty Tories presented claims for about £54,000 but the hard-boiled British inspectors scaled them down to just over £14,000.[63]

Making a new start, often in middle life and nearly penniless, in distant New Brunswick or Nova Scotia involved great hardships and heartbreak. When the war ended, a few Tories drifted back unobtrusively into Connecticut. In Redding the town directed the selectmen to eject summarily all Tories who had dared to return. In Norwalk over ninety citizens drew up a scorching indictment:

. . . these Miscreants . . . flew to the assistance of our Murderers and display'd their Talents against us in the most vigorous and Savage-like manner . . . yet while filial Tears are fresh upon our Cheeks and our murdered Brethren scarcely cold in their Graves, we have the mortification to behold these Wretches cringing back to our protection and living in our Country with Impunity —

The petitioners asked the Assembly to take effective steps against such returnees.[64]

In their overall effect upon Revolutionary Connecticut, the Tories must be classified chiefly as an irritant group who fled the state or were quickly disarmed. It is difficult to cite another state where the Patriots obtained such thorough political control so early in the conflict.

The First British Raid: Danbury, April 1777

FROM the outbreak of the war the Patriots in exposed towns along the Sound lived in great fear of a British attack. In October 1775 came the first important act dealing with coastal protection, which involved stationing seventy men at New London, thirty at New Haven, fifteen at Lyme, and forty at Stonington — all men to be paid the same as those serving elsewhere. Those at New London were to occupy themselves with completing the fort and mounting cannon on it. Contingents of such size, too weak to repulse a major British attack, could repulse minor marauders or give the alarm in a major attack. After the British secured control of New York and Long Island, fear of invasion vastly increased. Not until April 1777, however, did the long-dreaded British attack eventuate. [65]

General Howe, seeking a safe objective for a secondary raid, ordered Major General William Tryon, royal governor of New York, to attack Danbury and destroy the Continental military stores located there. Howe gave Tryon about 2,000 troops, a few dragoons, and some fieldpieces. The expedition sailed from New York, put into the mouth of the Saugatuck River, and landed at Compo on the afternoon of April 25, 1777. Marching inland they spent the night in Weston. The appearance of so many soldiers sent Patriot messengers fanning out to warn the countryside. Some surmised that the Danbury supply depot would be the chief target, and at 3:00 A.M. on April 26 a courier rode into Danbury with a warning. Another arrived at 6:00 A.M. to confirm the likelihood of attack. When word reached General David Wooster at New Haven, he promptly called out the militia there. Benedict Arnold, sulking at his sister's home in New Haven and "itching for a fight" as always, joined Wooster, and they hastened to Fairfield, where Wooster assumed command of counteroperations. Meanwhile General Selleck Silliman, in command of Fairfield County militia, had called his men to arms.[66]

On April 26 Tryon's little army marched unopposed to Danbury, where local forces amounting to only 150 men could do little but withdraw. Arriving in Danbury shortly before three that afternoon, Tryon set up his headquarters in Nehemiah Dibble's home on South Street. Six- and twelve-pounders sent cannon balls screaming through the town to intimidate any resisters, after which the British began a methodical destruction of all stores, though a few, including medical supplies, had just been removed to safety. The supplies in a barn belonging to Nehemiah Dibble were destroyed, but the barn was preserved because of Dibble's Tory inclinations. Those supplies in the Anglican Church were burned in the street, as the redcoats spared the church. A torch was applied to a large barn full of grain on Main Street, which burned furiously. Tryon ordered his men to destroy the rum stores, but soon hundreds of them were gloriously drunk! The inebriated bands, shouting, singing, and tumbling about, filled the town with terror as darkness fell. Luckily for Tryon, some of his men remained sober, and moved about marking crosses upon houses of known Tories so that these would not be burned.[67]

Meanwhile General Tryon suddenly realized that he was in a precarious situation. Seeing the majority of his troops helplessly intoxicated, he suspected that Connecticut militia in unknown numbers were closing in upon him. Probably he had hoped to spend the Sabbath quietly in Danbury, but a little after midnight he received word that the militia had reached Bethel and might attack soon. Immediate orders went out to evacuate Danbury and, by means best known to hard-boiled noncoms, the drunken soldiers soon found themselves capable of marching again! Before departure, however, picked soldiers spent an hour or so setting fire to accessible homes of Patriots, so that some nineteen homes, plus twenty-two storehouses and barns, were consumed. Against this fiery backdrop the redcoats took their departure![68]

It soon became apparent that the return march of the British would be much more difficult. The Connecticut militia were displaying that "swarming" tendency which characterized American militia in all states when their own neighborhood was invaded. Tryon sought to outwit the Americans by swinging farther westward through Ridgebury and Ridgefield for his return to the Sound, but this maneuver was anticipated. In Bethel at 2:00 A.M. on Sunday, Wooster, Silliman, and Arnold considered how best to employ their force of about 500 militia and 100 Continentals. They decided that Arnold and Silliman, with 400 men, should proceed to Ridgefield for an attack upon the retreating British. Meanwhile Wooster, with 200 men, was to harass the enemy's rear.[69]

Wooster's men, knowing the country intimately, broke out from woods upon an unsuspecting British rear regiment at breakfast and captured forty men. Later that morning Wooster's men struck again. This time the British jarred the Americans with artillery fire which caused them to hesitate in the attack. Observing this, Wooster turned in the saddle and called out, "Come on, my boys! Never mind such random shots!" At that instant an enemy musket ball struck his back and fatally wounded him.[70]

The British pushed on meanwhile and soon reached Arnold's roadblock in Ridgefield. Though outnumbered four to one, Arnold's men threw a heavy fire, but they were forced back when the British outflanked them. Arnold, the last man to retreat, suddenly spied a British platoon charging down upon him from a ledge. As he turned his horse to flee, the platoon fired. No less than nine bullets struck his horse, but Arnold miraculously escaped. As he tried vainly to disentangle his feet from the stirrups a redcoat, bayonet drawn, rushed him and shouted, "Surrender! You are my prisoner." Arnold replied, "Not yet!" and calmly shot his pursuer dead. Then, extricating himself from the stirrups, he sprinted into a nearby swamp, followed by a harmless shower of bullets.[71]

Determined to even the score with the British, who camped that night near Ridgefield, Arnold once more rounded up the militia. Artillery reinforcements under Colonel John Lamb and militia under Colonel Jedediah Huntington joined him. Monday's retreat proved to be a nightmare for Tryon's men. On a smaller scale it was another retreat from Concord to Boston. From behind convenient stone walls, trees, and buildings the militia fired continually at the redcoats marching on the road. Arnold, in the meantime, had stationed his forces so that they commanded both roads by which Tryon might try to gain the safety of his ships. The exhausted British now were outnumbered and might indeed have been captured, but timely reinforcements of hard-hitting marines from the fleet broke up the incipient American attack. Arnold rode furiously about the field, pleading with his men to repulse the marines and close in on Tryon. Another horse was shot under him and a bullet ripped through his coat collar. Although Lamb's artillery also fought valiantly, the bulk of the American forces fled. In the confusion Tryon's men slipped aboard their boats. Tryon had achieved his mission, but at a cost which would discourage a return visit! British casualties ran close to two hundred, including ten officers. The Americans lost about twenty killed and forty wounded.[72]

The Assembly's special committee upon personal damages in Danbury reported verified losses of over £16,000, and in May 1778 the Assembly appropriated one-third the amount of the losses for relief of the sufferers. In Ridgefield the selectmen noted that the British troops "did in their merciless rage consume with fire about six dwelling-houses . . . a corn-mill and other buildings together with a large quantity of household goods, cloathing, provisions &c. . . . amounting to the sum of £2625.1.8." Again the legislators voted one-third the damages. In view of such niggardly treatment, one can imagine that victims did not soon, if ever, recover financially from the losses, not to mention the terrors of the experience.[73]

War Brings Shortages

IN the basically agricultural economy of Connecticut, a lengthy war meant serious shortages of manufactured goods, both military and civilian. As colonials, people had relied upon England for powder, cannon, and other critical military materiel, as well as for fine cloth, glass, and many other items for the home.

Some of the greatest difficulties arose in nonmilitary items, such as *salt*, the common meat preservative of that age. In peacetime the colony had imported a substantial proportion of its salt from the West Indies and elsewhere — sources now largely cut off by the British navy. Hence Connecticut must manufacture most of its salt. As an incentive, the legislature in May 1776 voted a bounty of a hundred pounds to the first person who erected new saltworks and completed five hundred bushels of salt. Several saltworks were set up near the coast and apparently used sea water. Five New Haven men claimed the first prize in 1777 and were awarded the bounty. Meanwhile the General Assembly in October 1776 enacted a general bounty of one shilling per bushel, and in December doubled the rate, which held for the remainder of the war. The state also resorted to threats in an act of November 1776 which authorized town officials to seize the stores of "any engrosser or monopolizer" of salt and to distribute it to the needy at the legal price.[74]

In spite of all laws, the shortage persisted. Frequently permission was granted to export embargoed items if the shipper would bring back salt. In November 1777 the Council of Safety gave Governor Trumbull complete discretion in permitting out-of-staters who brought in salt to take away any kind of Connecticut produce; yet in September 1779 the Council of Safety noted that salt remained as scarce as two years earlier. Again and again the towns were asked for salt for the meat supplies of the armed forces, but the salt problem continued to plague the state to the end of the conflict.[75]

The manufacture of cloth and clothing provides an example of marked wartime stimulation in demand. One must not visualize, however, anything remotely like the huge textile mills of the twentieth century. Even during the war most clothing for both civilian and military use was fashioned within private homes. The militia and Continental troops required clothing and blankets on a huge scale, and under the rigors of duty these items wore out rapidly. These clothing needs were generally met by levies upon the towns, which in turn applied pressure to individual residents.

In January 1778 the General Assembly, upon Congress' request, ordered every town to procure for each of its soldiers in the Continental army one "hunting-shirt or frock, two linen shirts, two pair of linen overhalls, one pair of stockings and two pairs of good well made shoes, for each officer and

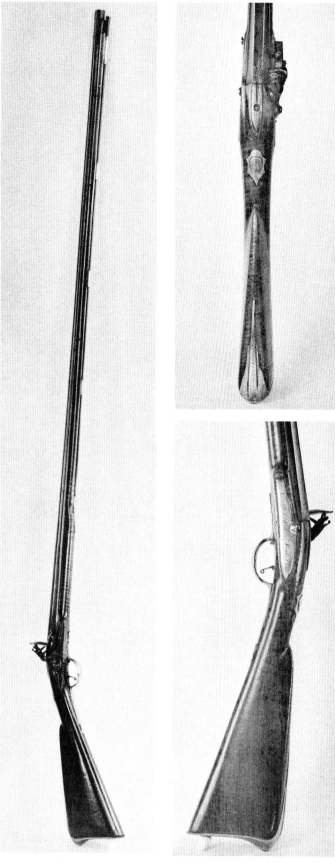

soldier . . . and also half as many blankets" as the total town quota. At the town level one finds that Norwich, in town meeting on March 23, 1778, set up a committee of nine men to purchase the clothing. On December 23 Norwich appointed a committee to inquire into the deficiency of clothing. The next June the town created a committee of eleven to handle the borrowing of money for purchase of clothing called for by the General Assembly Act of May 1779. On July 6 an emergency committee was chosen to exert every influence to procure clothing and report in eight days. To the end of the war Norwich continued to struggle with clothing quotas. In April 1781 a special town committee divided the town into sixty-six groups to facilitate collection of a threepence tax for obtaining "summer" clothing. The Revolutionary records of many Connecticut towns reveal the same preoccupation with this problem.[76]

There did exist "infant" industries, such as small establishments in the West Hartford–Farmington area where the French officer, the Marquis de Chastellux, noted in 1780 that woolen cloth was being made. At Norwich, Christopher Leffingwell manufactured cloth, and in Middletown, George Starr managed a small shoe and leather goods factory, important enough for George Washington, at the proprietor's request, to urge Governor Trumbull to exempt the employees from militia service.[77]

Forging the Sinews of War

CONNECTICUT experienced great difficulties in producing saltpeter and powder, products usually imported previously. Again sizable bounties were offered, and powder mills began operation at East Hartford, Windham, New Haven, Glastonbury, Stratford, and Salisbury. Setbacks occurred, as on August 23, 1777, at Glastonbury, when an explosion blew up the building, stock, and six employees! Although the state never obtained an adequate or uniformly good powder supply, the rate of production did increase greatly.[78]

In the field of gunmaking, Connecticut had a nucleus of skilled craftsmen who stepped up production to meet large wartime demands. The state helped by giving a bounty to every soldier who

Gun made by Benoni Hills of Goshen in 1757.
(owned by Ben F. Hubbell).

provided himself with a gun "well fixed with a good bayonet and cartouch box." In May 1775 the General Assembly offered gunsmiths a bounty of 5s. per gun and 1s. 6d. per gunlock. Perhaps the title of "most productive" goes to Hezekiah Huntington of Windham, who made and repaired guns in a shop at Willimantic. In May 1783 he presented a petition to the General Assembly showing he had produced 340 guns and had received a bounty for only 60, an oversight which the legislators tardily rectified the following October. In just over one year Uriah Hanks of Mansfield made 87 "double Bridle gunlocks" for which he asked and later received £17 8s. In Goshen three careful craftsmen, John Doud, Ebenezer Norton, and Medad Hills, collaborated in turning out fine guns. Occasionally state inspectors discovered "poor deficient arms, totally unfit for service," but normally Connecticut's soldiers possessed the requisite guns, if not always enough powder.[79]

The most interesting and probably the most important war industry of Connecticut was the Salisbury iron and cannon foundry. Thanks to extensive beds of iron ore in the vicinity, large expenditures, and energetic management, Salisbury became the leading Revolutionary cannon-making center of New England.

At the outbreak of hostilities Richard Smith, the owner of the foundry, suspected of Tory sympathies, journeyed to Britain "for the duration." Early in 1776 the Council of Safety dispatched "trouble-shooter" Jedidiah Elderkin to survey the area and report upon the condition of the works. Apparently he was optimistic and in March the Council selected Colonel Joshua Porter as overseer of the Salisbury project. Under his management fell the blast furnace, a "molding-house," a "Boring mill," a "Bridge house," a "Guard House," an "Upper Dam," and a barn. Before the cannon could be cast, however, and other products manufactured, Porter had to insure a steady flow of iron ore and limestone from nearby sources and of charcoal from neighboring towns, such as Cornwall, Canaan, Sharon, and Sheffield, Massachusetts. About sixty men, if "ore diggers" are included, worked in the project, and scores more were occupied preparing and hauling in necessary supplies. Governor Trumbull considered the work so vital that

he kept a special express rider almost constantly on the Lebanon-Salisbury route.[80]

In the first year of activity (1776) Salisbury produced cannon for the Connecticut coastal forts, for loans to New York, and for several ships. Late in 1776 the Continental Congress requested Salisbury cannon for the northern forts and the Continental ships. Thenceforth Salisbury served the American as well as the Connecticut war effort.[81]

To meet the greater demands, the legislature decided to reorganize the management and substi-

Advertisement of the Salisbury iron furnace.

A "pig" of iron made at Salisbury.

tuted for Porter alone a committee of three — Benjamin Henshaw, William Whiting, and Porter — to oversee the works. In January 1777 the Council voted to supply General Schuyler with thirty-nine cannon, ranging from three-pounders to eighteen-pounders, and necessary shot. Meanwhile Elderkin was sent to Boston and elsewhere to inquire about the latest and best techniques for boring and other steps in the manufacture. During the rushed months of 1777 several workers enlisted or were drafted for military service. Henshaw and Whiting begged the legislature to exempt sufficient men, and to their delight the legislators agreed to exempt fifty! Salisbury lay in a thinly settled portion of Connecticut, so that the managers found it necessary to advertise for workers.

From 1779 to 1783 Whiting served as active manager of the Salisbury enterprise on a lease basis and paid a modest rent. He obtained tools for boring cannon from ironworks at Colebrook.[82]

The contribution of the Salisbury works to the winning of the war must be reckoned as highly significant. Without these cannon Greenwich, Stamford, Norwalk, Fairfield, Stratford, Milford, New Haven, and New London would have been virtually defenseless. The Continental army in the north, the militia, the Connecticut and Continental navy, and Connecticut privateersmen all employed Salisbury cannon.[83]

Connecticut Fights in the Continental Army

IN addition to the two major categories of militia and Continentals, Connecticut organized a third type of organization called State Troops. These were special regiments drawn from the militia, for varying periods of time, to meet sudden emergencies. State Troops were sent to Boston in December 1775 to replace those coming home and stayed there until February 1776. The troops participating in the Northern Campaign of 1776, under Colonels Samuel Mott and Heman Swift, were State Troops. Official Revolutionary rolls list State Troops active in 1775, 1776, and 1777, but none after that, perhaps because of better organization of the Continental and militia troops.[84]

Even before the British evacuated Boston, Washington, foreseeing a probable attack upon New York, requested Connecticut to send men. As a result, 1,500 State Troops, called up under Colonels Andrew Ward and David Waterbury, spent a few weeks constructing fortifications on Brooklyn Heights and along the riverbanks, in accordance with plans prepared by General Charles Lee.[85]

On March 18, 1776, the Council of Safety considered a very urgent request for reinforcements from Washington, who feared that the British might proceed directly to New York. The Council ordered men detached from seven militia regiments and formed into two battalions of nine hundred men each, under Colonels Selleck Silliman and Matthew Talcott, for immediate service in New York. In June 1776 the Assembly voted to raise seven battalions of volunteers for service in New York under Brigadier General James Wadsworth. With an eye to the morale of the troops in New York, the Assembly also voted to send forward "four hogsheads of rum, two hogsheads of molasses and two barrels of sugar for each of their respective regiments . . . the embargo on West Indies goods . . . notwithstanding." In the summer, as the British invasion of New York materialized, the governor, on advice of the Council, ordered no less than *fourteen* regiments of militia "to march immediately to New York, and there put themselves under the command of General Washington until the present exigency is over." Before the end of the summer, the governor and Council ordered out nine more militia regiments and two cavalry regiments for New York service, which left the state largely denuded of troops.[86]

Colonel Selleck Silliman, who had gone to New York in March, had written his relatives that the American fortifications were almost "impregnable," but this optimism, shared by many American officers, proved to be unfounded. Under cover of overwhelming naval strength, Lord Howe landed and soon afterward met the American army at the Battle of Long Island. This battle holds special interest for Connecticut because Washington previously had given Putnam overall field command. Putnam, unfamiliar both with the terrain and with most of his troops, allowed himself to be surprised by a British flanking attack. It should be pointed out also that Washington's handling of his army in this battle has been widely criticized by military experts. In the earlier stages of the battle many Connecticut men under Samuel H. Parsons fought courageously in a holding action, while Connecticut regiments of Jedediah Huntington had heavy casualties.[87]

Putnam's later Revolutionary career failed to match the dashing promise of Bunker Hill. Though Washington did not criticize his leadership at Long Island, he seems to have decided that Putnam should be employed chiefly in posts not requiring battlefield command — first in Philadelphia and later in Peekskill. The younger officers meanwhile tended to regard "Old Put" as an outdated military leader. Any chance of further battlefield distinction was ended when he suffered a paralytic stroke in 1779 and retired to his farm for the remainder of his life.[88]

After the Long Island defeat and the skillful evacuation of Long Island, serious morale problems rose among poorly disciplined American troops, and desertions became rife. The faint-hearted left in droves, with perhaps 6,000 out of 8,000 Connecticut militia deserting. Silliman minced no words in discussing the deserters:

. . . for as Well the Officers as the Men belonging to the Militia, behaved extreamly ill; and Officers of all Ranks & Privates kept deserting & running off, in a Most Shamefull Scandalous Manner; and some were taken sick and a great Many more pretended to be so. Colonel John Mead's regiment from the Stamford area dwindled from 600 to 74 men! Much more training and experience would be needed to instill a professional attitude in American soldiers.[89]

After Howe's army landed upon Manhattan Island the American army retreated ignominiously; and possibly Mrs. Robert Murray's gracious hospitality to General Howe and staff accidentally saved many American troops, including Colonel Silliman's brigade. The next day Lieutenant Colonel Thomas Knowlton, with his picked body of 120 men, called Knowlton's Rangers, set out to reconnoiter the enemy's lines. They contacted a British outpost and lively firing ensued. When a superior British detachment of light infantry pushed forward, Knowlton ably withdrew his men. Washington decided to cut off the British detachment. In the ensuing Battle of Harlem the British were defeated. Connecticut lost one of its finest officers, however, when Knowlton was mortally wounded. Washington, deeply regretting this loss, extolled Knowlton as "a brave and Gallant officer."[90]

This loss was quickly followed by the tragic death of Connecticut's most famous and cherished Revolutionary hero, Nathan Hale. In September 1776 Washington badly needed information about British dispositions and plans and sought a highly courageous man to penetrate the enemy lines in disguise to obtain this information. Hearing of the Commander's desire, Hale discussed it with his good friend Captain William Hull, who tried to dissuade him from playing the spy. Hale's reply was forceful:

I am fully sensible of the consequences of discovery

Statue of Nathan Hale in capitol (Karl Gerhardt, sculptor).

151

and capture in such a situation. But for a year I have been attached to the army, and have not rendered any material service, while receiving a compensation, for which I make no return. Yet I am not influenced by the expectation of promotion or pecuniary reward; I wish to be useful, and every kind of service, necessary to the public good, becomes honourable by being necessary. If the exigencies of my country demand a peculiar service, its claims to perform that service are imperious.[91]

Disguised as a Dutch schoolmaster, Hale obtained a boat to Huntington, Long Island, and from there walked to New York. Under unknown circumstances he was "apprehended" on the night of September 21, 1776. Taken before General Howe for questioning, Hale readily admitted his objective. Howe ordered his execution the following morning. According to Hull, who obtained his information from British Captain John Montresor, a witness to the execution on Sunday, September 22, 1776, Hale was "calm, and bore himself with gentle dignity, the consciousness of rectitude and high intentions." Refused a Bible or a clergyman, he wrote two letters, then went to the gallows. Before dying, he uttered his unforgettable words: "I only regret that I have but one life to lose for my country."[92]

Connecticut troops of Colonel Webb's regiment played a significant role in the check to Howe at White Plains, October 28–29, 1776. Many Connecticut soldiers participated in the highly successful surprise attack of Christmas 1776 upon the Hessians in Trenton. The next year, 1777, a general reorganization of the Continental army occurred, largely as a result of Washington's persistent demands for long-term soldiers. It still proved impossible, however, to procure more than a minority of men needed for three years or for the duration. In 1777 Connecticut provided about ten and one-half regiments of infantry, one of cavalry, five artillery companies, and two Wyoming Valley companies; and with great difficulty it kept the Connecticut line at about this strength for most of the remainder of the war.[93]

Reluctant Soldiers

BOUNTIES and other devices were used in the difficult task of filling the state's quota. In May 1777 any two men who obtained a recruit for the Connecticut line for three years, or for the duration, would be themselves exempt from service for that period. In 1777, 1778, and 1779 bounties of such amounts as two, six, ten, and up to forty pounds, in addition to any Continental bounty and regular pay, were offered.[94]

The low rates of pay and dizzying inflation made the soldier's lot particularly unenviable. After six months' service in 1780, Oliver Boardman of Middletown wrote in his *Journal:* "My wages when Rec'd. would not pay the expence of food on My road to the North & back One of my Company Mates gave $100 Dollars for 10 lb Flax 3 Coppers would buy a [Paper] Dollar"[95]

Another powerful deterrent to military service was the inadequate care of the sick and wounded. As John Adams explained it, "Disease has destroyed ten men for us where the sword of the enemy has killed one." It is easy to understand why men with large families either stayed at home or deserted. Unfortunately, too many deserted without good reason; and a surprising number from all states carried home considerably more than their own belongings.[96]

The County Court records illuminate the problems of desertion and failure to report for duty, and the punishments meted out. At one session of the New Haven County Court early in 1777, sixty-eight men were tried for failure to march. Sixty were found guilty by the jury and were sentenced to pay a fine of ten pounds, plus costs, usually one to three pounds. Eight were declared not guilty and were released without payment of costs. In September 1777 the court was swamped by 167 cases. In 1778 the number of cases remained large, but after that they declined sharply.[97]

In Fairfield County the problem assumed greater magnitude. General Silliman, chief of the county militia and state's attorney for the county, noted in 1777 that on every militia call "all the Tories and great Numbers of others, would not march but stay at Home about their Business; and that it produced great Uneasiness among them that did March, that such as did not, were not punished off hand in some Way or other." On May 10, 1777, Silliman wrote Trumbull that there were about 1,200 "Military Delinquencies in the

County unprosecuted at Law." He proposed legislation whereby such deliquents in the future could be forcibly escorted to their duty! The proposal was approved in the Upper House, but failed in the Lower House. As Silliman clearly pointed out, the customary procedures hopelessly clogged the courts and still failed to deter many. Silliman's strong sentiments undoubtedly stemmed from the dismal militia turnout in the fall of 1777 when from 1,900 to 2,000 were called, with only 117 on duty in December and a maximum of 203 privates earlier. Silliman admitted that the recent British raid on Danbury, fear of future raids, and low pay were discouraging many from military life.[98]

Military Developments on Many Fronts

IN MAY 1777 Colonel Return Jonathan Meigs of Middletown led one of the most daring actions of the war — that against Sag Harbor, Long Island. From Sachem's Head, Guilford, he took four hundred men across the Sound in whaleboats. Meigs's force completely surprised the heavily armed British, scuttled twelve ships, killed six, captured ninety, and carried off large amounts of provisions. Meigs's men were back on Connecticut soil within twenty-four hours without a single casualty. An impressed Congress voted Meigs a sword and a memorial.[99]

Some Connecticut soldiers remained with the northern American army continuously after the unsuccessful Quebec attack of December 1775. In the army at Fort Ticonderoga in 1776 was Colonel Charles Burrell's Connecticut regiment. Many ship carpenters from Connecticut helped in building the small Lake Champlain fleet which Arnold used ably but unsuccessfully against a larger British fleet in October 1776.[100]

In 1777 Burgoyne's push southward spurred the gathering of militia in opposition. In the first Saratoga battle, at Freeman's Farm on September 19, 1777, Arnold's left wing included Connecticut militia under Colonels Thaddeus Cook and Jonathan Lattimer. Thanks to Arnold's zeal and courage, Gates's bungling leadership did not prevent an American victory. In the decisive battle at Bemis Heights, Connecticut men again fought in the thick of the fray. Arnold, after a bitter quarrel with

Gates, had lost his command prior to this battle; but the sight of violent fighting proved too much for Arnold, who galloped into the very center of the swirling battle. His appearance supplied the spark needed to ignite the American troops. Men from New London and Norwich in Learned's brigade, as they prepared to attack, spotted Arnold and cheered lustily. Waving his sword to acknowledge this tribute, Arnold responded, "God bless you! . . . Now come on, boys; if the day is long enough, we'll have them all in hell before night." After two daring but unsuccessful onslaughts against the enemy, Arnold then led Learned's men in an irresistible charge against Canadians and Indians screening Breymann's position. Next he placed himself at the head of some riflemen and infantry to spearhead a fierce charge against Breymann's entrenchments. As the Americans broke into the great redoubt the Germans fired one last volley. Arnold's horse was killed and, as he fell with the animal, a wounded German shot him in the same leg which had taken a ball in Quebec. Heedless of the excruciating pain, Arnold shouted to those following him: "Rush on, my brave boys." When an American started to bayonet the wounded German, Arnold protested, "He's a fine fellow — don't hurt him!" A little later, as evening came on, four soldiers picked Arnold up and carried him to shelter. Henry Dearborn, who had shared the privations of the march to Quebec, came up and asked Arnold where he was hit. Arnold replied, "In the same leg. I wish it had been my heart."[101]

Shortly after this engagement Burgoyne capitulated to Gates and jubilation reigned among the Americans. Oliver Boardman reflected this joy as he entered in his *Journal*:

The Hand of Providence work'd wonderfully In favor of America this Day. . . . It was a glorious sight to see the haughty Brittons march out & Surrender their arms to an Army which but a little before, they despis'd & called paltroons . . .

Many authorities have considered this American victory the turning point of the war, for it led directly to the decisive French Alliance of 1778.[102]

During the remainder of the conflict Connecticut men played a part in nearly all of the battles and movements of the Continental army, except for the southern campaigns. Six regiments were involved in the grim encounter at Germantown. The next year, 1778, General Jedediah Huntington's brigade fought well at the torrid Battle of Monmouth in New Jersey. In another sector, Rhode Island, Colonel Samuel B. Webb's regiment engaged in the battle of August 29, 1778, as did two militia regiments, those of Colonels Samuel Chapman and Samuel McClellan. In the winter of 1778–79 the main encampment of the Connecticut line was located at Redding. Although the next summer saw little fighting, two brigades were sent to the Connecticut coast in response to Tryon's second raid, but the British made good their escape.[103]

Fighting under "Mad Anthony" Wayne, Return Jonathan Meigs took a leading part in the midnight assault of July 15–16, 1779, against the strong British fort at Stony Point on the Hudson. Through the audacious direction of a hand-picked Connecticut light infantry regiment of four hundred men, Meigs contributed greatly to this important American victory.[104]

On November 21, 1780, Major Benjamin Tallmadge of Litchfield, leading two companies of Connecticut dismounted dragoons, about eighty men in all, set out in eight small boats on a raid against the British outpost at Brookhaven on Long Island. A violent storm precluded an attack the next day, but at dawn on the twenty-third the American raiders, with fixed bayonets, quickly captured the entire garrison and destroyed the works and stores at a cost of only one casualty.[105]

The disclosure, in September 1780, of Arnold's treason was a terrible shock to all Patriots — especially to those of Connecticut, his native state. Arnold's motivation was complex — frustrated ambition, burning anger at Congress' lack of justice and efficiency, the influence of his wife, Peggy Shippen, love of money, hatred of the French alliance, and above all, serious deficiencies of character. Fortunately the plot was discovered in time to save West Point, which Arnold planned to deliver to the British; but the treason of one of the country's most gifted generals brought profound gloom and anger to all, from Washington down. Arnold escaped to the British and received a high monetary reward from them. Later in the war he commanded British raiding expeditions against Virginia and New London, Connecticut.[106]

In the last years of the war Connecticut soldiers saw less of the enemy as the focus of fighting shifted to the south, although in 1781 ten companies from Connecticut were detached for service in Virginia under Lafayette. The fighting in Virginia proved difficult, and Lafayette's army was in grave danger more than once. In July a battalion of light infantry, under Major John Wyllys of Connecticut, took part in the hot engagement at Jamestown which was nearly disastrous for the outnumbered American army.[107]

In the north, meanwhile, Washington, seeking to strike a decisive blow, held important conferences at Joseph Webb's spacious home in Wethersfield. On Sunday, May 20, the General enjoyed "a good deal of private conversation with Govr. Trumbull," and in the next two days Washington and Rochambeau devised plans for a joint attack

Oliver Wolcott home at Litchfield (built 1753). It is believed that a gilded lead statue of George III was brought here in 1776 from New York City and melted down into about 42,000 cartridges for the Patriot cause.

Connecticut ship Defence.

against New York. The attack upon New York proved impracticable, and later in the summer Washington turned to plans for the Yorktown campaign, where, with the aid of De Grasse's fleet and French troops, he planned a pincers movement to trap Cornwallis' army in Yorktown.[108]

Washington's small army which now hastened southward to Virginia included some Connecticut light infantry. On the night of October 14, 1781, twenty soldiers from the Fourth Connecticut Regiment, led by Lieutenant John Mansfield, headed an impetuous charge against a British redoubt on the York River. Other forces followed and soon the redoubt fell. As a result of this capture and that of a nearby redoubt by the French, the besiegers were able to complete their second parallel of fortifications, which made Cornwallis' position extremely precarious. On October 19, 1781, the British commander surrendered his entire army, and American independence was at last assured.

Governor Trumbull's diary captured the Patriot mood:

Friday [October] 26th [1781] — About 7 o'Clo. in the eveng. recd The hand Bill from D. Govr Bowen, of the surrender of Ld Cornwallis & his Army — 9000 men, Seamen included — quantity of Warlike Stores — 1,40 Gun Ship — 1 frigate about one hundred Transports praised be the Ld of Hosts

No further large battles occurred, diplomatic negotiations began, the preliminary articles of peace were signed on November 30, 1782, and the definitive Peace of Paris on September 3, 1783.[109]

In proportion to its modest 200,000 population Connecticut's total military contribution had been very large. It appears that about 38,000 men saw military service of some kind, and about 40 percent of these became full-fledged Continentals. Because of the unreliable and incomplete condition of the Continental rolls and the great variety of lengths of service, it is virtually impossible to make a precise comparison of Connecticut's manpower contribution with that of other states. In proportion to population, however, there can be little doubt that Connecticut ranked among the leading states in manpower provided.[110]

Connecticut's State Navy

CONNECTICUT'S navy, having its inception in an act of July 1, 1775, grew as the war progressed until a total of thirteen ships saw service — the brigantines *Minerva* and *Old Defence*, the ships *Oliver Cromwell* and *Defence*, the sloops *Guilford* and *Schuyler*, the schooners *Spy* and *Mifflin*, the brig *America*, and the row galleys *Crane*, *New Defence*, *Shark*, and *Whiting*.[111]

The *Oliver Cromwell*, largest full-rigged ship built for the state, was constructed at Essex by Uriah Hayden, an experienced shipbuilder. The ship was launched on June 13, 1776, and on August

Shaw mansion in New London (built 1756).

18, under Captain William Coit, sailed out of the Connecticut River to New London. Under Captain Seth Harding, with a crew of 150 men, the ship began cruising in June 1777. Soon Harding brought in the first prize, the brig *Honour*, with a cargo valued at over £10,000. During the next two years eight more British ships were taken. Luck finally ran out in June 1779 when three British ships attacked the Connecticut vessel, and after a fierce two-hour battle, Harding's successor, Captain Timothy Parker, surrendered his battered ship.[112]

Even more successful was the state ship *Defence*, commanded first by Seth Harding. Scarcely a month after beginning its first cruise the *Defence* captured three British transports carrying 330 officers and men. Captain Harding's health forced him to retire temporarily and Samuel Smedley succeeded him. Lengthened and transformed from a brig into a ship, the *Defence* cruised over vast areas of the Atlantic, from Newfoundland to the Windward Islands. Intercepted by a vastly superior British squadron in March 1779, Captain Smedley tried desperately to reach New London's harbor, but in cutting across a reef, wrecked the ship — a sad finale for a ship which had captured thirteen enemy vessels.[113]

The schooner *Spy*, of only fifty tons, performed yeoman service in checking illicit trade on the Sound and seeking prizes. After taking rich prizes, the *Spy* sailed from Stonington in 1778 carrying a ratified copy of the treaty with France, and arrived safely at Brest in twenty-one days. Unfortunately, on the return voyage the little schooner and her crew of thirty fell victim to the British.[114]

In 1777, two ships were built for the Continental navy — the *Trumbull* and the *Confederacy*. The *Trumbull*, a thirty-six-gun frigate of 700 tons, was constructed at Chatham on the Connecticut River and had difficulty getting over Saybrook Bar. It sailed on its first cruise under Captain Dudley Saltonstall of New London. In June 1780 the *Trumbull* took part in a bloody three-hour battle with the British warship *Watt*, which ended with both ships nearly helpless from damages. Sometime later the *Trumbull*, disabled by a storm, was compelled to surrender by two British men-of-war. The *Confederacy*, a "jinxed" vessel fell victim to the first British warships she encountered.[115]

In July 1776 the Assembly appointed Nathaniel Shaw agent "for the purpose of naval supplies and for taking care of such sick seamen as may be sent on shore to his care." In October 1778 they made Shaw "Marine Agent," which involved equipping all state naval craft, giving sailing orders, and overseeing disposal of prizes.[116]

The little state fleet took forty-one British prizes with valuable cargoes and prisoners, supplemented the protection given the Connecticut coast by the coastal batteries, helped break up water-

156

borne illicit trade, and gave needed employment to many unemployed seamen. The men of Connecticut's little navy matched their skill against the experienced "tars" and officers of Britain's navy — the world's largest — and made a highly creditable record.[117]

David Bushnell of Saybrook attracted much attention by his invention in 1775 of a man-propelled submarine. Built of oak beams, it was dubbed "Bushnell's (American) Turtle," as it resembled the upper shell of two turtles joined together. He convinced the Council of Safety that his invention was practical and won strong support for several years. In trials the submarine worked well, but in three attempts against British warships it failed completely. Although Bushnell attributed the failure to incompetence of the operator, growing popular ridicule caused him to abandon the promising project. He well deserves the title "father of the American submarine."[118]

Connecticut Privateers Strike Heavy Blows

EARLY in the war privateering became a leading American weapon against Great Britain. The overwhelming size of Britain's navy made it virtually hopeless for the American navy seriously to challenge it, but the vast British merchant marine provided an alluring target. Hundreds of American vessels, moreover, idled by the disruption of commerce and the growing blockade, were available as privateers. The typical shipowner, faced by the grim choice of letting his ships rot at anchor or having them commissioned as privateers, often chose privateering.

In November 1775, and the following spring, Congress passed legislation authorizing itself and the states to commission privateers. In Connecticut the state normally took one-half the net proceeds of a prize, and the owner(s), officers, and crew split the other half. In May 1776 Connecticut passed an act permitting Trumbull to fill the blank commissions "for Private Ships of War and Letters of Marque and Reprizal" sent by Congress. The regular County Courts received jurisdiction over all cases involving captures.[119]

The British historian G. O. Trevelyan succinctly explained privateering's attractiveness: "they now fastened eagerly upon an occupation which had an appearance of reconciling the claims of patriotic duty with the attractions of an adventurous life, and the prospect of enormous gains."[120]

In the course of the war Connecticut sent out between two hundred and three hundred privateers. New London led, but New Haven, Wethersfield, Middletown, Hartford, Saybrook, and East Haddam also dispatched large numbers.[121]

The configuration of Long Island and nearby coasts made it easy to blockade New London and all Connecticut ports. On June 19, 1776, Nathaniel Shaw wrote in depressed vein to a Philadelphia friend that "Att Presst I think their is no Chance of Escaping the Men of Warr." Despite the blockade, many privateers were fitted out, enticing advertisements appeared, and crews were quickly signed up. Sir George Collier, Commodore of the British fleet in New England waters from 1776 to 1779, pictured New London's position: "The place was a famous receptacle for Privateers, and was thought on that account to injure the British trade as much as any harbour in America."[122]

Some privateers had a single owner, but often numerous individuals took up small "shares" to spread the risks. The blockade remained so tight in much of 1776 and 1777 that months passed without a single prize, and many privateers were captured. The *American Revenue*, owned by Nathaniel Shaw and Company, enjoyed fabulous success in taking thirteen prizes in 1777–79, but in August 1779 the British frigate *Greyhound* terminated the privateer's gaudy career. In May 1779 alone, eighteen prizes were carried into New London. In 1781 the state ship *Minerva* brought in the *Hannah* with a cargo estimated to be worth £80,000, the greatest single prize taken by a Connecticut privateer. Arnold's raid, in September 1781, caused great havoc, but it did not wipe out New London's privateer fleet.[123]

As the main British effort shifted southward in 1778 some relaxation of the New England blockade occurred. The years 1779 and 1780 saw the highest level of privateering. In 1781 the privateers continued quite busy, after which their numbers tapered off. Frequent newspaper notices of the sale of prize goods in the 1778–82 period attested the successes of Connecticut privateers.[124]

In the later years of the war privateering interfered with recruitment for the Continental army, navy, and the state forces. In May 1781 Colonel William Ledyard of New London wrote Trumbull that his two artillery companies had failed to fill up because "the great number of Privateers that have been fitted out this season with the great success they have had has taken almost all the men away that would leave home from this quarter." Privateering produced a strong impact in numerous port towns, where it brought excitement and, occasionally, rich earnings. No seaport, however, grew wealthy from privateering — not even New London, which languished below peacetime economic levels. It is probable that a majority of investors lost money, as privateering afforded a poor substitute for peacetime overseas and coastal trade. Connecticut's achievements, while far below Massachusetts', were impressive — nearly five hundred British ships brought into Connecticut ports, plus some taken to other friendly ports. The heavy British losses from American privateers undoubtedly hastened the war's end.[125]

Connecticut: "The Provisions State"

WHEN the Revolution broke out probably not one Connecticut leader foresaw that the state would become a leading source of provisions for the American forces. From the start able men played leading roles in the supply organization. Captain Joseph Trumbull provided highly efficient direction as first state Commissary General, and Elijah Hubbard of Middletown and Jeremiah Wadsworth of Hartford later held the leading commissary posts.

In May 1775 the Assembly took a step which deeply affected future supply problems. It adopted the following daily ration for each soldier: three-quarters of a pound of pork or one pound of beef, one pound of bread or flour, and three pints of beer to each man per day, also "one jill of rum to each man upon fatigue per day . . . milk, molasses, candles, soap, vinegar, coffee, chocolate, sugar, tobacco, onions in their season, and vegetables." Each week's ration should include, in addition, half a pint of rice or a pint of corn meal, six ounces of butter, and three pints of

peas or beans. These items would be the ones sought assiduously by the commissaries, who received a commission of 1½ percent upon all supplies purchased. Interestingly enough, Connecticut's ration strongly influenced that adopted by the Continental army in August 1775.[126]

In supplying the militia, the state held the selectmen of each town responsible for raising the town's quota. The state commissaries collected the town contributions, co-ordinated their efforts, and did additional purchasing. In December 1776 the Assembly selected Jeremiah Wadsworth as "Commissary of Supplies," with six principal assistants.[127]

In procuring supplies, fixed quotas were allotted to each town, based upon that town's assessed valuation. In October 1776, when the legislature ordered for the militia 2,000 tents, 2,000 iron pots, 4,000 wooden bowls, and 6,000 canteens, it requested of each town that it provide one tent, one pot, two bowls, and three canteens for each £1,000 on its general list. Late that fall a blanket shortage developed among the Connecticut soldiers in the Continental army, so that each town was asked for one blanket per £500 of the list. If necessary, impressment could be employed to obtain the quota. The following March the Continental army, desperately short of blankets, requested those collected earlier by the Connecticut towns, and the Council, without hesitation, ordered the selectmen to make them available for use by Connecticut Continentals.[128]

In May 1777 the Council selected Elijah Hubbard of Middletown as "Commissary and Superintendent of the stores of supplies and refreshments" for Connecticut's Continental troops. In elaborate instructions the Council directed Hubbard to load rum, sugar, molasses, and clothing from state stores and transport them to the Continental army at Peekskill. He could impress teams and boats as required and must keep careful accounts of all transactions.[129]

The records of town meetings indicate that most towns set up a special committee on the care of soldiers' families. Actually no charity was involved under the act of October 1777 which ordered towns to provide provisions and clothing at legal prices, since the individual soldier must deposit a sum up to one-half his pay, against which the town could draw. When necessary, officials could impress needed items at legal prices.[130]

In April 1777 Norwich voted to supply necessities to soldiers' families at legal prices if the committee received adequate funds from the men concerned. In December the town recommended to the local ministers that they call for a special offering of clothing, provisions, and money for the families of soldiers. In Middletown the size of the special committee corresponded almost exactly to the number of Continentals in service at the time, and each committeeman usually looked after one specific family.[131]

The supply effort was hampered by the difficulty of recruiting teamsters because of bad roads, severe exposure, and slow pay. The journal of Joseph Joslin, Jr., of Killingly, gives a vivid picture of the rugged life led by a state teamster in 1777 and 1778. For his back-breaking employment he received fifteen dollars monthly. Often it was difficult to secure enough oxen or carts, and the roads became impassable quagmires in late winter and early spring. Some teamsters, moreover, hauling valuable loads, yielded to the temptation of embezzlement, and vanished. Yet the teamsters, as a whole, made a vital contribution to the war effort.[132]

Food and clothing shortages of the Continental army were occasionally serious when Joseph Trumbull was Commissary General, but after his resignation in August 1777 conditions rapidly worsened under his successor, William Buchanan. Eventually, appalled at the chronic mismanagement, Congress turned again to a Connecticut supply expert. On April 9, 1778, Jeremiah Wadsworth assumed control as Continental Commissary General of Purchases, and served with distinction until December 2, 1779. Wadsworth's success stemmed in part from his excellent experience as a merchant and state commissary. He retained, moreover, many of the experienced deputy commissaries, such as Henry Champion, Peter Colt, and Jacob Cuyler, who had ably served earlier in Connecticut. Wadsworth and state authorities worked together smoothly and Wadsworth undoubtedly obtained more Connecticut supplies than any outsider could have done. Dur-

ing the winter of 1778–79 Washington reported that his troops were much better fed and clad than in the previous three winters.[133]

When French forces came to Rhode Island in July 1780 a new chapter in Connecticut's supply efforts commenced. Inevitably the French commissaries, well stocked with specie, turned to Connecticut farmers, who, offered gold by the French, and Continental paper money by Continental or state agents, reacted as one might expect![134]

A large number of skilled Connecticut commissaries resigned and flocked into French employment. Jeremiah Wadsworth led this defection and formed a highly lucrative partnership with John M. Carter of Newport.[135]

A picturesque chapter in French relations with Connecticut centered about the encampment at Lebanon of the Duke de Lauzun, four hundred hussars, and two companies of foot soldiers from November 1780 to June 1781. The location was chosen partly because the neighborhood was an excellent supply center. Very friendly conditions prevailed, and Lauzun found food and forage cheap and plentiful.[136]

For geographical reasons the largest profits in the French supply trade went to eastern Connecticut, with most supplies going by water from New London. The contractors and hundreds of individual farmers profited greatly from the French business. At times an unfortunate imbalance developed whereby the French were glutted with meat while Washington's army on the Hudson almost starved! Eventually, after several interstate discussions and Franco-American meetings, the rivalry between French and American supply agents was partially resolved.[137]

Perhaps the best indication of Connecticut's pre-eminent position as a supply state is found in Washington's very frequent appeals to Trumbull for help in provisions. The horrors of Valley Forge require no elaboration. Washington, in desperation, wrote Trumbull on February 6, 1778, that the army faced dissolution, since no provisions could be obtained in the middle states. Trumbull immediately ordered Commissaries Henry Champion and Peter Colt to take $200,000, earlier allocated to cattle purchases, and scour the countryside for live beef. The cattle were driven in herds by Champion and his son to Valley Forge. The first herd was devoured within five days by the ravenous soldiers![138]

The next two winters saw nearly as critical shortages. From Morristown, in January 1780, the Commander wrote Trumbull, referred to Connecticut as his chief meat source, and spotlighted the state's failure to meet its quota. In May he ascribed the state's deficiency partly to lack of money and a change in commissaries, but he still hoped that Champion would forward enough beef. The unhappy climax came a few days later when mutiny, induced chiefly by lack of food (meat especially), broke out among two regiments of the Connecticut line. Only the most determined efforts by officers prevented wholesale desertion.[139]

*Appalling Supply Deficiencies
Intermixed with Successes*

THE supply failures did not stem from any lack of legislation. An act of October 1778 bestowed upon commissaries and selectmen widespread powers in purchasing or impressing supplies. Almost every session from 1779 to 1782 saw at least one new act. In April 1780 Henry Champion was given general supervision over all food-buying for the Continental army. The winter of 1780–81 unfortunately brought another grave crisis, and on April 10, 1781, Washington wrote Trumbull that there was "no prospect of immediate relief, but from the salted provisions of Connecticut." Washington followed up his plea by dispatching to Connecticut General Heath, who described to the Assembly the dire lack of beef and climaxed his catalogue of hardships by noting that rum was so scarce that "men on the severest fatigue had nothing but water to drink." The solons responded by voting to send 1,000 barrels of salt beef and pork and twenty hogsheads of rum. In addition, they appropriated £2,000 for the purchase of beef cattle by Champion. The appalling situation of the Continentals was not really relieved, however, until shortly before the army began its famous march to Virginia.[140]

The Congressional requisitions of June 1780 give an excellent idea as to how Congress rated Connecticut's supply potential. These requisitions were laid upon ten states (excluding the Carolinas and Georgia). Connecticut ranked as follows: first in beef, salt, and oxen; second in bacon; and third in flour, grain, horses, and rum; which overall signified a position among the top two or three supply states![141]

Despite strenuous efforts, the inadequate delivery of foodstuffs persisted. Major reasons included: *1*] lack of basic authority by the central and state governments and consequent failures to enforce the supply laws; *2*] Congressional tardiness in making requisitions; *3*] slow payment to farmers; *4*] rivalry between Continental and state (and later French) commissaries; *5*] activities of profiteers; *6*] diversion of some supplies to the enemy — chiefly from Fairfield County; and *7*] serious currency depreciation. Peter Colt, an enterprising commissary, pleaded for greater powers, especially to seize hoarded supplies, and he described the shameful practices of shrewd speculators who bought up scarce supplies to heighten prices and boost profits.[142]

Connecticut appears to have been far more successful in providing clothing, which involved smaller costs, since much was made in the soldiers' homes at no cost to the state. Furthermore, Connecticut ordinarily clothed only its own men, whereas it raised and forwarded food for far more than its own troops.

Ordinarily the state assigned each town a quota of clothing, put the pressure upon the selectmen, and later reimbursed the towns at fixed prices for all clothing actually supplied. Even at Valley Forge Connecticut troops did not leave any bloody footprints on the snow! On March 31, 1778, Washington wrote Trumbull from Valley Forge:

Among the troops returned unfit for duty for want of clothing, none of your State are included. The care of your legislature in providing clothing and necessaries of all kinds for their men is highly laudable, and reflects the greatest honor upon their patriotism and humanity.

Although the amounts spent upon clothing and related items failed to approach that appropriated for provisions, a single action in January 1780 by the Pay Table (treasury) involved advancement of

£100,000 to Chauncey Whittlesey for purchase of officers' uniforms. On the whole, Connecticut troops, despite many complaints, were warmly and adequately clothed, thanks particularly to the Council of Safety.[143]

"The Financial Merry-Go-Round"

THE Revolution, like most wars, proved expensive and precipitated serious financial problems. In Connecticut the war entailed unprecedented financial burdens and necessitated the issuance of record-breaking quantities of paper money. The emission of paper money began on April 26, 1775, when £50,000 was ordered printed, to be paid off in two years by special taxes. The next month £50,000 more was voted, and the losing race between expenditures and paper money had begun. As the war dragged on paper issues skyrocketed, and the grand total for the 1775–83 period approximated £1,200,000 — a huge sum in an age when specie was very scarce. Bad as the situation became, Connecticut's total was exceeded by six states. Its neighbor, Massachusetts, issued over £13,000,000. In theory the issues were supposed to be retired quickly by taxation, but in practice very little was paid off during the war.[144]

Despite higher taxes and some aid from Congress, the state treasury remained in a sadly depleted situation. Taxes were raised considerably over the annual prewar average of one- to twopence on the pound. In August 1777 and again in October 1777 a tax of one shilling on the pound was levied, payable by November 1, 1777, and April 15, 1778, respectively. A vicious circle quickly developed. Large paper issues begat steady inflation; prices rose rapidly; the currency steadily depreciated; and, finally, higher taxes and more paper money were needed to cover even more inflated war expenses. Occasionally farsighted leaders, like Sherman, spoke up for much heavier taxation to curb inflation and currency depreciation, but their unpopular advice found few takers, especially in the Assembly.[145]

The depreciation of paper money gradually speeding up, despite severe laws, finally hurtled completely out of control in 1779 and 1780. On December 16, 1779, President Stiles reported that Yale students had been dismissed because the steward's allowance could not provide enough food at current prices. Little wonder, as the Continental paper had "fallen near a quarter within 3 Weeks or a month past." Finally Congress reluctantly recognized the financial chaos and, in March 1780, devalued the currency to one-fortieth of face value. The Connecticut Assembly adopted the Congressional table. This drastic devaluation promptly destroyed whatever public confidence remained. On May 2, 1781, President Stiles noted: "At Philad[elphi]a a Continental is 150 for 1. At New Haven 100 for 1. At Boston 130 for 1. — All running into Confusion & Crisis as to money!"[146]

In newspaper columns ardent laissez-faire advocates advised complete freedom, with prices finding their own level, while others saw one particular class or another as chief culprit. "Cato" in the *Courant* lambasted rich farmers, "those GREAT BUGS whose eyes stood out with fatness, and who have collops of fat on their flanks." Another writer vigorously denounced the legislature for voting expenditures of £500,000 but "totally neglecting to provide any means to furnish one half that sum to redeem it." Several noted the influence of the law of supply and demand, and others observed how debtors benefited from the rapid inflation. Illustrative of the price rise, the cost of both beef and wheat had multiplied about sixfold from 1775 to 1778.[147]

Persons on rigidly fixed salaries, such as clergymen, suffered greatly. This was vividly revealed in the Reverend Nathan Strong's letters to his Hartford parishioners in 1779. He explained that he was in dire financial straits because his salary had already fallen one-half in purchasing value. Unless speedy relief was given, he would be compelled to resign.[148]

From November 1776 on, the state resorted to sweeping control of prices of foodstuffs, labor, and so on, and as time passed, increased the scope and stringency of the regulations. Despite every effort, however, prices merrily climbed upward.[149]

At the very time that public expenditures rose steeply the assessment lists of Connecticut towns declined, as representative figures below reveal:

Town	Oct. 1774 List	Jan. 1782 List	Percent Change 1774–82	Percent Population Change 1774–82
New Haven	£ 72,395	£ 58,461	−19	−4
New London	36,424	29,052	−20	−3
Danbury	30,113	27,973	−6	+9
Fairfield	51,005	41,771	−18	+8
Salisbury	15,880	18,218	+15	+12
Litchfield	22,865	26,887	+18	+20
Hartford	49,036	42,846	−13	+8
Norwich	68,649	59,772	−13	0
	£346,367	£304,980	−12	+3

In the first four towns, those hit by British raids, the average of assessments fell nearly 18 percent; in the other four, less than 6 percent.[150]

The mode of assessment employed in Connecticut tended to bear most heavily upon the person of modest economic status. Heavy reliance was placed upon a poll tax (£18 per male, sixteen to seventy years old), and upon land and livestock. A 6 percent tax upon income of merchants, manufacturers, and craftsmen, and a penalty for engrossing (£50) passed in August 1777, seem to have been the only types of wartime tax aimed at tapping unusual profits.[151]

By 1781 paper bills had depreciated to such an extent that they nearly ceased to circulate. Philadelphia speculators brought a large amount of paper money into New England, where it had been worth more and, as a result, the paper money virtually became worthless. In newspaper advertisements of late 1781 and 1782 an increasing percentage of merchants demanded hard money.[152]

Interstate Wartime Trade

THE war produced a marked impact upon Connecticut's American and foreign trade. The British blockade of the Sound and Atlantic coastal waters created very dangerous conditions and inevitably curtailed trade sharply, especially with more distant points. The customs records of entries and clearances at New Haven for much of 1776–79 indicate that fifty-nine coasting ships entered the harbor, of which nearly one-half came from Massachusetts, slightly under one-fifth from Rhode Island, and one-third from other Connecticut ports. The main feature is the comparative *smallness* of the trade every year.[153]

Most of Connecticut's trade with her neighbors took a special form — that of the "permit" trade, which involved permits to export or import despite the embargo laws. Hundreds of petitions, usually from out-of-staters, to export embargoed provisions from Connecticut, were considered and a substantial proportion were approved. In the May 1779 Assembly session alone thirty-nine petitions were approved for export of embargoed goods to Massachusetts. A typical petition follows:

This Assembly do grant liberty to James Church to purchase in this State forty bushels of indian corn and rye for Henderson Inches, Esqr, and others of Boston committee for supplying the poor of that town, and transport the same, together with forty bushels of indian corn and eighteen bushels of rye already purchased . . . for the persons and purpose aforesaid.[154]

In the papers of Nathaniel Shaw of New London one finds evidence of considerable commercial activity with other states despite wartime hazards. In the last four months of 1776 his records reveal transactions with numerous firms in Massachusetts and Rhode Island, and with one each in Albany, Sag Harbor (New York), Philadelphia, and New Bern (North Carolina).[155]

For geographical reasons the Massachusetts trade almost entirely followed four routes: 1] to and from Long Island Sound ports by boat; 2] from Connecticut River towns upstream to Springfield and vicinity; 3] from these towns downstream and along the coast to Boston and other nearby coastal towns; and 4] a slight amount by land from northeastern Connecticut. It is very likely that most of the trade proceeded by water, with frequent interruptions by British warships.

Trade with Rhode Island chiefly involved Connecticut coastal towns east of the Connecticut River, and Connecticut and Thames River towns. Some goods were exchanged by land also. Among his far-flung operations, the prominent Nicholas Brown of Providence carried on important commercial transactions with Job and Samuel Taber of New London, who acted as his commission agents.[156]

After British seizure of New York City in 1776, legal trade with New York State shifted northward to land routes, over which supplies flowed to Washington's army. From Hartford, Middletown, and Danbury provisions went in a steady stream to Newburgh, Fishkill, Rhinebeck, and other Hudson River points. This supply business made up most of Connecticut's trade with New York, but civilian trade did exist too, particularly of the special "permit" sort, though less than with Massachusetts and Rhode Island.[157]

Trade with areas north of Massachusetts and south of New York ranked as slight in volume and significance. Occasionally Connecticut ships, such as those of Nathaniel or Thomas Shaw from New London, sailed to Philadelphia.[158]

Farther south only two states had any appreciable trade with Connecticut — North and South Carolina. The port of Roanoke (North Carolina) records reveal occasional clearances of Nutmeg ships. From July 1775 to July 1776, five ships stopped there, of which at least four were breaking a longer trip to the West Indies. Stops were infrequently made also in Charleston, South Carolina, usually to pick up rice. In 1779 Nehemiah Hubbard of Middletown organized such a trip.[159]

The Caribbean and European Trade

THE very prosperous West Indian trade was sharply curtailed by the British blockade, as the newspapers attested:

Last Sunday Evening, Capt. Bunnel in a Schooner belonging to New Haven; arrived here in 10 Days from St. Thomas's, with a Cargo of Rum and Sugar . . . Capt. Bunnel informs, That Capt. John Bulkley, belonging to Wethersfield, Capt. French from the western part of this State, and Capt. Brintnal in the Sloop

Wooster, from New Haven, are taken and carried into the West Indies.[160]

On the West Indian routes, ships, while keeping a sharp lookout for the Union Jack, carried cargoes similar to those of the prewar era. When the ship *Polly*, Master Timothy Tuttle, cleared New Haven harbor on January 11, 1777, bound for Martinique, it carried a typical cargo of lumber, horses, oxen, sheep, hogs, poultry, corn, and fish. In that entire year only about six vessels seem to have left New Haven for the West Indies, and a dozen to all foreign ports. War needs periodically required concentration upon import of critically needed articles, such as salt or powder. In 1776 and 1777 the state chartered at least eighteen ships to obtain salt in the West Indies.[161]

The chief West Indian ports visited by Connecticut mariners during the war included: French Guadeloupe, Martinique and St. Dominique; Spanish Grenada and Hispaniola; Dutch St. Eustatius; and Danish St. Croix and St. Thomas. The entry of France, Holland, and then Spain into the war, in 1778, 1780, and 1781 respectively, both aided and complicated the West Indian situation.

Advertisement of S. Austen and Company.

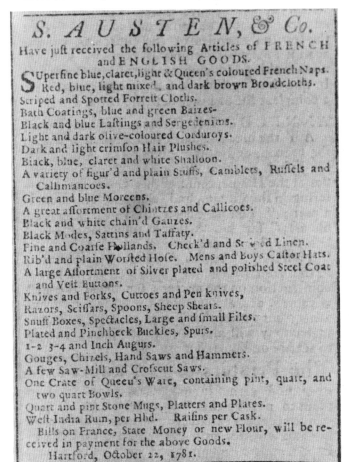

S. AUSTEN, & Co.
Have just received the following Articles of FRENCH and ENGLISH GOODS.

SUperfine blue, claret, light & Queen's coloured French Naps. Red, blue, light mixed, and dark brown Broadcloths.
Striped and Spotted Forrest Cloths.
Bath Coatings, blue and green Baizes.
Black and blue Lastings and Sergedenims.
Light and dark olive-coloured Corduroys.
Dark and light crimson Hair Plushes.
Black, blue, claret and white Shalloon.
A variety of figur'd and plain Stuffs, Camblets, Russels and Calimancoes.
Green and blue Moreens.
A great assortment of Chintzes and Callicoes.
Black and white chain'd Gauzes.
Black Modes, Sattins and Taffaty.
Fine and Coarse Hollands. Check'd and Striped Linen.
Rib'd and plain Worsted Hose. Mens and Boys Castor Hats.
A large Assortment of Silver plated and polished Steel Coat and Vest Buttons.
Knives and Forks, Cuttoes and Pen knives,
Razors, Scissars, Spoons, Sheep Shears.
Snuff Boxes, Spectacles, Large and small Files.
Plated and Pinchbeck Buckles, Spurs.
1-2 3-4 and Inch Augurs.
Gouges, Chizels, Hand Saws and Hammers.
A few Saw-Mill and Crosscut Saws.
One Crate of Queen's Ware, containing pint, quart, and two quart Bowls.
Quart and pint Stone Mugs, Platters and Plates.
West-India Rum, per Hhd. Raisins per Cask.
Bills on France, State Money or new Flour, will be received in payment for the above Goods.
Hartford, October 22, 1781.

At times the entire West Indian area was sealed off by British ships, but at other times it was comparatively safe.[162]

A small amount of direct trade with friendly European countries occurred. Our new ally, France, served as a magnet, though the British navy effectively discouraged any important expansion. In 1777, four ships did leave New Haven bound for Bordeaux, and occasional advertisements of French goods for sale in Hartford and elsewhere from 1778 to 1783 suggest that some French products came through the blockade.[163]

Goods from Holland also arrived in Connecticut in small quantities, though it is probable that they usually came indirectly, via Boston or other out-of-state ports. A mere trickle of goods came from other foreign countries, as illustrated by the arrival at New London in 1781 of the brigantine *La Impromateu* from Bergen, Norway.[164]

The Perplexities and Pains of Economic Regulation

UNDER the powerful impact of wartime problems Connecticut expanded economic controls until they far surpassed any level reached in her previous history. The first type of economic control instituted was the *embargo*, begun on April 26, 1775, forbidding export from the state of most basic foodstuffs. It represented definitely a "Connecticut first" policy — enough food for her civilians and soldiers before any supplies were exported. As time passed, many additional products were embargoed, including even tanned leather and shoes, and boats in December 1776.[165]

Many hundreds of hours were spent by Trumbull and his Council of Safety wrestling with the deluge of petitions in which each petitioner cited some compelling reason for an exemption from the embargo. Even with generous interpretation, the embargo acts caused sharp resentment in neighboring states. Philip Schuyler minced no words in expressing the official New York view that they "consider such a Law, under the present situation of this State as one of the greatest misfortunes that could befal them." Trumbull replied sympathetically but firmly that the embargo acts had exerted a "very salutary effect," especially in conjunction with price fixing. For legitimate cases permits were easy to obtain. The law, moreover, did not prevent articles from being brought *into* or *through* Connecticut. Schuyler wrote several times about New Yorkers' complaints, especially about the time and expense required to secure a permit. Most of the time to the end of the war, however, Connecticut tenaciously maintained its embargo. The legislature even closed up loopholes and directed the towns to appoint "Inspectors of Provisions," whose duty was to seize any embargoed goods being illegally taken through the town. In 1780 all old "permits" were abrogated, and the new permits carried short time limits.[166]

This tightening up occurred despite mounting demands from Rhode Island for discontinuance of the embargo. Governor Greene explained how Rhode Island in peacetime never had grown enough grain for its people. For two war years the British occupied one-third of the best farming land, and military service seriously reduced grain production. The state's commerce and fisheries also were largely ruined and, in addition, 2,000 refugees from the British-held area required care. Rhode Island sent two special spokesmen to describe in person their "deplorable circumstances" and to plead for immediate export of foodstuffs. Connecticut's lawmakers were moved, for they immediately gave Rhode Island agents liberty to buy a total of 7,000 bushels of grain (rye and corn) in specified amounts from each county.[167]

The Assembly gladly granted two former Rhode Islanders permission to solicit contributions for starving Patriot families of that state, and resolved that offerings be taken in all churches for "the relief and support of the unhappy persons suffering under the rigorous inhumanity and vindictive cruelty of our common enemy."[168]

Much evidence exists that the embargo laws were frequently disobeyed. Just below the surface much sentiment existed for complete repeal; and the governor himself admitted to Washington his low opinion of all regulatory laws, though officially he carefully upheld them.[169]

Early in the war three problems assumed serious proportions — hoarding scarce articles, charging exorbitant prices for scarce articles, and trading with the enemy — activities which stirred deep public resentment. The first act (1776) against hoarders, or "engrossers," neatly captures this sentiment:

Whereas many are so abandoned and lost to all the feelings of humanity as to prey upon the bowels of their country in this day of public distress and struggle by endeavouring to engross many of the necessary articles of life, especially of such as are more immediately wanted for the comfort and support of our armies, whereby much extortion and oppression arises upon the poor and the soldiery . . .

The legislators therefore authorized seizure of whatever the army needed from the hands of engrossers and payment of a just price set by two impartial appraisers.[170] .

One month later, in November 1776, the Assembly decided to set maximum prices and wages for basic foodstuffs and labor in an act aimed at "monopolizers, the great pest of society, who prefer their own private gain to the interest and safety of their country." Farm labor was set at a maximum rate of three shillings per day, with rates for all other labor to be in proportion. Wheat, rye, corn, wool, flax, pork, grass-fed beef, raw hides, salt, sugar, molasses, rum, tea, cheese, and butter — each had a stated maximum price.[171]

In all, twenty-two more acts followed in the next few years "to prevent illicit trade," "to prevent sharping and engrossing," and the like. In 1778 the state repealed the chief price-fixing act. Later, in line with the advice of the Hartford interstate convention of October 1779, the lawmakers reinstituted selective price controls and thereafter expanded them to include such items as cattle and other army supplies.[172]

The sharp rises in prices struck everybody. In town records one finds resolves to obey the latest law setting prices and prohibiting hoarding. The newspapers carried heated articles upon the persistent problems of spiraling prices, shortages, and notorious profiteering. The soldiers often felt bitter about the pyramiding of prices, which soon attained heights of five to ten times those of 1775:

I ask the question, will your army continue to defend you in the field, when their wives and their children are famishing and crying for bread at home, through your intolerable oppressions?

"Cato," who had a *Courant* series printed in December 1777, estimated that there were between one and two hundred engrossers whose *weekly* profits occasionally ran as high as £200 or £300. Although there were adequate supplies of foodstuffs, some farmers had hoarded their surpluses to stimulate rising prices. The small farmer who did not raise any substantial surplus faced a very bleak economic future — hurt by rising prices of the things which he must buy. "Cato" asserted convincingly that the credit of the paper money could be restored by "large taxation," coupled with a fair system of impressing hoarded goods.[173]

The enforcement of the regulatory laws was spread among several groups: local officials such as selectmen, constables, and justices of the peace; county courts and the Superior Court; and the governor and Council of Safety. More serious cases usually were taken before the county courts and a few reached the Superior Court.

The Profitable Illicit Trade

THE form of violation requiring the greatest enforcement effort was trade with the enemy, or the illicit trade, centered on Long Island Sound. British goods were purchased in New York City, often ostensibly for Tories, taken to Long Island, smuggled across the Sound to Connecticut, and traded for provisions. A second important route ran overland directly from New York to Fairfield County points and back. It is easy to find substantial data on the existence of a shocking amount of illicit trade:

[1777] A Mr. Fernandez, an Officer just released from Captivity by an exchange, informs me, that large and weekly supplies of fresh Provisions are brought into [New] York, which he was told by a Friend of ours, came from Connecticut . . . It is most probable, the most Common mode of Conveyance is by Water, and that the Supplies are from those, who live on the Sound . . .

[1780] The Trade to Long-Island, has been much talk'd of — it is now in every Body's Mouth . . . The Legislature of this State . . . have enacted severe penal Laws to suppress it . . . I am sorry to say, the diabolical Trade still stalks on with gigantic Pace . . . The Men who are pursuing the illicit Trade, are well known . . .[174]

Some of the whaleboat men, who were commissioned to prevent illegal trade, actively engaged in it. Forms of collusion were carefully executed whereby owners of Long Island stores "planned" to be robbed of goods, which mysteriously reappeared in Connecticut later! Lloyd's Neck and Port Jefferson on Long Island became notorious as bases of operations for illicit traders.[175]

In January 1780 Colonel John Mead of Greenwich gave a detailed description of illicit land operations along the border. During the preceding several months more fat cattle had been driven into New York than in any similar period. When local farmers were questioned as to sudden depletion of their herds, they reported that some

Proclamation of Governor Trumbull against illicit trade.

cattle had been stolen; but they seemed suspiciously unworried by these "thefts." Strangely enough, too, they quickly purchased more stock! In some places it required only twenty or thirty minutes to drive the cattle within the British lines. Though circumstantial evidence often was strong, local courts got nowhere in attempted prosecution.[176]

The "cowboys" and the "skinners" added further complications. The former were Tories who specialized in stealing cattle from farmers near the line and driving them to New York City markets. Hence the nickname "cowboys." The "skinners," theoretically American adherents, actually operated as vicious raiders, who indiscriminately robbed defenseless partisans of either side.[177]

The extreme seriousness with which state leaders regarded this illegal trade was shown by appointment in February 1781 of a special legislative committee of unusual caliber to recommend steps for checking these practices. Serving on this blue-ribbon committee were: Roger Sherman and Oliver Ellsworth from the Upper House; and General Selleck Silliman, John Hopkins, Stephen M. Mitchell, and Dr. Amos Mead of the Lower House. The Assembly decided not to change the laws against illicit trade, but did enact stricter laws against joining or aiding the enemy.[178]

The County Court records provide an excellent source of information as to cases involving illicit trade and the punishment incurred. Since the opportunities for illicit trade were greatest in Fairfield and New Haven counties, the largest number of cases occurred there. Most of these appear as "libels" against goods illegally imported or exported, and often against the ship involved. One such case involved George Monroe of Branford, charged with importing from Long Island "sundry Goods, Wares & Merchandize." He pleaded not guilty, but was adjudged guilty and sentenced to eighteen months in jail and costs of £11 12s. 6d. In most cases, however, treatment was far more lenient. Many found guilty suffered only payment of costs or perhaps forfeiture of bail if they failed to appear for sentencing or appeal. In December 1782, two Norwalk defendants were each fined £100 and costs for carrying on correspondence and commercial intercourse with the enemy. A third defendant, who pleaded guilty, was fined only £3 and costs.[179]

The general picture boils down to widespread infraction of the regulatory laws, with spotty and mild punitive measures — the logical result of a weak central government, inadequate, poorly paid enforcement officials, and a sizable segment of hostile public opinion. The scarcity of cases involving price infractions, a very prevalent practice, can be explained by the lack of public support. In 1780 Trumbull referred to a "Great Division of Sentiment . . . in both Houses" upon a price-fixing measure. After Cornwallis' surrender at Yorktown most Americans felt that the war was won. As a result, violations of the embargo acts and of price controls and trading with the enemy all increased markedly in the remaining eighteen months of the war. After the signing of the preliminary treaty of peace, Connecticut vessels often gained admittance to New York harbor, sometimes without flags of truce. Despite the gradual breakdown of economic regulation, it is difficult to see how this legislation could have been avoided, since it gave protection to those classes of the Patriot population which most needed such protection.[180]

Tryon Returns to Haunt Connecticut

ON February 26, 1779, the uneasy quiet on the coast enduring since April 1777 suddenly was broken by a small raid upon Greenwich, under General Tryon, principally to destroy the saltworks in the area. Despite brave but ineffectual resistance by greatly outnumbered militia under Putnam, the British raiders destroyed the saltworks, pillaged widely, and vanished with much livestock. Although the raid was briefer than most, it caused heavy losses. In May 1780 the Assembly's special committee listed 165 persons as incurring damages totaling £5,810 15s. 8d. The Assembly granted tax relief in that amount for taxes payable on the 1778 list.[181]

A much more devastating blow struck Connecticut in July 1779. General Clinton, British commander in New York, apparently hoped to lure Washington away from his safe position on the Hudson and defeat him decisively. Doubtless, too,

the active supply effort of Connecticut, and frequent attacks upon British commerce in the Sound by privateers, many based at New Haven, inclined Clinton toward a punitive expedition.[182]

On July 3, 1779, British troops — about 2,600 men in all, including one Tory regiment — embarked on transports. Early on the morning of July 5 the fleet, escorted by four warships, anchored off West Haven. A division under General George Garth, numbering perhaps 1,500 men, landed and marched toward New Haven. Hastily gathered volunteers, under Colonel Hezekiah Sabin, Jr., and a few Yale students, under Captain James Hillhouse, Jr., vainly contested the British advance. Garth's forces pushed ahead, harassed by snipers, and reached West Haven Green, where they paused for needed rest and nourishment. Meanwhile Captain Hillhouse, with members of the Governor's Guard, volunteers, and Yale students, crossed West Bridge and drove back Garth's advance guard. When the main British force appeared, the Patriots abruptly retreated under protection of Captain Phineas Bradley's artillery. West Bridge was quickly dismantled, and artillery discouraged British entry into New Haven by that route.[183]

At this moment the British were diverted by a solitary sniper on their flank, Napthali Daggett, septuagenarian president emeritus of Yale, who had been firing with a long fowling piece as antiquated as he was! "What are you doing there you old fool, firing on his Majesty's troops?" shouted an officer excitedly. "Exercising the rights of war," Daggett retorted. "If I let you go this time, you rascal," continued the officer, "will you ever fire again on the troops of his Majesty?" Unabashed, Daggett whipped back, "Nothing more likely." Angered by such uninhibited audacity, the redcoats beat him, removed his shoes, and forced him to march five miles into New Haven, which he reached more dead than alive.[184]

Garth decided to follow a more circuitous route, by way of the Derby highway. Some militia, under the direction of a visiting Princeton graduate, Aaron Burr, provided a harassing fire. As the British entered the town at Ditch Corner (where Whalley and Dixwell avenues meet), a sharp but short skirmish ensued, and the Americans, under

Colonel Sabin, were forced to retreat. Garth's men then began minor pillaging, committed atrocities upon several elderly citizens, and downed all the rum in sight.[185]

Tryon's men landed at two spots near Lightning Point and, under fire from militia, pushed inland, took Black Rock Fort and Beacon Hill, and began some unsystematic looting in East Haven. Tryon went on to confer with Garth and decide upon future action. How thorough destruction the British originally had planned is uncertain, but probably the ominous gathering of large militia forces with heavier cannon caused Garth and Tryon to forego a wholesale conflagration. Instead, their men destroyed some public stores and a few boats. In East Haven several houses were burned. Losses totaled nearly £14,000, of which Captain Thomas Wooster and Anthony Lamb suffered most, with losses of over £700 apiece. By threatening to fire the entire town, Tryon secured an unmolested evacuation for his expedition. They took some captives "and a few who chose to accompany them," and sailed away in search of easier prey.[186]

They did not go far — only to Fairfield, where on July 8 Garth and Tryon repeated the split landings and overran and burned the nearly defenseless town. The local fort, manned by twenty-three men under Lieutenant Isaac Jarvis, was stanchly defended. The local churches, the schoolhouses, nearly a hundred residences, and about the same number of other buildings were consumed. William Wheeler indicated in his *Journal* that only eleven houses survived the conflagration. Tryon's report defended this devastation as retaliation for "the fire of the rebels from their houses and to mask our retreat." Green Farms, near Fairfield, also lost most of its houses in flames.[187]

The British raiders crossed to Huntington, Long Island, to rest and to receive fresh supplies. Returning to Connecticut shores and again landing at separated points, they closed in upon Norwalk. A force of militia, under General Oliver Wolcott, and a few Continentals, under General Samuel H. Parsons, opposed the British, but were too few to provide serious opposition. Two churches, nearly 40 stores and shops, about 130 homes, flour mills, and saltworks, about 90 barns, and 5 ships were swept into the holocaust, after which Tryon made

a very speedy departure. The Assembly estimated over £8,500 damage to 105 persons. Direct military casualties on both sides were low at Fairfield and Norwalk.[188]

At the towns attacked, the British left copies of an "ADDRESS TO THE INHABITANTS OF CONNECTICUT," signed by Generals Collier and Tryon.

> Your towns, your property, yourselves, lie within the grasp of the power whose forbearance, you have ungenerously construed into fear, but whose lenity has persisted in its mild and noble efforts, even tho' branded with the most unworthy imputation.
>
> The existence of a single habitation on your defenceless coast, ought to be a constant reproof to your ingratitude....
>
> You who be so much in our power afford the most striking monument of our mercy, and therefore ought to set the first example of returning allegiance.

The proclamation promised that all who remained peacefully at home would be shielded from injury to person or property — an appeal which infuriated most Patriots.[189]

A Vicious Blow Against New London and Groton

THE final British assault upon Connecticut soil, against New London in 1781, proved to be the most brutal of them all. Ostensibly Clinton launched this attack mainly to distract the northern Franco-American forces from Cornwallis, seriously bogged down in Virginia; but his purpose was also to hit New London, a leading shipping and privateering center. Arnold received the command with a force of about 1,700 men.[190]

The expedition, thirty-two ships strong, appeared in Long Island Sound on September 5, 1781, the very day that De Grasse, in the Battle of the Capes, foiled Graves's attempt to rescue Cornwallis' beleaguered troops. Not until nine o'clock the next morning were the British able to enter New London harbor. One part, under Colonel Edmund Eyre, which included the crack Fortieth Regiment, veterans of Long Island, Fort Washington, Brandywine, and Germantown, landed in Groton and soon afterward received orders to take Fort Griswold. Arnold's division meanwhile experienced little opposition. The garrison of Fort Trumbull, commanded by Captain Adam Shapley, fired one broadside, then spiked their guns, hastened to the shore, and took boats across the harbor to reinforce Fort Griswold.[191]

In the meantime, Arnold himself after climbing the hill behind the town immediately recognized that Fort Griswold was much stronger than earlier described to him and that its garrison was being augmented by Shapley's men. Even worse, many vessels from the harbor were escaping up the river. Arnold immediately rushed word to Eyre to break off the attack on Griswold. Ironically, the message arrived a few minutes too late.[192]

Stephen Hempstead of New London, a survivor of the battle, described the fort as

an oblong square, with bastions at opposite angles . . . Its walls were of stone, and were ten or twelve feet high on the lower side, and surrounded by a ditch. On the wall were pickets, projecting over twelve feet; above this was a parapet with embrasures, and within a platform for the cannon and a step to mount upon to shoot over the parapet with small arms.

Even with Shapley's men, Colonel William Ledyard, the commander, mustered only about 150 militia to face the 800 veterans of Colonel Eyre. When Ledyard rejected a surrender demand, the British began a fierce assault from three sides. The Americans replied with enfilading cannon fire and caused heavy casualties. Finally the enemy, with a slashing bayonet attack, broke through the embrasures on one side. Both Eyre and Major William Montgomery, leader of the successful assault column, received fatal wounds.[193]

The British losses numbered approximately 40 killed and 100 wounded; the American, 6 killed and perhaps 20 wounded. Ledyard, realizing that his position was hopeless, ordered his men to ground their arms. A British officer shouted, "Who commands this garrison?" Ledyard promptly handed his sword to the speaker, replying, "I did, sir, but you do now." Instantly the sword was taken and brutally rammed through Ledyard's body. The wrought-up British soldiers butchered fourscore of the garrison before their officers finally halted the carnage. Major Stephen Bromfield, now in command, decided to blow up the powder magazine, so the American wounded were placed in an ammunition wagon. As the final act in this stark tragedy, the wagon got out of control on a hill, plunged wildly down the de-

clivity, and finally crashed into a tree, tossing the maimed about and killing several.[194]

In New London itself the British destroyed shipping and a huge quantity of goods — many on the ship *Hannah*, recently brought in by privateers. Warehouses and military stores, many shops, and some homes were set on fire. At the wrong moment the wind shifted and fanned the flames, spreading from explosion of powder magazines, through the heart of the town. Before the roaring fire died down, about 140 buildings were consumed.[195]

In its ruins New London counted 65 homes (leaving 97 families homeless), 31 stores and warehouses, 18 shops, 20 barns, 9 public buildings (including a church, jail, and customs), about a dozen ships, and 50 cannon. Not until the grant in 1793 of the appropriately named Firelands in the Western Reserve did victims receive adequate compensation. Nathaniel Shaw's handsome stone mansion barely escaped destruction, but he estimated other losses at £12,000. Particularly heartrending was the plight of the forty-odd widows of the battle and their children. Sarah Stedman, widow of John Stedman, survived with seven children under thirteen years and no estate. Another widow, Elizabeth Lebarry, with five minor children, reported no estate, their house burned, and nothing left but the clothing upon their backs.[196]

From the British viewpoint the expedition ranked as a very questionable victory. Their losses, 48 killed and 145 wounded, were high; and they failed to draw large American forces away from the attack upon Cornwallis.[197]

Troubled Times in Westmoreland

FROM 1769 to 1775 Connecticut's migrants rapidly filled the fertile lands of the Wyoming Valley. Despite constant danger from Pennsylvania claimants, the population, under the leadership of Zebulon Butler of Lyme, grew steadily until it reached 1,922 in 1774. That year the Assembly transformed its western outpost into the town of Westmoreland, a part of Litchfield County. Upon Assembly orders, the governor issued a proclamation on January 27, 1774, forbidding any person to enter the Connecticut lands west of New York without first obtaining permission.[198]

In 1775 Pennsylvania land speculators, under William Plunkett of Sunbury, an outspoken Tory, jauntily led seven hundred "Pennamites" northward with high hopes of crushing the Connecticut settlement. Captain Zebulon Butler and Lazarus Stewart quickly and efficiently organized the Westmoreland men for defense. As a result, the Pennsylvanians fell successively into three ambushes, the last on Christmas Day, 1775, after which they disconsolately backtracked to Northumberland. An undeclared truce between Yankees and Pennamites then developed, as they needed a common front against the British and their Indian allies.[199]

In October 1776 the Connecticut legislature changed Westmoreland from a town to a full-fledged county, perhaps to bolster the Connecticut position and the confidence of the settlers.[200]

Slowly Colonel John Butler, Tory chief of Mohawk Valley, gathered a powerful striking force, consisting of his Rangers, some of John Johnson's Royal Greens — about 400 whites in all — plus 700 scalp-seeking Senecas and Cayugas. As they approached Wyoming Valley late in June 1778, all available men, young and old alike, took up arms. After a council of war at Forty Fort, the Yankees, 300 strong, sallied confidently forth. A furious battle developed and the Yankees were doing well, driving the Tories before them, when Indians suddenly appeared at their rear in overwhelming numbers and completely turned the tide. Most of the fleeing Yankees were cut down ruthlessly, while others were caught along the Susquehanna River and later slowly tortured to death.[201]

This left the remainder of the settlers virtually helpless, and the surrender of Forty Fort followed. As was expected, Butler quickly lost control of the Indians, who pillaged promiscuously. The forlorn settlers, stripped of all possessions, their homes in flames, husbands lost, began a horrible pell-mell flight. Those who fell even slightly behind were scalped by sharp-eyed Indians. The pitiful refugees found temporary shelter in nearby Pennsylvania settlements, but many continued back to Connecticut.[202]

The Wyoming Massacre led to demands for retaliation, which culminated in General John Sullivan's destructive sweep through the Iroquois country of upstate New York. Moreover, the sturdy Connecticut refugees began the return trek to their farms in the fall after the massacre.[203]

As the end of the war approached, the Pennsylvania legislature, prodded by powerful land-speculating interests, asked Congress for a special court, under Article IX of the Articles of Confederation, to settle the long-disputed jurisdiction. A board of seven commissioners was appointed. As counsel, Connecticut had a distinguished trio: Eliphalet Dyer, Samuel Johnson, and Jesse Root. Pennsylvania likewise sent eminent legal talent. The board sat at Trenton in November and December 1782 and heard both sides at length. The final decision was unanimously in Pennsylvania's favor, and Connecticut peacefully, if unhappily, acquiesced — a fortunate step, contributing to greater interstate harmony. News of the decision reached the Assembly at its January 1783 session. After the names of the last two Westmoreland deputies (Captain Obadiah Gore and Jonathan Fitch) to sit in the Connecticut Assembly, the clerk jotted the lines:

> Annihilated and out of Sight; —
> If what the Court have done, is right.

Connecticut settlers, now numbering over 5,000, remained upon the banks of the Susquehanna, keeping it religiously and culturally a "little Connecticut." Finally, too, their individual land titles were confirmed by Pennsylvania.[204]

A "Conservative" Revolution

CONNECTICUT proceeded through the most radical epoch of its history in a conservative manner. There existed a considerable amount of deep-seated political tumult within the colony during the decade or so up to 1776. From 1776 on, however, once the Tory menace was quelled, the state operated politically under the strict control of a small group of Whigs, the so-called "Standing Order." Governor Trumbull, leader of this small clique, was regularly re-elected without strong opposition. He derived additional prestige from being the only Patriot governor to continue from prewar ranks, and from his trusted relationship with Washington.[205]

If one compares the personnel of the General

Assembly in May 1775 with that of May 1783, the elements of stability reveal themselves immediately. Of the twelve assistants elected in May 1775, eight were still chosen in May 1783: Abraham Davenport, Eliphalet Dyer, Jabez Hamlin, Samuel Huntington, William Pitkin, Roger Sherman, Joseph Spencer, and Oliver Wolcott. Even in the Lower House a large majority of the members were re-elected. In May 1783 about one-fourth of the 1775 members still were representing their towns. Other state officials remained throughout the conflict: Matthew Griswold as deputy governor, John Lawrence as treasurer, George Wyllys as secretary, and William Williams as House speaker.[206]

The picture of a tight "inner circle" emerges more clearly in the make-up of the Superior Court, the Congressional delegation, and the Council of Safety. The appointees to the Superior Court in May 1775 were: Matthew Griswold (chief judge), Eliphalet Dyer, Roger Sherman, William Pitkin, and Samuel Huntington — identical with the court of 1783! In October 1775 the Assembly elected Roger Sherman, Oliver Wolcott, Samuel Huntington, Titus Hosmer, and William Williams as representatives to Congress, any three to attend simultaneously. Three of the five were assistants, while Hosmer and Williams ranked among the leaders of the deputies. Eight years later Huntington and Wolcott still were being elected. The other 1783 delegates included Oliver Ellsworth, Benjamin Huntington, and Richard Law of the Upper House, and Jedidiah Strong and Stephen Mix Mitchell of the Lower House.[207]

Likewise, in the vital emergency Council of Safety, most members were selected from the Standing Order. The first Council of Safety, chosen in May 1775, contained the governor, four assistants, and five deputies. Eight years later the governor, six assistants, and sixteen deputies comprised the Council of Safety! One might conclude safely that the Standing Order in 1775–83 was composed of a "conservative" Patriot group of about two dozen persons, headed by Trumbull. John Adams neatly summarized the situation:

The state of Connecticut has always been governed by an aristocracy, more decisively than the empire of Great Britain is. Half a dozen, or, at most, a dozen families, have controlled that country when a colony, as well as since it has been a state.[208]

Connecticut's conservatism was demonstrated by her deep-seated attachment to the charter granted by Charles II in 1662. Aside from the fundamental step of breaking away from Britain, the state retained the charter of 1662 as a working instrument until 1818. In contrast, all the other states except Rhode Island drew up new constitutions, often incorporating numerous radical political changes. Connecticut's smooth transition was not surprising, because the functioning government for decades had been based mostly upon precedent and legislative enactments and not upon the charter.[209]

The Puritan (Congregational) Church continued as the Established Church. The Anglican Church, numbering perhaps 8 percent of the population, was placed in a precarious position by the war. Some of the Anglican clergy emigrated and others followed the counsel of William Samuel Johnson by settling into a tactful neutrality. Many of the Tories who fled from the state belonged to the Anglican Church. The strength of anti-Anglican feeling in the state was demonstrated in the special raid made into Westchester, New York, to apprehend the Reverend Samuel Seabury, Anglican clergyman born in Connecticut, a Yale graduate, and later chaplain of Colonel Edmund Fanning's Loyalist regiment. Seabury was imprisoned for six weeks in New Haven.[210]

Although the Anglican clergy suffered severe persecution, including bodily mistreatment, stubborn and venerable John Beach, missionary at Newtown and Redding, vowed that "he would do his duty, preach and pray for the King, till the rebels cut out his tongue." He preached until his death in 1782! In general, however, the Anglican Church in Connecticut barely survived the war.[211]

The other dissenting sects likewise lost ground. The Baptists continued to complain about being taxed to support the Congregational establishment and some did not wholeheartedly endorse the Revolution. Among the small group of Quakers in New Haven and elsewhere, Loyalist or pacifistic sentiment was common. The Sandemanians, a small sect in several western towns who believed in salvation for all who had unquestioning faith, retained their stanch loyalty to the Crown, but they were too tiny a group to pose a serious problem.[212]

The war years thus brought even tighter control by the Congregational majority. Yale, the citadel of the Established Church, under President Stiles adhered very strictly to orthodox faith. Stiles ascertained that every teaching applicant held rigidly orthodox beliefs before he received serious consideration. Throughout the war the elementary and secondary schools remained under careful supervision by the local Congregational societies.[213]

Religious faith played an important role in endowing both leaders and masses with the courage to persevere in the long discouraging war until victory was won. A sincere and powerful religious faith reveals itself in many public addresses and private letters. Almost any one of Trumbull's proclamations of a day of prayer and fasting serves to illustrate, as do many Assembly resolves and, above all, the Election Day sermons.[214]

One of the most controversial figures of the Revolutionary period is Silas Deane of Wethersfield. A prominent lawyer, trader, and politician, he served as one of Connecticut's delegates to the First Continental Congress. In 1776 Congress granted him the funds and sent him upon a difficult but highly important mission to France to buy and ship American produce and to use the proceeds of sales abroad to procure items needed at home. In addition, the Committee for Secret Correspondence instructed him to purchase arms and clothing for 25,000 men, also artillery and ammunition. He enjoyed much success and forwarded eight loaded ships in time for the Saratoga campaign. Many of the supplies were obtained ostensibly from Hortalez and Company, but really through efforts of Beaumarchais, the playwright.[215]

Unfortunately for Deane, he became involved in diplomatic affairs of great complexity and won the undying enmity of American commissioner Arthur Lee, who accused him of fraudulent transactions with Beaumarchais and Robert Morris, American banker. Although Deane engaged in some private trade on the side, there is grave doubt that he misused any government funds. On the other hand, his bookkeeping was extremely careless. The Deane-Lee quarrel grew into a major political battle. Seeing a chance to denounce the business interests in general, Tom Paine accused Deane of swindling his country of enormous sums in secret operations with Robert Morris. Deane felt it advisable to return to Philadelphia to have his accounts settled and his name cleared. In customary fashion, Congress procrastinated, and after a year of waiting, the frustrated Deane exploded in a public appeal over the head of Congress to the American people.[216]

In 1780 Deane returned to France, again as Morris' partner. His affairs went poorly, however, and Congress failed to pay his back salary. French and American friends and debtors all seemed to turn against him. Eventually he lost faith in the American cause and offered to help the British as a propagandist. Since he received no money from Britain, he went into exile nearly penniless and broken in health. Although considered by many a traitor, he had aided greatly in developing Franco-American commerce when its expansion was critically needed. In 1783 Deane prepared a pamphlet to defend his activities in France. He died in 1789 while en route to America. Many years later, when an impartial audit at last was made, Deane's protestations were vindicated, and in 1842 Congress made partial restitution by voting $37,000 to his heirs.[217]

The Heavy Load of a Wartime Governor

As the war dragged on, another Connecticut leader, Governor Trumbull, lost popularity and was accused of illicit trade. A story circulated about the state that a Trumbull vessel involved in illicit trade had been seized. Another story claimed that goods carrying Trumbull's label were seen on New York docks. These stories so embarrassed the governor that in January 1782 he requested a complete investigation. A special joint legislative committee discovered that a stranger had started the rumors at a tavern in Enfield. The committee concluded that there did not exist the slightest proof of any illicit trade by Trumbull and that the tale probably had been deliberately disseminated by "Partisans & Emissaries" of the enemy. The

Painting of Governor Jonathan Trumbull and Faith (Robinson) Trumbull by their son, John Trumbull.

charges deeply wounded the governor, who pointed out that he had not possessed one shilling's worth of British goods since before the war began and that during the conflict he had given up his private trade and neglected his lands.[218]

The popularity of Trumbull had sagged much, however, even before this episode. In May 1780, apparently for the first time, he failed to get a majority of the freemen's votes. The decision then fell to the Lower House, which gave Trumbull 107 votes against 9 for four others. In 1781, also, Trumbull fell below a majority, but he received 104 out of 122 Lower House votes. Though he apparently obtained the necessary majority in 1782, the following year he failed. Ninety-six deputies then voted for him, and twenty-six for all others — still a strong 79 percent support. Upon hearing the results, he submitted a written request for advice

about accepting the position. A special legislative committee conferred with Trumbull and urged him to serve. Trumbull consented and immediately was escorted to the Council Chamber, where he gave the customary address.[219]

The diminution of his popularity and the growing infirmities of old age, undoubtedly hastened by the heavy pressures of the war years, influenced Trumbull to announce his retirement late in 1783. Observing the noble prospect "of a happy establishment . . . in peace, tranquillity and national independence," he felt it an opportune time in his "advanced stage of life — a life worn out almost in the constant cares of office" to retire from further public service. He proceeded tactfully but firmly to state his "last advisory legacy," which included retention of "the happy constitution under which we have so long subsisted as a corporation."

173

Turning to the national scene, he expressed the opinion that Congress lacked "those powers which are absolutely necessary to the best management and direction of the general weal." He pleaded for an end to excessive jealousies among Americans which could only lead to "anarchy and confusion." The governor unflinchingly advised full redemption of all wartime public debts. Free and frequent elections he saw as "the great security and palladium" of the people. He exhorted his people "to love one another" and ground themselves in this "sure axiom, that virtue exalteth a nation, but that sin and evil workings are the destruction of a people." This message provides one of the clearest statements of Trumbull's conservative political philosophy and his stanch Puritan religious faith.[220]

Although the plea for stronger central government displeased some hearers, the Assembly gracefully thanked the governor for his distinguished services before and during the war. Especially noteworthy had been his intimate relationship with Washington who seems to have trusted him implicitly. Trumbull thus bowed out, after three years as deputy governor and fifteen years as governor. Though a quiet and unimpressive-looking man, he possessed strong qualities of industry, stability, courage, judgment, and religious faith, which made him one of the best of the Revolutionary governors. His partial loss of popular support late in the war came as the inevitable result of accumulating wartime restrictions and frustrations, which some freemen vented by voting against the governor as the symbol of these irritants. Some, too, who admired Trumbull, honestly felt that he had become too old. As it turned out, he enjoyed less than two years of well-earned retirement before his death on August 17, 1785.[221]

Glad Tidings of Peace

THE war gradually approached an end in Connecticut. The news of Yorktown convinced most leaders that it would be only a matter of time, but the United States still had to maintain its army. The year 1782 brought alternations of relaxation and reimposition of economic restrictions. Shipping at New Haven, depressed in 1781, picked up in 1782 and after April 1783 soared upward. Trade with the enemy increased considerably in 1782, as many felt that the regulatory laws *were* or *ought to be* dead letters! From a careful examination of the Assembly actions in 1782 it is obvious that the sense of danger and of urgency had disappeared.[222]

In April 1783 Connecticut joyfully received the long-awaited news of the preliminary Peace of Paris, ending the Revolution. After eight long and often sorrowful years Americans could concentrate upon the pursuits of peace. In May the Assembly repealed the principal wartime regulatory laws and began to wind up the extensive operations of the supply agents. The great majority of Connecticut's soldiers already were at home, and those with the Continental army soon would be back.[223]

A traveler passing through the state in the spring of 1783 would have seen few outward signs of the ravages of war. He might have observed a few blackened ruins at Fairfield or Norwalk, and some families could tell sad tales of lost or badly wounded sons. He would note a lack of bustle in many port towns. Inland, however, he would have found the farmers busily plowing and putting in crops, the town merchants again selling varied stocks of European goods, and a more optimistic spirit filling the hearts of the people. The experiences of the war had greatly broadened the horizons of many Connecticut citizens, especially those who, for the first time, had traveled widely and had fought with Americans of different sections and backgrounds. In the "Land of Steady Habits" the Revolution had cut deeply into the economic, social, political, and religious fabric. The relatively prosperous and healthy condition of Connecticut meant that it could move ahead easily to capitalize upon the expanding commercial and industrial opportunities of the next several decades.

CHAPTER 10

Federalism Reigns and Is Toppled

Readjustments to Peacetime, 1783–88 — The New Federal Constitution — The Fight for Ratification — Politics in the 1790's — Republican Challenge to the Federalists — An Unpopular War, 1812–15 — A Famous but Notorious Convention — Sheep and Woolens — Cotton and Other Manufacturing — Banks and Trade — A Political Revolution Brings a New Constitution

---

Readjustments to Peacetime, 1783–88

WITH the surrender of Cornwallis in October 1781 ending the fighting, the transition to real peace began. By the spring of 1783, with peace and independence assured, the Assembly repealed nearly all of the wartime economic and military laws, which public opinion, in practice, had repealed months earlier. On April 30, 1783, Hartford celebrated the joyous news that the final Peace of Paris had brought formal British acknowledgment of our independence.[1]

Other events marking the arrival of peace included the termination of Council of Safety meetings in October 1783, the adoption of a new seal in May 1784 to replace the colonial one, and the retirement of Governor Trumbull, effective May 1784. In accordance with Connecticut's conservative tradition of promoting the deputy governor to governor, the freemen replaced Trumbull by Matthew Griswold, deputy governor since 1769.[2]

For the port towns, peace meant the awaited revival of shipping, as in New Haven, where only four ships were registered in 1781 in contrast to forty in the June 1783–June 1784 period.[3]

The state changed its judiciary in 1784 by an act which barred the governor, lieutenant governor (title replacing "deputy governor" from 1784), assistants, representatives, or delegates in Congress from serving simultaneously on the Superior Court. The Assembly proceeded to create a new Supreme Court of Errors, composed of the lieutenant governor and Council, as the highest and final court of appeals from the Superior Court. The same year the legislature provided that no Negro or mulatto born in Connecticut after March 1 should be held a slave after reaching the age of twenty-five. In 1797 the Assembly dropped the age to twenty-one.[4]

Likewise, in local government there occurred an important deviation from the ancient pattern of townships. Undoubtedly aware of the increasing concentration of population in certain centers, accompanied inevitably by difficult political, social, and economic problems, the Assembly in 1784 incorporated the first five cities in the state: New Haven, New London, Hartford, Middletown, and Norwich. Freemen in each city could elect annually all municipal officers except the mayor, who, once elected, continued at the Assembly's pleasure. Each city received a city court of limited jurisdiction and a common council.[5]

In the 1780's the young nation, and especially New England, experienced severe economic difficulties, revolving about the chaotic currency and debt situation. The large quantities of wartime paper money, issued both by the central government and the states, had depreciated almost to complete worthlessness. As late as 1784 Connecticut citizens who had been burned out or pillaged by the British still were asking the Assembly for abatement of state taxes. Judging from the large number of bankruptcy cases and petitions of those seeking release from debtor's prison, one may surmise that business was stagnating. In Massachusetts desperate debtors staged Shays' Rebellion, which thoroughly alarmed Connecticut's conservatives. Governor Huntington issued a proclamation referring to "a horrid and unnatural RE-BELLION and WAR" and publicized the large rewards Massachusetts was offering for capture of Shays and his confederates. When rumors spread of a similar movement being organized at Sharon, the Assembly appointed Colonel Samuel Canfield to make a speedy investigation. Canfield, aided by Uriah Tracy, found some mob excitement but speedily apprehended ringleader William Mitchell and several others and took them to Litchfield for questioning. With the crushing of Shays' uprising, fears in Connecticut subsided, and the charges against the Sharon conspirators were dropped. Meanwhile, despite Connecticut's war debt of over $3,750,000, attempts to enact inflationary legal-tender legislation were defeated by the sound-money advocates.[6]

Treatment of Revolutionary officers became a "hot" issue in Connecticut after Congress passed its "commutation" act, granting them five years' full pay. Apparently this was unpopular in many circles, as several town meetings resolved that the act was unwise, unjust, and illegal. A convention in September 1783 at Middletown, with representatives from about fifty towns, prepared a protest. In December another convention indicated opposition to the new Society of Cincinnati — an organization of army officers. A final meeting in March 1784 resulted in an address to the people, again opposing the pay plan for officers and the

Cincinnati. Noah Webster felt that this convention was representative of a sizable segment of Connecticut opinion and constituted a nucleus for the future Jeffersonian party in Connecticut. In regard to its veterans, the Assembly followed the lead of the Confederation Acts of 1786 and 1788, which gave totally disabled officers pensions equal to one-half their service pay and awarded similarly afflicted enlisted men up to five dollars per month. The Connecticut laws established procedures for verifying claims and extended these benefits to any disabled in state service. Upon several occasions the state also implemented a Congressional resolution of 1780 giving half-pay for seven years to widows or orphans of officers lost in service.[7]

The New Federal Constitution

A GROWING feeling by numerous Americans, in many parts of the United States, that the Confederation was providing ineffective government led to the Annapolis Convention of 1786 and in turn to a call for a general interstate convention at Philadelphia in May 1787 to revise the Articles of Confederation. When the Assembly convened in May, Governor Huntington urged a prompt decision as to whether Connecticut should send delegates. After a vigorous debate the supporters of participation carried the day, and the Assembly chose Oliver Ellsworth, William Samuel Johnson, and Roger Sherman as delegates.[8]

This trio gave Connecticut a "superbly coördinated political team." Sherman, sixty-six years old, was a self-made man. Born in Massachusetts, he early learned the shoemaker's trade and then moved to New Milford, Connecticut. In 1754 he entered the practice of law, and in 1761 he moved to New Haven to engage in mercantile pursuits. Four years later he was chosen a judge of the County Court. Other honors quickly followed — elevation to the State Superior Court, membership in the Upper House, service in the Continental Congress, and election as first mayor of the city of New Haven. After adoption of the new constitution he served in the House of Representatives and, finally, the Senate. Sherman holds the unique distinction of being the only man to sign the Association of 1774, Declaration of Independence, Articles of Confederation, and the Constitution. Plain and blunt in speech and manner, he went to the convention a confirmed "Confederationist" and returned a devoted nationalist.[9]

Oliver Ellsworth attended Princeton, studied theology, then law, and was admitted to the bar in 1771. As a young man his financial resources were so slender that he supplemented his scanty legal income by farming and even chopping wood. Unable to keep a horse, he walked the ten miles from his home in Windsor to the sessions of the court in Hartford. After he moved to Hartford he soon rose to prominence as a leading lawyer, an assistant, and a representative in the Continental Congress. One of Connecticut's first two senators, he served as Chief Justice of the United States Supreme Court and special commissioner to France. A far more eloquent orator than Sherman, he, too, stanchly upheld the rights of the individual state.[10]

William Samuel Johnson, the third delegate, also enjoyed a notable career. Born in Stratford, a Yale graduate of 1744, with a Master's degree from Harvard in 1747, he early became a leading lawyer. A delegate to the Stamp Act Congress, the first Anglican ever elected to the Upper House, colonial agent in London, Judge of the Superior Court, he stayed quietly at home during the Revolution. From 1787 to 1800 he acted as president of Columbia College, and also enjoyed a brief term as senator from Connecticut. Conservative in outlook, he rounded out the very able Connecticut delegation at Philadelphia.[11]

Though Connecticut's delegates generally played a leading role at the convention, their most famous contribution was the so-called "Connecticut Compromise." When an impasse was reached between backers of the Virginia Plan, favored by large states, and those of the New Jersey Plan, urged by small states, Connecticut's delegates engineered the famous compromise by which representation in the Senate would be equal, and in the House of Representatives, proportional to population. When the convention completed its work, the proposed new Constitution was printed in full in newspapers, and a lively discussion began almost immediately.[12]

The Fight for Ratification

WHILE all three delegates enthusiastically endorsed the Constitution, perhaps the most effective broadside fired for it came from the pen of Ellsworth, who composed the anonymous letters by "A LANDHOLDER," thirteen in all, appearing in the *Courant* between November 5, 1787, and March 24, 1788. Writing in plain, clear style and aiming chiefly at farmers, still the state's majority group, Ellsworth stressed that "the prosperity and riches of the farmer must depend on the prosperity, and good national regulation of trade." Vigorously he asserted that "a foederal government of energy is the only means which will deliver us, and now or never is your opportunity to establish it, on such a basis as will preserve your liberty and riches." In later articles he specifically answered anti-Constitution arguments of Elbridge Gerry of Massachusetts and George Mason of Virginia. Roger Sherman joined the debate in a series of five letters to the newspapers in which he stressed the vital need of a strong central government.[13]

In October the Assembly unanimously voted to have the Constitution considered by a special convention, composed of delegates elected by each town in November. The delegates convened at the State House in Hartford on January 4, 1788, and quickly moved to the Meeting House of the First Society, where heat was available. The galleries were opened to the public, various persons took notes of the leading speeches, and the newspapers printed accounts of proceedings. The convention included many distinguished state leaders, of whom about one-third had served in the Revolution. The Constitution was read in full and then debated section by section, with an advance agreement that no vote could be taken until every section had been discussed. Ellsworth opened the debate by ardently defending the Federal Constitution, and he was followed by Johnson, who asserted that "Our commerce is annihilated, our national honour, once in so high esteem, is no more."[14]

The anti-Federalists, who disliked the large increase of powers bestowed upon the central government, were headed by General James Wadsworth of Durham. He objected especially to the provision for laying duties on imports and to the large financial and military powers. The opposition was centered chiefly in the rural towns of New Haven County and the northern, northwestern, and northeastern parts of Connecticut. William Williams expressed sorrow that a religious test was prohibited but later voted in favor of ratification. Apparently the opponents worried Ellsworth enough to precipitate a second major speech by him advocating the Constitution.[15]

After five crowded days of debate, the major question was moved and seconded. Then Governor Huntington, Lieutenant Governor Oliver Wolcott, and Chief Justice Richard Law successively delivered impressive pleas for ratification. Huntington declared, "There is at present an extreme want of power in the national government; and it is my opinion that this constitution does not give too much." After the desire for debate was exhausted, the fateful vote was taken on January 9, 1788, resulting in 128 favoring unconditional ratification and only 40 opposed — a decisive victory for the Federalists. Connecticut thus became the fifth state to ratify the new Constitution.[16]

Politics in the 1790's

DESPITE the fundamental change in the central government of the United States in 1789, politics in Connecticut for the next two decades largely moved along in the customary conservative channels. In the modern sense of vigorous two-party rivalry, political life scarcely existed, since the Federalists completely dominated the political stage and only a tiny minority, about 3 to 4 percent of the total population, bothered to vote at all. Gradually a few Democratic-Republicans, as followers of Thomas Jefferson were called, appeared in the Lower House, perhaps as many as fifteen or sixteen by 1799. In the 1790's, at least three local Democratic-Republican clubs, or "Democratic Societies," were organized at New Haven, Norwalk, and Stamford.[17]

In October 1788 Connecticut selected as its first two senators, Oliver Ellsworth and William Samuel Johnson. The election of representatives took place under a special act of October 1788, which provided for the preliminary choice of twelve candidates by the freemen in November and the election of five representatives on a state-wide basis in December. As a result of this polling, the initial delegation consisted of Benjamin Huntington, lawyer from Norwich; Roger Sherman; Jonathan Sturges, lawyer of Fairfield; Jonathan Trumbull, Jr., of Lebanon (son of the famed Revolutionary governor), later chosen second speaker of the House; and Jeremiah Wadsworth, wealthy Hartford businessman.[18]

For the first presidential election the Assembly chose as electors: Governor Huntington, Lieutenant Governor Wolcott, Thaddeus Burr, Matthew Griswold, Jedediah Huntington, Richard Law, and Erastus Wolcott. In February 1789 these electors met in Hartford, where they cast unanimous votes for Washington but divided in the vice-presidential ballot, five for John Adams and two for "local son" Governor Huntington. Not until 1820 did Connecticut provide for popular choice of electors.[19]

In 1789 the new Federal Congress proposed twelve amendments to the Constitution, ten of which protected vital individual rights. The two houses of the Assembly, although at times apparently favoring most of the proposals, maneuvered at cross-purposes and never could agree upon uniform action. Several prominent political leaders, including Sherman, Wadsworth, and Benjamin Huntington, threw their weight against the proposals, and Connecticut seemed content to leave to other states the honor of ratification. Not until 1939, the one-hundred-and-fiftieth anniversary of its promulgation, did Connecticut, in company with two other laggard states — Massachusetts and Georgia — belatedly ratify the Bill of Rights.[20]

In the 1790's, as emigrants flooded westward from New England, some Connecticut religious leaders began to feel an obligation to carry organized religion among the unchurched pioneers. In 1792 the General Association of the Congregational Church formally adopted a missionary program and called upon the Assembly for assistance. It responded with "an Act for the support of Missionaries to preach the Gospel in the Northern and Western parts of the United States," which requested voluntary contributions from every con-

Center (First) Congregational Church, Hartford (built 1806).

Portrait of Samuel Huntington, signer.

gregation. Although this measure was violently opposed by the Baptists as a sectarian contribution, the first collection brought gifts of over £382 from 165 churches. In 1798 the General Association voted to become the Missionary Society of Connecticut, and for several decades the new organization worked energetically on the frontier.[21]

The strong interest in missions was matched by a rekindling of religious fervor at home during the early 1800's. In 1802 President Timothy Dwight of Yale, an ardent Congregationalist clergyman, helped convert many college students. The revival movement soared to a peak in 1807 but continued strong until the 1820's. This powerful drive brought with it renewed emphasis upon strict observance of the Sabbath — much to the dislike of many people.[22]

In May 1791 a definite step away from religious toleration occurred when the Assembly curtailed the use of certificates whereby dissenters obtained permission to support their own church rather than the Established one. The new law required the certificate to be signed by two civil officers. Since such officers usually were Congregationalists, they might easily be tempted to reject the application. Dissenters immediately raised a storm of disapproval, headlined by the Reverend John Leland's tract, "The Rights of Conscience inalienable . . . ," which presented a vigorous case for disestablishment. Moved by such forceful opposition, leaders of the Standing Order in October 1791 effected repeal of the unpopular act and substitution of a measure enabling a dissenter to prepare his own certificate and merely file it with the local

180

Portrait of Jeremiah Halsey, Revolutionary officer, by Joseph Steward. Earliest known view of Old State House (completed 1796).

clerk of the Established Society. Even this law fell far short of satisfying dissenters and those religiously indifferent, so that toleration remained a hot politico-religious issue until 1818.[23]

The 1790's brought quick changes in the state's governors. Samuel Huntington of Norwich, a self-made man, lawyer, signer of the Declaration of Independence, president of the Continental Congress (1779–81), and one of the state's most outstanding Revolutionary leaders, was elected governor in 1786 and served in his usual efficient and conservative manner until his death in 1796. As his successor the electors chose Oliver Wolcott of Litchfield, another distinguished lawyer and Revolutionary leader, whose short term was terminated by death in 1797. The electorate then turned again to the Trumbull family by choosing

Jonathan Trumbull, Jr., who received nearly all of the votes cast. Literally "growing up" in politics, he had acted as a Continental paymaster and secretary to Washington during the war. Later he was elected representative in 1789 and senator in 1794. He voluntarily resigned his Senate seat in 1796 to assume the position of lieutenant governor.[24]

To Trumbull fell the difficult task of guiding the state through a turbulent period of national and international developments. His messages to the Assembly clearly reveal his intensely conservative philosophy. Like most ardent Federalists he viewed revolutionary France as a grave threat and in October 1798 warned that "an intimate connection with a nation of infidels and atheists . . . is to be avoided as the worst of evils." Although the

181

Reign of Terror had long since ended in France, to Trumbull and other leading pillars of the Standing Order the word France still signified "Jacobins"; and they enthusiastically used this frightening specter to create hysteria and repress all types of unorthodoxy in Connecticut — political, social, and religious. About 1801 a revised voting law, specifying oral nominations and the open standing vote by the freemen, tended to intimidate the minorities.[25]

Republican Challenge to the Federalists

IN the early 1800's Connecticut still remained under Federalist rule, but the Jeffersonian Republicans began to offer substantial opposition. Two newspapers, the *American Mercury* in Hartford and the *New London Bee*, became organs of the minority party. The *Mercury* carried articles sharply criticizing political practices in various towns, especially the "stand-up" law of 1801, which required that all nominations for assistants and Congress must be made by rising vote or show of hands. Since Federalists had ironclad control of most town meetings, this law greatly hurt any opposition. Charles Holt, *Bee* editor, running afoul of the national Sedition Act, was found guilty, and sentenced to a fine of three hundred dollars and three months in jail. Apparently freedom of the press was intended only for Federalist editors! A formal state-wide Republican organization may be dated from May 1800, when party leaders met in New Haven. They prepared a list of candidates — the first time such a general nomination had been made by any state party. Encouraged by Jefferson's candidacy for President in 1800, local Republicans, under Abraham Bishop, William Hart, and Gideon Granger, campaigned vigorously both for state and national offices. Although Republican votes increased sharply, Federalists still swept all Upper House and Congressional seats. In succeeding years the Republicans centered their attack upon the Established Church and vociferously demanded its disestablishment. Meanwhile the reign of Republicans in Washington resulted in substantial patronage for Connecticut's Republicans. The local Federalists bitterly criticized Jefferson's appointments, especially that of the

aged Samuel Bishop as New Haven Collector of Customs, but Jefferson stood firm.[26]

In the same period the Republicans campaigned actively for a new constitution, disestablishment, election of Congressmen by districts, the end of unfair taxation and of extravagance in local government. The year 1806 brought the largest gubernatorial vote yet, but Trumbull still scored a solid victory over his Republican opponent, William Hart, by 13,413 votes to 9,460. Passage of the Federal Embargo Act by a Republican-controlled Congress in 1807 proved a very unpopular measure in Connecticut, reduced local Republican strength, and brought vigorous resolutions of protest from the Assembly, as well as from a group of leading New Haven citizens. At a special session in February 1809, Governor Trumbull minced no words in calling the Embargo Act unconstitutional — a foreshadowing of strong local opposition to the War of 1812.[27]

Republicans finally obtained a limited victory as a result of a schism in the Federalist Party. In 1811, when the divided Federalists put forward two candidates — Governor John Treadwell (Trumbull's successor) and Roger Griswold — the Republicans decided to support Griswold as being more sympathetic to their program. Much Episcopalian sentiment also swung behind Griswold, so that he became the first nonchurch member elected governor. The Republicans quickly became thoroughly disenchanted with Griswold, because he rapidly proved himself a stanch conservative.[28]

An Unpopular War, 1812–15

IN June 1812 the United States declared war against Great Britain, officially because of numerous and prolonged British violations of our neutral rights, and unofficially because of hopes of expansionists that Canada and Florida could be acquired. In common with general New England sentiment, the entire Connecticut Congressional delegation voted against the declaration. From much of the press and the pulpit flooded forth scathing denunciation of "Mr. Madison's War":

Come on then, fellow citizens, cheerfully submit to the total destruction of your commerce, cheerfully submit to war-taxes, gird on your swords, fight manfully — the immortal honour of Madison and Co. is the *stake* you contend for!!!

A week later the *Courant* reported: "The dreadful tidings have just reached us, that on Thursday last Congress declared War against Great-Britain." The editor characterized the conflict as one in which the United States had everything to lose and nothing to gain. On the other hand, the pro-administration Hartford *Mercury* loyally supported the declaration:

ONCE more the standard is unfurled against our implacable and eternal enemy . . .

That the war commenced is just, honorable and necessary no *American* will deny. That it is popular and will be perseveringly supported, no doubt exists.[29]

When President Madison issued a call for use of militia troops against Canada, Governor Griswold refused to permit the Connecticut militia to leave the state and declared the request unconstitutional — a position which was approved by the next Assembly. The governor and Federalist Assembly did all possible to hamper Madison's administration in its prosecution of the war. As individuals, however, many Connecticut citizens served in the armed forces, including about 1,800 officers and men in the Regular Army alone. The Assembly considered local defense permissible, and the governor kept a large militia force alerted for duty.[30]

In a military sense the war did not affect the state directly until April 1813, when a strong British fleet under Captain Thomas Hardy established a tight blockade. On June 1, 1813, Commodore Stephen Decatur's squadron, the *United States, Macedonian,* and *Hornet,* arrived at the entrance to the Sound, and promptly was chased into New London harbor. So tight was the blockade of the harbor that Decatur was forced to move his ships up the Thames. When he attempted to escape on a dark night in December 1813, blue lights flashing at the harbor's entrance alerted the enemy. Not until November 1814, long after Decatur's assignment elsewhere, did one of the vessels, the sloop of war *Hornet,* finally run the blockade.[31]

In June 1813 an American schooner, *Eagle,* was cleverly fitted out as a torpedo vessel, her decks loaded as an innocent trader, and then was

allowed to fall into British hands off New London while the crew escaped. Three hours later, when a time fuse took effect, the schooner blew up and killed and injured many British seamen. A Norwich citizen devised a crude submarine, went under the British *Ramillies,* Hardy's ship, and on his

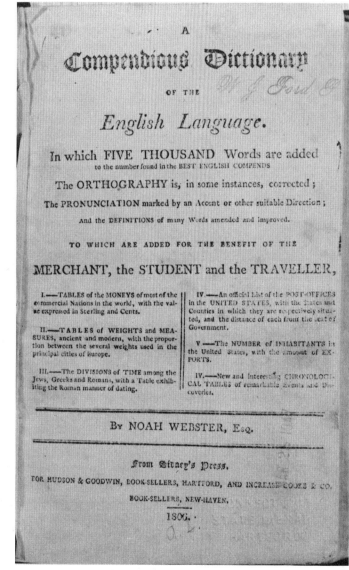

Title page of A Compendious Dictionary *by Noah Webster of West Hartford.*

third trip nearly succeeded in fastening a torpedo to its bottom when a screw broke and he was discovered; but he escaped. As a result of these efforts, Hardy tightened the blockade.[32]

Connecticut's coastal and overseas trade was drastically reduced, as the British ships carefully watched every inlet and river. Amazingly, the packet sloop *Juno* maintained its run from New London to New York throughout the war. Newspaper columns, however, were filled with accounts of vessels captured when bound to or from Connecticut ports, so that risks were high.[33]

Captain Thomas M. Hardy, forwarded this message:

Not wishing to destroy the unoffending inhabitants residing in the town of Stonington, one hour is given them from the receipt of this to move out of town.

Though the town possessed a battery of just

One of cannon which defended Stonington, and memorial marker.

Despite almost constant fear of a major British landing, only two genuine attacks were made. The first, in April 1814, consisted of a raid by about two hundred British sailors and marines up the Connecticut River at Pettipaug Point (North Cove), Essex, where they destroyed about twenty small vessels and a sail loft, inflicting perhaps $200,000 in damages.[34]

Far more serious was the attack launched against Stonington on August 9, 1814, when a small British fleet appeared, and its commander,

two eighteen-pounders and one four-pounder mounted at a small earthwork, the people chose to resist. By burning tar barrels as a signal, they summoned Colonel William Randall's regiment of militia, who repulsed British landing attempts both on August 9 and 10. The frustrated British then subjected the town to three days of furious bombardment from their five ships. According to the account of an eyewitness, Amos Palmer, the British shot at least sixty tons of metal into Stonington. However, they wounded only one man, while their own casualties reached several score, and one warship, the *Despatch*, was badly damaged. Through the years Stonington citizens have delighted in the closing lines of Philip Freneau's ballad on the Battle of Stonington:

> It cost the king ten thousand pounds
> To have a dash at Stonington.[35]

The war brought both fame and disgrace to some Connecticut men. William Hull of Derby, after achieving a distinguished record in the Revolution, entered law and politics in Massachusetts, and then went west, where he soon became governor of Michigan Territory. At the outbreak of war he was given command of the fort at Detroit. Perhaps advancing years had drained the initiative and resourcefulness of the old soldier, for he feebly surrendered Detroit to the British — a capitulation which deeply shocked Americans. Although Hull was not alone in responsibility, he made a convenient scapegoat for a court-martial, severe punishment, and disgrace.[36]

By a strange coincidence, just three days after Detroit's fall, a nephew, Captain Isaac Hull, also Connecticut-born, scored the first great American naval victory of the war when his ship, the frigate *Constitution*, destroyed the British frigate *Guerrière* in a brief, violent engagement. The victory sharply raised American morale and made Hull a national hero.[37]

Connecticut claimed an adopted son as a hero. Commodore Thomas Macdonough, though born in Delaware, in later years considered Middletown, Connecticut, as his home. Sent there in 1806 to assist in construction of some gunboats, he joined the local Episcopal Church and married a Middletown girl, Lucy Ann Shaler. At the memorable Battle of Plattsburgh on Lake Champlain in September 1814, he handled his fleet with such superlative skill as to defeat decisively a British fleet of approximately equal strength. This action forced the British to retreat to Canada and greatly strengthened the hand of American negotiators at the peace conference in Ghent.[38]

Despite the strong internal opposition to the war, marked by such amazing actions as a bill passed by Hartford's Common Council prohibiting Federal recruiting in Hartford, a few shipowners were willing to risk their vessels in privateering. It is estimated that Connecticut sent out approximately eleven different privateers.[39]

A Famous but Notorious Convention

ALTHOUGH Connecticut had many Republicans, the Federalists decisively won all state-wide elections during the war. When a Federal conscription law was passed in 1814, the Assembly voted 168 to 6 that it was unconstitutional. Meanwhile sectional disaffection reached such heights in Massachusetts as to produce a call from there for a meeting of delegates from all New England states to discuss grievances, measures of common defense, and possible changes in the Federal Constitution. Connecticut's Assembly voted 153 to 36 to participate.[40]

When the convention assembled in the old State House at Hartford on December 15, 1814, it consisted of official delegations from Massachusetts, Rhode Island, and Connecticut, plus a sprinkling of unofficial representatives from Vermont and New Hampshire. The Connecticut representatives chosen by the Assembly were all eminent Federalists: Lieutenant Governor Chauncey Goodrich, Calvin Goddard, James Hillhouse, Roger Sherman (nephew of the signer), Nathaniel Smith, Zephaniah Swift, and former Governor John Treadwell. Among the other delegates, Harrison Gray Otis of Massachusetts stood out as particularly forceful. The delegates voted to keep the proceedings secret — a decision which convinced many Republicans that treason was being hatched.[41]

The official report of the three-week convention appeared in an "extra" of the *Courant* on January 6, 1815. It vigorously condemned many Madison administration policies, restated New England's grievances, and recommended certain remedies, including individual state control of defense. The convention proposed seven amendments to the Federal Constitution, including a provision restricting a President to one term, and forbidding any state to provide two successive Presidents. The convention had expected its report to strike consternation into Madison's heart, but news of Jackson's victory at New Orleans, followed quickly by consummation of the Peace of Ghent, turned the

Hartford Convention into an object of national derision and disgrace. An opponent referred to the convention as "that foulest stain on our state escutcheon . . . an imperishable monument of infamy." Even full publication of the hitherto secret proceedings a few years later and a spirited defense in a long book by Theodore Dwight, secretary of the convention, failed to silence charges of treasonable behavior. The wisdom of holding the convention may be seriously questioned, but a close scrutiny of the proceedings reveals it as a purely partisan affair, involving burning grievances, not advocacy of secession nor disloyalty to the nation. The convention and unpatriotic Federalist policies during the war seriously damaged that party in Connecticut and helped produce a reinvigoration of ebbing Republicanism. The Republican vote increased sharply in 1815 and gave party leaders great encouragement.[42]

Many years after the Hartford Convention, a visitor to Hartford from the South strolled into the Old State House and requested to be shown the room where the Hartford Convention sat. It was the room used as the State Senate Chamber, and above the President's chair hung a portrait of Washington by Gilbert Stuart, now located in Memorial Hall of the State Library. This famous painting is brightly colored, and was probably more so then than now. The stranger turned his eyes to the painting and asked whether Washington hung there while the convention sat. "Certainly," replied the guide. "Well," said the southerner, looking at it again, "I'll be damned if he's got the blush off yet."[43]

Sheep and Woolens

DURING the decades of Revolutionary political battles the farmers of Connecticut continued practicing their accustomed conservative agricultural techniques, so that the inefficient methods of late colonial days were still prevailing in the early 1800's.[44]

Agricultural leaders, however, were beginning to demand reform, since only radical improvements would enable the state to compete with fertile western lands. The embargo and the war added a patriotic stimulus, and politicians, ship-

owners, editors, and others joined in the chorus advocating better agricultural techniques. The New Haven County Agricultural Society was launched about 1803, and the Connecticut Agricultural Society in 1817. General David Humphreys, as ringleader in the drive for agricultural reform, received powerful support from political leaders. The newspapers, by devoting increasing space to articles upon improved methods, hoped to check the emigration craze which had seized the state. At various times the Courant published articles upon the proper treatment of worn-out soils and other advanced agricultural practices. In 1818 the Hartford County Agricultural Society promoted its first field day, with prizes for livestock, plowing, and products of domestic manufacture. Meanwhile Humphreys made his farm an experimental center and widely advertised his results.[45]

Using knowledge of Spanish sheep growing gained while minister at Madrid, Humphreys single-handedly introduced the raising of merino sheep in Connecticut. When he left Spain he was permitted to bring back a flock of seventy-five ewes and twenty-five rams, from which came most of the early blooded sheep in America. With the sudden cutting off of foreign wool supply by the embargo, an insatiable demand for merinos developed. Whereas in 1806 Humphreys sold a ram and two ewes for $300, in 1810 he obtained $1,500 apiece for rams and ewes. The merino mania swept Connecticut, and optimists predicted that in wool New England at last had discovered a great staple. As a result of Napoleon's invasion of Spain in 1807–8, thousands of sheep were seized and exported to Britain, and many were shipped from there to America. Consequently their prices plummeted until the outbreak of war in 1812 steadied them.[46]

Sheep growing stimulated the establishment of woolen factories, and again Humphreys pioneered in Connecticut. In 1810 he and associates obtained a charter for the Humphreysville Manufacturing Company, capitalized at $500,000. Thomas Jefferson, hearing that Humphreys made the finest cloth in America, ordered a suiting from him. The Middletown Manufacturing Company was typical of many woolen concerns launched within a decade. Capitalized at $200,000, by 1815 it was operating in a five-story building, employing up to eighty hands, and producing $70,000 in cloth annually. Mills spread rapidly, and by 1818 Hartford County claimed nine woolen factories; New Haven, five; Fairfield, nine; Litchfield, eight; New London, sixteen; Tolland, four; Windham, ten; and Middlesex, five. Over two hundred fulling mills were spread over the state — another indication of Connecticut's booming woolen industry.[47]

Cotton and Other Manufacturing

THE years from 1807 to 1815 saw the birth of Connecticut's cotton industry, at a time when raw cotton was priced low and, in the absence of foreign competition, the demand for cloth was high. Windham County, blessed with ample water power and close to Rhode Island, the earliest center of cotton manufacturing, led in production, with important factories at Pomfret, Killingly, Plainfield, Thompson, and Woodstock. By 1818, sixty-seven cotton mills were operating in the state, and the value of their output ranked second only to agriculture. The industry served to absorb some of the surplus population and thus to check emigration.[48]

Manufacture in other lines was increasing rapidly too. Tanneries, ropewalks, flaxseed oil mills, and distilleries were thriving; and glass, pottery, small arms, tinware, iron, combs, clocks, paper products, silk, buttons, hats, and stockings, were being produced in substantial quantities in factory sites well scattered over the state. Most of the concerns were small, as in Danbury, where in 1810 there were fifty-six hat shops, none with over four employees. In May 1813 Governor John Cotton Smith told the Assembly:

Amidst the serious embarrassments occasioned by the war and the antecedent restrictions upon commerce, we have the consolation to witness a remarkable progress in manufactures, and in the cultivation of the useful arts.[49]

The rapid growth of industry attracted many people to the cities, while some small towns actually lost population. A sizable urban working class was appearing, as the 1820 census unmistakably revealed. In fact, only Rhode Island exceeded Connecticut in the percentage of population engaged in manufacturing.[50]

During the war years from 1812 to 1815 it was considered highly patriotic to open a new factory, and many were started. The Connecticut Republicans seem to have supported the factory movement more enthusiastically than the local Federalists, who tended to advocate home, or domestic, manufacturing.[51]

After the end of the war, British manufacturers seeking to regain old markets and to snuff out the infant American industries, promptly flooded our markets with low-priced goods. This procedure was a primary cause of the postwar depression which afflicted much of the United States. Cotton and wool companies perished in large numbers, and only technical improvements and able management enabled the stronger concerns to survive. An alarmed Assembly in May 1817 gave cotton and woolen factories whose sites did not exceed five acres in size a four-year exemption from taxation and their employees freedom from a poll tax and militia service. Both parties strove to make political capital out of the depression, while manufacturers struggled desperately to keep afloat.[52]

Banks and Trade

UNDERLYING the expansion of manufacturing in the state was the steady increase in banking facilities. Lack of banks and ready capital had severely cramped the growth of manufacturing throughout the colonial and early national periods and forced general resort to cumbersome barter trade. The typical country or town merchant had acted as financier in his colonial community by extending credit to many customers, but the need for banks became more pressing as population grew. By the 1790's revival of shipping, especially of the West India trade, had increased capital accumulations so much that the time seemed ripe to organize several banks. In 1792, therefore, two banks, the Hartford Bank and the Union Bank of New London, were incorporated. Three years later the New Haven Bank and the Middletown Bank were chartered, and within a decade banks were started in Norwich and Bridgeport. By 1818 the state had ten banks, plus the Middletown branch of the Second United States Bank, which made much money available for investment in factories, trade, turnpike companies, and western lands. Under an act of 1803 state funds could be invested in certain banks, which made the political-financial tie-up even closer. Later banking acts gave important privileges to the ecclesiastical societies and thus strengthened the alliance of Established Church and Standing Order.[53]

When the postwar depression hit, several of the banks failed, and bitter attacks were made by many averring that the banks oppressed the poor, speculated dishonestly, contracted the currency at whim, and helped precipitate the hard times. Since a majority of the bank directors were Federalists, the Republicans hammered away upon this theme.[54]

During the 1790's and early 1800's Connecticut's shipping reached new heights. Many small vessels traded with the West Indies, chiefly exporting surplus agricultural produce and importing sugar and molasses. A few ships, especially from New Haven, sailed for the East Indies and China, and the *Neptune* in a thirty-two months' cruise circled the globe and brought in a cargo of silk, tea, and chinaware which netted the owners profits of $240,000. Just before the embargo New Haven's port saw up to a hundred vessels clearing annually for foreign ports, and its famous Long Wharf was crowded with ships, shipping offices, ropewalks, and the produce of distant markets.[55]

The passage of the Embargo Act in December 1807 by Congress, and the later Non-Intercourse Act, severely reduced Connecticut's oceanic trade. Many heartily lambasted the "dambargo," and the *Courant* observed that because of it "the little finger of Thomas Jefferson is heavier than the loins of George the third." The shipbuilders still built many vessels during these years, but the future lay with manufacturing, as shipping never made a full comeback after the War of 1812.[56]

A Political Revolution Brings a New Constitution

POLITICAL affairs, like economic ones, were changing rapidly. The dramatic drive which shattered the Standing Order and achieved a new constitution began in February 1816 when a Republican-Episcopalian meeting took place in New Haven. Although Episcopalians generally had supported the Federalist Party earlier, many had become alienated by failure of the Assembly to vote part of the money available from the Phoenix bank bonus to the Episcopal Bishop's Fund. The participants shrewdly selected Oliver Wolcott of Litchfield as their candidate for governor. Son and grandson of governors, a Yale graduate, with service in the Revolution, lawyer, Federalist, friend of Washington, secretary of the treasury, Federal judge, merchant in New York, banker, and manufacturer, he offered eminence and complete respectability. In religious matters he held broad, tolerant views — an asset in the eyes of many. Furthermore, he had supported the War of 1812, but luckily had been out of state politics for years. A moderate in outlook, he was ideally suited to link Connecticut's conservative past with a more liberal future. For second place on the ticket, the new group, who called themselves Tolerationists, selected Judge Jonathan Ingersoll, a well-to-do and popular New Haven lawyer. The chief plank of the Toleration Party was ecclesiastical reform, that is, disestablishment; but they also advocated a new constitution and modernization of the entire governmental machinery.[57]

The Federalists responded by renominating Governor Smith and naming Calvin Goddard for the second place, and calling upon all voters to support the holy institutions of their fathers. Actually, the Connecticut Federalists had long possessed a formidable political "machine." It included the assistants, most of the Lower House, the sheriffs and deputies, judges of Superior, County, and Probate Courts, justices of the peace, most town officers, high militia officers, lawyers, and many teachers — forming a hard core of about 1,000 to 1,100 Federalists who normally could swing enough votes among close friends and relatives to carry the ticket. Yale College also was considered an integral part of the Federalist machine; and President Dwight, or "Pope" Dwight as his enemies called him, vigorously attacked every heresy, religious or political, which raised its head among faculty or students. The Congregational clergy, still a very powerful group, usually worked hand in glove with local and state Federalist leaders, and from their pulpits many openly supported Federalists. One of the greatest advantages of Federalism lay in its eminent respectability, whereas Republicanism usually connoted inferior social class and occupation.[58]

The 1816 elections gave the Federalist Governor Smith a close victory over Wolcott, but Ingersoll secured the second place. The Toleration party had run so well in gubernatorial and legislative elections that the frightened Federalist majority desperately tried conciliation in the fall of 1816 with an "Act for the support of Literature and Religion." It divided the Federal reimbursement (later amounting to $145,000) to Connecticut for war expenses as follows: Congregationalists, one-third; Episcopalians, one-seventh; Baptists, one-eighth; Methodists, one-twelfth; and Yale College, one-seventh; the remainder to stay in the state treasury. This bonus act satisfied no group, least of all the dissenters, who sharply criticized it as a piece of political chicanery. In the political campaign of April 1817, with the same gubernatorial candidates, the Tolerationists again proposed separation of church and state, no "religious test" for office, and a thorough revision of the taxation system. The Federalists stood firm upon the principles and institutions, religious and secular, of the past. Record-breaking balloting gave Wolcott 13,655 votes to 13,119 for Governor Smith. Though a close vote, it signified the triumph of new men and new principles. Governor Wolcott's broad, forward-looking proposals were largely blocked by the Federalist Upper House, but in 1818 the Tolerationists scored a landslide victory, re-electing Wolcott and capturing both houses. A political revolution had occurred![59]

The May 1818 legislature called for an August constitutional convention, whose delegates were to be elected in town meetings on July 4. As a result of these town elections, the Tolerationists secured a slight majority, but the delegates were broadly representative of all important segments of political opinion and economic class from ultra-Federalist through radical Republican. From such a body only a moderate constitution could emerge.[60]

On August 26, 1818, the convention met in the State House at Hartford to begin three weeks of intensive work. After vigorous debate they adopted a bill of rights which stated that "all political power is inherent in the people" and guaranteed many individual rights, such as freedom of speech and press, trial by jury, right of habeas corpus, and provided safeguards against excessive fines or bail, and against troop quartering in peacetime.[61]

While the charter of 1662 provided useful precedents, many new features were introduced into the new constitution, of which some of the most important were:

1] Clear separation of powers into three departments — legislative, executive, and judicial.

2] New election laws and revised suffrage requirements — twenty-one years of age, six months' residence; a freehold estate worth seven dollars a year, or militia service, or taxes paid within the year.

3] Reorganization of the court system, with number of judges reduced and tenure dependent upon age, record, and good behavior.

4] Annual elections and annual legislative sessions, alternating between Hartford and New Haven.

5] Governor given veto power, but a simple majority of legislature could override it.

6] Salaries of governor, lieutenant governor, senators (Upper House now called Senate), and representatives fixed by statute, and not alterable during an incumbent's term.

7] Amendments could be added through passage by two-thirds vote of both houses of the Assembly and approval by the voters.

8] The Congregational Church was disestablished and all religious bodies were placed upon a common basis of voluntary support.

This last provision loomed largest in the eyes of many delegates. Despite efforts of the supporters of the Established Church, the convention effected complete severance of church from state, the constitutional guaranty of the rights of conscience, and recognition of the complete equality before the law of all Christian sects. When the final vote came on September 15, 1818, the new constitution won decisive approval — 134 to 61.

Since there were at least seventy-one Federalists present and several Republicans voted negatively, obviously a few Federalists supported the document.[62]

It remained for the people to pass upon their handiwork — a new but moderate document which still preserved the old rights of the towns but guaranteed religious toleration. Many liberals were gravely dissatisfied, and conservatives felt that a catastrophe loomed ahead. The Toleration Party officially supported the constitution, while the Federalists fought it as full of dangerous innovations and an invitation to further radicalism. Returns of the October 5 vote showed 13,918 in favor and 12,364 against. In general, areas of strong religious dissent, such as New London and Fairfield counties, gave heavy majorities for ratification, while more conservative Litchfield and Hartford counties brought in substantial negative margins.[63]

The political revolution was rounded out under Governor Wolcott in 1818–19 by a reform of taxation which largely equalized the burden, by new election and judiciary laws, and by allocation of school funds to districts on the basis of children of school age (not taxable wealth). The victory of the Toleration Party signified a victory of nationalism over localism, and of democratic principles over aristocratic ones. At last Connecticut, politically, had joined the nineteenth century![64]

CHAPTER 11

Migrating Yankees

Early Wanderings — Northward into the Berkshires — Farther Northward to Vermont —
A "New Connecticut" in Vermont — Westward the Path of Empire — Connecticut's
Western Reserve — To Indiana, Illinois, and Beyond — Across the Mississippi to the Pacific

Early Wanderings

CONNECTICUT'S people were typical migrating Yankees. Hardly had the early pioneers settled when some of the more restless sought new homes. As already seen, Long Island and New Jersey were the objectives of seventeenth-century departures, but the eighteenth century brought far greater waves of migration.

While most of the earlier outpourings could be attributed largely to a spirit of adventure or to internal schisms, by the 1750's and 1760's weightier reasons for departure had developed. Connecticut's primitive agricultural economy, upon which the majority depended, no longer offered adequate economic inducements to many citizens, especially the young adults. Between 1730 and 1756 the population had jumped from about 38,000 to 130,611, and the 1774 census showed close to 200,000 persons. This amazing rate of growth resulted chiefly from a high birth rate, not from large immigration. Travelers of the period commented upon the large families which they observed everywhere. Connecticut's last frontier became virtually closed between the establish-

ment of Litchfield County in 1751 and 1774, when the census revealed over 27,000 inhabitants in that county. The pressure of the rapidly growing population in the colony meant that many families were being driven to cultivation of thin marginal lands, which under then current agricultural practices could not produce crops adequate for a decent standard of living. In the prevailing agricultural economy and with serious soil depletion quite evident, Connecticut already was approaching a population saturation point. When one also considers heavy taxes, restricted commerce, poor markets, inadequate transportation, and growing mania for land speculation, it is little wonder that the availability of far cheaper and more fertile lands on the frontier caused an explosive emigration movement by thousands of Connecticut Yankees.[1]

The final defeat of France in America in 1760 enabled Connecticut's pent-up populace to begin swarming out in all directions. Many turned their faces toward northeastern Pennsylvania, and the lands of the Susquehannah and the two Delaware companies — enthusiastic ventures initiated by Connecticut promoters. In 1774 other Connecticut

191

migrants settled in Lackaway and Bozrah, Pennsylvania, and though driven out in the Revolution, they returned afterward.[2]

A few enterprising Nutmeggers journeyed to faraway Mississippi. Their moving spirit was Phineas Lyman of Durham and later Suffield. Acting for a company called the Military Adventurers, veterans of the French and Indian War and the Havana Campaign, Lyman petitioned the British Government for a land grant on the Yazoo River in the present state of Mississippi. Whether Lyman actually obtained the grant is dubious, but he returned home enthusiastic about the venture and began energetic promotion. Rufus Putnam, surveyor for the company, and others visited the area in 1773, and their glowing report caused some families from Connecticut and Massachusetts to set out in 1773 and 1774 for the lower Mississippi. Despite setbacks from illness and other causes, many finally settled on the Big Black River, near the old French town of Natchez.[3]

A small number of adventurous spirits joined emigrants from Massachusetts who had settled in South Carolina and then in 1752 had obtained land grants in the Midway district of the Georgia frontier. After going to Midway these transplanted New Englanders retained strong interest in the struggle of their old homeland against Britain, and under Dr. Lyman Hall, a native of Wallingford, Connecticut, and a Yale graduate, they helped win Georgia to the Patriot side. Later Dr. Hall signed the Declaration of Independence for Georgia and was elected Georgia's governor in 1783. Another Connecticut son, Abraham Baldwin of Guilford, Yale graduate and tutor, moved to Georgia in 1783, served with distinction in Georgia's delegation to the Philadelphia Convention, fathered the public school system and state university, and served in the Federal House and Senate.[4]

Another small but interesting transplanting occurred far to the east in Nova Scotia. For about a decade beginning in 1759, ships from Norwich and New London carried eager immigrants to the townships of Amherst, Cornwallis, Dublin, Falmouth, and Horton — a movement which was instrumental in giving a strong New England tone to Nova Scotia on the eve of the American Revolution.[5]

Northward into the Berkshires

WITH the victorious ending of the French and Indian War, the hills and valleys of the Berkshires in western Massachusetts beckoned to the more adventurous Connecticut farmers. Although numerous pioneers to this region came from Massachusetts or other colonies, many of the Berkshire towns were settled primarily by Connecticut men. Pittsfield, the future metropolis of Berkshire County, affords a good example of a town whose mainstream of migration emanated from Connecticut. Pittsfield, or Poontoosuck as it was called until 1761, experienced many vicissitudes through the early years. The first settlement, made in the early 1740's, had failed because of the overwhelming French and Indian danger during King George's War. In 1752, with the war over, Solomon Deming of Wethersfield rode northward again, this time with his wife Sarah behind him on the pillion, and they established their home amidst the dense Berkshire forests. Charles Goodrich, also of Wethersfield, soon arrived with his cart and team, and for many years ranked as the wealthiest inhabitant of the infant town.[6]

The renewal of war with the French inspired such terror among the exposed settlers of the pioneer town that Connecticut sent armed men with extra horses to carry back all women and children. Indian prowlers became so numerous that all settlements north of Stockbridge were abandoned. A stockade, Fort Anson, was constructed at Pittsfield and garrisoned by a combined force of local men, Connecticut men, and others sent by Massachusetts' Governor Bernard.[7]

After the final French defeat, settlers flocked in from Wethersfield, Hartford, West Hartford, Litchfield, Lebanon, Lyme, Hebron, Ridgefield, and Stonington in Connecticut, as well as from Massachusetts towns. As with other pioneer settlements, Pittsfield soon organized itself at a proprietors' meeting and elected suitable officials. They faced the inevitable problems of roads, bridges, and taxes, and even voted that "hogs shall not run at large." True to best Connecticut (and Massachusetts) tradition, they promptly appointed a committee "to manage the whole affair of the meeting-house." The exertions involved in building the first meeting house proved to be quite strenuous and prolonged. Securing a minister offered an even greater challenge! After failing several times to obtain a permanently settled pastor they finally procured Thomas Allen of Northampton on the basis of a ninety-pound settlement and a salary of sixty pounds yearly, with an annual increase of five pounds to a maximum of eighty pounds. In April 1764 Allen commenced a long ministry, terminated only by his death in 1810. Among the fifty-two to join his church in the first year were Solomon and Sarah Deming.[8]

Pittsfield likewise wasted little time in tackling the problem of education. On March 11, 1765, the proprietors voted thirty pounds to "be raised to pay for Schooling this year." By 1773 the annual appropriation had jumped to a hundred pounds, and by 1775 the town boasted five schoolhouses. This educational expansion paralleled the rapid population growth — from perhaps 60 families in 1761 to 138 in 1772. One finds a typical early settler, William Williams, in a letter of 1767 boasting of the "goodness of our Air," the fine health prevailing, and the prosperity, and flatly asserting that "No man or Woman of but common Understanding, that ever came, and got Settled among us wished themselves back." Already, in fact, Charles Goodrich's land had appreciated fortyfold.[9]

When the Revolution broke out, the great majority of Pittsfield men ardently supported the Patriot cause, contributing generously of money and supplies, and participating in the Canadian expedition, the Boston siege, and the upper New York campaigns. When Tryon raided the Connecticut coast in 1779, fifteen men from Pittsfield rushed southward to help in the defense of their native soil.[10]

Williamstown provides another good example of a Berkshire town settled largely from Connecticut. The first settlement attempt, probably made in 1751 or 1752 by Fort Massachusetts soldiers, failed because of Indian threats. Nehemiah Smedley and William and Josia Horsford of Connecticut were involved in this abortive effort, and returned to the fort to help protect the frontier where they longed to live. Most of the small primary surge of settlers into Williamstown (1753–58) came from Massachusetts, but the far larger wave of the next

fifteen years poured forth mainly from Connecticut, and especially from Canaan, Colchester, Danbury, Litchfield, Middletown, and Wethersfield. These migrants purchased outlying lots from the proprietors, or earlier settlers, and helped to push Williamstown's population over 1,000 by 1776.[11]

The young town looked to Connecticut for its first regular minister and college president. The Reverend Whitman Welch (Yale 1762), a native of Milford, Connecticut, served a devoted parish for more than a decade, beginning in the fall of 1765. When Williams College was launched in the 1790's, the first president selected was the Reverend Ebenezer Fitch, born in Lisbon, Connecticut, Yale graduate (class of 1777), and later tutor there. He headed the struggling young college until 1815.[12]

The Berkshire County towns which had large, often dominant, infusions of Connecticut blood in the initial stages are located in every section of the county, both valley and mountain: Alford, Becket, Egremont, Great Barrington, Hancock, Hinsdale, Lanesboro, Lee, Lenox, New Ashford, New Marlboro, Otis, Richmond, Sandisfield, West Stockbridge, Wales, Washington, and Windsor.[13]

It is scarcely surprising that Berkshire settlers, largely of Congregational Connecticut background, frequently preferred a Connecticut-born, Yale-trained minister, as in Egremont, which called Eliphalet Steele (West Hartford native); Great Barrington, Samuel Hopkins (Waterbury); Lanesboro, Daniel Collins (Guilford); Tyringham, Adonijah Bidwell (Hartford); Hinsdale, Theodore Hinsdale — town named for him (Windsor); and Windsor, David Avery (Norwich). In other cases, towns chose Yale graduates not born in Connecticut. Out of 118 pastors settled in all of the counties of western Massachusetts up to 1800, Yale trained 87, as against only 31 from Harvard. Hence it is not surprising that orthodox Congregationalism dominated Berkshire County well into the nineteenth century with a vigor remarkable even for Puritan New England.[14]

Connecticut citizens played the leading role also in the beginnings of the Episcopal (then Anglican) Church in western Massachusetts — a story which revolves around the remarkable Gideon

193

Bostwick, born at New Milford in 1742 and graduated from Yale in 1762. Two years later he migrated to Great Barrington, where he soon became a lay reader in the Anglican Church. In 1769 he decided to travel to England for further training. He was ordained and sent back to New England as an Anglican missionary of the Society for the Propagation of the Gospel. His home church was the beautiful St. James, erected in Great Barrington by enthusiastic parishioners. For the next twenty-three years he toiled unremittingly over a vast area which included all of Berkshire County, upper New York, southern Vermont, and Canaan, Cornwall, Litchfield, New Milford, Norfolk, and Salisbury in Connecticut. During his long and dedicated career on the frontier he reputedly baptized 81 adults and 2,274 children! After his death another Connecticut clergyman, the Reverend Daniel Burhans of Sherman, took over his work, though in a more limited area. Within a short time seven Episcopal churches opened in Berkshire County, and Connecticut men had provided most of the generating power behind them.[15]

Connecticut also contributed Berkshire County's first highly effective Methodist circuit rider, "Billy" Hibbard. Born in Norwich in 1771, Hibbard migrated to Hinsdale, where he soon combined farming with preaching. He employed the fervent, highly emotional style of preaching so well that Bishop Francis Asbury once claimed that Hibbard "was heard distinctly half a mile"! He went on the Pittsfield circuit in 1797, and for forty-nine years he tirelessly preached the Gospel in Berkshire County, western Connecticut, Long Island, and the Hudson Valley.[16]

For many years the ties between Berkshire County and Connecticut remained even closer because the Hartford *Courant* circulated widely in the county and carried advertisements of runaway slaves and impounded cattle of that section. Until the age of the railroad arrived, Hartford also attracted much trade with the Berkshires.[17]

During the Revolutionary and post-Revolutionary periods, as a result of the frontier conditions, an almost open break occurred between Berkshire County and other western areas and the more conservative and class-conscious eastern part of Massachusetts. The westerners refused to admit the authority of the Massachusetts General Court or the judicial courts. Great Barrington, Richmond, and Lenox, towns thickly filled with Connecticut emigrants, in official votes protested violently against state policies, and Lenox once even petitioned "to be set off to be a part of a neighboring state" (presumably Connecticut!).[18]

Shays' Rebellion of 1786–87 arose out of the economic and political grievances of the yeoman farmers of western Massachusetts. Such political radicalism, however, was chiefly a surface manifestation, caused by immediate practical problems, and it failed to disturb the basic social, cultural, and religious conservatism of Berkshire County people.[19]

Farther Northward to Vermont

AS western Massachusetts rapidly filled up it was inevitable that the unsettled areas to the north would become the next target for intrepid Connecticut emigrants. It was the story of Berkshire County over again — but intensified. The factors which drove the younger adventurous element to new lands seemed ever more compelling as the Revolution brought widespread economic dislocations. A farmer, John Clarke, who later moved to Vermont, expressed the feelings of many:

About this time (1779) by reason of the war I began to be in trouble by heavy taxes and debts which I could not pay with Continental Money bills. The scarcity of provision distressed many and myself . . . and the scarcity of current money made it very difficult for me to procure provision. Neither my farm nor trade nor both together were adequate to procure a comfortable subsistence, especially in the years 1783 and 1784 when 12 acres of English grain harvested on my farm were not sufficient to bread my family 6 months.

For a few years during the Revolution and just afterward, Vermont levied no taxes on land, thanks to Ira Allen's ingenious scheme for running the government on money obtained from confiscated estates. Three basic factors sparked the Connecticut migration to Vermont: 1] economic dislocations caused by the Revolution; 2] the depressed state of agriculture; and 3] the desire of many to escape the religious and political restrictions imposed by the Standing Order. Land hunger, however, afforded the chief reason for migration.[20]

From 1749 to 1764 Governor Benning Wentworth of New Hampshire, hoping to pocket some extra money, freely granted townships, of which 129 in all were located in the future state of Vermont. A substantial number of the grantees or proprietors resided in Connecticut, and in many cases had no intentions of emigrating at all. The land rights of such speculators, however, often were sold to other Connecticut people, who promptly headed northward. Sometimes the proprietors provided special inducements, as in Hartford, Vermont, where they offered a premium for every bushel of wheat, corn, or rye grown.[21]

The settlement of Vermont was delayed for many years until the fall of Quebec and Montreal ended the French and Indian threat. Meanwhile numerous soldiers from Connecticut and other New England states saw the virgin lands of Vermont and realized their great possibilities. Hence the influx into Vermont commenced immediately after the war, though it proceeded more slowly than that into the Berkshire country.[22]

Two main streams of Connecticut migrants flowed northward into Vermont. The eastern branch, coming chiefly from upland areas of Tolland and Windham counties, especially Lebanon, Hebron, Coventry, Mansfield, and Canterbury, moved far up the Connecticut River and settled along its banks. These people held a conservative political and religious (Congregational) outlook. In contrast, the western stream, emanating from the newer hill towns of Litchfield County, Canaan, Cornwall, Goshen, Milford, and Salisbury especially, was decidedly less conservative politically and religiously, since many religious dissenters, as well as some deists and freethinkers, were found in their ranks. These broad differences actually colored the political and religious complexion of young Vermont so that east of the Green Mountains the people appeared as very traditional Yankees, west of the mountains, often as radicals. The Reverend Nathan Perkins of Hartford, Connecticut, who made a missionary tour up the western side in 1789, declared that half the people there "would chuse to have no Sabbath no ministers — no religion — no heaven — no hell — no morality."

When Ethan Allen wrote a book, *Reason the Only Oracle of Man*, defending rationalism in religion, he suffered no loss of reputation in western Vermont, though Connecticut Congregational leaders such as Stiles, Dwight, and Perkins sharply condemned it. It is scarcely surprising that nineteen out of twenty-one Congregational churches organized in Vermont by 1780 were located east of the mountains.[23]

In following the eastern flow of Connecticut settlers, one finds that the first charter given by Governor Wentworth after the close of the French and Indian War was granted in 1761 to John Baldwin and sixty-one others, mostly from Windham or Lebanon. They received full rights to a choice tract of land, six and one-half miles square, along the Connecticut River. The proprietors held their first meeting on August 26, 1761, at Windham, Connecticut, when they chose officials and a committee to view the land and lay out lots. The planning stage occupied about two years, and actual settlement of Hartford, Vermont, started probably in the spring of 1763, as the December 1763 proprietors' minutes refer to men "who have been at labor in said town this summer past, or fall." Very likely the pioneers followed the pattern common in new towns of coming up without families the first year, erecting crude shelters, clearing a small tract of land, and making other preparations for a permanent settlement. By the next summer the families of Elijah, Solomon, and Benajah Strong, Jonathan Marsh, Noah Dewey, and Benjamin Wright had settled in Hartford. In true Connecticut fashion, the first call was given in October 1764 for a town meeting to be held in December. Meanwhile, the last proprietors' meeting held in Connecticut took place at Lebanon in March 1765, after which future meetings were held at Hartford, Vermont. As was usually the case, only a few of the proprietors actually settled permanently in Hartford — probably not more than six — and the others generally disposed of their land rights to land-hungry neighbors of eastern Connecticut. Records of the town meetings for the next few years indicate the usual run of business as new settlers flocked in, obtained land, and settled down in the growing community. Each year it resembled more closely a Connecticut town, with the same basic institutions of town meetings, churches, and later, schools. One even finds the familiar inducements of land for those willing to build a sawmill or gristmill.[24]

The same general pattern can be found repeated in Norwich, Vermont, located just north of Hartford. Again Governor Wentworth made the initial grant, and the records reveal that the Norwich proprietors met "ye 26 Day of August 1761 at the House of Mr. Willm Waterman in Mansfield." The final meeting in Mansfield occurred March 2, 1767, after which presumably enough of the land proprietors actually lived in Norwich, Vermont, to make meetings there more practicable. Most of the early settlers of Norwich and of Hanover, New Hampshire, directly across the Connecticut River, came from the town of Mansfield, Connecticut. The pervasive influence of their old homeland comes out vividly in an action at the Norwich town meeting of March 9, 1779, aimed at co-operation and order:

Voted as Townsmen and Town officers are very n[ec]essary for the well being of said Town we hereby Covenant and agree to pay such respect to them and obey them in such manner and so far as was the case with respect to them in Connecticut in the year 1772 — and the said officers are to [ad]here to the Laws of Connecticut as they were inforce in the aforementioned year for the rule of their conduct in the execution of their said offices, to take cognisence of such breaches of peace and other offences as were cognizable by the Law of Said Connecticut and transact every other matter which appertains to the offices aforesaid so far as the circumstances of sd Town can possibly admit —

By 1790 Norwich numbered over 1,000 inhabitants, and it is claimed that every person possessed an eastern Connecticut origin.[25]

As one sweeps up the Connecticut River Valley he sees many towns which adventurous Connecticut pioneers helped to start, including Weathersfield, Windsor, Thetford, and Fairlee in Vermont; and Claremont, Plainfield, Lebanon, Hanover, Lyme, Orford, and Piermont in New Hampshire. Many Nutmeggers percolated well back into the hills on both sides of the River to settle at Marlboro, Pomfret, Sharon, Strafford, Northfield, Plainfield, Waterbury, Stowe, Wolcott, and Elmore — all east of the Green Mountains. To the eastward in New Hampshire the wave penetrated as far as Gilsum, Acworth, Newport, Canaan, Dorchester, Campton, Littleton, and Stratford.[26]

The second large Vermont-bound stream flowed from western Connecticut to western Vermont. In Salisbury, Connecticut, lived a large number of land-hungry persons who first hired an agent to find an attractive block of land and then applied to Governor Wentworth for a charter covering this land in the "New Hampshire Grants." On November 2, 1761, Wentworth issued the charter providing sixty-eight shares covering over six miles square in the Otter Creek area (Middlebury). Charter requirements included: 1] each grantee to plant and cultivate five acres within five years for every fifty-acre share and to preserve all suitable pine trees for the Royal Navy; 2] town lots to be laid out near the center of town for each grantee; 3] payment of one ear of Indian corn annually for ten years as rent; and 4] after that, one shilling annually for every hundred acres in lieu of all other rents. Single shares were ordered reserved for the Society for the Propagation of the Gospel, a Church of England glebe, support of the first settled minister, a school and last but not least, two shares for His Excellency! In general, this charter closely resembled the many others bestowed so freely by Governor Wentworth, who granted nearly 3,000,000 acres west of the Connecticut River between 1750 and 1764 — land which New York also strongly claimed.[27]

In the spring of 1773 Benjamin Smalley of Salisbury, one of the grantees, was the first person to settle with a family in Middlebury. During the next two decades many others followed, mostly from Connecticut towns such as Salisbury, Simsbury, Litchfield, Norfolk, Bolton, Glastonbury, Mansfield, and Voluntown, as well as from Massachusetts. The first meeting of Middlebury grantees took place at John Evart's home in Salisbury, so that it is entirely fitting to call Salisbury the "mother of Middlebury." With the outbreak of the Revolution the early families temporarily vacated their homes, but returned soon after the close of the war.[28]

Arlington, Vermont, represents another type of Connecticut migration — Anglican. Eleven families came from Newtown in 1764, and soon were joined by others from New Milford. Israel Canfield, a soldier in the French and Indian War, had passed through Arlington and admired it so much that upon his return home he persuaded neighbors to pack up and move northward to the fertile Vermont valley. In 1772, under Jehiel Hawley St. James, the first Anglican Church in Vermont was founded. When the Revolution came, Arlington, like its mother towns in Connecticut, contained many Tories.[29]

In their formative years many other towns of western Vermont enjoyed heavy infusions of Connecticut blood, including among others, Bennington, Dorset, Rupert, Pawlet, Wells, Tinmouth, Wallingford, Pittsford, Benson, Salisbury, Cornwall, Ripton, Addison, Panton, Vergennes, Ferrisburgh, Hinesburg, Shelburne, Williston, Essex, Castleton, Fairfax, Fairfield, Sheldon, Grand Isle, and North Hero. As is obvious, many Vermont towns took their names from Connecticut.[30]

A "New Connecticut" in Vermont

CONNECTICUT natives played the leading part in the formation of the state of Vermont. In the forefront were the Allen brothers, Ethan and Ira, from Salisbury. Land speculators on a gigantic scale, they explored in northern Vermont and then obtained title from Governor Wentworth to a huge tract, which they organized as the Onion River Company. Inevitably New Yorkers also cast covetous eyes on Vermont, and some moved in. All of the Connecticut settlers sooner or later were drawn into the lengthy and bitter battle between New Hampshire and New York for the possession of Vermont. As early as March 1775 Ethan Allen considered the possibility of an independent Vermont, but soon afterward he became the hero of the daring seizure of Fort Ticonderoga. It therefore fell to his brothers, Ira and Heman Allen, Captain Joseph Bowker, Thomas Chittenden, Dr. Jonas Fay, Colonel William Marsh, and Seth Warner to mastermind the plans which resulted in forming the independent republic of Vermont.[31]

The birth of independent Vermont resulted from a series of conventions beginning at Dorset in January 1776 and ending at Windsor in July 1777. At one of the intermediate conventions, held at Westminster in January 1777, the delegates first took a definite stand in favor of independence and voted to call their state "New Connecticut" — ample evidence of the key role Connecticut migrants had played in Vermont life. A later convention switched to "Vermont" when it was discovered that an area along the Susquehanna bore the same name.[32]

The new Vermont constitution, adopted at Windsor in July 1777, was a very democratic document which, although owing most to Pennsylvania's 1776 constitution, was strongly influenced by Connecticut institutions and practices. Presumably, at an earlier date, Oliver Wolcott, Sr., and others of Litchfield were requested to make suggestions as to organization of the Vermont government, and apparently they obliged. The Nutmeg influence was especially noticeable in the provision making the town the basis of representation in the legislature and requiring membership in the Protestant Church for members of the legislature.[33]

Many other similarities stand out. The Vermont criminal code of 1779, listing nine offenses punishable by death, is similar to, though not identical with, Connecticut's code. The journal of the first Vermont legislature contains an interesting entry: "*Passed* an act for the punishing high treason and other atrocious crimes, as said Act stands in the Connecticut law Book." In similar vein they "*Passed* an Act against treacherous conspiracies as said act stands in the Connecticut law Book." Other acts of the first session emulated Connecticut's example: instituting trainbands, or militia, to include all males from sixteen to fifty; and setting up Vermont's Superior Courts closely parallel to those of Connecticut. A Vermont jurist alluding to the state's indebtedness declared:

Especially were our jurisprudence and our judicial system and methods modelled after those of Connecticut. We inherited the common laws of England *per stirpe and not per capita.* We took it through Connecticut as applied by its courts and re-enacted by its legislatures. . . . For a long time in our earlier history Connecticut precedents were as paramount in authority as they were salutory in their results.[34]

The cherished institutions of old Connecticut — the Congregational Church (in creed and architecture), the town meeting, the village school, the university (in 1791 a charter was granted to the University of Vermont), free land tenure, and sturdy individualism — each found an esteemed place in the "New Connecticut."[35]

As a final indication of Connecticut's predominant influence, one needs only to note those elected to positions of leadership by the infant state. Thomas Chittenden from Salisbury served as Vermont's first governor (1778–97), and eight of the next fourteen incumbents claimed a Connecticut birthplace. Many of Chittenden's first Council came from Connecticut. Likewise, the mother state contributed such eminent figures as Thomas Chandler, Jr., from Woodstock, first secretary of state; Stephen Row Bradley from Cheshire, a Vermont senator; Nathaniel Chipman, a chief justice, and Gamaliel Painter, one of the founders of Middlebury College, both from Salisbury. In the white frame houses beside tree-lined streets, the village greens, and the meeting houses of many a contemporary Vermont town one sees architectural symbols of a common Puritan heritage derived from southern New England, and especially from Connecticut.[36]

Westward the Path of Empire

AS early as the 1740's and 1750's Connecticut migrants began to spill over into the eastern fringes of New York, especially Putnam and Orange counties, while Canaan pioneers journeyed a few miles westward into the area of Spencertown and Hillsdale.[37]

The big trek, however, did not start until after the Revolution, when, with the Iroquois threat dissipated, a large stream of immigrants rushed into largely unsettled upper New York. During the Revolution seven pairs of brothers from seven families in Plymouth, Connecticut, served in upper New York and developed a great liking for that section. When the war ended they lost little time in returning to found the town of Kirkland, New York. Neighbors and friends followed, including Judge Hugh White of Middletown, who left in 1784 with four grown sons. After founding Whitesboro, the Judge sent back samples of his finest New York wheat, potatoes, and oats — a display which caused many to pack up and move to

Oneida County. Others flocked farther westward into the Genesee country. In many cases the new settlers came from Berkshire County, Massachusetts, or Vermont, but had been born in Connecticut. Lowville and Binghamton attracted Connecticut pioneers, while Avon claimed Farmington as its mother. In 1740 a young couple left Northern Ireland and crossed the ocean to a new home in Plainfield, Connecticut, where they prospered. In 1765, with a family of nine sons and a daughter to support, they moved to the fresh lands of Windsor, Vermont. After the war, in 1793–94, four of the sons, lured by the virgin lands of New York, migrated to Marcy in Oneida County. Although the process of overrunning upstate New York was more a broad New England movement than a Connecticut one, the Nutmeg influence was great in many phases of life, especially religion and education. In 1804 Eliphalet Nott, a native of Ashford, assumed the presidency of Union College, and gave it vigorous leadership for sixty-two years. From the dedicated labors of Samuel Kirkland of Norwich, Hamilton College at Clinton, New York, made its start in the 1790's and Azel Backus, also of Norwich, served as first president.[38]

In 1798 the Missionary Society of Connecticut assigned missionaries to the Hudson and Mohawk river regions and the next year sent Seth Williston to Onondaga County. On the political front Connecticut's influence can be impressively seen in the New York constitutional convention of 1821: a majority of the 127 delegates were born in Connecticut or were sons of men born there.[39]

Connecticut men played a noteworthy part in the opening of Ohio and the whole Northwest Territory. The Reverend Manasseh Cutler, native of Killingly and Yale graduate, was a ringleader in the organization of the Ohio Company. An astute lobbyist, he persuaded the Treasury Board to sell very cheaply to the Ohio Company 1,500,000 choice acres in the Northwest Territory. Also, he offered several suggestions for the government of the Territory which were later incorporated in the Northwest Ordinance of 1787.[40]

This Company sponsored the first actual Yankee settlement in the future Ohio — that of Marietta in 1788. Two contingents — from Ipswich, Massachusetts, and Hartford — joined in carrying New

England's culture and creed into the wilderness. At the confluence of the Ohio and Muskingum rivers these Yankees quickly created a typical pioneer Massachusetts or Connecticut town, complete with town common, town lots, preaching, and within a few months, a school. When the Congregational church was formally organized in 1796, its rolls contained sixteen Connecticut names out of thirty-one members.[41]

Connecticut's Western Reserve

THE part of Ohio most intimately associated with Connecticut is the Western Reserve. When Connecticut yielded her claims to any Pennsylvania land by a deed of cession to Congress in 1786, the state specifically "reserved" a strip of land bordering upon Lake Erie and Pennsylvania, 120 miles wide from east to west and running from 41° to 42° 2′ north latitude. Congress accepted this reservation, and the area, called by such names as "New Connecticut," "the Connecticut Western Reserve," or most commonly, simply "the Western Reserve," was governed by Connecticut until 1800.[42]

Not until 1795 and after much controversy did the Assembly finally adopt a scheme for the settlement of the Western Reserve. It authorized a committee to sell the land, estimated at over 3,000,000 acres, for not less than $1,000,000. The net proceeds were to be placed in a special fund and the interest devoted to support of Connecticut schools (still in effect). The land was sold for $1,200,000 to thirty-five men representing themselves and others, with individual portions running from $1,683 to as high as $168,185 for Oliver Phelps. It was arranged that each investor should deposit with the state treasurer a bond and a mortgage on the lands. The purchasers and associates, numbering fifty-seven in all, organized a kind of syndicate called the Connecticut Land Company.[43]

The syndicate appointed Moses Cleaveland of Canterbury general agent to conduct the surveys of the land. Moving westward with a party of fifty, Cleaveland reached the Western Reserve July 4, 1796. After a salute of sixteen rounds, he ordered grog poured for everybody and happy toasts were drunk to the President, to "The State of New Con-

necticut," and "The Connecticut Land Company," among others. A few days later Cleaveland selected an attractive and strategic spot near where the Cuyahoga River emptied into Lake Erie as the site for the chief settlement in the Reserve. In typical New England fashion Cleaveland paced off a spacious ten-acre public square, and then his surveyors commenced laying out the town. Thus was born a tiny village in the wilderness, from which grew the great metropolis appropriately named Cleveland.[44]

At the western end of the Reserve was a strip twenty-five miles wide known as the Firelands. This area was linked with Connecticut by bonds of suffering and destruction. As a result of severe British raids upon Danbury, New Haven, Fairfield, Norwalk, and New London in the Revolution, many families incurred great losses. After years of petitions for relief, the state finally took decisive action in 1792 to reimburse the victims and their heirs by turning over to them 500,000 acres in Ohio for equitable division according to losses. These years of delay had been caused by lack of policy, legal delays, a careful study of the claims, an appraisal of losses made, and publication of an official list. Eventually, about 1,870 persons with claims amounting to more than $500,000 were recognized. Unfortunately it required many more years — until 1805 to be exact — before the Indians in the area agreed to cede their lands. Several more years were devoted to a survey, so that a full thirty years elapsed between the first British raid and the opening of the Firelands. By this time most of the sufferers were too old to migrate there, and actual settlement progressed slowly.[45]

The pioneers from Connecticut to the Western Reserve, coming in small numbers in the late 1790's and early 1800's, suffered great privations in their lonely cabins amidst the great wilderness. Because of the system of drawing lots for their land the early immigrants tended to be much scattered and were hampered by primitive roads and lack of available markets for their produce. After the War of 1812 ended, "Ohio fever" hit Connecticut, and one of the largest and most homogeneous group migrations in American history ensued. Many took the route by the Mohawk Valley and overland to Buffalo, then to Ohio by boat or by rough trail through Erie to Conneaut and on to their land. Others crossed Pennsylvania, ascending the mountains and dropping down to Pittsburgh, and then followed pack trails to Youngstown and the Reserve. Land agents in Connecticut, such as Uriel Holmes and Ephraim Root of Hartford, advertised freely, predicting quick fortunes for the ambitious, and offered easy terms. As the Indians withdrew and markets developed, Ohio began to grow rapidly, and western lands appeared to be both a safe and profitable investment. Many emigrants of means left for Ohio. Cheap land, low taxes, but still a New England way of life, offered an irresistible combination to young couples in Connecticut tired of high land prices, impoverished soil, and limited opportunities.[46]

Connecticut families rushed into all parts of Ohio and especially into the Western Reserve, which was populated almost entirely by Connecticut stock. By 1800 over thirty Connecticut names dotted the map: Berlin, Bloomfield, Bristol, Brookfield, Chatham, Chester, Colebrook, Danbury, Fairfield, Farmington, Franklin, Greenwich, Guilford, Hartford, Hartland, Huntington, Litchfield, Lyme, Middlebury, Monroe, Montville, New Haven, New London, Norwalk, Saybrook, Sharon, Southington, Thompson, Trumbull, Vernon, Warren, Windham, and Windsor. The exodus to Ohio and other states was so great that it caused fear and alarm in the mother state, whose census figures revealed an appalling depletion. Forty-five towns actually were larger in 1790 or 1800 than in 1820, and Connecticut's rate of population growth in the 1790–1820 period was only about one-seventh that of the United States. In 1817 Governor Oliver Wolcott's message to the Assembly evinced deep concern over the heavy emigration, and he suggested that steps such as tax relief be taken to render Connecticut more attractive.[47]

Despite everything, the Nutmeg tide rolled westward. David Hudson of Goshen named his Ohio town in his own honor, and in 1802 built a Congregational church and a schoolhouse. An early arrival there was Owen Brown of Torrington, who established a tannery, where his son John, later to be very famous, worked for a dozen years. A large group of Episcopalians from Plymouth founded Plymouth, Ohio, while pioneers from old Norwalk created a new Norwalk. Samuel Huntington of Norwich, adopted son of the signer of the Declaration of Independence and a Yale graduate, went to Ohio in 1800 and was elected second governor of the state. Another Connecticut man, Ethan Allen Brown of Darien, migrated to his Promised Land in 1804 and by 1818 was chosen governor of Ohio. James Kilbourne of New Britain organized an expedition to form the settlement of Worthington, near present Columbus. Kilbourne started the first newspaper in central Ohio, organized one of the earliest abolitionist societies, and got elected to Congress in 1812.[48]

Western Reserve College (now University), chartered in 1826, took Yale as its model; and naturally its board called as first president, Dr. George E. Pierce, a Yale graduate. For many years Western Reserve continued to look toward New Haven for inspiration in matters of organization, curriculum, and administration.[49]

It is scarcely an exaggeration to say that Connecticut created a "New Connecticut" in the Western Reserve, and also contributed large numbers of its citizens to other parts of Ohio. In the Reserve today one may see towns such as Aurora, Gates Mills, and Tallmadge, which appear to have been magically transported *in toto* from early Connecticut. Despite the grinding impact of modern civilization, the Reserve in many places clearly displays its Connecticut origins and heritage.[50]

To Indiana, Illinois, and Beyond

INDIANA attracted a far smaller number of New Englanders, although scattered flocks could be found. Wolcottville, Indiana, was named for an influential settler, George Wolcott from Torrington. Both LaGrange and LaPorte counties drew many Connecticut families. A colorful figure, Solon Robinson from Tolland, ran a country store in Lake County, Indiana. In 1836 he set up and directed the "Squatters Union," which aimed to preserve his own and neighbors' rather dubious land claims against speculators. After much publicity and agitation, Robinson and associates secured their land at government, not speculators', rates.[51]

Illinois proved to be more of a Mecca for New Englanders. Four Collins brothers from Litchfield in 1817 laid out Collinsville near St. Louis, put up a sawmill, a gristmill, and several shops, as well as a distillery. When some of Dr. Lyman Beecher's temperance literature reached Collinsville, the brothers read it and abandoned their distillery! They even carried their new prohibitionist sentiments to the extreme of naming a steamship, which they built for Mississippi trade, the *Cold Water!* When their father went to Illinois in 1824, he contributed the first large subscription to Illinois College. This school owed its origin to the Yale Band, a small group of seven missionaries who left New Haven in 1829 to set up Congregational churches and a college in Illinois. Edward Beecher, a son of Lyman Beecher and graduate of Yale, left the famous Park Street Church of Boston to assume the presidency of the infant college. This school quickly became a powerful influence upon the state, especially as an antislavery center and later as a station on the Underground Railroad. In Chicago, at least one Nutmegger rose to great prominence in the early years: Walter L. Newberry of Windsor made a fortune out of Chicago land and bequeathed much of it to enrich Chicago's public library.[52]

In Michigan, too, the Yankees left a deep imprint. Among the first (1832) settlers in Niles was Rufus Landon of Falls Village, while Rodney C. Paine from New Milford was an early mayor. Berrien County, in the southwestern corner, lured a sizable influx of families from New Milford, Norwich, and Stamford. In 1835 John Perrin of Woodstock greatly swelled Michigan's population by bringing his wife, five sons, and four daughters to the promised land. Traveling by boat to Albany, Erie Canal to Buffalo, and steamer to Detroit, they found exactly the right piece of land in Jefferson, Michigan. Connecticut also provided its share of early political leaders, including William Woodbridge of Norwich, the second governor, and James W. Gordon of Plainfield, a lieutenant governor. Perhaps the most fundamental Nutmeg contribution came in the work of Isaac Crary, chairman of the committee on education in Michigan's constitutional convention. Educated at Bacon Academy, Colchester, and Trinity (then Washing-

ton) College, he played the primary role in shaping Michigan's public school system. Crary, who had served as territorial delegate, also won election as the first representative sent to Congress from Michigan.[53]

In Wisconsin and Minnesota, Connecticut immigrants comprised only one of many sources of new settlers but provided some early influential leaders. Louis Harvey from East Haddam started an academy in Kenosha and later moved to Waterloo, where he objected so strongly to a new distillery that he purchased it, tore it down, and used the timbers to build a gristmill. In 1862 Wisconsin voters honored him by election to the governor's chair, but he died by drowning the same year while personally delivering food and supplies to Wisconsin troops in the Union Army. Congregational churches dotted the landscape of Wisconsin, and many a pulpit was filled by a minister born and trained in New England. These churches led a drive resulting in creation of several colleges in the state. Wisconsin's first governor, Nelson Dewey, and three of the next eleven incumbents started life in Connecticut. In Minnesota one finds towns such as New Haven, New Hartford, and Winsted proclaiming their Connecticut background. A "gnawing need" in Minnesota was filled admirably by Horatio Lillibridge from Connecticut who established the first cracker factory in 1856, to the great delight of all true New Englanders, never entirely happy without their cracker barrel! Cyrus Northrup, born in Ridgefield, devoted twenty-seven years (1884–1911) of his life to the presidency of the University of Minnesota, which he built into one of the great educational institutions of the country.[54]

Across the Mississippi to the Pacific

THE beginnings of the Texas Republic may be traced to the restless ambitions of Moses Austin, native of Durham, Connecticut. Migrating first to Philadelphia and later to Richmond, Virginia, in 1784, Austin operated a dry goods store and later a lead mine. Searching for more lucrative mining possibilities, he moved to southwestern Missouri, where he founded the town of Potosi and set up a lead mining and manufacturing enterprise. For a few years Austin prospered, but gradually the financial tide turned against him and his fortune vanished in 1819 with the collapse of a St. Louis bank in which he had heavily invested. Still seeking his golden land, Austin next went to San Antonio in Spanish Mexico, where he secured a permit to establish a colony of three hundred American families in Texas. Unfortunately Moses Austin died suddenly before his dream materialized, but his son, Stephen, in 1822 energetically pushed the actual settlement — the beginning of a notable movement which brought Texan independence and later incorporation into the United States.[55]

Farther northward there moved into Iowa, the Dakotas, and Kansas a large stream of Connecticut emigrants, along with those of other states and foreign countries. A group of seven Yale divinity students, the Yale-Dakota Band, who had pledged themselves to do missionary work in the Dakotas, arrived there in 1881 and began a long and influential ministry. When Kansas became the scene of a fierce struggle between "free" and "proslavery" settlers, Connecticut, in common with other New England states, was deeply stirred. In New Haven on March 31, 1856, a company of seventy men, recruited under Charles B. Lines, departed for Kansas with the cheers of thousands ringing in their ears. Henry Ward Beecher on behalf of his Brooklyn congregation had pledged to this company twenty-five Sharps' rifles along with twenty-five Bibles. Hence, armed antislavery emigrants were said to be equipped with "Beecher rifles." With the encouragement of public opinion and the Emigrant Aid Society, other Connecticut bands followed the long route to Kansas.[56]

The most famous Connecticut man who ever settled in Kansas undoubtedly was John Brown. Born at Torrington in 1800, he was the perennial migrant, living and failing financially in ten places. Soon after five of his sons went to Kansas in 1855 they begged their father to send guns and ammunition for defense against the slave forces. Never one to shirk such a challenge, Brown loaded a wagon with the needed supplies and, dressed as a surveyor, pushed out to Kansas, where he quickly took over leadership of a small band of local militia. Dissatisfied with the progress of the campaign against slavery advocates, the mentally

unbalanced Brown decided to wipe out some of their leaders. On the night of May 24, 1856, he and six others attacked and killed five men — the so-called "Pottawatomie Massacre" — an action which inflamed feelings in Kansas and the nation.[57]

As the westward movement carried the frontier across the high plains to Colorado and the Rockies, Connecticut emigrants became much rarer, but a few rose to early positions of trust. Wilbur Fisk Stone, born in Litchfield in 1833, almost qualified as a permanent migrant, since his parents took him in turn to New York, Michigan, Indiana, and Iowa. At age twenty-seven he abandoned his law practice in Omaha, purchased an ox team, and journeyed to Colorado. Soon he was editing a newspaper, the *Chieftain*, at Pueblo, and promoting the Denver and Rio Grande Western Railroad. After taking a prominent part in drafting the Colorado constitution, he was elected to the State Supreme Court. Later he served as editor of a four-volume history of Colorado. Another Connecticut son, Frederick W. Pitkin of Manchester, distinguished himself by election as first Yankee governor of the young state in 1879.[58]

Out in sunny California, a few early Connecticut wanderers arrived in the 1830's during Spanish rule. The bulk of the state's emigrants, however, arrived during the "gold rush of forty-nine," though Connecticut supplied fewer persons than many other states, including Massachusetts, Maine, and Vermont. By 1860 the census revealed 2,950 California residents who claimed Connecticut as their old home. Although a tiny percentage of the whole, some Nutmeggers found places of leadership. Stephen J. Field from Haddam went to California in 1849, sat in the first legislature, wrote the bill creating a judiciary system, and codified the laws. After attaining the position of chief justice in California, he was appointed to the Supreme Court by President Lincoln. Collis P. Huntington of Harwinton caught the California fever in 1848, tried mining for one day, and then set up a store in Sacramento. Later he made a vast fortune as an aggressive official and promoter of the Central Pacific Railroad — an important link in the first transcontinental railroad.[59]

The expansive energies of thousands of Connecticut men and women thus spanned the continent by the mid-nineteenth century and transported some of the Connecticut spirit of intense concern for religion, the church, representative government, the school, and the college. In many cases this spirit was merged into the broader New England stream, but in any event it helped mightily in shaping the early development of many states, from Vermont and New York all the way to California.

One outstanding historian, Charles M. Andrews, claimed that Connecticut in its first half-century as a state, proportionate to size and population, furnished more prominent leaders of government, business, and education than any other state. In 1831, unbelievably, one-third of the United States Senate and one-fourth of the House of Representatives had been born in Connecticut. Alexis de Tocqueville included Connecticut in the itinerary of his famous 1831 tour of America. Upon his return to France he was invited to attend a Fourth-of-July party given by some Americans in Paris. There he made some observations about Connecticut, which were reported delightfully as follows:

Connect-de-Coot. Vy messieurs, I vill tell you, vid de permission of de president of dis festival, von very leetle story, an den I vill give you von grand sentiment to dat leetle state you call Connect-de-Coot. Von day ven I was in de gallery of de House of Representatives, I held up von map of de Confederation in my hand. Der was von leetle spot dey called Connect-de-Coot. I found by de Constitution he was entitled to six of his boys to represent him on dat floor. But ven I make de acquaintance person*elle* of de member I find dat more dan tirty of de Representatives on dat floor was born in Connect-de-Coot. And den ven I was in de gallerie of the house of de Senat I find de Constitution permit Connect-de-Coot to send two of his boys to represent him in dat legislature. But once more ven I make de acquaintance person*elle* of de senator I find nine of de senator was born in Connect-de-Coot. So gentlemen I have made my leetle speech. Now I vill give you my grand sentiment.

"Connect-de-Coot, de leetle yellow spot dat make de clock-peddler, de schoolmaster, and de senator. De first give you time, de second tell you what to do with him, and de tird make your law and your civilization."

De Tocqueville sat down amidst laughter, but he quickly rose again, and shaking his finger over his auditors, exclaimed loudly, "Ah, gentlemen, dat leetle yellow state you call Connect-de-Coot is one very great miracle to me."[60]

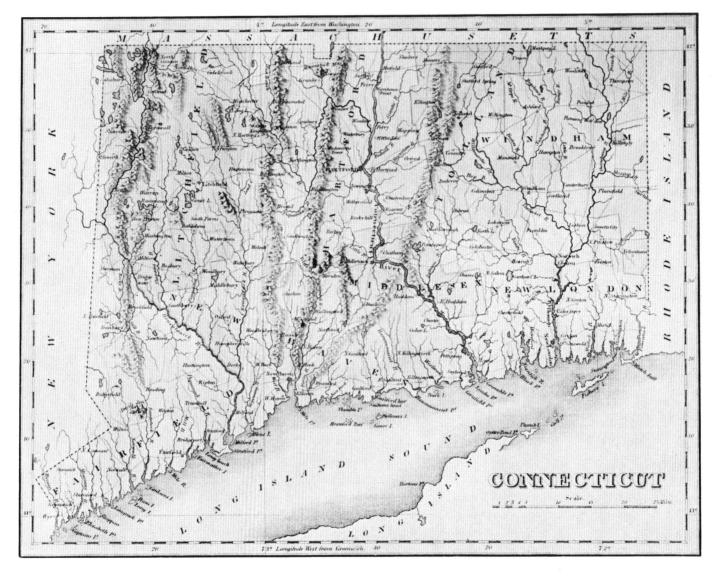

Map of Connecticut (c. 1824) by A. Finley.

CHAPTER 12

Under the New Constitution, 1818-50

A Return to Conservatism, 1818–27 — Appearance of the Democratic Party — Opening of
a Humanitarian Era — Antislavery and Temperance Drives — Politics from 1833 to 1850

A Return to Conservatism, 1818–27

IN 1818, after Connecticut had adopted its new constitution, more attuned to the needs of the times, many asked the question: Would the new constitution be followed by further large steps in a liberal direction, or would the lawmakers complacently settle back with the feeling that no more reform was desirable?[1]

It soon became apparent that the Federalist party had lost too much strength to offer more than token opposition to the Republicans during the next few years. On the other hand, the Republicans generally seemed interested chiefly in rigid economy rather than any broad reform program. A few Republicans wished to introduce some of the democratic reforms adopted by frontier states, but they found themselves greatly outnumbered.[2]

The Republican Assembly leaders displayed conservatism in several ways, such as altering the poor-relief laws so as to shift more of the burden upon the towns. Oliver Wolcott, Republican governor from 1817 to 1827, strongly recommended a revision of the tax laws, and a new system was devised in 1819 which reduced the grand list and placed a heavier load upon the wealthy. It also served to reduce the state's revenues, and thus rendered impossible any subsidies to agriculture, roads, canals, or manufacturing. Even the state's school system suffered from the stinginess of the Assembly. During the economy campaign, salaries of public officials were pared and the costs of the state prison slashed. A general depression over the United States in the 1819–21 period helped strengthen the economy drive.[3]

Governor Wolcott himself usually urged vigorous action for encouragement of agriculture, improvement of schools, and other forward-looking measures, but his recommendations normally fell upon deaf ears. When he vetoed as unconstitutional a steamboat law which aimed at protecting Connecticut concerns against New York competition, the Assembly rode roughshod over his veto. After the Supreme Court declared that Congress alone held the right to regulate interstate commerce, the steamboat law was repealed. Farmers and traders alike rejoiced in the action, since the act had obstructed the vital traffic between New York City and Connecticut.[4]

The presidential campaign of 1824 in which Andrew Jackson narrowly missed being elected President caused much excitement in Connecticut. The large majority of Connecticut citizens seem to have opposed Jackson, although they evidenced no powerful enthusiasm for John Quincy Adams, who finally won. The Reverend Thomas Robbins, a confirmed Federalist, who kept a valuable diary, reflected prevailing conservative opinion when he expressed gratitude that none of the other candidates had won, since they were all disrespectable characters. A brief revival of the almost moribund Connecticut Federalists resulted, but David Daggett, their candidate, polled less than one-fifth as many votes as Governor Wolcott.[5]

The governor repeatedly urged his party to resume a reform program, and advocated that Connecticut emulate neighboring states by creating a comprehensive scheme of canals and turnpike roads; but, as usual, the standpat Republican politicians ignored their leader. Even the popular issue of districting the Senate to replace the prevailing system of elections-at-large was blocked by Republican leaders, who feared that it would favor Federalists or other minorities.[6]

In his message to the Assembly Wolcott emphasized the need for a better banking system — a proposal which events only too amply pointed up late in 1825 when two Connecticut banks failed, with large losses. The Derby Bank actually had voluntarily wound up its business, but a group of swindlers secured the dormant charter and issued $80,000 worth of fraudulent notes, which the legal managers could not meet. The Eagle Bank of New Haven overextended credit dangerously and finally went into bankruptcy in September, with heavy losses to numerous depositors. The shock of these failures may have influenced the legislature to reject no less than eight petitions for new bank charters.[7]

The Republicans did manage to push through just one significant reform measure during these barren legislative years — that exempting women from imprisonment for debt. A bill to this end had been discussed in 1823 but failed to pass. In the 1826 session a genuine liberal, Samuel A. Dana of Middletown, vigorously denounced the old statutes as a degradation of women, and the Assembly responded by an act forbidding the imprisonment of any woman for debt.[8]

A political era came to an end in 1827 when Oliver Wolcott was defeated for re-election as governor. This happened because the Republican party caucus decided to abandon him and support Gideon Tomlinson instead. The reasons for this switch have never been clearly explained, but Wolcott's sturdy independence and frequent differences of opinion with the Republican "machine" undoubtedly had not increased his popularity. Even so, strong support for Wolcott developed, especially in Hartford and New Haven. The final vote was: Tomlinson, 7,681; Wolcott, 5,297; and 627 scattering. Thus ended the political career of a man of unusual integrity, culture, and ability, who never had hesitated to express his views clearly and forcefully and to emphasize the growing need for progressive measures.[9]

Appearance of the Democratic Party

AFTER ten years in power the Republicans could point to only a few positive achievements — reforms of finance and of the judiciary, a new poor-relief law, liberalization of alien land holding, and end of female imprisonment for debt. Actually their handling of most of these and other problems was characterized by a niggardly, penny-pinching approach, ill-suited to the growing wealth of the state. It looked very much as if Connecticut merely had exchanged Republican standpatters for Federalist standpatters![10]

The new governor, Gideon Tomlinson, a Yale graduate and lawyer from Fairfield, had served eight years in Congress, and while not a radical, leaned toward the more liberal wing of his party. Like Wolcott, he, too, soon found that his serious proposals for encouragement of industry, improvement of schools, and attention to problems of crime and poverty were ignored by the Assembly. Instead, the solons turned to an old political problem, that of districting the Senate. The reformers advocating districting equated their program with anti-Jacksonianism, which undoubtedly aided them in the 1828 election. That year the new Assembly pushed through an amendment which provided for a Senate of from eighteen to twenty-four members, with each county entitled to at least two senators, no town to be divided, but the state divided into districts. During the summer of

1828 this proposed amendment was warmly debated. The amendment ran into strong opposition in small towns, but was ratified by the narrow margin of 8,630 to 7,873.[11]

In 1828 Andrew Jackson won the Presidency, an event which the *Courant* lamented as "a foul

the national trend. The Federalist party had been completely dead for a number of years, but it was foolish to think that Connecticut voters would be satisfied for long with a one-party (Republican) system. The success of Jackson proved too much for conservative Republicans, many of whom went

Aquatint of New Haven green in 1830 by Illman and Pilbrow, showing Trinity Episcopal Church, State House, Center Congregational Church, and United Church, with Yale College in background.

stain on the character of our country," an opinion undoubtedly shared by the majority in the state, since Adams carried Connecticut by a large margin. Jackson supporters, taking the title "Democrats," decided to run candidates in the April 1829 state elections, but the Republicans won easily. The dominance of the Republicans was threatened, however, by the appearance of another party in Connecticut known as the "Antimasons." They substituted for the old caucus method of choosing candidates the new nominating convention — an innovation quickly adopted by the other parties. In 1830–31 a realignment of parties occurred in Connecticut which roughly paralleled

into a newly organized party called the "National Republicans," forerunners of the Whig party. This group enthusiastically endorsed Henry Clay's "American system," which especially advocated a protective tariff. In the 1831 state elections the National Republicans triumphed, and since Tomlinson had gone to the United States Senate, a new governor, John S. Peters, was elected.[12]

In 1832 the overconfident National Republicans ran into a well-organized Democratic campaign. The latter nominated Henry W. Edwards and adopted a progressive platform favoring an unrestricted franchise, limited judicial terms, rotation of offices, and taxation reforms to aid labor.

The National Republican candidate, Governor Peters, received more popular votes than Edwards, but because of the presence of an Antimasonic candidate, he fell short of an absolute majority. Hence the election was thrown into the Assembly,

Statue of Thomas H. Gallaudet and Alice Cogswell.

which the Democrats had captured, so that Edwards was declared governor. His victory marked the end of a long conservative era of politics as Connecticut began to share more fully in the liberal tendencies sweeping through most of the nation.[13]

Opening of a Humanitarian Era

IN the second quarter of the nineteenth century a sudden and powerful interest in social reform swept across the United States, generating much enthusiasm as well as solid achievement. This phenomenon was visible in Connecticut, where reform projects were accorded a much more cordial reception than earlier.[14]

A start in this direction was made shortly before 1818 by the creation of four private charitable organizations in New Haven — the Female Humane Society, the Female Charitable Society, the Episcopal Female Charitable Society, and the Society for the Relief of Poor Female Professors of Religion. One wonders what fate befell indigent males in New Haven![15]

A notable philanthropic enterprise, the American School for the Deaf, was started almost by accident in 1817. Dr. Mason F. Cogswell of Hartford had an infant daughter who caught spotted fever in 1807 and became completely deaf. Stirred by his daughter's plight, Dr. Cogswell appealed to the General Association of the Congregational Church to help him in determining the number of deaf persons in the state. Their special committee made a report in 1812 which indicated the crying need for a school for deaf children. Dr. Cogswell called together a small number of his friends, and they decided to send a man to Europe to learn proper means of instructing the deaf. After adequate funds were raised, the sponsors persuaded the Reverend Thomas Gallaudet to undertake the study abroad so that he could head a school here. In Paris he studied under the Abbé Sicard, head of a famous school for the deaf. While Gallaudet was there his friends in Connecticut prevailed upon the legislature to grant a charter in 1816 for the desired school. In August 1816 Gallaudet returned with Laurent Clerc, a deaf and dumb pupil of Sicard, and they toured the United States, soliciting funds for the new school. Backed by these funds and a state appropriation, the institution opened in Hartford on April 15, 1817, with Dr. Cogswell's daughter among the first pupils. Under Dr. Gallaudet's able leadership, and with the devoted assistance of Clerc, this pioneer American school grew rapidly, acquired larger quarters in 1821, and furnished an inspiring example which many other states soon followed. Today the school operates in West Hartford under the name American School for the Deaf, and some of the graduates enter Gallaudet College in Washington, D.C., a unique institution of higher learning for deaf students.[16]

In this period a growing concern for better care of the insane made the harsh colonial precedents seem inadequate. Colonial laws of 1699 and 1727 made relatives or the estate of an insane (or feeble-minded) person liable for his support, and that of

Fortunately, at least one Connecticut doctor was seriously enough dissatisfied with the callous treatment of the insane to fight for changes. He was Dr. Eli Todd. A native of New Haven and Yale graduate (class of 1787), Dr. Todd practiced in Farmington for many years before moving to Hartford. In 1821 he became aware of the large number of insane and the demoralizing difficulties

Early view of the Hartford Retreat.

1727 authorized confinement of the neglected insane in the workhouse when not cared for by relatives and unfit to go at large. Apparently many towns shirked their responsibilities toward the insane, as the Assembly in 1793 ordered towns to confine all dangerous insane in a suitable place, which might even be the local jail. No longer, however, could authorities commit an insane person to the workhouse, and in 1797 incarceration in jail also was prohibited. For years no further action was taken until an 1824 law provided for compulsory confinement by a town upon verified complaint that a dangerous person was wandering freely. The general attitude reflected in all of these laws was that of protecting the community, not of helping the unfortunate. After passage of this law, the state dodged any major responsibility for care of the insane until 1866, when a state hospital for the insane was finally voted.[17]

which relatives and friends experienced in caring for them. Many insane, he learned, were wandering about the state, half-clothed, wretched, and ill-treated. Dr. Todd vividly pictured their plight before the State Medical Convention, won approval for a campaign to establish a new institution, and personally led the drive for funds. As a result, the famous Hartford Retreat (now Institute for Living) opened its doors in 1824, with Dr. Todd as first superintendent. Through methods of gentleness and sympathy, modeled after those of Philippe Pinel in France and William Tuke in England, and attempts to keep patients constructively occupied, Dr. Todd and his overseer, Dr. Mason F. Cogswell, enjoyed enough success to attract national and international attention. The insistence upon kindness even when dealing with violent maniacs deeply impressed those studying mental illnesses. Within a few years several of the staff trained by Dr. Todd went to other states as heads of similar newly opened institutions.[18]

Although the Retreat provided excellent facilities for those who could pay, the indigent insane, who numbered perhaps one-half the total, posed a major problem. For years the Assembly sidestepped the issue and evinced willingness to spend only a very small sum annually to keep a few poor insane at the Retreat. By 1846 the state was paying for about a hundred patients, but they represented only a minority of those needing treatment. Not until 1866 did the Assembly belatedly authorize construction of a state asylum for the insane at Middletown.[19]

In treatment of the poor the state followed the very economical policy of placing nearly all of the burden upon the towns. While local selectmen were often more familiar with the details of individual cases, abuses crept into the system. In 1820 the Assembly passed an act allowing selectmen to farm out the poor at public auction when they did not wish to use regular almshouses. Thus the lowest bidder received a state contract for the maintenance of the poor in a particular town. Although some overseers treated their charges humanely, the system offered tempting opportunities for mistreatment of the poor. Luckily for Connecticut the number of paupers still was quite few, as its local system certainly was gauged only to small numbers.[20]

The growing national interest in prison reform affected Connecticut markedly. The state's ancient prison at Newgate was an unbelievably horrible place, in which some of the prisoners were housed aboveground in crowded buildings, while others huddled underground in the abandoned shafts of the old copper mine. Modern visitors who climb down the ladder into the mine are appalled by the damp, foul atmosphere and the water trickling down the grimy walls. In view of the revolting physical and moral conditions at the prison, and the high cost of operation, the Assembly in 1826 ordered erection of a new prison at Wethersfield.[21]

The new prison, opened in 1827, was modeled largely after an Auburn, New York, prison, which stressed keeping prisoners busy with productive labor rather than permitting them to brood over their situation. Physical conditions at Wethersfield represented a vast improvement, and the products made by the prisoners brought in enough income to create a net profit.[22]

The women's rights movement also came forcefully to the attention of Connecticut's populace. The legislature beat down all attempts to repeal the 1826 act forbidding imprisonment of women for debt, and in the 1830's and 1840's considered various measures to give married women some rights over their own property. Current laws placed a wife's property completely under her husband's control. After years of discussion the Assembly finally, in 1845–46, enacted laws which, among other things, gave protection to property a woman brought into marriage or inherited later. The personal effects of the wife, however, remained legally unprotected.[23]

Several of the most famous American feminist leaders were born in Connecticut or worked there, including Catherine Beecher, Sarah Porter, and Mrs. Emma Hart Willard. Mrs. Willard was born at Berlin, Connecticut, and grew up there. In 1821 she founded a famous girls' school at Troy, later called the Emma Willard School. In her later life she traveled widely, working for the cause of public education. Sarah Porter in 1843 launched her girls' finishing school at Farmington. Catherine Beecher, oldest child of the Reverend Lyman Beecher and sister of Harriet Beecher Stowe, has been overshadowed by her more famous relatives. Yet in her modest but determined way she worked indefatigably for the advancement of women in society. In 1823 she and her sister Mary founded the successful Hartford Female Seminary, which she headed until 1831. From this she expanded her interests into a broad campaign for greater feminine social rights. She left the state in 1832 and moved to Ohio, where she opened a school and wrote several influential books, such as *The Duty of American Women to Their Country* (1845). She urged more women to prepare carefully for the teaching profession, but as an antisuffragist she felt that for most women the proper place was in the home.[24]

Antislavery and Temperance Drives

THE antislavery movement made little progress

in the state prior to the 1830's and 1840's, although a few spokesmen for this cause were heard much earlier. One was the Reverend Levi Hart of Preston, who in September 1774 was invited to preach an antislavery sermon to his native town of Farmington. The next year Aaron Cleveland of Nor-

men formed a club called the "Anti-slavery Association," which aimed especially at improving conditions of life for New Haven Negroes. The same group organized the Connecticut Colonization Society, which aimed at resettling in Africa free Negroes who desired to go there. Through the

View of Newgate prison by Richard Brunton.

wich published an antislavery poem. Perhaps the most influential antislavery figure of Connecticut after the turn of the century was the Reverend Leonard Bacon of New Haven. Early concerned by the miserable status of freed Negroes in Connecticut and elsewhere, and active in the African Colonization Society, Bacon delivered from his pulpit in New Haven on July 4, 1825, a sermon, "Plea for Africa," which was printed and widely circulated. Two days later he and a few young

years he attacked slavery as a moral wrong, though he advocated gradual emancipation in contrast to the abolitionists, who demanded immediate emancipation.[25]

In 1833 a proposal to establish a Negro school in New Haven caused the Assembly to hasten passage of an act permitting establishment of institutions for colored persons only when town authorities agreed. It is probable that some public opinion reacted against Negroes because of the very fervor of William Lloyd Garrison and other abolitionists.[26]

Much anti-Negro sentiment rose to the surface as a result of a famous case in the quiet town of Canterbury. In 1831 Prudence Crandall, as a young woman of twenty-seven and a graduate of the Friends' Boarding School in Providence, was invited by Canterbury residents to head a school there for local young ladies. She accepted and soon the school was flourishing. When Sarah Harris, a Negro girl, applied for admittance, Miss Crandall accepted her. Very soon afterward the schoolmistress was told by some of the local citizens that the colored girl must leave or the school would be greatly damaged. Stung by the growing hostility of the townspeople, Miss Crandall decided to convert the school into one for training Negro girls to become teachers of their own race. Seeking advice as to ways and means, she turned to William Lloyd Garrison, noted abolitionist, who gladly gave her much assistance.[27]

When her plans became known locally, a delegation of town leaders called upon her and strongly urged the abandonment of the scheme. Apparently much of the opposition arose from fear that the Negro students would attend the local church services. The Reverend Samuel May, pastor of the Unitarian Church in nearby Brooklyn, Connecticut, vigorously supported Miss Crandall throughout her long battle. A special town meeting solidified the opposition and sympathizers were not allowed to speak. Undaunted by the efforts at intimidation, Miss Crandall on April 1, 1833, received twenty Negro girls, recruited largely by Garrison and his friends. Almost immediately, local shopkeepers refused to sell food to the school, and a general boycott developed.[28]

So determined and influential were Miss Crandall's opponents that they secured passage by the May 1833 Assembly of a measure sometimes called the "Black Law." It stated that no colored person from outside the state should be permitted instruction in any but the free public schools unless a town gave specific approval. Undaunted, Miss Crandall continued her instruction and sought additional pupils. Finally on June 27 she was arrested and placed in the county jail. Although she stayed only one night (and friends could have arranged her bail to avoid that), her imprisonment received national publicity, especially since she was placed in a cell recently occupied by a criminal hanged for murdering his wife. Garrison's *Liberator* thundered against this mistreatment, and an abolitionist newspaper, the *Unionist,* was launched at Brooklyn that month to give further publicity to the Crandall case.[29]

Her trial opened in Windham County Court on August 23, 1833. A brilliant panel of lawyers — Calvin Goddard, Henry Strong, and W. W. Ellsworth — defended Miss Crandall on grounds that the law was unconstitutional. Three times the jury failed to agree, and the case was transferred to the Superior Court. Here it was tried on October 3, 1833, before Judge David Daggett, a confirmed supporter of the "Black Law." The verdict went against Miss Crandall, who appealed to the Court of Errors, which in July 1834 set it aside on technical grounds. Miss Crandall was given banquets by abolitionist friends in Boston, and gifts arrived from admirers abroad.[30]

Despite the legal victory, the school came to a sudden end in September 1834, soon after Miss Crandall's marriage to the Reverend Calvin Philleo. A series of continued persecutions was climaxed on the night of September 9, 1834, when some men ruthlessly smashed the windows of the front rooms. It seemed hopeless to go on, since no protection was offered against further attacks. The girls were sent home and the great experiment ended.[31]

Many years later, in 1886, the legislature made belated amends by voting Mrs. Philleo an annuity of four hundred dollars. Appropriately enough, the petition for such an annuity was initiated in Canterbury and promoted by Andrew Clark, a nephew of Andrew T. Judson who had been Miss Crandall's chief local enemy. The elderly woman, then a widow living in Kansas, was still keen of mind, and she penned a gracious reply thanking those who had sponsored her cause. Among these was Mark Twain, who had wanted to reinstate her in her Canterbury home.[32]

A few years later another famous incident involving Negroes attracted nation-wide attention to Connecticut. In July 1839 a meeting occurred on a Spanish slave ship, the *Amistad,* where after killing some of the crew, the slaves gained control of the ship. They allowed two Cubans, owners of the slaves, to survive, and ordered them to steer the ship to Africa. Employing stratagems, the owners tried to reach Cuba while ostensibly aiming for Africa, but they accidentally came into Long Island Sound, where the *Amistad* was seized on August 26 by Federal authorities. Disposition of the ship and the Negroes proved so highly complicated that the affair became an international incident. While numerous legal moves were in process the Negroes, including their leader, Cinquè, were kept in the New Haven County jail. Many New York and New Haven citizens, moved by the plight of the Africans, brought gifts of clothing and other necessities and contributed funds for their legal defense. Although President Van Buren agreed with claims of the Spanish Government that our Federal courts had no jurisdiction, and that the slaves should be returned to their Spanish owners, sufficient public opinion in favor of the Negroes was aroused so that Roger Sherman Baldwin, a leading New Haven attorney, was engaged as chief defense counsel. The high point of the trial came when Cinquè testified, through an interpreter, as to how he had been shanghaied from his wife and three small children in Africa. On the basis of this and other evidence, Judge Andrew T. Judson ordered the slaves released to the President, who should return them to Africa. The Federal government filed immediate notice of appeal, so that the case was carried to the Supreme Court, and the *Amistad* Negroes spent many more months in captivity. In the Supreme Court trial, former President John Quincy Adams supplemented Baldwin's efforts with an eloquent and bitter attack upon the legalistic position of the Federal government. In March 1841 the court turned down the government's appeal and directed that the Negroes be freed immediately. Although abolitionists and other sympathizers were delighted by the verdict, the future of the liberated slaves was clouded with uncertainty. After a year of exhibitions over the country for some, and employment and instruction at Farmington for others, they were returned to Sierra Leone, accompanied by missionaries who planned to work with their tribesmen. In 1846 the American Missionary So-

ciety was formed by four societies, of which one was originally created to help the cause of the *Amistad* Negroes. In 1848 slavery finally was abolished in Connecticut.[33]

Another reform drive which generated much power was the temperance movement. It appears to have been chiefly a result of the general re-

Lighthouse at Stonington (built 1823).

forming spirit of the times rather than of any increase in drunkenness and related problems. As early as 1810 several ministers in the state preached sermons advocating total abstinence from strong drink. In 1812 and 1813 the General Association of the Congregational Church considered the problem of intemperance, but little was achieved, as judged by the increase in distilleries from 232 in 1819 to 384 in 1820. Liquor continued to be extensively advertised in the newspapers, and habitual drunkards seemed to find it easy to procure too much liquid refreshment. In

1825 Lyman Beecher made a frontal attack upon the problem with a series of six sermons delivered at Litchfield, in which he vividly stressed the moral ruin facing inebriates, advised individual abstinence, and called for a great crusade against intemperance. Almost simultaneously the Rever-

behind the movement, as did the Reverend Samuel May of Brooklyn. These and other temperance advocates organized the Connecticut Temperance Society in 1829, and within a year it claimed 22,532 members pledged to abstinence. The society's first report in 1830 gave statistics revealing very heavy

Congregational Church, Litchfield (built 1828–29).

end Calvin Chapin of Rocky Hill wrote thirty-three temperance articles, which appeared in the *Connecticut Observer.*[34]

After Beecher left the state, the Reverend Nathaniel Hewit of Fairfield assumed leadership and spoke widely in all parts of Connecticut. President Jeremiah Day of Yale threw his prestige

liquor consumption, especially in Hartford and Litchfield counties. Nevertheless, state-wide figures indicated that there may have been some overall reduction in amount of drinking. Regulation of liquor sales varied from year to year, but the liquor laws generally lacked any real teeth. The Whig party veered toward tighter legal controls, while the Democrats maintained that liquor was a personal matter, to be divorced from politics. Hence Whig-dominated legislatures usually enacted more stringent laws, and the Democrats quickly weakened or repealed them when the opportunity arose. In 1841 John G. Cooley of Norwich launched a monthly paper, whose title, *Total Abstinence,* clearly revealed its aims. In 1849 the temperance movement was enlivened by the appearance in the state of Father Theobald Mathew, a Catholic priest noted as an energetic temperance crusader. He made many temperance converts throughout the state. Two years later, in 1851, Maine passed the first state prohibition law, and three years afterward Connecticut enacted its first prohibition law, which forbade sale of liquor, with a few minor exceptions, and contained strict search and seizure provisions.[35]

Politics from 1833 to 1850

ALTHOUGH social reform activity burgeoned, Connecticut politics drifted along in the customary conservative channels. From 1833 to 1850 the two major parties, Democratic and Whig (originally National Republican), alternated in power, and neither achieved any sustained program of reform. An important factor in the political conservatism was the growing overrepresentation of the small towns, who more and more dominated the House of Representatives. By 1850 towns of under 3,000 population made up about 55 percent of the state's population but held 76 percent of the seats in the legislature. Probably also contributing to political conservatism was the lack of any sizable immigration in the entire first half of the century, as the population remained overwhelmingly of English stock up to the Civil War.[36]

The 1830's brought some significant legislation as the political pendulum swung back and forth between Democrats and Whigs. While writing to a friend in 1832 Governor John S. Peters boasted of the tidy finances of the state, which owed no money and avoided state-supported internal improvements. The governor declared that "the enterprise of our Citizens will continue the Onward March of the American System without the aid of the State, or General Government." Henry W. Edwards, Democratic governor, 1833–34 and 1835–38, in 1835 called for a variety of progressive measures, such as abolition of property requirements for voting, the single ballot, and a geological survey of the state. As usual, most recommendations met with a cool reception. In an effort to give the legislature greater control of the Superior Court, an amendment was approved by the Assembly for popular consideration whereby the Superior Court was limited to five members chosen for five-year terms. The Assembly also approved a geological survey and the division of the state into separate congressional districts. A mechanics' lien law was passed in 1836, as well as one ending the requirement that jurors must be freeholders.[37]

In 1836, for the first time in its history, Connecticut gave a majority to a Democratic presidential candidate, Martin Van Buren. The next year the Assembly Democrats, under pressure of growing economic problems, pushed through an act abolishing imprisonment for debt and also a general incorporation law which made it easier for small companies to obtain a charter. The same year, Governor Edwards achieved something which no other Connecticut governor had been able to do under the new constitution — he vetoed an act repealing the charter of the City Bank of New Haven, and the Assembly failed to override the veto. Undoubtedly this temerity ended Edwards' gubernatorial career, as he was not renominated. Both parties seemed to prefer a weak executive.[38]

In 1838 the Whigs, aided by a national depression which hurt the party in power, returned to control, with William W. Ellsworth as governor. An experienced and very conservative political leader, he approved a policy of economy so severe as to ignore internal improvement subsidies and to cripple even the state's small program of aid to unfortunates and indigents. The complacency of many citizens with the status quo was epitomized by Governor Ellsworth's inaugural address statement in 1841 that Connecticut presented "a republic which secures more good, and avoids more evil, than any other political community of ancient or modern times."[39]

In 1842 Chauncey F. Cleveland, by a tiny mar-

gin, regained the governor's chair for the Democrats. Many constitutional and other kinds of reform were proposed, and some progress was registered, though attempts to change the basis of representation in the Lower House failed. The Assembly passed a labor law, however, which prohibited employment of children under fourteen for more than ten hours daily in cotton or woolen mills. The next year the Democrats won again and pushed through several social reforms, including extension to Jews of the protective laws covering Christian churches, and liberalization of divorce laws. Previously all petitions for divorce were considered, often with long delays, by the legislature; but the new law permitted the Superior Court to grant divorces in cases of intolerable cruelty or habitual drunkenness.[40]

From 1844 on, political campaigns in Connecticut began to be marked by more mass enthusiasm than ever before, as noisy parades and mass meetings attracted large numbers. Nativism, an anti-immigrant and anti-Catholic movement, also began to make inroads. Late in 1844 one New Haven newspaper, the *Morning Courier*, openly espoused this cause, which nationally became organized as the Native American party. In 1844, meanwhile, the Whigs won the state elections, but Democrats found consolation in a spirited celebration over Polk's election to the Presidency. The Reverend Thomas Robbins, a confirmed Whig, commented that "the clamor and firing in the streets [of Hartford] last evening continued late, and was most disgraceful, and we have reason to fear very offensive in the view of heaven." The state Whig politicians in 1844 seemed more concerned with national than with state and local problems, so that little was achieved. In 1845 Governor Roger S. Baldwin again sought action on numerous problems such as prison labor and temperance, but little progress occurred. The year 1845 brought acceptance, over Baldwin's opposition, of a constitutional amendment ending property requirements for voting.[41]

The annexation of Texas and subsequent declaration of war against Mexico were unpopular in Connecticut, since these actions were widely regarded as aiding the expansion of slavery. The Assembly even censured the state's representa-

Four towns west of Connecticut River — Fair Haven, Meriden, Middletown, and South Cornwall — from original pen-and-ink sketches by John Warner Barber (made about 1835).

tives, as well as Senator Niles, for voting to annex Texas, and passed resolutions denouncing any resort to war. In 1846 Mexican-American differences precipitated the outbreak of war. In May, when Governor Isaac Toucey informed the Assembly of President Polk's nation-wide call for 50,000 volunteers, the legislators, confronted by the *fait accompli* of war, unanimously voiced approval of the administration's actions and authorized formation of three regiments of volunteers. More than fifty officers and six hundred enlisted men from Connecticut saw Army service in this conflict. General Joseph G. Totten of New Haven, attached to General Winfield Scott's army, won distinction as the engineer in charge of siege operations at Vera Cruz. The war years generally affected Connecticut far less deeply than had those of the Revolution or the War of 1812.[42]

From 1845 to 1850 the internal political scene in Connecticut produced much partisan warfare but little solid achievement. Governor Toucey's election bribery act, passed by the Democrats in 1846, was repealed the next year by the Whigs. The nominal state Whig leader, Clark Bissell, governor from 1847 to 1849, found it impossible to unite his party on any comprehensive legislative program. A proposal to give Negroes the suffrage, presented to voters in November 1847, failed by a wide margin to pass. Meanwhile the Native American party gained little strength, despite the existence of considerable anti-Catholic sentiment. The Irish, as the chief recent immigrant group, were singled out for special attack. Several newspapers, including the *Courant* and the New Haven *Palladium,* vigorously criticized the deluge of immigrants. Connecticut had so few naturalized voters in the 1840's, however, that neither the Whigs, who opposed the immigrants, nor the Democrats, who were friendly toward them, could capitalize on the issue. By 1848 the Native American party had virtually disappeared, both nationally and in Connecticut, while the major parties turned to more significant problems.[43]

In 1849 Joseph Trumbull, a Whig and nephew of the Revolutionary governor, was chosen chief executive by the Assembly, since the Free Soil party had won enough votes to prevent either major party's candidate from attaining an outright

Four towns east of Connecticut River — Norwich, Enfield (Shaker Village), Thompson, and Willimantic — by John Warner Barber.

majority of all votes cast. Trumbull proved such an inept leader that little was achieved except an act establishing a state normal school, sponsored by John D. Baldwin, founder of the Free Soil party in Connecticut. The Whig party demonstrated such slight capacity for leadership that it already was entering its fatal descent to oblivion, both in Connecticut and nationally. As Connecticut reached the mid-century the electorate returned the Democrats to power, with Thomas H. Seymour as governor. While his party seemed more concerned with some of the complex problems growing out of industrialization, railroad expansion, and the like, neither party was yet prepared to break away from the iron grip of deeply rooted standpattism.[44]

CHAPTER 13

The Civil War Era, 1850-65

The "Feverish Fifties" — State and National Elections in 1860 — Bright Hopes for a Quick Victory — Connecticut Becomes a Union Arsenal — The Boom in Textiles and Shipbuilding — Connecticut's Men in Blue: The Fourteenth Regiment of Connecticut Volunteers — General Military and Naval Contributions — Heated Politics During the War Years

The "Feverish Fifties"

THE dramatic and tragic decade of the 1850's opened with an intense Congressional political debate producing the Compromise of 1850, which consisted of five acts dealing with territorial expansion and slavery. One of these measures, the severe Fugitive Slave Act, helped create deeper antislavery feeling in Connecticut and the North generally than had ever existed previously. Symptomatic of the trend was the launching in January 1849 by William H. Burleigh at Hartford of the newspaper the *Republican* as an organ of the Free Soil party.[1]

Some Connecticut abolitionists played an active role in the famous Underground Railroad, which enabled many Negro slaves to escape from southern masters, often to the safety of Canada. Fleeing slaves who stowed away on vessels engaged in the West Indian trade often left the vessels at such places as Greenwich, New Haven, Deep River, and Norwich. Once in Connecticut, the fugitives, moving chiefly by night, used wagons, horses, boats, railroads, or proceeded on foot from one "station," or hiding place, to another. For about forty years prior to the Civil War the

Railroad functioned with considerable success. A barn behind the home of Francis Gillette in Hartford, for instance, served as one station for slaves who came concealed in a wagon from Middletown or up the river by boat. The next night the fugitives usually were carried away, again hidden under hay, to the station at Bloomfield or Farmington. The latter town seems to have been the most important junction in the state for Underground routes. There were many routes, touching most parts of the state: from Greenwich and Norwalk to Wilton and northward to New Milford, Washington, Torrington, and Norfolk, on a western route; from New Haven or Deep River northward by some combination of stops at Southington, Meriden, Middletown, Rocky Hill, Wethersfield, and Hartford, on the central routes; and at Norwich, Hanover, Lebanon, Willimantic, Hampton, Brooklyn, Canterbury, and Killingly, on the eastern routes. Most of the slaves hoped to reach the safety of Canada. Passage of the Fugitive Slave Act stimulated abolitionists to redoubled efforts for the Underground Railway and also frightened some former slaves already settled in Connecticut into fleeing northward. Increasing numbers of runaways were forwarded from New York City through Connecticut. Farmers of Middlefield, led by William Lyman, reflected the growing sense of outrage at the law by declaring:

This Fugitive Slave Law commands all good citizens to be slave-catchers: good citizens *cannot* be slave-catchers any more than light can be darkness. you tell us, the Union will be endangered if we oppose this law. We reply, that greater things than the Union will be endangered, if we submit to it: Conscience, Humanity, Self-Respect . . .

General public reaction was unfavorable enough to the law so that in 1854 the Assembly passed "an act for the Defense of Liberty in this State" which provided drastic penalties of five years in prison and $5,000 fine for falsely representing a person to be a slave, or for seizing a free person with intent to make him a slave.[2]

In Connecticut, as nationally, the 1850's were characterized by confused, shifting party lines and political alliances. In 1850 the principal issue in the state gubernatorial election — the exclusion of slavery from the western territories — found the Free Soilers vigorously antislavery, the Whigs in an intermediate position, and the Democrats advocating States' rights. No candidate received a majority, so that the General Assembly made the choice. Here the Free Soilers, who held the balance of power, leaned toward the Democrats, who had co-operated with them in naming some common candidates in several local elections. As a result, the Assembly chose Thomas H. Seymour of Hartford, Democratic candidate, as governor.[3]

The next year temperance edged out slavery as the principal issue. Whigs and Free Soilers supported state control of liquor traffic, whereas the Democrats declared that such control deprived citizens of their liberty. Again no candidate obtained a clear majority, and once more the Assembly chose Seymour. Passage of the first state prohibition law, that of Maine in June 1851, insured that temperance again would be the dominant issue of the 1852 campaign. The Connecticut Temperance Society and many clergymen strongly supported the Maine act. The Reverend Samuel W. Dutton of North Church, New Haven, asserted that "there are more than two hundred places in this city where drunkards, criminals and paupers are made, and widows and orphans, too." Both

Whigs and Free Soilers took a strong pro-Maine law stand, while the Democrats simply ignored it. Apparently the pro-Maine law position hurt the Whigs, for the Democrats, under Seymour, swept the gubernatorial and Assembly elections. In the 1852 presidential race, in which antislavery and antiforeignism played leading roles, Franklin Pierce, the Democratic candidate, carried Connecticut and the nation over Winfield Scott, the Whig, whose poor performance foreshadowed the coming demise of his disunited party. The next spring, 1853, Seymour and his ticket easily triumphed in the state election.[4]

Politics is ever an uncertain game, however; a truism never illustrated better than by Connecticut political trends in the 1854–60 period. Just when the state Democrats seemed to be firmly ensconced in power, Stephen Douglas' Kansas-Nebraska Bill passed the Senate in March 1854. This measure, which applied Douglas' principle of popular sovereignty to Kansas and repealed the Missouri Compromise, outraged large numbers of northerners in a way that cut across party lines. Among other things it soon killed the Whig party and precipitated the launching of a new national party, the Republican, in 1854.[5]

At the state level, the act hurt the Democrats by temporarily uniting Whigs, Free Soilers, and Prohibitionists and by reviving strong ministerial participation in politics, which was called "pulpit politics" and lasted until 1865. The Reverend Leonard Bacon of New Haven, through public addresses and editorials in the *Independent*, spearheaded this ecclesiastical drive against the Douglas compromise on Kansas. In the 1854 state elections the anti-Democratic coalition secured control of the Assembly and placed Henry Dutton, a Whig, in the governor's chair. Intense disapproval of the Kansas-Nebraska Act led the Assembly to pass a joint resolution condemning it and censuring Connecticut's Democratic senator, Isaac Toucey, for supporting it. The same session also brought passage of a prohibition act which outlawed all traffic in spirituous liquors except for medicinal purposes. Some New Havenites anticipated the act by carefully laying in a supply for a year, while others staged a final celebration by staggering down a main street beside a cart carrying a barrel of rum! Public enthusiasm for the prohibition experiment quickly faded, and within a decade the law became a dead letter.[6]

In the meantime the complicated political situation in Connecticut was plunged into deeper confusion by the resurgence of nativist sentiment, sparked in part by heavy Catholic immigration. In 1852–53 various nativist groups in the North gradually fused into a single party, popularly called the "Know-Nothings." This party capitalized on growing dissatisfaction with the older parties and on the strong fears felt by many native-born of the huge Catholic immigration from Ireland and Germany in the 1840's and 1850's. In July 1853 the Know-Nothings launched their local invasion under the innocent-sounding title of "State Council of Connecticut." Their constitution bluntly stated:

Its object shall be to resist the insidious policy of the Church of Rome, and all other foreign influences against the institutions of our country, by placing in all offices in the gift of the people, whether by election or appointment, none but native-born Protestant citizens.

The Know-Nothings quickly demonstrated their growing appeal in the New Haven city election of June 1854, when, in alliance with the Whigs, they swept Chauncey Jerome, a clock manufacturer, into the mayor's office. Early the next year the party claimed 22,000 members in 169 lodges throughout the state. The Know-Nothings operated first as a secret order, with the full panoply of secret signs, passwords, grips, and so forth. "Have you seen SAM today?" for instance, meant that a brother was asking another brother the purposes of a meeting of the order. Eventually the inner workings of the order were exposed by the Hartford *Times*, and it henceforth was called "Sam" by many people. Most Know-Nothings were antiforeign and anti-Catholic persons who had disgustedly left the dying Whig party. In addition, a few converts came from Free Soilers and Democrats. In 1855, as a result of a very confused political campaign, the Know-Nothings succeeded in getting their candidate, William T. Minor, elected governor.[7]

After denouncing many immigrants as unfit to be citizens, Minor advocated a longer residence before an alien could be naturalized, and also the disbanding of militia companies consisting entirely of foreign-born persons. The legislature showed its close sympathy with this nativistic program by passing an act which struck directly at the Catholic system of holding by bishops, requiring that all church property be held by individual congregations. The act specifically exempted the Episcopal, Methodist Episcopal, Methodist Protestant, Shaker, and Jewish churches, the other groups which would have been affected. Despite strong Democratic opposition, a proposed amendment restricting suffrage to men able to read the constitution or laws also passed easily and received popular approval that fall. Another nativistic act forbade the state courts to naturalize aliens. After Assembly adjournment Minor quickly ordered dissolution of six militia companies composed of foreign-born men (Irish). When Adjutant General Hodge flatly refused to comply he was removed by the governor and replaced by a more compliant official who carried out the assignment, to the great bitterness of the Irish.[8]

Although the Know-Nothings appeared strong, they had risen to the top by side-stepping slavery — a fundamental issue which soon destroyed them and helped spawn a far more significant party. Before the spring state elections rolled around in 1856, the new Republican party had appeared in Connecticut. It had its unofficial origin in an informal meeting on February 4, 1856, held at Joseph R. Hawley's office on Main Street, Hartford. Hawley and his friends then called a general meeting for February 11, which attracted two hundred persons, including some prominent politicians. The guiding spirit of the assemblage was Gideon Welles, who clearly enunciated the group's unalterable opposition to any extension of slavery. On March 12 the Republicans held their first state convention at Hartford. Many Know-Nothing members were present, but the convention wisely passed over Minor as its nominee in favor of Welles. The pathetic remnant of Whigs held their last convention and named John A. Rockwell as standard-bearer. The Democrats, hopeful of victory, again chose Samuel Ingham, and the Know-Nothings once more backed Governor Minor. The campaign which followed was marked by much abusive language. Democrats were pictured as upholders of "Rum, Romanism and Slavery," while Democratic campaigners lumped all their opponents together as "Irish-haters and negro-worshippers," and spoke disparagingly of the "Black Republicans." In the vote, Ingham received the largest total, but not a majority. Again the Assembly, with Democrats in the minority, elected Minor as governor.[9]

Inveighing violently against immigrants in his message to the Assembly, Minor strongly advocated a longer residence for naturalization. A proposal to make the term twenty-one years received little support. The far more fundamental question of slavery rapidly pushed the nativist issue into the background. Undoubtedly, too, public opinion gradually was becoming more friendly to the Irish immigrants as closer contact reduced the earlier fears and Irish laboring skills steadily became more necessary to the growing industries.[10]

In 1856 the Republican party offered its first presidential candidate, John Fremont, who carried Connecticut by a sizable plurality over James Buchanan, Democratic candidate — 42,715 to 34,995 — while Millard Fillmore, Know-Nothing-Whig standard-bearer, obtained only 2,615 votes. Buchanan won the Presidency, but in Connecticut, Republican strength was impressive. The party was not yet ready to try to win alone in the state elections, however, and in 1857 its managers joined with the Know-Nothings in backing Alexander H. Holley. Again the Democrats nominated Ingham. While the campaign was in process the Dred Scott decision was announced, as well as Buchanan's appointment of former Senator Toucey as Secretary of the Navy, and both apparently affected the Democrats adversely. Holley squeaked through, and the newly elected Assembly clearly was dominated by the Republican-Know-Nothing coalition.[11]

In the 1858 convention the Republican and Know-Nothing leaders split irrevocably over nativist measures, and the latter walked out. The Republicans, faced with a difficult choice of a gubernatorial candidate, passed over Governor Holley and Gideon Welles in favor of William A. Buckingham of Norwich, a man known for integrity as well as great business success. Since no-

body would accept the separate Know-Nothing nomination, their leaders finally reluctantly supported Buckingham too. The Democrats chose General James T. Pratt to run for governor, but factionalism within the party hurt it seriously. As a result, Buckingham's vote topped that of Pratt by 2,754. The Know-Nothing appeal, as indicated in votes for their separate candidates for two other state offices, fell to an almost negligible level. After many years Connecticut at last was settling down to a basic two-party situation — Democrats versus Republicans. The next year, 1859, made this clearer as Buckingham again defeated Pratt, though by only a small margin. The Republicans at last felt they had won without the assistance of a minor party.[12]

State and National Elections in 1860

THE SPRING election campaign attracted national attention since it was considered by seasoned political observers as a weather vane for the presidential race in the fall. The state Democrats chose as their gubernatorial standard-bearer, Thomas H. Seymour, a lawyer of tall stature and pleasing voice who had traveled widely and displayed an urbanity which his opponent, Governor Buckingham, lacked. Seymour's record included service as a colonel in the Mexican War and six years as minister to Russia. Beyond this, he commanded the firm allegiance of leaders and rank and file in his party, in contrast to Buckingham, who still had to bridge a formidable gap between the conservative and radical wings of his party.[13]

The platforms of the two parties as adopted in their respective conventions pointed up their basic differences. The Republicans condemned "John Brownism," that is, forcible abolition, condemned any further extension of slavery, and called for a protective tariff and a homestead act. Earlier, Democrats had emphasized the large amount of Connecticut business with the South, especially that of the New Haven carriage industry, which sold most of its carriages there. Aware that the slavery issue threatened to wreck their party, nationally and locally, they cautiously skirted it, denounced Brown's "invasion," and advocated the ever-popular idea of cheap postage.[14]

Torchlight parade of "Wide-Awakes" in Hartford.

National Democratic leaders especially wanted a Democratic victory to bolster sagging party prestige, and sent Fernando Wood, mayor of New York, and Caleb Cushing to address local rallies. Cushing attracted no less than 5,000 persons to his address at Hartford on March 22. The Republicans responded by dispatching several nationally known figures, including Abraham Lincoln, already famous despite his defeat by Stephen Douglas in the 1858 Illinois senatorial race. In speaking at Hartford on March 5 Lincoln dealt forthrightly with the slavery issue:

We understand that the "equality of man" principle which actuated our forefathers in the establishment of the government is right; and that slavery, being directly opposed to this, is morally wrong.

Looking ahead hopefully to a national Republican victory in the fall, Lincoln expressed the view:

If, then, we of the Republican party who think slavery is a wrong, and would mould public opinion to the fact that it is wrong, should get the control of the general government, I do not say we would or should middle [sic] with it where it exists; but we could inaugurate a policy which would treat it as a wrong, and prevent its extension.

The *Courant,* a Republican paper, noted that the speech had "humor and fun interspersed" and that "there could not have been even a ten year old boy in that crowd at the City Hall, who did not leave the room satisfied that Mr. Lincoln was right, and

had argued his points man-fashion." At Meriden, Lincoln was greeted by a torchlight procession and 3,000 heard his speech. During this swing Lincoln also addressed audiences in New Haven, Middletown, Waterbury, and Norwich. Large amounts of money, much of it from outside sources, were thrown into the campaign, and partisan presses whipped up popular feeling. Large mass meetings and rallies were held by both sides. The Republicans enjoyed unusual success with a young men's club called the "Wide-Awakes," which specialized in dramatic torchlight parades and stirred up great enthusiasm.[15]

In the largest vote yet cast in a gubernatorial contest, Buckingham eked out a narrow victory over Seymour by 44,458 to 43,917. His victory stemmed from his own strong record, considerable business and farm support, exasperation with President Buchanan's indecisive national policies, Lincoln's speeches, and a vigorous, highly efficient Republican organization. Although the Republicans also carried both houses of the Assembly, the small gubernatorial margin revealed very clearly how evenly the two parties were matched.[16]

In Connecticut, as nationally, the torrid presidential campaign of 1860 generated great excitement. Most Republicans enthusiastically supported their candidate, Lincoln. For Democrats the choice was more difficult because of their party's split into northern and southern wings, which nominated Stephen Douglas and John Breckenridge respectively. A fourth party, the Constitutional Union, further complicated the situation by offering a candidate, John Bell, an ambiguous middle-of-the-road man upon all critical issues. Connecticut Democrats were hopelessly split between Douglas and anti-Douglas factions, which fought each other viciously. It is not surprising that Lincoln won a landslide victory, polling 43,792 votes — more than Douglas, Breckenridge, and Bell, combined. The state had registered a clear mandate for Lincoln and for stopping the spread of slavery.[17]

Bright Hopes for a Quick Victory

THE furious bombardment of Fort Sumter on April 12, 1861, opened the Civil War. In Connecticut, huge crowds besieged newspaper offices for the latest information, and extra editions quickly sold out. Political partisanship temporarily vanished, as did organized opposition to the war. Public opinion nearly everywhere in the North seemed to support Lincoln's proposition that the Federal Union must be preserved intact.[18]

When the President called for 75,000 three-month volunteers, which meant one regiment as Connecticut's share, Governor Buckingham issued a special proclamation urging a patriotic response. Within six days two regiments of 780 men each were enrolled and equipped, thanks especially to large and enthusiastic "war meetings" held in many places. Hartford, Meriden, and New Britain moved especially rapidly in recruiting, with the Hartford Volunteer Rifles being the first volunteer company accepted.[19]

Public enthusiasm assumed many forms. After the Thames Bank of Norwich voluntarily offered the state a loan of $100,000, other banks followed suit, and private citizens made smaller contributions. In New Haven, Pease and Foster, dealers in heavy dry goods, pledged continued pay during war service and positions on return to all employees who volunteered. The Adjutant General was swamped by enlistment applications from towns too small to fill up an entire company.

Women offered their help in preparing uniforms, bandages, and other equipment. At Buckingham's urging, the Irish were welcomed back into the militia after the Assembly rushed through a bill repealing the 1855 act of dissolution. In September, recruiting began for the first Irish regiment, the Ninth Connecticut Volunteers, and before the war ended nearly 8,000 Connecticut Irish saw military service.[20]

Although the political truce did not even last through the first wartime session of the Assembly in May 1861, preparedness drew bipartisan support. In response to the governor's request for creation of a well-trained militia immediately available in all emergencies, the legislators unanimously passed a bill authorizing enlistments up to 10,000 men, payment of ten dollars monthly in addition to Federal pay, and an expenditure of $2,000,000 to pay the new troops. The Democrats soon resumed sharp criticism of Republican policies, state and national, and their organs, such as the Hartford *Times,* fired salvo after salvo of criticism. The *Times* expressed the view that Lincoln's policies signified an overturn of the American governmental system and establishment of a new, highly centralized type. The paper advocated withdrawing all Federal fleets and armies from the South and making a sincere effort to woo back the South. If some states refused to return, the North should "let them go *in peace.*" Former Governor Seymour presented a resolution to the Assembly supporting the Crittenden Compromise, and flatly warned that conquest of the South would be impossible. His resolution was overwhelmingly defeated, 173 to 18. State Democrats, however, continued to plug the peace theme, but carefully avoided taking an openly disloyal position.[21]

Connecticut's three regiments of volunteers meanwhile began training. The First and Second Regiments, stationed at New Haven, were deluged with gifts of food, supplies, and reading matter by the well-intentioned public. Most soldiers received Sharps' Rifles (made in Hartford) before they departed by boat on May 10 and 18, amidst cheering crowds. The Third Regiment, mustered into service at Hartford, was equipped with Springfield smoothbore muskets. On May 20, after the governor presented them with their colors in an eloquent speech before the State House, they marched through dense crowds to the railroad station, boarded the train for New Haven, and then traveled via boat toward their rendezvous with the Confederates. Despite the great haste with which these three-month regiments were organized, they left the state unusually well equipped.[22]

After several minor skirmishes Connecticut's three regiments and the Fourth Maine Regiment, organized as a brigade, were thrown into action

down and destroyed by Unionists. At Stonington on August 9, 1861, and at Saybrook a week later, peace meetings were taken over by war supporters, who then conducted a rally of their own.[24]

The *Bridgeport Evening Farmer* ranked as the most uninhibited peace paper in the state. When war broke out it firmly opposed the struggle and openly exulted in the Union defeat at First Bull Run. The editors, Nathan S. Morse and William S. Pomeroy, defiantly editorialized that the rebels, like the Revolutionary fathers, were fighting for their proper rights. The *Farmer's* position caused

Sharps' carbine (Model 1859) (owned by Floyd L. Atkins).

with McDowell's army at First Bull Run in Virginia. Here, amidst great confusion and mismanagement on the Union side, Connecticut's volunteers fought remarkably well; and after the battle was lost, they courageously and firmly held the Union rear against attacks by some Confederate cavalry. The brigade suffered sixty-eight casualties, including six killed. Soon afterward, with the expiration of their ninety days approaching, the three regiments returned home to receive the plaudits of the state. Most of the men re-enlisted, five hundred later held commissions in the Union Army, and seven became generals.[23]

Emboldened by the severe Union defeat at First Bull Run, peace advocates held meetings in many Connecticut towns during the summer of 1861. Masterminding this activity was William W. Eaton of Hartford, a leading lawyer, debater, and politician. At Sharon a meeting resolved "that the cost of this unnatural war will entail upon the people a system of taxation too intolerable to be borne." In New Fairfield peace supporters flew a white flag, which precipitated a sharp melee, and several persons were seriously injured. At Ridgefield a man who expressed satisfaction over the Bull Run disaster was thoroughly ducked under the town pump! In several towns Confederate flags were run up, but usually they were quickly pulled

intense anger among pro-Union citizens, which reached a boiling point on August 24. That day many of the three-month soldiers, just back from service, helped to break up a peace meeting at nearby Stepney. On returning to Bridgeport they met cheering crowds. When somebody shouted, "To the *Farmer* office!" a large number of ex-soldiers and others rushed toward it. Meeting no opposition, they easily broke into the newspaper office, threw all light equipment out the window, and smashed the presses beyond repair. Editor Morse escaped by the roof, found shelter with friends, but soon was almost literally hooted out of the state. Eventually he ended up in Georgia as editor of a Confederate newspaper. In 1862 Pomeroy quietly resumed publication, but he avoided provocative editorials. The Bridgeport mob action may well have persuaded the governor that strong measures must be taken to avert further clashes. On August 31, 1861, he issued a proclamation warning of the perilous state of the nation and calling upon all citizens "to abstain from every act which can tend to encourage and strengthen this conspiracy." Law officers were to arrest those guilty of sedition, treason, or obstructing the laws. Apparently this proved adequate, as peace demonstrations and serious public disorders ceased.[25]

The stinging defeat at Bull Run, with its severe

casualties, convinced most citizens that winning the war would require far greater efforts. Soon afterward, news arrived of the death of General Nathaniel Lyon at the Battle of Wilson's Creek, Missouri. A native of Eastford, Lyon graduated from West Point and served with marked distinction in the Mexican War. When the Civil War broke out he was stationed in Missouri — a border state of sharply divided loyalties. Lyon proved to be a tower of strength for the Union side, as he

arms industry. Endowed with ample capital, managerial know-how, and modern plants, they at first lacked only enough skilled workers to meet booming production schedules.[27]

Colt's Armory at Hartford, completed in 1855, was located on former marshland along the Connecticut River. After purchasing this land in 1852, Samuel Colt built a dike nearly two miles long to protect his investment, and drained the land. Then he erected a three-story brick armory crowned by

Ætna Insurance Company poster — burning of Colt's pistol factory in 1864.

quickly fought and won several battles against secessionists. Finally, in the fierce action at Wilson's Creek on August 10, 1861, he audaciously led his outnumbered troops forward and was mortally wounded. The first Union general to perish in battle, Lyon was considered a northern hero, and from 10,000 to 15,000 persons, including many notables, attended his funeral at Eastford.[26]

Connecticut Becomes a Union Arsenal

WITH actual fighting in progress, another kind of campaign — to speed up arms production — was being pushed in Connecticut. Fortunately several important small-arms companies already were active in the state and could quickly expand to meet unprecedented demands. Four principal companies — two in Hartford, Colt's and Sharps'; the Whitney and Winchester firm in New Haven; and the Middletown establishment of Alsop and Savage — constituted the nucleus of the state's small-

an onion-shaped blue and gold cupola supporting a large colt. A mechanical genius and tireless worker, Colt applied the interchangeable-parts principle and used the best machine tools obtainable, including some which he personally designed. In 1861 the company produced 72,848 revolvers and rifles, and a large addition was under way which would double productive capacity. He negotiated separate contracts for each part of his rifle through different middlemen, and provided the space, power machinery, and samples. Colt himself oversaw only the assembly of the standardized components into a finished weapon. Through overwork Colt brought on his premature death in 1862. Despite the great diversity of operations at Colt's Armory, breakdowns were rare and production exceeded all records. Even the loss of half the works in a spectacular, oil-soaked fire in 1864 caused only a temporary setback. During the Civil War the Colt's Armory turned out 387,017 revolvers, 6,693 rifles, and 113,980 muskets.[28]

Other companies also boosted production of rifles far beyond previous records. During the war Sharps' working force of about 450 men produced about 30,000 rifles yearly. In New Haven, the Winchester Arms Company far surpassed previous production levels and, in addition, developed a vastly improved weapon, the Henry repeating rifle. Although more rapidly loaded and far more accurate than conventional rifles, as evidenced in official trials, it still was considered experimental, and because of official conservatism, only small orders were given to Winchester during the war.[29]

In the related industry of making gunpowder Connecticut also ranked very high, especially in Hartford County. From colonial times onward, various small companies in East Hartford, Canton, and Enfield had engaged in this enterprise. Among the giants of the industry was the Hazard Powder Company of Enfield, launched in 1843 by Augustus Hazard. Prior to the Civil War Hazard's concern sold much powder in the South. After the war came it secured large state and Federal contracts and carried on production in 125 buildings.[30]

Connecticut iron furnaces of the Salisbury district made much of the armor for Union ironclads and provided the Alger works in Massachusetts with metal used in guns cast by it for the Union Army. In 1862 the Ames Iron Works at Falls Village produced a few wrought-iron cannon able to fire a fifty-six-pound projectile five miles. Although it received a favorable Ordnance Committee report, it never was used in the field. The Ames Company ranked first in production of side arms, especially sword and saber blades. However, Ames had invested so much money in producing the cannon that he went bankrupt. Meanwhile the Collins Company of Collinsville, world's largest makers of axes and edged tools, prospered on orders for sabers and similar ordnance materiel. New Haven carriage companies, facing bankruptcy when cut off from southern customers, soon found a profitable alternative in heavy orders for Army wagons. In the Naugatuck Valley at Waterbury, Ansonia, and Naugatuck, millions of brass buttons were made for Union uniforms, as well as a wide variety of artillery accessories and rolled and drawn brass products. The war's impact upon Hartford is well captured in a letter written by State Librarian Charles J. Hoadly on October 4, 1861:

Probably Hartford has suffered less in its business than most other places, on account of the large manufactories of arms here, — I suppose not far from 3000 men are employed at Sharps Rifle and Colt's Pistol works . . . a large number are busy in making clothing, leather work, and boilers and machinery for the new gun boats, &c. . . . Peace meetings are stopped in this region now, we have had a small band of secession sympathizers, but to counteract them there is an association called the Patriots' League having head quarters in this city and extending over the state . . .[31]

The Boom in Textiles and Shipbuilding

CONNECTICUT's large textile industry possessed the plant capacity and managerial skill in the cotton, wool, thread, and silk fields to meet an important proportion of the wartime needs of the armed forces. The high tariffs of 1862 and 1864 generally raised the amount of protection for woolen manufacturers, among others, and thus increased profits. In 1860 the state had eighty-four woolen factories, employing an average of 14,840 workers and producing over $40,000,000 of goods annually. Before the war they specialized in coarse cloths, which were sold chiefly in the South. The Connecticut cotton industry had its real beginning with mills at Vernon and Pomfret in 1803–6, and rapidly expanded into New London and Windham counties, especially in and around Jewett City, Thompson, Killingly, and Norwich. By 1860 there were 129 establishments, producing goods valued at about $9,000,000.[32]

The war caused severe dislocations and wild speculation in the cotton industry. Anticipating serious trouble, cotton manufacturers late in 1860 stocked up with southern raw cotton, so that they had bulging warehouses in 1861. At first with the disappearance of southern orders business was slow, but a good northern market soon developed. By the next year demand rose sharply and cut deeply into existing stocks. Raw cotton virtually vanished, and prices of cotton cloth skyrocketed. Conditions appeared nearly hopeless until Union victories in 1863 at Vicksburg and elsewhere on the Mississippi meant that some of the 1863 crop would find its way northward, and probably still more would the next year if Union victories continued. The combination of increased tariff protection, pent-up civilian demand, and the prospect of large future profits led many capitalists to invest heavily. Heavy pressure was brought upon the legislature to grant flowage privileges similar to those already effective in Massachusetts and Rhode Island. Such rights would permit textile concerns to condemn private property for water-power purposes, which essentially meant using eminent domain for private profits rather than public use. The Assembly's flowage law of 1864 conceded all that the lobbyists had demanded.[33]

In the last two years of the war much new capital was invested in cotton manufacturing. Water rights on the Quinebaug, Shetucket, and other rivers in eastern Connecticut were hurriedly acquired. By 1865 Lorenzo Blackstone had 46,000 spindles in his mills. At Thompson, Dr. William Grosvenor from 1854 to 1865 had increased the capacity of his mills from 2,700 to 19,000 spindles. The Willimantic Linen Company, prospering from heavy demand for cotton thread, sharply expanded its capacity. In many cases profits from other types of wartime business were being invested in cotton, until eastern Connecticut's landscape became dotted with mills. After 1862, because of raw cotton shortage, the industry played a minor role in the war effort, except for thread, which remained in ample supply. Silk-making firms, especially at Manchester, meanwhile found the war years very lucrative.[34]

For Connecticut's woolen industry the war brought boom times, with large government orders and strong civilian demand. With state and Federal agents bidding against each other, the better broadcloths, cassimeres, and blankets vanished, and soon only coarse items remained. This low-quality material — coarse satinette and cassinette — was worked up from worn-out fabrics into "shoddy" and sold to the Army. Such huge profits were made in the shoddy business that old mills expanded and new ones entered the field. One of the largest and wealthiest operators was Colonel Francis Loomis of New London, who owned numerous mills in New London, Windham, and Tolland counties and had over 1,200 workers engaged upon government orders. In 1864 he dis-

played his patriotism and wealth in a dramatic offer to the President. In order to free the Fort Trumbull garrison at New London for service with Grant's army, he pledged that he would personally obtain volunteers and maintain them for a hundred days at his own expense. Lincoln graciously acknowledged this remarkable offer, but for military reasons declined acceptance.[35]

The coarse satinette uniforms which were issued to most Connecticut troops at the start of the war caused a furor in the state. The evil of cheap material was compounded by careless workmanship and failure to give the individual soldier a well-fitting uniform. A special joint committee of the Assembly investigated the loud complaints about poor and misfitting uniforms. The committee reported that the broadcloth uniforms were excellent, and only a small portion of satinette uniforms were seriously defective. The poor fitting resulted mostly from the rapid turnover of recruits. The committee uncovered no evidence of excessive profiteering.[36]

In another important field, shipbuilding, Connecticut played a leading role, and strangely enough the center of this vast effort was the small settlement of Mystic. This village, blessed with excellent shipbuilding sites along a five-mile stretch of the Mystic River, had produced many sloops in the early part of the century. After the War of 1812 the revival of sealing and whaling and the increase in southern trade highly stimulated Mystic's growth. The town's phenomenal rise largely paralleled that of Charles Mallory. After finishing an apprenticeship to a New London sailmaker in 1816, he set out on foot for Boston. On Christmas morning he walked barefoot into Mystic and joined some boys playing ball. An observant youth, he spotted a fleet of ships moored close by and had a sudden inspiration to seek work there. He obtained work, and in a few years he rose to a high place among Mystic's shipbuilders and shipowners. Capitalizing upon a rising demand for whale oil, Mallory built up a fleet of nine whalers in the late 1830's and acquired a fortune from their voyages.[37]

Another firm, George Greenman and Company, forged rapidly to the front rank of Mystic shipbuilding concerns. Operating in an area within the present Mystic seaport, this firm constructed many of America's most famous packets and clipper ships, including the *David Crockett* of 1,679 tons. This and other Mystic ships regularly ran the very difficult Cape Horn route to San Francisco, and nearly 11 percent of the notable clipper voyages of 110 days or less were made by Mystic-built vessels.[38]

The Civil War greatly accelerated the demand for shipping, with Mystic garnering the largest single share among all New England ports except Boston. At the nearby Maxson and Fish shipyard was built the *Galena*, the first seagoing ironclad of the Navy. By the end of the war the humming Mystic shipyards had built for the Federal Navy fifty-six steamers, many of which measured 230 feet or more in length. Altogether over 30,000 tons of shipping were launched in a town whose population reached only 3,600.[39]

Shipbuilders elsewhere shared richly in the boom. At Portland, Sylvester Gildersleeve used his facilities to construct the steam gunboat *Cayuga* in 1861, and the steamship *United States* (1600 tons) in 1864. At Fairhaven, near New Haven, Cornelius S. Bushnell, who had accumulated a fortune as a New Haven grocer, established a shipyard in which he turned out more steamships than any other builder in the country. He also built eight monitor batteries — all improvements upon the original model.[40]

Connecticut's Men in Blue: The Fourteenth Regiment of Connecticut Volunteers

THOUGH many Connecticut regiments compiled distinguished wartime records, space limitations preclude a study of each regiment. By tracing the activities of one regiment, the Fourteenth, which encountered long and unusually sanguinary experiences, it is possible to visualize better what service in the Union Army meant. In May 1862 the War Department announced that it would accept one additional Connecticut regiment for inclusion in a fifty-thousand-man "Camp of Instruction" at Annapolis, Maryland. In response to this call the governor on May 22 ordered the raising of three-year volunteers, to be called the "Fourteenth Regiment of Infantry," and appointed

Dwight Morris of Bridgeport as colonel. At the time, a series of recent Union victories — Forts Henry and Donelson, New Bern, and New Orleans — had engendered overoptimism in the North, thus slowing down recruiting. When the Confederates in the Seven Days' battles repulsed McClellan's attack upon Richmond and punctured

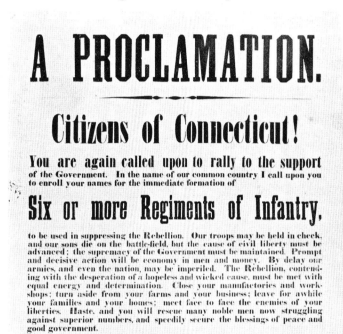

Proclamation of Governor Buckingham calling for six or more regiments.

hopes of quick victory, President Lincoln quickly called for 300,000 additional men, of which Connecticut's quota was six regiments (7,145 men). In reply, the governor phrased a forceful appeal. The Union's grave situation and an energetic recruiting drive quickly attracted many volunteers. The Fourteenth suddenly found large numbers flocking to its training grounds at Camp Foote, two miles south of Hartford. The regiment reached a strength of 1,015 men, who were soon armed with Springfield rifles, except for two companies equipped with Sharps' rifles. The regiment broadly represented the whole state, as it had recruits from eighty-six towns.[41]

After a few inadequate weeks of training, the Fourteenth received orders to break camp and proceed to Washington. On August 25 the men marched through dense, cheering Hartford crowds to embark upon two ships. As the vessels slipped slowly downstream into a peaceful, moonlit night few of the raw recruits could have visualized the inferno ahead. After a tedious rail journey from New Jersey to the capital, they passed in review before President Lincoln, General Scott, and Secretary of War Stanton. As the B Company passed by, noting that the President seemed preoccupied with other business, they began singing loudly, "We are coming, Father Abraham, three hundred thousand more." At this, Lincoln turned, straightened up, faced them, doffed his silk hat, and bowed repeatedly.[42]

The soldiers fully expected a lengthy period of thorough training before seeing any serious frontline duty. On September 7, however, the Fourteenth was incorporated with two other "green" regiments (from Pennsylvania and New York) into the Second Brigade of the Third Division of the Army of the Potomac, and Lieutenant Colonel S. H. Perkins took command of the Fourteenth. The brigade was rushed into Maryland to help stem General Lee's first northern invasion. As the Connecticut men marched by an old engine house in Frederick City, Maryland, where Confederate prisoners were held, one prisoner inquired, "What regiment is that?" "The 14th Wooden Nutmeg," came the reply, to which a rebel answered boldly, "You will soon get your heads grated."[43]

On September 17, 1862, only three weeks after leaving Connecticut, the raw, untrained Fourteenth was thrown into one of the most fearful battles of the entire war — Antietam. In the rolling hills of Maryland, McClellan's Army of the Potomac met Lee's army in a titanic collision, causing staggering losses on both sides. There the Fourteenth received its baptism under the murderous fire of veteran Confederate infantry and artillery. The regiment was moved several times during the battle, fighting near the Roulette Farm and "Bloody Lane," and ended up hugging the furrows of a plowed field. The scene, as the harrowing day drew to a close, was well described by Major William B. Hincks of the Fourteenth:

It was very trying to have to lie inactive under fire and listen to the hideous howling of the shell varied only by their crash in exploding and occasionally the shriek of some one who was struck. I lay closer to the ground than ever before in my life, although it was a plowed field and an exceedingly dirty place, and I never prayed more fervently for darkness than then.

The next day brought an exchange of sharpshooting which pinned down much of the Union Army, including the Fourteenth. In the battle, the regiment suffered substantial losses: 21 killed, 88 wounded, and 28 missing. Colonel Morris, who had been assigned command of the brigade, said in his official report:

The men in my brigade were all new troops, hastily raised, and without drill or experience, and although under fire for the first time, behaved with great gallantry. In front of the last position held by the Fourteenth Connecticut more than 1,000 of the enemy lie slain.

Other Connecticut units also incurred heavy casualties, especially the Eighth Regiment, which lost nearly one-half of those engaged. Among the many Connecticut officers who lost their lives was Major General Joseph K. F. Mansfield of Middletown, a West Point graduate with a distinguished record in the Mexican War. Total Connecticut casualties were 136 killed and 466 wounded — the largest for any engagement in the entire war. While the battle can be classed as a draw, it ended Lee's invasion, and more important, it paved the way for Lincoln's Emancipation Proclamation.[44]

After Antietam, the Fourteenth marched to Bolivar Heights across the Potomac from Harper's Ferry. During the stay there President Lincoln inspected the camp and received a hearty welcome. Sergeant E. H. Wade noted that Lincoln appeared haggard and careworn and seemed by his appearance to have a harder time even than the troops. Late in the fall the regiment rejoined its division at Falmouth, Virginia, for the Fredericksburg attack. There General Ambrose Burnside ordered the Union Army to attack Lee's army, which had heavily fortified the almost impregnable Marye's Heights above the town. On December 13, 1862, the regiment participated in the desperate charge against a stone wall from which heavy Confederate artillery and infantry fire mowed down both officers and men. Despite the utmost bravery, the men in blue were forced back with terrible losses, and the Fourteenth counted 122 casualties, including its commanding officer, Lieutenant Colonel Perkins. The apparent senselessness of the attack puzzled many Union soldiers, including Sergeant Wade who commented: ". . . why our corps were sent on such a murderous errand or desperate undertaking, no one could tell." The Fourteenth was the only Connecticut regiment heavily engaged in this seriously mismanaged battle, though the Twenty-seventh also charged the stone wall, incurring heavy losses. This costly defeat produced consternation in the North and caused Lincoln to remove Burnside from his command.[45]

After spending the winter of 1862–63 near Fredericksburg, the regiment moved with the Army of the Potomac under General Joseph C. E. Hooker into the unhappy Chancellorsville campaign. Theodore G. Ellis had succeeded Perkins as commander of the Fourteenth and gave his unit intelligent leadership. Chancellorsville was another of the many battles in which General Robert E. Lee thoroughly outfoxed his Federal rival. On May 2 the Fourteenth was moved with its brigade to try to check the Confederates who had surprised and routed the Union Eleventh Corps. While the fight was at its height the Fourteenth's band marched out between the Union and enemy lines, and with shot and shell landing around them, played "The Star-Spangled Banner," "The Red, White and Blue," and "Yankee Doodle." A Pennsylvanian who witnessed this affair later wrote: "It was undoubtedly the first and only band concert ever given under such conditions. Never was American grit more finely illustrated. Its effect upon the men was magical." On the next day, May 3, the Fourteenth was violently attacked upon its front and right flanks simultaneously and forced to fall back. The regiment suffered over 30 casualties out of the 219 men thrown into the battle. Again the men openly wondered why an army with superior numbers had suffered another stinging defeat. Sergeant Wade commended Hooker for his personal bravery, but lamented:

Oh, it seemed dreadful to think that with all the advantages we had and everything in our favor, we should be whipped, — whipped so easy too, by a party of men, even dirtier and worse looking than we were, with not half the fighting qualities or discipline that the army of the Potomac possessed.

The defeat was particularly galling because of the large number of soldiers captured by the Confederates — about 8,000 Yankees, including 503 from Connecticut. The Connecticut Twenty-seventh, surrounded by the enemy and forced to capitulate, had 282 men taken prisoner. Fortunately, after a short stay at Libby Prison and Belle Isle, they were exchanged.[46]

After the stunning victory at Chancellorsville, General Lee had perhaps his greatest opportunity of the war to strike a decisive blow against the Union. After much discussion with his top generals, Lee rejected a western expedition to restore the Confederacy's position there in favor of a bold invasion of the North. A smashing victory deep within Union borders might very well effect the peace upon Southern terms which Lee and all Confederate leaders so ardently sought. Lee's army invaded Pennsylvania, and General George G. Meade, who had just taken command of the Union Army, cautiously moved on a somewhat parallel course to the east. At Gettysburg advance detachments of the two armies accidentally collided on July 1. Then began the most dramatic and probably the greatest battle of the Civil War.[47]

Into this awesome battle the Fourteenth moved with its effectives — only 160 men — and took up a position at the Union left on Cemetery Ridge. On the third day of the battle the Fourteenth found itself right in the path of the greatest charge in American history — that of 15,000 Confederates under Pickett and Pettigrew. Preceding this charge the Confederates launched the greatest massed artillery attack yet seen in the war, but most of the missiles passed over the heads of the Union infantry, massed along a stone wall. Sergeant Wade, an eyewitness of the famed Confederate charge which followed, gives a vivid account:

About 3 o'clock the enemy's fire died away, and we could see in the distance about a quarter of a mile, extending across the plain, and coming towards us, two rebel lines of battle, preceded by a line of skirmishers, and a third line in the rear. The spectacle was magnificent. On they came, with colors flying, and bayonets shining in the sunlight. . . . When the enemy had advanced their first line to within two hundred yards our fire spread almost simultaneously along the whole line. The enemy's first line was broken and the second line came on in the same good style as the first did. They fired into us, but they could not stand the raking fire we gave them, and so they too fell back . . . Detached portions of their lines then rallied, and for a while maintained their ground, but being cut down by our terribly destructive fire, they commenced falling back. By this time the 14th was all excitement. They remembered Antietam, and Fredericksburg, and Chancellorsville, and over the wall they went, nothing could stop them, and soon they were fighting hand to hand with the rebels. We captured 6 battle flags and forty prisoners, and over one hundred prisoners came in and surrendered to us afterwards, including 2 Colonels, 3 Lieut. Colonels, majors and any number of line officers.

In the entire battle the regiment suffered 66 casualties, small compared with some units but over one-third of those engaged.[48]

Four other Connecticut regiments, the Fifth, Seventeenth, Twentieth, and Twenty-seventh, participated in the great battle. The Fifth and Twentieth were involved in the heavy fighting on the Union right flank at Culp's Hill, the Seventeenth in the right center on Cemetery Ridge, and the Twenty-seventh close to the Fourteenth on the left center. All regiments except the Fifth incurred heavy losses. The Seventeenth, which came under strong artillery and musket fire all three days of the engagement, lost over one-half of its strength. The Second Connecticut Light Battery participated in the tremendous artillery exchange on the third day but suffered only minor casualties.[49]

In the bloody battles of Grant's 1864 hammering campaign — the Wilderness, Spotsylvania, and Cold Harbor — the Fourteenth fought hard. In the fierce Battle of the Wilderness, the soldiers endured the frustrations of an indecisive battle and heavy losses. At Spotsylvania, participating in the surprise of the Confederates at the "Bloody Angle," the regiment helped stem a violent counter-attack. Undismayed by the stupendous losses of his army in these battles, Grant swung his forces around to the east of Richmond. At Cold Harbor on June 3, 1864, Grant spent his men recklessly and lost 12,000 men in two hours of fruitless attack. Here the Fourteenth lost over 20 men, and the

Second Connecticut Artillery endured the heaviest casualties of any Connecticut regiment in any single battle of the entire war — 75 killed and 184 wounded.[50]

This campaign brought death to one of Connecticut's highest-ranking officers, Major General John Sedgwick, killed by a sharpshooter's bullet at Spotsylvania. A native of Cornwall, Connecticut, he graduated from West Point in 1837 and won

General John Sedgwick (at left) *and two of his staff officers, at Harrison's Landing, Virginia.*

high laurels for gallantry in the Mexican War. In the Civil War he helped save the Army at Fair Oaks, was wounded grievously at Antietam, but recovered in time to lead his troops at Chancellorsville and Fredericksburg. Always highly popular with his troops, who called him "Uncle John," Sedgwick twice was offered command of the Army of the Potomac and twice he declined. A good corps commander, he did not seek higher honors and responsibility.[51]

The month of intense fighting from the Wilderness through Cold Harbor cost the Fourteenth 185 casualties — about one-half of its strength. Long marches and occasional fighting followed as the regiment moved with Grant's army to the east and south to attack Petersburg, the southeast bastion of Richmond's defense. On August 25 the Fourteenth, after destroying the railroad track at Ream's Station, was attacked in force and suffered 51 casualties, or over 30 percent of the 167 men who went into the encounter.[52]

In comparison with the intense fighting of the preceding spring and summer, the winter of 1864–65, even with minor actions at Hatcher's Run, seemed relatively peaceful to the men in the intrenchments outside of Petersburg. The nine months spent before Petersburg involved much fatigue duty and a vast amount of pick-and-shovel work but very little fighting. Sergeant Charles G. Blatchley of the Fourteenth commented:

If there was one thing more than another that became indelibly impressed upon the men's minds of the Fourteenth in their peregrinations with the Army of the Potomac it was plodding through this everlasting Virginia mud.

The rout of the Confederate Army came with startling suddenness early in April. The Fourteenth fought its last engagement with the Confederates at the High Bridge crossing of the Appomattox River on April 7. When rumors of Lee's surrender reached the regiment late on the morning of April 9, the majority of the men refused to believe it. Only when General Meade moved through the lines to congratulate the men did they break into unrestrained exhibitions of joy.[53]

With the surrender of Lee, the men of the Fourteenth eagerly anticipated their return home. Prior to that they participated in a grand review in Washington on May 23. Finally, after a steamship trip from New York, the 18 officers and 210 men left in the regiment reached Hartford on June 8, where they paraded with their torn battle flags and received a vociferous welcome. Similar joyous scenes greeted the other Connecticut regiments as they returned and were separated from the service.[54]

The Fourteenth had paid a high price in its service. Some 1,015 men had departed in 1862, and 697 additional volunteers and substitutes had served with the regiment for varying periods, so that over 1,700 men were enrolled. Of this number about 200 were killed or died of wounds, 186 perished from disease in camp or in prison, and 552 were nonfatally wounded. Others are unaccounted for in the official records and presumably died. The official figures give a total of 1,467 casualties, including those "discharged for disability" — the highest total for any Connecticut regiment.[55]

General Military and Naval Contributions

ALTOGETHER Connecticut sent into the Army one regiment of cavalry, two of heavy artillery, three battalions of light artillery, and thirty regiments of infantry of which two were Negro. These units saw action in far-flung theaters of war. The Fifth endured heavy losses at Cedar Mountain, Virginia, in August 1862 and fought in over twenty engagements, including Chancellorsville, Gettysburg, and Sherman's Georgia campaign. The Sixth and Seventh regiments took part in Sherman's 1861 expedition to South Carolina, and after the naval battle of Port Royal, the Seventh's flag was the first Union one to wave over South Carolina soil. The Eighth, Tenth, and Eleventh comprised part of Burnside's expedition to Roanoke Island and were involved in the Battle of New Bern, North Carolina. The Ninth or "Irish" Regiment and the Twelfth were active in the Lower Mississippi, and later in the Shenandoah Valley, contributing their efforts in the hard-fought battle of Cedar Creek. Concurrent with the siege of Vicksburg was that of Port Hudson, Louisiana, in which the Twelfth, Thirteenth, Twenty-fourth, Twenty-fifth, Twenty-sixth, and Twenty-eighth regiments participated. Port Hudson fell on July 8, 1863, four days after Vicksburg, which conquests together opened the Mississippi to Union ships and control. In General Sherman's army which drove relentlessly to Atlanta and then made its "March to the Sea" were Connecticut soldiers of the Fifth and Twentieth regiments.[56]

Students from Connecticut's colleges — Yale, Trinity, and Wesleyan — flocked to the colors. The attack upon Fort Sumter occurred during Yale's spring vacation, and only one Southern student remained on campus — to tell his friends good-by. Each class organized a drill company. In all, 1,044 students and alumni served in the Union forces, and at least 206 for the Confederacy. From Wesleyan's campus 133 students went into the Union Army, while a few joined the Confederates. In 1862 the Wesleyan Guards joined Company G of the Fourth (later First) Connecticut Artillery.[57]

On the roster of state heroes, General Alfred H. Terry deserves a very high position. As colonel of the Second Regiment (1861), which fought well at First Bull Run, through command of the hard-hitting Seventh Regiment (1861–62), to larger responsibilities as First Division commander, Terry forged a brilliant record. Grant selected him for the very difficult task of capturing the supposedly impregnable Fort Fisher, which protected Wilmington, North Carolina, a center of blockade-running. Moving in close and effective co-operation with Admiral David Porter's powerful fleet, Terry's infantry, including the Sixth and Seventh Connecticut, stormed the fort, and despite bitter resistance, captured it on January 15, 1865. So pleased was the President that he nominated Terry as Major General of Volunteers and a Brigadier General in the Regular Army — which the Senate promptly confirmed.[58]

One of the most appealing stories of the war involves the Sixteenth Regiment, which in March 1864 was part of a garrison of 1,600 men at Plymouth, North Carolina. This detachment was attacked by a Confederate army of 12,000, and after a furious siege was finally overwhelmed. When all hope of escape had vanished, the color guard of the Sixteenth ripped each flag from its staff and tore each into tiny strips, which were distributed among many soldiers with injunctions to keep them hidden. Of the 423 men captured, one-half died in southern prisons. Years later, in 1879, many of the remnants were finally collected, made up as a shield surmounted by an eagle, and sewn upon a white silk banner. This handsome banner was placed with the Connecticut battle flags in the collection at the capitol on Battle Flag Day, September 17, 1879.[59]

Connecticut cavalrymen and artillerymen also played a worthy role in the struggle. An organization, known originally as the First Squadron Connecticut Volunteer Cavalry, recruited in 1861, soon was merged into a New York outfit and lost its separate identity. Successful in maintaining a separate identity was the First Regiment Connecticut Volunteer Infantry. From April 1862 to April 1865 it took part in eighty-eight engagements — all in Virginia. At Cedar Creek it played a decisive role in checking the enemy, and at Appomattox it had the honor of escorting General Grant when he went to accept Lee's surrender. The First and Second regiments of heavy artillery each saw service from 1862 to the war's end. The First was active almost entirely in Virginia, including the siege of Petersburg. Among its engagements the Second saw fierce action at Cold Harbor and in the Shenandoah Valley. Altogether it suffered 1,306 casualties, the second highest of any Connecticut unit.[60]

Connecticut men also represented the Union ably in the naval aspects of the Civil War, including Gideon Welles as Secretary of the Navy and over 250 officers and 2,100 men who served in the United States Navy. Undoubtedly the most renowned state naval officer was Commodore (later Rear Admiral) Andrew Hull Foote from New Haven, who commanded the Navy's flotilla in the highly successful joint operations with Grant in 1862 against Fort Henry on the Tennessee River and Fort Donelson on the Cumberland River. Foote also provided the flotilla vital to the reduction of Island Number Ten on the Mississippi the same year. The next year his gunboats and transports co-operated smoothly with Grant in his complicated operations against Vicksburg, which were climaxed by the close siege and capture of the Confederate stronghold.[61]

Connecticut citizen Cornelius S. Bushnell played a vital role in getting the *Monitor* built. After he had met John Ericsson and found that the inventor could not get a hearing with Navy officials, he worked upon Welles and won his support and Lincoln's. Bushnell later persuaded Ericsson to appear before the Naval Board and won Navy approval. Bushnell was one of those who advanced the money for Ericsson's *Monitor*. Thus the strange-looking little ironclad was built and completed in the nick of time to stop the Confederate ironclad *Merrimack* in the famous encounter at Hampton Roads in March 1862.[62]

Altogether about 55,000 Connecticut men fought under the Stars and Stripes, and over

*Men of Thirtieth Connecticut Volunteer Infantry. At Camp Douglass,
near Washington, D.C.*

*Thirteen-inch sea coast mortar used by First Connecticut Heavy Artillery in front of Peters-
burg, 1864–65, widely known as the "Dictator" or "The Petersburg Express." (Mortar now
on state capitol lawn believed to be this one.)*

20,000 of these became casualties. Among the Connecticut Volunteers 2,088 men were killed, reported missing, or died of wounds. In addition, 2,801 died from disease, and 689 more perished in prison camps. Connecticut thus made a huge sacrifice for the preservation of the Union and the destruction of slavery.[63]

Heated Politics During the War Years

THE unusual political conditions of the war period helped to produce a new political coalition known as the Union party. This organization provided a tolerable solution for many war Democrats who could not happily support the Republican party but sought escape from the peace Democrats. The Union party organized on December 10, 1861, with a call for "the true friends of the Union" to "rally as one man, irrespective of past party lines and party issues" in subduing the rebellion and restoring peace. Holding its first state convention at Hartford in January 1862, it approved a platform which expressed strong Union feelings and unqualified support to the Federal government in crushing the rebellion.[64]

State Republican leaders moved adroitly to secure this group's support without sacrificing Republican strength. At a convention in Hartford they endorsed the Unionist ticket and confidently prepared for the spring elections. Dismayed by the coalition against them, the Democrats renominated James C. Loomis for governor and took a stand favoring support of the war but opposing emancipation. The party also vigorously attacked the issuance of irredeemable paper money and the suspension of habeas corpus. As usual the Democrats pictured Republicans nationally and locally as riding roughshod over the Constitution. This view was reflected in a Democratic campaign slogan: "The Union as it was and the Constitution as it is!" Republicans argued that a vote for Governor Buckingham was a vote for President Lincoln. The real campaigning occurred mostly in partisan newspapers, while the populace, preoccupied with wartime activities, displayed little interest. The vote gave the Union party a landslide victory, with Buckingham polling 39,782 votes against 30,636 for Loomis. An analysis of the returns suggests that an unusually large number of Democrats failed to vote. The General Assembly was overwhelmingly Republican, which in turn insured the re-election of Senator James Dixon by that body.[65]

As a result of McClellan's failure to take Richmond in 1862, Lincoln called for 300,000 new men, of which six regiments were desired from Connecticut. Much of the enthusiasm of 1861 was still evident as towns competed in voting bounties for volunteers. Some would-be soldiers even moved from town to town, seeking the best offer! Both in cities and rural districts the volunteers flocked to enlist, and partisan politics seems to have temporarily evaporated. In August 1862, when Lincoln asked for 300,000 more men for nine months, and ordered a draft if a state failed to meet its quota, large numbers of men turned out. Many apparently preferred volunteering to being drafted, while some sought medical exemptions, and a few suddenly took a Canadian vacation! After several postponements, Buckingham, in September, ordered a draft to complete the quotas. This first draft caused much criticism of the governor and failed miserably to meet the needs. Out of 1,212 men conscripted only 76 conscripts and 142 substitutes actually were mustered into service, and 81 of these deserted.[66]

The truce in Connecticut's political wars, weakened by the draft, was abruptly broken by Lincoln's announcement in September of the forthcoming Emancipation Proclamation. Democratic leaders, who had vigorously opposed emancipation before and during the war, now took the position that the Proclamation was unconstitutional. Whatever the political ramifications, Lincoln's action gave to the war a new humanitarian objective — the freeing of the Negro and the abolition of slavery. To large numbers of New Englanders this new policy transformed the war into a moral crusade.[67]

In December 1862 the sickening slaughter at Fredericksburg cast a pall over the North and caused strong criticism of the Lincoln administration. State Democrats, sensing the mood of defeatism which continued into 1863, chose as their gubernatorial standard-bearer the pronounced peace advocate, Thomas H. Seymour, and called

236

openly for termination of the war. Their platform castigated a long list of Administration actions as highly unconstitutional. Buckingham again received the support of the Union-Republican coalition. Just at the psychological moment to provide political ammunition to the opposition, Lincoln signed the Conscription Act of March 1863. This divided the country into districts and gave each a quota, based upon population, to be completed by conscription if volunteering fell short. Democratic spokesmen called this military dictatorship. This was the prelude to a hard-hitting campaign in which outside speakers were used by both sides. Clarence Vallandigham, famous pacifist Democrat from Ohio, spoke at Stamford, while Miss Anna Dickinson of Philadelphia spoke effectively for the Republicans in a dozen towns. Despite energetic efforts by the Democrats, Buckingham won by about 2,600 votes. Republican majorities in both houses were considerably reduced. Democratic leaders, bitter over the unexpected defeat, publicly attributed it to furloughed Republican soldiers, extensive bribery, and direct political intimidation. It is doubtful that any of these charges could have been clearly proven, but the results showed a close balance of political power in the state.[68]

During the summer of 1863 the application of the new conscription law stirred up much interest as it struck close to home. While resistance was less than in 1862, again the trains northward were so crowded with draft-dodgers, according to the *Courant,* that extra coaches were used! Despite intense excitement, the public drawing of names started peacefully in New Haven and Hartford on July 13, 1863. When news of the terrible conscription riots in New York City spread through Connecticut, state officials were apprehensive. Buckingham took extreme precautions, including removal of rifles from arsenals and arming responsible citizens to intimidate would-be rioters.[69]

This conscription law offered various legal methods of avoiding military service, of which payment of $300 commutation or provision of a substitute were the principal ones. While the average laboring man could not possibly raise $300, many young men living in what was probably the wealthiest state per capita in the Union could easily find this sum. To make it easier, numerous towns raised substantial sums for commutation payments. In some cases the town aid permitted a man with a large family to avoid service. New Haven and Hartford each voted $200,000 for commutation purposes. Some men preferred the more personal action of procuring a substitute, which in addition seemed to offer a more permanent exemption than commutation, which might apply only to one particular draft. At first a substitute cost $200 to $300, but later the price rose to $400 or more. Some men set up as brokers dealing in substitutes and collected a percentage of the price. Many substitutes were men of dubious character who deserted at the first opportunity and had to be taken to Army camps under strict guard. Total expenditures of towns for bounties, commutations, and support of families probably exceeded $5,000,000; while individuals spent estimated totals of over $1,000,000 for substitutes and about $300,000 for commutations. Even with commutation and substitutes, by October 17, 1863, Connecticut had obtained only about one-third of its quota of 7,691. Prosperity at home and continued heavy losses at the front undoubtedly played major roles in this changed outlook. In November the Assembly forbade towns to offer bounties and set a state-wide bounty of $300 to volunteers. A companion bill authorized setting up of Negro regiments and batteries. Also, on a straight party vote, the majority Republicans passed a proposed constitutional amendment permitting soldiers on active service to vote.[70]

As the 1864 state elections approached, the only real danger to the Republican cause came from within their ranks — a lingering factional conflict between Radicals, led by Buckingham and friends, and Conservatives, led by Senator Dixon. The intrigues of Dixon's clique claimed most of the Federal patronage but completely failed to unseat Buckingham, who won renomination and faced Origen S. Seymour. Again national issues overshadowed local ones, and Buckingham won much more easily than the previous year, while his party increased its legislative majority.[71]

The 1864 presidential election, pitting Lincoln against McClellan, stirred up intense state-wide interest. Lincoln and his Union party sought the peace of clean-cut victory, while the Democrats

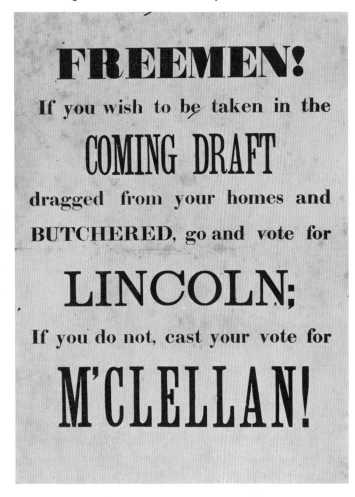

Broadside issued by Democrats in 1864.

advocated a peace of negotiation and compromise. Republican managers were quick to point out the contradictory nature of the Democratic peace

platform and McClellan's known warlike views. In rebuttal, a leading Democratic paper saw a choice between Democrats offering peace, re-union, no draft, and lower taxes, and Lincoln's administration offering more war and butchery, drafts, bankruptcy, and possible permanent separation. The events of the summer played into the hands of the opposition. Grant's army suffered staggering casualties without capturing Richmond or crushing Lee's army. A draft in July further lowered morale, and war weariness grew. Then came the electrifying news that Sherman had captured Atlanta, a victory which caused a noticeable uplift in northern spirits. Both Republicans and Democrats held numerous rallies, but popular excitement fell below that of 1860. When the votes were counted, Lincoln edged out McClellan by 44,691 to 42,285.[72]

In the next few months events moved swiftly to the dramatic collapse of southern resistance. Leaving Atlanta in mid-November, Sherman presented Savannah to Lincoln as a Christmas present. Then his army struck northward through South Carolina, steadily destroying the area's economic resources. Grant's army meanwhile was threatening to crack through Lee's weakening lines. Against this backdrop of Union successes, the 1865 state election brought a rematch of Buckingham and Origen Seymour. On the very morning of election day, April 3, 1865, a telegram arrived from Lincoln with the dramatic news that Grant had taken Richmond. Undoubtedly this aided Buckingham in achieving an easy victory — 42,374 to 31,339. It was a nice tribute to Buckingham for a strong record in difficult times. Upon news of Richmond's fall, the populace rang bells, fired cannon, and displayed flags. Within a few weeks the bloodiest war in American history finally was ended.[73]

CHAPTER 14

Political, Social, & Economic Developments, 1865-1914

Prosperity Resulting from the War — Politics from 1865 to 1868 — Politics and a New Capitol — Growing Interest in Political Reform — Social Changes — The Changing Farm Scene — A New Agricultural College Makes Good — Development of Intensive Agriculture — The Industrial Worker — Growing Volume of Labor Legislation — Politics in the 1890's — Constitutional Problems to the Fore — The Changing Nature of Early Twentieth-Century Politics — A Heavy Immigrant Tide

---

Prosperity Resulting from the War

THE Civil War pumped a vast amount of money into Connecticut's economy and produced a general economic boom which even long periods of military reverses did not discourage. Although the state and the towns incurred heavy expenses in raising and equipping the volunteer regiments, the tax burden was kept relatively light. In the first half of the war neither the governor nor the Assembly nor business interests in general would tolerate a real pay-as-you-go financing of the war effort, so that the state resorted to heavy borrowing, especially through long-term state bonds. Not until 1864 was the base of the state's taxes broadened by imposing new taxes on savings banks, railroads, the telegraph system, banks, insurance, and all other incorporated companies. Even with these new levies, expenses far outran income.[1]

Since the Federal government had financed itself during the war largely by loans and paper money, inflation inevitably swept over the entire country and prices zoomed upward. With the issuance of large amounts of paper money, or "greenbacks," by the Federal government, this cheaper money rapidly drove gold, and then frac-

tional currency, into hiding. By the summer of 1862 change was so scarce in Hartford that postage currency was used as a substitute. As the shortage grew worse, private firms and individuals issued their own fractional notes, or "shin plasters," which fluctuated wildly in value. Eventually the Federal treasury distributed ample amounts of paper currency in small denominations to relieve the situation.[2]

The war period brought into existence the new national banking system, which aimed to bring order and stability out of the general banking chaos. Under Federal supervision a series of banking associations were to be set up which could issue banknotes backed by United States bonds and guaranteed by the United States Government. Connecticut bankers for several years tended to distrust the new system, and by May 1864 only three banks had joined it. The next year the bankers, realizing that with victory achieved the national system would have many advantages, brought twenty-three banks into the fold. During the four years of conflict the banking community generally followed conservative policies, eschewed tempting speculation, and with booming deposits and fairly high interest rates on loans,

239

they made excellent profits. Unsound speculation was rare, and no bank failures occurred. At the war's end, Connecticut's funded debt amounted to $18,000,000 — a large total, but not excessive considering that the grand list in the state had risen nearly $60,000,000 from 1860 to 1865.[3]

In addition to manufacturing which benefited from the wartime boom, another sector of the state's economy — the railroads — also prospered greatly. In the 1850's the New Haven nearly collapsed under the twin catastrophes of the Norwalk River accident, which cost forty-five lives, and the revelation of enormous graft by the company's president. During the Civil War the railroads found freight and passenger traffic sharply expanding — an increase aided by a dearth of competing steamships. The governor in 1865 reported that the state's railroads had carried almost 1,000,000 more passengers than during any previous year, and that their net earnings had risen more than 25 percent. Unfortunately, as profits shot upward the quality of maintenance and service drastically declined. A number of wrecks, attended by the injury or death of many passengers, emphasized the deplorable condition of most lines. Not only did the railroad officials fail to reinvest adequate funds in maintenance but they raised rates and tried to do away with the commutation fare.[4]

Such railroad practices created demands for giving stronger regulatory powers to the Railroad Commission. The fight for regulation was led by P. T. Barnum. After a hard battle the Assembly passed a law which provided removal from the Railroad Commission of any member "employed by any railroad corporation in this state, either directly or indirectly." A further bill prohibited railroads from abolishing commutation fares or disproportionately raising them.[5]

The end of the war found the fiercely competitive railroads with badly deteriorated equipment but well endowed by wartime surpluses available for future expansion. By the late 1860's the New York and New Haven Railroad was one of New England's most prosperous enterprises. The railroads' great rivals — the shipping interests — had enjoyed a temporary boom, but they faced a declining future.[6]

Politics from 1865 to 1868

STATE politics in the postwar decade were characterized by much intraparty squabbling on the Republican side, and by a very even balance of power between Republicans and Democrats. The gravity of the fight to preserve the Union, appeals to patriotism, and Buckingham's able, adroit leadership had held the Republicans together during four war years. Buckingham stepped down in 1866, and radical and conservative Republicans immediately began a savage struggle for party control. On the other side, the Democrats, lean and hungry from years of defeat, were solidly united.[7]

As the war was ending, the Assembly's May 1865 session unanimously ratified the Federal Constitution's Thirteenth Amendment, prohibiting slavery. When the radical Republicans proposed to grant suffrage to Negroes by the simple device of striking the word "white" from the voting qualifications, a lively political battle resulted. The Assembly approved the amendment, but in a popular referendum the proposition was solidly defeated, with an adverse vote in seven of the eight counties.[8]

As 1866 rolled around, the intra-Republican struggle attained a feverish pitch. Leading the radicals was General Joseph R. Hawley of Hartford, a war hero and one of the party founders in Connecticut. At his right hand was Charles Dudley Warner, a talented writer, who had co-operated with Hawley in making the Hartford *Press* a widely read Republican paper. Conservative Republicans, skeptical about Hawley, could offer no candidate of equal appeal and went along reluctantly with his nomination. Several conservatives were put on the ticket, and a compromise platform was adopted. The party reflected well the deep split in Washington between President Johnson, a moderate, and the radical Republican Congressional leadership, which wanted harsh reconstruction in the South and a rapid, uncompromising advance of Negro political and social rights.[9]

The Democrats sought as a candidate a man of clearly patriotic war record, since the party everywhere during the war had suffered from charges of "copperheadism," or peace at any price. They found their candidate in James E. English, a self-made, New Haven clock manufacturer, and congressman during the war. The party upheld Johnson's theory of presidential reconstruction and asserted that suffrage should be granted or withheld by the individual states. President Johnson seemed to be more in sympathy with English's attitudes than those of Hawley — which further complicated an exciting campaign already full of crosscurrents. The final vote showed the virtually equal strength of the two parties, as Hawley obtained a bare majority of 531 votes out of over 87,000 cast.[10]

Republican dominance was short-lived, however, in part due to the deep conservative-radical schism in the party. This split reflected not only political outlook but also the deep-seated rivalry between Hartford and New Haven. Leading the New Haven forces was Nehemiah Sperry, postmaster and bitter enemy of Hawley. Hartford was a financial and insurance center with strong national interests, New Haven more of an industrial center. Conservative Republicans were stronger in New Haven; radicals, in Hartford. The intraparty split, as well as this strong political and economic rivalry — an almost permanent feature of Connecticut life — played important roles in the Republican defeat in 1867. The 1867 campaign involved a rematch of English and Hawley, but certain special factors, including an economic recession, hurt Hawley. Again the spring elections were very close, but this time English won by nearly 1,000 votes. In a broad sense it was a personal triumph for English — a thoroughly honest, gentle, and personable man, who had risen on his own merits from a poverty-stricken youth to a highly successful businessman, well liked by most groups, including the New Haven working class. During the war he had unhesitatingly put country before party in his enthusiastic support of Lincoln's policies. The 1868 elections, pitting English against Marshall Jewell, an able and conservative Hartford businessman, brought re-election to English, but again the Republicans controlled the Assembly.[11]

After the 1868 election, leaders of the Republican-controlled Assembly, eying the great success of the Democrats in enrolling large numbers of recent immigrants, decided to push through a new law on electors and elections. This law required naturalized citizens to prove naturalization by appropriate documents. If any elector in a town requested proof of such a citizen, the latter was required to obtain an elector to testify as to his identity or requisite age and residence. The entire act was cleverly conceived to take full advantage of the living conditions of the immigrants. To be made a voter one had to register in person three weeks prior to the election, and registry boards as well as polling places closed at 5:00 P.M., a distinct hardship for workers, who could lose considerable pay by any absence during working hours. Also, an employer could make it difficult for the worker to leave at all. A second act stated that no alien would be allowed to declare his intent of becoming a citizen before any city or probate court, but must appear before the Superior Court in the county where he had resided for the past four months. In emphatic vetoes Governor English denounced both acts as unjust and unconstitutional. Since the constitution permits a governor's veto to be overridden by a simple majority vote, the Assembly immediately repassed both measures amidst open jubilation by Republican leaders.[12]

One of the hardest fought and most important postwar politico-economic battles was that between the shipping and railroad interests. The chief issue was whether or not railroads could obtain legislative approval to bridge the navigable rivers. Whenever the question had arisen before the war, the shipping magnates had effectively blocked the railroad aims. As a result, rail lines were operating with slow, clumsy ferries for both freight and passenger service. The shipping interests, representing a very wealthy and firmly entrenched group, could afford to spend lavishly to defeat the railroads. They found allies in the cities of Hartford and Norwich, which feared that their river and Sound shipping would be ruined by competition from shore railroads with bridges. Although such a speeded-up transport offered no competitive threat to the water transport of bulky articles of low value per unit of weight, they might capture much of the market for the very valuable products of specialized industries. New Haven,

Bridgeport, and New London, however, blessed by direct rail communications with New York and Boston, saw a much greater future in rail transportation.[13]

From 1866 to 1868 a titanic railroad bridge battle dominated the Assembly sessions. In 1866 a

from New York to Boston by many miles. Vital to this project was a bridge across the Connecticut River at Middletown. This proposal caused some realignment of economic interests, with New Haven, Middletown, and rural Middlesex and Windham counties enthusiastically supporting the

Spectacular wreck on Central Vermont Railroad at Eagleville in December 1896, caused by engine blowing up.

bill to permit the Shore Line to bridge the Connecticut River at Lyme precipitated a fierce debate, which culminated in defeat for the railroad in the House. A major factor in the railroad defeat was the failure to demonstrate and emphasize that by use of the drawbridge the railroads would not interfere with river vessels.[14]

The next year another powerful array of lobbyists descended upon the capitol — this time to fight for or against the reincorporation of the Air Line Railroad, which would reduce the rail distance

venture. A new charter was obtained in 1867, but the bridge at Middletown was defeated. In 1868 the showdown came. William Eaton of Hartford, an extremely able orator, pleaded for the anti-bridge forces, while Thomas M. Waller of New London argued the advantages of the bridge. Eaton was the more eloquent, but Waller had mastered the facts proving that a drawbridge would not obstruct traffic. On June 3, 1868, the House approved the Shore Line bridge by 136 to 92, and that of the Air Line the next day. Better railroad service soon would be available to meet the transport needs of a rapidly expanding economy.[15]

Politics and a New Capitol

IT is probable that the new naturalization and election laws aided the Republicans in winning the 1869 elections, which gave them a large edge in the Assembly and a narrow victory for Jewell over English. The Republican leadership moved promptly toward consideration of the proposed Fifteenth Amendment to the Federal Constitution, guaranteeing the right to vote. On May 7, 1869, the Senate approved the amendment, and the House followed suit May 13.[16]

The next year, 1870, brought a dull campaign, with the same candidates, and English won a narrow victory. As it turned out, 1870 was the calm before a great political storm — that of 1871. That campaign opened in traditional form, with Governor English facing his usual rival, Marshall Jewell, but at the end it became a very brutal, "no holds barred" slugging match. Issues were forgotten amidst a clash of personalities. The Republicans obtained a copy of a telegram sent from English to the notorious Boss Tweed of New York saying, "Do not disappoint us. Nothing could be more disastrous." Actually it referred merely to the inability of Richard O'Gorman, a New York Democratic leader, to campaign in Connecticut. Only the presence of Tweed's name on the telegram made it "red-hot" campaign material. To make matters worse for the Connecticut Democrats, their high command, including Governor English, had accepted the extravagant hospitality of Tweed at an outing in Greenwich the previous summer — an affair criticized by the Republican press at the time. Democrats fought back hard, but "smear" charges have always been hard to overcome. After a heavy vote the official returns gave English 47,496 and Jewell 47,473. Both sides claimed the victory and looked for frauds in the count. An extremely acrimonious debate took place before the convening of the Assembly, which had a Republican majority in both branches. A highly partisan Republican legislative committee examined the returns, claimed serious tampering with the votes,

especially in New Haven, and finally reported that Jewell had won by 100 votes. By almost a straight party vote of 123 to 100 in the House and by a voice vote in the Senate, with Democrats abstaining, Jewell and the Republican slate were declared elected. Democrats claimed bitterly that it was a "stolen" election.[17]

This election unmistakably mirrored the shoddy

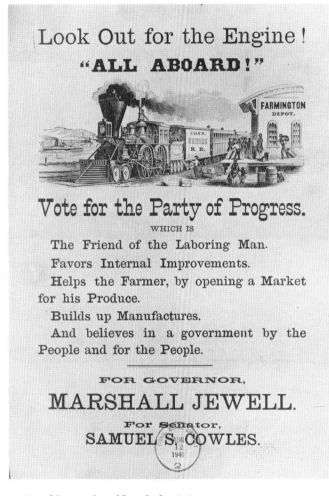

Republican political broadside of 1872.

state of politics locally and throughout the nation. As a result of the Civil War, there had been an enormous growth of national and state wealth, accompanied by an alarming breakdown in moral standards. The special-interest groups had almost unlimited funds available for use in influencing legislators. Luckily Connecticut never had a political ring so brazenly unscrupulous as that of Boss Tweed in New York; yet neither major party in the state during the postwar decade held to high ethical standards or made any sincere attempt to meet the pressing political, social, and economic problems of the times.[18]

The early 1870's brought to the center of the political stage an issue fraught with emotion: Should Connecticut have one capital city? If so, Hartford or New Haven, or some third city? The 1818 constitution had preserved the colonial scheme of having both Hartford and New Haven as capitals. By the late 1860's many persons were criticizing this cumbersome arrangement as inefficient in an age of steadily expanding governmental functions. Hartford boasted of its central location as a convincing reason for being sole capital, while New Haven emphasized its larger population, industry, and wealth. The poor condition of the state houses in the two cities, moreover, added a sense of urgency to the debate. In 1870 the city of Hartford took the initiative by offering the state $500,000 toward a new capitol. In a referendum vote in October 1873 Hartford won by 36,853 to 30,685, with only New Haven and Fairfield counties rejecting the proposal. After Hartford was selected, the legislature authorized Hartford to issue $1,000,000 in bonds toward costs of the land and the building. The city purchased Trinity College and gave its site as a location for the new capitol. From May 1875 on, all Assembly sessions were held at Hartford, but the imposing Gothic-style capitol building, designed by Richard Marshall Upjohn, was not ready until 1879.[19]

Growing Interest in Political Reform

AN interesting outgrowth of the capital controversy was the stimulation of demands for constitutional reform. In New Haven and Fairfield counties, where rapid industrialization had caused heavy population growth, many felt that the overrepresentation of country towns had assured Hartford of being capital. Certain it is that the contrasts were striking. In 1872 the ten smallest towns with a population of 5,696 and grand lists of $2,744,797 elected eleven representatives to the Lower House, while the ten largest cities with 191,207 population and grand lists of $157,669,534 had only eighteen representatives. This meant one

representative per 518 persons for the smallest towns, and one per 10,622 for the largest cities. Aroused by this modern "rotten borough" system, a number of citizens from New Haven and Bridgeport in January 1873 organized a nonpartisan group, the Constitutional Reform Association. They desired a constitutional convention which would redistrict the state. The Democratic platform called for a constitutional convention, while the Republican platform ignored the problem.[20]

The greater interest of the Democratic leadership in political reform undoubtedly contributed to a six-year period of dominance in the gubernatorial seat — a length of control not again equaled until the 1930's. Assuredly the deep factionalism of the Republicans strongly aided the Democrats, as did the noisome scandals of the Grant administration, and a severe national economic depression beginning in 1873. With Charles R. Ingersoll, a well-known New Haven lawyer, as candidate for governor, the Democrats, aided by some liberal Republican votes, rolled to lopsided victories in 1873 and 1874. In 1875 Ingersoll's plurality approached an unprecedented 10,000, and the Democrats even captured *both* houses of the Assembly. This meant, too, that Senator Buckingham, whose record in Congress had been a decided "letdown" from his brilliant wartime gubernatorial performance, was replaced by a Democrat, William W. Eaton, in 1874. The next year, when Republican Senator Orris Ferry died, Governor Ingersoll appointed English to the Senate. As it turned out, the Democratic leadership, though pledged to reform, was nearly as conservative as the Republican, so that no sharp changes in policies occurred. The much-criticized election and registry laws of 1868 were deliberately ignored by the new leadership, and no real attempt was made by either party to cope with the serious human problems created by rapid industrialization.[21]

The 1870's brought small constitutional reforms, although the overrepresentation of small towns remained essentially undisturbed:

ARTICLE XV (adopted 1874)

Every town which contains or shall contain 5,000 or more population shall be entitled to two repre-

View of the State Capitol, with the State Library and Supreme Court Building in the background.

sentatives, and all others entitled to the present number.

ARTICLE XVI (1875)

Elections for state officials and members of Assembly changed from April to November. One-year terms retained for representatives, but state officials and senators to have two-year terms. The Assembly's annual sessions to begin in January.

ARTICLE XVIII (1876)

Newly incorporated towns not to have one representative until population reaches 2,500.

ARTICLE XXII (1876)

Compensation of Assembly members not to exceed three hundred dollars per annum. Also, to be allowed one round-trip mileage at twenty-five cents per mile for each session.

ARTICLE XXIII (1876)

The word "white" stricken from Article VIII: "Every white male citizen of the United States . . . shall . . . be an elector."

ARTICLE XXV (1877)

No county, city, town, or borough permitted to

245

subscribe to capital stock or purchase bonds, or make donations or loans to any railroad.

No drastic changes were effected except for Negro male suffrage, but at least the political inertia of the late sixties and early seventies had finally been routed.[22]

Social Changes

THE burgeoning prosperity and rapid population growth of the war and postwar years literally

span, registered an amazing 162 percent increase. Meriden, with its booming silver industry, shot up from 3,559 to 10,495, a 195 percent rise.[23]

The 1870 census revealed important changes in the composition of Connecticut's population of 537,454. Overwhelmingly English in stock throughout the colonial and early national periods, the population began to receive large non-English infusions around the mid-nineteenth century. Growing economic opportunities, and closeness to New York City, principal port of entry for immigrants, helped explain heavy immigration. By 1870 the

LEFT: *Mark Twain's Nook Farm home in Hartford.* RIGHT: *Mark Twain's "Expert Columbia" bicycle made by the Pope Manufacturing Company.*

changed the face of Connecticut, and especially of the cities. When Gideon Welles came home in 1869 from eight years' service as Secretary of the Navy he noted:

Hartford itself has greatly altered, — I might say improved, for it has been beautified and adorned by many magnificent buildings, and the population has increased. . . . A new and different people seem to move in the streets. Few, comparatively, are known to me.

Hartford had jumped in population from 13,555 in 1850 to 29,152 in 1860 and 37,743 in 1870 — an increase of 178 percent for the twenty-year period. In the same period, New Haven grew from 20,345 to 50,840 — an impressive 150 percent rise. Bridgeport, in going from 7,560 to 19,835 in the same

foreign-born, totaling 113,639, constituted 21 percent of the populace. The Irish-born were far in the lead with 70,630; followed by English, Scotch, and Welsh, 16,527; German, 12,443; and Canadian (chiefly French) 10,073. The foreign-born groups tended to concentrate in urban centers, where expanding factories offered employment opportunities. Irish flocked into New Haven, where they made up nearly one-fifth of the city's population of over 50,000. French-Canadians found employment in the textile centers of eastern Connecticut. The new immigrants, often with markedly different cultural and religious backgrounds, brought sharp changes to the "land of steady habits."[24]

Connecticut's population growth from 1850 to

1870, jumping from 370,792 to 537,454, represented a 45 percent increase — about the same as neighboring Massachusetts and Rhode Island, but below the United States percentage rise of over 70 percent. Connecticut's urban areas, thanks to heavy immigration, were growing lustily. Many agricultural towns, however, were virtually standing still, and sixty-nine had actually suffered a decline in population over the two decades as the young people moved to fertile western lands or to cities.[25]

The unparalleled spurt in urban population was

accompanied by a land and building boom, especially noticeable in such cities as Hartford. In 1870 the Connecticut Mutual Life Insurance Company, then the largest in the state, erected a huge Italian Renaissance building. Hundreds of new homes dotted the spreading streets of the city, and attractive shops sprang up to serve the growing populace. For the *nouveaux riches*, magnificent estates were built on Asylum and Farmington avenues. From the Colt mansion, "Armsmear," built in the 1850's on Wethersfield Avenue, Mrs. Colt reigned over Hartford's high society and gave lavish parties. In Bridgeport, P. T. Barnum built a sumptuous estate, "Waldemere," amidst magnificent grounds overlooking the sea.[26]

During the postwar era Hartford, in line with its strong literary tradition, enjoyed an impressive literary renaissance. Back in the 1780's an eminent group of writers known as the Hartford or Connecticut Wits attracted national attention. That circle included Joel Barlow, who attempted an American epic in *The Columbiad;* Theodore Dwight, ardent Federalist partisan and editor; Timothy Dwight, Yale's president and author of *The Conquest of Canaan;* David Humphreys, agricultural reformer; Lemuel Hopkins, picturesque physician and sharp satirist; Richard Alsop, merchant; and John Trumbull, author of *M'Fingal,* a clever Revolutionary caricature of the Tories. In 1819 another coterie, the Knights of the Round Table, gathered around Samuel G. Goodrich, a publisher. Later, Lydia H. Sigourney, a prolific and sentimental poet, formed her literary salon. Hartford's last great literary colony was that at Nook Farm, an attractive piece of rolling and partly wooded land, lying then just outside the city's western limits. In 1851 lawyer John Hooker of Farmington and his brother-in-law, abolitionist Francis Gillette, purchased the Nook Farm property.[27]

Within a decade or two an unusual number of eminent persons, both literary and nonliterary, came to live in the Nook Farm area. Undoubtedly, Mark Twain, Harriet Beecher Stowe, and Charles Dudley Warner were the most famous literary residents. In many ways Nook Farm became one big and usually happy family, where doors were always unlocked and residents freely went in and out of each other's homes. While Twain lived on the Farm, first in a leased house, and then from 1874 to 1891 in the imposing house he had built at the Farmington Avenue end of the Farm, there appeared in print many of his most significant and delightful works, including *Roughing It, The Gilded Age* (with neighbor Charles Dudley Warner), *Mark Twain's Sketches New and Old, The Adventures of Tom Sawyer, A Tramp Abroad, The Prince and the Pauper, Life on the Mississippi, Adventures of Huckleberry Finn,* and *A Connecticut Yankee in King Arthur's Court.* The distinguished poetry of Wallace Stevens in recent years indicates that Hartford's literary tradition remains important.[28]

Although the masses did not live as comfortably as those on Nook Farm, many innovations were improving conditions for the majority of people. The railroad now brought in fresh milk from the dairy farms, as well as meat, butter, cheese, and other products from Connecticut farms. Piped water was introduced in Hartford in 1855 and in New Haven in 1861. Some of the principal streets of the larger cities were being paved, and horse-

tremendous social dislocations from extremely rapid industrialization and urbanization were largely ignored by political parties, while public and private welfare agencies were not yet prepared to cope with them. As a result, many people lived in great insecurity.[30]

The Panic of 1873, followed by five or six years of national depression, hurt Connecticut's business badly and caused serious unemployment. The un-

Corner of Church and Chapel streets, New Haven, c. 1880.

drawn rail cars, with far larger capacities than the earlier omnibuses, served the people. New Haven introduced the first municipal transportation system, and on May 7, 1861, horsecars started running on a schedule from New Haven to Fairhaven. Soon afterward Bridgeport, Hartford, and New Haven citizens enjoyed regular service by "horse trolley" along their principal streets. In New Haven the world's first commercial telephone exchange was opened on January 28, 1878, and within a month there were enough subscribers to justify the issuance of a directory.[29]

Many aspects of the postwar urban scene were less pleasant. Although the building of factories, business establishments, and homes for the wealthy boomed, there existed a serious shortage of housing for persons of modest and low incomes. After the great depression of 1873 hit, large numbers of unemployed wandered about. In Hartford they were numerous enough to cause the police much concern. In Connecticut, as elsewhere, the

stable textile industry was badly shaken. The state's banks, which had been charging high interest rates on loans and paying usually 6 to 7 percent dividends, were not well prepared for hard times. In 1872 the Staffordville Savings Bank went into receivership, with heavy losses to depositors. Unlawful investment in western railroads and illegal loans to bank officers precipitated its downfall. On January 1, 1873, just before the economic "storm" hit, 201,742 Connecticut people, or 39 percent of the populace, had on deposit in state savings banks over $68,000,000. The great majority of depositors were persons of very modest means. In the spring of 1873 the E. S. Scranton Bank of New Haven failed after much unwise speculation. Evidences of banking irregularities caused the 1873 Assembly to appoint special bank commissioners for a thorough examination of every savings bank in Connecticut. Their careful report, appearing in 1874, revealed that the large majority of banks were honestly conducted and in sound condition.

They uncovered, however, serious malpractices in a few banks. The illegal purchasing of railroad bonds and loans to bank directors were cited, as well as simple bad judgment. One bank in Winsted, which had illegally purchased Illinois mortgages, openly defied the Assembly to withdraw its charter and refused to provide some information required. The worst offender was the Townsend Savings Bank of New Haven, which had about 12,000 depositors. It became involved in a labyrinth of unsound investments which proved largely worthless, and it tried to stave off bankruptcy by concealing its plight. Eventually the bank commissioners penetrated the financial jungle and bankruptcy followed in 1874. The "panic" caused serious runs upon all banks, so that they generally ceased making loans for a time, and some closed their doors temporarily against all demands. Luckily nearly all of them weathered the storm without resort to bankruptcy. The special commissioners' report had some impact, as the Assembly passed an act limiting maximum interest rates to 7 percent and dividends to 6 percent. This, however, was only one of the large number of the commissioners' recommendations for tightening up banking laws. It would be many years before either Federal or state banking laws would give adequate protection to depositors.[31]

Since the war undoubtedly had stimulated drinking, this decade also saw a revival of the temperance movement. Connecticut had several active temperance organizations, such as the Connecticut Temperance Union, the Good Templars, the Good Samaritans, and the Sons of Temperance. By 1872 the Good Templars claimed 10,000 members. The prohibitionists wanted a strengthened Maine law, with strict enforcement, while the moderates took a middle-of-the-road, "moral suasion" approach. At Meriden, in April 1871, a small group formed the Union Temperance League of Connecticut to serve as a kind of clearing house for all temperance groups. It declared its intention of raising adequate funds to promote the temperance cause. It was apparent that temperance reformers, who had usually been Republicans, now felt that both major parties were avidly seeking support of the "rum vote." They felt that local officials feared to prosecute offenders, and therefore they wanted appointed state police placed in charge of enforcement. Stung by failure of the state constabulary bill to pass in 1871, the temperance advocates met in December to establish the Union Reform party of Connecticut, and nominated Francis Gillette, Hartford reformer, as their gubernatorial standard-bearer. Gillette polled only 1,549 votes — too few to influence the outcome of the election, since Jewell was re-elected in 1872 by 2,001 votes plurality. The Republican-controlled Assembly of 1872 enacted a stricter liquor-licensing law, which, among other things, forbade liquor sales to minors and known drunkards, and established stricter controls for granting licenses; but it failed to satisfy the Prohibitionists. In 1874 the legislature amended the 1872 law by adding some restrictions on liquor sales by licensees. Prohibitionists undoubtedly were influential in effecting state action to reduce some of the worst evils associated with irresponsible sale and excessive consumption of liquor.[32]

The Changing Farm Scene

BY the late nineteenth century Connecticut agriculture was shifting sharply away from the pattern which had largely prevailed since the 1630's. Colonial farming had been subsistence farming, in which the farmer and his family raised corn, rye, hay, and livestock and depended almost entirely upon their own labor for food, shelter, and clothing. This pattern changed little until the early 1800's, when the Industrial Revolution began to be felt in the state. As cities showed rapid growth, an expanding market for farm products developed. Commercial agriculture increased, and many farm families, enjoying much larger cash incomes, no longer made their own clothes and other domestic items as much as formerly. The subsistence farm was disappearing as the advantages of specialization and division of labor became apparent.[33]

Between 1840 and 1870 an industrial boom, tremendous urban growth, sharp competition from very fertile western farms, heavy westward migration, and a great influx of immigrants deeply affected Connecticut's agriculture. Commercial farming upon the better soils showed profits. Western competition, however, largely spelled doom for the flourishing sheep industry of the 1840's, with the result that dairy farms largely supplanted sheep raising.[34]

In the drastic readjustment of the last thirty years of the nineteenth century the Connecticut (and New England) farmer experienced heart-breaking times, and no governmental subsidies were available to cushion the staggering blows which fell. Not only did the states of the Mississippi-Missouri valleys possess far more fertile and more easily cultivated soils but constant transportation improvements, especially in the railroad systems, enabled western agricultural products to tap eastern markets. Local cheese- and butter-making industries could not match the western competition. When G. F. and E. C. Swift shipped their first carload of fresh beef to Boston in 1879, it signaled the imminent downfall of New England's beef industry. The acreage of improved land reached a peak in 1860, dropped slowly to 1880, and then entered upon a precipitous decline which resulted in a reduction of over one-half from 1880 to 1920. The hay and pasture lands formerly used for sheep and cattle gradually reverted to brush and forest. For the Connecticut farmer who loved his occupation these must have been decades of almost unrelieved gloom.[35]

Some citizens saw hope for future farmers in better agricultural education. The Cream Hill Agricultural School, set up in May 1845 by Dr. Samuel Gold and his son, Theodore Gold, on their farm at Cream Hill, West Cornwall, offered agricultural education. The school stressed practical training in agriculture upon the two-hundred-acre Gold farm, though many nonagricultural subjects as well seem to have been taught. Altogether the school enrolled 272 pupils during its period of existence from 1845 to 1869. One of these was George J. Brush, later director of the Sheffield Scientific School. To the end of his life in 1906 Theodore Gold remained a powerful force in all moves for advancement of agricultural education, including the founding and expansion of Storrs Agricultural School.[36]

Actually, in the state the late nineteenth century was a period of great significance in the fields of agricultural education and organization. In 1866 the Assembly created the State Board of Agricul-ture. The board was empowered to oversee bequests for promoting agricultural education and to employ a secretary who should actively study and promote improved methods of husbandry. Through public meetings and lectures this board stirred up great interest in improved techniques. In 1870 the board was abolished, only to be replaced the next year by a new board with increased powers and staff. This board was a clearing house for exchange of scientific information, and helped encourage the rise of new agricultural educational institutions as well as expansion at Yale.[37]

During the 1840's Professor Benjamin Silliman of Yale was one of the American leaders in interpreting and popularizing new chemical studies in reference to agriculture. In 1846 John P. Norton, a former Connecticut farm boy and, later, collaborator of Silliman, was appointed professor of agriculture and agricultural chemistry — the first such in the country. He quickly set up a laboratory for giving "practical instruction in the applications of science to the arts and agriculture." From this humble start developed the Sheffield Scientific School of Yale University, which was generously endowed by Joseph E. Sheffield. In Yale's laboratory, Professor Samuel W. Johnson carried on the first analysis of commercial fertilizers. Johnson also lectured widely upon the necessity of applying scientific knowledge to agriculture. Two of his books, *How Crops Grow* . . . , published in 1868, and *How Crops Feed* . . . , published in 1870, were highly influential.[38]

The next step came with the establishment in 1875 of the first American agricultural experiment station, the result chiefly of strong advocacy by Johnson, Professor W. O. Atwater of Wesleyan, and Orange Judd, an agricultural editor. In July 1875, after much study, the Assembly passed a resolution appropriating $700 per quarter for two years to be used by Wesleyan University for employing scientists to man the new station. Professor Atwater brilliantly directed the program, which began with intensive examination of fertilizers. By 1881 he had concluded that free atmospheric nitrogen was assimilated by leguminous plants. Atwater headed the station for only two years, 1875–77, after which it was moved to New Haven; but he continued his fundamental research, for which he won international recognition and the title, "father of American agricultural chemistry." He became vitally interested in calorimetry, or measurement of quantities of heat, a field in which he pioneered. With the help of Professor Edward B. Rosa of Wesleyan he developed the famous Atwater-Rosa calorimeter.[39]

In the meantime the Assembly in 1877 created the Connecticut Agricultural Experiment Station "for the purpose of promoting agriculture by scientific investigation and experiments," and granted it $5,000 annually. Professor Johnson was appointed the first director, and the Sheffield Scientific School provided quarters until 1882, when the state opened its own facilities at New Haven. Largely as a result of Professor Atwater's advocacy, Congress in 1887 passed the Hatch Act, which granted each state $15,000 yearly for at least one agricultural experiment station. As the high economic value of the Connecticut station became apparent the Assembly gradually raised its appropriations. The station carried out an impressive program which included: *1*] study of each serious insect pest and fungus pest and development of methods for combating it; *2*] mosquito elimination programs; *3*] exposure of frauds in foods and fertilizers; *4*] trials of spraying field crops and orchards; *5*] studies on the composition and properties of vegetable proteins; *6*] studies in nutrition; *7*] discoveries in plant breeding, resulting in improved varieties of corn and tobacco; *8*] introduction of successful shade-grown tobacco, and other improvements in the tobacco industry; and *9*] introduction of a fairer method (by butter-fat content) of paying dairymen for cream.[40]

A New Agricultural College Makes Good

MEANWHILE, in 1881, two brothers made a small gift to the state out of which eventually grew the huge University of Connecticut. Charles and Augustus Storrs offered the state $6,000 and 170 acres of land with several buildings on it, located in Mansfield, for an agricultural school. According to Theodore Gold, the brothers strongly desired to do something for their town, and

above all impressed with a sense of the want, of young men, of opportunities to obtain an education that should better fit them for the business of life, especially for farm life, and from their own experiences of the want of intelligent farm labor, conceived the plan of a farm school . . .

The Assembly, moved by this generous gift, passed an act creating the Storrs Agricultural School to educate young men "in such branches of scientific knowledge as shall tend to increase their proficiency in the business of agriculture." Fortunately, empty buildings, once used by the Connecticut Soldiers' Orphans Home, were available on the property. On October 7, 1881, the school was formally opened, with Solomon Mead of New Haven as principal, H. P. Armsby as vice-principal and professor of agricultural chemistry, B. F. Koons as professor of natural history, and thirteen students in attendance.[41]

The school first offered a two-year course either in "Agricultural Practice," or in "Agricultural Science." The daily schedule would make many modern students shudder:

Rising bell	6:30 A.M.
Breakfast	7:00 A.M.
Prayers	Immediately after breakfast
Lectures, recitations	8:00 A.M. to noon
Dinner	12:15 P.M.
Work	2:00–5:00 P.M.
Supper	6:00 P.M.
Study hours	7:00–9:00 P.M.

Manual labor remained an important part of the program for nearly twenty years. Hardly had the school been launched, however, before its very existence was seriously challenged. Some argued that Storrs was too isolated, the soil too poor, and the title to the land too uncertain. As a result, special Assembly committees in 1884 and 1885 considered moving it. The 1885 committee went beyond immediate problems to the fundamental question: Why have a state agricultural school? In their report dated February 2, 1886, they answered this question by citing the great economic value such an institution could have. Although a move to a site near Willimantic was recommended, Augustus Storrs presented a new deed in 1886 which gave the Storrs land to the state without restrictions. So Storrs kept its school. An increasingly friendly public opinion was reflected in the 1889 legislative appropriation of $50,000 for new buildings. By 1891, ten years after its inception, the school had sixty-three students and a graduating class of thirteen.[42]

Haven and Storrs. The new Morrill funds offered a prize well worth a fight. Yale fought vigorously, and finally went to court to obtain the Federal funds. After a lengthy legal battle Yale was awarded damages, but the legal relationship with the state was severed. This left Storrs the victor. In 1893 the Assembly changed the school's name

Storrs Agricultural College in the 1890's.

The future of the school still was clouded, however, by a storm which blew up over the allocation of Federal funds and became known as the "Yale-Storrs Controversy." The State Grange for several years had been unhappy over Yale's entrance requirements, which disbarred most farm youths, and joined in widespread criticism of the "classical" nature of the Yale curriculum. Immediately at stake was the disposition of Federal funds under the Hatch Act of 1887 ($15,000 per year) and the Morrill Act of 1890, which authorized Federal payments of $25,000 per year for agricultural education. Yale and the state had reached contractual agreement in 1863 which seemed to make Yale the land-grant college of Connecticut. In May 1887 the Assembly compromised by splitting Hatch Act income between the experiment stations at New

to Storrs Agricultural College and made it full beneficiary of the 1862 and 1890 Federal acts. Six years later, in an attempt to indicate better the college's service relationship to the entire state, the Assembly changed the name to Connecticut Agricultural College.[43]

The Storrs Agricultural Experiment Station, like its counterpart at New Haven, compiled an impressive record. The school's farm conducted experiments under the supervision of Professor C. S. Phelps, agriculturalist and vice-director. Professor Atwater served as director but spent nearly all of his time in basic research at Middletown. Early studies of significance at Storrs included those in dairy bacteriology, poultry, feeding of sheep and dairy cattle, the fixation of free nitrogen by leguminous plants, and nutrition.[44]

Development of Intensive Agriculture

IN the late nineteenth and early twentieth century, Connecticut farmers shifted slowly from an extensive to an intensive agriculture — a change plainly reflected by the simultaneous sharp drop

of the best soil in the state. Farms were small, land values high, and agriculture highly developed.

3] *Vegetable and fruit areas* — starting near Bolton and Marlboro, running west to Wethersfield, and thence through the Central Lowland to New Haven, there turning along the coast to

Bringing in a load of tobacco at Canton in 1902.

in acreage and steep rise in value of product per acre and per farm. Even with adjustment for the changing value of the dollar, over the four decades the value of farm products per acre rose from $10 in 1880 to $48.57 in 1920, and per farm from $536.40 to $1,726.50. By 1920 tobacco was by far the most valuable cash crop, with vegetables, fruits, and potatoes also important. One could classify Connecticut agriculture as follows:

1] *Chiefly woodland areas* — including northeastern Litchfield County, southern Middlesex, southwestern New London, northeastern Tolland, and northwestern Windham. Only a small percentage of the land was in farms at all, crop acreage was low, and most farmers found it very difficult to obtain a decent living by farming alone.

2] *Tobacco areas* — in the Connecticut (mostly) and Housatonic valleys, including much

New York. Vegetables and fruits dominated but often were combined with dairying.

4] *Dairying areas* — spread over the remaining parts of the state, including the three eastern counties, Litchfield, and northern Fairfield.[45]

Despite fierce competition from the West, Connecticut farmers gradually discovered that they could still compete profitably in certain lines. These included highly perishable items, such as tomatoes, berries, lettuce, and so on; crops of a bulky nature and low value per unit of weight, such as market hay, potatoes, and late cabbages; crops with clear seasonal advantages, such as local peaches in season; high quality tobacco; and finally, dairying, the chief farm industry. Dairying, competitive because of high perishability and heavy demand in the large eastern cities, brought in more income in 1919 than any other form.[46]

The heavy immigration into Connecticut sharply affected agriculture. By 1920 just over one-third of the state's farmers were foreign-born. In Fairfield and Hartford counties many Irish owned farms, while Italians settled close to and northward of New Haven and became largely fruit and vegetable growers. Farmers classified as "Slavic" by the census, often Jewish, concentrated in such areas as Colchester and Lebanon and in Hartford County. French-Canadian farmers showed a preference for the eastern lands. Germans were scattered along a broad band through south central, central, and western portions of the state. Only at the northwest and southeast corners of Connecticut were the farmers overwhelmingly native-born. For a large percentage of the immigrant farmers, able to buy only abandoned and inferior farm lands, the struggle to earn a good living must have been quite difficult. Yet by and large, Connecticut farmers had learned by the early twentieth century to prosper under radically changed conditions.[47]

The Industrial Worker

THE Civil War period had been a difficult one for the average industrial worker, who had enjoyed only a surface prosperity of full employment and rising wages. This illusory prosperity concealed a drop in real wages caused by the great increase in living costs. Realizing that they were losing ground, wage earners nationally and locally evinced greater interest in labor unions. In Connecticut, from December 1863 to December 1864 the number of local unions jumped from two to six. After the war, state labor leaders actively participated in the national drive for a shorter working day. In opposition to the prevalent eleven-hour day, the National Labor Union, organized in 1866, took a strong stand for an eight-hour day. This objective apparently became a political issue in Connecticut, where longer working days were common. A ten-hour-day law had been enacted in 1855, but being loosely drawn it had been violated frequently. In 1867 the Democratic platform declared that no employer should work children over ten hours daily. The Republicans said that the laboring classes would receive whatever remedies

they needed from the Assembly. In response to direct questions from a New Haven union about the eight-hour day and related issues, Hawley (Republican) gave vague, ambiguous responses, while English (Democrat) clearly stated his unqualified support of the eight-hour day.[48]

It is very possible that labor votes insured English's victory, although this cannot be documented. In June 1867 the Assembly passed an innocuous act declaring that eight hours "shall be deemed a lawful day's work, unless otherwise agreed by the parties; *provided*, this law shall not affect in any manner existing contracts." The same session enacted a law prohibiting political coercion of workers or bribery of any person, but it was phrased vaguely and carried no provisions for enforcement. Certainly it was an era of fairly complete dominance of labor by management.[49]

Although the 1870's brought Connecticut no capital-labor bloodshed and property destruction comparable to that in the railroad strike of 1877 at Baltimore and elsewhere, much unrest existed. In January 1872 a bitter eruption occurred at the brownstone quarries in Portland and Cromwell, where the laborers felt that their pay of $1.50 daily in the winter season was lower than that of any class of day laborers in New England. Many workers lived in company homes or had built homes on company land. For company-owned homes rent was collected in advance, semiannually. During the warmer part of the year the men worked ten hours daily. A union was formed to seek better conditions and higher pay. When they asked to have the earlier rate of $1.60 daily restored, the quarry companies effectively staged a lockout simply by locking up all their employees' tools. The Cromwell quarry granted a wage increase, but the Portland quarries remained obdurate. One even advertised that it would not employ any man who belonged to the quarrymen's union. Despite such labor turbulence, there seemed to be little disposition by laboring men to vote for a special labor party. The Labor Reform party was organized in the spring of 1872, but it polled only 399 votes for its gubernatorial candidate out of over 93,000 cast.[50]

Another strike vividly illustrative of conditions prevailing in the textile industry occurred in 1875 at the state's largest cotton mill, in Taftville. Working sixty-seven hours weekly, the mill hands averaged only $8.25 to $9.00 per week. Many of them lived in nearby company-owned tenements or boarding houses. There was only one store in Taftville, which employees said was company-owned. Whether or not this was true, the company carefully deducted store bills from the workers' pay. It is not surprising that such conditions of virtual industrial peonage led to a strike for higher wages.[51]

The growing labor movement of the early 1870's may well have influenced the Assembly enough to cause it to create a bureau of labor statistics in 1873, with very limited funds and a staff of two. James F. Babcock of New Haven was appointed the first chief of the new bureau. Despite lack of co-operation from some companies, Babcock and his deputy collected much significant data on industrial working conditions. They found that a considerable number of children who should have been in school were employed in factories. The Windsor Locks school superintendent reported "about thirty children out of school who work in factories." Information from the town of Thompson indicated the shocking fact that 245 children were not attending school. In regard to excessive hours of labor, Babcock wrote with indignation that some Connecticut cotton mills employed women and children for a working week of sixty-six to seventy hours.[52]

Growing Volume of Labor Legislation

THE 1880's and 1890's brought a large volume of labor legislation, including a few acts with teeth in them. The growing power of the Knights of Labor (a national labor group started in 1869) in the state, and the continued close balance of power between the major parties, made labor legislation seem more attractive to both parties. The two decades since the Civil War had seen creation of at least fifty-one labor unions which were destined to last into the present century. In 1886 the Assembly enacted a law stating that "no child under thirteen years of age shall be employed in any mechanical, mercantile or manufacturing establishment." This represented a compromise be-

tween the State Board of Education, backing twelve years as the minimum age, and the Knights of Labor, fourteen. To the State Board of Education fell the onerous task of enforcing the act through special agents. Though a distinct advance over earlier laws, this one had loopholes, and was deliberately violated by some parents and factory owners. The 1888 report of the State Board of Education charged:

. . . the rapacity of parents has impelled them to false statements concerning the ages of their children. The reports indicate extensive, deliberate and unqualified lying for the sole purpose of securing the money which their children can earn.

The previous year the board had found 1,602 children under thirteen employed in state factories, and even 153 only eight or nine years old. As usual, cotton factories were the worst offenders, although many textile owners were swinging to the view that children provided unprofitable labor and would be better off in school. The 1886 law helped so greatly in checking child labor that by 1894 only six cases of employment of children under thirteen years of age could be uncovered. In 1895 the Assembly raised the minimum age to fourteen. The 1900 census revealed 393 children under fourteen employed in Connecticut factories — perhaps chiefly due to dishonest statements in the required certificate stating the age of a child working in a factory. As a result, a 1901 law tightened up on the method of obtaining certificates. In the next few years enforcement agents still found cases of unlawful child labor, but its prevalence was markedly reduced from a decade or two earlier.[53]

Many other aspects of capital-labor relations were covered in laws of the 1880's and 1890's. In 1887, maximum hours of labor were set at ten daily and sixty weekly for women and minors under sixteen. Actually, most factories already had established the ten-hour day before the law appeared. Since the law was little enforced, some employers when pressed by heavy orders often kept their operatives longer hours. The State Bureau of Labor Statistics, however, noted definite progress over the years. In 1860, sixty hours was a minimum in all industries, and one-fifth worked more than that, including *all* cotton and woolen mill employees. By 1904, only 40 percent worked a sixty-hour week, and over one-fifth were down to fifty-five hours or less. In cigar making and the building trades an eight-hour day already was general. The labor unions, moreover, continued to battle for legislation guaranteeing shorter hours.[54]

Labor union influence on labor legislation reached a high point in 1885–86, when no less than thirty-seven members of the Assembly belonged to the Knights of Labor. At that time the Knights had an estimated membership of 60,000 in Connecticut, of whom 40,000 were voters. They strongly influenced both major parties to pass important labor legislation — re-establishment of the Bureau of Labor Statistics (1885); child labor law (1886); prohibition of discounting wages for payment before the regular payday (1886); factory inspection act (1887); ten-hour act for women and children, already cited; and weekly payment act (1887).[55]

With the sudden decline of the Knights nationally and locally in the late 1880's, the newly formed American Federation of Labor (organized 1881) began to exert a growing influence. Mainly through efforts of the Central Labor Union of Hartford, the Connecticut branch of the American Federation of Labor, later called the Connecticut Federation of Labor, was founded in 1887. Its avowed objectives were: 1] assistance in establishing national and international trade unions; 2] formation of local trade unions and association of them in a state federation; 3] influencing public opinion and obtaining legislation for the workers; and 4] aiding the labor press of Connecticut. Starting in 1888 the Federation stationed a "watch-dog" committee at the capitol during Assembly sessions to work for enactment of labor measures and to block antilabor action. During the next fifteen years the Federation undoubtedly influenced the passage of numerous labor laws:

1893 — Union label law.
1895 — Prohibition of prisoner employment in manufacture of food, medicine, cigars, tobacco, and so forth.
1895 — Establishment of State Board of Mediation and Arbitration.
1895 — Minimum age of fourteen for child labor.
1895 — Employees' right to join labor unions secured.

1897 — Blacklisting of employees forbidden.
1897 — Inspection of bakeries.
1901 — Employers' liability act.
1901 — Barbers' license law.
1901 — Establishment of free public employment bureaus.
1905 — Sanitary facilities in foundries.

As a whole, this body of legislation undoubtedly benefited not only the working man and woman but also all Connecticut citizens.[56]

It was through strikes that organized labor best displayed its growing power. Taking 1904 as a fairly typical year, one finds that thirty-six strikes occurred, most of them lasting only a few days, involving from a handful of workers up to 360. The employees usually struck for at least one or more of these reasons: 1] objection to wage reduction; 2] demands for increase in wage rates; 3] demands for reduced hours but same total wages; 4] demands both for shorter hours and higher wage rates; 5] objections to hiring of nonunion men; 6] refusal to work with nonunion men; 7] lockout by employers.

Assessing the outcome of the thirty-six strikes, the State Bureau of Labor Statistics classified about one-fourth as settled clearly in favor of labor, approximately the same for management, another fourth compromised (sometimes arbitrated), and the remainder unsettled or falling into other categories. By 1901 the Connecticut Federation of Labor had affiliated with it ninety-one unions and central bodies representing between 9,000 and 10,000 members. Thanks particularly to the national unions, labor had progressed far from its weak position of a few decades earlier.[57]

Politics in the 1890's

AFTER two decades of very close elections, the famous state elections of 1890 produced an incredible political deadlock which lasted two years. This election pitted Republican Samuel E. Merwin of New Haven against fellow townsman Judge Luzon B. Morris. The latter had also run in 1888, when he actually polled 1,415 more votes than Morgan G. Bulkeley of Hartford. Since Morris lacked the required overall majority, it fell to the Republican-controlled Assembly, under constitutional provision, to elect a governor from the two candidates with the highest totals. So Bulkeley was declared elected. The presence on the 1890 ballot of two minor parties, Prohibition and Labor, seemed inconsequential, but this precipitated a strange and bitter legislative stalemate.[58]

The official 1890 returns of the State Board of Canvassers showed the following results: Morris (Democrat) 67,662; Merwin (Republican) 63,976; Augur (Prohibition) 3,413; Baldwin (Labor) 209; scattering, 38. These returns gave Morris an absolute majority of twenty-six votes. Almost immediately a bitter battle broke out as to the legality of a number of the ballots. At that time each party provided its own ballots. The Prohibition party's ballots had the word "for" printed before a candidate's name, while a number of Republican ballots had a large speck on them. In Bridgeport, 126 such "specked" ballots were disallowed; if counted they would have prevented Morris from obtaining the needed absolute majority. The Hartford papers, the *Courant* (Republican) and the *Times* (Democratic), quickly launched a vitriolic political campaign in their columns, which foreshadowed the more serious legislative struggle of 1891–92.[59]

When the Assembly convened in January 1891, the Republican House and Democratic Senate immediately took diametrically opposed positions. The Democratic Senate declared that the Assembly possessed no power to go behind the official Board of Canvassers' returns, while the Republican House insisted that the legislators could do so. The Senate quickly resolved that the entire Democratic ticket, having polled an absolute majority according to the official returns, was thereby elected. Trying to meet the constitutional requirement that the Assembly on the first day of its session declare those elected, the House extended the official first day indefinitely by taking recesses from day to day instead of adjourning. When a Senate committee called on Governor Bulkeley to invite him to the inauguration of Morris as his successor, Bulkeley firmly replied, "I give you notice that I regard such action as revolutionary and unauthorized." Defying Bulkeley, the Senate later the same day swore into office the entire Demo-

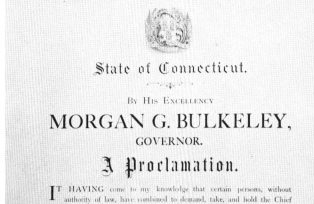

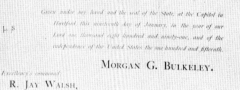

TOP: *Proclamation of Governor Bulkeley in 1891.*
BOTTOM: *Cartoon depicting Governor Bulkeley enjoying the 1891 political deadlock.*

cratic ticket. Republican officeholders, however, revealed no intention of surrendering their offices. Meanwhile, on January 19, 1891, Governor Bulkeley issued a forceful and famous proclamation in which he denied the right of the Democratic candidates to assume office and boldly announced his intention of holding his office until a constitutional finding and declaration should be made by the entire Assembly. Soon afterward a special House election committee reported that all the Democratic candidates, except Nicholas Staub for comptroller, lacked overall majorities. In jocose vein, a New York reporter described Connecticut's situation:

> Sing a song of governors,
> One, two, three;
> Samuel E. and Luzon B. and Morgan
> G.
> Talk about a small state, gracious
> me!
> There's New York with only one
> and we've got three![60]

The two conflicting houses seemed unable to work out a compromise; and the only progress made was in permitting Staub to take over as new comptroller, since he had a clear overall majority whether all disputed ballots were counted or thrown out. Late in March a dramatic incident occurred involving Staub and Bulkeley. In response to a request by a Democratic committee for exclusive use of an anteroom adjoining the governor's office, Staub persuaded the building superintendent to secure the door between that room and the governor's office with a large padlock. When Bulkeley found this door locked, he ordered a crowbar, and with the aid of a clerk succeeded in breaking the lock! For this feat he won the nickname, the "Crowbar Governor."[61]

When the legislative deadlock persisted, Judge Morris and Dr. Joseph W. Alsop, Democratic candidate for lieutenant governor, in April brought *quo warranto* proceedings in Superior Court at New Haven against Governor Bulkeley and Lieutenant Governor Merwin, with the hope of forcing them to vacate their offices. Long and involved legal maneuverings followed. Meanwhile, because of the refusal of the Assembly to vote adequate appropriations, the state ran out of money. Governor Bulkeley, apparently pledging his entire fortune

as a guarantee, arranged with the Ætna Life Insurance Company, of which he was president, to cash all claims against the state. Apparently Ætna advanced nearly $300,000 — a substantial sum, but less than 10 percent of total state government costs for the period. In November the Supreme Court, to which the *quo warranto* case had been passed, heard arguments by counsel for both sides. On January 5, 1892, it handed down a unanimous decision that Governor Bulkeley, in the absence of a constitutionally chosen successor, remained the *de jure* as well as *de facto* governor. The two houses of the Assembly were unwilling even to cooperate in voting money for state participation in the 1893 World's Fair, so that Bulkeley invited citizens to contribute money. The plea produced enough and Connecticut was represented by a very impressive exhibit. Governor Bulkeley carried on the state's business meanwhile until early 1893. The 1892 elections produced a clear-cut victory for Judge Morris — one not to be nullified by legal or political moves. Fortunately Connecticut had avoided outright violence, but the will of the majority had been thwarted for two years.[62]

The new administration and Assembly saw to it that all of the accounts and acts of Bulkeley were declared valid. Public opinion seems to have been deeply aroused, however, by the frequent spectacle of the Assembly electing as governor a man who had received fewer votes than an opponent. At the turn of the century the Assembly proposed, and on October 7, 1901, the people overwhelmingly approved an amendment which stated that the candidate receiving the highest popular vote for a state office would be elected.[63]

In the 1890's national politics exerted an unusually heavy influence on state politics. Although the two major parties entered the decade fairly evenly matched, as they had been for years, they left it with the Republicans far ahead. What caused the sudden Republican rise to clear dominance? In 1892 the Democrats won, but in 1894 the tide turned to the Republicans. A severe economic depression struck nationally in 1893, and the Democrats, as the party in power, reaped the unpopularity of bad times. The Democrats in 1894 claimed that Republicans worked with the nativist, anti-Catholic American Protective Association. This and other cultural issues, such as the rural-urban and Yankee-immigrant tensions, seem to have been quite significant both in 1894 and 1896. On basic, economic, "bread-and-butter" issues such as the tariff and currency, there was little to choose between the major parties prior to 1896, even though Democrats claimed a lower tariff position. By 1894 a general drift of large groups toward the Republican party was evident. Aiding this was a rising stress between Democratic city bosses on one side and the conservative pro-

more dangerous. Bryan was a colorful campaigner and superb orator who attracted a diverse following. Alexander Troup, a Connecticut labor leader, enthusiastically backed him. Although McKinley seemed colorless by comparison, his clear stand for a gold standard and a high tariff attracted wide support from those alarmed by Bryan's relative radicalism. The state and Congressional races were completely overshadowed. Election day brought Republicans their greatest landslide since 1860. Both McKinley and Lorrin A. Cooke, Repub-

Factory workers at Seymour demonstrate in 1896 for "McKinley and Protection."

Cleveland party leaders and big party contributors on the other.[64]

In 1896 youthful William Jennings Bryan of Nebraska stampeded the Democratic National Convention into nominating him on a "free silver" platform. This marked the party's capture by western agrarian interests. This development shocked and dismayed most of the top Connecticut Democrats, who ardently believed in a gold standard. Many middle-class Democrats were convinced by Republican arguments that Bryan's election might mean loss of their property. The income tax, anti-injunction, and antijudiciary planks also antagonized many middle-class voters. To the unemployed, "free silver" and agrarian reform meant very little. Connecticut farmers, who had developed a very different type of agriculture from that in the West, found almost nothing appealing in Bryan's program and much that was threatening. Bryan's proposed reforms, they felt, would serve simply to make western farm competition even

lican gubernatorial candidate, nearly doubled their opponent's vote, while the Gold Democrats (a separate Democratic ticket advocating the gold standard) and Prohibition candidates received trifling support. Bryan ran poorly in all areas. Although Cleveland carried Hartford in 1892, for example, Bryan lost it badly — 9,123 to 4,180. In 1898 and 1900 the Republicans scored decisive victories, though Bryan's vote increased considerably in 1900. For years after 1896 the Democratic party seems to have suffered from the deep split in leadership and ranks produced by what some called the "Bryan blight."[65]

Scarcely had the dark economic clouds lifted when the nation became involved in a war with Spain. At the declaration of war in April 1898, the state had four organized regiments of the National Guard. In meeting Connecticut's share of the 125,000 volunteers requested by President McKinley, Governor Cooke chose the First Regiment. One light and two heavy artillery batteries were added, and all of the men enlisted for two years. In response to the next presidential call of May 25, the Third Regiment also was designated for active duty.[66]

Ordered to Camp Haven at Niantic, they passed a long, wet, and boring spring. Officials at Washington, fearing a possible Spanish attack upon the northern coast, ordered the two regiments held in Connecticut for coastal defense. Early in July the

weak power. Although the war's effects were great in marking the "arrival" of the United States as a world power with an overseas empire, the immediate effects upon Connecticut were small.[67]

Constitutional Problems to the Fore

AFTER the war, reformers and some politicians again focused attention on constitutional prob-

Scene at Camp Alger, Virginia, in 1898.

First Regiment, after being split up for duty at Fort Knox, Maine, and other places, was ordered to Camp Alger, Virginia, and the Third to Camp Meade, Pennsylvania. In these camps many were struck down by disease, but neither regiment ever faced the enemy, although the men were eager to do so. Meanwhile, in June, Connecticut's naval battalion, 188 enlisted men and 17 officers, was mustered into active service. For many of these men the call resulted only in a monotonous summer on the *U.S.S. Minnesota,* tied to a wharf in Boston. Virtually the only Connecticut men to engage in actual combat with the enemy were the few already in the regular Army and Navy when war broke out. In addition to these regulars it is estimated that about 3,400 Connecticut volunteers officially entered service. The Spanish-American War proved to be short and easy, as Spain was a

lems, especially the enormous overrepresentation of many small towns. The most extreme contrast involved New Haven, with 108,027 inhabitants, and Union, with 428, each having two representatives in the Lower House! Though the Senate's districts were more even, the most populous district had over nine times the number of inhabitants of the least populous. Both in 1896 and 1900 the Democrats had called for reform of the Assembly representation scheme. In October 1901, voters approved an amendment setting the Senate's size at a minimum of twenty-four and maximum of thirty-six. This prospect had failed, however, to satisfy those desiring House reform. In the spring of 1901, after some hesitation, Governor McLean and other Republican leaders had finally endorsed the proposed constitutional convention and persuaded the Assembly to call it. At a special state-wide election in November 1901, each town elected one delegate. In the able group selected were such men as former Governors Charles B. Andrews and Thomas M. Waller. The small towns had both the skilled politicians and the votes to prevent major changes. The convention met from January 1 until May 15, 1902, and painfully hammered out a constitution involving a few important changes. The most controversial issue was that of House representation. Three main groups developed: those wanting drastic change in favor of real democracy; those who would accept minor modifications; and those opposing any change. Eventually, on May 5, the delegates agreed upon the compromise Bissell Plan. Towns were to be represented in the House as follows:

Under 2,000 population	1 member
From 2,000 to 50,000	2 members
From 50,000 to 100,000	3 members
100,000 or more	4 members
One extra for each 50,000 in excess of 100,000.	

Other changes included a Senate of forty-five members, elected by districts of contiguous territory and as nearly equal in population as possible, provided that no county had less than two; a simpler amendment process; a small salary raise for legislators; and ten days instead of three for the governor to act upon bills. Unfortunately, political feuds became involved in the proposals. The key Bissell Plan was pushed through by the McLean-Fyler-Clark faction of the G.O.P., so that other Republican factions, plus the Democrats, were determined to discredit the plan. Even so, the proposed constitution received much publicity in the press. Proponents there and elsewhere argued that the new constitution contained many highly desirable improvements and could be easily amended when necessary. Opponents stressed the greater cost of the Assembly because of salary increases and the great difficulty in calling future constitutional conventions. They also claimed that the new representation formula satisfied neither towns nor cities. Somehow the document failed to capture broad public interest. Whereas 74,062 people had voted in 1901 for holding the convention, only 31,611 voted on the constitution. The large cities overwhelmingly rejected it, and most small towns also defeated it, though Litchfield

County approved it by a narrow margin. Altogether 10,377 favored and 21,234 opposed it. The defeat seems to have resulted from such factors as the fierce inter- and intraparty rivalries, the unwillingness of city leaders to accept the Bissell Plan, and the understandable fear by small-town inhabitants that they would lose most of their political influence. A few years later a writer half seriously labeled Connecticut, "The State Ruled by its Uninhabited Country Towns."[68]

The Changing Nature of Early Twentieth-Century Politics

IT is interesting to contrast the evolution of Democratic and Republican party organizations and policies from the late 1890's to 1914. The Democratic party required many years to recover from the 1896 defeat, especially because of the deep split produced by Bryanism. Part of the conservative leadership of the 1880's and early 1890's had accepted Bryan (some without enthusiasm), but others, like Lynde Harrison, walked out permanently. Some Gold Democrats gradually drifted back. The money issue, however, continued to divide the party, illustrative of the tendency of Democrats at this period to split over *issues*, while Republicans split mostly over personalities, patronage, and the like. Hence the latter could unite easily for a campaign, whereas Democratic internecine conflict usually carried over into campaigns, with detrimental results. Alexander Troup, editor of the *New Haven Union* and ringleader of Bryanism, powerfully backed the "Great Commoner" in his unsuccessful 1900 and 1908 bids for the Presidency. The unyielding advocacy of Troup and other Bryanites helped perpetuate the 1896 schism even beyond Troup's death in 1908. The few Democratic successes between 1896 and 1910 came in city mayoralty elections, where such men as Thomas Reilly of Meriden and Bryan Mahan of New London scored victories. In 1910 Reilly was elected to Congress from the Second District — the first Democratic congressman chosen since 1894.[69]

Ethnic factors added to the party's problems, as considerable rivalry developed between the Irish and the old-line Yankees who had controlled the party so long. The city Irish, mostly Democrats, fared poorly at state conventions, where the overrepresented rural areas consistently effected nomination for governor of Yankees who could attract sizable party contributions. Not until 1918 did Democrats nominate an Irish-American, Thomas Spellacy, for governor. The growing Irish influence was apparent, however, in 1912, when five Irish Democratic Congressional candidates — Reilly, Mahan, Jeremiah Donovan of Norwalk, William Kennedy of Naugatuck, and Augustine Lonergan of Hartford — were elected. A comparison of the rolls of state committeemen in 1896 and 1914 clearly reveals growing Irish influence. Although tensions existed, they should not be exaggerated, as political parties have normally been alliances of diverse groups.[70]

In an era when the nation and state were predominantly Republican, the G.O.P. could count

Orsamus R. Fyler, Charles H. Clark, Robert O. Eaton, Congressman Ebenezer J. Hill, and J. Henry Roraback (dominant in Litchfield County after Fyler's death in 1909). In 1911 Roraback helped McLean to wrest from Bulkeley his Senate seat. Leaders of both factions usually were lawyers and often lobbied for corporations. Aside from the Irish, the ethnic groups seem largely to have gravitated to the Republicans, who organized special clubs for the Italians, Poles, and Swedes. There also existed a Sumner League for Republican Negroes.[71]

The first decade of the century showed a strong Republican trend in Connecticut, as well as nationally. In presidential years, Republican state candidates could safely ignore or de-emphasize state issues and still ride to easy victory on the broad coattails of McKinley, Roosevelt, and Taft, as the figures below clearly reveal.[72]

MAJOR PARTY VOTES, 1900–1908

	1900	1902	1904	1906	1908
President	McKinley (R) 102,572 Bryan (D) 74,014		Roosevelt (R) 111,089 Parker (D) 72,909		Taft (R) 112,915 Bryan (D) 68,255
Governor	McLean (R) 95,822 Bronson (D) 81,421	Chamberlain (R) 85,338 Cary (D) 69,330	Roberts (R) 104,736 Robertson (D) 79,164	Woodruff (R) 88,384 Thayer (D) 67,776	Lilley (R) 98,179 Robertson (D) 82,260

on winning state elections if it could avoid serious factional battles. There were few ideological disputes in these years, but keen rivalry for nominations existed. Morgan G. Bulkeley and Samuel Fessenden, each wanting a Senate seat when Hawley or Platt should retire or die, led opposed cliques working for state and national offices. When Hawley's seat became vacant in 1905 Bulkeley prevailed. When Platt suddenly died three months later, Fessenden decided the feeling against him was too great, he supported Frank E. Brandegee, who was successful and enjoyed a long career at Washington. The old Bulkeley-Fessenden split gradually evolved into a different division. On one side were Bulkeley, Brandegee, Michael Kenealy, Isaac Ullman, Everett Lake, and Frank Healy. Opposed were George P. McLean,

In 1910 a sudden change in Democratic fortunes occurred. That year Simeon Baldwin, a distinguished lawyer, Yale professor, and author, retired as Chief Justice of the State Supreme Court. A Democrat of impeccable personal and professional reputation, Baldwin evinced interest in the Democratic nomination for governor, though he had never held a political office before. Despite a somewhat cold personality, he easily won the nomination. At the Republican convention, adherents of Charles A. Goodwin, executive secretary to Governors Lilley and Weeks, and followers of former Lieutenant Governor Everett J. Lake fought a bitter battle before Goodwin won. The split helped the Democratic candidate.[73]

The two parties offered almost identical platforms, each advocating a public utilities commission and workmen's compensation legislation, though the Democrats took a stronger stand on a corrupt-practices law. In his campaign Baldwin stressed national issues and sharply attacked the Republican high tariff. As Baldwin had hoped, his high-level approach appealed to many independent voters, so that he won by about 3,700 votes, although Republicans captured the other state offices and both Assembly houses. The new governor proved successful, nevertheless, in getting the Assembly to enact some of his proposals, including a corrupt-practices act and establishment of the long-overdue public utilities commission.[74]

Renominated by acclamation in 1912, Baldwin faced not one but at least two, perhaps three, major opponents. The Republicans nominated John P. Studley of the New Haven Probate Court. National events had their repercussion in Connecticut. When President Taft was renominated, many Republican supporters of Theodore Roosevelt held a separate convention to nominate him as a Progressive, or Bull Moose, party candidate. In Connecticut, State Senator Joseph W. Alsop of Avon, angry over Republican rejection of Roosevelt, began organization of a Connecticut Progressive party in June 1912. He found willing allies in such men as Frank Butterworth of New Haven, Edward Roszelle, labor leader, John C. Brinsmede of Washington, President Flavel S. Luther of Trinity, and Gutzon Borglum of Stamford, famous sculptor. The new party chose as its gubernatorial candidate Herbert K. Smith of Hartford, who had resigned a high Federal position to work for the Progressives. At this time the Socialist party, with Eugene Debs as presidential nominee and Samuel E. Beardsley running for governor, was expected to do well. Since the Progressive leaders mostly were from the liberal wing of the Republican party, it seemed likely that they would draw their major support from Republicans. An unusually interesting state race was largely overshadowed by the torrid presidential race in which Woodrow Wilson (Democrat) competed with Taft, Debs, and Roosevelt. Wilson won nationally and in Connecticut, thanks to the huge vote Roosevelt drew away from Taft. State results closely paralleled the national ones:

Baldwin	78,264
Studley	67,531
Smith	31,020
Beardsley	10,236
Bassette (*Prohibition*)	2,096
Wells (*Socialist Labor*)	1,247

Although polling only 41 percent of the total vote, Baldwin won easily. Democrats took all Congressional seats and the State Senate, but lost the House. Though the Progressives ran more poorly than in most states, they undoubtedly insured Democratic victory by their deep inroads among Republicans.[75]

At the 1913 Assembly, Baldwin's prodding helped in securing passage of a workmen's compensation bill, which declared industrial accidents the employer's liability and set terms and rates of compensation for injured workers. The law permitted establishment of mutual insurance associations by employers to finance payments. Most of Baldwin's recommendations for constitutional reforms, however, were completely ignored.[76]

Despite opposition in 1914, Baldwin won nomination for the United States Senate to oppose Brandegee. Since this was the first popular election of a senator under the Seventeenth Amendment, the campaign attracted special interest. Baldwin soon found himself on the defensive, trying to answer Republican attacks on Wilson's administration. Moreover, he could expect little help from the Progressives in drawing away votes from the Republicans. The Progressives had declined into a noisy, squabbling group, largely deserted by their 1912 following. They did nominate former Professor Willard C. Fisher of Wesleyan for governor, on a platform of tax reform, including abolition of the two-dollar personal tax. The G.O.P. drafted for governor an unwilling candidate, Judge Marcus Holcomb of the State Superior Court. Their platform advocated the high protective tariff and a balanced budget. Holcomb's Democratic opponent, Lyman T. Tingier, was a conservative lawyer. The Progressives attacked "bossism" in the Republican party and denounced Roraback, new state chairman, as a mouthpiece for corrupt railroad interests. Apparently in Connecticut, as elsewhere, most Progressives returned to their old Republican faith, as Holcomb routed

Tingier by 91,262 to 73,888 votes, while Fisher polled only 8,030. Brandegee won over Baldwin by 89,983 to 76,081.[77]

A Heavy Immigrant Tide

THE early years of the present century brought not only exciting political shifts but also major changes in the composition of the population. From 1900 to 1910 occurred the heaviest immigration in American history, and Connecticut, close to

After a full century during which its rate of growth lagged behind the national average, Connecticut from 1890 to 1910 slightly exceeded the average rate. The state was rapidly becoming an "urban" area; by 1910 some 89.7 percent of the population fell into that category, placing the state third in percentage behind only Rhode Island and Massachusetts. Between 1890 and 1910 New Haven and then Bridgeport passed the 100,000 mark. The latter, thanks chiefly to expanding industry, had registered a 109 percent growth since

Country of Birth	Connecticut	Bridgeport	Hartford	New Haven
1. Ireland	58,457	5,085	7,048	9,004
2. Italy	56,953	5,021	4,521	13,159
3. Russia	54,120	4,116	6,647	7,980
4. Germany	31,126	2,811	2,424	4,114
5. Austria	23,642	3,858	1,865	1,109
6. England	22,422	3,264	1,653	1,867
7. Canada (French)	18,889	499	792	461
8. Sweden	18,208	1,677	2,185	1,446
9. Hungary	13,855	6,975	328	473
10. Canada (not French)	7,797	771	1,285	855
11. Scotland	6,750	606	759	724
12. Denmark	2,722	374	592	265

the principal immigrant entry port, New York City, received an avalanche of newcomers. By 1910 foreign-born numbered 329,574, or about 30 percent of the state's 1,114,756 people. The numbers from principal foreign nations and their distribution in the three largest cities as indicated in the 1910 census afford a significant study. Nations represented by 1,000 to 2,619 persons were France, Greece, Norway, Switzerland, and Turkey. In common with national immigration trends, the largest flow into Connecticut came from southern and eastern Europe, especially from Italy, Austria-Hungary, and Russia.[78]

1890. The census revealed also that 161,921 of the 175,523 children six to fourteen years of age were attending school regularly — a rate of 92.3 percent as against the national rate of 81.4 percent. Illiteracy, on the other hand, also reached considerable proportions — some 53,665 persons, or 6 percent. Not surprisingly, the foreign-born whites, often having had no educational opportunities, were 15.4 percent illiterate, while the native-born, with far greater opportunities, registered only one-half of one percent. The overall picture in the state by 1910 thus showed a rapidly growing and highly urbanized and industrialized population.[79]

CHAPTER 15

Connecticut During World War I

Politics from 1915 to 1917 — Mobilizing Public Opinion — Making the Weapons — In Training and On to France — Fighting a Formidable Enemy — Labor Problems and Achievements — Victory and Politics, 1918–19

Politics from 1915 to 1917

THE Assembly's 1915 session brought some measures of broad significance. The legislature combined two separate bureaus — labor statistics and factory inspection — into a single State Department of Labor and Factory Inspection, under one commissioner. It also created a commissioner of banks, who was to inspect and oversee all banks, savings societies, and related organizations. The 1913 act establishing a State Civil Service Commission was revised so that the civil service fell into three categories — classified, unclassified, and exempt. The second group included all elected officials, heads of departments, and teachers, among others; while the exempt service involved those for whom tests would be impractical.[1]

In September 1916 a special session of the Assembly was called to insure the ballot for the increasing number of Connecticut men in the armed forces who were not members of the Regular Army. A new law enabled such men to vote by absentee ballots, which had to be received from ten to thirty days before election day. Another act carried a small appropriation to reimburse towns for payments to soldiers' dependents. These acts reflected the growing impact of the national preparedness program.[2]

In the late nineteenth century the state had developed a chaotic assortment of taxes on public service companies. To bring some order out of the confusion, a special commission was appointed by the governor under authority of an Assembly act of 1911. Largely following the commission's suggestions to substitute a simple tax on gross earnings for the previous complicated provisions, the Assembly in 1913 imposed this type of tax upon express, private railroad car, telegraph, and telephone companies. In 1915 it levied a tax of 3½ percent on the gross earnings of steam and electric companies and 4½ percent on street railways, and lower rates on certain other enterprises.[3]

In 1916 the state political campaign approached in the lengthening shadows of World War I. This highly sanguinary struggle alarmed and depressed many thoughtful Americans, who wondered whether this nation could continue to stay out. The war and the broad sweep of the Wilson reform program since 1914 combined to push the state elections into the background as compared with the national campaign pitting President Wilson against Republican Charles Evans Hughes.

The *Courant* vigorously condemned Wilson's tariff policies (the Underwood Tariff especially), the Adamson Eight-Hour Act, Democratic foreign policies, and also alleged vacillation and inefficiency; while the *Times* stanchly defended Wilson's entire domestic and foreign program.[4]

As expected, the Republicans renominated popular Governor Holcomb, although he seemed genuinely indifferent as to whether or not he was chosen again; while Frank E. Healy of Windsor Locks fought desperately to get the nomination. Again the Republicans proclaimed their faith in the high protective tariff, called for stronger foreign policies, for state preparedness measures, tighter bookkeeping and accounting practices, and a continued reduction of the state's debt. The Democrats selected Morris B. Beardsley of Bridgeport as candidate for governor and Homer S. Cummings of Stamford for the United States Senate. Their state platform, among many planks, called for amendment of the workers' compensation law, and more and better roads. Democrats in Connecticut urged re-election of President Wilson so "that the nation may be saved from war." A Democratic paper declared, "Hartford regards the European war as terrible, and is glad it has no part in it." Although Wilson was re-elected by a narrow margin, Connecticut went Republican, giving Hughes 106,514 votes to Wilson's 99,786. George P. McLean won the United States Senate seat, while Holcomb was re-elected by about 12,500 plurality over Beardsley. The Progressive party did not offer a candidate, and the other minor parties received insignificant votes. Except for the election of Democrat Augustine Lonergan to Congress it was a Republican sweep.[5]

The Assembly's 1917 session clearly reflected mounting concern over the international situation and the need for preparedness. On February 20, 1917, it approved a bill requiring an inventory of men and materials available in case of war. Every male sixteen years of age and older was expected to answer a questionnaire, giving information as to residence, citizenship, marital status, dependents, occupation, health, and special skills. Governor Holcomb personally wrote to every selectman in the state asking for full co-operation. Unpaid volunteer workers in the various towns collected the needed data and forwarded it to Hartford. About 2,800 business establishments provided information, which was tabulated and placed on file in the State Library, where it was available to state and Federal officials.[6]

The industrial survey made on the eve of our entrance into World War I revealed that thirty-four Connecticut firms, employing over 40,000 workers, already held government contracts. Among the more prominent were Maxim Silencer, Hartford Machine Screw, Veeder, and Colt's, of Hartford; Waterbury Manufacturing and Scoville, of Waterbury; Ansonia Manufacturing of Ansonia; Foster, Merriam of Meriden; Russell of Middletown; and Hopkins and Allen of Norwich.[7]

About two years before American entrance into the war several Connecticut arms makers began to accept foreign orders. In 1915 a Bridgeport company concluded a contract with the German Government for making shrapnel shell. After Germany had provided money to construct the plant and a small number of shell were produced, it became obvious that the products could not be delivered, because of the British naval blockade of Germany. As a result, the United States took over the shrapnel and the plant as the Liberty Ordnance Company, which became an important center of arms production. Meanwhile large, secret orders began coming in from Canada late in 1914, and soon several Hartford companies, including Colt's, were booming. This was the beginning of a steady stream of British, Canadian, and French orders, which brought great prosperity to numerous Connecticut defense industries, especially in the Bridgeport and Hartford areas.[8]

Mobilizing Public Opinion

PROBABLY the key agency in co-ordinating Connecticut's home-front mobilization was the State Council of Defense. As in other states, its organization came in response to a request by Newton D. Baker, Secretary of War. Governor Holcomb moved speedily to appoint the Council under an Assembly act of March 14, 1917, granting him wide discretionary power to meet wartime emergencies. He chose Richard M. Bissell as chairman and added other prominent citizens, representing industrial, financial, insurance, munitions, medical, legal, labor, farm, and military groups. The wide scope of its activities is apparent from the list of committees which functioned actively: finance and ways and means, publicity, legal, coordination of societies, food supply and conservation, industrial survey, manpower and labor, military and naval, state protection, transportation, and sanitation and medicine. Late in September 1917 a women's committee was added, and it quickly became highly active.[9]

The publicity committee strove to make the public aware of the nation's and state's wartime needs. In the fall of 1917 it sponsored over two hundred war rallies at which teams consisting of one man and one woman spoke and attempted to whip up greater enthusiasm for the war effort by describing our war aims, the price of defeat, and related topics. A second series of small rallies followed in January and February 1918, and a third, or "Victory War Rallies," began in March. Separate rallies in June 1918 emphasized the thrift stamp savings program, while a united war work campaign in November 1918 featured 274 meetings, at most of which a priest, a rabbi, and a Protestant clergyman spoke. Connecticut initiated the "liberty chorus" in a rally at Foot Guard Hall, Hartford, on October 17, 1917, when four hundred high school students sang impressively. Other states enthusiastically copied this idea. To supplement the public rallies, the publicity department sponsored the showing of several specially prepared movies.[10]

Another exceedingly active program was that to increase the food supply. Every effort was made through a "Junior Food Army" and the "Connecticut Canning Corps" to enroll large numbers of children and adults in raising extra food and canning part of it. In May 1917 the Assembly passed a law enabling high school pupils over fourteen to volunteer for farm work. The experience of that year indicated the need of special training for the inexperienced, so training camps at Loomis and Connecticut Agricultural College were established in 1918. Home gardens increased so greatly in size and number that Connecticut women exceeded their quota of 5,000,000 quarts of canned fruits and vegetables. A valuable by-product of the food drive came in a careful survey, county by county, of the state's farms.[11]

In common with other states which had large numbers of recent immigrants, including some from enemy nations, Connecticut worried about the loyalty of its melting pot. Governor Holcomb wrote to a selected list of the foreign-born in seventy-five towns and urged an educational program to stimulate patriotism. By April 1918, twenty-one towns had formed "American loyalty" committees, which worked on the Americanization program with apparent success.[12]

The Americanization efforts tied in closely with the work of the Committee on Education, which encouraged teaching of citizenship and American war objectives. A pamphlet entitled *Why We Are at War with Germany* was prepared, and 45,000 copies were printed and distributed. The sponsors suggested its use in the seventh, eighth, and ninth grades and advised teachers to encourage students to take it home and try to interest their parents in reading it. Written in strongly patriotic tones, the twelve-page pamphlet briefly sketched the origins of the war and quoted President Wilson on Allied war aims. Other publications included *What We Are Fighting For* and *Beware of German Trickery at the Bargain Counter of Europe.*[13]

The Council of Defense carried on many other activities. The Women's Division displayed great energy along such lines as Americanization, publicity, food conservation, and rallies. Attention was devoted to fuel conservation, health and sanitation, legal matters, employment, recreation, historical records, manpower and labor, and even military matters. In many of these fields the Council worked very closely with Federal agencies. Altogether it did much to help successfully mobilize Connecticut's home front.[14]

Making the Weapons

WITH American entrance into World War I in 1917, Connecticut's munitions industry, already partially mobilized, quickly slipped into high gear. The "Big Five" — Remington Arms and Ammunition and Remington Union Metallic, of Bridgeport; Winchester Repeating Arms and Marlin-Rockwell, of New Haven; and Colt's Patent Firearms, of Hartford — had been working on foreign and American contracts prior to our entrance. They found it relatively easy to step up production. Scores of other companies also soon obtained government contracts. The vastness of the expansion showed itself clearly in employment increases, such as that at Colt's from a prewar figure of 800 to over 8,000, and at Winchester from 5,000 to over 21,000. All of Connecticut, plus four counties in western Massachusetts, was placed in the Bridgeport Ordnance District by the Federal government. Only the New York Ordnance District surpassed the Bridgeport District in value of contracts relative to area.[15]

In line with its lengthy experience Connecticut specialized in small-arms making. The Winchester Company, for example, turned out about 466,000 Enfield rifles by Armistice Day — nearly 20 percent of the entire national production for the Army. Remington primarily, and Winchester secondarily, together made all the bayonets — about 2,000,000; while the Jewell Belting Company of Hartford supplied a majority of the scabbards for these bayonets. Colt's was one of only two American companies which made revolvers for the government. The Colt .45 official service pistol, invented by Colt employee John M. Browning, was made almost entirely by Colt's, although Remington produced a few thousand. Landers, Frary and Clark of New Britain manufactured 113,000 trench knives (Model 1918) for the armed forces. In the line of ammunition Connecticut also ranked very high. It is estimated that about 45 percent of all small-arms cartridges (.30 and .45 caliber) came from Remington, which eventually employed 12,000 in this effort.[16]

For outstanding individual contributions to the war effort one must cite John M. Browning of Colt's, who developed, among other weapons, three types of guns: 1] the heavy Browning water-cooled machine gun, 2] the light Browning automatic rifle, and 3] the Browning synchronized aircraft gun. These guns were highly reliable and simple in design. So great was the demand for these weapons that Colt's could not possibly produce quickly enough all the armed forces required. Hence the government reached an agreement

whereby Colt's, for the duration of the war, surrendered its exclusive rights in return for a royalty plan. By Armistice time the government had accepted over 52,000 Browning automatic rifles, of which Colt's produced about 9,000, Marlin-Rockwell, 16,000, and Winchester, 27,000. This weapon and the heavy machine gun were widely used by front-line American troops.[17]

In the field of big guns only one Connecticut firm played an important part — the Bullard Engineering Company of Bridgeport. In a new plant built with government funds the company made and assembled 155-mm. guns, of which it completed 265 by 1919. At production peak, 1,050 employees, including 150 women, labored upon this project.[18]

Although one might not connect the making of woven and elastic goods with vital defense needs, the Russell Manufacturing Company of Middletown proved the intimate relationship. Ranking second nationally in this field, Russell produced about 1,500,000 woven articles for the armed forces, including machine-gun belts (a rate of 3,000 daily attained), cartridge belts, haversacks, pistol holsters, canteen covers, bayonet scabbards, elastic cord for airplane snubbers, and elastic braid for aviators' goggles and gas masks. Other varied state defense products were silk for parachutes by Cheney Brothers, Manchester; fuse casings by Waterbury Brass Goods; hand grenades by Bassick Company, Bridgeport, and P. and F. Corbin of New Britain; and trench-mortar fuses by Ansonia Manufacturing Company in Ansonia, and Russell and Irwin Manufacturing Company of New Britain. At Danbury, thousands of service hats were made. Altogether about 80 percent of the state's industries were directly or indirectly involved in producing arms or supplies for the Army and Navy.[19]

In Training and On to France

BEFORE American entrance into World War I some Connecticut troops obtained a taste of limited military activity in the Mexican border troubles of 1916. Among the troops which actually went to the Mexican border were the First and Second Infantry regiments under Colonels Richard J. Goodman and Charles F. McCabe respectively. These units, stationed near Nogales and Arivaca, Arizona, from July to October 1916, found burning heat and torrential downpours more formidable foes than the Mexicans. In the absence of any actual fighting, daily drill, border patrol duty, and tactical problems kept the men busily occupied until the welcome orders came in October to entrain for Connecticut. It is likely that the mobilization provided some useful experience for the grimmer work which lay ahead in France.[20]

Before the formal American declaration of war on Germany, April 6, 1917, mobilization of Connecticut National Guard troops had started with a call late in March for the First Infantry Regiment. Soon afterward other units received their calls, with the Naval Militia going to the Boston Navy Yard. Four cavalry troops, after muster into Federal service, were formed into the One Hundred First Machine Gun Battalion (Companies A, B, C, D) and saw active service at Île de France, Lorraine, Champagne-Marne, Aisne-Marne, St. Mihiel, and Meuse-Argonne. Connecticut's Coast Artillery was divided, part going to batteries in France and part to companies on duty at Fort H. G. Wright (Fishers Island) and elsewhere on the American coast.[21]

The bulk of the First and Second regiments of infantry were combined into the new One Hundred Second United States Infantry. The surplus of the two regiments, called the Fifty-eighth Pioneer Infantry, went to Camp Green, North Carolina, and later to Camp Wadsworth, South Carolina. The First Separate Company (colored infantry) was ordered to Camp Stuart, Virginia, as Company M, Three Hundred Seventy-second Infantry. Thousands of Connecticut volunteers and draftees in addition were scattered through many Army units, some of which saw front-line duty.[22]

Since the organized militia was largely taken into Federal service, there was immediate need of organizing a Home Guard. Under authority of an Assembly act of March 9, 1917, Governor Holcomb appointed a Military Emergency Board, which within three months had 10,000 men enrolled, organized, and armed in the new Home Guard. These men guarded transportation lines

and were available to meet any major emergency.[23]

Particular interest attaches to the One Hundred Second Infantry, since it was originally wholly a Connecticut organization serving in New England's "Yankee" Division, the Twenty-sixth. The combining of a large part of the old Connecticut First and Second regiments into the One Hundred Second Regiment resulted from the War Department's plan to bring state regiments up to a strength of 95 officers and 3,604 men. The new Twenty-sixth Division was organized in August from the National Guard troops of the six New England states. Besides the One Hundred Second, two batteries of field artillery became part of the One Hundred Third Field Artillery; the squadron of Connecticut Cavalry went into the One Hundred First Machine Gun Battalion; the Connecticut Field Signal Troops were designated as Radio Company A, Three Hundred Twenty-sixth Field Signal Battalion; and the First Ambulance and Field Hospital companies were merged into the One Hundred First Sanitary Train — moves which completed the state's roster in the Twenty-sixth Division.[24]

As the Nutmeggers trained in camps at New Haven and Niantic they wondered when overseas orders would come. Meanwhile, on August 22, 1917, the division acquired its commander, Major General Clarence R. Edwards, a Regular Army officer, who was to lead the division ably through most of its action in France until finally relieved by Brigadier General Frank E. Bamford on October 24, 1918. General Edwards quickly won the confidence and affection of his men.[25]

Orders to leave the friendly confines of Camp Yale at New Haven came suddenly, and on September 6, 1917, two companies rolled their packs, marched quietly to the West Haven railroad station, proceeded to New York, and soon boarded the camouflaged liner *Adriatic* for the dangerous Atlantic crossing. Soon Camp Yale and Camp Niantic became ghost towns as all remaining units moved either to New York or Montreal for embarkation. The first Connecticut soldiers arrived at Liverpool on September 22 and at Le Havre on September 24. Others followed, and by early November all Connecticut combat units of the

Twenty-sixth Division were in France and had gone to their prescribed training area near Neufchâteau in the foothills of the Vosges Mountains.[26]

Intensive training for trench warfare began almost immediately, with guidance from experienced French and British troops. The infantry and engineers around Neufchâteau even constructed a model system of fire, cover, and support trenches for practice. On January 11, 1918, Colonel John H. Parker succeeded Ernest L. Isbell in command of the One Hundred Second. The new commander, nicknamed "Machine Gun" Parker, was a handsome giant of a man, who had great black mustachios and smoked a curved black brier pipe. Assembling a battalion at a time on a hillside, he harangued his men in army-style language. Challenging them to prove true to their Yankee heritage, coming from "the best fightin' stock in the world," he declared, "Now I want just one thing, — Spirit!" With the realization that his men were sick of training, he promised them that they soon would be fighting. Though a very popular commander, Colonel Parker pulled no punches in promising drastic action against men absent without leave. As a result, the café at nearby Épinal, a notorious rendezvous of A.W.O.L.'s, lost its patrons from the One Hundred Second.[27]

Fighting a Formidable Enemy

EARLY in February 1918 the Twenty-sixth entered the front lines in a relatively quiet sector north of Soissons, called the Chemin des Dames. At first the infantry companies were interspersed with French troops, and received thorough training from French officers and noncoms. Gradually the French withdrew, leaving a sizable section of the front in American hands. Each infantry regiment had one battalion on the front, one in support, and the third in reserve. The Germans soon tested the new arrivals with two raids, which were beaten off, and followed with a heavy gas attack in mid-March. On March 18 a small mixed force of French and Americans of the One Hundred Second attempted to cross a canal on rafts, but "friendly" artillery-fire fell short and broke up the first offensive action of the regiment. Right after this abortive attempt orders came for the division

to move to the southern end of the line. As the last of a Waterbury company pulled out, a comradely French soldier called out, "Bon soir, bon soir, crazee Americains!"[28]

The division, originally scheduled for refitting and further training, was urgently rushed to the La Reine, or Boucq, sector near Toul, formerly held by the First Division. This proved to be a highly active area marked by almost constant skirmishes and several serious engagements. On April 20 the German command loosed a frightful artillery barrage around Seicheprey and Remières Woods, followed by an advance of 1,500 *Sturmtruppen*, or hand-picked shock-troops, through the fog to seize Seicheprey and heights nearby. Companies C and D of the One Hundred Second were largely overrun, fought back ferociously under orders to hold their front line at all costs, and were nearly annihilated. Under Major George J. Rau and other officers, an effective counterattack was mounted which forced the Germans to abandon the attack. Deeds of extraordinary heroism were quite common. Typical was that of First Lieutenant Charles E. Lockhart, whose platoon held a sector over 1,800 feet in length for thirty-six hours against overwhelming odds. Lockhart brought out eight survivors. Every other man fell at his post of duty! Seicheprey was the genuine "baptism by fire" for many Connecticut soldiers — an action which General Pershing described as "violent, causing heavy losses on both sides."[29]

Early July found the Twenty-sixth moved to the Château-Thierry sector, not far from Paris — the center of a dangerous German penetration. Relieving the Second Division, the Yankee Division helped stop a German attack July 15–18, after which it joined in the Aisne-Marne offensive — a bitterly fought affair. Although the division had received numerous inexperienced draftees to replace casualties, the newcomers, steadied and guided by the battle-hardened veterans, performed creditably. The One Hundred Second Regiment actively participated in helping to reduce the enemy salient north of Château-Thierry. In Épieds and Trugny large elements of the One Hundred Second, exposed to withering enemy fire, suffered enormous losses, largely because of the enemy's excellent defensive position and the lack of supporting artillery fire. On July 23–24, after intensive artillery preparation, other units of the division drove the enemy back, but the One Hundred Second was too shattered to take part in the advance. It had suffered 1,200 casualties, including 137 killed in action. Despite the desperate enemy resistance, the division as a whole advanced about eleven miles. General Edwards cited no less than 112 officers and men of the One Hundred Second for "marked gallantry and meritorious service" during this Aisne-Marne offensive of July 18–25, 1918.[30]

The Twenty-sixth was next moved into a reserve status at Rupt, south of Verdun, where it received training in open fighting. During this interim the popular regimental commander, Colonel Parker, was replaced briefly by Colonel H. P. Hobbs, July 31, and by Colonel Hiram I. Bearss (U.S.M.C.), August 10. In September the newly organized American First Army under General Pershing obtained its first important assignment as a large separate army — the reduction of the St. Mihiel salient, a piece of German-held territory near the Meuse River, jutting far into Allied lines. In this great battle, involving 550,000 American troops, the One Hundred Second Infantry and the One Hundred First Machine Gun Battalion were at first held out as reserves. As the battle developed, however, they too were thrown into it with orders to take the village of Vigneulles. Colonel Bearss, believing in the adage that a straight line is the shortest distance between two points, ordered a daring nighttime advance down a road called La Grande Tranchée, which led directly to the village. In the very early morning hours of September 13 the One Hundred Second entered Vigneulles — to be joined later by elements of the First Division. The One Hundred Second and the entire division, which captured nearly 1,000 prisoners, could take pride in this successful offensive.[31]

During a brief period under French command in the Troyon sector in late September, the division staged a successful diversionary raid at Marcheville and Riaville, despite heavy enemy resistance. The next move of the division was to the Verdun area, where it relieved the French Eighteenth Division. Here the Germans held extremely strong positions, protecting vital steel pro-

duction areas. Plagued by influenza, heavy rains, and insufficient shelter, the Twenty-sixth in late October advanced slowly and with frightful casualties. The failure to get replacements and the removal of General Edwards and other popular high officers did much to damage morale of the entire

Three men of Company K, One Hundred Second Infantry Regiment in trench at Seicheprey, France, in 1918.

division, which soon literally was "shot up" and "done up." One battalion which had gone into the line 1,000 strong could muster only 93 effectives a few weeks later. Despite the exhausted and depleted condition of the division, it fought on under its new commander, Brigadier General Frank E. Bamford, with offensive action occurring even on November 11, as the artillery continued heavy firing right up to the Armistice at 11:00 A.M. As the blessed but unreal quiet of peace descended over the battlefields the men were too exhausted to display much outward emotion. Finally that evening the troops began firing all available pyrotechnics in celebration of the war's end. At Verdun four of the division's bands participated in a victory parade before cheering crowds.[32]

The end of fighting came just in time for the decimated Twenty-sixth. In gaining slightly more than three miles in the Verdun offensive, the One Hundred Second suffered nearly 1,500 casualties, and the entire division nearly 4,700. The division finally got the rest it so badly needed after nearly ten months of continuous service. On Armistice Day less than 30 percent of the nearly 28,000 New Englanders who crossed the Atlantic remained with the division. Casualties had included over one-half the original strength, and the division had received over 14,000 replacements. Altogether it captured over 3,100 German troops. Connecticut's One Hundred Second Regiment recorded more than 4,100 casualties for the war. Its ambulance company, mostly Bridgeport men, lost an appalling 85 percent wounded or gassed as it ministered to the casualties of fighting units, and from February to November 1918 transported over 20,000 wounded. The division as a whole was cited or commended in at least fourteen general orders of the French Army as well as in five by A.E.F. headquarters. More than 250 won the American Distinguished Service Cross and over 65 won the French Croix de Guerre for conspicuous gallantry above and beyond the call of duty.[33]

In World War I the airplane for the first time served as an important weapon of reconnaissance and offense. Connecticut's interest in this new dimension of warfare was heightened by the exploits of Major Raoul Lufbery of Wallingford. As a restless and adventurous young man he had run away from home, had traveled into distant corners of the world, and had served in the United States Army. After learning to fly he joined the French Foreign Legion. Soon after the war broke out he succeeded in entering the French air service and later secured a transfer to the American section, called the Lafayette Escadrille. After the United States entered the conflict, Lufbery received a commission as a major in our small Air Force. Here he added to his already brilliant record by running his official total of German planes

shot down to eighteen, though he probably accounted for many more. When he was killed in action on May 19, 1918, he ranked as the leading American ace.[34]

Labor Problems and Achievements

"ROSIE THE RIVETER" of World War II fame had her counterpart in World War I. A careful survey of some women workers at Remington Arms Union Metallic Cartridge Company in Bridgeport revealed much about the typical female worker. Mostly single, and boasting previous experience in factory work, usually at some other plant in Bridgeport, she nearly always worked on a single product — cartridges. Since no lengthy training period was required, and speed and manual dexterity were prime needs, the women workers filled these jobs admirably. When questioned about the hazards of their work, they said they felt that conditions generally were safer as a result of the Workmen's Compensation Act of 1913. The act failed, however, to protect against industrial diseases, or disabilities of less than ten days' duration, and granted only 50 percent of regular wages. The combination of limited benefits available if injured and the dangerous nature of materials processed constituted a psychological hazard for many of the feminine operatives. Most of the women were unorganized and offered little resistance to the lengthening of the workday to nine and even ten hours in many cases, and often they accepted night work. Although wages of women were reputed to be extremely high, the group surveyed had a median weekly wage of only about eleven dollars! Actually, many families in the Bridgeport area had two to five persons employed in defense work, and total family income ranged generally from twenty to sixty dollars weekly.[35]

The need for more effective legislation preventing night employment of women and minors seemed obvious to such groups as the State Federation of Labor, the Consumers' League of Connecticut, and the State Department of Labor. As a result of their efforts, four bills were introduced at the 1917 Assembly session. Apparently, however, the legislators did not believe the problem urgent, as none passed. The Assembly contented itself with an act prohibiting employment of women and minors under sixteen in any public restaurant, café, barber shop, hairdressing or manicuring establishment, or photographic gallery between 10:00 P.M. and 6:00 A.M.[36]

Housing provided a major headache for cities swollen by a huge influx of new workers at companies with large military contracts. One author ranked Bridgeport as among five American cities suffering from "intolerable overcrowding of industrial workers." Bridgeport's plight did not primarily stem from lack of foresight or civic interest. As early as 1916, when a city planner characterized the situation as already "desperate," the local Chamber of Commerce launched a campaign for better housing. The Bridgeport Housing Company, capitalized at $1,000,000 and backed by several leading citizens, outlined plans for housing 1,000 families at modest rents of $15.00 to $25.00 monthly. In 1915 the Remington Union Metallic Cartridge Company and the Remington Armory of Bridgeport invested over $2,000,000 in housing facilities for employees. Several dormitories were constructed for young women, who paid only $1.75 to $3.00 per week for rent.[37]

At Waterbury in 1915 the Scovill Manufacturing Company, specialists in brass products, had about 150 brick houses built and offered for sale to employees at prices of $4,200 and $4,700, payable in easy monthly installments. In addition to making these and other homes available at low cost, the company also constructed barracks for male workers and charged only fifty cents weekly rent. These and other efforts in Waterbury and Bridgeport were badly needed, as wartime rent increases averaged about 60 percent there — apparently higher than average. Chiefly because of bad housing conditions in war production centers, the labor turnover rate was extremely high, especially at Bridgeport, where some plants reported rates of 200 to 400 percent annually. The Federal government in July 1918 finally established the United States Housing Corporation to provide emergency housing in shortage areas. Several of the nineteen projects authorized were in Connecticut, but only those in Bridgeport, Groton, Waterbury, and New London were completed.

The housing shortage was heightened by a marked slowdown in new building. In 1917–18 only 343 tenement construction projects were reported in Connecticut, compared with 1,524 in 1915–16. The Federal government felt that scarce building materials were more needed for direct contributions to the war effort, and it prohibited new residential construction except in clearly pressing circumstances.[38]

Shortage of labor in war production centers posed a serious problem in 1917 and 1918. Although wages rose to as much as $4.00 or $4.50 per day for unskilled labor and job openings were advertised widely, the War Industries Board found it necessary late in 1918 to send 1,000 draftees from Camp Devens, Massachusetts, back to the brass mills of the Naugatuck Valley. Many agencies cooperated in trying to lure women into the factories, with an especially aggressive campaign occurring in Bridgeport in September 1918. Airplanes dropped leaflets, newspapers and movies spread the story, and 100 "minute women" canvassed house to house. The results were impressive, as many school teachers and others took part-time jobs. Some 6,000 entered the factories on their own initiative, and 2,000 more came through referral from the Federal Employment Service. Some factories even provided nurseries. The women performed a variety of tasks, from polishing small parts of guns to filling office jobs. By early 1918 Stamford had developed an extremely serious labor shortage, which caused an estimated cut of at least one-third in war production. Manufacturers, the Employment Service, and local authorities co-operated in an energetic drive to reduce turnover in the factories and to find more workers among local citizens who normally would not seek factory employment. As in Bridgeport, great ingenuity was displayed in making this appeal.[39]

Considering the highly abnormal labor market of the war years, one could reasonably expect some serious capital-labor strife. Bridgeport, as the center of the state's burgeoning munitions industry, experienced a large amount of labor trouble. Out of 422 Connecticut strikes and lockouts in 1915–16, 73 occurred in Bridgeport. In 1917–18 Connecticut suffered 183 strikes involving 33,400 workers, of whom 5,073 were in munitions factories. The gravest wartime strike, from a defense viewpoint, was that of 5,000 machinists of the Bridgeport Machinists Union (affiliated with the American Federation of Labor), who demanded higher wages, an eight-hour day, and an end to alleged discrimination against union members. Employers responded by asking the Federal government to institute criminal proceedings against the union. When management rejected the workers' demands, a strike started at Remington Arms, Liberty Ordnance, and twenty-two subcontracting shops. Very bad feeling between management and union representatives made negotiations difficult. Since production of vital war products was being delayed, the War Labor Board entered the dispute, but failed to solve it. Eventually an arbiter handed down a decision which appeared to satisfy both sides, but the execution bogged down. Again the workers walked out. This time President Wilson entered the dispute with a stiff letter to the union ordering the men back to work on penalty of being barred from defense employment in Bridgeport for one year, with military deferments lifted. Faced by this ultimatum, the strikers on September 17, 1918, voted a return to work. They received a pay increase and recognition of collective bargaining rights, among other gains.[40]

Despite this and other strikes, the overall labor picture was not dark. Speaking of labor's role in the war, Governor Holcomb praised the service of women workers and observed:

The loyalty and patriotism of Connecticut labor has been a valuable asset. The prevailing sentiment is that differences between employers and employees can well be postponed until we secure a safe peace. Backing up the Government in this war comes first, all other matters being sidetracked.[41]

Victory and Politics, 1918–19

THE state political campaign in 1918, fought against the fiery backdrop of the climactic battles of World War I, attracted slight interest. The major parties held their state conventions in June, earlier than usual, so that ballots could be distributed early enough to the more than 10,000 servicemen. The Republicans renominated Gov-

ernor Holcomb and Lieutenant Governor Wilson. Their platform pledged all Republicans to the task of winning the war and scored the "chronic incapacity of the democratic party to govern the country." Upon the two "hot" issues of the day — women's suffrage and prohibition — it deliberately took an ambiguous position. In vague phrases carrying an intimation of support, it cautiously advocated leaving the feminine suffrage problem to the people, and it boasted about the reduction of the state's debt from $10,960,000 in 1914 to $2,600,000 on September 30, 1917. Both parties vowed their utmost dedication to the task of winning the war. Upon the key domestic issues the Democrats adopted much more explicit positions. They strongly endorsed the proposed feminine suffrage amendment and asked for a public referendum on the prohibition amendment as a guide for future Assembly action. As candidate to oppose Governor Holcomb they selected Thomas J. Spellacy, United States District Attorney for Connecticut.[42]

On October 25, President Wilson injected an appeal to the nation for election of a Democratic Congress — an act shattering the campaign lethargy. In Connecticut, Republican newspapers almost unanimously denounced this partisan plea, while the Hartford *Times* argued that it was one's patriotic duty to support the President by electing the Democratic state and Congressional slate. Indeed, President Wilson himself seemed to become a major campaign issue. It appears doubtful that either prohibition or women's suffrage stirred up enough public interest to aid either party substantially, though the clearer Democratic support of the latter may have attracted some voters sympathetic to feminine voting. The Republicans possessed the heavy advantage of a two-term governor who had demonstrated vigorous wartime leadership. This may well have been decisive in Holcomb's polling 84,891 votes to 76,773 for Spellacy. In addition, Republicans won commanding majorities in both houses of the Assembly and took four out of five Congressional seats. National election returns likewise revealed large Republican gains.[43]

Scarcely had the election passed before news came of the false Armistice. On November 7 reports reached the United States that hostilities had ceased, tidings which precipitated wild demonstrations. In Hartford workers poured out of factories and offices and thronged the streets, causing great traffic jams. Then came a letdown as the public learned that war continued. Finally, at

sixth Division the honor of a visit on Christmas Day, 1918. The Chief of Staff, General Drum, explained this choice as resulting from the division's having the longest period of service in France. The President spoke eloquently to the soldiers of his pride in them and of his desire to win a lasting

Homecoming parade of One Hundred Second Infantry Regiment in Hartford, April 30, 1919.

11:00 A.M. on November 11, 1918, the bloodshed officially ceased. This time an almost spontaneous parade erupted in Hartford, with about 10,000 marchers celebrating the arrival of peace by beating drums and tin pans, blowing horns, and throwing confetti, in their unrestrained jubilation. In other cities similar dramatic demonstrations greeted the Armistice.⁴⁴

As might be expected, the Armistice turned soldiers' thoughts to the prospect of returning home and resuming normal family life and jobs. Hence the remaining months, especially for those in France, tended to drag considerably. Fortunately there were ceremonial occasions to break the monotony. President Wilson paid the Twenty-

and just peace, worthy of their great efforts and sacrifices. On January 14, 1919, Marshal Pétain visited the Twenty-sixth to decorate the One Hundred Second Regimental Colors and the First Battalion, One Hundred Second Infantry, for their brilliant operation at Marcheville and Riaville. A few weeks later the division was very thoroughly reviewed by General Pershing, who highly praised General H. C. Hale (Bamford's successor) and his entire command. Late in March the vanguard of the Twenty-sixth sailed for home. On April 4 the transport *Mount Vernon* steamed into Boston harbor with 5,824 veterans of the Twenty-sixth, who received a tumultuous welcome. Other ships followed closely, including the

Agamemnon, which made port on April 7 with all of the One Hundred Second Regiment. On April 25 Boston gave its official reception for the Yankee division, which marched through the heart of downtown Boston before hundreds of thousands of wildly cheering onlookers. For the Connecticut soldiers there remained one final parade before the home folks. Marching along Hartford's jammed streets on April 30 were 1,500 men of the One Hundred Second and 225 of the One Hundred First Machine Gun Battalion, soldiers of the Three Hundred Fourth Infantry of the Seventy-sixth Division, Colonel Richard J. Goodman with the remnants of the old First and Second regiments who had gone into the Fifty-fifth Pioneers, nattily uniformed men of the naval reserve, and sailors, colored soldiers, and marines. Jubilant crowds, estimated at 200,000, from every corner of the state, let the Connecticut service men know clearly that they were back home![45]

CHAPTER 16

Life in the "Golden Twenties"

The "Red Scare" — Fall Election in 1920 — Rapid Changes in Daily Life in the Decade of "Flappers, Flivvers, and Flickers" — The Prohibition Experiment Runs into Opposition — Violaters Find a Plentiful Liquor Supply — A Long Debate Climaxed by Repeal — Republican and Democratic Leadership — Politics from 1921 through 1924 — Politics from 1925 through 1928

The "Red Scare"

WITH the end of hostilities, the nation eagerly entered the postwar period confident that happy times lay ahead. The Army was demobilized very rapidly and economic demobilization proceeded even more rapidly. Within four weeks after November 11, 1918, the War Department canceled over one-half the outstanding defense contracts, and in December Congress ordered termination of United States Housing Corporation projects not over 70 percent completed. The curtailment of Connecticut defense contracts meant that 20,000 to 30,000 workers lost their jobs by mid-January of 1919, with Winchester Arms in New Haven alone laying off 7,000 employees. For some time skilled workers experienced great difficulty in finding new employment. In defense centers such as Bridgeport the wholesale dismissals caused serious unrest. Fortunately some war production facilities could be used for peacetime purposes. Winchester Repeating Arms in New Haven decided to keep its small-arms plant and expand into

the field of sporting goods. Remington at Bridgeport sold its small-arms plant to the General Electric Company, which soon was producing electrical equipment. In Hartford many manufacturers agreed upon a policy of dismissing women not supporting families and giving ex-soldiers job preference. Meanwhile certain major sectors of the American economy — construction, automobiles, shipbuilding, and export trade, among others — operated at such a high level as to help prevent any immediate slump.[1]

While Americans in general seemed disinclined to assume large international responsibilities after the war, there was growing concern over the progress of the Bolshevik Revolution in Russia. The "Red scare" of 1919 — one of the most dramatic outgrowths of the war — advanced beyond the early stage of fearing Bolshevism to an attack by certain self-appointed superpatriots upon radical and even liberal thought of all kinds. Pressures for conformity were so great that one writer declared bitterly, "America is the land of liberty — liberty to keep in step." Certain events in 1919, such as steel and coal strikes, a Boston police strike, bomb outrages, and various radical meetings and parades contributed to growing public alarm. Capitalizing upon this near panic, the Attorney General of the United States, A. Mitchell Palmer, moved far more ruthlessly against radicals than would have been possible had not his chief, President Wilson, been gravely ill.[2]

In Connecticut, intimations of a "Red scare" were visible as early as 1918, when a Bridgeport Socialists' meeting and a Hartford radicals' meeting apparently excited some alarm. Connecticut papers generally played up Bolshevik "plots" and activities, whether local or foreign. A Ukrainian Socialist party meeting in Hartford on January 12, 1919, for instance, was headlined "MASS MEETING HAS BOLSHEVIK TENDENCY." Actually the meeting was concerned primarily with improvement of working conditions and not at all with encouraging a "Red" revolution. In February 1919 the chief of police at Ansonia told the Assembly committee on military affairs of a local plot to send $2,600 to the Russian Bolsheviks. Another prominent Ansonia citizen estimated that half the city's population belonged to "cheap" foreign laboring elements, an obvious insinuation as to their probable lack of patriotism. This "scare" testimony was given as part of a barrage aimed at getting a state armory in Ansonia.[3]

On March 2, 1919, a mass meeting of 2,000 persons at the Grand Theater, Hartford, heard speakers of the Industrial Workers of the World (I.W.W. or "Wobblies") praise the Bolsheviks and condemn capitalists. Similar gatherings occurred in Waterbury and New Haven. In Waterbury, all participants were carried off to police headquarters and charged with breach of the peace. Forgotten were constitutional provisions about freedom of speech and of assembly! The police did not discriminate between members of the I.W.W. and those who merely happened to attend from curiosity. When Governor Holcomb was asked about I.W.W. activities in Connecticut, he declared that none of the I.W.W.'s lawlessness would be tolerated.[4]

In March 1919 the Hartford Board of Aldermen unanimously voted to make it unlawful for Bolsheviks and I.W.W. members to display the red flag, conduct public meetings, or distribute radical literature. A fine of a hundred dollars and six months in jail awaited violators. Local action soon was overshadowed by a series of raids in November by the Federal Department of Justice under Palmer, aimed primarily at the Federated Union of Russian Workers — a loosely organized immigrant organization — with the prime purpose of deporting as many radical aliens as possible. Agents struck in Hartford, New Britain, Ansonia, Waterbury, and New Haven, with the largest haul, sixty-seven, being made in Bridgeport. Newspapers referred to the prisoners as "alleged anarchists." Although some were quickly freed, others were held for five months under heavy guard in Hartford jail until Federal authorities decided upon further action. Enterprising reporters told of anarchists' plans to flood the state with subversive literature.[5]

In Hartford the Federal agents struck again on November 19, capturing twenty-six persons, including one woman, at a "Notorious Local Hotbed of Radicalism." The following Sunday the *Courant* presented a lengthy feature article, "How Connecticut Is Checking Bolshevism." It cited the large number of foreign-born and the seeming complacency of local authorities as major factors favoring the spread of Bolshevism. Then followed a city-by-city analysis evaluating the penetration of radicalism, which indicated that Hartford was the principal "Red" center and that "Red" activities in other cities had largely been curbed.[6]

The November raids were merely preliminary to more wide-sweeping ones on January 2, 1920. Palmer's agents, armed with individual warrants, hit simultaneously all over the country. Again several score were taken in Connecticut cities and brought under heavy guard to Hartford. Every person taken was supposed to be affiliated with the Communist or Communist Labor party. All were aliens, either Lithuanians or Russians. With a carry-over from the November raids, Hartford's jail was crammed with more than a hundred aliens awaiting hearings on possible deportation. Amazingly enough, some persons who went to the jail only to visit prisoners there were themselves incarcerated! When asked about this by a Congressional committee, Attorney General Palmer declared that such visits were like attendance at a revolutionary group's meeting, that is *prima facie* evidence of membership. While vigorously denying charges of severe mistreatment of some Hartford prisoners, Palmer admitted that some had been arrested at Bridgeport in November without warrants, and that many aliens were held for five months at Hartford under a very strict regime before transfer to Deer Island, Massachusetts, with eventual deportation for some. In retrospect it seems likely that certain civil rights guaranteed in the Federal Constitution had been seriously violated in regard to at least a number of these Hartford prisoners.[7]

Fall Election in 1920

AS the months passed in 1920 the "Red scare" subsided rapidly in Connecticut and nationally. In preparation for approaching national and state elections, attention turned primarily to politics. Thanks to ratification of the Nineteenth Amendment, made absolutely certain by action of Connecticut's legislature on September 21, 1920, the women of Connecticut enjoyed their first opportunity to vote. In preparing for the campaign, the Republicans renominated Senator Brandegee as expected, but split over the gubernatorial candidate. Boss Roraback apparently favored Attorney General Frank E. Healy of Windsor Locks, who could not win the necessary votes. Hence the delegates turned to a "dark horse," former Lieutenant Governor Everett J. Lake. The president of a lumber company in Hartford, Lake well represented a conservative businessman's point of view toward government. The party's platform included a ringing endorsement of Harding and Coolidge as men whose election would "give assurance of sound and progressive administration and a sane solution of the perplexing questions now before the country." As to state issues, the platform on one hand advocated more concern for child welfare, better salaries for public school teachers, and improvement of housing conditions, and on the other hand, strict governmental economy.[8]

At the Democratic convention the faithful heard Thomas Spellacy call the League of Nations the outstanding issue of the national cam-

paign. To run for governor, the delegates selected lawyer Rollin U. Tyler of Haddam, and for the United States Senate, Augustine Lonergan of Hartford. The platform approved Wilson's administration as well as a soldiers' bonus, and advocated an eight-hour day for women and children, adequate health and social insurance, increased teachers' salaries, creation of a labor advisory board to help settle capital-labor disputes, and economy in government. On state issues it was difficult to discern any major differences in program, but the Democrats were more clearly committed to the League of Nations. When Franklin D. Roosevelt, Democratic vice-presidential candidate, spoke in Hartford on September 17, 1920, he strongly advocated American participation in the League.[9]

The 1920 campaign revolved largely around national and international issues. Republican candidates and papers displayed vigorous opposition to the League of Nations, and their high command brought in Senators Henry Cabot Lodge (Massachusetts), William Borah (Idaho), and Hiram Johnson (California) to attack the League, President Wilson, and the Democratic party while urging re-election of Brandegee. Meanwhile a Democratic paper, the Hartford *Times,* quoted a withering *New York Times* editorial which hit Brandegee as a "defiant and cynical opponent of women's suffrage, the vociferous enemy of the league of nations." It depicted him also as heavily antilabor in his voting record. Finding no basic change in the senator's ultraconservative views during his senatorial career, the Hartford *Times* concluded that the "leopard does not change his spots." This sharp attack precipitated a series of full-page advertisements in the *Courant* from the Republican State Committee, picturing the Democratic party as unfairly partisan against Brandegee, just as it had been against Lincoln in 1864. The *Times* refused to carry the advertisements, and the political feud between the Hartford papers reached a fever pitch. In support of their candidates the state Democrats imported such well-known national figures as James Cox, presidential candidate, Newton D. Baker, Secretary of War, and A. Mitchell Palmer, Attorney General. Senator Brandegee declared flatly that the League would mean war and promised, "So help me God I will vote against going in [the League] if I am re-elected to the senate."[10]

In Connecticut, as nationally, November 2, 1920, brought a Republican landslide for Harding and Coolidge; Brandegee, Lake, and the state ticket; and all five Republican candidates for the House of Representatives. Harding and Lake each polled over 60 percent of the popular vote. In assessing the results, it seems probable that the general climate of public opinion rather than specific issues turned the tide. Harding and his party seemed to suit perfectly the postwar mood of the nation, which was utterly tired of reform and war, of Wilson's demands for assumption of heavy international responsibilities; worried by "Reds," the Russian Revolution, strikes, the high cost of living; and yearning for the "return to normalcy" promised by Harding. The popular vote in Connecticut reached more than 365,000, far above the previous 1916 high of about 214,000. Upon this historic occasion approximately 150,000 women exercised their newly won right to vote.[11]

After the "Red scare" subsided and the elections were over, the most significant national manifestation of intolerance came in the resurgence of the Ku Klux Klan. This organization violently opposed Catholics, Jews, Negroes, and immigrants in general, while setting itself up as the best interpreter of "Americanism" and as the protector of the older Anglo-Saxon stock of the nation. In July 1924 a Klan speaker delivered an address at Manchester which attracted about three hundred persons. Advocating "white supremacy" the speaker played skillfully upon the racial and religious prejudices of many hearers to win fervent applause. A reporter at the scene felt, however, that very few of those present evinced any strong interest in joining the Klan. In the 1928 presidential election there is ample reason to believe that the Klan for religious reasons threw its weight strongly against Alfred E. Smith; but again there is no indication of any large-scale Klan campaign in Connecticut. The New York *World* printed a letter which it claimed John W. Perry, Klan leader of Rhode Island and Connecticut, had mailed to hundreds of present and former Klansmen, calling for a crusade to save "Protestant America." Although such an approach may have swayed many voters in rural areas of the South and West, there is no reason to think that it influenced any large number of Connecticut citizens.[12]

Rapid Changes in Daily Life in the Decade of "Flappers, Flivvers, and Flickers"

FOR Connecticut as for the nation the decade after the war brought revolutionary changes in everyday life. Patterns of home life, recreation, clothing, and travel all were changing abruptly under the impact of new inventions and living conditions. A dramatic aspect of the era was the improvement in the status of women. Thanks to the Nineteenth Amendment, a substantial number of women voted in the 1920 elections and thereafter. Here as elsewhere large numbers of women worked, and the censuses of 1920 and 1930 reflected a shift away from the older occupations, often menial in nature, to the more attractive service and professional occupations. Women earlier had largely captured the fields of schoolteaching and clerical work. During the 1920's serious attempts were made by various reform groups, such as the Consumers League and the Federation of Labor, to obtain a minimum wage and reduce the maximum working hours for women, which were then set at ten hours daily and fifty-five weekly in manufacturing and mechanical establishments, and fifty-eight in mercantile firms. At hearings of the Assembly's labor committee, management spokesmen vigorously opposed any reduction in hours or setting of a minimum wage, which attitude undoubtedly influenced the committee in reaching its negative decision upon all bills calling for reduced hours and a minimum wage. Only in the area of child labor did the decade produce significant legislation. Laws enacted in 1921 and 1923 established a maximum eight-hour day for children employed in manufacturing and allowed school officials to refuse employment certificates to children from fourteen to sixteen years who lacked sufficient schooling to warrant their leaving. In 1927 the Assembly prohibited children under sixteen and women from working at night.[13]

During the 1920's one of the burning questions for the young woman was: "Marriage, or a career, or both?" For many Connecticut women the answer clearly was both! The 1920 Federal census revealed that Connecticut had 141,181 women gainfully employed. In Bridgeport, Hartford, and New Haven the proportion of women sixteen and over who were gainfully employed averaged almost one-third as against a national average of 24 percent. Approximately one-tenth of Connecticut married women and nearly six-tenths of the unmarried held jobs. In New Haven there were 18,281 gainfully employed in such fields as: the clothing industry, 892; iron and steel, 859; textiles, 107; telephone operators, 316; store clerks, 304; saleswomen, 695; teachers, 1,030; trained nurses, 529. Factories employed nearly 57,000 of the 141,181 total, or about 40 percent. One of the newest, rarest, and most important feminine occupations was that of state *legislator,* a status which one senator and nineteen representatives had achieved by 1929 — the end of the first decade of women's suffrage.[14]

For the average housewife the 1920's brought an important reduction in the time-consuming drudgery of housekeeping. Houses were being built smaller and floor layouts improved, while many lived in apartments which required minimal housekeeping. The telephone, vacuum cleaner, electricity, washing machines, electric irons, increased use of canned and baked goods, and ready-made clothing — each gave the American woman enlarged opportunities to "live her own life." For city dwellers, who now constituted a majority of Connecticut's population, the home was steadily losing its earlier position as the center of closely knit family life. Both parents and children turned increasingly to the highly developed and well-advertised commercial recreations — movies, night clubs, dancing, football, baseball, boxing, golf, and other sports — or found much relaxation in motoring. Among the newer recreations only the radio tended to keep the family at home. It is highly probable, too, that the great popular interest in and frequent misinterpretation of Sigmund Freud's writings, with their emphasis upon sex, sometimes helped to loosen family ties.[15]

During the 1920's, Americans became a "nation on wheels." Before World War I the "horseless carriage" was considered a luxury; after the war,

a necessity. Passenger auto registrations jumped from around 100,000 in 1920 to about 338,000 by 1936. The development of the closed car and the steady improvement of roads, partly a result of matching Federal aid, made driving far more pleasurable in the 1920's. By the end of the decade drivers could enjoy some 472 miles of concrete highways and a system of state and local improved roads, totaling about 4,200 miles. Even among working class families, ownership of an auto was common by the late twenties, though great sacrifices often were made to purchase it. By 1931 over 400,000 persons were licensed to operate motor vehicles. As a symbol of social status the auto took high rank, especially for teen-agers, whose social rating often was equated with ownership of an auto, preferably expensive. For the high school and college crowd, social life and courtship often centered around the auto.[16]

The auto was a prime factor, too, in the explosive expansion of cities outward into suburbia and the countryside. While Hartford, for example, was enjoying a healthy 19 percent growth from 1920 to 1930, six suburban towns — East and West Hartford, Windsor, Wethersfield, Newington, and Manchester — showed an average jump of about 65 percent. West Hartford nearly tripled its population as it rose from 8,854 in 1920 to 24,941 in 1930![17]

A new invention, the radio, helped to transform life. Broadcasting, which began in 1920 with simple headphone listening sets, expanded very rapidly until by the late 1920's hundreds of stations broadcast into millions of homes. Connecticut listeners found varied fare: the national political conventions and campaigns of 1924 and 1928, religious programs, educational talks, news reports, children's stories, serious music, and, increasingly, jazz and advertising. In combination with the telephone and better roads, the radio radically reduced the isolation of farm life. Special farm radio programs, moreover, offered valuable weather and crop reports as well as information upon improved techniques. On December 10, 1922, station WDRC at New Haven inaugurated radio broadcasting in this state, and by 1928 four other stations were on the air: WTIC, Hartford; WCAC, Storrs, dividing time with WDRC; and WCWS, Danbury, dividing with WICC, Bridgeport. The 1930 census revealed that nearly 55 percent of all state families owned radios.[18]

Another form of entertainment, motion pictures, or "movies," began to have a major impact in the 1920's. Going to the movies became one of the nation's most popular pastimes, with many making it at least a weekly habit. Movie-goers saw a wide variety of stories, though most dealt with love, sex, or crime, chiefly among the wealthy. Since Hollywood already dominated the huge industry, Connecticut audiences saw the same pictures as those seen elsewhere. Exciting entertainment without effort helped make the movies extremely popular, but the moral and educational possibilities of this medium largely went unrealized. In October 1927 the first feature-length talking picture, *The Jazz Singer,* starring Al Jolson, scored a great success. Connecticut movie-goers first saw this film at Bridgeport on January 21, 1928, with openings a few days later in Hartford and New Haven. Within two years most theaters were wired for sound and "talkies" henceforth were the rule. There can be little doubt that Hollywood in the 1920's exercised a heavy influence upon American manners, morals, fashions, and general outlook on life. Experts differed as to whether this influence was basically beneficial or harmful. The Payne Fund studies, which were made with great care, suggested that both children and adults often were adversely affected, while a reply by Raymond Moley gave the movies a fairly clean bill of health. Certainly the fabulous salaries paid top movie stars and producers and their fantastically expensive scale of living in a sort of "diamond fishbowl" created widespread interest, admiration, and condemnation.[19]

The Prohibition Experiment Runs into Opposition

ON January 17, 1920, the nation entered upon what was undoubtedly its most remarkable modern social experiment — prohibition. The Eighteenth Amendment to the Federal Constitution, passed by Congress in 1919 and ratified quietly by the necessary three-fourths of the states, made unlawful "the manufacture, sale, or transportation of intoxicating liquors within, the importation there-

of, into, or the exportation thereof from the United States . . . for beverage purposes." Over President Wilson's veto Congress passed the Volstead Act, which defined "intoxicating" liquor as any beverage containing in excess of one-half of one percent alcohol. The amendment and the Volstead Act resulted from an organized drive by "dry" forces, especially the Anti-Saloon League; and stemmed from the unsavory reputation of the saloon, wartime problems such as food production needs and the necessity of keeping shipbuilders and servicemen sober.[20]

Connecticut's hostile attitude toward prohibition was revealed by the fact that it was one of only two states (Rhode Island, the other) which *never* ratified the Eighteenth Amendment. Yet once the amendment became effective the Assembly, at its 1921 session, enacted a statute for "the Enforcement of the Eighteenth Amendment to the Constitution of the United States." This was a very comprehensive law which outlawed the sale or transportation of liquor except for strictly medical needs and provided penalties of a fine up to $2,000 or two years imprisonment, or both.[21]

Just prior to prohibition Connecticut had demonstrated much "wet" sentiment. Under the local option law prevailing for many years before prohibition, the 1919 town elections resulted in seventy-six towns "wet" and ninety-one "dry." The "wet" towns contained a large majority of Connecticut's population. Little sentiment for the amendment existed among political leaders or the press. In March 1918 Simeon Baldwin characterized the amendment as "contrary to the fundamental principles of our constitution," and the next year the *Courant* called it a "highly dangerous invasion of the rights of the individual states." When the State Senate in February 1919 rejected the amendment by a vote of twenty to fourteen, the New Haven *Journal-Courier* declared that "Connecticut is alone entitled to raise the flag of freedom in her hands and wave it aloft." Professor Irving Fisher of Yale, however, saw freedom to drink as "the thralldom of society to drunkenness, poverty, vice, crime and degeneracy." For the Connecticut Temperance Union, the W.C.T.U. (Women's Christian Temperance Union), the Connecticut Grange, and the Connecticut Dry

Alliance, among others, the national ratification of prohibition produced great celebration.[22]

On January 16, 1920, the final day before the prohibition amendment took effect, the *Courant* predicted that many would subscribe to the philosophy "Eat, Drink, etc., For Tomorrow We Go Dry." How well this was practiced may be gleaned from headlines of the next day: "Last Rites for John Barleycorn"; "Glasses Clink and Diners Make Merry on Final 'Wet' Day"! For police, the Federal amendment, plus the state law, posed a formidable enforcement problem. Connecticut lay within the "wettest" belt in the nation — a broad band stretching from Baltimore to Boston. Large numbers of the state's population, moreover, especially among those who had recently immigrated, were accustomed to the regular imbibing of alcoholic beverages. Would they still demand their drinks? Would the local police and Federal agents enforce the law strictly, or "wink" at violators?[23]

It soon became apparent that violations of prohibition were common and involved organized "rings" and even gang warfare. In October 1920 a man named Joseph Renaldino was found murdered in his auto. He had told his wife that he was going to collect $2,000 in "booze money" at Farmington, but apparently his enemies intercepted him. The police surmised that Renaldino belonged to a Hartford liquor gang which had connections in New York City. Similar to this was the shooting at West Haven in 1927 of Harry Kitone, a bootlegger, who apparently had double-crossed his gang by setting fire to a still at Ansonia. Earlier, a notorious Waterbury bootlegger, "Big John" Costanzo, was found shot to death in his auto — again the "mob's" vengeance for a double-cross.[24]

While such shocking crimes were rarer in Connecticut than in some of the large cities elsewhere, it was obvious that large numbers of citizens decided that the law need not be obeyed. In the gubernatorial message to the 1923 Assembly, Templeton expressed "grave concern" over the tendency for citizens, otherwise law-abiding, to violate the prohibition law. Declaring that as long as the law was on the books it ought to be enforced, he asked co-operation from all citizens.[25]

Judging by State Police reports, many ignored this plea. The average number of violators reported for the period of July 1, 1924, through June 30, 1929, was 489 — nearly double the average number per year in the 1913–17 period. State Police Commissioner Robert T. Hurley noted in his 1923 report that nearly all of the $163,342 in value of liquor seized and destroyed the past year consisted of goods in transit, mostly from outside of the state. Hurley felt that there had been a sharp decrease in liquor manufacturing within Connecticut. State Police statistics, however, failed to include hundreds of cases handled by local or Federal authorities.[26]

Violators Find a Plentiful Liquor Supply

VIOLATORS of prohibition were especially prevalent among four classes of people: 1] a small number of chronic alcoholics; 2] recent immigrants, who considered beer or wine a normal part of the daily diet and knew little or nothing of the evils of the saloon; 3] the fashionable wealthy, who felt that a "gentleman" must serve fine wines and liquors; and 4] the natural rebels and thrill seekers, who found it enormously satisfying to break the law. Many collegians and other young people belonged in the last category. Yale's *Daily News* of April 21, 1926, contained a student poll voting three to one in favor of the proposition that prohibition had failed to reduce drinking at the university. Two student leaders testified that any student could obtain all the liquor he desired by simply going off the campus. Statistics compiled by James H. Barnett in a scholarly, nation-wide study of attitudes and practices of college seniors in 1932 respecting prohibition revealed that most Connecticut collegians replying to the questionnaire favored either repeal or the use of light wines and beer and that a large majority indulged in drinking.[27]

The most comprehensive study of prohibition was made by the Wickersham Commission from 1929 to 1931. Its special committee on welfare agencies declared in reference to workers' attitudes:

. . . the great mass of testimony is to the effect that the prohibition laws, as they are enforced, are not regarded in the same light as other laws; that the prevailing attitude is one of defiance, resentment, or merely indifference ... A violation in itself does not involve a sense of guilt; the only shame consists in getting caught, and successful violation is rather a matter of boasting.[28]

Where did Connecticut's liquor come from? The Federal enforcement chief, Frank T. Putney, claimed in 1925 that much of it originated in New York, probably starting as denatured alcohol diverted from legitimate commercial uses. Large quantities were seized in Connecticut from trucks bearing New York licenses. Since Connecticut lacked commercial distilleries, Putney believed that Connecticut could be "dried up." Unfortunately for Mr. Putney's theory, illegal stills sprang up around the state. Near Stafford Springs, in May 1923, the State Police surprised three moonshiners operating four hundred-gallon stills on an old farm. They paid fines totaling $808.26 and lost all their equipment and liquor. One source estimated that by 1923 Connecticut bootleggers already owed the Federal government $1,000,000 in unpaid income taxes.[29]

Some liquor was made right at home in the cellar, using small stills, as the necessary ingredients were readily available. Those who preferred a more professional job obtained theirs through well-established bootleggers. Over half the alcoholic beverages obtainable probably came from illegally diverted and redistilled industrial stocks, but concealed commercial stills and foreign liquors also contributed. Since Connecticut had no border with Canada and only a limited seacoast, there probably was relatively little foreign stock brought directly into the state. Occasionally small boats landed cargoes, often obtained from larger vessels in the "Rum Row" offshore. This furtive trade was well illustrated by a small schooner seized in December 1927 on the Branford River. State Police reported a cargo of a hundred barrels of Scotch malt and forty cases of gin, valued in all at $40,000.[30]

Those who drank risked death from wood alcohol or poisonous liquor, as the death of a nineteen-year-old girl at New Haven from poisonous gin indicated. Earlier incidents caused the Assembly in 1925 to pass an act against making, transporting, or selling any liquors or imitations which were adulterated with any harmful or poisonous substance.[31]

A Long Debate Climaxed by Repeal

THROUGHOUT the 1920's debate raged as to whether prohibition was proving successful. Advocates on each side offered barrels of statistics to defend their case. The Vital Records of Connecticut, for example, indicate that the death rate from *alcoholism* fell sharply in the first three years of prohibition as compared with the average for 1910–18, but then climbed to new peaks in 1927–30. Admissions to state hospitals for alcoholic psychoses exceeded the national average and showed a steady increase after the first two years of prohibition. Yet even liquor industry spokesmen admitted that the total national per capita consumption had fallen by the mid-twenties to about one-half the 1918 rate, while "dry" leaders contended that it was only 5 to 10 percent as much. Ernest V. Claypool, retiring superintendent of the Connecticut Anti-Saloon League, asserted in his final 1926 report that the worst of liquor violations had passed and popular acceptance of the Eighteenth Amendment was growing. The *Courant* replied editorially that "never before since the coming of the prohibition laws has there been such an uprising against them as in 1926."[32]

An illuminating study made under the direction of Martha B. Bruère, who did much research on the subject, included reports from social workers and public officials upon effects of prohibition on the family life in four Connecticut cities. At Danbury, factory workers seemed better dressed and fed, and many had automobiles. Drunkenness on the streets had declined sharply, as had absence from work on Monday mornings. In Waterbury the police chief attributed a current crime wave to bad liquor, while social workers saw both improvement and deterioration. At Hartford the police docket revealed a steady decline in arrests for intoxication. A spokesman for one of the largest industries claimed that there was less time lost from drunkenness, and steadier work done. At Willimantic the selectmen who handled welfare claimed that few aid cases stemmed from excessive drinking. Another town official reported more places to get a drink, but reduced expenditures.[33]

A special study of state-wide conditions was made for the Wickersham Commission by Palmer Canfield, an experienced agent of the Federal Prohibition Bureau. He emphasized the need for much greater local effort, since there were 2,047 local and state police officers in the state and only 13 Federal prohibition agents. The author cited statistics on the alcoholism death rate, claiming that it was less than half as much in 1920–27 as in the period 1912–19. He called the experiment a "limited success," and contended that if "premature impatience" could be "suppressed" prohibition finally would receive general acceptance. Statistics in another section of the Wickersham report giving figures for the state's five largest cities on arrests for intoxication and liquor law violations revealed a steep rise from 6,314 to 13,774 in comparing 1920 with 1929.[34]

Some experts stressed changes in spending habits caused by prohibition. With the price of alcoholic beverages far above preprohibition levels, the sale of milk increased by 50 percent from 1917 to 1924, while ice cream, candy, and soft drinks registered huge gains. Savings, attendance at moving pictures and theaters, patronage of lunch rooms, soda bars, and coffee shops showed unusual increases. Among the working class there was an impressive increase in savings bank deposits, and far less pauperism. Professor Irving Fisher claimed that prohibition had added the equivalent of six billion dollars yearly to the national income, but other authorities hotly disputed this. Questionnaires filled in by members of national social work organizations bolstered the view that less drinking occurred among working families, the children were fed and clothed better, and street disorders were fewer.[35]

Only a Solomon could accurately strike a balance on the total impact of prohibition. Although the final recommendation of the Wickersham Commission definitely opposed repeal or any restoration of the saloon, its findings had little influence. In any case, the public support for it steadily weakened, especially after 1929. The depression proved to be the decisive factor in terminating the "noble experiment" (as Hoover had designated it). In 1932 the Democratic national platform said

plainly, "We favor repeal of the Eighteenth Amendment," a position strongly endorsed by their candidate, Franklin D. Roosevelt. Soon after the Democratic victory, Congress modified the Volstead Act to permit beer of not over 3.2 percent alcoholic content. By late in 1933 the necessary number of states ratified the Twenty-first Amendment repealing the Eighteenth, and the "noble experiment" was ended.[36]

Republican and Democratic Leadership

FROM 1921 until 1930 Connecticut politics hewed closely to the conservative pattern set in the 1920 elections. The dominant figure of the entire decade was J. Henry Roraback. "J. Henry," as his friends and the press called him, came from a rural background in Massachusetts and North Canaan, Connecticut. Too poor to attend college, he taught school and read law. Soon he gravitated into local politics, and at the ripe age of twenty-four became chairman of the North Canaan Republican town committee. Four years later he won a place on the State Central Committee. In 1901 the New York, New Haven and Hartford Railroad lured Roraback from direct party politics by hiring him as counsel, with the special task of lobbying at Hartford — a position he held for nine years. In 1912, two years after resignation from the railroad position, he managed by an eighteen-to-seventeen vote to unseat Michael H. Kenealy as chairman of the Republican State Central Committee. This was the year of the Bull Moose defection from the party and of large Democratic victories. The Progressive leaders were an odd group, whose earlier influence among the G.O.P.'s "inner circle" apparently had been quite small. There is little evidence that their bolt ever greatly affected the G.O.P.'s conservative leadership. From 1912 to 1924 Roraback was occupied in building up the party and consolidating his personal control. He could compromise, as in 1922, when he accepted as gubernatorial candidate, Charles A. Templeton, whom he personally opposed.[37]

Boss Roraback preferred to work quietly behind the scenes from a third-floor office in the Allyn House, Hartford, state Republican headquarters. From the early 1920's onward for many years virtually every candidate and every patronage position in state politics had to be "cleared" with "J. Henry"! Apparently important legislative bills sometimes received his approval or disapproval as a necessary preliminary to action at the capitol. Yet Roraback drew a very strict line between normal political spoils and political graft, and he gave strict orders against misuse of any state funds. He ruled by shrewdly distributing the spoils available — from the highest paid appointive offices down to justices of the peace in the towns. Roraback claimed that he never picked a candidate for an office and described himself as "simply a clearing house." Obviously his influence was greatly heightened by the overwhelming Republican majority in the legislature, plus control of the governor's chair from 1915 to 1931. Even the large cities, whether Republican or Democratic, hesitated to oppose Roraback upon any major issue, as Connecticut cities are corporations created by the Assembly and therefore subject ultimately to it. Though many Republicans were restive under "J. Henry's" autocratic rule, the party continued to win election after election. As a successful businessman he strongly appealed to business leaders, who felt that he understood their problems.[38]

Throughout his long reign Roraback maintained his intimate connections with the dominant private power interests, and especially with the Connecticut Light and Power Company, of which he had served as first president. In 1923 the company obtained authority from the Assembly to divert waters from the Housatonic River to the Rocky River, despite protests from some Democrats in the Senate. Four years later the company sought authorization from the legislature to manufacture gas, build pipe lines to carry it, and sell it in all parts of the state not previously allocated to others. The Speaker of the House defended this measure and claimed that the interest of the people would be fully protected by the Public Utilities Commission. Not mentioned was the fact that all appointments to this commission were first screened and "cleared" by Roraback. As was to be expected, the bill easily passed![39]

The Democrats, enjoying a few crumbs of patronage from Roraback's table, lacked vigorous leadership and any clear-cut program as a genuine alternative to the Republican one. Democratic failure in rural regions guaranteed Republican control of the Lower House. In fact, the Democrats scarcely tried to court the farmers and residents of small towns. Since there was no state Democratic boss comparable to Roraback, the party operated as a loose coalition of city machines, which occasionally won a city election and tried to deliver votes to the state candidates. The backbone of the party was the Irish, who generally cold-shouldered the other major immigrant group, the Italians. If the Irish had successfully courted the Italian vote and retained the sprinkling of Yankees in the party, their party would have won more state elections. A low-tariff stand drove off most industrialists and even some labor votes. As a minority party the Democrats almost completely failed to capitalize upon weaknesses of the Republicans or to push that party into more progressive legislation. Even among the Republicans some wished that the Democrats would show more life, as did John Trumbull, who as governor in 1927 declared that "a more even balance of power . . . between the two parties would tend to liven up affairs."[40]

Politics from 1921 through 1924

FROM 1921 to 1923, under Governor Everett Lake, the state followed very conservative policies. The governor devoted much of his message of January 1921 to a review of what he considered the deplorable financial condition of the state, with its net debt of some $6,500,000, and he recommended not added taxes, but rather a "policy of retrenchment and of economy." Despite this plea, the steady growth of the state and inadequate 1919 appropriations made budgetary increases essential. In spite of rejection of nearly $10,000,000 in building projects and salary increases, the regular budget for the 1921–23 biennium topped $26,000,000. To meet this figure some old taxes were expanded and new taxes were levied upon gasoline, admission tickets, and gross income of wholesale and retail establishments. Other significant legislation included abandonment, after eight years' trial, of the civil service system for state employees, and a new requirement that all public school teachers must be certified by the state board of education.[41]

In 1922 most of the political warfare preceded the actual campaign. Republican dissidents, led by Frank Healy of Windsor Locks, John T. King of Bridgeport, and Colonel Isaac M. Ullman of New Haven, tried desperately to unseat Roraback. In the showdown, Republican town caucuses voted three to one for Roraback. Later the Healy-King-Ullman combine attempted to secure approval of a moderately liberal report as a basis for the party's platform. This manifesto called for extension of child welfare, re-establishment of civil service, legislation requiring "certain power interests to pay their just taxes," and forbidding the use of Connecticut's natural resources by private interests. This opportunity to modernize the party was completely defeated, undoubtedly at Roraback's bidding. Instead, the keynote convention speech of Senator Brandegee and the official party platform were ultraconservative. As principal candidates the convention selected Charles A. Templeton, Waterbury hardware merchant, for governor, and renominated Senator McLean. Governor Lake, who had won Roraback's enmity, had no chance of renomination. During the campaign Vice-President Calvin Coolidge was to address a party rally, and Roraback invited scores of state leaders to grace the platform. Governor Lake, however, was completely ignored and sat forlornly alone in the balcony.[42]

In the Democratic party an alliance of New Haven's mayor, David E. Fitzgerald, and Thomas J. Spellacy, the party's unsuccessful gubernatorial candidate in 1918, dominated the scene. The convention adopted a plank calling for modification of the Volstead (prohibition) Act to permit sale of light wines and beers; whereas the Republicans made no reference to prohibition. The Democrats nominated Fitzgerald for governor and Spellacy for the United States Senate. The state races awakened only ripples of interest, but the McLean-Spellacy contest generated considerable heat, especially on the tariff issue. McLean, as a member of the Senate Finance Committee, had strongly supported the drawing up and passage of the high Fordney-McCumber tariff of 1922. Prominent

manufacturers extolled him for this work; and Democrats gained little by pointing to his large-scale absenteeism and unimpressive senatorial record. The Republican tide continued running as McLean and Templeton won easily, while four of five Federal House seats and the General Assembly went strongly Republican.[43]

The two years of Templeton's administration were relatively quiet ones. The governor's message to the Assembly drew a bright picture of state financial conditions but cautioned against trying any of the costly innovations of other states. Apparently Templeton believed that Connecticut had achieved that "normalcy" which Harding had proposed as a national goal in 1920![44]

The economy mood made hard sledding for state educational institutions. The appropriations committee reported adversely upon a proposal for a $150,000 dormitory at the Agricultural College in Storrs, though it meant future admissions would be sharply reduced. Joseph W. Alsop, a college trustee, pointed out that some 3,000 Connecticut students were being forced to attend colleges outside the state. A sharp legislative battle which had begun on the issue terminated only when college trustees voted to yield peacefully to the legislative fiat. Later, $100,000 for a dormitory at Danbury Normal School was defeated by a veto of Governor Templeton, who saw no present or future need for such accommodations. The House rejected a school-aid bill for a group of towns, despite a favorable Education Committee report. A bill to permit local option on professional baseball or football on Sunday afternoons, killed in 1921 by Governor Lake's veto, passed the Senate, but was killed in the House, which action may well have been influenced by Templeton's promise of a veto. Two years later, however, a similar bill did become law, and Hartford was the first city to legalize Sunday baseball under the local option provision.[45]

As usual in presidential election years, national conditions in 1924 heavily influenced state political trends. The Republicans, favored by the continuing prosperity of the country, nominated Calvin Coolidge, who had become President in August 1923 upon Harding's sudden death. The Democrats, rent by a bitter split between supporters of Alfred E. Smith and William G. Mc-Adoo, compromised by nominating a conservative New York lawyer, John W. Davis. With conservatives representing both major parties, the Conference for Progressive Political Action nominated Robert M. La Follette, Republican of Wisconsin, for the Presidency. The party's platform espoused government ownership of railroads, abolition of injunctions in labor disputes, and farm relief programs, among other items. As it turned out nationally and in Connecticut, both major parties concentrated their fire upon La Follette and the Progressives as being dangerously radical.[46]

The Republican Convention, firmly under Roraback's control, dropped Governor Templeton and nominated Hiram Bingham for governor and John Trumbull for lieutenant governor. The Democrats chose Charles G. Morris of New Haven to run against Bingham. The Republicans opened their state campaign with a rally at Foot Guard Hall on October 17, at which Bingham claimed that the chief issue of the current campaign was "Coolidge and common sense versus demagoguery and bunkum." At New Haven, Bingham attacked the spending record of the last Democratic (Simeon Baldwin) administration and promised lower taxes and economy. Morris vigorously denounced "special privilege" and the high tariff which he felt encouraged monopoly.[47]

On October 14, just as the campaign warmed up, Connecticut was shocked by news of the suicide of Senator Brandegee. Poor health and other personal problems apparently lay behind the action by the political veteran, whose legislative career stretched back to 1888. As United States Representative (1902–5) and Senator (1909–24) he had won a reputation as a hard-working, independent-minded person, often an obstructionist, bitterly opposed to President Wilson's internationalist policies.[48]

As election day approached, Republican orators loudly denounced La Follette, who they feared might prevent Coolidge from receiving an Electoral College majority. Nonetheless, 1924 marked another Republican landslide nationally and in Connecticut. Coolidge received 246,322 votes, Davis, 110,184, and La Follette, 42,416. Equally decisive was the state vote, as Bingham more than doubled Morris' vote, and the G.O.P. swept the five Congressional districts. At a December special election to fill the Senate seat vacated by Brandegee, Governor-elect Bingham handily defeated Democrat Hamilton Holt.[49]

Politics from 1925 through 1928

THE election of Bingham to the Senate automatically elevated Lieutenant Governor John H. Trumbull of Plainville to the governor's chair. Trumbull epitomized the complacent, conservative outlook of the 1920's. President of the Trumbull Electric Manufacturing Company, he held the full confidence of business leaders.[50]

The 1925 Assembly had the distinction of receiving messages almost identical in tone and approach from two governors — Bingham, just before he formally quit his office for the Senate, and his successor, Trumbull, later in January. Both called for restraint in undertaking new programs and continued conservative financial policies. As it turned out, the Assembly made a thorough study of the state's financial resources and then drew up a budget which neatly fitted the probable tax return available upon the existing structure — a fact which Trumbull heartily extolled in his brief closing message. Less admirable was the Bridgeport "Ripper" Bill, illustrative of the "ripper" type of legislation which involved the Assembly's "ripping" away some of the normal powers of a city. In this case the governor was empowered to appoint a special board to control the assessment and collection of Bridgeport taxes. Granted that tax reform was needed in Bridgeport, the act still constituted a serious blow against the principle of municipal home rule. In the House a plan to drop part of the projected trunk highway system stirred up an immediate revolt among the towns affected. As a result, the administration restored nearly all of the roads. With the total number of autos increasing very rapidly, "good roads" were becoming an appealing political issue.[51]

The off-year elections in 1926 pitted Governor Trumbull against Charles G. Morris and Senator Bingham against Rollin U. Tyler. The Republican state platform praised the party's record statewide and nationally, reaffirmed pay-as-you-go financing and strong States' rights, and promised a moderate program of social welfare. Democrats emphasized "decentralization" (States' rights) and sharply attacked prohibition as "an indefensible curtailment of personal liberty." With the advantages of holding office, Roraback's well-lubricated state machine, and continuing high pros-

(Republican) faced Governor Alfred E. Smith (Democrat) of New York. At the Republican convention, Boss Roraback largely wasted Connecticut's influence by stubbornly supporting President Coolidge until the day of the vote, when Coolidge reasserted his well-known intention not to run again. Finally the Connecticut delegation

Election results of 1924, reported in the Hartford Times.

perity, Republican candidates again rolled to easy victory, with Trumbull and Bingham each obtaining pluralities of about 85,000.[52]

At the 1927 session the Assembly voted a record budget of more than $42,000,000, which included a number of new buildings for the state institutions. Sunday afternoon recreation was broadened to include hockey, movies, and trapshooting. The Assembly provided a small appropriation for public health nursing in small towns. Perhaps the most significant step taken was a detailed amendment of the workers' compensation law. This achievement resulted from an agreement reached outside the capitol by business and labor representatives.[53]

The most exciting national political campaign since 1912 took place in 1928 as Herbert Hoover

switched solidly to Hoover, the famous engineer, relief expert of World War I, and Secretary of Commerce. A vice-presidential boom for Representative John Tilson, Connecticut's Third District congressman and floor leader of the House, stirred interest, but Charles Curtis easily won the nomination. The Democratic delegation to the Houston convention, under Thomas Spellacy's leadership, gave complete support to Smith's candidacy. The Republican Hartford *Courant* editorialized that the Democratic party "has made a first-rate nomination, a nomination that unquestionably makes a strong appeal to the popular imagination." Certainly in the poor boy who rose from the Fulton Fish Market on the lower East Side of New York City to be four times governor of New York, the country had a new kind of presidential candidate.

Smith's Tammany Hall, "wet," Catholic background, plus the continuing prosperity of the country, and Hoover's own strong appeal as an orphaned farm boy who climbed a steep ladder to success made Hoover a decided favorite.[54]

At the state level, Governor Trumbull won renomination, while Frederic C. Walcott obtained the senatorial spot. In opposition, the Democrats chose Charles G. Morris for governor and Augustine Lonergan for senator. The Republican platform pledged a continuance of the Trumbull and Coolidge administrations' policies, the high tariff, sound road expansion, and an adequate social-welfare program. Democrats called for more rapid expansion of state parks (especially through acquisition of salt-water frontage), agricultural relief, reorganization of state government, and wholehearted support of Governor Smith's position upon prohibition.[55]

The 1928 campaign was a lively one nationally, marked by a widespread "campaign within a campaign," or a whispering campaign against Smith by "dry," anti-Catholic groups who appealed to bigotry and prejudice. In Connecticut, with its heavy immigrant and Catholic population, there could be little profit for either party in raising the specter of religious prejudice; nor did Smith's "wet" position change any large number of voters in either party. Connecticut's antiprohibition sentiment has already been noted.[56]

From a study of campaign speeches and editorial comment in the state it seems likely that *prosperity* constituted the major issue working for the Republicans. Trumbull followed Hoover's lead in attributing the booming economy to the wisdom of party policies, including the high tariff, and both predicted even greater prosperity ahead if Republican rule should be retained. During the fall a parade of prominent national leaders visited the state, including Governor Ritchie of Maryland, Franklin D. Roosevelt and Ferdinand Pecora of New York for the Democrats, and in opposition, Charles Curtis, Republican vice-presidential candidate, Senator Borah of Idaho, Senator Wadsworth of New York, and William MacCracken, an assistant secretary of commerce. Strong public interest in the presidential campaign and determined efforts by party workers to get possible voters registered brought unprecedented crowds to registration places.[57]

With Roraback's blessing, Hoover omitted Connecticut from his campaign itinerary, but Smith made rear-platform stops at a number of cities on October 25. Only in Hartford did he leave his train for a drive through the downtown section. Hartford's deep affection for the governor was overwhelmingly apparent, as the leading Republican paper of the city carried banner headlines "THOUSANDS ACCLAIM SMITH IN HARTFORD'S GREATEST OF OVATIONS." Smith's automobile crawled through choked streets to the frenzied welcome of 100,000 to 150,000 persons.[58]

On November 6, 1928, Connecticut gave the Republican party an overwhelming mandate to continue in control. Hoover, Trumbull, and Walcott each carried the state by about 45,000 votes plurality in a total vote of over 550,000. Roraback called it a triumph for "protective tariff and good government." The Democratic Hartford *Times*, observing that Hoover's prosperity theme had been highly effective, declared that the Democratic party was in serious trouble. A searching analysis by Lane Lancaster offered these principal reasons for continued Democratic defeats: 1] Bryanism had driven out many future leaders and gravely weakened the party; 2] the state's powerful business leaders were almost entirely Republican and considered the Democratic party turbulent and disorderly; 3] unfavorable press; 4] incompetent party leadership; 5] mediocre candidates; and 6] inability to criticize effectively. Generally overlooked amidst Republican rejoicing and Democratic lamentations was the fact that Smith, Morris, and Lonergan had polled far more votes than any other Democrats in the state's history and had convincingly carried New Haven, Hartford, Bridgeport, and Waterbury — the four largest cities. By hitching itself so firmly to the star of prosperity the Republican party, moreover, was laying itself open to possible voter repudiation if economic depression were to strike.[59]

CHAPTER 17

The Depression Decade and Connecticut's "New Deal"

*The Economic "Crash" Hits Connecticut — An Exciting Political Race — 1931 Assembly
Session — 1932 Election Campaign — The Banking Crisis — Aid for the Unemployed —
Achievements of the 1933 Assembly Session — Federal Relief and Reform — Strikes and
an Election — Political Reform Battles in 1935 — Celebrating a Three-hundredth Birthday
— The Great 1936 Flood — Serious Strikes Plague the State — The 1936 Landslide —
Reform on the Heels of the Landslide — More Political Reform (1937) — The Great
Hurricane and Flood of September 1938 — Political Scandals — The 1938 Campaign*

The Economic "Crash" Hits Connecticut

DURING the 1920's the United States seemed to grow more prosperous year by year. In 1928 Herbert Hoover declared optimistically: "We in America today are nearer to the final triumph over poverty than ever before in the history of any land." It came as a stunning shock to optimistic Americans in October 1929, when the stock market nose-dived in the great "crash" and was followed by ever-widening waves of depression.[1]

How could a nation plunge so quickly from unparalleled prosperity into black depression? Experts and the general public have been arguing ever since about this question. In retrospect, danger signals were clearly flying as early as 1927, when the booming construction field — bellwether of prosperity — began to decline, as did consumer spending and the rate of growth of incomes. Wage earners in factories decreased between 1925 and 1927, the housing shortage disappeared, and employment in the construction industry slackened. Perhaps even more ominous was the beginning of a reduction in private capital investment. Moreover, both national and local governmental spending fell off slightly. Many farmers continued to be hard-pressed financially, and per capita farm income by 1929 averaged less than one-third of the national average. Despite domestic warning signals and economic weaknesses in Europe, the speculative boom in stocks continued at a feverish pace through 1927, 1928, and into the fall of 1929. Sales on the New York Stock Exchange jumped from 236,000,000 shares in 1923 to 1,125,000,000 shares in 1928 — a situation in which large numbers of Connecticut investors were certainly involved.[2]

A decline in prices started in September, but few investment counselors foresaw a serious "break." On October 24, "Black Thursday," prices took the sharpest plunge in the Exchange's history, and on October 29 they fell sharply again. Despite reassuring statements from governmental and business leaders, the tail spin continued through 1930, 1931, and into 1932. Industrial stocks stood at an average of 452 in September 1929, at 224 two months later, and by July 1932 they finally scraped bottom at 58. The cold figures fail to reflect the vast human tragedy involved. Thousands of homes and farms were foreclosed, uncounted businesses went bankrupt, several thousand banks were closed, and unbelievable numbers of people became unemployed, especially in the larger cities.[3]

The great Wall Street "crash" was the horrible symbol of the depression rather than its explanation. As already noted, American agriculture was distressed through most of the decade, so that the average farmer had little purchasing power. Large reductions in Federal income tax, pushed through shortly before at the request of Secretary of the Treasury Andrew Mellon, had given the largest benefits to the wealthiest. Meanwhile huge gains in industrial productivity went largely into profits for the stockholders rather than into generous raises for factory workers or into lower prices for the general public. For manufacturing as a whole, output per man-hour from 1923 to 1929 increased 32 percent, but average hourly earnings advanced only 8 percent. Railroads and express companies registered a 58 percent rise in profits, while the amount of traffic declined. It appears that profits on the whole were yielding a greater surplus than could be utilized for genuine investment under existing conditions in the late 1920's.[4]

Connecticut, as a very highly industrialized state, could not possibly escape the economic debacle. Yet the highly diversified nature of the state's industries made the impact less sudden and severe. As early as October 1, 1929, however, Hartford was experiencing enough increase in welfare costs to require an extra $75,000 appropriation. In the October "crash," stocks of Hartford area concerns fell sharply to the approximate levels of January 1, 1928. Business, financial, journalistic, and governmental leaders joined in a reassuring chorus that 1930 would bring better times. In response to President Hoover's appeal for public expenditures to stimulate business, Governor Trumbull cited the extensive building and highway construction programs already in progress. The president of the Connecticut Chamber of Commerce claimed that underlying business conditions were sound — an opinion echoed by Governor Trumbull just before Christmas 1929, when he forecast a prosperous year ahead. Connecticut economic statistics — in regard to building operations, savings bank deposits, post-office receipts, and weekly payrolls — tended to support assertions of generally good business late in 1929 as compared with a year earlier.[5]

In December 1929 the mayors of the principal cities all expressed optimism about the outlook for 1930. Unfortunately, national and state economic indicators continued their downward slide throughout 1930. The number of paupers — individuals who had not lived in a locality long enough to qualify for regular relief (four years) — began to rise noticeably in November 1929. Nationally, 1930 was a year of spreading unemployment, exhaustion of cash reserves by many families, borrowing, and even serious undernourishment. In Connecticut as everywhere the relief programs of cities and towns were geared to the care only of a small number of unemployables, not to the catastrophe of mass unemployment.[6]

An Exciting Political Race

AGAINST the stern backdrop of depression, Connecticut's politicos prepared for the 1930 state elections. After fifteen solid years of control of the governor's chair and the Assembly, the potent Republican state machine, under Roraback, understandably exuded strong confidence. The Democratic leaders, on the other hand, discouraged by repeated defeats, searched desperately for a winning candidate and winning issues. Some party workers, led by Archibald McNeil of Bridgeport, were interested in Wilbur L. Cross, distinguished scholar, English professor of the Yale faculty for many years, Dean of the Graduate School, and editor of the *Yale Review*. After a rather bitter battle between old- and new-guard factions at the Democratic State Convention in September, the new guard, supporting Cross, triumphed, and the convention unanimously chose him. In his acceptance speech Cross called unemployment the nation's gravest problem, sharply attacked Roraback as the man who made and controlled governors, and spoke forcefully for repeal of prohibition.[7]

Since Governor Trumbull already had declined to run again, the Republican convention turned for its gubernatorial standard-bearer to an able public servant, Ernest E. Rogers, the lieutenant governor and a past president of the Connecticut Chamber of Commerce. The platform called for a balanced budget, better rural roads, and improved institutional care for the sick and helpless. At Roraback's insistence the platform straddled the pro-

State of Connecticut

OUI TRANSTULIT SUSTINET

By His Excellency WILBUR L. CROSS, Governor: a

PROCLAMATION

Time out of mind at this turn of the seasons when the hardy oak leaves rustle in the wind and the frost gives a tang to the air and the dusk falls early and the friendly evenings lengthen under the heel of Orion, it has seemed good to our people to join together in praising the Creator and Preserver, who has brought us by a way that we did not know to the end of another year. In observance of this custom, I appoint Thursday, the twenty-sixth of November, as a day of

PUBLIC THANKSGIVING

for the blessings that have been our common lot and have placed our beloved State with the favored regions of earth—for all the creature comforts: the yield of the soil that has fed us and the richer yield from labor of every kind that has sustained our lives—and for all those things, as dear as breath to the body, that quicken man's faith in his manhood, that nourish and strengthen his spirit to do the great work still before him: for the brotherly word and act; for honor held above price; for steadfast courage and zeal in the long, long search after truth; for liberty and for justice freely granted by each to his fellow and so as freely enjoyed; and for the crowning glory and mercy of peace upon our land;—that we may humbly take heart of these blessings as we gather once again with solemn and festive rites to keep our Harvest Home.

Given under my hand and seal of the State at the Capitol, in Hartford, this twelfth day of November, in the year of our Lord one thousand nine hundred and thirty-six and of the independence of the United States the one hundred and sixty-first.

Wilbur L. Cross

By His Excellency's Command:

John Satt

Secretary.

Famous 1936 Thanksgiving proclamation of Governor Wilbur L. Cross.

hibition issue by asking for return of control to the states, while unemployment relief and old-age pensions were ignored. The Democrats called for repeal of prohibition, while advocating old-age pensions, a commission to study unemployment, improved rural roads, and a better Public Utilities Commission.[8]

Although the Democrats had failed to elect a governor since Simeon Baldwin in 1912, Cross entered the campaign with restrained optimism. After studying the 1928 returns, he decided that neither major party controlled a majority of the state's voters and that the independent voter probably would determine the outcome and should be assiduously courted. Several recent events aided Cross. In 1929 the United States Senate had censured Republican Senator Hiram S. Bingham for employing as an aide a man still on the payroll of the Manufacturers' Association of Connecticut. Another, earlier, incident involved misconduct by State Treasurer G. Harold Gilpatric, who shot himself in 1924. Freshest of all in the public mind was the legal action taken by Albert G. Levitt of Redding, a dissident Republican, against the New Haven Railroad for failure to eliminate grade crossings as scheduled. Since the Public Utilities Commission had failed to act, Levitt's attack really was aimed at Roraback as the power behind the commission. The case still was being argued during the 1930 election campaign.[9]

Although a neophyte in politics, Cross took to campaigning with great zeal and skill. Blessed by a lively sense of humor of the homey, cracker-barrel variety, he capitalized fully on his simple rural background in tiny Gurleyville, in the town of Mansfield. To captivated audiences he recounted in native dialect incidents from his early days as a farm boy. He vividly likened the state Republican machine, and Roraback in particular, to an old hen who had been "settin' on rotten eggs for fifteen years without hatching out any chickens." He observed tartly that "the only way you can get rid of this old hen is to throw her out into the snows or cold rains of next November."[10]

Republican strategy at first was to downgrade Cross's challenge. While on the stump against him Boss Roraback condescendingly referred to his opponent as "the dear old gentleman down at Yale who, I understand, is for old-age pensions, and if I were in his place, I'd be too." The remark backfired badly, with Cross using it effectively as an illustration of Republican indifference to the welfare of the aged. "The dear old gentleman down at Yale" campaigning vigorously despite his age (sixty-eight) made about 170 campaign speeches. He pressed hard for repeal of the Volstead Act and prohibition amendment, while his opponent consistently refused to take a clear stand. Cross criticized the bad condition of the dirt roads, and he condemned the grossly inadequate facilities for treatment of tubercular patients in state sanatoriums. Republicans struck back hard at Cross's inexperience in elective office and inserted huge advertisements contrasting Rogers' political achievements with Cross's lack of any.[11]

Election day in November 1930 produced a startling upset when Cross won by a margin of over 5,000 votes. How had he managed it while Republicans were winning all of the other major state offices? His rural background and unusual ability to talk to the farmers and other rural dwellers helped to reduce the usual Republican majorities in these areas. "Bossism" proved an effective issue too — probably chiefly among independent voters. A clear stand for repeal of prohibition also won Cross some votes. Roraback himself, among others, attributed Rogers' defeat to heavy unemployment and unsatisfactory business conditions. The *Courant*, which had supported the Republican ticket, explained Cross's victory in terms of the depression, his "more forceful personality," and his introduction of a "new and refreshing sense of political independence."[12]

1931 Assembly Session

ON January 7, 1931, a new era in state politics opened with the inauguration of Wilbur L. Cross. In the inaugural address Cross offered a comprehensive and progressive program which emphasized:

1] Court reform, with gubernatorial power to nominate minor court judges.

2] A constitutional amendment requiring a

two-thirds vote of each house, instead of a simple majority, to override the governor's veto.

3] Various measures to cope with rising unemployment, such as an emergency committee with broad powers to co-ordinate relief work; a special appropriation for work in the state forests; and speed-up of the state institutional building program.

4] A program for improving dirt roads, with

cool reception from the Republican legislature. The Republican high command considered Cross's election a "fluke" and vowed not to let the governor disturb the prevailing patronage pattern. On January 30 a Republican bill was introduced providing that each nomination by the governor for appointment of any commissioner or other state officer must be submitted by April 1. If such nomination were not confirmed by the Senate within

Election results of 1930, reported in the Hartford Times.

gasoline tax and motor vehicle registration fees allocated to it.

5] Increase in power of Public Utilities Commission.

6] Old-age pensions endorsed in principle, and special study commission recommended.

7] More liberal teachers' pension fund.

Cross also stated his personal preference for repeal of the Eighteenth Amendment and the Volstead Act.[13]

On the first day, the Assembly approved the governor's request for $10,000 for continuation of the unemployment commission's work and also $100,000 for work during the winter, clearing brush and deadwood in the state forests. Cross's broad program, characterized by the *Courant* as "forward looking" and mostly "conservative," drew a

fifteen days, the office should be filled by concurrent votes of both houses. Since the Republicans controlled both the Senate and House by wide margins, it meant that Cross could easily be prevented from making any appointments which he desired or from removing Republican officeholders of the previous administration. This measure was only one of a series which Cross characterized as "The Art of Hamstringing a Governor."[14]

Shrewd as was the design of the bill, it ran into violent attack from the press of both parties. It quickly became apparent that the Roraback forces had overreached themselves. After the bill to destroy the governor's power of appointment was pigeonholed, Cross made future co-operation easier by including many Republicans in his appointments of judges and commissioners. As a result, all but one of Cross's appointees won confirmation.[15]

In line with the recommendations of the Judicial Council of Connecticut, a nonpartisan group of legal experts, Cross asked for the abolition of the politics-ridden local, town, borough, and city courts and that they be replaced by a system of thirty-six district courts. This controversial act met quick defeat, probably chiefly because it would result in heavy patronage losses.[16]

The Assembly, however, approved creation of a commission to study the subject of old-age pensions. A dirt-roads bill involving expenditure of $3,000,000 was passed, with the money being divided equally among all the towns — a reflection of the tremendous power exerted by the thinly populated, overrepresented small towns. Other enactments provided for a substantial building program in the state's humane, educational, and penal institutions. In addressing the Assembly just before adjournment, Cross with tongue in cheek declared, "And now, as I bid you good-bye with best wishes for the future, I hope that I may see some of you back here two years hence."[17]

Because of the unceasing pressures and problems created by the growth of the state and by the worsening economic depression, Cross made of the governorship a full-time position — a view taken by all successors. He met weekly with the Board of Finance and Control, which operated in a nonpartisan manner. Another innovation was his address to the state convention of the American Federation of Labor at Bridgeport; he was the first governor ever to accept such an invitation. When he announced strong support for collective bargaining, he received tumultuous applause. Yet Cross had virtually no success in getting laws governing labor relations changed during the decade.[18]

1932 Election Campaign

IN 1932, with both presidential and state races scheduled, the political pot came to an early boil. The Democratic old guard succeeded in committing Connecticut's delegation to Alfred E. Smith against the wishes of the large new-guard minority, who preferred Governor Franklin D. Roosevelt of New York. Cross himself wanted the delegates to split their strength between the two men.

At the national convention in Chicago the Connecticut delegation remained loyal to Smith. Soon after Roosevelt won the nomination, however, he telephoned Cross and obtained a pledge of full support.[19]

In preparation for the state races both parties laid careful plans. The Republicans, stung by the unexpected loss to Cross, were determined to regain the governor's chair. Early in the spring Roraback and Senators Bingham and Walcott decided to present an unequivocally "wet" platform. John Trumbull, three-term winner in the 1920's, was drafted to oppose Cross, while Bingham was nominated for another term as senator. The platform took the "dripping wet" position planned and stated strong opposition to any new taxes. A small dissident group, "dry" and vigorously anti-Bingham because of his conspicuously "wet" position at the Republican National Convention, nominated Albert Levitt for governor on the Independent Republican ticket.[20]

For the Democrats the chief problem was the factional split. The old guard, with blood in their eyes, demanded the renomination of Daniel J. Leary for lieutenant governor, while Cross and the new guard were determined to replace him. After a stormy scene the delegates chose Thomas Hewes for lieutenant governor, as well as the other candidates desired by Cross. Then the governor was enthusiastically renominated and ran on a platform calling for relief to depositors in closed banks, direct aid to distressed communities, and repeal of the Eighteenth Amendment.[21]

The Democratic high command brought in several prominent party leaders — Governors Ritchie of Maryland and Ely of Massachusetts as well as Al Smith — to urge solid support of the state and national tickets. Roosevelt passed through the state, but could campaign very little because of heavy rain. Cross ran chiefly upon his record and emphasized the obstruction of his plans by the Republican legislature. Trumbull played up his three administrations as governor (1925–31), marked by pay-as-you-go policies and a treasury surplus. Roraback concentrated on thorough preparation of his party to get out the vote. Late in the campaign Cross proposed a five-point program advocating stringent governmental economy, sales tax for unemployment relief, old-age pensions, reorganization of state government, and revision of public utilities laws.[22]

On November 8, 1932, many Connecticut voters again indulged in the practice of ticket-splitting. Governor Cross won over popular former Governor Trumbull by an official margin of 10,844 votes, while Hoover defeated Roosevelt by 6,788. Though Cross triumphed, Republicans swept the other state offices and took four of six seats in the Federal House of Representatives. Senator Hiram Bingham, however, lost to Augustine Lonergan, the first Democratic senator elected since the 1870's. After eighteen years of waiting, the Democrats finally captured the State Senate, though only by a margin of one seat. Despite the mixed results, the trend clearly was toward the Democratic party. Connecticut newspaper editors generally agreed that the depression had hurt the Republicans badly. Here as elsewhere, radical "third" parties — the Socialist, Socialist Labor, and Communist — made little appeal, garnering 4 percent of the presidential vote. The Independent "Dry" Republicans' gubernatorial candidate polled only 5,125 votes. Even under the worst economic conditions within memory, Connecticut voters remained overwhelmingly within the traditional two-party framework.[23]

The Banking Crisis

BEFORE and after the election the banking situation caused much concern to many persons in the state. From 1929 to early 1933 several thousand American banks failed, causing staggering losses to their depositors. In Connecticut, strict banking laws and close supervision by the State Banking Commissioner held bank closings to a very low number. Although the first failures, involving banks in New Haven and New Britain, occurred in December 1930, the year 1931 proved to be the worst. About a dozen banks experienced very serious difficulties, and at least nine ceased doing business under agreements whereby deposit liabilities were assumed by banks in sounder condition. Two other banks were closed, placed in receivership, reorganized, and reopened. In 1932 the position of additional banks became so distressed that at least twenty-nine required loans from the new Federal Reconstruction Finance Corporation (RFC). Even so, the Bank Commissioner's report for the year 1932 listed twelve banks which had gone into receivership, only two of which ever reopened. The one bright spot was that not a single savings bank failed during the entire banking crisis.[24]

In March 1933 a banking holiday, which began in Michigan, quickly spread to all of the states. On March 6 Cross met in emergency conference with bankers and political figures to decide what action to take. Out of this meeting came ideas which resulted in speedy enactment of seven key banking acts. Senator John M. Wadhams, a Torrington banker, provided important leadership in setting up the program. Under the new legislation, bank mergers could be effected, and the powers of the Bank Commissioner were drastically strengthened. The amount of capital necessary to open a bank was doubled, and the governor could declare bank holidays and standardize the laws on deposit-withdrawal notices. These acts and major Federal banking measures prevented any major breakdown of the state's banking system, as only three more banks failed in 1933.[25]

For the unfortunates with funds deposited in the closed banks, the situation often was very tragic. At first, liquidation was placed with private receivers, but it soon became apparent that they were charging excessive amounts. As a result, an act of June 1935 appointed the Bank Commissioner receiver for all closed banks. A special liquidation division handled the cases of seventeen banks, whose deposits and other liabilities at date of closing were appraised at $68,912,403.17. The dividends finally paid ranged from 44 to 100 percent for commercial departments of the closed banks, and from 83.6 to 100 percent for savings departments. Depositors in the Pawcatuck Bank and Trust Company and the Windsor Locks Trust and Safe Deposit Company eventually received 100 percent return![26]

Aid for the Unemployed

THE most tragic aspect of the early 1930's was the tremendous increase in unemployment and the accompanying deprivations. The Federal census of unemployment made in 1930 showed 50,809 persons out of work, or 7.5 percent of Connecticut's labor force — slightly above the national average of 6.6 percent. In the next two years economic conditions deteriorated so rapidly that unemployment vaulted to unprecedented heights, reaching a conservatively estimated 140,000 to 150,000 by the spring of 1932. Among the large cities, Bridgeport estimated 15,500 to 16,500 were jobless, Hartford 13,500 to 14,500, New Haven, 12,000 to 13,000, and Waterbury, 10,600 to 11,200. In the textile centers of eastern Connecticut, conditions were relatively even worse, with fourteen cities and towns experiencing a decrease in employment of 40 to 50 percent. West of the Connecticut River, five localities, Bristol, New Britain, Plainville, Plymouth, and Windsor Locks, ranked in the same critical category.[27]

The impact of the depression, while serious in all parts of the state, was very uneven as to type of work and worker. White-collar positions held up far better than factory jobs. A deliberate "spread-the-work" program in many industries kept additional workers on the job, but meant reduced take-home pay for the other employees. Frightful as were conditions of unemployment or underemployment early in 1932, they grew even worse later that year and early in 1933. From January 1932 to the nadir in April 1933 employment fell 14.5 percent, and payrolls a staggering 32.1 percent. Little wonder that unemployed "hunger marchers" invaded Hartford and surrounded the capitol! They carried a petition requesting the Assembly's Judiciary Committee to approve a bill providing $12,000,000 for direct relief for the unemployed and their families. In Cross's absence a delegation of five were allowed to confer with his executive secretary, Kenneth Wynne. Later they spoke at the committee hearing. Meanwhile the state's cities and towns were staggering under the sharply increased relief load.[28]

The traditional American approach to relief was on the verge of complete collapse by early 1933. Predicated upon reasonably stable economic conditions, it expected the local community to take care of a relatively small number of persons unemployed because of misfortunes, layoffs, or un-

willingness to work. Public and private welfare agencies therefore were swamped in 1931 and 1932 by a vast army of unemployed. It is interesting to speculate how Connecticut at the local and state level would have found the tax money to provide minimal care for the 150,000 or so unemployed in 1933 or for the large numbers affected later. Before large Federal aid began, most cities and towns were already so strained as to be at or

Hunger marchers go to capitol. From the Hartford Times, *March 22, 1933.*

near their statutory borrowing limits. The 1933 Assembly created a Municipal Finance and Unemployment Relief Commission, which placed local relief and finances under strict state supervision and authorized the commission to apply to Washington for any emergency aid made available by Congress.[29]

Fortunately Congress moved with striking speed to tackle unemployment and relief. On April 5, 1933, under Congressional authorization President Roosevelt set up the Civilian Conservation Corps (CCC) — an investment in America's unemployed young men. Connecticut's first quota was 3,250 men, generally from seventeen through twenty-eight years of age. They were quickly selected and sent to camps, mostly located in state parks or forests. There they undertook useful work of many kinds, including reforestation, building of roads, bridges, foot and horse trails, fire-hazard reduction projects, and tree and plant disease control. The men fought fires and floods, while many participated in voluntary educational programs after regular working hours. In the period from April 1933 to the end of 1936 about 18,000 Connecticut men enrolled in the CCC. A substantial part of their wages was reserved for needy dependents.[30]

Far larger Federal programs soon materialized. After passage of the Federal Emergency Relief Act of May 1933, Cross ordered the new state Relief Commission, under Chairman Newton Brainard of Hartford, to obtain figures for first-quarter relief expenditures from each town. The Federal act had authorized payments equal to one-third of those made locally. The Commission found many towns unco-operative and apparently unable to believe that the Federal government would make direct cash payments for relief of local unemployment. As a result, the commission could collect data from only 78 towns for submission to Washington. Since most of the data was unverified, Cross's emissaries, James Hook and Newton C. Brainard, set out for Washington with some doubts as to whether Relief Administrator Harry Hopkins would approve the application. Their fears proved groundless. In ten minutes Hopkins gave his approval and promised that payment would be sent to the governor the following week. Ten days later Cross received a check for $858,526! Brainard was so appalled at the casual manner in which large sums were disbursed by Hopkins that only Hook's pleas kept him from immediate resignation. He continued, however, and developed a very efficient state organization. In a summary report to the governor on December 31, 1936, Brainard noted that his commission had administered grants to Connecticut communities of $34,137,560 in cash and $2,735,616 in commodities.[31]

Achievements of the 1933 Assembly Session

IN state politics, meanwhile, thanks to a Democratic Senate majority of one, the governor enjoyed

far more success in making appointments in 1933 than in 1931. Under heavy pressure from party leaders he made more "political" appointments than earlier, though the *Courant* commented favorably upon the quality of the men chosen. On the minor court judgeships, a violent struggle preceded a brazen "deal" between parties in the Assembly whereby the spoils were evenly divided. As expected, the lower house defeated a bill for a system of district courts to replace the traditional local court system. Likewise, an old-age pension bill failed, as did attempts at reorganization and a merger of the four teachers' colleges and the setting up of a sort of "supercommissioner" of education over teachers' colleges and the state college at Storrs.[32]

Probably the most torrid political engagement of the 1933 session centered about future beer and liquor control. With the end of the Volstead Act and the Eighteenth Amendment clearly imminent, it seemed wise to have a state law ready for the new situation. A special commission of seven, headed by John Buckley, prepared a bill covering major aspects of liquor traffic and sales. A bipartisan state commission of three, appointed by the governor, would be in general charge. The old-fashioned saloon was forbidden, for in no tavern where beer was available could liquor be sold. A countermove by certain Republicans in the House resulted in a measure permitting town control of beer. Feeling that such a plan would dangerously link local politics with drink, Cross took to the airwaves twice, pleading vigorously for public support of the Buckley commission program and rejection of the so-called "Alcorn beer bill." Public response came swiftly in an avalanche of letters, telegrams, and petitions descending upon Cross and legislators, urging enactment of the state-control plan. On April 18 a bitter four-hour showdown debate raged in the House. When the vote finally was taken, the Buckley plan won by 138 to 120. More than sixty Republicans defied party leadership in bolting to Cross's position! The *Courant* observed: "Nothing more heartening has happened for a long time in the General Assembly . . . It shows how effective can be the force of public opinion once it is aroused." In the Senate the Buckley plan easily passed by a vote of twenty-seven to seven, with nine Republicans joining in support. On June 20 the voters of Connecticut overwhelmingly chose "wet" delegates to the convention, which voted July 11 for the Twenty-first Amendment repealing the Eighteenth.[33]

One of the worst evils afflicting Connecticut during the depression was an invasion of sweatshops fleeing from the stricter labor laws of New York. These unsanitary establishments, usually located in lofts or abandoned factories and equipped with a few machines for finishing dresses, shirts, or underwear, paid semistarvation wages, frequently only three dollars weekly and sometimes less — and this for a working week of fifty-five hours or longer! There were several hundred of these inhuman sweatshops in Connecticut. Labor Commissioner Joseph Tone moved energetically to eradicate them, but soon found that weak laws largely nullified his campaign. In November 1932 an article in *Collier's*, "Robbing the Working Girl," gave national publicity to Tone's efforts against the vicious sweatshops. The Assembly finally voted that all manufacturing firms must register with the Labor Commissioner and that none could open without his written approval. The commissioner or his agents could enter freely into any establishment covered under the act. Armed with the new weapon, Tone renewed the battle, with such success that within a year nearly all sweatshops were wiped out. Meanwhile, late in the 1933 session, the Deputy Labor Commissioner, Senator William J. Fitzgerald of Norwich, renewed the fight for a minimum-wage law. He cited specific examples of wages as low as fifty cents weekly as an argument for a wage board in the Department of Labor and Factory Inspection. Though a minimum-wage bill seemed dead, suddenly the day before adjournment it cleared both houses. The new wage board could set and enforce a decent minimum wage in any industry. Obviously women and minors — the worst-exploited groups — stood to gain most by this humane reform act.[34]

Federal Relief and Reform

THE Federal work relief program for the winter of 1933–34 (CWA) provided work for over 40,000 persons; yet this met only part of the enormous unemployment problem. Bridgeport's mayor reported that 18,000 applied for the 4,000 to 5,000 places available there in CWA projects. New Haven's mayor revealed that his city was feeding more than 14,000 — a load gravely straining the local resources. The strong, steady infusion of Federal funds, however, gradually revived the economy. By July 1934 it was estimated that New Deal agencies had pumped about $90,000,000 into Connecticut, work relief making up $24,000,000. Home owners needing mortgage refinancing had obtained over $22,000,000 from the Home Owners' Loan Corporation (HOLC), while the RFC had loaned over $20,000,000 to banks and other businesses. The Public Works Administration (PWA) advanced $3,500,000 to the New Haven Railroad for improving passenger cars and other equipment. The Commissioner of Labor reported that by April 1934 the state's employment index (January 1932 equals 100) had risen to 117.8 from 85.5 one year earlier, and payrolls to 118.7 from 67.9.[35]

A key New Deal recovery measure, the National Industrial Recovery Act (NRA) of June 1933, attempted to spur prosperity through sweeping price agreements and production quotas. In turn, business was to accept wage agreements taking the form of codes of fair practice which set a floor under wages and a ceiling over hours. Section 7A of the act guaranteed labor the right of collective bargaining. A placard with a blue eagle was granted to all businessmen who adhered to the prescribed standards. Heading the entire program was the energetic, ebullient, and often profane General Hugh S. Johnson. Apparently some NRA leaders in Washington felt that the state was dragging its heels, as one of Johnson's aides supposedly said, "We have done all we can in Connecticut. The state can now go to hell." Cross responded with a telegram protesting this aspersion and received a very pleasant letter from General Johnson containing an apology and a statement that Connecticut's co-operation had been excellent. Many Nutmeggers, however, remained far from enthusiastic about the seemingly high-handed approach of some NRA officials. Yet public opinion generally strongly approved the NRA's objectives. Whatever the misgivings, by August 31, 1933, some 26,021 employees had enrolled under the Blue Eagle, leaving only a relative handful of recalcitrants.[36]

Strikes and an Election

IN a period of great changes in the national laws governing relations between capital and labor, it was virtually certain that there would be much agitation and unrest among industrial workers. Early in September 1934 the United Textile Union called a national textile strike which quickly re-

settlement effective September 24. Textile strikers in Connecticut and elsewhere gladly streamed back to their looms, even though the agreement was indecisive.[37]

Meanwhile September convention time had arrived. The Democratic old guard again tried to wipe Cross off the ticket, but once more he easily prevailed. A week later Republicans by acclamation nominated Hugh M. Alcorn, the hard-hitting State's Attorney for Hartford County. Alcorn charged the New Deal was making "paupers and mendicants" of the people. As Cross wrote later,

Textile strike produces violence. From the Hartford Courant, September 13, 1934.

sulted in thousands of Connecticut textile employees' leaving their looms. In the border towns of eastern Connecticut flying squadrons of pickets jumped from mill to mill, attempting to persuade operatives to join the strike. The national demands called for union recognition, a thirty-hour week, higher wages, and establishment of a board empowered to settle future disputes by decisions binding upon both parties. By the end of the week forty-eight plants employing 19,201 were completely closed. Serious clashes between police and strikers occurred at Putnam and Danielson. When Cross returned from a short trip, he found that Lieutenant Governor Wilcox, on his own initiative, had called out the National Guard. He immediately conferred with strike leaders and dispatched Tone to calm troubled waters, which he did very successfully. Meanwhile Federal mediators worked feverishly and obtained a national

he felt that this remark "was a cruel insult to a hundred thousand workers in the state who had lost their jobs during the industrial depression through no fault of their own."[38]

During the campaign Cross found that "bossism" was an ineffective issue, because there was little evidence that Boss Roraback had played any important role in the nomination of Alcorn, who was widely known for his highly independent attitude. To complicate the situation, Jasper McLevy, popular mayor of Bridgeport, decided to run for governor on the Socialist ticket. Some thought that McLevy might draw enough votes away from Cross in the Bridgeport area to give victory to Alcorn. As the campaign progressed, the 1933 liquor law and the low prices received by farmers for milk received much attention from Cross and Alcorn. Actually little difference developed between the two on these issues, as both agreed that some changes were needed, especially in the liquor law. The sharp language of Alcorn, however, riled Cross enough to spur him to more vigorous campaigning. In a speech at Willimantic he charged Alcorn with planning a clean sweep of Democratic officeholders, having no genuine regard for the state's welfare, and being a person whose "egotism is colossal."[39]

While Cross carried almost the entire load of discussing state issues and defending his record, the other Democratic candidates, including Representative Francis T. Maloney of Meriden, opposing United States Senator Frederic C. Walcott, largely tied their kites to the popularity of Roosevelt and the New Deal. Organized labor as a whole was pro-Democratic, and the A. F. of L. openly opposed Senator Walcott on the basis of his voting record. A puzzling facet of the campaign was the inactivity at state Republican headquarters in Hartford. One veteran Republican told a Hartford *Times* reporter that "Mr. Roraback . . . is not interested in electing Mr. Alcorn governor. His only interest is in the success of Senator Frederic C. Walcott."[40]

On November 6 the electorate gave an overall victory to the Democrats. Although McLevy polled over 38,000 votes, Cross still won by a margin of 8,599, and the entire Democratic state ticket easily prevailed. Maloney unseated Walcott, and Democrats took four of the six House seats. In the Assembly the House remained Republican, but the Senate lacked a majority because of the election of three Socialists from Bridgeport. In analyzing the Democratic triumph it seems probable that Cross's personal popularity, his strong record as governor, and the broad appeal of the New Deal were the decisive factors.[41]

Political Reform Battles in 1935

GOVERNOR CROSS's third term opened inauspiciously with a bitter political wrangle over organization of the State Senate. This unseemly contest stemmed from the election results — seventeen Democrats, fifteen Republicans, and three Socialists, which meant a majority for no party. Ignoring the governor, the Democratic old-guard leaders drew up their own slate of officers for the Senate, and with promises of patronage favors won over a majority of the Democratic senators. When the Assembly convened on January 9, 1935, each of the three parties presented a separate slate of Senate officers, and the senators stubbornly voted all day — seventeen for the old-guard Democrats, fifteen for the Republican slate, and three for the Socialists. After sixty-two roll calls the Senate adjourned in disgust, and the governor's inauguration was postponed. The next day, amidst much excitement, the battle resumed. The three Socialists visited Cross to inform him that they could not support the Democratic ticket as then constituted, and intimated that they might go over to the Republicans. On the second day the balloting deadlock persisted through a hundred nine roll calls. Suddenly, on the hundred tenth ballot, the Socialists voted with the Republicans and thus gave them an eighteen-to-seventeen majority. As later became evident, a limited agreement had been struck between Republicans and Socialists under which the Socialists votes were obtained in return for Republican support for certain measures benefiting Bridgeport. The situation placed the Socialists in a very strong position to influence all major legislation of the session. The Democratic old guard was badly hurt by its failure, and Cross found it possible to work fairly smoothly with all three Senate groups.[42]

In comparison with previous legislatures the 1935 Assembly achieved an impressive record of accomplishment, especially in matters of social reform. After spirited discussion the first old-age pension was enacted, allowing a maximum of seven dollars per week to qualified persons sixty-five or over. Action came also upon the long-agitated question of maximum hours of labor for women and minors under eighteen — now reduced from fifty-five to forty-eight per week. The Assembly prohibited nightwork for such persons and struck further blows at sweatshops. A child-labor bill outlawed employment of children under sixteen in industry (except agriculture and newspaper delivery) and forbade the hiring of those from sixteen to eighteen in certain dangerous jobs. The ease with which this labor-reform legislation cleared both houses indicated strong bipartisan and public backing. On the other hand, the proposed Federal child-labor amendment, defeated in 1925, once again met rejection.[43]

One of Cross's pet projects — a major increase in powers of the Public Utilities Commission — received approval. Likewise, favorable action occurred on the proposal to merge the two existing welfare departments into a single one. The governor astounded many political observers by naming former Republican United States Senator Walcott as first commissioner of the new department. Most of Cross's reorganization and merit system proposals, however, met quick death, primarily because of patronage losses involved. He obtained a bill permitting him to appoint a commission to prepare a comprehensive plan for reorganization of the state government.[44]

The state liquor bill — a subject of much criticism since 1933 — was amended to legalize the sale of alcoholic liquor by the drink, in hotels, restaurants, clubs, railroads, and boats, and to provide temporary beer permits for picnics. In March legalized race-track betting, an old favorite of those seeking an easy method of increasing state revenues, was rushed through both houses. Cross sharply vetoed it. For the first time the House sustained his veto![45]

Unfortunately the legislature showed a lack of similar courage in facing up to the state's growing financial needs. As the state's population grew and its citizens demanded expanded services, old taxes had to be raised or new taxes imposed or a combination of the two effected. Extra money, also, was urgently needed so that the state could meet rising welfare costs and give tax relief to real estate owners in cities and towns. Various proposals were advanced, of which two proved to be especially controversial — a 2 percent general sales tax and a tax on income from dividends and interest. Cross tried to break the tax deadlock by a special message on May 22 in which he strongly urged implementing the recommendations of a special state tax commission. These included the retail sales tax, the tax on interest and dividends, one on cigarettes, and a revision of existing taxes on businesses and insurance companies. In order to restore salary cuts of state employees, restore the teachers' pension funds, and undertake capital improvements, he also urged diversion of money

from the highway fund. The State Grange, the Connecticut Merchants Association, Chambers of Commerce, consumer organizations, trade unions, and the Socialist party all joined in opposing the sales tax and expressing preference for an income tax. Democrats in the Assembly refused to support the sales tax unless food was exempted and the tax on dividends and interest also was levied. After a spirited debate the Senate narrowly defeated the sales tax, probably chiefly because a dividends-and-interest-tax rider was attached, which made the bill unacceptable to Republicans. In the House the sales tax also failed to pass, largely because it lacked the Senate rider and therefore was unacceptable to the Democrats. The resulting deadlock therefore deprived the state's cities and towns of aid for urgent welfare programs. The Assembly finally agreed only on a package of minor taxes. In a closing address to the Assembly, Cross admitted his keen disappointment about tax matters but called the session as a whole "a happy experience" because of the large body of progressive legislation enacted.[46]

Celebrating a Three-hundredth Birthday

DURING the year 1935 Connecticut celebrated its tercentenary in impressive fashion, with 3,000 exhibitions and events attracting about 4,000,000 people. The purpose of the tercentenary was to focus attention on the state's rich historical heritage of 300 years and to remind its citizens of some of the highlights of its evolution from three tiny wilderness villages of the 1630's to a bustling, prosperous, industrialized state in the 1930's. Five years of careful planning by the Tercentenary Commission resulted in a celebration outstanding for variety, extent, and quality. The program opened auspiciously on April 26, 1935, with an impressive joint meeting of the General Assembly and Supreme Court to commemorate the first meeting, 299 years earlier, of the General Court of the three tiny Connecticut River towns. Throughout the state, local committees organized parades, pageants, and unusual exhibits of interest. On October 5 and 6, special state-wide religious services memorialized the powerful role of religion in the founding and development of Connecticut. Finally, on October 12, a gigantic tercentenary parade, replete with magnificent floats depicting famous historical events, wound its way through Hartford.[47]

Far less dramatic but more permanent in nature was the work of the Tercentenary Committee on Historical Publications, under the successive direction of Professors Charles M. Andrews of Yale and George M. Dutcher of Wesleyan. This committee brought out sixty pamphlets on many important phases of Connecticut's history — pamphlets which in many cases are still useful sources of information for students of Connecticut's past.[48]

The Great 1936 Flood

FOR Connecticut the year 1936 wrote into the pages of history a series of dramatic extremes — in politics, in labor relations, and most of all in an unforgettable demonstration of Mother Nature's awesome power. January and February were cold and snowy months in Connecticut, while even heavier snows piled up to great depths on the mountains of northern New England. Then suddenly early in March came a pronounced thaw accompanied by torrential rains.[49]

Since much of the rain and melting snow of northern New England could go only into the Connecticut River, it began to rise with appalling speed. All through Wednesday, March 18, 1936, it rose, and by Thursday at 12:30 P.M. it passed the all-time previous high record of 29.8 feet above the normal river level (United States Army base) set in the May 1854 flood. The Connecticut River bridge was closed, and businessmen and families on Front Street and other east-side streets began to evacuate. National Guardsmen in the area were called to duty and worked side by side with Naval Militia, Coast Guardsmen, and State Police. A fleet of Coast Guard whaleboats wound through the "canals" of Hartford's east side, removing hundreds of persons, often from second-story windows of their homes. On Thursday the utilities began to experience trouble as the electric plant and the telephone building gradually became partially inundated. By early Friday many Hartford residents lacked both telephone service and electricity, and Bushnell Park and the east side formed

one great lake. All roads out of Hartford to the north, east, and south were impassable, while authorities were giving food and shelter hourly to new hordes of dazed flood victims: Meanwhile the Connecticut River surged higher and higher, passing 32 feet, then 33, reaching 34 feet on Thursday night and 35 on Friday. Late that afternoon a general power failure occurred and 40,000 telephones were "dead." Two feet of water covered the Bond Hotel's lobby and page boys splashed about in hip boots! Guests arriving by train walked out of the railroad station, stepped into boats, and were rowed directly to the registration desk of the hotel! Hundreds of salesmen and other businessmen, completely stranded by the murky waters, "took philosophic refuge in bottled goods."[50]

In Hartford and other cities along the great River the night of March 20–21 was one of eerie darkness, driving rain, and stark terror. The water lapped higher and higher, engulfing block after block of the downtown section. Frightening rumors spread that the inmates of Wethersfield Prison were rioting and might break out. On Saturday morning, with the rampaging Connecticut climbing above 37 feet, normal activity in Hartford was virtually paralyzed. With 5,000 people flooded out, the city was far more crippled than ever before in its entire three hundred years of existence. In East Hartford one-third of the town was under water, 1,000 people were homeless, and the Red Cross was giving shelter to some

Scene at the Hartford railroad station.

Aerial view of flooded Hartford in March 1936.

2,000 victims in all. In Middletown most of the families below Main Street evacuated their homes, the Middletown-Portland bridge was closed, and thousands of feet of lumber in Portland were carried away. Damage in that area reached about $2,000,000. Even as Hartford flood effects were still growing more serious the river at 8:00 A.M. on Saturday reached its all-time record height of 37.56 feet, and then almost imperceptibly it began to fall.[51]

As the flood waters slowly subsided the gigantic operations of clean-up and reconstruction began immediately. Over 1,000 CCC and WPA men moved into Hartford on March 25 to begin disinfecting buildings affected by the flood. The state Health Commissioner, Dr. Stanley H. Osborn, reported that over 3,000 Connecticut homes had been evacuated (Hartford, 1,000, East Hartford, 500, and Middletown, 550) and 1,700 more residences were flooded but still occupied.[52]

Sheer physical destruction, pushing losses into the millions of dollars, posed a critical financial problem. When east-side merchants finally returned to their premises, they were stunned at the complete ruin of their stocks, often a lifetime investment. A large group of Hartford's business leaders met and pledged themselves to raise $2,000,000 for reconstruction, but even this sum was inadequate. Governor Cross, in company with Attorney General Edward J. Daly and Welfare Commissioner Frederic Walcott, went to Washington for a conference with WPA Administrator Harry Hopkins. As a result, Hopkins promised an immediate allocation of $3,000,000 for work projects in the stricken zone. While admirable courage and splendid co-operation marked the battle of Connecticut men and women against the overpowering flood waters, thoughtful observers saw a pressing need for long-range measures to prevent a repetition of any similar catastrophe. This one had cost several lives and at least $25,000,000 in property losses.[53]

Serious Strikes Plague the State

IN 1936 and 1937 Connecticut was plagued by several unusually bitter and difficult strikes. What was probably the worst strike of the entire decade broke out in May 1936 at the Middletown plant of the Remington Rand Company, an enterprise devoted to making office equipment, especially typewriters. Workers in five other company plants, located in New York and Ohio, also struck. Attempts by the State Board of Mediation and Arbitration to bring together company and union representatives failed. Likewise Federal mediation efforts were fruitless. The strike dragged on for weeks, and tempers grew strained. On the night of July 7–8 a savage fight broke out between strikers and strikebreakers, during which a few workers' homes and buses carrying workers were stoned. Cross soon dispatched telegrams to Governors Lehman of New York and Davey of Ohio, and President James Rand of Remington Rand, requesting that a conference be held in New York City. Rand refused to do this, but he did talk with Cross in Hartford. He seemed so genial that Cross

Early in 1937 a new technique in striking, the "sit-down strike," appeared. In this procedure, first used at many General Motors plants, the strikers stayed inside the plants beside their machines, but refused to work. The first Connecticut test of the new strategy occurred at the Electric Boat Company in Groton, which was building sub-

"100,000 Hail Roosevelt,"
from the Hartford Times.

felt optimistic about settlement of the strike. When Rand later defined his position in a telegram, it indicated clearly, however, that he had not budged from his original position. He refused to negotiate at all with the union leaders or strikers and would consider re-employing strikers only when and if it pleased him.[54]

The bitter Middletown strike thus dragged on, with further violence in late August. In 1940 the strike finally culminated in the closing of the plant amidst much bad feeling. The National Labor Relations Board charged that the company closed the Middletown plant and transferred its operations elsewhere in order to discourage membership of employees in labor unions. The company claimed the closing was in accord with its long-range policy of concentrating its operations to improve production efficiency.[55]

marines for the Navy. Feeling that the sit-down strike was illegal, Cross sent in police holding bench warrants charging the strikers with trespassing on company property. They evicted the "sit-downers." When strike leaders visited the governor the next day, he declared flatly: "There will be no sit-down strikes in Connecticut as long as I am Governor" — a stand which won widespread approval. The Groton strike soon ended, and no further important sit-down strikes occurred within Connecticut.[56]

The 1936 Landslide

AFTER some uncertainty, punctuated by rumors that Cross would not run for a fourth term, he announced that he was available once again. Lieutenant Governor Hayes of Waterbury was warmly interested in succeeding Cross, but once again Cross was renominated, this time by acclamation. The Republicans turned to Arthur Brown, State's Attorney for New London County, as a candidate to oppose Cross. The most unusual occurrence at the Republican convention was a speech by J. Henry Roraback bestowing much praise on the Democratic governor. The Republicans in their platform and campaign centered their attacks on the New Deal and intentionally subordinated state issues. Since 1936 was a presidential year, the contest between President Roosevelt and Republican Alfred Landon, governor of Kansas, easily pushed state campaigns into the shadows. When President Roosevelt toured the state on October 22, some 700,000 to 800,000 persons turned out to accord him a tumultuous welcome. In Hartford alone about 100,000 enthusiastic persons thronged the streets and Bushnell Park to see and hear the President. Brown saved his harshest criticisms for Roosevelt, whom he charged with betraying his party and the democratic principles of the nation. He called the Social Security Act "the chicanery superb of the Roosevelt Administration." Only three days before the election, State Representative Noah H. Swayne of Darien, a member of the State Commission on Unemployment Compensation, loosed a blast against Cross charging that the governor pressed the Commission and him personally to include an additional one percent deduction from workers' pay envelopes as a contribution to unemployment compensation. In reply, Cross vigorously denied exerting any such pressure. In a campaign speech at Willimantic, Cross discussed the Social Security Act and the proposed adoption of a state unemployment insurance act. On October 31 Cross made an unexpected radio address opposing employee contributions. Thus, at the very end of the state campaign, the proposed tax for unemployment compensation became the liveliest issue.[57]

Election Day, November 3, 1936, brought the greatest Democratic landslide in American and Connecticut history. Roosevelt took the state by the enormous plurality of 103,444 votes (382,129 to 278,685). The governor telegraphed the President: "Returns show that you have carried Connecticut by a majority so large as to strain my knowledge of arithmetic." Cross defeated Brown by a 95,763 plurality, despite McLevy's candidacy on the Socialist ticket. All third-party candidates fared very poorly in the presidential race, Norman Thomas, Socialist, polling only 5,683 votes; William Lemke, Union party, 21,805; John Aiken, Socialist Labor, 1,228; and Earl Browder, Communist, 1,193. Democrats captured all six Congressional seats. In the Assembly, Democrats easily won the Senate, twenty-six to nine, and increased their House seats by fifteen. For state Republican leaders the debacle occasioned much soul searching and helped spark a demand by insurgents for reorganization. Some pointed to Raymond E. Baldwin of Stratford as the new type of leader needed.[58]

Reform on the Heels of the Landslide

AT a special session, beginning two days after the election, the Assembly passed three significant measures. One established an earlier date for presidential electors to cast their votes, which was to conform to the new twenty-second Federal amendment. A second act authorized establishment of housing authorities in municipalities of the state. The third, and most vital, created an unemployment compensation system, probably the most fundamental social reform act of the 1930's. The act covered the majority of workers and levied a compulsory tax on employers of five or more workers. Beginning January 1, 1938, eligible unemployed persons could draw a benefit of $7.50 to $15.00 weekly for a maximum time of thirteen weeks in any one year's period. The usefulness of the act as a financial cushion during unemployment was demonstrated during the 1938 recession when nearly 260,000 initial claims were filed in the first six months of that year. In passing this act the Assembly tacitly acknowledged that unemployment was often not the individual's fault and that management must carry at least part of the cost of lessening its baneful effects.[59]

More Political Reform (1937)

IN his January 1937 opening message, Cross reiterated many of his earlier recommendations, including administrative reorganization and a district court system. He also called for new legislation to cope with the severe depression in the milk industry, complete co-ordination of all state and local relief programs, a state office building, and a new institution for the feeble-minded. The message stressed state financial problems and proposed that an ambitious building program be launched, financed by borrowing and new taxes.[60]

The 1937 Assembly tallied an impressive record of significant legislation. Foremost was its favorable action on important reorganization proposals as developed by the special reorganization commission, with Thomas Hewes of Farmington as chairman and Dean Charles E. Clark of the Yale Law School as vice-chairman. The commission found a chaotic system in the executive agencies, many of which operated quite independently. As a result of lengthy study, the commission recommended consolidation of 116 separate administrative departments into eighteen, each under direct supervision of the governor. Only the governor and lieutenant governor would be elected by the people. Other recommendations included a four-year term for governor and increased gubernatorial veto powers. Cross and several commission members stumped the state and gave radio talks asserting that the reorganization scheme would save money and simultaneously provide more efficient government. After lengthy debate many reorganization measures passed. The old Board of Finance and Control, which formerly had controlled budgets and expenditures, was abolished and a new Department of Finance and Control created, with a commissioner appointed and controlled by the governor. Under the commissioner would serve a director of the budget and a supervisor of purchases. Another major innovation was creation of a Department of Public Works. A new Personnel Department also came into existence, along with a broad Civil Service Act. The latter covered all classified state employees and included a provision prohibiting such employees from participation in political campaigns. There was created a gubernatorial advisory cabinet, consisting of the heads of eleven executive departments. The governor's weak veto power, however, remained unchanged, requiring only a simple majority of

both houses to override it. Altogether 107 separate reorganization acts were passed — the most sweeping change since 1818.[61]

The 1937 Assembly also made women eligible for jury duty. Finally, long steps were taken toward meeting the critical need for additional buildings at state institutions. The Assembly authorized an appropriation of $11,000,000 for new facilities at hospitals, sanitariums, or schools, in Newtown, Mansfield, Rocky Hill, Meriden, Shelton, Norwich, Hartford, Middletown, Mystic, Storrs, and East Lyme. Serial bonds would cover the state's share; and since the program presumably would be approved by the PWA, a Federal contribution of 45 percent of the total cost would insure completion of all thirteen projects. In line with Cross's recommendation, all of the normal schools were raised to the level of four-year teachers' colleges. When it came to passage of a district court bill to replace the local courts, the House killed the bill passed by the Senate. Then a bitter stalemate developed between the parties over appointment of the local judges, so the governor was able to appoint the entire list of judges on an interim basis. Symptomatic of the needs of a growing population and the expansion of state services was adoption of a $100,000,000 budget for the 1937–39 biennium.[62]

In what was destined to be his last adjournment message to the legislature, Cross declared, "I have been reasonably happy with you," and congratulated them upon passage of much positive legislation, including the vital reorganization measures. He closed with the remark: "As for me, I intend to sit for a while under the gilded dome and look myself over to see what damage I may have received during the last few months."[63]

Several weeks before legislative adjournment, Connecticut was deeply shocked by the suicide of J. Henry Roraback. Early in 1936 Roraback had suffered a serious illness and had never recovered his earlier great physical vigor. During the 1936 fall campaign, newspaper reporters commented upon his rather lackadaisical attitude and comparative inactivity as well as his obvious admiration for Governor Cross. Though he remained clearly the G.O.P. state boss until his death, four consecutive defeats weakened his position measurably. The ample patronage which had lubricated his machine for so many years was much reduced in the 1930's. Probably Roraback had enjoyed his happiest years during the 1920's — a decade when his "machine" operated victoriously and when dominant state and national political trends harmonized nicely with his own beliefs. He once summed up his personal credo in these words: "Good business is good politics. Good politics is good business." To such a man, whose entire career epitomized the theory of rule by big busi-

The Great Hurricane and Flood of September 1938

ON September 4 an unobtrusive, weak, low-pressure area was noted at Bilma Oasis in the south central Sahara. By the seventh this disturbance had formed a whirl over French West Africa, after which it moved westward into the Atlantic and drifted slowly toward the Caribbean islands. By the evening of September 16 American weather experts recognized this storm as a full-fledged hur-

Devastation caused by hurricane at Point O'Woods in Old Lyme.

ness in intimate alliance with political leadership, the increasing popularity of the New Deal must have been gall and wormwood. Although some of Roraback's lieutenants became involved in graft, he scrupulously avoided it. Apparently ill health was the prime cause of his suicide.[64]

On July 1, 1937, the reorganization bills took effect, and Cross worked enthusiastically upon the task of implementing them. In line with his earlier claims, the centralized purchasing system saved large sums, as did the much tighter control of the general budget. He appointed Robert A. Hurley, an engineer and then head of the WPA in Connecticut, as first Commissioner of Public Works. Since large matching Federal grants flowed in during 1938, Hurley directed the largest state construction program yet undertaken.[65]

ricane, but no special alarm was felt, since most Atlantic hurricanes completely miss the American mainland. On September 17 and 18 the storm moved slowly westward, and then on September 19 and 20 it began to curve northward. A huge North Atlantic high-pressure area was located too close to the shore to permit the customary northeastern curve. Meanwhile another high-pressure area was moving eastward across the United States. This left a narrow intervening corridor of warm, moist air pointed straight at New England. On September 21 the hurricane suddenly accelerated and began racing toward an unsuspecting New England. By 11:00 A.M. the storm center lay east of Norfolk, by 1:00 P.M. it was off New Jersey and speeding at perhaps seventy miles per hour directly toward Long Island and southern New

England. Unfortunately, accurate reports were lacking, as ships generally had moved clear of the storm.[66]

Virtually oblivious to the threat of the onrushing hurricane, New Englanders were worrying about very heavy rains of the past four days which were already causing an alarming rise in the upper reaches of all rivers and thoroughly saturating the ground in many sections. Newspaper reports referred to a tropical storm in the Atlantic and storm warnings from Wilmington, North Carolina to Atlantic City.[67]

of seafront, their total fortune, which they planned to sell at auction in a few days. The hurricane left them just two acres![69]

Early in the afternoon the crack New Haven passenger train, the *Bostonian,* passing through Stonington, ground to a halt as a tower man flashed a danger signal. Ahead the track was still intact but unable to carry a full train. The engineer uncoupled his engine and slowly pushed a cabin cruiser and then a house off the track! Next he backed up and coupled onto a single coach and a diner. All of the passengers crowded into the two

The *Bostonian and the trawler*
Ruth *share the track!*

September 21 in New England was an oppressively warm and muggy day, even salty, and the rapidly falling air pressure made one's ears feel peculiar. By 1:00 P.M. winds on the shore attained gale force, and at 2:00 P.M. the rain began to fall in torrents. Soon after this a gigantic wall of black-green sea water, pushed by the storm, smashed against the shores of Connecticut, Rhode Island, and Massachusetts, reducing thousands of shore cottages to kindling wood and drowning scores of persons.[68]

The violence of the storm pushed the ocean tides ten to seventeen feet above normal, drowned many people, demolished even large shore houses, destroyed or damaged the majority of the pleasure craft on the Sound, and cut chunks out of the coast. Three Connecticut sisters owned fifty acres

cars, dined well, drank beer, and entertained one another through a long isolated night. The last two coaches of the train turned on their sides, coming to rest very close to the flood waters. Nestling on the track against the rear coach was a small trawler, *Ruth.* By a happy miracle not a single casualty occurred on the famous "Lost Train"![70]

The New London water front was blown into a chaotic mass of broken boats and shattered buildings. The storm caused a fire which swept through the business district, with fire and wind causing about $4,000,000 damages. At nearby Ocean Beach most cottages were shattered beyond repair. At Mystic, Noank, Cornfield Point, Old Saybrook, Old Lyme, Crescent Beach, Clinton, Madison, and Westbrook, to name only a few places, the destruction was appalling. Among the storm victims were Mrs. Helen Lewis, Republican Secretary of State candidate, and her husband, drowned on Thimble Island in the Sound.[71]

Scarcely diminished at all, the storm roared inland during the afternoon and cut a terrible swath of destruction many miles wide before moving into Massachusetts and northern New England. At Durham, hundreds of huge trees fell across the main road — a scene duplicated in nearly every town of central and eastern Connecticut, the area of highest winds in the state. In Glastonbury, residents saw large pieces of buildings literally sailing through the air. At Middletown, the Wesleyan Chapel steeple was blown down into the interior. The entire faculty and student body had just completed the annual Matriculation Service, and fortunately the large majority had left the building. Inhabitants of Hartford and vicinity, bracing for the flood from the north, suddenly were struck from behind by the howling hurricane. Shrieking in at about 4:00 P.M., the storm left the city a shambles, with streets full of fallen trees, poles, wires, crushed autos, and debris from buildings. A garage collapsed, killing a youth inside. Altogether five perished in Hartford during the storm and twenty-two were injured. All bus, trolley, and railroad transportation was halted, and telephone service was badly disrupted. A seventeen-foot bronze statue atop the capitol dome, called "The Genius of Connecticut," already in a weakened state, amazed everybody by riding out the fierce winds unscathed. Yet these same winds turned pine needles brown forty miles inland and smeared leaf pulp over thousands of white houses, turning them green! Connecticut was virtually isolated because of blocked roads and broken telephone and electrical lines.[72]

After the hurricane passed, Hartford returned to the struggle against the rising Connecticut River. An army of 1,000 men, and 100 trucks worked feverishly to strengthen the Colt and nearby dikes and save the South End. Army engineers estimated only a fifty-fifty chance that the river could be held. There seemed to be a repetition of 1936 as refugees jammed the Old State House, the National Guard sprang into action, and the river continued its relentless rise throughout September 22 and 23. This time Hartford, hard-ened by the 1936 experience, took the crisis much more in its stride. To those throwing fifty-pound bags on the Colt Dike — the small army of city workers, WPA men, college students, and other volunteers — the swollen river seemed likely to break through. At 5:30 P.M. on Friday, September 23, it attained a height of 35.10 feet and held there until 10:00 P.M., when it fell to 35.09! At midnight it dropped farther to 35.02. The "Battle of the Colt Dike" was won, and Hartford had escaped with far less damage than in 1936! Even so, it created a critical situation for many east-side merchants, once more wiped out, in many cases still owing on loans taken out after the 1936 flood. Luckily the Federal Disaster Loan Corporation stood ready to grant rehabilitation loans on generous terms.[73]

In eastern Connecticut the Quinebaug River rose to unprecedented heights and dealt a severe blow to several communities, and especially to Norwich. There the surging river reached the ceilings of stores in the city's center and pushed eleven feet of water into the wholesale food firms. As a result, grocery stores were forced to ration food strictly for several days.[74]

One early estimate of direct hurricane and flood damage in Connecticut placed it at $58,000,000 — a stupendous total, which did not include the severe losses of the railroads and utility companies. Localities with losses of $1,000,000 or more included Hartford, Manchester, Rockville, New Britain, Norwich, Putnam, New London, New Haven, West Haven, Greenwich, Stamford, Norwalk, and Middletown. In addition, a six-town coastal area, comprising Westbrook, Madison, Guilford, Branford, Old Saybrook, and Lyme incurred at least $7,000,000 in damages. Future losses in property taxes would be very heavy in scores of Connecticut towns. The tobacco crop suffered a $20,000,000 blow, while fruit and potato growers also experienced heavy losses. The United States Weather Bureau placed the state's property destruction at $100,000,000 and the loss of life at eighty-five.[75]

Political Scandals

A SERIES of political scandals involving both major parties undoubtedly affected the results in the

November elections. In the spring of 1937 Attorney General Daly discovered that unduly high prices were being paid for land purchased for the projected Merritt Parkway. Highway Commissioner John Macdonald told Cross that land prices had jumped sharply as soon as the general route of the parkway became known. Daly instituted a thorough investigation of the land purchase transactions, and after his appointment to the Superior Court, Charles McLaughlin completed the study. In a report of January 3, 1938, they indicated existence of criminal collusion between G. Leroy Kemp, state purchasing agent, and various real estate men. Cross immediately asked for a Fairfield County grand jury probe.[76]

Late in March 1938 the Fairfield County Grand Jury brought in indictments against Kemp and two real estate brokers on a charge of criminal conspiracy and in April recommended Macdonald's immediate removal. On the basis of this report, Cross asked for and received Macdonald's resignation, and immediately, before political pressures could appear, appointed William J. Cox, a professor of mechanical engineering at Yale, as the new highway commissioner. After a lengthy legal battle, Kemp finally went to Wethersfield State Prison. On June 29, 1938, Governor Cross officially dedicated an eighteen-mile stretch of the Merritt Parkway, from the New York line to Norwalk. It immediately took rank as one of the most beautiful and best-engineered highways of the time. Over two decades later, motorists by the thousands from all parts of the Union still enjoy the scenic beauty of the Parkway, and especially its spring displays of dogwood and its rich-hued autumn foliage.[77]

Hardly had the Merritt Parkway land-purchase scandals broken when a greater conspiracy came to light in Waterbury. For over seven years a "reform" administration, under Mayor T. Frank Hayes and Comptroller Daniel J. Leary, had run the city and reduced taxes. In the 1937 fall elections a coalition ticket defeated Leary and nearly unseated Hayes. The new comptroller, Sherwood L. Rowland, quickly uncovered evidences of large-scale misuse of city funds by the Hayes machine. In March an extraordinary grand jury was impaneled by the Superior Court and Hugh Al-

corn was named as special prosecutor. On May 19, 1938, the grand jury issued a shocking report. It called for the arrest and prosecution of twenty-seven persons for conspiracy to defraud the city of Waterbury of millions of dollars through a carefully planned and disguised series of dishonest financial transactions. Mayor Hayes, his executive secretary, Thomas Kelly, Carl Olsen, a banker, and Comptroller Leary were named as ringleaders. Also seriously implicated were Charles E. Williamson of Darien and Harry Mackenzie, then Boss Roraback's right-hand man. Cross urged Hayes to resign from his position as lieutenant governor, but Hayes refused. A long and hotly contested court suit ensued, and finally in August 1939 Hayes and twenty-two others were convicted of conspiracy to defraud Waterbury. In March 1941 the Connecticut Supreme Court unanimously affirmed the convictions of Hayes and nine others, who soon began serving their sentences. This scandal, involving members of both parties, had a great impact upon the 1938 state elections, and has indeed had an important effect upon the general course of state politics ever since.[78]

The 1938 Campaign

AS nominating time in 1938 approached, Cross again indicated his willingness to run, as he wanted to continue the fight for minor court and other reforms. He easily won renomination, while Thomas Hewes, after a sharp fight, won the nod for lieutenant governor. On the Republican side, the convention, after considering as gubernatorial possibilities President James L. McConaughy of Wesleyan, William J. Pape, who broke open the Waterbury mess, and William H. Blodgett, a Roraback henchman, turned to lawyer Raymond E. Baldwin of Stratford, an experienced and liberal politician. McConaughy was named as his running mate. For the United States Senate, Republicans chose John A. Danaher to oppose incumbent Augustine Lonergan. Both major parties adopted rather progressive platforms. Republicans denounced the increasing centralization of power under the New Deal as well as "the prostitution of relief for political purposes." The platform pledged improvement in humane institutions, support of flood-control measures in Congress, and new legislation prohibiting dual job-holding by state legislators. Democrats sounded a call for expanded social legislation, stricter regulation of public utilities, strengthening of the governor's veto, a direct-primary law, and a constitutional convention. Both parties agreed on the need for a separate juvenile court and further legislation to protect labor.[79]

With the two major parties suffering black eyes from the Waterbury and Merritt Parkway revelations, the Socialists gleefully raised high their banner for Jasper McLevy, with the slogan "Don't let the raiders raid again!" In his acceptance speech as gubernatorial candidate McLevy cited chapter and verse from grand jury findings and charged the Cross administration with not even trying to find out about the serious misconduct occurring. With public indignation at a high pitch, the aggressive Socialist campaign which followed seemed likely to win votes from both major parties, especially from the Democrats. In a hard-hitting campaign, McLevy attracted large crowds and much enthusiasm. Speaking to 1,600 persons at Bushnell Hall in Hartford, he bitingly cited the Waterbury and Merritt Parkway scandals as "Connecticut's disgrace, a record of betrayal of both old political parties." All over the state McLevy attacked the "double machine" — a corrupt Democratic-Republican alliance — and promised if elected to give Connecticut the same type of efficient government enjoyed by Bridgeport.[80]

Sensing that Cross was on the defensive, Baldwin and McConaughy planned and pressed an aggressive campaign. The latter made sharp and often personal attacks on Democratic leadership and policies, while Baldwin devoted principal attention to the broad positive aspects of his party's program. As he saw it, the chief problems facing Connecticut were these: 1] the need for more jobs in private industry, or "a job for every home"; 2] the state's bad financial situation (he promised a balanced budget and no new taxes); 3] prohibition of dual job-holding; 4] need for "good news" from Connecticut (to replace the recent diet of scandals); 5] an anti-injunction bill. An energetic campaigner, Baldwin had able support from his campaign manager, James B. Lowell of

Canton, who had wide contacts in the state.[81]

The campaign hit a rather high level, as the candidates talked issues instead of slinging mud. State finances received much attention as Republicans charged undue extravagance and deficits and Cross countered with the claim that most of the deficit was incurred by a Republican-dominated Board of Finance and Control. McConaughy charged that because Cross could not cope with grasping politicians in his own party Connecticut had become famous for "waste, extravagance and corruption." Cross was particularly irritated by his opponent's charges of needless delay on building projects. When some doubts were voiced regarding efficiency at Cross's age (then seventy-six), he replied that he felt undamaged by governmental service, came of a long-lived family, and had no intention of resigning in favor of the lieutenant governor if he were elected.[82]

Other issues discussed included general economic conditions and auto inspection. The Republicans presented as a slogan, "For Recovery — Bring in the Republicans," to which Cross replied that Connecticut economic conditions had greatly improved while he was governor. The required semiannual inspection of automobiles gave Republicans an opportunity to capitalize upon an irritant. Cross answered that auto inspection was worthwhile if it saved one life.[83]

Mother Nature's hurricane-flood rampage of September gave Republicans an issue of great emotional impact — flood control. The *Courant* bitterly attacked Congressmen Herman Kopplemann (First District) and William Citron (At-large) for their "unreasonable, not to say demagogic, opposition to the Flood Control Compact," while Republican William J. Miller, running against Kopplemann, told Hartford east siders, "The New Deal fiddles while we get flooded." Cross reiterated his support of the proposed flood compact plan for the Connecticut River Valley, but Kopplemann, Citron, William Fitzgerald, and Alfred Phillips had all opposed the compacts. Attempts in Washington to get flood-control work under way in the fall of 1938 came too late to help Democratic candidates who were vulnerable because of their votes on flood-control bills for the New England area.[84]

The approach of election day found the leaders of the political parties deep in uncertainty about the outcome. At the eleventh hour a group calling themselves the "Union party" succeeded in placing candidates on the ballot. For a ticket they listed Baldwin, McConaughy, and a mixture of Re-

is a happy fact that since 1938 Connecticut has not experienced any major political scandal remotely comparable to Waterbury's![86]

After eight eventful years as governor, it was the end of the political road for Cross. By his skilled efforts at responsible government he had given

"Baldwin Elected Governor . . . ," from the Hartford Courant *of November 9, 1938.*

publicans and Democrats for other state offices. Although this party had no connection whatever with the Union party of 1936 (William Lemke, supported by Father Coughlin), it obviously hoped to attract some votes from supporters of that movement.[85]

On November 8, Connecticut voters reversed the New Deal tide, and by a narrow margin elected Baldwin and the Republican state ticket, as well as Danaher and four of the six Republicans seeking House seats. The Union party label attracted 3,046 votes to Baldwin, whose plurality was only 2,688 votes. The huge McLevy vote, 166,253, represented an impressive protest vote.

Undoubtedly the election returns demonstrated that large numbers of voters would not tolerate serious corruption in important public offices. It

"the Republicans a chance to become progressive without losing face." An especially graceful tribute came from the *Courant:*

And now just a word for Governor Cross to whom we say, "Hail and Farewell!" He has been . . . a good Governor, a popular Governor, and he has wrought much for the State during these last eight years. He has brought great distinction to Connecticut by his erudition, by the fine literary qualities of his official proclamations, by the charm that his presence has lent to public occasions here and elsewhere, and by his mellowed philosophy and excellent sense of humor. The election figures indicate that if it had not been for the inroads made by Mr. McLevy he might have achieved his ambition to be the first Governor since Oliver Wolcott's day, back in 1817, to serve ten years in that office. As it is, he goes down to an honorable defeat with few personal enemies and with a multitude of friends and well-wishers.[87]

314

CHAPTER 18

Trade, Transportation, and Industry

Revival and Decline of West Indian Trade — Whaling Attracts Stanch Mariners —
Turnpikes and Canals — Steamboats on Rivers and the Sound — Railroading in Connecticut
— Brass Making and the Miracle on Mad River — Firearms, Another Typical Industry —
Insurance: One of the State's Greatest Industries — Diversification of Industry

---

Revival and Decline of West Indian Trade

AFTER the Revolution, Connecticut merchants sought to regain and expand the profitable oceanic trade routes of late colonial times, including the highly lucrative West Indian route. Since the United States was now a foreign nation to Britain, they treated us as such. Although sugar, molasses, and rum could be freely exported to the United States, timber, grain, flour, bread, and livestock could be imported from us *only* in British ships, and American meat and fish not at all. Since whale oil no longer could be imported into Britain, the New England whaling industry declined. Americans still could and did trade with non-British West Indian ports, and through various stratagems traded with British West Indian interests. Americans also smuggled goods in and out, but the British regulations severely restricted the total trade. After the signing of Jay's Treaty with Britain in 1795, American vessels of up to seventy tons were permitted, but the West Indian trade still fought heavy odds. Other outlets for surplus produce were New York and the southern states,

but these were heavily competitive markets which New England merchants found difficult to exploit.[1]

During the post-Revolutionary era Norwich, contrary to the general trend, seems to have enjoyed a boom in its West Indian trade. Better protected than New London and Sound ports and free of damaging wartime raids, Norwich resumed its oceanic trade more quickly in the 1780's. Livestock, provisions, and lumber still constituted the chief exports, with the livestock usually being put aboard at New London. Two round-trip voyages yearly was the average. An analysis of exports to the West Indies from Norwich in a fourteen-month period from January 1, 1788, indicated the principal items to have been: horses, mules, horned cattle, sheep, hogs, beef, pork, butter, cheese, ham, grain, hoops, and staves. Imports were mainly coffee, molasses, rum, sugar, and salt. "European goods" were imported, but it is probable that they came chiefly from Boston and other American ports rather than directly from Europe.[2]

Some enterprising Norwich shipowners developed a very profitable trade with northern South

America. Typical of these voyages was that of the *Enterpriser,* clearing for Demerara, British Guiana, on November 2, 1789, with provisions of bricks, lumber, horses, cattle, mules, sheep, swine, geese, and turkeys. On the return voyage it carried rum, molasses, sugar, wine, pimento, pepper, limes, tamarinds, sweetmeats, aniseed, coffee, cotton, tobacco, indigo, and salt, as well as some spirits, cotton, sugar, and cocoa, not declared but discovered by the eagle-eyed customs![3]

Throughout the 1790's the head of the Thames at Norwich must have been a scene of bustling activity. Several packets ran regularly to New York City, one to Newport, and another to Boston. There were several small vessels plying the Thames and nearby coasts. In 1795 the port of Norwich claimed seven ships, nine brigs, nine schooners, and seventeen sloops, exclusive of the purely river craft and regularly scheduled packets. The largest vessel listed was the ship *George,* 364 tons; the smallest, the sloops *Patty* and *Bud,* 35 tons apiece. Norwich's golden era of foreign commerce apparently reached its peak in the late 1790's, as judged by unusually high customs duties paid by some vessels. Other ports, such as New London, Middletown, and New Haven, also participated in the West Indian trade during the 1780's and 1790's. In 1793 war broke out between Britain and France — a struggle which raged almost continuously until Waterloo in 1814. The Caribbean area was ravaged, islands changed hands, and the belligerents preyed upon neutral American ships in the Atlantic and Caribbean. By the early 1800's Connecticut's West Indian trade had begun the long decline from which it never recovered. Jefferson's embargo, passed late in 1807, gravely hampered oceanic trade. Soon afterward the War of 1812, with an accompanying British blockade, struck further grave blows at all ocean-borne trade. After the war some Caribbean trade reappeared. New Haven, for instance, in a one-year period from October 1825, reported shipments to that area valued at $344,000 and imports of $336,000. By this time, however, except for whaling, the golden age of Connecticut's oceanic trade had long since passed. Manufacturing offered far greater investment opportunities, made easier by a growing volume of bank credit.[4]

Whaling Attracts Stanch Mariners

ALTHOUGH whaling's great age was in the middle third of the nineteenth century, it engaged a few Americans from the early colonial period. The first organized whaling in America began about 1650 among the eastern Long Island inhabitants, who then traded their whale oil with Boston and

Andrew Jackson, *clipper ship built in Mystic (1855) by Irons and Grinnell. It set three unbroken records for merchant ships of the sail.*

Connecticut. In May 1647 the Connecticut legislature gave William Whiting and associates a monopoly of whaling rights for a period of seven years, provided that they indicated a desire to continue after two years' trial. Apparently the project failed. Early interest in whaling undoubtedly arose from the fact that whales often appeared in the Sound, and occasionally one was stranded on shore, to the delight of the nearby settlers.[5]

Eighteenth-century American whaling changed radically because of an accidental discovery. Around 1712 Captain Christopher Hussey, while on a whaling expedition in Nantucket South Shoals, was blown far out to sea, and when the storm subsided he sighted a school of sperm whales, the aristocrat of whales, with oil of un-paralleled richness, especially in its bulky head. Thus was inaugurated deep-sea whaling. After this, New England whalemen, paying less attention to offshore whaling, began to voyage farther and farther into the North Atlantic, and eventually into the Arctic, searching for whales. Apparently

The whaler Charles W. Morgan, *now at Mystic Seaport.*

eighteenth-century Connecticut vessels made occasional whaling voyages, as the sloop *Greyhound* of Nantucket, bound for Davis Strait in the Arctic, hailed a whaling sloop from Saybrook in 1753. Indication of the growing interest in whaling was the advertisement in which Caleb Trapp of Norwich sought "raw Hands for Whaling."[6]

During the heyday of American whaling, the 1840's and 1850's, New London ranked third among American ports, behind only New Bedford and Nantucket, in number of whalers plying the Seven Seas. New London's postwar rise was gradual from May 20, 1784, when the sloop *Rising Sun* sailed for the Atlantic whaling grounds. The next Connecticut voyage reported was that of the *Commerce,* owned in East Haddam but clearing from New London in February 1794 for southern

latitudes. In 1806 whaling became well established, as three vessels cleared, and others followed through 1808, mostly going into the South Atlantic. Then came the Embargo Act and the war, which completely stopped all Connecticut whaling for a decade.[7]

In 1819 whaling resumed and quickly attracted increasing numbers of enterprising businessmen to finance the voyages and adventurous mariners to man the ships. In 1832 a new record was set when twenty whalers cleared from New London, of which thirteen proceeded to South Atlantic grounds. Other Connecticut ports entered this exciting industry. Stonington's first whaler, the *Hydaspe,* cleared in 1822; while the first American sealer to Antarctica, the *Hersilia,* sailed from Stonington in 1819. In 1822, three years after New Haven entered whaling, the *Thames* cleared for the Pacific grounds and carried some missionaries to Hawaii. In 1832 Mystic's first whaler, the *Aeronaut,* set out for the South Atlantic, followed closely by the *Bingham,* from the same port. The demand for illuminating and lubricating oil was increasing as the nation grew in population and prosperity. Wealthy families demanded the best spermaceti candles, while whalebone found increasing use in corsets, stays, and umbrella ribs. In the 1840's Connecticut whaling attained its peak, with the record number, forty-one vessels, leaving New London in 1844.[8]

The whaling industry developed a distinctive pattern. Until the 1820's the crews were mostly composed of New England Yankees — men of sturdy physique and good intellect who found in whaling the realization of their dreams. Beginning as a cabin boy or foremast hand, a young New Londoner through diligence might work up to a mate and eventually to captain, with all the honor and huge responsibility involved. As the infirmities of age appeared, a captain often retired to a career as a merchant, perhaps selling the cargoes of the very ship which he once commanded or of others like it. After 1830 the industry lost its ethnic homogeneity, and because of the demand for whalemen, diverse elements crowded the forecastles — Indians, Portuguese, Negroes, mulattoes, South Sea Islanders, and western Europeans. An increasing number of hardened criminals, irresponsible drifters, and rough adventurers also joined the crews, and efficiency suffered. The whaling industry's greatest expansion came when the ablest young New Englanders were heading westward or going into eastern factories. In addition, whalers' compensation was very low, food bad, illness prevalent, and brutality by captain and mates proverbial. Realistically, whaling at its height was a sweated industry.[9]

Whaling employed a unique system of wages. The whaleman did not receive a set wage by the day, week, month, or year, or a prescribed sum for each barrel of oil or pound of bone. Instead he was assigned a fractional share, called a "lay," of the total net return of a voyage. The captain might receive as high as 1/8 or 1/10, or as low as 1/16 or 1/18. Mates, boat steerers, and coopers averaged 1/38 to 1/50, while able and ordinary seamen and the cook took 1/100 to 1/160 apiece. The new "green" hands and "boys" could expect 1/160 to 1/200 and sometimes even less. Fluctuations in the size of the lay occurred because of varying owner policies, prevailing shortage or surplus of hands, the general market, local custom, probable length and danger of voyage, and other factors involved. Usually the whaleman went into debt to the owner for various items, including clothing, and then incurred further debits for purchases from the ship's stores (the slopchest). If a voyage were unsuccessful an individual might end up owing money and be put under heavy pressure to sign on again. On the average, foremast hands earned far less on a per diem basis than unskilled laborers ashore. Undoubtedly many men signed on whalers because they loved the life despite its grim hardships; others were caught up in a web of debt, and some sought an escape from the arms of the law.[10]

The logs of whalers record many accidents. The ship *Connecticut* of New London, after clearing in 1831 for the Pacific, lost Captain Paul Burgess, "killed while fast to a whale." The ship *Armata*, also of New London, whaling in the Indian Ocean, lost a mate and a boat's crew, "taken down by a whale, 1837." In 1843 Captain Edwin J. Ames and one man of the ship *Clematis*, New London, were killed by a blow from a whale's flukes. In Arctic or Antarctic regions, whalers faced grave

perils from extreme cold, fog, ice floes, and uncharted coasts.[11]

During the 1850's the ninety-one-ton *Amaret* of New London wrote an eventful chapter in Arctic whaling. The first voyage to Davis Strait in 1853–54 went successfully enough, with 369 barrels of whale oil and 8,000 pounds of whalebone being secured. On the second voyage the vessel was frozen in the ice from October 1854 to July 1855, and came home empty. Returning again to Davis Strait in 1856, the brig enjoyed a successful hunt. Sailing again in September 1857, the *Amaret* promptly became locked in ice for eight months. On July 1, 1858, the crew took its first whale and captured others so rapidly that the hold was full by July 22! On April 13, 1859, the *Amaret* left New London for the Cumberland Strait, where she was lost on September 27, 1860. In the period 1784–1876, at least 820 whaling voyages began at New London.[12]

Stonington was a distant second to New London among Connecticut's whaling ports, as it sent out over 130 voyages from 1830 through 1860. Mystic took third place, with 105 voyages during the 1832–60 period. Occasional vessels cleared from other ports such as Bridgeport, New Haven, and East Haddam. The Civil War apparently closed down all Connecticut whaling except New London's, which persisted for several decades more. Various factors operated to doom the American whaling industry. As new oil wells were discovered in Pennsylvania and improvements were made in oil refining, petroleum gradually overcame its competitor. Meanwhile whales became less numerous, thus necessitating longer voyages. Costs of ships, supplies, and crews increased sharply. The earlier gold rush to California had diverted men, ships, and capital from whaling. It is a fitting memorial to the intrepid Connecticut whaling captains and crews that the last of the great American whalers, the *Charles W. Morgan*, is now permanently berthed at Mystic Seaport, Mystic, Connecticut, where it is visited yearly by thousands of Americans.[13]

One of the most dramatic whaling voyages in New London's history began uneventfully enough on May 29, 1855, when the bark *George Henry*, under Captain James M. Buddington, sailed for

Davis Strait. In September, Captain Buddington spotted a vessel near Cape Mercy, Baffin Island, listing badly. Close inspection revealed that it was the British six-hundred-ton bark *Resolute,* abandoned in the ice sixteen months earlier and 1,100 miles away! Buddington decided to try salvaging the vessel — a formidable task. Finally, however, the captain and ten men, plus the ship's carpenter, put the vessel in condition to attempt sailing. The bark was short-handed, poorly rigged, lacked chronometer and maps, had burst its tanks, and was buffeted by a series of gales. Yet Captain Buddington somehow finally brought the *Resolute* into New London harbor on Christmas Eve, 1855.[14]

After delicate negotiations the *Resolute* was purchased by the United States Government, carefully refitted, and then sent to Queen Victoria in England as a gift and token of friendship from the President and people of the United States. In December 1856 the queen formally and graciously accepted this gift on behalf of an appreciative British nation. When the *Resolute* was broken up in 1880, Queen Victoria directed that a piece of furniture be constructed from the timbers and presented to our President. Thus a teak desk was made, sent to Washington, and presented to President Hayes. This beautiful desk still stands in the White House in a second-floor office used by the President when he is delivering a speech to the nation. It serves as a fitting memorial not only to Anglo-American amity but also to the courage of an intrepid Groton whaling Captain, James Monroe Buddington.[15]

The Civil War added the special peril of Confederate raiders. The famous *Alabama* captured and burned the New London bark *Alert.* Another Confederate vessel, the steamer *Shenandoah,* claimed two New London victims, the bark *Peril,* off Ascension Island, and the ship *General Williams* in Bering Strait. Other Connecticut whalers came to an unusual end as part of the great "stone" fleet purchased by the Federal government in 1861 and sunk in Charleston Harbor to block Confederate traffic.[16]

The most profitable whaling voyage ever recorded was that of the *Pioneer* of New London (valued, with equipment, at $35,800), which sailed June 4, 1864, for Davis Strait and Hudson Bay. On September 18, 1865, she returned to New London with 1,391 barrels of whale oil and 22,650 pounds of bone, then worth a fabulous $150,060.[17]

After the war American whaling steadily declined, mostly for solid economic reasons. This decline was hastened by an Arctic disaster of unprecedented magnitude in 1871. Early in September ice suddenly closed in on a large fleet of New England whalers. The masters wisely abandoned their ships on September 14. After a terrifying trip all the fugitives safely reached seven vessels farther south. In this disaster New London lost two of its whalers, the *Monticello* and the *J. D. Thompson.* Rising costs and declining demand, however, were more damaging than natural hazards or hostile natives. New London's impressive fleet of forty-eight whalers in 1848 had declined to twenty in 1873 and only five in 1880. In 1909 the final Connecticut whaling voyage began from New London, and a thrilling chapter of history drew to an end.[18]

Turnpikes and Canals

A VITAL ingredient in the development of an advanced civilization is provision of good transportation facilities. The roads of the colonial period, including Connecticut's, had been incredibly rough and sometimes impassable. After the Revolution, Virginia in 1785 authorized the first toll, or turnpike, road in the United States. The word "turnpike" meant literally a form of gate composed of four crossed bars sharpened at their outer ends and turning on a center. Hence any road with such a gate blocking progress was called a turnpike.[19]

As Connecticut grew, the complete dependence upon each town keeping its roads in decent repair, a holdover from colonial days, became impractical. As through traffic increased, towns located on main routes felt increasing reluctance to pay for the wear and tear on their roads caused by "strangers" on long trips. Hence it is noteworthy that the second and third American turnpikes were authorized by Connecticut's Assembly — the Mohegan Road between New London and Norwich in May 1792 and the Old Post Road in Greenwich in October 1792. These turnpikes followed an ancient English type of organization involving management by public authority; in this case the officials were commissioners, responsible to the County Court. All later Connecticut turnpikes were privately operated after incorporation of a company by the Assembly. The lawmakers usually specified the general route and the exact amount of toll permitted for each type of conveyance or traveler. Normally the company improved and straightened an existing route and erected toll gates at certain places. A typical Assembly turnpike company act usually exempted certain classes from toll payments:

Provided that persons travelling on the Lord's day and other public days to attend public worship, persons traveling to attend Society Town, and Freemens meeting and funerals, and persons belonging to the Town where any Gate shall be Established passing through the same to attend their ordinary Farming business, persons going to mill with a Horse and Militia going to attend military Exercises and Reviews shall not be liable to the payment of said Toll.[20]

In some parts of the nation plank toll roads became very popular. In Connecticut during the 1850's seven plank road companies were incorporated, but probably only one, the Waterbury and Cheshire Plank Road Company, actually constructed such a road.[21]

Connecticut developed a very extensive turnpike system, chartering 121 companies by 1853, although many never actually operated a turnpike. The rapid expansion of railroad lines hastened the breakdown of the turnpike system after 1850, though the last of the old order, the Derby Turnpike, lingered on, collecting tolls until 1895.[22]

Even shorter lived in Connecticut's transportation history was the age of canals. The proposed projects included these:

1] *Saugatuck and New Milford Canal* — running from the Sound at Saugatuck to New Milford on the Housatonic River. Incorporated in 1829 but never constructed.

2] *Ousatonic Canal* — the length of the Housatonic River to the Massachusetts line. Incorporated in 1822 but never built.

3] *Sharon Canal* — which would connect with a canal in New York running from either the Hudson or Harlem River. Incorporated in 1826 but never built.

4] *Quinebaug Canal* — to run from Norwich to the Massachusetts line with connections to Worcester and other towns. Incorporated in 1826 but not built.

5] *Enfield Canal* — a by-pass around the rapids of the Connecticut River. Charter granted in 1824 and actually built.

6] *Farmington Canal* — the first and most important project.[23]

Connecticut's first canal charter went to the Farmington Canal group, which hoped to build a canal from New Haven via Farmington to the Massachusetts line. There it would connect with the Hampshire and Hampden Canal going to Northampton. Beyond that, dreamers visualized a canal to the St. Lawrence River via the Connecticut River, Lake Memphremagog, and the St. Francis River Valley! Despite much opposition to the Farmington Canal idea from Hartford people, New Haven interests, under the skillful leadership of James Hillhouse, secured a charter in 1822. After herculean labors both in raising needed capital and in conquering engineering problems, the canal opened for limited traffic late in 1828. From New Haven, boats hauled such items as sugar, molasses, salt, coffee, flour, and hides. They returned laden with upcountry produce, such as apples, cider, cider brandy, butter, and wood.[24]

The Farmington Canal seems to have been born under an unlucky star. In 1829 excessively dry weather interfered with navigation. In 1830 the canal appeared to be flourishing when in June a bad break in a bank occurred. Later that fall a drought forced closing of a section for three months. In July 1835 the canal finally was open the entire length to Northampton, using the Hampshire and Hampden Canal in Massachusetts. On July 30 the boat *Northampton*, drawn by five horses, completed the first through journey from Hillhouse Basin, New Haven, via Northampton to the Connecticut River. For several years communities on the canal prospered, but freshets caused heavy damages to the "fill" composing much of the canal bank. As a result, the company in 1836–40 spent over four times its total revenue. The great depression beginning in 1837, moreover, discouraged the settling of industrial plants along the canal where they could get water power and transportation.[25]

In 1838 a line of packet boats offered passage and meals from New Haven to Northampton in twenty-four hours, for which they charged $3.75. Two years later energetic Joseph E. Sheffield of New Haven obtained control of the canal. The year 1844 was the canal's best, with record-breaking tonnage hauled, no days lost, and a good season's profit. The following July brought an unusually severe drought, closing the entire canal for over two months. This caused the new owners of the canal to have a survey made to determine the possibility of building a railroad along the canal towpath. On the basis of a favorable report the owners obtained authorization to build a railroad as far as Canton. They had hoped to operate railroad and canal simultaneously, but at the end of the 1847 season the canal closed down, never again to operate over the full route. The Farmington Canal, though sound in conception, always lacked adequate capital. A depression, financial rivalries, frequent rampages of Mother Nature, and above all the advent of railroads, sealed its doom. Even so, in its brief life it stimulated sharply the mercantile growth of New Haven.[26]

Steamboats on Rivers and the Sound

THE introduction of steam brought a nineteenth-century revolution to water and land transportation. Although John Fitch of South Windsor successfully operated a steamboat on the Delaware River as early as 1788, and Samuel Morey of Hebron ran one on the upper Connecticut in the early 1790's, it was Robert Fulton's *Clermont* which convinced the public of the steamboat's utility by its successful trip from New York to Albany in 1807.[27]

The first steamboat appearing on the Sound and the lower Connecticut was the *Fulton,* which steamed from New York to New Haven in March 1815 in eleven hours. In May it ascended the Connecticut, reaching Hartford on Election Day and creating a sensation among the 7,000 or 8,000 persons visiting the boat. The *Fulton* and a slightly larger steamboat, the *Connecticut,* soon provided regular service from New York to New Haven and New London.[28]

In 1813 another steamer, the *Juliana,* after being towed through the Sound operated briefly, as a *Courant* advertisement testifies:

STEAM-BOAT JULIANNA.

The public are respectfully informed that this boat has commenced running from Hartford to Middletown. The Julianna will leave Hartford every day at 8 o'clock, A.M. and arrive at Middletown at 11 A.M. Returning, leave Middletown at 30 minutes past, 1 P.M. and arrive at Hartford at 6 P.M. — Fare of each passenger 75 cents — children half price; — way passengers to pay at the rate of twelve and a half cents for every three miles.

The *Juliana* typifies the early era of experimentation. In 1819 the newspapers advertised that a steamboat, the *Enterprize,* of Hartford, was making regular runs to Saybrook and return. Builder of the *Enterprize* was the Connecticut Steam Boat Company, incorporated in 1819, which pioneered organized steamboat operations in the valley. In 1824 this company introduced an impressive new vessel, the *Oliver Ellsworth,* measuring almost 230 tons. Containing separate cabins for ladies and gentlemen, staterooms, offices, baggage rooms, and so on, this steamer ran successfully from New York to Hartford until 1833.[29]

Business was so good that a rival, the *McDonough,* entered the Hartford–New York run, leaving Hartford on Wednesdays and Saturdays. The *Ellsworth* departed Mondays and Thursdays. Within a short time new competitors, challenging the older steamboats, precipitated a rate war. Fares which had reached five dollars for the run from Hartford to New York plummeted to as little as one dollar plus meals. Needless to say, profits were slim or nonexistent. As the years passed, older steamboats were transferred to other routes, met accidents, or otherwise disappeared from Connecticut waters.[30]

Terrible accidents punctuated the early years of steamboating. Early on the morning of October 9, 1833, the *New England,* a side-wheeler of 261 tons, stopped at Essex. Suddenly her two boilers exploded almost simultaneously, killing or injuring fifteen of seventy passengers. Greater catastrophes occurred on the more exposed Sound. Early in the evening of January 13, 1840, the *Lexington,* bound to Stonington, caught fire and soon was engulfed in flames as her cargo of cotton ignited. Complete panic seized crew and passengers, and only four persons survived.[31]

Fortunately engines were radically improved and safety measures taken, so that steamboat travel gradually became far safer, faster, and more comfortable. On the Connecticut River after 1850 the chaotic competition of early years gave way to stabilization. One of the principal ships of that era was *City of Hartford* (later called *Capitol City*), a side-wheeler of 970 tons, licensed to carry 977

out ceremony, started on its last trip down the Connecticut. Thus ended regular steamboat service on the river.[33]

In a sense the Sound was New York's "down East," as Bridgeport, New Haven, Hartford, New London, Norwich, and Stonington all carried on an important freight and passenger business with the metropolis. Whereas sloops and schooners dominated this traffic early in the century, steamboats decisively triumphed by the 1830's. Because

Scene at Norwich, featuring side-wheeler steamboat Connecticut *(built 1861). It operated on New York–Norwich run in conjunction with Norwich and Worcester Railroad. From painting by Sandy Adams.*

passengers and 1,400 tons of cargo. Her career of thirty-four years on the river was marred by a spectacular accident. On March 29, 1876, she ran straight into the Middletown bridge! Apparently the pilot confused a light on shore with one at the opening. Luckily the ship could be repaired. Thenceforth bridge lights were required to be red.[32]

Completion of the Connecticut Valley Railroad from Hartford to Saybrook in 1871 posed a formidable threat to the very existence of steamboats. Eventually a reorganization was achieved through the Hartford and New York Transportation Company, so that steamboats continued service for many years. In the present century the New Haven Railroad completed its acquisition of the steamboat lines of the Sound and the Connecticut River. Better roads, increased use of autos, and finally the depression soon ended Connecticut River steamboating. On October 31, 1931, the *Hartford*, with-

of long delays in getting goods through rail routes from New York to Boston, steamboats dominated passenger and freight traffic until late in the century. When a railroad line was built from Providence to Stonington in 1837, it revolutionized the quiet Connecticut town. On November 10 the first steamboat, the *Narragansett*, arrived from New York. Soon the Stonington boat line was organized to connect with two trains daily in each direction from Providence. Since this route avoided the often rough-water passage around Point Judith into Narragansett Bay, it became very popular. Stonington's wharves teemed with activity, and her railroad yards filled the air with noise and smoke. In 1880 the two steamboats on this line, *Narragansett* and *Stonington*, collided in a dense fog, the former caught fire, and many lives were lost. Service was resumed later and continued with interruptions until 1909, when it was permanently abandoned.[34]

Norwich served as a vital connector between a steamboat line from New York and a railroad to interior cities. Boasting a "protected" route, this boat line prospered for many years despite bitter competition, principally from the Fall River Line and the Stonington Line but also from shorter-lived lines operating out of Providence, Newport, Bristol, and New Bedford. In 1881 the Norwich line launched the *City of Worcester*, the first large iron steamer on the Sound. All of the Sound lines eventually were absorbed by the omnivorous New Haven Railroad. As faster through trains were introduced in the 1890's on the New York-Providence-Boston run, travelers more often preferred railroad to steamboat. Even after boat passenger traffic fell to low levels, freight remained very profitable, especially for the Norwich line. As the twentieth century advanced, improved rail service, the huge increase in private automobiles, and trucking competition did great damage; finally the depression killed all regular steamboat service on the Sound.[35]

Railroading in Connecticut

EVEN after Massachusetts, Vermont, and Maine were in the throes of railroad-promotion excitement, Connecticut remained passive. Blessed by a coast with many good harbors, navigable rivers, grandiose canal plans, and an unusually complete turnpike system, the state in the eyes of most business leaders did not yet require railroads.[36]

A few New Haven capitalists, however, had caught the railroad "bug." From the Assembly in 1833 they obtained a charter which authorized construction from Hartford to New Haven. When books were opened for subscriptions, investors in New Haven, Hartford, and New York pledged over $1,400,000. When the depression of 1837 threatened the entire venture, energetic James Brewster of New Haven retired from his successful carriage-making firm to campaign for money. Thanks largely to his efforts, the railroad was completed and the first train entered Hartford on December 14, 1839.[37]

For the next several decades railroad expansion brought concurrent and often competing projects, out of which emerged some short railroad lines. Us-

ing the Farmington Canal route, Joseph E. Sheffield of New Haven pushed the New Haven and Northampton Railroad through to Northampton in 1856. The Housatonic Railroad — Bridgeport's dream child — was completed up the Housatonic Valley in 1842 to a connection with Massachusetts' Western Railroad. It became one of the first railroads to ship milk to New York City in large quan-

Advertisement for Hartford and New Haven Railroad.

tities. Alfred Bishop, Bridgeport's leading railroad promoter, almost single-handedly pushed rails from his city up the Naugatuck Valley to Winsted — a line which prospered from the booming brass industry. Meanwhile the New Haven and Hartford line achieved a logical extension to Springfield in 1844. Also, in 1844 a number of Connecticut and New York bankers and businessmen obtained a charter for the New York and New Haven Railroad. Under the driving leadership of Sheffield and Samuel J. Hitchcock this railroad became a reality in 1848. Earlier, in November 1837, the first railroad trains in Connecticut's history had operated from Stonington to the nearby Rhode Island line as part of the line to Providence. Expansion in eastern Connecticut in the 1840's and 1850's created a network of lines, tying together such points as Hartford, Manchester, Willimantic, New London, Norwich, Plainfield, and Putnam. Total railroad mileage in the state, jumping from 102 miles in 1840 to 402 in 1850 and 601 in 1860, made Connecticut's concentration one of the densest in the nation.[38]

From the Civil War to 1900 Connecticut's railroad history revolved about the creation of a unified New York, New Haven and Hartford Railroad and the attempt of that line to devour all competitors. The first step, marriage of the New York and New Haven Railroad with the Hartford and New Haven, stirred up intense opposition, organized by hard-hitting Henry L. Goodwin, *Courant* editor. After years of complicated political and financial juggling, in 1871–72 W. D. Bishop of Bridgeport and his forces succeeded in winning legislative approval for creation of the New York, New Haven and Hartford Railroad, called popularly for many years the "Consolidated." From 1872 to 1888 in geography and leadership it remained primarily a Connecticut institution, one which reaped rich profits, especially from its heavy passenger traffic.[39]

Some of Goodwin's criticisms of railroad management finally resulted in appointment of a special legislative committee to investigate alleged frauds. This committee found that nearly every railroad in Connecticut had watered its stock, concealed true earnings, and in other ways misled the public. Even the reports of the state railroad commission were found to be incomplete and misleading. Undoubtedly Goodwin's vigilance helped insure an improvement in the honesty of railroad management.[40]

The next two decades of the Consolidated's history centered about the elimination of competition in southern New England. Since revenues from passenger traffic, the main source of income, were especially heavy on the New York to New Haven runs, the Consolidated worried over schemes for rival parallel lines between New York and New Haven. Under the energetic leadership of Charles P. Clark, who assumed the presidency in 1887, acquisition or leasing of rivals in southern New England proceeded rapidly. Jabez A. Bostwick put up a titanic battle defending his New York and New England line, but the Consolidated triumphed in the legislature. In 1889 the legislature authorized it to issue $35,000,000 in new securities, and in 1893 it was permitted to increase its capital to $100,000,000. The Consolidated by the early 1890's controlled over twenty other lines and had won a through route from New York to Boston. Next came a peace treaty in which the Consolidated and the Boston and Maine divided New England along an east-west line drawn through central Massachusetts. By 1900 its southern New England empire totaled over 2,000 miles of trackage. Accompanying the octopuslike expansion was a huge program of rebuilding the main line, equipping it with four tracks, and eliminating grade crossings.[41]

The New Haven's checkered history in the present century affords a striking illustration of the tragic effects of mismanagement. For about forty years before 1900 the line had paid high dividends — never less than $7.50 per share — and ranked as the East's strongest system. In 1903 the J. P. Morgan interests of New York, who gradually had wrested control away from Connecticut men, selected Charles S. Mellen, president of the Northern Pacific Railroad, for the New Haven's presidency. In the Northwest, Mellen had enjoyed success through an aggressive policy of *expansion* and *monopoly*. He vigorously applied the same principles to New Haven management. Buying up every sort of transportation line available — streetcars, interurban lines, coastal freight and passenger boat lines — within a decade he had loaded the New Haven down with an amazing collection of "white elephants." Late in 1913 the New Haven missed its usual dividend. By 1914 the railroad's service had declined seriously, maintenance was neglected, and frequent wrecks occurred. The Interstate Commerce Commission held sixty days of public hearings. President Mellen admitted that the railroad regularly employed political bosses, including Roraback, as lobbyists to prevent unfavorable legislation. Roraback was paid $5,000 per session. The New Haven had over three hundred subsidiary corporations, many for deliberate concealment of certain operations. The management resorted frequently to collusive purchasing, and deliberately purchased lines which already were running deficits. In 1903 the New Haven was capitalized at $93,000,000; in 1913 at $417,000,000. The Mellen leadership had invested $120,000,000 of the difference in solid improvements in the railroad, but it put $204,000,000 into nonrailroad operations! The I.C.C. denounced the management for an "indefensible standard of business ethics and an absence of financial acumen," and scathingly criticized the New Haven's board of directors for gross ignorance and indifference.[42]

Despite its parasitical appendages, the New Haven, under new management, succeeded in avoiding bankruptcy. During World War I, in common with all railroads, the New Haven went under government management and carried the additional freight and troops required. Entering the postwar period with badly worn equipment, the New Haven quickly suffered the twin blows of a shopmen's strike and the coal strike. On top of this came the extremely frigid winter of 1922–23. In 1923 a state legislative committee investigated complaints of poor New Haven service. Although verifying a deterioration in service, the legislators attributed it largely to the special circumstances already mentioned, over which railroad management had little control. In the next five years the New Haven staged a comeback, resuming payment of dividends in 1928, only to stop in 1931 as the depression deepened and truck competition increased. Despite great efforts to retrench, the long-term debt of $257,000,000 proved fatal. An income of $142,000,000 in 1929 fell to $72,000,000 in 1935, while fixed costs remained at the 1929 level. Final collapse came in 1935, when a New Haven application for an additional $5,000,000 loan was flatly rejected by the I.C.C. Pointing out that the line had recently borrowed over $30,000,000 from the RFC, PWA, and banks, and still had suffered heavy losses in 1934 and 1935, the examiners felt that the road should be reorganized. So the New Haven, now "only a hollow shell," was put through the wringer of bankruptcy and reorganization.[43]

Once again, as the line was painfully regaining strength, a great war came along. It brought a temporary stimulus to business and earnings, but the postwar period again proved brutal. Connecticut expanded its system of superhighways and improved others, so that people usually preferred driving their automobiles. Passenger traffic, particularly important to the New Haven, declined seriously. Lower traffic necessitated higher fares, which drove still more passengers away. Meanwhile the expanding and aggressive truck industry bit deeply into freight traffic. The Connecticut commuter into New York whose pattern of living is tied to New Haven service has endured fare boost after fare boost. In the late 1950's state-wide complaints about undependable service, dirty equipment, and inadequate maintenance grew in volume. Early in 1960 the State Public Utilities Commission conducted lengthy hearings on the New Haven. Company spokesmen asserted that the line could not much longer endure its heavy losses on passenger operations and must have speedy relief through higher fares and tax reductions. In March the I.C.C. highlighted the grave situation by ordering a sweeping investigation of the line. The State Commission's report of May 4, 1960, recommended, among other things, joint action by Connecticut, Massachusetts, Rhode Island, and New York to provide tax relief adequate at least to eliminate the road's deficits. At the same time the commission charged the line with imprudent managerial policies. Tax relief of some sort seems inevitable, as Connecticut and neighboring states badly need a healthy New Haven Railroad.[44]

Brass Making and the Miracle on Mad River

THE American brass industry arose humbly about 1790 out of the making of pewter buttons by Silas, Henry, and Samuel Grilley in Waterbury, much of the output being sold by the famous itinerant Yankee peddlers. In 1795 Abel Porter, Revolutionary War veteran, settled down to the tinner's trade in Southington, where for the next few years he carried on a thriving business.[45]

In 1802 Abel Porter and his brother, Levi, discussed with Daniel Clark and Silas Grilley of

Waterbury the possibility of a partnership. The Porters could offer experience, capital, tools, and equipment from the Southington tin shop; Silas Grilley was well known for his invention of a practicable wire-eye pewter button; while Daniel Clark, active in Waterbury real estate circles, could arrange for the acquisition of vital water-power rights on Mad River in Waterbury. They reached an agreement in 1802, resulting in the establishment in Waterbury of Abel Porter and Company, out of which later emerged the Scovill Manufacturing Company. Abel Porter and associates early decided that the best metal for button making was brass rather than pewter. A process of alloying copper with zinc to form brass had been developed by James Emerson of England in 1781.[46]

After experimentation, Abel Porter and associates, sometime between 1806 and 1809, achieved the first successful American castings of brass bars. Using tiny molds, they produced bars of metal, each approximately one pound in weight, which were cold-rolled into brass strips. The power source used for this early cold rolling probably came from a water-powered mill operated by Frederick Wolcott and Company near Litchfield; but by 1815 the water-power facilities on the Mad River at Waterbury were made suitable for both casting and rolling operations. In 1811 Abel Porter sold the entire enterprise to Frederick Leavenworth, James Scovill, and his son, James Mitchell Lamson Scovill. During the War of 1812 the new owners benefited from the increasing demands, heightened by temporary elimination of English competition. When Lafayette revisited America in 1824, Scovill presented to him as a token of affection a complete set of solid gold buttons, which are collector's items today.[47]

During the early nineteenth century English brass interests, still pre-eminent in the world, jealously guarded their secrets by forbidding export of rolls and skilled brass workers. Despite this situation, Scovill interests succeeded in 1821 in obtaining the services of James Croft, a skilled English metalworker and toolmaker. The invention of the one-day brass clock in 1837 by Chauncey Jerome created a substantial demand for sheet brass. By 1850 the brass industry of the Naugatuck Valley

was firmly established and even had begun exporting brass to Europe. [48]

In 1850 the Scovill Manufacturing Company was formed. The same year marked another major decision: to introduce steam power. The engine, quaintly named "Sally Ann," was installed in 1852 and developed 125 horsepower. Water power still was used, however, for many years.[49]

Scovill enjoyed favorable national post–Civil War conditions, such as the rapid growth of population and home markets, a protective tariff, a growing labor supply, and agreements (probably informal) among producers. Starting work at Scovill in 1862, Chauncey P. Goss and Mark L. Sperry soon infused new vigor into the organization. Other favorable local developments had occurred, among which the chartering of the first Waterbury bank in 1848 and the arrival of the railroad in the Naugatuck Valley in 1849 stood foremost.[50]

Technological improvements came rapidly in the late nineteenth and early twentieth centuries. The turn of the new century saw the beginning of the shift to electric power generation which, in a few years, replaced steam. The great value of the new power source in conjunction with numerous other technological advances, such as giant 4-hi rolling mills, is reflected in Scovill's rapid increase in production from a brass sheet output of about 3,000 pounds in 1815 to 663,000 in 1860 and 100,000,000 in 1952.[51]

World War I necessitated rapid expansion. Scovill made and delivered to our Allies 2,000,000,000 brass cups for cartridge shell, 443,000,000 bullet jackets, 21,000,000 completely assembled time fuses for shrapnel, and 19,000,000 75-mm. shell cases, as well as a half billion other metal items for various armament requirements. To meet war orders Scovill expanded its labor force from 3,600 in 1915 to a wartime peak in 1918 of 13,500. A large number of new employees were immigrants, who as a group proved to be satisfactory workers. About this time, new automatic machinery was introduced, though the innovations were made gradually so as not to impede output.[52]

After the prosperous 1920's, the depression hit Scovill severely, causing a sales slump from $37,000,000 in 1929 to $15,700,000 in 1932. Even so, the company showed an operating profit, before depreciation, in every year from 1930 through 1939.[53]

In 1940 Scovill accepted an American educational order for 15,000 fuses of the new M-54, 25-second type. After the entry of the United States into the Second World War, it speeded up production so that by the end of 1945 it had delivered

forces, of firemen, and of railroad conductors across the country. At the same time the company produces an enormous amount of brass — rod, wire, sheet, and tube — and uses a substantial part of its total mill output in its own fabricating plants.[55]

Continued technical progress is exhibited in the

LEFT: *Mill house on Mad River in 1836.* RIGHT: *Modern Scovill plant at Waterbury.*

over 24,000,000 M-54 fuses. Scovill also filled contracts for artillery shell cases, aircraft radios, lifeboat equipment, gas mask fittings, explosive rivets for aircraft, medical equipment, helmet hardware, and flare pistols. Sales in 1940–45 reached $510,000,000 as compared with $208,000,000 in 1915–19. Technical developments, such as the adaptation of the Junghans continuous casting machine, use of substitutes for scarce materials, and improvement of powder blending, greatly aided it in fulfilling its contracts.[54]

The postwar period has continued the plant expansion program, which has entailed expenditures of over $75,000,000 from 1940 to 1957. Production at Scovill ranges from common pins (4,700 per pound) to brass strip in coils of 3,000 pounds apiece. The firm has demonstrated remarkable financial stability, maintaining a continuous dividend record for over a century. Today Scovill uniform buttons still adorn the coats of the armed

Rossi-type continuous brass alloy casting machine. In February 1960 the company announced plans for a $5,500,000 continuous-casting aluminum plant, which will double capacity and produce flat aluminum strips at a minimum cost. Thus in a century and a half Scovill has grown from Abel Porter's partnership of four owners and nine employees in 1802 to a modern international firm of about 10,000 employees and over 18,000 stockholders, with annual sales of about $146,000,000. Although it operates important manufacturing facilities in other states and foreign countries, it still centers operations at Waterbury.[56]

While the bulk of the state's brass industry is concentrated in the Naugatuck Valley from Ansonia to Torrington, there are other important centers, such as Bristol and Bridgeport. Bristol early entered the field when local clockmakers grew tired of the delays in hauling their brass by ox team over the mountain from Waterbury.

Among the primary producers in Connecticut's brass industry today are American Brass, Chase Brass and Copper, Plume and Atwood, Waterbury Rolling Mills, all in the Waterbury area; and elsewhere, Bridgeport Brass, Bridgeport Rolling Mills, Bristol Brass, Miller, New Haven Copper, Olin Mathieson Chemical, Seymour Manufacturing, and Stamford Rolling Mills. Though located far from sources of raw materials and facing serious foreign competition using much cheaper labor, Connecticut remains in the forefront in value of brass goods produced annually.[57]

Firearms, Another Typical Industry

IN creating the new industrialized America no man played a more influential role than Eli Whitney. Born in Massachusetts, he received his college education at Yale. After graduation he accepted a position as tutor on a southern plantation, and soon found that southern plantation owners desperately needed a machine to clean the short-staple, green-seed, upland cotton. In a brief period of concentrated activity Whitney invented his cotton gin, which met enthusiastic response. It enabled southern planters for the first time to help fill the enormous demands of the British and northern textile plants. Yet this epochal invention brought to its inventor chiefly expensive litigation and heartbreak. Others pirated the invention, and Whitney spent years vainly attempting to win his rights.[58]

Learning much from these bitter experiences, Whitney in 1798 decided to enter the small-arms industry, provided he could secure a government contract. In a letter to Secretary of the Treasury Oliver Wolcott, Whitney offered to make 10,000 to 15,000 stand of arms (musket, bayonet, ramrod, wiper, and screw-driver). Seemingly, imminent war with France made Whitney's application timely. The application represented a giant gamble, based on Whitney's conviction that he could attain quantity production through the use of machines yet to be invented, at a factory yet to be acquired, with workers yet to be secured and trained! At wit's end as to where to secure enough arms, the Federal administration eagerly embraced Whitney's proposals. Within a few weeks

Whitney signed a contract with Wolcott to make 10,000 complete stand and deliver them by September 20, 1800.[59]

Whitney encountered formidable difficulties in getting his project launched. There was a millsite near East Rock in Hamden, just north of New Haven, which seemed ideally suited. The water supply was excellent, and a thirty-five-foot fall over the dam assured ample power. Heavy barges could navigate the stream to the foot of the dam, while a new turnpike to Hartford passed nearby. A farm by the river, included in Whitney's purchase, offered space for living quarters for employees and himself. Unavoidable delays in completing purchase of the site, followed by a severe winter, caused Whitney to fall far behind in his plans. Slow delivery of raw materials and credit difficulties further hampered him. Finding many unsolved problems involved in tooling up for quantity production, Whitney requested an extension of time, which Wolcott granted.[60]

Whitney's system of manufacture necessitated the separation into basic parts of the article which he intended to produce and the subsequent invention of a machine, or machines, to produce each part accurately. The old system of having a workman fashion parts by hand meant that each piece varied slightly from every other. Moreover, since skilled arms workers were very scarce, mass production of arms by individual custom methods was impossible. Whitney's plan of relying upon precision tools more accurate than the best craftsman's hands would guarantee unprecedented uniformity. His machine tools thus would make the parts of his musket fully interchangeable.[61]

Although he had already invented a number of machines, Whitney as yet had failed to deliver a single musket when Wolcott retired in November 1800. Hence it was necessary to convince the new administration at Washington that his principles would result in good muskets. In January 1801 Whitney dramatically pleaded his cause. Spreading out parts on a large table, he picked up pieces at random and quickly assembled a complete lock and then promptly disassembled it. Before the gaping witnesses he demonstrated that the parts were completely interchangeable and that any man present could easily follow his example. The outgoing President Adams and the incoming Jefferson, as well as other officials, became converts. Elizur Goodrich, Connecticut congressman from the New Haven district, reported that Whitney's arms "have met universal approbation." As a result of the triumph, Whitney obtained more favorable

rotating on its own axis, possessed an edge irregularly shaped to conform exactly to that required for a particular component. He immediately placed the new invention at the disposal of the Federal armories. Whitney's influence upon arms making extended also to principles of cost account-

TOP: *Eli Whitney gun factory, from a painting by William Giles Munson.* BOTTOM: *Eli Whitney Charleville model gun.* (*owned by Floyd L. Atkins*).

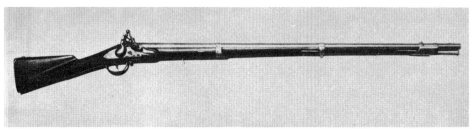

financial terms and a considerable extension in delivery date. Although he fell far behind the new schedule, his completed arms generally received solid approval by government inspectors.[62]

During the War of 1812 era Whitney continued to produce muskets for the government. A serious running conflict with Captain Callender Irvine of the War Department, who had interests in a rival (and inferior) musket, ended finally in Whitney's complete victory. Soon afterward Whitney removed one of the last bottlenecks in making the Charleville musket by creating a mechanized cutter or milling machine. This device enabled Whitney's operatives to shape metal parts with an accuracy heretofore unknown. The cutting tool,

ing, which other manufacturers and the government eventually adopted. While other Connecticut arms makers, such as Simeon North of Middletown, made significant contributions, Whitney's paramount influence on the modern arms industry, through the system of interchangeable parts, is unchallenged. Samuel Colt's revolver, Isaac Singer's sewing machine, and Cyrus H. McCormick's reaper represented famous applications of Whitney's principles. This principle of interchangeable parts helped pave the way for America's future economy of abundance.[63]

The Winchester Company of New Haven evolved in part out of the Smith and Wesson Company, founded by Horace Smith and Daniel Wesson of Norwich, who were also pioneers in improvements on repeating firearms. The "Winchester" became a great favorite of sportsmen, explorers, and adventurers throughout the world, though the company also filled large government contracts in the Spanish–American War, as well as in World Wars I and II. Winchester, now a division of Olin Mathieson Chemical Corporation, at present produces sporting arms and ammunition, traps, targets, and certain tools.[64]

Connecticut's tradition of making fine small arms was carried on by many inventors and com-

Colt's "Peacemaker" revolver.

panies. At Middletown, Simeon North operated the first important pistol factory in America. Obtaining his first government contract in 1799, he expanded into a three-story factory in 1813. His company from 1799 to 1853 filled contracts for about 50,000 pistols and 33,000 rifles and established a notable record for quality and dependability. Samuel Sharps, inventor of a breech-loading rifle, established the Sharps' Company in 1851. This rifle, with its enormous superiority to the muzzle-loading weapons, helped the North to win the Civil War. As already seen, the Colt's Patent Fire Arms Manufacturing Company made hundreds of thousands of revolvers during the Civil War. The famous Colt "Peacemaker" model, the "Cowboys' Friend," greatly speeded up conquest of the West after the Civil War. The Remington Arms Company of Bridgeport, which held important government contracts in the Mexican and the Civil wars, was famous for many technical improvements in rifles.[65]

Today Connecticut holds first rank nationally in

value of small arms produced. The major firms now active besides Winchester and Colt's are Marlin Firearms (New Haven) and High Standard (Hamden). Recently Colt's began production of the AR-15 automatic rifle, a new infantry weapon of light weight which offers full automatic fire of 720 rounds per minute.[66]

Insurance: One of the State's Greatest Industries

HARTFORD is widely known as the "insurance capital" of the United States. How Hartford gained this insurance leadership is a typical story of Yankee ingenuity and perseverance. It began in the closing decade of the eighteenth century, when Hartford merchants engaged in considerable sea-borne trade involving heavy risks from storms, pirates, and depredations of supposedly friendly nations involved in a desperate European war. Gradually there evolved in Hartford a plan for spreading the risks of a voyage among a group rather than letting the vessel's owner bear it alone. In return for this obligation the insurers received a specified share of the profits, if any. These early policies were handwritten. On February 8, 1794, the oldest known *printed* insurance policy was drawn up by the firm of Sanford and Wadsworth of Hartford. It provided £800 worth of fire insurance on the house of William Imlay of Hartford for one year at a rate of one-half percent.[67]

Soon afterward there occurred the next logical step forward — the formation of an insurance corporation to replace individual underwriters. In May 1795 the Mutual Assurance Company of the City of Norwich was incorporated. Providing protection against losses by fire, the company issued policies only through its Norwich home office and an agency in New London. In 1838 it decided to insure only residences, and then to a maximum of only $1,000. This company (now called the New London County Mutual Insurance Company), still a small mutual-type organization, carries on its business in the same conservative tradition.[68]

The second company, incorporated by the legislature in 1797, was the New Haven Insurance Company, a stock-type company confined strictly to marine policies. In its early years this company enjoyed large profits, but it ceased operations in

1833. Other marine insurance companies were incorporated at Hartford, Middletown, and Norwich in 1803, and at New London in 1805. The serious deterioration of shipping during the Napoleonic Wars and the War of 1812 imposed strains which helped terminate the marine insurance companies as such by the 1830's.[69]

Connecticut's oldest active stock fire-insurance company is the Hartford Fire Insurance Company, incorporated in 1810. Although fire insurance was held to be a matter of chance, the Hartford firm followed certain common-sense principles. Both the property and the owner received a thorough examination before a policy was issued. Their first, great test came in the terrible New York fire of December 1835, which destroyed nearly seven hundred buildings. When the news reached Hartford, Eliphalet Terry, president of Hartford Fire Insurance Company, rushed to the Hartford Bank, obtained a blanket promise to honor all drafts which he might make on his company, and in turn pledged his personal fortune as security. Going to New York on a sleigh in below-zero temperatures, he found that most insurance companies had collapsed and the populace was demoralized. Terry immediately announced that his company would pay every just claim in full. He also opened his books for new business. In response, he was deluged with applications. The Hartford Company was well on the road to booming prosperity. In the process, it had greatly boosted Hartford's reputation as the best place to obtain insurance. This confidence was strengthened when a second fire swept New York in 1845, causing heavy claims on Hartford's Ætna (Fire) Insurance Company — claims which were promptly honored. From 1845 to 1871 almost a score of new fire-insurance companies appeared in Connecticut, and the future seemed assured for all. Then came the 1871 Chicago fire, which destroyed $140,000,000 worth of property. Eleven Connecticut companies were involved in the fiery catastrophe, and only the Hartford, Ætna, Phoenix, and Fairfield County companies managed to pay in full their claims. This time it was Marshall Jewell, a director of Phoenix, who stampeded crowds of despairing Chicagoans by standing on a dry-goods box and promising to pay Phoenix policyholders on the spot. In the San

Francisco earthquake and fire of 1906 Connecticut fire-insurance companies again came through — this time to the tune of $18,000,000! Today fire insurance remains a major factor in Connecticut's insurance business.[70]

The mid-nineteenth century saw new types of insurance offered. In 1846 the Assembly chartered the state's first *life*-insurance company, the Connecticut Mutual. Managed from the start by able men, this company served as a successful example for many other life-insurance companies. In 1851 the temperance drive manifested itself in the formation of the American Temperance Life Insurance Company, with bylaws requiring each insurance applicant to sign a total-abstinence pledge. Officers theorized that abstainers would have greater longevity. Unfortunately, a decade of experience proved that the inadequate numbers willing to sign the pledge could not maintain the company, so it was dropped and the company's name changed to Phoenix Mutual Life. The new company pioneered in the thorough training of agents and in insistence that they devote full time to the company. In 1853 an outgrowth of the Ætna (Fire) Insurance Company was started on an independent career as the Ætna Life Insurance Company. Blessed by unusually enterprising presidents — Eliphalet A. Bulkeley (1853–72), Thomas O. Enders (1872–79), Morgan G. Bulkeley (1879–1922), Morgan B. Brainard (1922–55), and Henry S. Beers (1956–   ) — the Ætna has grown into one of America's largest multiple-line insurance companies. At the end of 1959 Ætna and its affiliated companies had $22,952,000,000 worth of life insurance in force![71]

Usually the formation of the Travelers Insurance Company is ascribed to the European trip of Hartford businessman James G. Batterson. In 1863, while in England, he purchased an "accident ticket," which would pay £1,000 if he were killed in a train while on a journey from Leamington to Liverpool. While in England, Batterson made a thorough study of the Railway Passengers Assurance Company and sent an immediate report to Hartford. From this letter it seems very probable that Batterson had seriously considered accident insurance before his trip to England. On his return home he attempted to interest friends in founding a company offering similar coverage to American travelers. One day, a friend, James Bolter, president of the Hartford Bank, asked Batterson what he would charge to insure him for $5,000 against accidental death on the way home to dinner and return. "Two cents," replied Batterson. Bolter paid the two cents, which now hang framed at the Travelers Insurance Company.[72]

As originally set up, the company insured only

1959, Travelers premium income exceeded $1,100,000,000, and total life insurance in force climbed above $25,000,000,000.[73]

In common with many industries, insurance suffered from mismanagement and graft during the turbulent rise-of-big-business decades of the nineteenth century. Some companies recklessly underwrote risks and then divided profits to the last dollar, leaving no reserve fund. The new mush-

Main office building of Ætna Life Affiliated Companies. Largest colonial-style building in the world.

against travel risks, but in the next year, 1864, the charter was expanded to permit protection against other hazards. Despite a lack of statistics and experience as a sound basis for determining rates, the Travelers quickly enjoyed marked success. Soon offering other types of insurance, it became America's first multiple-line insurance company. The Travelers wrote the first automobile policy in 1897. Seven years later it organized the first department of engineering and inspection to reduce accidents. In 1913 it pioneered with group life insurance and in 1919 with the first aircraft insurance policy, issued to President Woodrow Wilson. Recent decades in the company's history have been marked by large expansion in old lines and introduction of new lines, such as windstorm, earthquake, fire, and inland marine. In the year

rooming cities of the country were built mostly of wood and lacked well-organized fire protection. When the decade of reckoning came in an epidemic of great fires, some very large companies, such as the Protection Insurance Company of Hartford, collapsed into ruin. The soundly managed Ætna took over much of the former business of the Protection Company. In the case of the State Fire Insurance Company of New Haven, incorporated in 1855, brazen deception was practiced. In an inventory made in 1862 the real assets of the bankrupt company amounted to exactly $83.49! Likewise, the Charter Oak Life Insurance Company of Hartford, starting out very promisingly in the 1850's, became hopelessly entangled in losing railroad, mine, and other speculations, and failed in 1886, with huge losses to many.[74]

The twentieth century has brought enormous expansion in the volume and scope of Connecticut's insurance business. As of mid–1959 there were 35 Connecticut licensed insurance companies, 3 fraternal benefit societies, 13 savings banks issuing life-insurance policies, one medical and one hospital service corporation. On December 31, 1958, these companies claimed assets of about $14,000,000,000. Also licensed to operate in Connecticut were 471 nonresident and foreign companies and 59 fraternal benefit societies. As of December 31, 1958, the eight Connecticut life-insurance companies possessed admitted assets of $10,820,212,926. As of January 1, 1960, according to the *National Underwriter*, Connecticut had three companies in the top ten for total life insurance in force: Travelers, fourth; Ætna Life, sixth; and Connecticut General, eighth.[75]

While several out-of-state companies far surpass the major Connecticut companies in volume of life insurance written, the state companies still hold the lead nationally in *fire* and *casualty* lines. As of December 31, 1958, Connecticut's nineteen fire and casualty companies had admitted assets of $3,076,795,664. A recent significant development generally introduced in 1960 is the issuance of low-cost automobile policies under safe-driver rating plans. Connecticut's insurance laws are very strict, involving thorough periodic examination by the insurance commissioner of every company doing business within Connecticut. The enormous importance of the insurance industry to Hartford has been demonstrated anew by the recent decision of the Travelers and the Phoenix Mutual to erect huge buildings in the city's new downtown redevelopment area. In 1959, according to Alfred N. Premo, State Insurance Commissioner, insurance companies poured about $250,000,000 into the overall economy of the state.[76]

Diversification of Industry

ONE of the major characteristics of Connecticut's industry has been its great diversification, running the gamut from pins to helicopters. Skilled craftsmanship has always been Connecticut's answer to a glaring lack of natural resources. In many fields, such as silverware, hats, and clocks, Connecticut

TOP: *The Travelers first "home office" (from 1864 on) — two rooms on second floor of second building (with one prominent chimney), on Main Street, Hartford.* BOTTOM: *The Travelers (today) at 740 Main Street, Hartford.*

Moon's age clock. Made by Daniel Burnap.
(Owned by Philip Hammerslough.)

pioneered. Beginning with Job Prince of Milford and René Grignon of Norwich, both active around 1700, a long line of eighteenth-century silversmiths, numbering in the scores, established a tradition of making fine silverware, including spoons, silver dishes, communion sets, jewelry, and other items. Norwich, New Haven, Middletown, and Hartford were centers for colonial silversmiths, though many also worked in smaller towns.[77]

The modern era in silver making began at Hartford in 1847. Three brothers, Asa, Simeon, and William Rogers, building upon knowledge of methods already used in England, developed in a small cellar a practical method of silver plating. After much experimentation the brothers decided in 1847 that their product should be advertised as Rogers Brothers silver-plated flatware. It found ready public acceptance. In Meriden a group of manufacturers specializing in britannia ware formed the Meriden Britannia Company in 1852. Their product, "britannia," was a silver-white alloy consisting of tin, antimony, and copper. In 1862 this company acquired Rogers Brothers, who then moved to Meriden. Several decades of high prosperity in the industry reached a climax with the organization in 1898 of the giant new firm called the International Silver Company, which absorbed most of the important Connecticut silver companies. The other major company still operating in Connecticut is Wallace Silversmiths Company of Wallingford, which now employs about 1,000 persons in making flatware and hollow ware, both sterling and plated. The International Silver Company concentrated on vital military contracts during World War II, but it quickly returned to its original work afterward. Today it employs approximately 4,000 persons and turns out a varied line of sterling and silver-plated flatware and hollow ware as well as stainless steel. Connecticut ranks first in the United States in the value of its silverware and plated ware.[78]

In clockmaking, likewise, Connecticut has held a pre-eminent place. Eli Terry of East Windsor did for clockmaking what Eli Whitney had done for the small-arms industry. As a youth Terry served as an apprentice to Daniel Burnap, a very skilled and dedicated craftsman who had learned the business from Thomas Harland of Norwich. Terry launched his own shop at Plymouth in 1793, making both brass and wooden clocks, which, with a case, retailed at eighteen to eighty dollars, the brass clocks being more expensive. Acting as his own salesman, Terry strapped one clock in each saddlebag, one forward of the saddle and one back, and set forth in search of customers. As business improved he erected a building on a small stream where a wheel provided water power. Inventing new machinery to which the power could be applied, he signed a contract to make 4,000 clocks — a number so large that contemporaries ridiculed him. Most of the first year was devoted to improving the machinery, but the second year saw about 1,000 clocks completed, the third year 3,000 more. Thus mass production of clocks was introduced.[79]

By 1808 Terry was using machine power to perform many steps formerly done by hand. In 1814 he introduced the short, or shelf, clock and obtained a patent for it in 1816. This thirty-hour wood-movement clock, with later improvements, became so popular at the lower prices then possible that Terry amassed a large fortune from their manufacture. In first applying the system of interchangeable parts to clockmaking, Terry paved the way for others to exploit more fully the enormous potential national market.[80]

The clock industry was further revolutionized by the development of the cheap brass clock. Between 1818 and 1832 Joseph Ives of Bristol carried on the basic experiments resulting in a workable, eight-day, rolled-brass movement. Chauncey and Noble Jerome soon realized the great commercial possibilities of the cheaper and superior brass clock. Profitable production, however, required large concentrations of capital, mass production, and expanded markets. In the 1850's the American industry was dominated by four Connecticut firms: Seth Thomas of Plymouth, William L. Gilbert of Winsted, E. N. Welch of Bristol, and the New Haven Clock Company of New Haven, which together produced about 400,000 rolled-brass clocks in the single year of 1855.[81]

A century later Connecticut still ranked among the leading clock manufacturing states. Five of the companies organized in the first half of the nineteenth century still operate: William L. Gilbert Company of Winsted (organized by Riley Whiting in 1807), Seth Thomas of Thomaston (1813 — now a division of General Time Instruments), New Haven Clock Company (1824), Sessions Clock Company of Forestville (1833), and the E. Ingraham Company of Bristol (1842). Contemporary major clock and timing producers are General Electric Company of Bridgeport, Waterbury Clock Company (now a division of U. S. Time Corporation), and Lux Clock Manufacturing Company of Waterbury. In 1939 there were 7,563 employed in the industry; in 1947, 10,552; and in 1954, 7,220. Most companies have widened their production to include timing instruments of various types. Commemorating the state's great clockmaking tradition is the famous clock museum at Bristol containing Connecticut clocks of several centuries.[82]

The extreme inventiveness of Connecticut citizens has been remarkable. From the beginning of the American patent system in 1790 to the 1930's Connecticut regularly led all states in the number of patents granted relative to population. Since the 1930's Connecticut has slipped slightly to third place, but the 1959 figure of one patent per 1,556 persons was far better than the national average of one per 3,808 persons. The list of epochal inventions is almost endless, and only a few can be cited. Charles Goodyear's vulcanizing process tamed rubber and made its use practical. Eli Whitney Blake, a nephew of Eli Whitney, developed a stone-crusher which revolutionized road building. Francis A. Pratt and Amos Whitney founded a company for making machine tools and trained a whole generation of toolmakers, many of whom founded new companies elsewhere. Through the development of a "standard inch" Pratt and Whitney opened the way for its standard measuring machine, accurate to .00001 of an inch. In its new museum the century-old West Hartford company now displays such mechanical marvels as a numerically controlled jig borer; a numerically controlled Keller (milling) machine, which can make large dies with unbelievable accuracy; numerically controlled rotary tables; and tape-controlled turret lathes. Major inventions today are more likely to stem from large research programs

The Nautilus, *world's first nuclear-powered submarine. Built by General Dynamics Corporation's Electric Boat Division at Groton.*

manned by teams of experts rather than from the efforts of a solitary genius. Engineers at the Pratt and Whitney Division of United Aircraft at East Hartford, for instance, recently have developed several types of extremely powerful engines for jet aircraft. At Maromas, near Middletown, other scientists are working on an atomic aircraft engine. Connecticut thus remains in the forefront of the technological revolution of the mid-twentieth century.[83]

POSTWAR ECONOMIC GROWTH[84]
as Reflected in
Total Value Added by Manufacturing

	1947	1954	1958
Durable Goods Industries			
Transportation equipment	$120,142,000	$432,597,000	$619,968,000
Machinery, except electrical	384,826,000	568,320,000	575,743,000
Electrical machinery	166,134,000	247,798,000	288,086,000
Fabricated metals	244,876,000	283,477,000	311,284,000
Primary metals	164,506,000	218,461,000	230,490,000
Instruments and related products	83,973,000	105,796,000	126,223,000
Stone, clay, and glass products	28,473,000	32,683,000	51,389,000
Lumber and wood products	5,494,000	8,640,000	8,825,000
Nondurable Goods			
Food and related products	44,380,000	95,462,000	129,207,000
Chemicals	52,329,000	125,565,000	127,113,000
Textiles and mill products	174,497,000	139,481,000	120,448,000
Printing and publishing	67,081,000	92,163,000	112,596,000
Rubber products	56,266,000	94,207,000	103,667,000
Apparel and related products	60,938,000	74,726,000	80,891,000
Pulp and paper products	41,446,000	61,112,000	68,795,000
Furniture and fixtures	8,918,000	15,279,000	25,369,000
Leather and leather goods	6,358,000	9,655,000	12,037,000
Petroleum and coal products	(not available)	5,633,000	3,750,000
TOTAL	$1,896,711,000	$2,877,486,000	$3,219,770,000

336

Religion and Education in Modern Connecticut

The Congregational Church Since 1818 — Brief Sketch of the Protestant Episcopal
Church — Baptists, Methodists, and Other Protestant Sects — Rise and Expansion of the
Roman Catholic Church — The Jews in Connecticut — Henry Barnard Symbolizes Growing
Interest in the Public Schools — Academies and High Schools — The State Board of
Education and State-wide Educational Problems — Connecticut's Preparatory Schools
— Development of a Catholic School System — The "Collegiate School" Evolves into
Yale College — Yale's Development into a National University — Trinity, Wesleyan,
Connecticut College for Women, and Other Institutions — Impressive Growth of The
University of Connecticut

The Congregational Church Since 1818

AFTER the disestablishment of the Congregational Church in 1818, it was forced to work thenceforth on its own. Congregational clergy, fearing a general slump in religion, a sharp growth in other sects, and the fall of their own church, launched a striking revival during the next few years. Many churches reported sharp increases in membership. Spearheading the revival was the Reverend Lyman Beecher of Litchfield, a stirring evangelist, who preached tirelessly throughout the state and won many converts.[1]

In a few years a serious challenge to Congregationalism arose from its liberal wing in Massachusetts, the Unitarians. The election of a liberal candidate in 1805 as professor of divinity at Harvard occurred despite the bitter opposition of conservatives led by Jedidiah Morse (Yale, 1783). The Unitarians emphasized the "unity" of God, rejected the Holy Trinity, and declared that no man was inevitably damned. By the 1820's many leading Massachusetts Congregational churches had gone over to Unitarianism. When Unitarian ministers invaded Connecticut, Beecher and other

orthodox clergy struck back hard and effectively. A Unitarian church was set up at Hartford about 1830, but by 1850 the *Connecticut Register* listed only three Unitarian ministers in Connecticut. Congregationalism still was far too firmly established to yield much ground.[2]

Although Beecher did not advocate the popular preaching style of Baptists and Methodists, he did urge Congregational clergy to give up the dull pedantic preaching then in vogue and indulge in some emotional exhortation. The Reverend Joel Hawes of Hartford's First Church well exemplified a growing tendency toward dealing in simple language with everyday problems. This approach strengthened the bonds between pastor and church members. About 1830 Professor Nathaniel W. Taylor of Yale threatened a schism by offering a milder sort of Calvinism, which denied that God was the author of sin and rejected the doctrine of election. Taylor believed that man is responsible for his personal sins and his salvation; therefore he depends on his own free choice of good or evil. Taylor's avowed purpose was to train for the ministry young men capable of defeating Unitarianism and winning converts to liberalized Congrega-

337

tionalism. He quickly ran into vigorous opposition from most orthodox clergy. As a result, the conservatives founded a new theological seminary at East Windsor, which later developed into the Hartford Theological Seminary. In 1840 the Reverend Leonard Bacon penned a strong appeal to Congregationalists to take a tolerant view of their differences and not allow a serious schism to occur. None did, and Congregationalism remained the most influential Connecticut sect for several more decades.[3]

Later in the century Connecticut Congregationalists found a leader, Horace Bushnell, who gained national renown and influence. In 1847 his first book, *Views of Christian Nurture*, appeared. In it he attacked the Calvinistic teachings concerning the depravity of children and stated the simple proposition "that the child is to grow up a Christian, and never know himself as being otherwise." Bushnell felt strongly that with the proper family training a child could eventually enter into religious experience without any great suffering. In a rather mystical second book, *God in Christ* (1849), he carried his ideas further and so enraged the conservatives that they wanted to try him as a heretic. Bushnell's *Vicarious Sacrifice* (1866) represented a sort of culmination of his own religious experiences and thinking. In this work he enunciated his moral-influence theory, which stated that men are saved not by a legal transaction but by a spiritual living union with God through Christ.[4]

More of a prophet and preacher than a deep theologian, Bushnell's influence on Protestantism in general, on many young preachers, and especially on religious education, was profound. The Young People's Society of Christian Endeavor, organized by the Reverend Francis E. Clark and enlisting thousands of young people, owed much of its original inspiration to Bushnell. He influenced several great Sunday-school leaders. Likewise, the more rational approach to foreign missions owed much to Bushnell's criticisms of the contrasting methods so popular earlier. Luther Weigle, of the Yale Divinity School, evaluated Bushnell's leadership in these terms:

The modern movement for the better religious education of children owes more to Horace Bushnell, doubt-less, than to any other one man. His "Christian Nurture" was in sober truth an epoch-making book. In it he sharply criticized the extreme individualism, the reliance upon emotional revivals, and the one-sided supernaturalism which had characterized the thought and practice of American churches throughout the second half of the eighteenth and the first half of the nineteenth centuries; and he vindicated for childhood its normal place in the Kingdom of God, and for the family its function as the instrument, by God's grace, of Christian nurture.

It was very appropriate that Hartford citizens decided in 1876, just before Bushnell's death, to name in his honor the large park below the new capitol, which he had conceived and made a reality.[5]

Another religious development of great importance in nineteenth-century Connecticut was the rise and expansion of the Sunday-school movement, which began around 1820. In 1824 the Connecticut Sunday School Union was organized as an auxiliary of the American Sunday School Union. In 1826 the General Association of Congregational churches recommended that every church should establish a Sunday school. Nathaniel Taylor and Timothy Dwight were leaders in the new state Union. By 1830 there were two hundred active Sunday schools, with 4,470 officers and teachers and 23,825 students. Study materials and special libraries were developed for the children. Many pupils, moved by the "revivals" of the period, joined the church. Connecticut as a whole contributed substantially to the interdenominational national program of the American Sunday School Union. In the late 1850's Henry Clay Trumbull, in the position of Sabbath-school missionary for Connecticut, generated great interest in reviving older Sunday schools and stimulating establishment of new ones. In 1861 he reported 914 Sunday schools, 13,366 teachers, and 84,697 students. By that time Sunday schools, with the blessing of churches and public schools, had clearly assumed the function of religious education outside the home.[6]

It is interesting to compare 1859 statistics for the Congregationalists with those of a century later. In 1859 there were 284 churches with 47,109 members. In 1959 the Congregational Christian Churches (united in 1931) had 136,955 members, served by 264 pastors. As in the past, it remains the largest of the Protestant sects in Connecticut.[7]

Brief Sketch of the Protestant Episcopal Church

AS was seen earlier, the Anglicans, many of whom were Loyalists, suffered much persecution in Revolutionary days. With the war's end, ten of the fourteen Episcopal clergymen in Connecticut met in March 1783 at the Glebe House in Woodbury to choose their candidate as head of an American episcopacy. When their first choice, Jeremiah Leaming, declined because of inadequate health, the group named Samuel Seabury, a Groton native, who had been chaplain of a Loyalist regiment during the war. After cooling his heels in England for many months while English bishops hesitated over the propriety and legality of consecrating him, Seabury journeyed to Scotland. There he received a cordial reception, and on November 14, 1784, he was consecrated by three nonjuring Scottish bishops.[8]

Under Bishop Seabury's leadership the Episcopal Church expanded steadily, with new churches appearing at East and Middle Haddam, Portland, Granby, Southington, East Plymouth, Harwinton, Northfield, Bethany, East Haven, Hamden, and Meriden. In 1789, Seabury actively participated in a general convention at Philadelphia, where the Protestant Episcopal Church in the United States was formally established as a national church. In 1794 provision was made for an Episcopal school in Connecticut, and two years later John Bowden was chosen principal. That same year Bishop Seabury suddenly died. In his eleven years as bishop he had presided courageously and effectively over a Church which had grown considerably despite general popular dislike. The fact that so many Anglicans had been Loyalists during the Revolution had nourished popular suspicions of the Episcopal Church. These sentiments did not weaken markedly until after the War of 1812.[9]

A diocesan convention chose the Reverend Abraham Jarvis of Middletown as successor to Seabury. Although the Church continued to grow steadily, by 1808 it had only twenty-six clergy to care for seventy-three parishes. Meanwhile strenuous efforts had resulted in actual incorporation and launching of its school as the Episcopal Academy of Connecticut. By 1819 it had sixty students, and twenty-eight graduates were Episcopal cler-

gymen. As already seen, the Episcopalians joined wholeheartedly in the successful battle to overturn the Standing Order in 1817–18 and insure a new constitution guaranteeing separation of church and state. The new outlook was dramatically illustrated when Governor Wolcott asked an Episcopal clergyman, the Reverend Harry Cros-

St. Michael's Episcopal Church, Litchfield.

well of Trinity Church, New Haven, to preach the election sermon in 1818.[10]

After the death of Bishop Jarvis in 1813, the Church had experienced a trying period of uncertainty until the selection of Thomas C. Brownell as bishop in 1819. Under his far-seeing direction the Episcopal Church registered impressive growth in size and influence. Doctrinal differences and religious revivals occurred during Bishop Brownell's long tenure, but the Church continued to grow. His primary role in founding and heading the new Washington College will be discussed later. During his first twenty-five years as bishop, Brownell ordained 120 priests and 125 deacons, consecrated 66 churches, and confirmed 11,353 persons. Since the bishop was growing old, his request for an assistant was granted. In 1851 the Reverend John Williams was chosen for the position. When Trinity College's theological department was separated and moved to Middletown, Bishop Williams took over leadership of the institution, known as the Berkeley Divinity School. In 1865 the death of Bishop Brownell ended an era which had seen expansion from a weak, struggling band of 40 scattered clergy, ministering to small flocks, to a strong Church with about 12,500 communicants and 150 clergy. Missionary and charitable contributions ran over $200,000 yearly.[11]

During the near century since Brownell passed away, the Episcopal Church has strengthened its position as the second largest of Protestant groups in Connecticut. By the early 1930's the Church had 220 clergy ministering to almost 60,000 members. In December 1959, under Bishop Walter H. Gray, total membership numbered 129,337. From the birth of the Episcopal Church at the Glebe House to the present the Church in Connecticut has placed major emphasis on complete separation of church and state, social welfare, church schools, loyal citizenship, overseas missions, and a well-educated clergy. Since 1886, Episcopalians have been leaders in the drive for Church union, though their insistence upon episcopacy has so far proven an insurmountable obstacle to union with any other major American Protestant group. In common with other denominations the Church is deeply concerned with ministering to the "unchurched" and to those of its own communion who constantly are moving into Connecticut.[12]

Baptists, Methodists, and Other Protestant Sects

DESPITE the presence of an Established Church up to 1818, the Baptists already were strongly entrenched in the colony long before the Revolution broke out. The first Baptist society was that set up at Groton in 1705. Thanks chiefly to the Great Awakening, the number of Baptist churches between 1740 and shortly before the Revolution jumped from four to twelve.[13]

After the Revolution the democracy of the Baptists and their uneducated clergy appealed powerfully to those of humble rank in country and town. By 1800 they were estimated to have fifty-nine societies and 4,663 members; and by 1820, seventy-three societies and 7,503 communicants. With the coming of religious freedom under the constitution of 1818, the Baptists still found large expansion difficult — partly because their creed called for public baptism by complete immersion, a rite which large elements of the populace found unacceptable. In 1823 the Baptist State Convention was established, but the Church in Connecticut remained largely unconcerned with the problem of educating its ministry. The only educational step taken was the establishment in 1835 of an academy at Suffield called the Connecticut Literary Institute, intended primarily for very poor students. The Baptists used an evangelical approach which appealed primarily to country people. As country districts lost population the Baptist Convention was hard pressed to keep some of its rural churches alive. The *Register* for 1848 put the Baptists in second place numerically among all sects, with 18,061 members, 746 baptisms, 109 churches, and 96 pastors and stated supplies. By 1860 the Convention reported 117 churches, 90 pastors, 18,358 members, and 2,067 baptisms. The failure of the Church to grow, despite a baptism rate almost three times that of 1848, may have resulted mostly from the steady depopulation of rural areas and continued heavy migration out of the state. In 1890, Baptists numbered 22,600; 1916 — 26,243; 1936 — 26,521 white and 6,626 Negro; and 1959 — 36,054.[14]

The fourth of the major Protestant sects in Connecticut, the Methodists, appeared rather late. In May 1789 the Methodist Conference appointed Jesse Lee to the "Stamford Circuit" in Connecticut — the start of organized Methodism here. He quickly organized a circuit for preaching, and at Stamford established the first Connecticut Methodist society. Later that year Lee started a society at Redding. He preached at New London in September 1789 and June 1790, and Francis Asbury, first American Methodist bishop, was there in 1791. Their labors led to organization in 1793 of a New London preaching circuit and a local society. The New London society flourished, enjoyed a highly emotional revival in 1808, and had 321 members by 1819. The aggressive tactics of Methodist preachers resulted in much petty persecution by authorities. Some magistrates refused to acknowledge Methodist preachers as legitimate pastors, and one was fined for performing a marriage ceremony. Despite such persecution, the Methodists claimed 1,201 members by 1796. To the Established ministers, the uneducated exhorters, frequent camp meetings, and other highly emotional phenomena seemed revolutionary. Thomas Robbins observed that the "Methodists go great lengths in fanaticism." Fully aware of Congregational opposition, the Methodists enthusiastically joined Baptists and Episcopalians in the battle for disestablishment.[15]

By 1818 the Methodists had organized over fifty societies in all counties and parts of the state. Thirty years later the *Register* gave the Methodists 111 churches and 14,069 communicants. While the Church in Connecticut did not enjoy growth comparable to that in the South and West, it did climb past the Baptists into third place among Protestant sects. The religious census figures were : 1890 — 30,815; 1916 — 41,090; 1936 — 45,640; and 1959 — 51,966 (estimate). In their recent history, Connecticut Methodists have shared in the trends and movements which have characterized Protestants as a whole, including the battle between Fundamentalism and Modernism, the social gospel, peace movements, and interdenominationalism.[16]

Among the important small Protestant sects were the Universalists, who long preceded Unitarians in boldly challenging the Established Church. Universalists rejected Calvinist doctrines of eternal punishment and stressed such beliefs as the love and eternal fatherhood of God, the mission of Jesus as reconciler of man to God, the certainty of punishment for sin, and the final salvation of all souls. As early as 1792, Universalism appeared in Southington, where a society soon was organized. The movement generally scored its greatest successes among rural and small-town inhabitants. It won many unchurched persons as well as some Baptists. The orthodox ridiculed Universalism, and the Assembly in 1820 rejected a

lottery plan to raise funds for a Universalist church. Nevertheless, the *Register* for 1829 listed four Universalist ministers in the state, while that for 1848 gave eighteen ministers and thirty-one societies. In the many decades since then the Universalists have remained a small sect, having only ten active clergymen in 1960.[17]

The appearance of many other religious sects since 1818 undoubtedly has been greatly influenced by the heavy immigration which has brought in persons of diverse faiths. The largest Protestant denomination not already discussed is the Lutheran — actually there are at least seven separate Lutheran sects in Connecticut — totaling over 46,000 members in 1952. Since the Lutheran Church is strongest in Germany and Scandinavia, it is probable that a large percentage of members have immediate or distant backgrounds from those areas. Beyond the Lutherans, the Protestant picture is a very scattered one, with most sects numbering adherents only in the hundreds. Mention should be made also of the presence of the Armenian Orthodox Church, the Russian Orthodox Greek Catholic Church, the Polish National Catholic Church, the Greek Orthodox Church, and the Ukrainian Catholic Church. The Salvation Army also maintains clergy and an active program in the principal cities. The Church of Christ, Scientist has churches in nearly thirty Connecticut cities. Thus Connecticut, in accord with the Federal and state constitutional principle of freedom of religion, affords its citizens the right to worship freely as each sees fit.[18]

Rise and Expansion of the Roman Catholic Church

LONG before there was an organized Catholic Church in Connecticut there were Catholics here. It is certain that a few Catholic Irishmen, such as John Dyer of Windsor, a fighter in the Pequot War, came to the infant colony. The first Catholic priest recorded as visiting Connecticut was a Jesuit, Father Gabriel Druillettes, who was engaged in a diplomatic mission for the government of New France. He visited New Haven in September 1651 and may well have celebrated Mass there. The presence of twenty-one Irish names among New

Haven settlers in 1639–45 suggests the early arrival of a few Catholics. In colonial records one finds Irish in small numbers scattered through all parts of Connecticut. From early times New London seems to have had the largest percentage of persons of non-English and often of Catholic faith,

Church of the Holy Trinity, Hartford, the first Catholic church in Connecticut.

including some Spanish. A few Irish were transported to Connecticut as convicts or as redemptioners. The latter, too poor to pay for passage, were required to serve a master here for a specified term of years, perhaps three or four. As already seen, several hundred Acadian Catholic exiles lived in Connecticut for some time also.[19]

During the Revolution the excellent behavior of French (Catholic) troops in Connecticut during

marches across the state, as well as in winter encampments, undoubtedly tended to reduce anti-Catholic feeling. Connecticut Revolutionary records reveal that many Irish Catholics served the American cause. Not until 1789, however, did American Catholics have a bishop. In that year the Right Reverend John Carroll was appointed bishop to the new see of Baltimore, which included Connecticut in its far-flung jurisdiction. In 1791 Bishop Carroll visited New London, where the local Catholics warmly welcomed him. In 1808 the diocese of Boston was created to include all of New England. The new bishop was John Cheverus, a native of Brittany, a noted scholar, and a profoundly moving orator. In May 1823 Bishop Cheverus celebrated Mass in the State House. From Hartford he went to New Haven and New London. Events in France led to the assignment of Bishop Cheverus to a see in his native country — a transfer greatly mourned by all Catholics and many Protestants in New England. William Ellery Channing, famous Unitarian minister, wrote glowingly of Bishop Cheverus' devoted and able ministry to his small and scattered flock.[20]

Bishop Benedict J. Fenwick, Cheverus' successor, assigned Father Robert D. Woodley as a resident priest to cover all of Rhode Island and Connecticut. Meanwhile the building of the Enfield Canal and other economic developments gradually brought increasing numbers of Irish Catholics. In July 1829 Bishop Fenwick came to Hartford to purchase a church which the Episcopalians had outgrown. There Episcopal Bishop Brownell and Bishop Fenwick amiably consummated the deal:

"Well, Bishop Fenwick," said Bishop Brownell, "as we have a fine new church building we will let you have the old one."

"Yes, and you have a fine new religion, and we will keep the old one," [replied Bishop Fenwick.]

Almost simultaneously the first Catholic newspaper appeared on July 11, 1829, as the *Catholic Press*, ancestor of the present *Catholic Transcript*. After Bishop Fenwick's visit the first Catholic Sunday school started in the rooms of the *Catholic Press*. Bishop Fenwick moved rapidly to give Hartford its first resident pastor, Father Bernard O'Cavanaugh, who arrived on August 26, 1829. After a short pastorate Father O'Cavanaugh went west, and in 1831 Father James Fitton, an enthusiastic missionary, replaced him.[21]

Under Father Fitton's energetic leadership the Hartford parish, as well as the missionary field of Connecticut, prospered. In September 1832 he obtained as assistant the Reverend James McDermot, who later that year received promotion to a pastorate at New Haven. By 1835 there were an estimated 720 Catholics in Connecticut, and by 1844 over 4,800.[22]

In 1843 Bishop Fenwick's urgent requests for a division of the diocese of Boston resulted in creation of a new diocese of Hartford, with jurisdiction over Connecticut and Rhode Island. On April 12, 1844, the new bishop, the Very Reverend William Tyler, a native of New England, was installed at Hartford. Finding that Providence had a much larger Catholic populace, Bishop Tyler petitioned Rome to have the seat of the diocese moved there, and this was soon effected. Under Tyler the diocese remained small, lacking in priests, and enduring dire poverty. In 1849 Bishop Tyler died, and his successor was Bishop Bernard O'Reilly. By this time Irish immigrants were flocking into Connecticut by the thousands, but they had few priests to serve them. Bishop O'Reilly journeyed to Dublin in 1852 and found several young men willing to serve here. Despite much anti-Catholicism, especially among Know-Nothings, the Church grew steadily until there were twenty-seven churches and twenty-six priests in the mid–1850's.[23]

In the century since Bishop O'Reilly's death the Catholic Church has enjoyed an unparalleled growth. In 1872 the diocese of Hartford was set off from Providence as a separate see, with Francis P. MacFarland as the bishop. Under his leadership St. Joseph's Cathedral was begun, though it was not completed and consecrated until 1892. In 1882 the fraternal society of Catholic men called the Knights of Columbus was incorporated in Connecticut. From here the society spread into every state and many foreign countries. The immigrant flood reached even greater levels in the late 1800's and early 1900's as thousands of Italians, Irish, French-Canadians, Poles, and Slavs settled in Connecticut. In many cases the newcomers preferred priests fluent in their native tongues. A great shortage of priests remained a serious problem, so that those available often worked beyond safe physical limits in serving widely scattered parishioners. By 1890 there were over 150,000 Catholics in Connecticut, or more than the combined membership of all Protestant sects.[24]

Bishop Michael Tierney (1893–1908), devoting special attention to the problem of training priests, decided that the diocese should have its own preparatory seminary. From this seminary graduates could go to advanced seminaries abroad to complete their training and also develop a fluency in the language of many of their future parishioners. In 1898 St. Thomas Seminary opened for classes with thirty-seven students. It has grown steadily until in the fall of 1958 it enrolled 115 young men from Connecticut and 30 from out of state. Through the years many of its graduates have continued their studies at higher seminaries in America and abroad. Another monument to Bishop Tierney's energies is Hartford's St. Francis Hospital, which opened in August 1897, staffed by the Sisters of St. Joseph of Chambery. Just before Bishop Tierney passed away in 1908 he presided over 167 parishes, as against 98 in 1894, and 342 clerics as against 204.[25]

Under successive bishops — John J. Nelan (1910–34), Maurice M. McAuliffe (1934–44), and Henry J. O'Brien (1945–   ) — the steady growth of the Church has continued unabated. In 1953 Hartford was made an archdiocese, flanked by the diocese of Bridgeport (Bishop Lawrence J. Shehan), and the diocese of Norwich (Bishop Bernard J. Flanagan). Recent official Catholic statistics give these totals:

JANUARY 1, 1960

	Active Clergy	Parishes	Members
Archdiocese of Hartford	634	183	705,225
Diocese of Bridgeport	303	73	278,876
Diocese of Norwich	184	60	154,560
Total	1,121	316	1,138,661

These figures indicate that in Connecticut there are more Catholics than members of all other sects combined.[26]

On December 31, 1956, one of the most spectacular fires in modern Connecticut's history swept St. Joseph's Cathedral, Hartford, and gutted the huge brownstone structure. Experts found the

of New York's Jewish colony, Assur Levy, traveled to Hartford to plead for a fellow Jew, Jacob Lucena, a trader who had become seriously involved with the law. As a result, the General Court in a token of respect for Levy reduced the fine from ten pounds to five; originally it had been twenty pounds.[28]

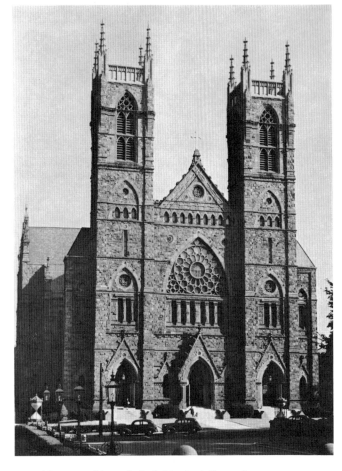

Old St. Joseph's Cathedral, Hartford (burned December 1956).

Artist's drawing of the new St. Joseph's Cathedral (under construction).

shell left in unsafe condition, so a new cathedral is now rising on the same site.[27]

The Jews in Connecticut

NO Jew is recorded in colonial Connecticut until November 9, 1659, when "David the Jew" appears in the legislative records. A little later, a Hartford town meeting of September 2, 1661, voted that the Jews presently living at John Marsh's house could continue there for seven months. In 1670 a leader

British occupation of New York City and Newport during the Revolution caused a few Jewish families to flee into the supposed safety of Fairfield County. At Stratford there were soon enough adult men (ten) to hold a religious service. Other refugees settled at Stamford, Norwalk, Danbury, and Wilton. A distinguished company gathered at Norwalk, including Samson Mears and Solomon Simson, merchants, Myer Myers, silversmith, and Asher Myers, coppersmith. To a limited degree Mears managed to continue trade with Aaron

Lopez, famous Rhode Island merchant. Tryon's invasion of Norwalk in 1779 caused heavy losses to the Jews in the area — depredations vividly described by Samson Mears in a letter to Lopez. Another Jew, Michael Judah, a long-time Norwalk merchant, lost disastrously because he trusted and held onto the wartime paper money which eventually became virtually worthless.[29]

Only with the heavy migration of German Jews to the United States in the 1840's did Connecticut begin to receive any substantial numbers. This wave undoubtedly was encouraged by passage of an Assembly act in 1843 giving Jews the complete freedom of worship already accorded all Christians in the 1818 constitution. The scattering of Spanish and Portuguese (Sephardic) Jews already in Connecticut soon were swamped by the German influx. The Jewish community in Hartford, which first assumed large importance in the 1840's, affords an excellent case study. In July 1847 the Congregation Beth Israel was formed, and by 1851 it boasted fifty members and twenty-five pupils in its religious school. In 1856 the congregation acquired the former First Baptist Church and renamed it Touro Hall. Isaac Mayer, the first rabbi, was a prominent Hartfordian who also served many years as drama critic of the Hartford *Times*.[30]

Some of the Hartford Jewish community in 1851 established the Ararat Lodge of B'nai B'rith, an international Jewish brotherhood, both social and benevolent in nature. Membership carried with it warm fellowship as well as certain definite assistance in time of illness or death. Aid was often also sent to persecuted Jews abroad. Meetings were marked by democratic and often heated discussion. As new immigrants poured into the city the lodge helped them to get settled and adjusted to their new environment. In recent years B'nai B'rith has developed new programs, such as the Hillel Foundations on over two hundred college campuses and the Anti-Defamation Leagues.[31]

Almost from the start Jews became prominent in Hartford's business life. From the Hartford city directories of 1850 and thereabouts, one finds Jews active as merchants, peddlers, grocers, butchers, barbers, bookkeepers, watch repairers, clerks, tailors, tobacconists, opticians, horse dealers,

nurses, and boardinghouse proprietors. In 1847 Gershon Fox opened a small store which by painstaking direction and scrupulous honesty he built into a mercantile landmark before his death in 1880. Descendants have further expanded the store until today G. Fox and Company is the largest independently owned department store in the world.[32]

The Americanization of the German Jews proceeded rapidly. In 1857 one of the two Jewish schools was still giving instruction in German as well as Hebrew; but after 1873 the city directory listed only a Hebrew-English school. Jews also began to join numerous American social organizations such as the Odd Fellows and the Masons. During the Civil War one frequently heard special prayers for the Union's safety offered in Beth Israel Synagogue. In politics, too, Jews occasionally won election to the City Council. For the New Haven area, Jacob Ullman became Republican "boss" in the early twentieth century. In 1932 Herman P. Kopplemann was elected congressman from the First (Hartford) District and secured reelection several times. In 1954 Abraham A. Ribicoff of Hartford was the first Jew elected governor — an honor repeated in his landslide victory of 1958.[33]

In the 1880's a radical change in Jewish immigration began. From Lithuania, Russia, the Ukraine, Poland, Hungary, Rumania, and Galicia, Jews fled from bitter persecution and often grinding poverty to seek a better life here. So great was this tide that the east European Jews in Hartford by 1910 outnumbered the earlier German group by five to one. The newcomers tended to cluster together according to ethnic background. As a result, there was a Polish synagogue, a Lithuanian synagogue, a Ukrainian synagogue, and so forth. Recent refugees from Nazi Germany formed their synagogue, Tikvah Hadasha ("New Hope"). The east European arrivals, along with their faith and their dreams, brought a host of skills. From Pinsk in Russia came expert furriers Samuel Glotzer and Julius Bassevitz, who quickly established a sound fur trade. The newcomers formed a variety of social, charitable, and religious organizations, as well as the Hartford Yeshiva, a day school.[34]

The diverse ethnic groups required time to

learn how to work together, but as the newer arrivals became better adjusted co-operation increased. In 1912 the United Jewish Charities was organized to administer more efficiently a wide variety of welfare activities. It started with a budget of $8,000 — a decided contrast to the 1959

raised millions of dollars for Jewish colonization in Palestine. At one mass meeting in May 1921, attended by Albert Einstein and Chaim Weizmann, $75,000 was raised. After World War II, in 1945, the State of Israel became a reality. Immediately it had to fight the Arabs to maintain its very exist-

Temple Beth Israel, Hartford.

budget of the Jewish Social Service of Hartford, amounting to $107,558.91. A current area of this vital co-operative Jewish effort is represented by the Hartford Jewish Federation.[35]

In the present century Hartford has been a center of Zionism, the movement to create a Jewish state in Palestine. After a Jewish congress in Switzerland in 1897 the Zionist movement spread quickly to this country. In Hartford a few Zionists early organized the B'nai Zion Society to work for the cause. World War I helped focus attention on Palestine and encouraged Hartford Zionists. Abraham Goldstein was appointed state director for the Zionist movement, and his dynamic leadership helped make Connecticut a leading contributor. Hartford provided the genesis of the Keren Hayesod (Foundation Fund), which was adopted nationally in 1921 and since then has

ence. From the beginning, Connecticut Jewry has contributed generously in helping the new nation to get on its feet. The Hartford office for the State of Israel bonds has sold about $10,000,000 in bonds since 1948.[36]

Today the Jewish community in the Hartford area is the largest in Connecticut, numbering nearly 30,000 persons. There are sixteen synagogues, representing the Orthodox, Conservative, and Reform branches of Judaism. As Jews, in common with all Americans, move increasingly to suburbs, they form close to their new homes a new congregation, often the "child" of a city congregation. In that sense Emanuel Synagogue (Conservative), for example, can claim seven "children." The Jews of Hartford increasingly have worked together not only for Jewish causes, such as the Hartford Jewish Federation, but also for community, state, and national causes of all kinds. The Jewish record for organized social welfare work and for philanthropy has been so outstanding as to influence strongly Americans as a whole. The chief problem of the contemporary Jew, as it appears to some spokesmen, is how to preserve the traditional spiritual values of their religion and their way of life and at the same time make the maximum contribution to the spiritual and general welfare of their nation and society.[37]

The evolution of the Hartford Jewish community has been paralleled by that of Jewish groups in many other Connecticut cities and towns. In New London, for instance, there existed the same general immigration pattern — first, a handful of Sephardic Jews (1654–1825); second, German Jews (1825–76); third, Russian, Polish, and Rumanian Jews, in the largest wave (1881–1914); and fourth, refugees from Nazi oppression (1933 and on). The most unusual aspect of the New London community is that many of its members are descended from Russian-Jewish dairymen who first settled at Chesterfield, ten miles away. Mostly dairy farmers, they organized a congregation at Chesterfield in 1892. Eventually the poor soil and other factors led most of them to move to New London or Norwich. A similar dairying community of Russian Jews at Colchester — begun in 1893

with some initial help from the Baron de Hirsch Fund — created a profitable dairying industry. There are still Jewish dairy farmers active in Colchester. The majority of the Jewish farmers in Connecticut, however, have turned to poultry raising in recent years.[38]

As in other states, the three principal branches of Judaism are well represented. The latest available Connecticut figures show this division: 1] Orthodox congregations: twenty-eight; 2] Conservative congregations: thirty affiliated with United Synagogue of America and having estimated family membership of about 8,000 (perhaps 28,000 individuals), also eight to ten Conservative congregations not affiliated; 3] Reform congregations: fourteen (nine affiliated with the Union of American Hebrew Congregations) with a total membership (August 1, 1960) of 3,400 families, or 11,900 individuals. The 1960 Jewish Year Book estimates the total Jewish population in Connecticut at just under 100,000 living in over thirty communities. According to the same source the ten largest Jewish communities are as follows: Hartford, 26,000; New Haven, 20,000; Bridgeport, 14,000; Stamford, 7,500; Norwalk, 4,900; Waterbury, 4,700; New London, 3,000; New Britain and Norwich, 2,500 apiece; and Westport, 2,450.[39]

GENERAL TREND IN MEMBERSHIP OF THE CHIEF SECTS[40]

CHURCH	1890	1906	1916	1926	1936	Latest Estimate 1959
Leading Protestant						
Congregational (to 1931)	59,154	65,657	71,244	81,142	—	—
Congregational Christian (from 1931)	—	—	—	—	87,790	136,955
Protestant Episcopal	26,652	37,466	48,854	89,434	83,317	129,337
Methodist	30,815	34,603	38,650	41,323	45,640	51,966
Baptist	22,600	27,834	26,243	28,391	33,147	36,054
Roman Catholic	152,945	352,368	483,834	557,747	635,750	1,138,661
Jewish Congregations	1,621	1,733	8,688	90,165	90,614	99,100

Henry Barnard Symbolizes Growing
Interest in the Public Schools

IN the 1790's Connecticut entered a new era in its educational system as a result of two revolutionary pieces of legislation. The first, in 1795, as previously explained, set aside the income from sale of lands in the Western Reserve as a perpetual Connecticut School Fund. In 1798 the Assembly transferred control of the schools from the ecclesiastical society of the town to a new and distinct unit, the school society. This society was authorized to "Institute a School of a higher Order for the Common benefit of all the Inhabitants . . ." — phraseology which foreshadowed the rise of the high school. Latin and Greek no longer were required but could be offered "on particular desire."[41]

Although the new system appeared to have important advantages, in practice it worked badly. Many school societies regarded the School Fund as a means of avoiding local taxation rather than as a way of improving the schools. Public opinion generally seemed indifferent to the quality of education provided. At a teachers' convention in Hartford in 1830 Heman Humphrey, president of Amherst, declared that a doubling of expenditures was required to provide "a tolerable education." The next year Governor Peters noted that public apathy, inadequate teachers, and parental indifference had caused serious damage to the common schools. The Assembly, however, turned a deaf ear to his recommendation for a small tax to benefit the school districts. In 1836 Governor Edwards' annual message emphasized the lack of qualified teachers, those "capable of communicating, as well as learning."[42]

At the end of 1836 the state came into a windfall when a budget surplus of the Federal government was divided among the states. The legislature divided Connecticut's share among the towns and provided that one-half of the income from said fund in each town (known as the town deposit fund) should be used for education. In 1837 the legislature asked that the school visitors prepare a report on conditions in every school society. As a result 104 out of 211 societies submitted reports the next year. The picture which emerged was shocking: 1] parents exhibited very little interest in the public schools; 2] teachers were poorly qualified and received only an average of $14.50 monthly for men and $5.75 monthly for women (exclusive of board); 3] many school committees and visitors failed to perform their duties; 4] a hodgepodge of books was used; 5] many schoolhouses were poorly constructed and equipped; 6] many school-age children were not in school — probably at least 6,000 of them; 7] in most towns a private school operated, and these private schools, serving less than 10,000 children of the wealthier classes, cost more than was appropriated for the other 60,000 to 70,000 children in the state.[43]

On the basis of this report the legislature passed an act "for the better supervision of Common Schools." This established a board of commissioners for common schools, which had to submit an annual report to the Assembly on the condition of each common school and educational progress in general. The board could require detailed information from local school societies. On the basis of information collected the board would make recommendations for future improvements.[44]

The new board chose as its first secretary Henry Barnard, the legislator responsible for introducing the new education bill. A Hartford native, Yale graduate (1830), and lawyer by profession, Barnard brought enormous energy and high vision to the new position. In a determined drive to lift Connecticut teachers out of their provincialism, Barnard began publication of the *Connecticut Common School Journal*. In 1839 he sponsored a state teachers' convention in Hartford, and later in the year a teachers' institute. Though he won approval of the board for establishment of a normal school, this and other major plans were wrecked by the Assembly's frankly partisan political action of 1843 in repealing much of the basic 1839 act. Undaunted by this stunning setback, Barnard accepted a comparable position in Rhode Island, where he effected substantial improvements in the public schools. Connecticut's legislators, undergoing a change of heart in 1849, appropriated a small sum to establish a normal school at New Britain, which actually opened its doors to thirty-five students on May 15, 1850. Barnard returned as the first principal of this school, as well as superintendent of common schools for the state. After a few years temporary ill health forced his resignation. Later he headed in turn the University of Wisconsin and St. John's College, Maryland. In 1867 he became the first United States Commissioner of Education, a position he held for three years. In the final thirty years of his life he devoted his time to an amazing variety of projects aimed at improvement of public education. For many years he edited as well as wrote voluminously for the *American Journal of Education,* which he had launched in 1855. His influential educational philosophy is well epitomized in his famous saying that the United States should have "schools good enough for the best and cheap enough for the poorest."[45]

Academies and High Schools

AFTER 1800 a new type of college preparatory school, the "academy," began to replace the "grammar" school of the colonial era. The academy usually offered a curriculum of wider scope than the narrow classical one of the grammar school. Thanks to a legacy left by Samuel Staples, the Staples Academy, or "Free School," was founded at North Fairfield in 1781. Another excellent early academy operated at Greenfield Hill from 1783 on, under Timothy Dwight's direction. In eastern Connecticut, academies were founded at Plainfield and Woodstock in 1770 and 1801 respectively. In 1803 one of the state's most famous schools, Bacon Academy in Colchester, was launched. The founder, Pierpont Bacon, stipulated in his will that the school should exist "for the instruction of Youth in Reading, and writing English, in Arithmetic, Mathimaticks, and the languages, or such other branches of Learning as said Inhabitants shall direct." The academy quickly earned a good reputation, including among its distinguished alumni such men as William A. Buckingham, Civil War governor; Morgan G. Bulkeley, Connecticut governor and senator; Edward S. Bartholomew, sculptor; and Lyman Trumbull, senator from Illinois. Another early academy with unusually distinguished alumni was the Cheshire Episcopal Academy, founded in 1794.

Admiral Andrew H. Foote, General Joseph Wheeler, Gideon Welles, and J. Pierpont Morgan, Sr., were among its famous sons. Altogether thirty-three academies obtained legislative incorporation from 1801 to 1840, though none received any state financial assistance.[46]

For the public schools, meanwhile, Barnard advocated a system of graded schools crowned by a high school. Actually, college preparatory subjects were being taught in the ungraded public schools by the late 1830's but in a very ineffective manner. In 1840 Middletown set up the state's first permanent high school. Authorities took all children from nine to sixteen out of the old district schools and placed them in the new high school. In Hartford a long campaign for a public high school finally won approval in 1847. The ancient Hopkins Grammar School in Hartford was absorbed as the Classical Department of the new high school. This school offered three programs: *1*] the "English Course," aimed at giving a student a practical four-year course; *2*] the "Partial Course," running two years, for those wishing to go to work earlier; and *3*] the "Classical Course," concentrating on Latin and Greek in affording a preparation for college. Despite severe criticism and much experimentation in its early years, the Hartford High School quickly won an important place, from the start serving a large number of students. Within a few years New Haven, New Britain, New London, and Waterbury established high schools. Thus the high school developed as a graded school under public control and administration, open freely to all boys and girls from every social class, and offering preparation for everyday life, as well as for college. The course of instruction at Hartford High School in 1872 indicates that a few electives already were available in the general or "English" course. Freshmen could choose a year of one language from Latin, French, or German, and could select a term of botany or physiology. Sophomores had the same language alternatives. On the other hand, the Classical Department, which prepared students for college, offered a rigid four-year curriculum, including arithmetic review, algebra, geometry, grammar, Latin reader, Caesar, Cicero, Virgil, either the *Anabasis* or *Goodwin's Reader,* the *Iliad,* Phaedrus, Ovid, physiology, physical geography, Greek history and Roman history.[47]

By 1868 all elementary public schools in Connecticut were free and by 1872 virtually all public high schools also. Under an 1856 law each town controlled its public schools and supported them as well as possible. Sources of income included some state aid from the sale of the western lands, the town deposit fund, and often a town or district

schools totaled seventy-six, while six localities maintained a six-year junior-senior high school program.[48]

At this time there also existed eight endowed academies which provided high school education. This mixture of the old academy system with the new high school found its best illustration in the Norwich Free Academy, which still operates today as a privately endowed institution, offering

East Hartford High School.

tax, which might be a capitation tax or a direct tax on property. Although taxes for educational purposes undoubtedly seemed high, the salaries of teachers and principals were quite modest. In 1872, Hartford County male teachers' salaries ranged from $29 to $200 monthly, with the most common salaries in the $50–$70 bracket. Female teachers had a salary scale of $27.19 to $46.86 monthly. While only a minority of Connecticut's children of high school age were actually attending high school, the steady increase in the total attendance was encouraging. Moreover the high school was serving a relatively broad cross section of the population, including children of farmers, common laborers, and artisans. In 1904, forty-nine of Connecticut's seventy-seven high schools offered a four-year course. By 1927 the State Board of Education's list of approved four-year high

the high school program for Norwich. The school owed its start largely to the energetic drive for funds led by the Reverend John P. Gulliver, pastor of Norwich's Broadway Congregational Church. Receiving a charter in 1854, the Free Academy opened in 1856. In the 1880's the Academy received from William A. Slater, prominent Norwich industrialist, the gift of a large building, in honor of his father, John F. Slater. Blessed by good leadership and strong public support, the Academy grew rapidly. In the late 1880's each Norwich student paid five dollars per term for incidentals, and outside students paid ten dollars extra. Scholarship aid was available for any pupil "of high character and scholarship." The school offered three programs of study: 1] classical, aiming at college; 2] scientific, leading to scientific schools such as Sheffield at Yale or Massachusetts

Institute of Technology; and 3] general, offering "a good training for practical life." In 1891 the Academy rounded out its offerings with a two-year course in manual training.[49]

At present there are three other endowed and incorporated private academies approved as high schools by the State Board of Education for the attendance of pupils whose tuition has been paid from public funds: Bacon Academy in Colchester, the Gilbert School in Winsted, and Woodstock Academy in Woodstock.[50]

The State Board of Education and State-wide Educational Problems

IN 1865 the Assembly established the State Board of Education and gave it "general supervision and control of the educational interests of the state." At first this board consisted of four members chosen by the Assembly on a basis of one per Congressional district. These members in turn selected a secretary to perform a multitude of duties. Later, under the board's general supervision, the governor and lieutenant governor as well as the secretary were made ex officio members. In 1919 membership was enlarged to nine, with the county becoming the unit of representation and the governor making the appointments. In 1931 all ex officio members were removed, so that at present there are nine members — one per county plus one at large. Although gubernatorial selection would seem to favor political leverage, strong tradition has worked in favor of able, non-partisan choices. The present board consists of five men and four women, and the secretary of the board is Dr. William J. Sanders.[51]

The board supervises the work of the entire State Department of Education. Though primary responsibility for providing public education falls upon local boards of education and local government, the State Department of Education conducts many highly significant activities. During 1959–60 it administered grants totaling $51,407,291.69 for local school needs. It operates four teachers' colleges, one technical institute, fourteen vocational-technical schools, and the Mystic Oral School (for the totally deaf); supervises directly all school systems with thirty-five or

fewer teachers; grants certificates to teachers, supervisors, and administrators; operates a program of vocational rehabilitation and one for handicapped children; oversees the state school-lunch program; and maintains various services to librarians.[52]

With a rapidly growing school population and the ever-increasing demands upon the schools in the training of children for a very complex society, Connecticut, in common with other states, has faced very difficult educational problems, especially since the end of World War II. Among the most stimulating studies of this era was that made in 1950 by the Governor's Fact-Finding Commission on Education. A small group of public-spirited citizens, appointed by Governor Bowles and headed by Norman Cousins, enlisted the aid of local school boards, as well as several out-of-state specialists, in their intensive survey. Most of the conditions and problems uncovered then still exist. Although the commission found Connecticut education in a healthy condition relative to other states, it also found serious deficiencies. Despite the fact that Connecticut usually leads all states in per capita income, it ranked far down the list in proportion of income devoted to education. The commission felt that the problem of making education beyond high school available to young men and women regardless of financial resources was the number one educational challenge. It recommended a system of state scholarships for higher education, earlier recommended by Education Commissioner Alonzo G. Grace, but the 1950's have passed without legislative action. Likewise, the commission advocated a state four-year medical and dental school and a veterinary school — which were also rejected in the Assembly. For The University of Connecticut, whose leadership under President Albert N. Jorgensen received strong commendation, the commission envisaged further large growth and a great opportunity for advanced scholarly research.[53]

Asserting that the disease of "janitoritis" had afflicted most levels of school administration, the commission felt that noneducational problems tended to crowd out basic educational ones. It recommended that the responsibilities of the local school boards be more sharply defined and that they be independent of the local board of finance, with power to levy a school tax. On the problem of financing public education, the commission criticized the current flat grant basis of state help and advocated instead aid inversely in proportion to a town's ability to finance its own program. An equalized grand list for the entire state would be essential in implementing this program.[54]

One of the major postwar educational problems has been the construction of new schools or additions to old schools to meet the needs of a rapidly growing school-age population. Although communities differ in the ability to finance such construction, it generally has been difficult. In 1945 the Assembly passed the first act to aid in building new schools or enlarging or remodeling old ones. The state would help to a limit of $150 per pupil or one-third of the total cost, up to a maximum of $50,000. Later acts of 1947, 1949, and 1957 liberalized the formula. Under the 1957 act the state may pay up to one-half the total cost of new buildings (excluding site acquisition costs), and one-third the cost of major alterations. A hardship clause, providing extra aid, covers town and regional school districts unable to make the usual financial contributions. From 1945 through 1959 the school building program has cost communities over $307,000,000 in addition to nearly $93,000,000 in state aid. Population statistics suggest that building demands will remain very high in the decade ahead.[55]

In 1956 the State Department of Education issued a study reviewing major developments of the period since 1900 and evaluating the current situation. In 1921 the state had 653 one-room schools, and by 1956 only twenty-three remained. A study of comparative expenditures for secondary education is revealing:

Year	Total Expenditures (Except for Vocational-Technical)	Expenditure per Pupil
1900	$ 366,053.96	$ 45.05
1925	4,242,896.85	131.41
1940	11,290,773.26	113.38
1950	24,138,516.70	327.24
1955	37,230,186.86	404.87

The recent sharp upward spiral of costs could be explained by: 1] far larger number of students served; 2] wider services provided; 3] public demand for higher quality service; 4] inflation. Most schools averaged eleven to twenty rooms in size and conducted classes averaging 29.66 students apiece. The survey indicated that a large percentage of high school students had outside employment (55 percent of seniors), and about 10 percent had the heavy load of over twenty hours weekly. This report noted the great shortage in science equipment and trained science teachers. A few television courses were being offered, but major expansion remained for the future.[56]

This study noted the steady increase in enrollments of colleges — a figure close to 40,000. Interestingly enough, Connecticut was not doing its full share, as about 15 percent more Connecticut young people went out of the state for higher education than came into Connecticut from other states for college training. Also, Connecticut was failing by far to train enough teachers for its public schools. About one-third of the elementary teachers and over 45 percent of the high school teachers beginning work in Connecticut schools in September 1954 had received their training elsewhere.[57]

There have been many significant changes in programs during recent years. The National Defense Education Act of 1958 paved the way for the use of Federal and state funds for education to strengthen the defense needs of the nation. In the fiscal year 1958–59 the Federal government allotted $395,350 to Connecticut public schools on a matching basis for the improvement of science, mathematics, and modern language instruction. Federal funds also were advanced under this act for expansion of guidance and counseling work. Meanwhile the advanced placement program has expanded and in 1958–59 included fourteen high schools. Under this arrangement superior students may take courses in certain fields which carry college credits. For help at the other end of the intelligence scale, a 1959 Assembly act required all towns to provide special classes for the retarded by September 1961. By 1958–59, fifty-five towns already offered such a program.[58]

To improve instruction generally, the State Department of Education has recently prepared curriculum bulletins in most subjects for grades seven through twelve. Local systems may or may not use these guides as they see fit, but the hope is that they will stimulate local curriculum studies. The Education Department feels that the guides have already exerted a large influence.[59]

The problem of sheer numbers and impressive numerical increase is clearly demonstrated in official enrollment figures for the public schools.

These registration figures indicate a 21-percent increase in five years. Closely related has been the sharp rise in staff, salaries, and total costs.

The 1958–59 public school enrollment of 460,132 may seem large, but the Department of Education forecasts a rise to 543,292 in 1963–64, and 602,150 in 1968–69. Quite obviously there will have to be a large increase in educational expend-

itures just to maintain quality at the present level, without considering improvements.[60]

During the past decade the state teachers' colleges likewise have experienced rapid growth. The oldest, Central Connecticut State College at New Britain, which began instruction in 1850, registered an increase in total full-time and part-time undergraduates from 1,511 in September 1950 to 2,829 ten years later. Southern Connecticut State College at New Haven enrolled 1,668 undergraduates in September 1950 as compared with 2,854 a decade later. In the same span Danbury State College rose from 874 to 1,090, while Willimantic State College declined from 632 to 551. At all four colleges the period brought a major increase in *full-time* undergraduates, with the total gain amounting to nearly 90 percent. In recent years the legislature has appropriated substantial sums for new facilities.

	1954–55	1955–56	1956–57	1957–58	1958–59
Estimated Total Population	2,222,000	2,271,000	2,313,000	2,362,000	2,423,000
Number of Schools					
Elementary	736	757	768	759	774
Junior High	42	41	55	53	69
High	99	96	99	104	111
Registration					
Elementary	283,074	292,228	302,487	312,884	321,235
Junior High	24,251	30,370	35,263	35,647	37,696
High	72,676	76,953	82,398	93,296	101,201
Total Registration	380,001	399,551	420,148	441,827	460,132

	1954–55	1955–56	1956–57	1957–58	1958–59
Classroom teachers	14,148	14,780	15,462	16,306	17,240
Teachers' average salary	$ 4,283	4,463	4,737	5,117	5,460
Current expenses*	$101,000,000	113,000,000	128,000,000	146,000,000	163,000,000
State grants for current expenses*	$ 26,000,000	27,000,000	38,000,000	40,000,000	42,000,000

* To nearest million.

Connecticut's Preparatory Schools

CONNECTICUT has one of the most distinguished groups of private preparatory schools in the nation. The oldest of these in active service is the Hopkins Grammar School of New Haven, founded in 1660 as a result of a bequest by Edward Hopkins, "to give some encouragement in those

Founded in 1833, Suffield Academy has enjoyed a long and influential career reaching to the present. The oldest girls' school was that launched at Litchfield by Miss Sarah Pierce in 1792. It won a high reputation during its nearly forty years of existence. Among the girls' schools still operating, unquestionably the most famous is Miss Porter's School in Farmington, begun in 1843 by Sarah

The Hopkins Grammar School —
replica of 1660 building.

Aerial view of The Hopkins
Grammar School in 1960.

forrayne Plantations for the breeding up of hopefull youths both at the Grammar Schoole and Colledge for the publique service of the Country in future tymes." Modeled after the great English grammar schools, Hopkins trained thoroughly many of the colonial and national leaders of Connecticut and the nation. By the early 1920's Hopkins' roll of famous graduates included 3 cabinet officers, 8 United States Senators, 20 United States Representatives, 4 Connecticut governors and 3 of other states, 3 New Haven mayors and 4 of other cities, 2 Supreme Court judges, 4 Chief Justices of the State Supreme Court, 17 college presidents, 141 ministers, and 126 college professors — as well as many other distinguished leaders in business and other callings.[61]

Next oldest is the Cheshire Academy, originally known as the Episcopal Academy of Connecticut and later as the Roxbury School. Its difficult early years have already been discussed.

Porter, who gave it fifty-seven years of dedicated leadership. Rounding out the list of schools over a hundred years old is the Gunnery School for boys at Washington, founded in 1850 by the renowned educator and abolitionist, Frederick William Gunn, who insisted upon hard work in an atmosphere of informality and intimacy.[62]

The last hundred years has seen the opening of many excellent preparatory boarding schools, but space allows mention of only a few. The late nineteenth century brought into being a notable group of private schools: Westminster, founded at Simsbury in 1888 by William Lee Cushing; Taft, at Watertown, launched in 1890 by Horace Dutton Taft, who felt that spiritual growth was as important as intellectual growth; Hotchkiss, founded at Lakeville in 1891, with a gift from Mrs. Maria Harrison Hotchkiss; the Pomfret School, at Pomfret, founded in 1894; and the Salisbury School, at Salisbury, established in 1901 by the Reverend

George E. Quaile. Members of the Loomis family in Windsor procured a charter in 1874 for the education of Loomis children and others nearby, twelve years or older. Actual operations began in the World War I period when Nathaniel H. Batchelder (headmaster, 1912–49) developed Loomis into a strong college preparatory school. Connecticut's present largest preparatory boarding

Charles Phelps Taft Hall at The Taft School, Watertown.

Aerial view of The Kent School.

school, Choate, at Wallingford, also dates from this era. Judge William G. Choate founded the school in 1896 with the objective of combining the benefits of family life with those of a first-class boarding school.[63]

Among the most distinguished schools opened in the last five or six decades is the Kent School at Kent, on the Housatonic River. In 1906 the Reverend Frederick H. Sill founded it as an Episcopal Church school and placed heavy emphasis upon simplicity, purposefulness, and self-reliance. In 1960 Kent opened a co-ordinate girls' school nearby. Other additions to the roll of significant preparatory schools were Westover (girls) in 1909, Ethel Walker (girls) in 1911, Canterbury in 1915, South Kent in 1923, Wooster in 1926, and Avon Old Farms in 1930. There are also a number of excellent elementary private boarding schools and a strong group of private country or city day schools such as Kingswood in West Hartford.[64]

Development of a Catholic School System

A CATHOLIC educational system developed late in Connecticut's history because few Catholics lived here until about 1850. Desperate economic conditions in Ireland in the late 1840's precipitated a large migration to America. By 1850, census figures indicated 26,689 foreign-born Irish in Connecticut, and by 1860 the number jumped to 55,445, over 12 percent of the state's entire population.[65]

Although the first Catholic Sunday school in Hartford started in 1829, apparently it was some time in 1830 before Father James Fitton launched the first Catholic elementary school in the basement of the new Holy Trinity Church. Miss Agnes Whiting from Boston provided the instruction. Until the early 1850's, however, Catholic educational opportunities were confined to intermittent sessions by lay teachers.[66]

The rapidly growing Catholic population, estimated at over 50,000 by 1853, consisted mostly of unskilled laborers. They generally supported the Catholic principle that Catholic children should be taught in Catholic schools so that their faith would be strengthened. This belief met strong opposition from prominent Protestant leaders, especially Horace Bushnell of Hartford, who evinced genuine alarm at the likelihood of a large Catholic school system. Bushnell feared that the movement for parochial schools, whether Catholic or Protestant, inevitably would gravely weaken or even destroy the publicly supported schools. This would be probable, he asserted, if each denomination were permitted to petition for a proportional share of public school funds. Bushnell

(1852), Ansonia (1853), Norwalk (1854), Meriden (1855), Danbury (1860), Stamford (1860), New Britain (1862), and Winsted (1865). Most of these schools were taught by lay teachers. By the 1860's the Sisters of Mercy expanded their work at New Haven and Hartford into the secondary level.[68]

From 1866 to 1886 a period of steady growth marked the Catholic school system. For the first

Northwest Catholic High School, West Hartford.

did not seek Protestant common schools but did demand common schools for all children, regardless of sect, as a fundamental American principle. Catholic leaders objected vigorously to the use of the King James version of the Bible in the public schools and demanded use of the Douay version for their children. They also pointed to the heavy burden of double taxation of Catholics for two sets of schools. The political climate of the 1850's, as already seen, was marked by much anti-immigrant and anti-Catholic feeling, which added greatly to the difficulty of reaching any mutually satisfactory solution on educational differences.[67]

In any event, a rapid expansion of Catholic parochial schools occurred. In 1852, five Sisters of Mercy came to Hartford from their mother house in Providence to begin educational and charitable work. By 1857 they were in complete charge of a school with 550 pupils. Parochial schools appeared in many places, such as New Haven (1834), Middletown (1849), Wallingford (1851), Derby

time a community of religious men, the Brothers of the Christian Schools, taught within the diocese of Hartford. In 1866 a few of the Christian Brothers on invitation took charge of the boys' department at St. Patrick's school in Hartford. In general, most graduates of the Catholic schools who wished further schooling seem to have been prepared and able to enter the public high schools. The Sisters of Mercy expanded their work and were joined by nuns of other orders, such as the Sisters of Notre Dame (at Waterbury), the Sisters of the Third Order of St. Francis (at Winsted), and the Sisters of Charity of Our Lady (at Baltic and Willimantic). By 1879 the Catholic population of about 156,000 was supporting forty-three schools, and by 1884 over 13,000 of the estimated 40,000 school-age children were in Catholic schools.[69]

From 1886 to 1906 the parochial schools became better organized, and greater efforts were made to implement decrees of synods at Hartford in 1878 and 1886 which, among other things, strongly urged a Catholic education for Catholic children. In 1886 a diocesan school board was created with the purpose of supervising and improving the schools. Slowly the parochial schools were graded and made more uniform in curriculum, length of year, and use of religious teachers. In 1914 an eight-grade school became the standard. Gradually, too, the Catholic schools, except for religious

special emphasis to more thorough training of teachers. His successor, Father William J. Fitzgerald (supervisor, 1910–20), concentrated on development of a well-balanced curriculum — an effort continued by Father Edwin Flynn (supervisor, 1920–28). In the 1930's summer schools first appeared, especially for Catholic children who did not regularly attend parochial schools. Since the

St. Teresa School, Trumbull.

education, patterned their curriculum closely after that of public schools. Hence it became reasonably easy for their students to proceed into the public high schools. Since parochial graduates generally fared well in competitive examinations, many Catholics felt that they should not have to support both the public schools and their own. Some charges of discrimination against parochial elementary graduates wishing entrance to public high schools were aired, but by 1925 graduates of fourteen parochial schools were admitted to the local high schools without examination. Efforts to secure public funds for parochial schools from funds paid by the state to the towns under the 1871 law failed.[70]

The appointment of Father Patrick J. McCormick as supervisor of schools for the Hartford diocese in 1906, replacing the earlier board of diocesan examiners, ushered in a period of thorough reorganization of parochial schools. Father McCormick, working on many problems, gave

Catholic population of Connecticut continued to rise rapidly, great efforts were made to expand the parochial system proportionately. By the mid-1930's, however, less than half the parishes in the state had a parochial school. In a study of eighty-one parishes with such schools, it was found that for the 1934–35 school year, one out of three Catholic children was in a public elementary school. At that time (October 1934) 44,506 children were enrolled in the entire diocese. Most of these were in elementary schools, as Catholic high schools remained scarce.[71]

As the system operated in 1958–59 it consisted of 149 parochial schools, with official registrations as follows: kindergarten, 2,693; elementary, 63,761; high schools, 1,537; or a total of 67,991 pupils under instruction by 1,635 teachers. Recently plans were completed and funds pledged for three large high schools in the metropolitan Hartford area — each to serve 1,200 students — scheduled for opening in September 1961.[72]

At the college level there are a number of Catholic institutions: Albertus Magnus at New Haven (281 students in September 1958); Annhurst College at South Woodstock (204); Diocesan Teachers College, Hartford (180); Fairfield University, Fairfield (1,580); Holy Apostles Seminary, Cromwell (35); St. Basil's College, Stamford (33); St. Joseph College, West Hartford (552); St. Mary's Seminary, Norwalk (72); and St. Thomas Seminary, Bloomfield (145).[73]

The "Collegiate School" Evolves into Yale College

FROM the early decades of New Haven Colony's history, leaders dreamed of founding a college. It was expensive to send young men to Harvard, and many felt that Harvard was becoming too liberal. After much discussion, a group of clergymen petitioned the October 1701 Assembly session for a college charter. In line with Puritan tradition, the legislators granted a charter for "a Collegiate School . . . wherein youth may be instructed in the arts and sciences, who through the blessing of Almighty God, may be fitted for publick imployments both in church and civill state." The trustees selected Saybrook as the site and chose the Reverend Abraham Pierson of Killingworth as first head. Tuition was set at thirty shillings yearly, a few regulations were adopted, and for all situations not otherwise covered Harvard's rules would apply. Since all trustees except one were Harvard graduates, this tendency to copy Harvard was normal. In March 1702 Jacob Heminway of East Haven presented himself to Pierson as the first student. Fourteen had graduated before Pierson's death in 1707.[74]

The young school, poverty-stricken and rent by internal conflict, nearly broke apart in the next few years. In 1716 the trustees finally voted five to two for a move to New Haven, which promised more financial aid than the principal rivals, Saybrook or Hartford, could offer. There ensued a period of several years of amazing confusion, during which students studied at several places. In 1717 and 1718 there were separate commencements at New Haven and Wethersfield. The locale of the school became a heated legislative issue, with the two houses differing, but the New Haven

group finally won out. The victory was confirmed by an unexpected act of philanthropy. Elihu Yale, born at Boston in 1649, grew up in England and later made a vast, if tainted, fortune in India. Cotton Mather directly appealed to Yale for assistance and held out the bait of naming the infant college in his honor. In 1718 Yale responded by sending three bales of valuable goods to be sold for the school, a portrait of George I, the royal coat of arms, and a case of books — worth in all about £800. It clinched New Haven's case, and Yale College had its permanent name. However, it required almost a pitched battle to get the books from Saybrook. Saybrook partisans destroyed bridges and broke down carts, but most of the books got through to New Haven.[75]

Yale College grew slowly but steadily from the 1720's to the Revolution. Perhaps the greatest sensation of the half-century came in 1722, when Rector Timothy Cutler and several tutors deserted the Congregational Church for the Episcopalian. Needless to say, Cutler and his aides resigned and were replaced by orthodox Congregationalists. In fact, Yale became far more conservative than Harvard in religion, while maintaining curricular emphasis on the classics. Under the energetic drive of conservative Rector Thomas Clap (1739–66), Yale grew rapidly, having more students than Harvard from 1753 to 1760. Clap persuaded a tight-fisted legislature to appropriate funds for a new building, known as Connecticut Hall. Never intended exclusively as a college to train ministers, by 1750 it had 306 graduates in the ministry and 336 laymen.[76]

In college life, the lowly freshman was even lowlier two centuries ago! He could not wear a hat in the college yard (except in stormy weather), run or shout in the yard, had to perform all reasonable errands for any superior, and respectfully accept instructions from seniors! All undergraduates were forbidden to wear hats (except in a storm) in the front yard of the president or a professor, or within ten rods of the president, eight rods of a professor, and five rods of a tutor. Commencements were joyous occasions — sometimes too much so, with drunkenness and rioting not uncommon.[77]

President Napthali Daggett (1766–77) provided

less forceful leadership than Clap. Some democratic tendencies became evident in 1768, when, for the first time, students were listed alphabetically in the catalog, and not by social rank. Although the classics remained the backbone of the curriculum, in 1772, for the first time, the college laws were printed in English instead of Latin. The stormy days of the Revolution retarded but did

of students from southern and western states increased sharply. Typifying this trend was the presence of John C. Calhoun of South Carolina, B.A. class of 1804, one of scores of graduates who went on to positions of national leadership.[79]

During the tenure of President Jeremiah Day (1817–46) Yale grew steadily despite chronic financial struggles. In 1822, when the school requested

Connecticut Hall, Yale University (completed 1752).

not destroy Yale — perhaps largely due to the heroic efforts of President Ezra Stiles (1777–95).[78]

Yale's Development into a National University

UNDER President Timothy Dwight (1795–1817), Yale deliberately began to move toward the position of a *national* institution. Illustrious professors such as Benjamin Silliman, Jeremiah Day, and James Kingsley contributed much to the school's prestige. After a period of disagreement and discussion between the Connecticut Medical Society (incorporated 1792) and Yale, the Assembly in 1810 passed a bill founding the Yale Medical School, under joint control of the Medical Society and Yale. In October 1813, thirty-one students began their medical studies — a far cry from the more than five hundred students studying in the School of Medicine and using its elaborate facilities today. Under Dwight's administration the number

aid from the legislature, it stated that its capital was only $50,000, it still owed $11,000 for the new North College building, and endowment income was only $2,300 yearly. State aid to Yale dwindled in the nineteenth century, but fortunately gifts from alumni and other friends grew rapidly. In 1834, for example, Dr. Alfred E. Perkins of Norwich bequeathed $10,000, with the interest to go for purchase of library books. This was the largest single gift since Elihu Yale's. While Day was president a separate department of theology was established in 1822 — the genesis of the Divinity School, which granted the first Bachelor of Divinity degree in 1867. Judge David Daggett (class of 1783) and Samuel J. Hitchcock (class of 1809), in 1824 assumed control of a private law school which by 1826 became officially connected with Yale when Daggett was appointed a professor of law. Yale conferred its first Bachelor of Laws degree in 1843.[80]

In Day's regime, Yale, through unusual circumstances, acquired the first collegiate art gallery in the nation. John Trumbull, the "painter of the American Revolution," fell into poverty during his later years. He proposed to his nephew, Benjamin Silliman, that Yale take his large paintings and many miniatures, erect a building for them, and pay him an annuity of $1,000. An agreement was reached; Trumbull designed the building and presented Yale with eight large paintings of the American Revolution and nearly two hundred fifty portraits — a collection of great artistic and historical value. Relieved of financial worry, Trumbull lived to a ripe old age![81]

During the lengthy administration of Day's successor, Theodore Dwight Woolsey (1846–71), Yale made great advances in its science program. In 1846, professorships of agricultural chemistry and applied chemistry were created, largely as a result of Benjamin Silliman's work. In the 1850's other scientific positions were set up, especially in engineering. In 1858 Joseph E. Sheffield of New Haven gave a building and scientific equipment to Yale. Hence it occasioned little surprise that Yale's new school of science, in 1861, took the name, Sheffield Scientific School, which it still holds. Until 1919 the school offered both graduate and undergraduate courses, then only undergraduate courses until 1945, when it once again offered graduate work.[82]

Under Woolsey, other notable developments occurred, such as the large gift for the Peabody Museum of Natural History, a benefaction of George Peabody, banker and philanthropist. In 1869 the pioneer American college art school began classes. Yale also set up several new professorships, including chairs in modern languages and history. Growing emphasis on graduate work resulted in Yale's granting the first American Ph.D. in 1861.[83]

College students of a century or more ago apparently acted much like those of today, and as relief from the "bookish grind" found outlets in many forms. In 1819 Yale freshmen and sophomores staged a three-day revolt against bad food. In 1828 the "Bread and Butter Rebellion" occurred, involving a wholesale refusal to patronize the commons until the fare improved. There was great excitement, and four students were expelled

before peace was re-established. In 1830 a refusal to recite in the prescribed form for a mathematics course led to the expulsion of forty-four students. Irrepressible youthful energies found more harmless expression in pranks, such as putting a cow on the top floor of a dormitory or painting the president's house a patriotic red, white, and blue! Town-gown (community versus college) episodes also erupted periodically, for instance, in fights with sailors in 1811, 1815, and 1819. In some of the town-gown battles the students marched under a chosen leader called "Major Bully." On March 17, 1854, a sharp battle between a town mob and students, developing out of minor differences, resulted in one student being stabbed to death. Similarly, in March 1959, a bad town-gown fracas followed student snowballing of a St. Patrick's Day parade.[84]

Student energies, fortunately, have usually gone into more desirable extracurricular activities. As early as 1826 Yale appropriated money for an outdoor gymnasium. In the 1840's the first rowing occurred, and in 1852 the first Yale-Harvard boat race took place on Lake Winnepesaukee. Meanwhile, in 1836, undergraduates launched the *Yale Literary Magazine*, the first of its type in any American college. The first real glee club was organized by the class of 1863. In 1878 Yale rowed against Harvard on the Thames River — the first of a long series continuing to the present. After several years of informal baseball Yale had its first intercollegiate game in 1865 with a Wesleyan group, winning 39 to 13.[85]

Since Yale had expanded its program far beyond that of a classical undergraduate college, it seemed logical that Yale authorities in 1872 should recognize that the school had four separate faculties — Divinity, Law, Medicine, and Philosophy and the Arts — and was, in fact, a university; though the name, Yale University, was formally adopted only in 1887. James Dwight Dana, Silliman Professor of Geology and Mineralogy and an ardent champion of the Sheffield School, in 1871 wrote a very significant pamphlet outlining in bold terms Yale's future needs. He advocated thorough reorganization of the school, with greater emphasis on an expanded graduate program, and a formal graduate school. He also called for larger funds for every department, so that a "true university" could be achieved. But the conservatives were strongly entrenched and found an articulate leader in Noah Porter, Professor of Moral Philosophy and Metaphysics. A fervent believer in the traditional, classical system of education, Porter felt that Yale was not yet ready for full-fledged graduate work and its professional training. During Porter's long presidency (1871–86) Yale remained essentially a strong college, which obtained nearly all of the funds, prestige, and staff; while Sheffield, Law, Art, Divinity, and Medicine struggled along on leftovers.[86]

Even Porter could not indefinitely ignore the demand for a more flexible curriculum, or the elective system, which was sweeping American higher education in the last quarter or more of the century. He gave very little ground however until 1884, when a determined faculty almost literally browbeat him into acceptance of a modest elective system. With the retirement of Porter in 1886 the mantle passed to Timothy Dwight, grandson of the earlier President Timothy Dwight. The new president led Yale through a period of rapid growth and moderate change. In 1870 Yale had 64 teaching faculty and 755 students; in 1899, 260 and 2,684 respectively. One of Yale's prides in the nineteenth-century lay in its many distinguished alumni. In higher education, for example, Yale graduates were chosen as first presidents of Princeton, Columbia, Dartmouth, Williams, Hamilton, Kenyon, Illinois, Wabash, Beloit, Cornell, Johns Hopkins, and the Universities of Georgia, Missouri, Mississippi, Wisconsin, Chicago, and California.[87]

Though still addicted to gradualism in the new century, Yale managed to combine steady growth in facilities, faculty, and student body with careful attention to the larger demands of a steadily more complex society. Under President Arthur Twining Hadley (1899–1921) the institution broadened its scope, while still carefully preserving the ideal of a liberal-arts education. In 1900 the School of Forestry was created, and in 1908 the Yale University Press began its notable career. Several agonizing studies of such basic problems as overall university organization and curriculum took place. A sweeping revision of the university's

organization brought greater unity and efficiency. Students had a far greater choice of subjects in 1921 than in 1899, but Yale College still insisted on training and proficiency in languages (though no longer Greek), mathematics, and the physical and social sciences. Good teaching, lofty ideals,

Entrance to the Sterling Memorial Library.

and rigorous moral standards remained cornerstones of the university's objectives. The earlier feeling of outside educational leaders that Yale's athletes were too good and her professional schools too poor was certainly far less justified in 1920 than it might have been several decades earlier. Already the schools of Divinity, Law, Medicine, and Forestry had attained top-level stature.[88]

During President James Rowland Angell's administration (1921–37) Yale continued its amazing growth, helped greatly by an enormous bequest of $39,000,000 from John W. Sterling (B.A., 1864). The Sterling Memorial Library, completed in

1930, ranks as one of the largest in the world. Schools of Nursing (1923) and Engineering (1932) were created. In 1933 the university, through gifts from Edward S. Harkness, launched its famous residential college plan, which attempted to preserve for undergraduates the educational and so-

President Alfred Whitney Griswold (1950–) significant new ventures include: a Master of Arts in Teaching program; reorganization of the Nursing and Music schools; the magnificent new art gallery; a new Department of Biophysics; and an impressive physical expansion, especially for sci-

The Famous Yale Bowl.

cial values of small groups amidst a large university.[89]

Despite the depression, Yale's enormous material growth was mirrored in the endowment increase from $25,677,000 in 1921 to $107,585,000 in 1937; while student enrollment and faculty figures climbed from 3,808 and 382 to 5,490 and 504 respectively. At the same time, President Angell succeeded in raising standards, attracting and holding an excellent faculty, strengthening the graduate offerings, and maintaining the centrality of the liberal arts.[90]

During President Charles Seymour's administration (1937–50) much of Yale's efforts centered about aiding the war effort through specialized programs for servicemen. In 1946 a Scholars of the House program, providing independent work for able seniors, was introduced. Yale set up new institutes for medical research and Far Eastern languages and a labor-management center. Under

ence departments. Yet Yale's needs keep far ahead of her great resources. In May 1960 President Griswold announced that Yale would seek $69,500,000 in new funds by 1963, to meet the school's urgent, immediate needs. This is the initial phase of a drive for $147,000,000 in ten years. Within its own family Yale has tremendous resources and loyalty, as the 1959–60 Alumni Fund Drive revealed in its resulting contribution of over $2,300,000 from more than 33,500 alumni and friends.[91]

Trinity, Wesleyan, Connecticut College for Women, and Other Institutions

EARLY in the nineteenth century, meanwhile, Connecticut acquired its second and third colleges — Trinity and Wesleyan. For many years Episcopalians had hoped to establish a college, but circumstances were unfavorable until after the adoption of the 1818 constitution. The moving spirit in the project was Thomas C. Brownell, who was elected Bishop of Connecticut in 1819. In May 1823 the Assembly considered a petition of Bishop Brownell and other Episcopalians to found a college at Hartford, Middletown, or New Haven. It passed easily. Since Hartford offered the greatest

since 1845, remained a small liberal-arts college. In 1872 the trustees sold the campus to Hartford, which desired it as the site for the new state capitol. With the proceeds the trustees purchased eighty acres on Rocky Hill, a traprock ridge at the western edge of Hartford. Gradually a new cam-

The chapel and Downes Memorial of Trinity College.

financial inducements, the trustees voted to settle the new college there. Vigorous opposition to the college quickly appeared. A series of anonymous *Courant* articles and two pamphlets, apparently written by Roger Sherman Baldwin or Chauncey Allen Goodrich as spokesman for the opposition, vigorously objected to a second college in Connecticut as a dangerous scheme which would inevitably injure Yale. Despite such misgivings, the new institution, first called Washington College, opened its doors on September 23, 1824, to nine students. Bishop Brownell, as first president, nursed the infant school along tenderly but firmly. Discipline was strict. In summer, classes began at 5:00 A.M., in winter at 6:00 A.M.! No student was permitted to attend "any festive entertainment in the city of Hartford or its vicinity." At the first graduation, in August 1827, ten young men received their Bachelor's degrees.[92]

For many decades Washington, called Trinity

pus took form as William Burges created the first collegiate Gothic buildings in America. Enrollment still was small late in the century, numbering only 122 in 1892–93. The present century has brought Trinity large benefactions, an expanded campus, and the means of serving a much larger student body. Under President Remsen B. Ogilby (1920–43) the buildings doubled, endowment went up 250 percent, faculty increased from 25 to 62, and students from 167 to 530. The magnificent Gothic-style chapel was erected in a position dominating the campus. Under Ogilby's successor, Keith Funston (1943–51), the college expanded its enrollment to 900 to meet the needs of returning veterans, and decided to maintain enrollment at approximately that figure. In 1953 Albert C. Jacobs, former Chancellor of the University of Denver, accepted a call to the presidency. Undergraduates in September 1958 numbered 999, graduate and evening students 449.[93]

In common with Yale and Trinity, Wesleyan, the third college founded in Connecticut, had a religious inception. Among Methodist leaders in the East, the desire for a Methodist institution of true college rank had been growing for a number of years. Such a school could serve the graduates of Methodist secondary schools such as Wilbraham Academy in Massachusetts. By sheer good luck at this juncture Captain Alden Partridge decided to move his American Literary, Scientific, and Military Academy from Middletown to Norwich, Vermont. This left a campus of several buildings, located on a hill 150 feet above the Connecticut River, completely vacant. The New York Conference of the Methodist Church was interested but decided to hear from all possible cities wishing to submit proposals. Troy, New York, Wilbraham, Bridgeport, and Middletown all made bids. Middletown's was the most attractive, and a ready-made campus beckoned. As a result, the New York Conference chose Middletown and selected trustees, who in turn asked the Reverend Willbur Fisk, head of Wilbraham Academy, to be first president.[94]

After its opening on September 21, 1831, Wesleyan experienced a bitter struggle against poverty, but it gradually grew stronger. Like Trinity's charter, Wesleyan's provided that subscribing to any specific religious tenet should not be a condition for admission. Fisk himself was nonsectarian in attitude, and the college, while enjoying Methodist support, did not insist that faculty and students belong to that church. In 1870 a new charter provided that a majority of trustees and faculty and the president should be Methodists — a sectarian stipulation finally abolished in the 1907 charter. President Fisk inveighed against the narrowness of the classical curriculum and espoused the primacy of modern literature and the sciences. Yet Wesleyan's course schedule throughout the early decades was very similar to that of most colleges. The first real liberalization came under President Joseph Cummings, when a true elective system was introduced in the fall of 1873. The previous year the first woman had been admitted as an undergraduate, and coeducation remained a fact until 1912. Significant curriculum changes, offering more diversification and electives, were made in 1885, 1892, and 1907.[95]

From 1839 to 1908, under Fisk's successors, Stephen Olin (1839–41, 1842–51), Nathan Bangs (1841–42), Augustus W. Smith (1852–57), Joseph Cummings (1857–75), Cyrus D. Foss (1875–80), John W. Beach (1880–87), and Bradford P. Raymond (1889–1908), Wesleyan remained essentially a small, struggling liberal-arts college. Only dur-

"Old Brownstone Row,"
Wesleyan campus.

ing William A. Shanklin's tenure (1909–23) did the school first enjoy a rapid physical and educational growth. Endowment tripled, passing $4,000,000, new buildings were erected, and faculty increased from 35 to 58. When 1919 enrollment reached a new peak of 594, the trustees voted to set a future

Studies programs. Also, the college recently established a Department of Publications, which issues a wide variety of educational materials for public schools as well as scholarly books for adults. The college plans a gradual expansion of the undergraduate body from 800 to 1,250. To preserve the

Artist's drawing of general classroom building, The University of Hartford.

limit of 500. Under Shanklin's successor, James L. McConaughy (1925–43), there occurred great physical and endowment expansion. McConaughy successfully maintained the well-established traditions of a strong faculty and student body, intimately bound together and working in a genuine liberal-arts atmosphere.[96]

World War II service for the Federal government necessitated McConaughy's resignation. In 1943 the trustees chose Victor L. Butterfield as eleventh president. Under his imaginative leadership the college has won an enviable reputation nationally for its unusually distinguished faculty and high academic standards. Thanks to recent large endowment increases, the college in 1960 had available for educational purposes more funds per student than any other college or university in the nation. A student-faculty ratio of seven to one prevails, insuring on the whole very small classes. With its great resources, Wesleyan has found it possible to expand its graduate work considerably, especially the relatively new Master of Arts in Teaching and Master of Arts in Liberal

important values of the "small college" environment, several undergraduate colleges within Wesleyan are being planned. A College of Letters operated on an experimental basis during the 1959–60 academic year.[97]

Although Connecticut possessed a trio of outstanding men's private institutions of higher learning, it lacked a similar women's college. Various citizens determined to remedy this lack and secured a charter from the Assembly in 1911. Though various communities wanted the college, New London made the greatest efforts. In September 1915 Connecticut College for Women welcomed its first class. Under the presidencies of Frederick H. Sykes, Benjamin T. Marshall, Katharine Blunt, Dorothy Schaffter, and Rosemary Park, Connecticut College has grown steadily in size, academic prestige, and influence. In September 1959 a faculty of about 120 was teaching nearly 1,000 students, who came from a majority of the states and several foreign countries.[98]

In the present century a number of additional four-year colleges have appeared, including The

University of Bridgeport (Bridgeport); The University of Hartford (Hillyer College, Hartt School of Music, Hartford Art School, and Ward School of Electronics); and Quinnipiac College (Hamden). For graduate training, in addition to Yale, Wesleyan, and Trinity, the following offer programs: Berkeley Divinity School (New Haven);

mately 800. At his formal inaugural on June 12, 1936, President Jorgensen stated:

The State has no more important asset than its human resources and it would be truly false economy to do other than to guarantee the maximum development of these resources through education.

The College needs as a condition of success that pro-

Entrance to the United States Coast Guard Academy, New London.

Diocesan Teachers College (Hartford); The University of Hartford; The Hartford Seminary Foundation; St. Mary's Seminary (Norwalk); and St. Thomas Seminary (Bloomfield).[99]

Impressive Growth of The University of Connecticut

IN the past two decades or so The University of Connecticut has expanded into the largest institution of higher learning in the state. This era of remarkable growth coincides almost exactly with the tenure as president of Albert N. Jorgensen, who assumed his duties in October 1935. In that year Connecticut State College was still primarily an agriculturally oriented school, with a faculty of about 100 and a student enrollment of approxi-

vision should be made for its reasonable growth and development. In this prosperous and cultural area which has produced wealth and culture at so high a level, the demands on the State College must constantly increase. . . . If it is not continually improving its facilities for instruction so as to keep abreast of other first-class institutions in the quality of its work, then it is relatively, if not absolutely, falling behind and bringing discredit on itself and on the State.

Looking toward the future, the Assembly in 1939 vastly widened the possible future scope of service through legislation creating The University of Connecticut. During World War II the university conducted a special program for apprentices at Pratt and Whitney Aircraft. The Extension Division, as part of the National Defense Training Program, offered many courses in such fields as mathematics, chemistry, physics, drafting, me-

Aerial view of Connecticut State College campus in 1935.

chanics, management, and engineering. Beginning in July 1943 there was a unit of the Army Specialized Training Program stationed on campus.[100]

Since 1945 the university growth has been phenomenal. Several score new educational, recreational, and dormitory buildings have been constructed, many at no net cost to the state because of the self-liquidating bond principle. Even with this vast physical expansion, it has proven impossible to provide adequate facilities for all of those qualified and seeking higher education there. At the undergraduate level over 7,700 applied for admission, and about 2,600 were admitted in September 1959. Comparable (tentative) figures for September 1960 indicate even greater pressure — nearly 9,500 applications for about 2,900 places. About 2,000 qualified and admissible students had to be rejected because of inadequate housing and educational facilities and insufficient staff. President Jorgensen and the trustees have fought hard in recent years to hold costs for students at a low level. The current general university fee of $150 ($550 for the few out-of-state students admitted)

Aerial view of The University of Connecticut in 1960.

per school year is remarkably low. For total yearly costs of resident students, university officials suggest as a median estimate a figure of $1,160, which covers general fee, student union and student government fees, room, board, and books. This $1,160 total compares with charges in most private institutions for these items ranging from $2,000 to $3,000. Despite the modest costs, it is estimated that in 1959–60 about 90 percent of the undergraduates earned part of their way, and approximately 19 percent, the entire amount.[101]

In the fall semester of 1959–60 there were 7,400 students taking courses at Storrs, and a total of 11,313 for all campuses. Branches at Hartford, Stamford, Torrington, and Waterbury offer two years of undergraduate work, thus enabling students located nearby to live at home. The schools of Insurance, Law, and Social Work are located in Hartford. In its role as a university, Connecticut offers graduate work for the doctorate in nineteen fields, with further expansion imminent. There have been proposals to the legislature for medical and dental schools, but no positive action has been taken yet. In common with state universities nationally, the university will require sharply increased state support in the decade ahead if it is to provide quality education for the rapidly increasing numbers who will need and want this opportunity.[102]

In a recent address President Jorgensen outlined some of the problems and challenges facing state universities everywhere.

A state university exists for no other purpose than to advance the interests of the state and nation now and in the future.

· ·

As one contemplates the state university of the future, he will be impressed with its enormous responsibilities in *first,* conserving, and *second,* strengthening the democratic way of life. He must come to the inevitable conclusion that the great objectives of life must be reflected in the curricula and in the service programs of the state university.

To plan wisely the undoubted expansion and sound qualitative development of our state colleges and state universities, with general public and legislative understanding and support, is a need in every state.

· ·

When people say they cannot afford more for education, they mean that they value other things more. To say that we cannot afford more for education — in a country with the highest standard of living in the world — is just not true.[103]

CHAPTER 20

Connecticut, an "Arsenal of Democracy," 1939-45

1939 Legislative Session — 1940 Campaign — Politics and Preparedness, 1941–42 — First Wartime Assembly Since 1917 — A Mobilized Home Front — Connecticut Servicemen Fight All Over the World — From the November 1944 Election to the End of the War

1939 Legislative Session

THE defeat of Governor Cross by Baldwin ushered in a new era in Connecticut's state politics. Baldwin's inaugural address, reflecting a liberal approach, called for a broad legislative program involving such matters as minor court reform; constitutional amendments banning dual job-holding and recommending a merit basis for state office-holding; abolition of auto inspection; a larger highway patrol; immediate rehabilitation of state parks (from hurricane damage); a fair anti-injunction bill; improved laws to protect women and child workers; increased workmen's compensation benefits; the combination of various independent agricultural agencies under the Department of Agriculture; reforms in the liquor act; new highways and bridges; and reorganization of the state military establishment. He emphasized that a "friendly relationship between labor and capital will encourage business to come to Connecticut." He saw the proper solution for unemployment in a genuine recovery of private industry, with government giving a friendly hand. On fiscal matters Baldwin stood unequivocally for a balanced budget and stern economy to attain it.[1]

Although the Senate was divided — seventeen Democrats, sixteen Republicans, and two Socialists — through a "basic understanding" with the Bridgeport Socialists, the Republicans managed to organize and control it for the session. After prolonged wrangling the two houses adopted resolutions for a constitutional amendment permitting the governor to nominate all minor judges. A measure prohibiting dual job-holding also was started through the drawn-out amendment process.[2]

The perennial attempt to legalize pari-mutuel betting on horse and dog races failed because of reliable reports that Baldwin would veto the bill. Legalized bingo, however, cleared both houses and became law. Baldwin insisted upon a balanced budget, but not by legalizing pari-mutuel betting! After a hard battle and without levying new taxes he got a legislative budget promising a slight surplus.[3]

Education, transportation, and labor also received major attention. Connecticut State College was made The University of Connecticut, an augury of greatly expanded future service to the state. Economy proposals to close two teachers' colleges and two trade schools were rejected. Construction of the Wilbur Cross Parkway as a limited-access highway, and new Connecticut and Thames River bridges were authorized, with tolls and highway fund money used in financing them. The Assembly enacted a very impressive body of labor and welfare legislation: *1*] "kickbacks" prohibited; *2*] old-age pension increased; *3*] an eight-hour day on state contracts put into effect; *4*] minimum-wage law revised in line with Federal Fair Labor Standards Act of 1938; and *5*] anti-injunction law passed. As a step toward attracting new industries the legislature created the Connecticut Development Commission.[4]

In his closing message Baldwin praised the Assembly for its work, especially that on minor court reform, labor legislation, and budget balancing. He expressed pride in the achievement of nearly all of his party's 1938 platform.[5]

1940 Campaign

THE 1940 fall campaign pitted Governor Baldwin against a man who had never held an elective office, Robert A. Hurley of Bridgeport. A Navy veteran of World War I, Hurley headed an engineering and construction firm for a number of years. In 1936 he served as special Federal representative in co-ordinating flood relief at Hartford. Later that year he was appointed state director of the Works Progress Administration. When a new State Department of Public Works was established in 1937, Cross chose Hurley as first commissioner. Both candidates were liberal in outlook and ran on liberal platforms. To oppose incumbent Senator Maloney, the Republicans chose Paul Cornell, retired advertising executive and private school head, of Washington, Connecticut. Such was the strong interest engendered by President Roosevelt's decision to break tradition and run for a third term that his race against Wendell Willkie largely overshadowed the state races. In his campaign Baldwin hammered hard on the thesis: "There is no substitute for a good job — a good job in private industry." Running basically on his administration's record, he cited the bal-

anced budget with no new taxes, the coming of new industries to Connecticut, increased highway activity, and preparedness measures such as the first State Council of Defense. The state set up a job-training program, involving schools in most industrial centers, which soon was turning out 850 beginners monthly for industry. The National Guard was strengthened and a Home, or State, Guard organized long before the President requested it.[6]

Both gubernatorial candidates deliberately linked their appeals closely with their party's presidential aspirant. Baldwin had been a seconder for Willkie at the Republican National Convention and worked hard for his election. Political observers found it difficult to predict the outcome of the state races. As it turned out, Roosevelt's coattails, even if reduced to a 55,802-vote margin, proved wide enough to carry the full Democratic state ticket and the five Congressmen. Popular Senator Maloney won on his own, with a majority exceeding Roosevelt's. Even Governor Baldwin met defeat, though only by 13,780 votes. Both Hartford newspapers agreed that Baldwin really lost to Roosevelt. This result sparked much post-election discussion about a possible constitutional amendment to separate state and presidential elections by having state officers elected for a four-year term at the off-year elections.[7]

Politics and Preparedness, 1941–42

THE 1941 Assembly session took place against the grim backdrop of a rapidly worsening world situation and stepped-up preparedness measures in Washington. Hence it is not surprising that defense problems received much attention. Former Governor Baldwin, under executive order, had created a defense council. Hurley proposed a new defense council, which would have a paid administrator appointed by the governor. After some partisan disagreements, a compromise measure was enacted for the new State Defense Council. Governor Hurley appointed Colonel Samuel H. Fisher as first administrator and named as members eminent representatives of the judiciary, police, business, labor, utilities, agriculture, and women's organizations, among others.[8]

The legislature enacted a variety of major bills. Under a new act for aid to dependent children, Connecticut joined in a noteworthy Federal program. A state-wide juvenile court bill passed, as did a savings bank life-insurance bill. The Assembly authorized a substantial land purchase program for state forests and the acquisition of Sherwood Island for a park. A new milk control act and a rural electrification bill were signed into law. Amendments to the unemployment compensation act and workmen's compensation act were passed, but Hurley failed in his principal labor recommendation — a state labor relations board, or a "baby Wagner" act, as many dubbed it. Another significant measure provided for annual independent audits of the public utilities. The House rejected the proposed amendments concerning dual job-holding and gubernatorial nomination of judges — a great disappointment to Hurley and many others. On the other hand, it approved amendments for four-year terms for state officials and annual sessions of the Assembly. Overall, it could be classified as a moderately productive session.[9]

On December 7, 1941, the Japanese attacked Pearl Harbor, and we were at war. For Connecticut it brought sweeping changes in the lives of most citizens. Soon Federal economic controls were put into effect. Many thousands of young men volunteered for service or were drafted. A survey of the state's production facilities had been made earlier and proved useful. Defense orders poured into the state, and factories hastily recruited workers to man second or third shifts. Home building construction ceased and housing shortages appeared. Again Connecticut was called upon to give freely of her men and her arms.[10]

The 1942 state elections involved a rematch of Hurley and Baldwin. The Democratic platform offered an unusually comprehensive labor plank, including a labor relations act, a commission on fair employment practices, and liberalization of existing legislation. It also pledged a constitutional convention after the war, court reform, expansion and equalization of educational opportunity, and an extensive social welfare program. The Republicans eschewed specific promises and placed major emphasis on winning the war. Baldwin

devoted most of his acceptance speech on September 11 to an eloquent plea for nonpartisan dedication to the war effort. He also advocated saving part of the state's war-inflated revenues for postwar purposes. In the campaign he emphasized that "business as usual" and "politics as usual" were out for the war's duration and exhorted, "Let's stop fumbling." Noting that Connecticut had set up the nation's first state defense council when he was governor, he promised a comprehensive Connecticut plan for more energetic prosecution of the war. Hurley, declaring that the state had the men and machines to fill all war orders, likewise stressed the theme of all-out effort to win the war. He hit the Republicans as avoiding vital issues and threatening an economy so severe as to strangle vital state services. The election results strongly favored the Republicans. Baldwin won by 26,196 over Hurley and helped carry the entire Republican state and Congressional ticket to victory, as well as both Assembly houses. Mrs. Clare Boothe Luce, noted playwright and victor in the Fourth District, was the first Connecticut woman ever elected to Congress.[11]

First Wartime Assembly Since 1917

IN his message to the Assembly in January 1943, Baldwin challenged it to meet the war crisis, saying:

This war is the first concern of the people. It has been said that America is the Arsenal of Democracy and it has also been said that Connecticut is the Arsenal of the Nation. . . . Our Federal Government is already heavily burdened with the affairs of this war and we will increase our support by doing all that we can to help ourselves.

Throughout the speech he emphasized war problems and means of handling them.[12]

Connecticut's first wartime Assembly in a quarter century implemented many of the governor's recommendations. Highlights of its achievements included the following:

Agriculture: 1] Appropriation of $100,000 to the University of Connecticut's Agricultural Extension Service for recruiting farm workers (in short supply) and housing them; *2*] release of school children to aid farmers for a period not exceeding thirty days in a school year, authorized when county agents certified a shortage; 3] slaughterhouse inspectors to be appointed by local authorities but licensed by the Domestic Animals Commissioner.

Appropriations: 1] Bipartisan Finance Advisory Committee established to recover for legislature some control over postsession expenditures lost in the 1937 reorganization bill; 2] balanced budget voted lower than in 1943, and a special segregated budget of $5,000,000 for war-incurred expenditures adopted.

Banking: Savings Banks' Deposit Guaranty Fund of Connecticut, Inc., created to give full protection to deposits in mutual savings banks.

Constitutional amendments: 1] House approved proposals for four-year terms for state officials and annual sessions of legislature, among others; 2] rejected a constitutional convention and gubernatorial nomination of minor court judges.

Election laws: Revised absentee ballot law to aid servicemen.

Labor: 1] Women in war work permitted 55-hour work week; 2] maximum workmen's compensation increased to $30 weekly.

Parks and Forests: Commission on Forests and Wild Life allotted $400,000 for land purchases.

Public utilities: Because of crowded public transportation, various regulations relaxed — for example, permitting auto owners once daily to transport workers to and from work.

State employees: 1] Residence requirements eased for merit system appointments; 2] cost-of-living increases granted and improvements in retirement system made.

Taxes: Servicemen exempted from payment of old-age assistance tax and given $1,000 property tax exemption.

Welfare: 1] Interracial commission established to work against discrimination; 2] discrimination for color specifically forbidden in merit system law amendment.

Emergency wartime measures: 1] Broad powers given governor, including suspension of statutes — in effect to February 1, 1944; 2] former State Defense Council changed to Connecticut War Council, with increased authority and no limit on membership; 3] postwar planning commission created.

Although the session achieved much, both the *Courant* and *Times* criticized the unseemly patronage struggle and general excess of partisanship displayed during critical war days. In speaking at the Assembly's end, Baldwin called it a "win the war" session and praised the legislators for their action on many pressing problems.[13]

In January 1944 a special session took place. In addressing the legislators Baldwin indicated that he had used his emergency powers a total of eight times to meet special war conditions and needs. His war orders included authorizing night work for women in manufacturing plants and restaurants, hiring workers beyond seventy years of age as state employees, increasing the number of standees on buses, and suspending an amendment to the rent eviction law. The principal actions of the five-day session were an extension of Baldwin's emergency war powers, enactment of a liberal absentee ballot for servicemen and women under which they could vote anywhere in the world up to the eve of the election, and a memorial to the President and Congress urging the necessity of immediate relief to milk producers.[14]

A Mobilized Home Front

THE enormous needs of the Allied military forces, plus the minimum needs of the civilians, posed a formidable challenge. Fortunately Connecticut, through its very early organization of a State Defense Council, later reorganized and strengthened as the State War Council, and through well-coordinated efforts with local and Federal bodies, was able to handle both war production and civilian needs quite efficiently. The State War Council, in fact, won an award of merit from the Federal Office of Civilian Defense. The Council operated both on a state-wide basis and through local war councils in every town and city. Early in the war, when invasion and/or bombing seemed probable, it organized over 50,000 men and women as air-raid wardens, 12,000 men as auxiliary firemen, and about 5,200 men as local or state auxiliary police-men. It worked out a state-wide communications system, which proved helpful in the 1944 hurricane. Likewise, about 1,000 volunteers were on hand almost immediately after the dreadful Hartford circus fire of July 6, 1944, in which 168 persons, many children, lost their lives and over 500 were injured.[15]

Industrial manpower provided the most difficult broad problem facing the state government and the War Council. With many factory workers in service, and far more needed than in peacetime, many thousands of new workers had to be recruited and decent living conditions provided for them. Co-operation with the Federal Housing Authority helped secure proper housing. The War Council originated the plan of having stores remain open one night weekly for the special benefit of day factory workers, many of whom worked far longer hours than were required in typical peacetime schedules. It encouraged school teachers to take summer war work, and tried to locate branches of defense plants outside critical labor shortage areas. It promoted courses in industrial safety and industrial training, which were given at Yale and The University of Connecticut. Those completing such courses in turn supervised similar programs in their own plants. The War Council met a critical fuel-oil shortage in January 1943 by establishing emergency offices and handling 80,000 emergency cases. The next winter a shortage of anthracite coal brought prompt assistance through emergency fuel depots. To increase the food supply a large war-gardens program was started; for example, 160,000 gardens were planted in the summer of 1944. A nutrition committee sponsored an educational program which helped many companies provide better lunches for war workers. When many farmers faced a critical shortage of grain in 1943 and 1944, the War Council and state administration worked hard to obtain priorities, especially for milk and egg farmers. Many vital steps were taken to secure additional farm labor. In co-operation with the State Department of Education, child care centers for children of working mothers were established. Sales of war savings bonds were pushed hard through special bond rallies and benefits, payroll deduction plans,

and tireless individual efforts. Mrs. Raymond Baldwin, the governor's wife, for example, visited almost every public school on behalf of the program. From May 1941 through June 1946 sales of series E, F, and G bonds totaled over $1,100,000,000, and Connecticut oversubscribed its quota in all war-loan drives.[16]

Industrial production during the war exceeded all expectations, thanks to intensive use, often around-the-clock, of Connecticut's great manufacturing facilities. The job-training program, started under Governor Baldwin and first directed by Carl Gray, trained 30,000 persons for defense positions before Pearl Harbor and about 66,000 afterward. Industrial employment zoomed from 350,000 in 1939 to 550,000 in 1944 — a new high point. Many industries converted entirely or largely to defense production. In May 1944 it was reported that 147,800 workers in essential industry were women.[17]

The total volume of war contracts placed in the state through May 1945, when cutbacks started, was over $8,000,000,000, or more than 4 percent of the nation's total. Of the contracts, aircraft accounted for over $4,000,000,000; ordnance, nearly $2,400,000,000; ships, about $294,000,000; communications equipment, about $146,000,000; and other categories, over $1,100,000,000. Although a few states exceeded Connecticut in total volume of contracts, Connecticut clearly ranked first in per capita value of such contracts. Connecticut firms made over 80 percent of all precision ball bearings. The aircraft industry turned out over 500,000 engines and 1,000,000 propeller blades. At Groton, the Electric Boat Company built more than seventy-five submarines. As already seen, the brass, small-arms, and silver industries made huge contributions to the war effort. In World War II, as in World War I, Connecticut became truly an arsenal of democracy.[18]

Connecticut Servicemen Fight All Over the World

FROM the sneak attack on Pearl Harbor until the final Japanese surrender in 1945, over 210,000 Connecticut men — soldiers, sailors, marines, and coastguardmen — saw action in many parts of the world. About 75,000 of these voluntarily enlisted:

roughly 33,500 each in the Army and Navy; close to 6,000 in the Marine Corps; and nearly 2,400 in the Coast Guard. In addition, at least 136,000 were inducted through the Selective Service System, which had sixty-five local boards covering the state. As in other states, the majority of the able-bodied men from eighteen to about thirty-five years of age were under arms during the conflict. The most reliable figures available on the distribution of men and women among the services show:

Army (including the Air Force)	145,294
Navy	54,445
Marine Corps	8,561
Coast Guard	2,591
TOTAL	210,891

It is virtually certain that more servicemen came from Connecticut than our records indicate. In war periods record-keeping is done under enormous difficulties, and an absolute, accurate record undoubtedly never will be achieved. Out of the 210,891 servicemen and women known to have come from this state, about 5,700 gave their lives in the great battle against the German, Italian, and Japanese dictatorships. In addition, thousands more were wounded — some to be crippled for life. World War II differed from earlier wars in that there were distinct feminine branches of each service, WACS, WAVES, SPARS, and Women Marines. Although reliable statistics are lacking as to Connecticut's total feminine enlistment, the Army reported that 3,308 Connecticut women had entered the WACS between November 1, 1940, and June 30, 1945.[19]

Since Connecticut servicemen were scattered among those of other states in countless units of the armed forces, it is impossible to call any outfit a "Connecticut" one. The closest approach to this would be the Forty-third Division, which prior to the war consisted of National Guardsmen from Connecticut, Maine, Vermont, and Rhode Island. Connecticut then provided the personnel for all of the Eighty-fifth Brigade (One Hundred Second and One Hundred Sixty-ninth Infantry), part of the Sixty-eighth Field Artillery, the Division Headquarters, the Special Troops, part of the One Hundred Eighteenth Medical Regiment, and all

of the Division Aviation. On February 24, 1941, the Forty-third was formally inducted into active Federal service. There followed intensive training, the addition of men from all over the United States, and participation in the Louisiana maneuvers of August and September 1941, and the Carolina maneuvers of that fall. Further training at Camp Blanding, Florida; Camp Shelby, Mississippi; and Fort Ord, California, preceded shipment in October 1942 to the Southwest Pacific Theater of Operations.[20]

Most of the division went to New Zealand, where it was stationed as a strategic reserve against possible Japanese invasion. Later the division moved to New Caledonia, and then to Guadalcanal in January 1943, just prior to that campaign's end. The Forty-third's savage baptism of fire came later that year when it joined a special Army-Navy-Marine task force which hit Rendova Island, New Georgia, early in the summer of 1943. Many weeks of unceasing jungle warfare at its worst followed. At one time the Forty-third was in a precarious situation facing entrapment by the Japanese, but timely reinforcements saved it. The division played a major role in the final capture of the Munda airfield, which fell on August 5, 1943. The division killed about 4,000 Japanese and had 581 men killed in action and 2,059 wounded.[21]

In July 1944 elements of the Forty-third were rushed to Aitape, New Guinea, to aid an offensive already in progress. Their contribution was sharply limited by their worn weapons, many of which were unserviceable. During this period Major General John H. Hester, commanding officer since August 1941, was replaced by Major General Leonard F. Wing, who held the position until demobilization.[22]

The Forty-third elements continued patrolling Aitape until late in 1944, when Australians relieved them. The Forty-third prepared on Aitape for the far-reaching Luzon (Philippines) operations. In January 1945 it joined the huge invasion force which struck at Lingayen Gulf, Luzon, Philippine Islands. The Forty-third's mission was to take the left flank of the assault on the Gulf and seize the hill masses and road network, thus cutting off Japanese troops in the mountains near Baguio. For a month the division engaged in constant action with the enemy and inflicted very severe casualties. Later it moved into the Fort Stotsenberg area of Luzon, then southward to destroy the Japanese line in the Antipolo-New Bosoboso sector east of Manila. The Forty-third helped capture Ipo Dam, and then spent June and July 1945 in mopping-up operations. The Philip-

third arrived at San Francisco in October 1945 on six transports, though most of the original National Guardsmen had come earlier. In its proud record of achievement, the Forty-third could point to unit citations awarded to the First, Second, and Third Battalions of the One Hundred Sixty-ninth Infantry. Individual decorations were very numer-

Twelve-inch Japanese gun captured by Forty-third Division in Luzon, Philippines.

pine operations exacted a dreadful toll — 952 killed and 3,921 wounded. With Japanese surrender, the Forty-third landed at Yokohama for occupation duties northwest of Tokyo, but soon afterward it was ordered home. Many of the Forty-

ous in the battle-scarred division, which had spent over 9,000 hours in front-line duty.[23]

In the following tabulation are listed a few of the Army divisions in which sizable numbers of Connecticut men served:[24]

Division	Campaigns or Major Actions	Notes	Number of Connecticut Men Listed in Commemorative Booklet
SECOND	D-Day plus one Landing Normandy Brittany (Brest) Belgian Bulge Germany	Total of 320 days fighting: 2,999 killed, 10,924 wounded, 109 missing. Ended war at Pilsen, Czechoslovakia.	222
FOURTH ("Ivy")	D-Day Normandy Belgium Luxembourg Germany	Occupied Cherbourg; helped liberate Paris; drove through Ardennes Forest; penetrated Siegfried Line; suffered 21,550 casualties.	209
FIFTH ("Red Devils")	Viederville, France Metz Relief of the Belgian Bulge Luxembourg Czechoslovakia	Took 7,800 prisoners in drive across France and capture of Metz. In 10 months of fighting had 564 officers and 11,822 men casualties.	236

Division	Campaigns or Major Actions	Notes	Number of Connecticut Men Listed in Commemorative Booklet
EIGHTH ("Pathfinder")	Normandy (D plus 28) Brest Crozon Peninsula Luxembourg Germany	Helped take Brest. Fought in Hurtgen Forest.	204
TENTH ("Mountain")	Mt. Belvedere Apennines Lake Garda–Brenner Pass	Dislodged Germans permanently from Mt. Belvedere and many other mountain peaks.	225
THIRTEENTH (Airborne)	Italy Southern France (517th Parachute Inf. Regt. only)	Except for 517th Parachute Inf. Regt. the Division sent to ETO too late.	240
THIRTIETH ("Old Hickory")	Normandy (D plus 9) St. Lo Breakthrough Belgium and Belgian Bulge Germany	Near Mortain, France, attacked by 5 German armored divisions and held. While in ETO took 50,374 prisoners and destroyed 434 enemy tanks.	261
FORTY-FOURTH	Vosges Mountains Saar Austria	2d Battalion, 114th Inf. Regt. saved Division by stand at Schalbeck, France, Nov. 25, 1944.	117
EIGHTY-FIFTH ("Custer")	Gustav Line Relief of Anzio Rome Alps	Captured several German divisions intact near Brenner Pass.	66 (low estimate)
EIGHTY-SIXTH ("Black Hawk")	Rhine Ruhr Pocket Bavaria	Captured 79,698 prisoners in Europe and liberated over 100,000 allied prisoners of war.	208
EIGHTY-SEVENTH ("Acorn")	Saar Belgium-Ardennes Luxembourg Siegfried Line Moselle and Rhine rivers	Captured over 31,000 prisoners in combat; took Coblenz.	156
NINETY-FIRST ("Powder River")	Gothic Line (Italy) Livergnano Po, toward Trieste	Completely destroyed a section of Gothic Line; ended war near Trieste.	104
NINETY-FIFTH ("Victory")	Metz Saar (Saarlautern) Cleanup of Harz Mountains	Took part of deepest section of Siegfried Line (West Wall).	186

Division	Campaigns or Major Actions	Notes	Number of Connecticut Men Listed in Commemorative Booklet
NINETY-SEVENTH ("Trident")	Ruhr Pocket	Reached Czechoslovakia by end of war.	243
ONE HUNDRED FOURTH ("Timberwolf")	Holland Roer Remagen and 350 miles eastward	Seized Lamersdorf-Indent-Lucherberg; called by Gen. J. Lawton Collins the finest single piece of work in VII Army Corps since D-Day.	142

During the war nine Connecticut men were awarded the very rare Congressional Medal of Honor. Each medal represents heroic action far above and beyond the call of duty. In performing these virtually unbelievable feats of valor, four of the men made the supreme sacrifice.[25]

Name of Recipient	Date and Place of Valorous Action
Captain Michael J. Daly (Southport)	April 18, 1945, at Nuremberg, Germany
Sergeant William G. Fournier (Norwich)	January 10, 1943; killed at Guadalcanal
Pfc. John D. Magrath (East Norwalk)	April 14, 1945; killed at Castel d'Aiano, Italy
Pfc. William J. Johnston (Middletown, Hartford)	February 17, 1944, near Padiglione, Italy
Captain Robert P. Nett (New Haven)	December 14, 1944, near Cognon, Leyte, Philippines
Radio Electrician Thomas J. Reeves, U.S.N. (Thomaston)	December 7, 1941; killed at Pearl Harbor
Captain Herbert Schonland, U.S.N. (New London)	October 11–12, November 12–13, 1942, Savo Island
Pfc. William A. Soderman (West Haven)	December 17, 1944, near Rocherath, Belgium
Pfc. Frank P. Witek (Derby) U.S.M.C.R.	August 3, 1944; killed at Guam

From the November 1944 Election to the End of the War

IN preparation for the November 1944 elections the Republicans prevailed upon Governor Baldwin to make a fourth run, even though he had signified a desire to retire. John A. Danaher was renominated for senator. The platform emphasized the war record. Democrats named Hurley for the third time and chose Brien McMahon as senatorial candidate. The party's platform called for a direct primary, a labor-relations act, and vigorous prosecution of the war. The presidential race, matching Roosevelt, seeking a fourth term, against Thomas Dewey, as usual tended to attract more interest than the state races. Although Roosevelt's name was still very influential, Hurley had helped create sharp factionalism in his party organization. Election results revealed that many Connecticut voters split their tickets to vote for President Roosevelt and Governor Baldwin, as both won handily. Democrats captured four of the six House seats, and McMahon unseated Danaher.[26]

From relatively early in the war, Governor Baldwin devoted much thought to the problems of conversion to peacetime, and especially to the Connecticut Re-employment Commission, with Carl Gray, a manufacturer, as chairman. Gray had earlier gained valuable experience in administering the job-training program. Basic in the re-employment plan was the principle of individual counseling for veterans and displaced war workers, to ascertain what further education or job-training each needed. To increase effectiveness, local re-employment committees were organized.

Tied in with this broad effort were two other agencies — the Postwar Planning Commission and the Development Commission, both striving to stimulate future economic expansion in Connecticut. The Postwar Commission assembled detailed job availability information, which would be useful in planning for the future. In addition, the War Council and a recently organized Industrial Reconversion Commission contributed to the preparation for readjustment to a prosperous peacetime society. The overall setup, often referred to as the "Connecticut Plan," attracted wide interest nationally and helped boost the morale of Connecticut's fighting men, who were pleased at the careful planning for their future. One article on the program bore the expressive title, "Jobs, Not a Dole, for the Veteran."[27]

The Assembly which convened in January 1945 was remarkable for having thirty-nine women members, the most it had ever had — a direct result of the long war. Baldwin called upon the legislators to enact a far-reaching program involving judiciary reforms, extension of the war-powers bill, unification of four separate aeronautic agencies into one, approval of the constitutional amendment setting four-year terms for state officers, establishment of a recreation commission, amendment of the milk-control act, expanded facilities for chronic and mental illnesses, active postwar planning, large increase in the Soldiers', Sailors', and Marines' Fund, labor-relations act, liberalized workmen's compensation, and a balanced budget, among other items. The session was marked by bitter wrangling between the Democratic Senate and the Republican House, especially over patronage matters. Finally, late in May, the governor asked the legislature to concentrate on the major business at hand. The savage battle over minor court judges, after consuming much time, ended in an impasse, so the governor was able to appoint all of them on an interim basis. Since nearly all the important bills were passed late in the session, it was right in character for this Assembly to stop the clock at midnight and run four hours beyond compulsory adjournment time![28]

Despite intense and prolonged politicking, the legislators passed many important bills, including a comprehensive labor-relations act, a goal of organized labor for years; a sharp increase in the Soldiers', Sailors', and Marines' Fund from $2,500,000 to $15,000,000; several veterans' benefit bills; renewal of the governor's war powers; passage of a $130,000,000 state budget and a $1,500,000 war budget, with an overall balance expected. On the last day Baldwin personally appeared in the House to ask it to start on its way an amendment providing that minor court judges be appointed by the governor and confirmed by the Assembly. After a stormy debate the House did so. The aviation bill failed, as did Senate confirmation of five state officials appointed by Baldwin. For this Assembly, as the *Times* editorialized, "Even Adjournment Was Hard."[29]

The last months of the war were in many ways extremely trying. By early spring it was obvious that Germany and Italy were tottering, and early in May they surrendered. Yet most young men still were away in service, and home-front problems such as housing shortages and the black market in scarce articles continued to plague a war-weary people. The poultry farmers, for example, were caught in a bad squeeze between high feed prices and low OPA ceilings on eggs and chickens. Some farmers were selling their eggs on the black market in New York. According to the *Courant* of May 12, 1945, broilers with an OPA ceiling of 30.7 cents per pound were bringing 50 cents on the black market! The OPA broiler price ceilings apparently were calculated on production costs of large producers in Maryland and Delaware, which created an unfair situation for the Connecticut small farmer. This led Baldwin to ask the OPA for an increase in the ceiling. The governor used his emergency war powers to seize poultry and eggs for institutional use, especially for hospitals, which were in desperate need of them. The poultry situation well illustrates the extremely complex problems involved in wartime price fixing.[30]

Late 1945 and 1946 were essentially a period of transition from war to peace. With the surrender of Japan on September 2, most of Connecticut's servicemen soon were veterans in "civvies" returning to old jobs, seeking new ones, or resuming interrupted educations. Thanks to the elaborate plans made for industrial reconversion and for state and Federal aid to veterans, the readjustment proved far less painful than generally expected. As was inevitable, the total labor force in factories dropped considerably when war contracts were terminated. Many women workers returned to homemaking. Peacetime production resumed quickly enough so that no serious unemployment developed. Connecticut had come through the ordeal of war in a healthy condition, prepared and eager to meet the challenges and promises of peacetime. Certainly Governor Baldwin's dedicated and efficient wartime leadership contributed enormously to Connecticut's fine war record and established him firmly in the great tradition set by Trumbull, Buckingham, and Holcomb.

CHAPTER 21

A Brief Survey of Postwar Connecticut

Postwar Readjustments and Politics, 1946–48 — Political Campaign of 1948 — Two Stirring Years of Political Strife — The 1950 State Campaign — A Brief Sketch of the Lodge Administration, 1951–55 — Politics and Two Disastrous Floods in 1955 — The 1956 Republican Sweep, the 1957 Legislature, and a Recession — The 1958 Democratic Landslide — The 1959 "Reform" Legislature — Undemocratic System of Representation in the General Assembly — The Battle for Urban Renewal — Our Past, Present, and Future

---

Postwar Readjustments and Politics, 1946–48

THE immediate postwar period was filled with difficult readjustments to peacetime living — national, state, local, and individual. As the servicemen gladly became civilians again — by March 1, 1946, over 152,000 of them were discharged — they found many kinds of assistance available. Draft boards now reversed their roles and helped veterans to recover their old positions, if desired, or to secure other jobs. The state maintained offices for veterans' assistance in thirty-seven towns. Regular employment offices were instructed to make every effort to place veterans, and many firms followed a policy of veterans' preference. Both the Federal and state governments gave veterans an automatic bonus on civil service examinations. Of particularly high value to honorably discharged veterans were the educational benefits in the famous G.I. Bill. Under this act a veteran could continue his education at Federal government expense (a reasonable allowance provided) for one year plus the length of time in service. Connecticut colleges, universities, and vo-

cational schools have had 91,500 World War II veterans, many married, taking courses under this act during the postwar period. College teachers in Connecticut found these vets, who averaged several years older than the average undergraduate, unusually conscientious, serious, and high-ranking students. For those wanting technical training, the G.I. Bill was equally valuable.[1]

Since there had been very little new housing permitted during the war, a severe housing shortage plagued postwar Connecticut. Although both builders and prospective buyers or renters had common interests in accelerated construction, a severe shortage of building materials greatly hampered efforts. The housing problem constituted the most important item recommended to the Assembly by the governor at the special session, called for May 1946. The legislators agreed to make funds available for housing and authorized towns to take necessary action. At the same session an aviation commission was created and money appropriated for improvements at Bradley Field and Trumbull Airport. Since prices were rising rapidly everywhere because of the relaxation of national price controls, a cost-of-living increase was voted to state employees.[2]

The governor envisaged a co-ordinated local, state, and Federal attack on the housing shortage in a comprehensive nine-point program, which he announced in the spring. The Federal Housing Authority (FHA) insured mortgage loans for thousands of new homes and rental housing in the state, as well as for property improvement of old homes. In addition, the State Housing Administration in November 1946 allocated $2,174,000 for veterans' housing from the housing act appropriation. Even with strenuous efforts, however, the housing problem remained acute, locally as nationally, for several years more.[3]

In politics, both major parties were also having their postwar adjustment problems. In June 1945 Governor Baldwin declared his intention to retire from politics and accept a position with an insurance company, and he publicly reiterated these plans in January 1946. Throughout the spring and early summer, heavy pressure was put on Baldwin by both state and national Republican leaders to run for the United States Senate. Finally, in August, the governor yielded to the enormous pressure and agreed to make the Senate race. Meanwhile a scramble for the gubernatorial race developed, with James L. McConaughy emerging the victor over his chief rival, Joseph Talbot, of Naugatuck. McConaughy had served as president of Wesleyan, 1925–43, headed China Relief during much of the war, and held an important position with the famous Office of Strategic Services (OSS). In 1939–41 he had been lieutenant governor. After Hurley's two consecutive defeats, the Democrats were seeking a new gubernatorial candidate. Wilbert Snow, English professor at Wesleyan and a noted poet, succeeded in winning the nomination from his principal rival, Chester Bowles. Snow was lieutenant governor at the time. Joseph Tone was nominated to face Baldwin for the full six-year Senate term.[4]

Both party platforms took liberal positions on such matters as welfare programs, labor, antidiscrimination measures, and education, while promising increased veterans' benefits, including a cash bonus, and efforts to improve housing conditions. On the housing problem, the Democrats offered a much more specific plank, promising a vigorous state-level program for homes and low-cost rentals. After an energetic campaign the Republicans scored a resounding victory, their greatest in two decades. Baldwin amassed a spectacular vote of 381,328 to Tone's 276,424, while McConaughy easily won over Snow by 371,852 to 276,335. Republicans swept all six Congressional seats and took both houses of the Assembly. The extent of the Republican victory may be partly explained by the unusual strength of the Baldwin-McConaughy team at the top — especially Baldwin's impressive record as war governor — and by a general Republican tide running strongly in Connecticut, as nationally.[5]

On December 27, 1946, Baldwin resigned as governor in order to take his seat in the Senate. This in turn meant that Snow became governor for the term of thirteen days until McConaughy's term started on January 8, 1947. Governor Snow with keen gusto celebrated his record-breaking tenure by appointing a governor's military staff![6]

In his recommendations to the 1947 Assembly, Governor McConaughy presented a broad program, much of which could be classified as postwar readjustment. Since the special postwar fund was virtually exhausted, revenues were down, and expenses were rising in an inflationary period, the governor advised a serious study of means to effect wise economies. Many of his specific recommendations, however, entailed substantial new expenditures: increased state aid to schools and the state university; a group life-insurance plan for state employees; a bonus for veterans; an increased Soldiers', Sailors', and Marines' Fund; a fair employment practices act; serious consideration of a report on care of the chronically ill, aged, and infirm; an increase in the gasoline tax, to help finance the expanding highway system, including secondary roads; and a strengthened labor program. Since the governor's party firmly controlled both houses, a favorable situation existed to secure action on the proposed program.[7]

Much to McConaughy's evident surprise and pleasure, the legislature enacted into law practically all of his recommendations: larger educational grants to towns and cities; Fair Employment Practices Act; Rent Control Act; more liberal workmen's unemployment benefits; larger old-age benefits; limited housing program (called "a drop in the bucket" by many critics); veterans' bonus based on length of service, with a minimum of thirty dollars and a maximum of three hundred dollars; increase in the Soldiers', Sailors', and Marines' Fund; group life insurance for state employees; limited reorganization of agricultural agencies; and an expanded highway and institutional building program. Sharp controversy developed over several measures. McConaughy's fair-employment proposal precipitated violent debate in the House and was nearly defeated by rural Republican members. As always, the hardest assignment was that of finding means to pay for the expanded services to be offered, and this occasioned lengthy debate. Democrats uncompromisingly fought the sales tax. The resulting tax package, jammed through by high-handed, eleventh-hour legislative tactics, included a new 3 percent sales and use tax, expected to produce a heavy yield, and increases in old taxes such as those on gasoline, cigarettes, and corporate income. The Assembly dropped the old-age-assistance tax. Certainly Governor McConaughy's influence was large in the achievement of so much progressive legislation.[8]

On the constitutional side, four major changes received final approval before submission to the electorate: 1] setting four-year terms for state officers; 2] setting the same for probate judges; 3] permitting the Assembly to establish its own methods for restoring forfeited rights; and 4] having minor court judges nominated by the governor, with confirmation by both houses. The Assembly also started on its way an amendment requiring a two-thirds vote to override a governor's veto.[9]

During the remainder of 1947 there was much criticism of the sales tax, especially by Democrats. Also, the housing situation remained bad despite increased construction. As it turned out, the sales tax and other tax yields were so good that McConaughy called a special Assembly session for February 1948. It reduced the sales tax from 3 to 1 percent for fifteen months from April 1, 1948, after which it would be 2 percent. It exempted from the sales tax restaurant meals under one dol-

lar and materials consumed by farmers and manufacturers in production. Only a few days after the special session, on March 7, 1948, the state was deeply shocked by the sudden death of Governor McConaughy. Apparently in excellent health and relishing the challenges of his job, he was well on his way to achieving a distinguished record.[10]

James C. Shannon, the lieutenant governor, automatically succeeded McConaughy. Shannon, a Bridgeport native, Yale Law School graduate, World War I aviator, and judge in Bridgeport's municipal court system, had been counsel for the Connecticut Federation of Labor since 1939. In August of 1948 he summoned the Assembly to a special session on housing. The legislature passed the program he advocated. It increased the state's local housing authority bond guarantee total from $15,000,000 to $45,000,000, lengthened the bond amortization period so that rents could be reduced slightly, and provided a virtual moratorium for seven months on evictions. Democrats vainly fought for a direct-subsidy housing program as drawn up by Chester Bowles. Other measures passed included an increase in the old-age pension maximum from forty-five to fifty dollars monthly.[11]

Political Campaign of 1948

FOR the Democrats, who had lost three consecutive state elections, the need for finding a winning gubernatorial candidate was urgent. When the Democratic State Convention met in August 1948 there were two leading candidates, Thomas J. Dodd and Chester Bowles. Dodd, a Yale Law School graduate, served from 1938 to 1945 in the Federal Department of Justice. In 1945–46 he earned distinction as Chief Trial Counsel at the Nuremberg International Trial of Nazi war criminals. Bowles entered politics after a highly successful career in the advertising field. During part of World War II, he headed the OPA — an extremely difficult job. In 1946 President Truman appointed him head of the new Office of Economic Stabilization. Later that year when Congress passed a price-control act full of loopholes, Bowles resigned in protest. The next year he accepted an appointment as chairman of a United Nations relief operation for children. In 1946, perhaps partly due to Brien McMahon's opposition, he lost his gubernatorial nomination bid to Wilbert Snow.[12]

To the 1948 convention Bowles brought powerful labor and other backing and quickly won the nomination. As a unity gesture he asked Dodd to run for lieutenant governor, but he declined. The convention then named William T. Carroll of Torrington as Bowles's running mate. Bowles insisted on a highly liberal platform, calling, among many items, for this broad program: 1] immediate construction of 65,000 permanent low-rent housing units; 2] modification of the eviction law; 3] a seventy-five cents hourly minimum wage; 4] extension of workmen's compensation insurance; 5] revision of constitution to provide more equal system of representation; 6] direct primary system for state and local offices; and 7] repeal of the sales tax. In mid-September the Progressive party candidate, Professor Thomas I. Emerson, fearing that he would draw votes away from Bowles, withdrew from the race. Early in the campaign, Philip Murray, C.I.O. leader, and William Green, A.F. of L. head, enthusiastically endorsed Bowles.[13]

The Republican convention, as expected, nominated Governor Shannon and chose Meade Alcorn as running mate. The platform, less specific than the Democrats', stressed the party's recent achievement. It pledged a balanced budget without new taxes, "dynamic action" on housing, elimination of river and beach pollution, a study of state employee pay schedules, and continuation of many current programs, such as unemployment compensation, workmen's compensation, educational subsidies, care and treatment of the aged, infirm, and chronically ill (by inference, therefore, no increase was advocated). The platform condemned communism, urged a stronger United Nations, and endorsed economic aid for Israel. Keith Shonrock of the *Courant* pithily compared the platforms: "Democrats Long on Promises; Republicans Review Performances."[14]

As the state campaign unfolded, an interesting difference in party strategies was evident. This stemmed largely from a view among informed political observers of both parties that Shannon would easily win. Pointing to their record of the past two years, Republicans asserted that every

1946 platform pledge had been "delivered." The 1946 elections, nationally and in Connecticut, had gone heavily Republican, and the state G.O.P. felt that the trend would continue. For the Democrats, however, a spirited and slashing offensive seemed to be the only hope to overcome adverse initial odds, made worse by the fact that for the first time in sixteen years they could not ride on Roosevelt's popularity. Republicans decided to let Bowles start his hard-hitting attack early, on the assumption that he would wear himself out prematurely. Republicans then would take over, with Alcorn answering Bowles, while Shannon concentrated on G.O.P. achievements and desirability of a renewed mandate. Jack Zaiman, *Courant* political writer, called this a dangerous strategy to employ against Bowles.[15]

As it turned out, Bowles campaigned so vigorously and dramatically that he became more of an issue than the issues themselves. Speaking on the radio several times weekly and stumping the state furiously, he kept up the race all the way. Billboards claimed, "Bowles Kept Prices Down; He Can Get Housing Up." On one radio program Bowles had five New Haven residents tell about shocking housing conditions they endured. Bowles claimed that the Republican program, involving 920 units under construction, was grossly inadequate at a time when there existed a waiting list of 5,500 families at the Hartford housing office alone. Besides emphasizing housing shortages, he hammered away at such issues as salary raises for state employees, needed labor legislation (platform planks), increased funds for education, reduced prices, retention of old industry and attraction of new. At least twice, Bowles challenged Shannon to debate the leading issues, but in vain.[16]

In return, Governor Shannon vigorously defended his housing and other programs and charged his opponent with giving "a one-sided, distorted caricature of the real truth." In another sharp attack, Shannon called the election "a contest between the Republican party and a group of men who, having snarled things up in Washington, have now moved in on the Democratic party in Connecticut and taken over." The governor also frequently flagellated the Truman administration, and he described Bowles as advocating "a hybrid mixture of Trumanism and Wallaceism in Connecticut."[17]

The last month of campaigning became even more heated. Meade Alcorn surpassed Shannon in attacking Bowles as not meeting the issue of communism, as being dishonest on prices, and as making a "sinister" deal to obtain the withdrawal of Emerson as Progressive party candidate. Alcorn also repeatedly warned against believing the glamorous promises of Bowles. The latter replied, accusing Republicans of "smears, innuendoes and distortions." The final weeks of the campaign grew torrid enough to overshadow the presidential race between Truman and Dewey. Late in October both presidential candidates made hurried trips across Connecticut, and each received a warm welcome. The state candidates continued, meanwhile, to pummel each other mercilessly, right down to the closing bell.[18]

The 1948 fall elections brought profound shock to poll-takers and Republicans. One famous pollster warned Bowles that he faced crushing defeat by over 200,000 votes, and there was general agreement that Truman was doomed! Dewey managed to carry Connecticut, though losing nationally, but Bowles triumphed by the narrow margin of 2,225 votes. While the House remained Republican by a reduced margin (179–93), Democrats captured the Senate (23–13). Stunned Republican leaders found the defeat difficult to accept or explain. The *Courant* thought that Emerson's withdrawal had been decisive. Since Henry Wallace, as Progressive party presidential candidate, polled 13,713 votes, this theory has plausibility. State labor leaders claimed that the labor vote had turned the tide. In a close contest any one group can consider themselves decisive, but to this observer the main cause of victory appears to have been the dramatic and dynamic campaign which Bowles waged. It stirred deep interest and apparently attracted many "independent" voters.[19]

Two Stirring Years of Political Strife

BOWLES's term as governor produced more political fireworks than any comparable period in the century. Immediately after the election, Republicans challenged the validity of the returns, and complicated legal moves and countermoves continued for several weeks. Bowles, however, took office on the scheduled day in January 1949, and in his inaugural address called for a program implementing the Democratic platform.[20]

In April Connecticut's political world was rocked by Bowles's announcement that he had nominated Senator Baldwin as an Associate Justice of the Supreme Court. This cleared the road for an interim appointment of Democrat William Benton to the vacated Senate seat and simultaneously eliminated Baldwin as a gubernatorial possibility. Many Republicans charged that Baldwin had let his party down. Baldwin stated recently that he accepted the judicial seat primarily because it represented the cherished realization of a lifelong dream. He also felt that he had served his state and party for a long and trying period.[21]

Two other of Bowles's actions also sparked much interest: 1] his call for ending segregation in the Connecticut National Guard, and 2] suspension of James T. Dunn as chairman of the State Liquor Control Commission. The antisegregation bill passed and he signed it on March 16 — the second such law in the nation. Since Dunn was a prominent Republican, cries of partisanship went up. After a trial, Dunn was found guilty of neglect and incompetence and removed. Major John C. Kelly, a Republican and head of the State Police, was Bowles's choice as successor.[22]

The Assembly session became more hectic as time passed. Bowles did succeed in getting Assembly enactment of an extended workmen's compensation act, a bond issue for new dormitories at the University of Connecticut, an expansion of the Interracial Commission's powers to examine complaints of discrimination in public housing, hotels, and restaurants. On most items in Bowles's program, however, a complete impasse developed. The Democratic Senate decided to pass the program and let the Republican House pass or defeat each measure. Republican House leadership then buried the measures in committee. In return, Democrats refused to consider any private "pet" bills of individual Republicans. The latter retaliated by avoiding discussion of compromise on the chaotic situation until the "pet" bill ban was lifted. Bowles's budget, calling for over $355,000,000 and including $75,000,000 in capital construction, abolition of sales tax, and substitution of an income tax, ran into violent Republican opposition. The Republicans refused Bowles's offer of substantial concessions, and the mandatory adjournment date found the state without any budget at all for the new biennium just weeks away![23]

On the thorny housing problem, the Assembly compromised on a bill authorizing construction of 9,500 unsubsidized homes, of which 3,000 would be for sale and 6,500 for rent. Earlier in the session the legislators agreed on a compromise aimed at checking the torrent of evictions. Both laws gave Bowles only part of what he had recommended.[24]

The special session called by Bowles to consider the budget, school building aid, and mental hospitals expansion exceeded the regular session in explosiveness. The Senate reluctantly accepted the House-sponsored budget of $239,342,900. Then a bitter fight developed over school building and University of Connecticut proposals, and the House staged a walkout on June 16. When Bowles adjourned the legislature on June 30, the House defied him and met on July 6, with only one Democrat present, to pass bills which would never become laws.[25]

Governor Bowles did not make any appointments of minor court judges in the regular session. Under a new constitutional amendment, the governor appoints these judges and they are confirmed by the Assembly. At the end of June, while the House was on its "walkout," Bowles made the appointments, to be effective July 1. When some Republican incumbents refused to vacate their seats on July 1, the matter went to the courts. A month later the Supreme Court unanimously ruled the appointments legal. For Bowles and Bailey it was a great patronage victory, which undoubtedly deepened the rift between the governor and the House.[26]

In the fall the second and third special sessions occurred. The second, called to remedy a defect in the housing law, coincided with the start of the World Series. Baseball-conscious solons moved with amazing speed to complete their business!

The third session in November rekindled the wrangling — in this case beginning with the proposed agenda. Bowles and the Senate leadership apparently hoped to concentrate on school aid, while the House received bills on many subjects. Bowles had requested bond issues up to $25,000,000 for aiding local school boards in building new schools. Finally, in early December, a compromise bill was passed permitting state assistance to towns in redeeming local bond issues for elementary and secondary schools. Meanwhile a national recession had caused heavy unemployment, which by mid-July reached 106,200 — an eleven-year peak in Connecticut. By December, when many unemployed began to exhaust benefit payments, labor leaders urged the governor to call a special session to make a temporary extension of compensation benefits from the current twenty-six-week limit to March 1950. Bowles was willing to call such a session if Republican leaders would promise in advance to co-operate on a definite plan. When they refused, Bowles decided against a special session.[27]

The early part of 1950 was famous for the violent battle over state reorganization. Alarmed by the sudden rapid growth of governmental agencies and their pyramiding costs, public-spirited citizens generally welcomed the Assembly action authorizing a nonpartisan study of the state government aimed at discovering means of increasing efficiency and reducing costs. A five-man commission, headed by Carter W. Atkins, chairman of the Connecticut Public Expenditures Council, worked intensively with the help of many expert associates, and submitted its report on February 27, 1950. It broadly summarized the basic problems in these terms:

1] The management of the functions of the State government is so decentralized and so illogically divided among nearly two hundred separate departments, boards, commissions and agencies, as to lead to uncontrolled State expenditures, without any means under this system of producing an efficient and economical government.

2] The citizens are not getting one hundred cents' worth of government service for their dollar.

3] . . . Too often the agencies under this decentralized system respond to interests which are special and local rather than to the larger interests of the people of the State as a whole.[28]

The commission made sweeping recommendations, including *1*] abolition of election of all state officials except governor and lieutenant governor; *2*] annual legislative sessions; *3*] substantial salary increases for Assembly members; *4*] redistricting of the Senate every ten years; *5*] ban on dual job-holding by legislators; *6*] consolidation of 202 departments and agencies into 20 streamlined departments, the heads of all but three appointed by and responsible to the governor, with no legislative confirmation required; *7*] substantial salary increases for the governor, department heads, and their chief assistants; *8*] an amendment guaranteeing towns and cities true home rule; *9*] further study at a later date of reapportionment plans for the House, but an interim reduction of total size to 169 — one member per town; *10*] nominations by direct primary; *11*] creation of an office of legislative services; *12*] a unified court system completely replacing the current system; *13*] submission by the Assembly of a revised constitution including many points listed above as well as initiative, referendum, and recall. The commission even drew up the necessary enabling acts and a completely rewritten constitution.[29]

The battle began immediately. Such groups as the American Legion, public utilities companies, Connecticut Public Expenditures Council, farm and sportsmen's groups, the Connecticut Chamber of Commerce, and the Connecticut Manufacturers Association opposed various proposals. The Legion, for example, did not want the Soldiers', Sailors', and Marines' Fund placed under tight centralized control within the Welfare Department. Presidents of four large insurance companies spoke against the proposed strong Commerce Department, which would absorb the Insurance Commissioner. Bowles took the issues to the people by radio, and he noted that those who had shouted loudest about waste and inefficiency in government were leaders in opposing the reforms needed to remedy those evils. It soon was obvious that the Assembly was prepared to accept at best only a small fraction of the plan. On March 26, 1950, a *Courant* editorial advocated laying aside the extremely controversial portions of the report and concentrating on areas of possible agreement. Seeing the handwriting on the wall,

Bowles offered a compromise which omitted legislative reapportionment, the new constitution, left alone the Insurance Commissioner and Public Utilities Commission, and tried to meet objections of labor, farm, and veterans' groups. The Republican leaders rejected this and offered their own plan — seven bills which ignored most of the reorganization report. They would support only home rule, the dual-job ban, a separate public works department, centralized purchasing of state supplies, and some minor agency consolidations. Finally party leaders reached an agreement upon enactment of a minimal program, which Bowles felt merely scratched the surface of reorganization needs. Even the minimal program fell short when politics got the upper hand. On May 23, the Democratic Senate leader, Alfred F. Wechsler of Hartford, mentioned that Bowles might call another special session, after the Republican convention in August, to test the sincerity of the Republican platform. Using this statement as a convenient pretext, all Republicans simply walked out. An hour later Bowles took to the radio, asking them to return and enact the remainder of the acts agreed upon. There was no answer.[30]

Other factors, too, caused the failure: opposition of powerful special-interest groups, especially insurance and utility companies; the poor timing of the report — not enough time for public discussion and too near the election; excessive radicalism in the eyes of many people; poor press relations and much misrepresentation; and, finally, a strong feeling of negativism toward a "strong governor." When it came to the showdown, many special-interest groups preferred the power they currently enjoyed to the greater efficiency possible under reorganization. Although it is probable that under more favorable circumstances added state governmental reform could have been achieved in 1950, the titanic battle waged nine years later — when the Democrats were far more powerful — to obtain basic reorganization points up the huge opposition to reformers in Connecticut.[31]

The 1950 State Campaign

WORRIED by Bowles and by party disunity, the Republican high command decided to hold their convention early. Meeting in mid-June, delegates adopted a liberal platform, advocating such items as increased state aid to education, more benefits to labor, a ban on dual job-holding, redistricting of the Senate, a House of 169 seats, and more home rule. John Davis Lodge, a Westport lawyer and grandson of the famous Senator, Henry Cabot Lodge of Massachusetts, easily won the gubernatorial nomination. He offered an unusual background, including a brief Hollywood acting career, distinguished wartime Navy service, and two terms as congressman from the Fourth District. As Lodge's running mate Republicans chose Edward N. Allen of Hartford, a man of wide experience in politics and business. For the Senate, the convention selected Joseph Talbot (for full term) and Prescott Bush (unexpired term).[32]

Democrats renominated Bowles and Carroll as well as Senators Brien McMahon and Benton. On state affairs, the platform supported the full reorganization plan, including a constitutional convention. Since the Korean War had begun, strong support of the Truman administration and firm opposition to communism were stressed. On the Socialist ticket, McLevy was making his thirteenth try.[33]

Before the campaign could start Bowles called his fifth and final special session for September 5 to consider expansion of the state housing program. Feeling that the housing shortage still was critical, the governor asked for an additional $60,000,000, to be divided equally between new houses for sale and rental housing. Aware that housing was an explosive political issue, both parties handled it gingerly. The Republicans finally decided to accept the $30,000,000 new-homes program but rejected the rental one. After vetoing pay increases for state employees through all of the 1949 and 1950 sessions, suddenly, a few hours before this session ended and with an election imminent, the legislators voted small, across-the-board pay increases. Prompted by the Korean War, the Assembly also passed a civil defense bill which gave the governor extensive emergency powers until June 1, 1951.[34]

The fall campaign generated more heat than enlightenment, as each side deplored the abuse practiced by the other and then resorted to the same thing. Even so, some issues did emerge clearly. Republicans attacked Bowles on these points, among others: 1] failure to keep his pledges, especially that of bringing down prices; 2] failure to provide efficiency and economy; 3] allowing dual job-holding; 4] waste in the state housing program; and 5] "softness" on communism. Soviet aggressiveness, the Korean War, spy scares, and Senator McCarthy's efforts all had contributed to unusual concern over Communist infiltration domestically, and each party sought to capitalize on this.[35]

Democrats struck back hard, emphasizing such matters as: 1] G.O.P. obstructionism — a G.O.P. House had used every means to block virtually all of Bowles's program; 2] Lodge was almost totally unfamiliar with state problems; 3] Lodge could not implement his pledges against opposition from a G.O.P. House; 4] Korea would be a victory, not a defeat as Republicans claimed; and 5] Republican "softness" on communism.[36]

The campaign proved painfully short of real discussion of problems, though Lodge and Bowles did agree to a face-to-face debate, under League of Women Voters' sponsorship, on the topic, "Modernization of the State Constitution." The speeches were calm, but a spirited question-and-answer period followed. Bowles interjected the charge that Republican State Treasurer Joseph Adorno had blackmailed him by refusing to pay state employees unless Bowles gave him authority to borrow. The Adorno-Bowles feud, centering about differing views on the state's fiscal situation, remained "hot" throughout the campaign. Late in October McLevy joined Bowles and Lodge in a triangular discussion at Bridgeport. Lodge won applause for his statement that the chief issue was "promises versus performance," while Bowles hit back that the G.O.P. lacked "integrity" in adopting a platform advocating the very measures which the Republican House had recently defeated. Lodge and his wife spoke Italian fluently, and they used this ability in appealing to the large Italo-American population. Lodge also could speak Polish — another political asset.[37]

In mid-campaign, Republicans seemed to switch tactics. They stopped trying to "sell" Lodge, who was not well-known, and strengthened their attacks against Bowles. Pollsters employed by the Democrats reported that much anti-Bowles feeling existed. Frequently they heard, "I think Governor Bowles will be re-elected, but I'm not voting for him." Republicans learned from their poll-takers of this anti-Bowles trend, accompanied by a lack of knowledge and enthusiasm concerning Lodge.[38]

Senatorial races also were conducted at a torrid level, especially the McMahon-Talbot contest. Talbot received much aid from retired General Groves, wartime head of the Manhattan atomic bomb project. Groves vigorously flayed McMahon as incompetent in the atomic field, even though McMahon had won much fame for his senatorial work in that area. Talbot charged McMahon with being a virtual "tool" of Moscow. McMahon spared no efforts in leveling a withering counter-attack against Talbot. The hard-pressed Democratic state ticket received a helping hand from Vice-President Barkley, who spent a day vigorously campaigning at Bridgeport, Waterbury, and Hartford. Late in October, a Washington columnist, Thomas L. Stokes, complimented Connecticut upon the high level of candidates, but expressed the view that only Congressman Ribicoff (First District) appeared certain of re-election.[39]

Thus a furious campaign, in which both camps spent lavishly, finally ended on election eve in an aura of uncertainty. Could Bowles overcome the normal off-year Republican dominance? Would the united backing of organized labor prove effective? As in 1948, Bowles himself had proven to be the major issue. The voters defeated Bowles by 436,418 to 419,404, but elected McMahon by a wide margin and Benton by a razor-thin margin. Republicans won four of the six Congressional seats and gained in the Assembly, though Democrats kept the Senate, nineteen to seventeen. Bowles, the most liberal governor in Connecticut's history, undoubtedly seemed too radical to a large number of voters. Bowles himself felt that his reform drive had stepped upon too many toes too fast, that he had been "too much of an amateur," unwilling to make "deals," and that he needed four years to "sell" his program. Others cited personality factors, "overselling," too many special sessions, and use of a sort of "brain trust," as help-

ing to defeat him. Apparently, two years was too short a time for Bowles to learn how to harness together smoothly his crusading idealism and realistic party politics. Perhaps, also, the electorate had simply swung back to its normal Republican tendency.[40]

A Brief Sketch of the Lodge Administration, 1951–55

THE four years of Governor Lodge's administration may well be characterized as ones of moderate progress in terms of legislative action, of a violent Republican intraparty schism, and of general prosperity, sparked in part by the Korean conflict.

The Korean War vitally affected thousands of Connecticut men and their families. Although the exact number who served will never be known, the state bonus already has been paid to over 67,000 veterans or next of kin. Veterans were eligible who served in the armed forces for ninety days or more between June 27, 1950, and October 27, 1953, and received honorable discharges. Obviously, many receiving the bonus never served in Korea, but a large number did. The Forty-third Division (still Connecticut, Rhode Island, and Vermont men) was federalized on September 5, 1950. Though the division as a whole never was ordered to the Korean theater, about 3,400 of its men were detached for service there. The remainder of the Forty-third and replacements went to Bavaria, in Germany, to strengthen NATO forces. Service there involved intensive training, but fortunately no fighting. In 1952 the Forty-third's two-year tour of duty ended.[41]

For Connecticut's industry the Korean War meant heavy defense orders. The value of military procurement and construction contracts during the period of July 1950 to September 1954 amounted to nearly $5,000,000,000 — the seventh highest among all states. As usual, Connecticut ranked first in per capita value of military contracts. In the first year of the Korean conflict, for example, contracts averaged about $860 per capita as against about $470 for the second highest state.[42]

The 1951 Assembly, with a Democratic Senate and Republican House, granted to Korean veterans the property exemption and to their families eligibility for aid from the Soldiers', Sailors', and Marines' Fund. It continued the sales tax, housing, and defense programs. Large bond issues insured new buildings at several state institutions. Colored oleomargarine became legal. A minimum wage of seventy-five cents hourly was voted for all workers not covered by Federal laws. An especially important and controversial issue was that of the dual-job ban applied to state legislators. Apparently many legislators, especially Republicans, vigorously opposed this cutting off of lucrative patronage for themselves; yet both parties were pledged to it. Democrats in the Senate held out for and got the House to accept a strong bill prohibiting a legislator from accepting and holding any other paid state, county, or local administrative or judicial government position during the term for which he was elected to the Assembly. The Assembly also started a constitutional amendment to this end, as well as one for annual sessions.[43]

During the second year of Lodge's term he helped precipitate a bitter intraparty fight, which persisted for a long time. William Brennan, leader of the powerful Fairfield County organization, was also national committeeman for Connecticut. Although Brennan had been one of Lodge's first supporters, he decided that Brennan must step down as committeeman. An undercover campaign against Brennan was followed by an open attack led by Clarence Baldwin, state chairman. Among the differences between Lodge and Brennan was that caused by the governor's support of Eisenhower, and Brennan's championship of Taft. Fred Zeller of Stonington and other Republican leaders belonged to the pro-Brennan, pro-Taft faction. After a bitter struggle which caused a deep party rift, Brennan was deposed and Shannon named in his place. This in turn guaranteed an overwhelmingly pro-Eisenhower delegation to the Republican National Convention. Lodge became known as a leading eastern Eisenhower supporter — a reputation enhanced at the convention.[44]

As both parties considered plans for the 1952 fall elections, Lodge decided not to run for the United States Senate. This cleared the way for the Republican choices of incumbent William Purtell

for the full term and Prescott Bush of Greenwich for the unexpired term of Brien McMahon, who had died earlier in the year. The Democrats named Senator William Benton for the full term and Representative Abraham A. Ribicoff of Hartford for the short term. Because of the recently approved four-year amendment there would be no gubernatorial race until 1954. The presidential race between the very popular General Eisenhower and the highly articulate Adlai Stevenson largely overshadowed the state races. As it turned out, the General's great personal appeal, combined with such issues as "time for a change," the Korean War, corruption, and suggested softness toward communism produced a landslide. Eisenhower polled 611,012 votes; Stevenson, only 481,649. The General's prestige carried in Bush, Purtell, and five of the six congressmen. Only Thomas Dodd in the First District survived the Republican sweep. Republicans easily captured both Assembly houses. For victory-starved Republicans it meant the first Federal patronage since Hoover's Presidency. Even though Ribicoff lost the Senate race, his feat in running about 49,000 votes ahead of Stevenson marked him as a leading Democratic gubernatorial possibility for 1954.[45]

The 1953 legislature was moderately productive in measures of broad public significance. Major items included: extension of civil defense program for two years; increase in number of Superior and Common Pleas Court judges; four-year term for minor-court judges; increase of state educational aid to local communities by four dollars per pupil; revision of state election laws; redistricting the Senate; authorization of a toll superhighway from New York to Rhode Island line; increase in workmen's compensation and unemployment compensation benefits; large bond issues for institutional building programs; extension of state veterans' benefits to Korean War veterans; creation of the State Department of Mental Health; and recodification of the constitution and its forty-seven amendments into one continuous document. To finance state services, the Assembly raised the sales tax from 2 to 3 percent, the corporation tax from 3 to 3¾ percent, and the unincorporated business tax from one to two dollars per $1,000 of gross income over $50,000. Lodge experienced great difficulty in getting the tax increases, the local court change, and the increased labor benefits approved by his party. He continued to ignore Brennan and to cold-shoulder the Zeller wing of the party, yet managed to achieve most of his program.[46]

In preparation for the 1954 elections, both parties did the expected. The Republicans renominated Governor Lodge, and the Democrats chose former Congressman Ribicoff, who had demonstrated unusual vote-getting ability in 1952. Both parties adopted highly liberal platforms, and the Republicans strongly praised the Lodge administration's achievements. The chief differences lay in the far more detailed Democratic planks on education and labor, and their call for sweeping constitutional reforms, such as abolition of county government, equitable legislative representation, and reorganization of the court system. A hard-fought campaign was climaxed by an extremely close gubernatorial race. It was fairly late on election night before it was clear that Ribicoff had won by the narrow margin of 463,643 to 460,528. It was a lonely victory for Ribicoff, as every other elected state official was a Republican. Assuming that other factors between Lodge and Ribicoff were about even, it appears likely that the Republican schism defeated Lodge. He ran 10,539 votes behind successful Fred Zeller, comptroller, prominent in the Brennan faction. Otherwise, Republicans fared rather well, taking five of the six Congressional seats, and the House, but losing the Senate.[47]

Politics and Two Disastrous Floods in 1955

IN his inaugural message Governor Ribicoff requested measures to aid the state's economic growth — an objective which he stressed continuously. Part of the comprehensive program which he laid before the Assembly was enacted despite one of the most disgraceful session-end jams in history. Achievements included establishment of the first adult probation system in Connecticut's history, tightening up of the absentee-ballot law, extension of rent controls to March 31, 1956, when they would automatically expire, consolidation of the care of all neglected and abandoned children

under the state, a stepped-up highway program, small pay raises for state employees, liberalization of unemployment and workmen's compensation benefits, beach erosion controls, a Korean War veterans' bonus, and a revised system of assessing charges against patients in state institutions. A direct-primary bill precipitated intricate political maneuvering and crossing of lines by members of both parties, but no bill passed both houses.[48]

Since many key measures, including vital tax bills, were lost in the chaotic closing hours on June 8, Ribicoff called a special session for June 22. The sales, corporation, and unincorporated business taxes were continued at the current rates, while the gas tax was raised from four to six cents per gallon. The overlooked bill raising state education grants by an average of twenty-one dollars per pupil yearly was passed. The legislators voted substantial bond issues for humane and welfare institutions and vocational-technical schools. The Assembly also initiated three constitutional amendments covering annual sessions, greater home rule, and a claims commission. Most important of all probably was passage of a limited direct-primary act. In analyzing reasons for passage of this act, Duane Lockard (a senator in the 1955 sessions) expresses the view that leaders of both houses hoped to "improve" the direct primary bill to death, but finally neither party dared face possible voters' retribution for killing it.[49]

The summer of 1955 brings vivid and often terrifying memories to thousands of Nutmeggers. July and early August were unusually hot and dry. On the night of August 18–19, a dying hurricane, "Diane," dumped torrential rains of an intensity and duration never before experienced in many parts of the state. In Burlington an almost unbelievable 12.77 inches fell within a twenty-four hour period — a new state record. For a thirty-hour period many places had fourteen inches of rain. The Mad and Still rivers rushed through Winsted, leaving Main Street a rubble-strewn horror similar to wartime bombed areas. The Naugatuck River, breaking all previous records for height and volume of water, tore apart low-lying sections of Torrington, Thomaston, Waterbury, Beacon Falls, Naugatuck, Seymour, and Ansonia, and partially or entirely destroyed many factories and retail establishments. The Farmington River went on a similar rampage, especially in New Hartford, Collinsville, and Unionville, while the Park River struck Hartford serious blows. In eastern Connecticut the Quinebaug River cut a fearful path of destruction through Putnam, Danielson, Thompson, and other localities. Numerous other streams in many sections

for immediate and long-range reconstruction. This committee, whose survey showed a total statewide loss of $202,801,832, worked at high speed upon its broad assignment.[50]

Aid to stricken families and business came from many sources: private gifts, the Red Cross, the Salvation Army, a merchants' Disaster Committee, United Service Clubs, local drives, and loans from

Main Street, Winsted, during 1955 flood.

Main Street, Winsted, after the flood.

inflicted enormous damage. The waters climbed so rapidly that some homes were carried away even before residents could evacuate them, and about eighty persons were drowned. During the night of August 18–19 Ribicoff assumed personal control of an around-the-clock mobilization for immediate aid and long-range rehabilitation. The magnitude of the disaster was great: about 200 seriously injured, in addition to approximately 100 fatalities; about 15,000 families affected; 668 homes destroyed and 2,460 subjected to major damage; 507 industrial firms with physical losses of over $88,000,000; 1,436 commercial establishments with $45,500,000 damage; 922 farms reported $2,500,000 in losses; public property suffered to the estimated extent of $36,800,000; and there were 70,000 temporarily unemployed. Some of the smaller communities like Winsted and Putnam suffered the greatest relative losses. Ribicoff quickly named a Flood Recovery Committee under Sherman R. Knapp, president of the Connecticut Light and Power Company, to devise plans

the Federal Small Business Administration and numerous banks. While Connecticut was still recovering from the more than $200,000,000 loss of August, another flood struck on October 15–16, causing over $20,000,000 in damage, mostly in western and southwestern Connecticut, and taking a toll of seventeen lives. Danbury and Norwalk seem to have suffered the most, though over sixty towns reported some damage, including thirty-nine hit in August. Particularly unfortunate was the fact that some small merchants, especially in the Naugatuck Valley, grievously hurt in the August floods, were flooded out again. By mid-November, recovery from both floods was well advanced, though far from complete. Loans reaching over $17,000,000 had been approved by the Small Business Administration, private bank loans exceeded $6,000,000, and Red Cross direct aid to 625 of the worst stricken families and businesses totaled over $9,500,000. The Army Corps of Engineers had spent over $15,000,000 on rehabilitation work. The American Brass Company, whose plants in Waterbury, Ansonia, and Torrington suffered savage blows, expected to spend about $15,000,000 in rehabilitation. United States Rubber in Naugatuck estimated its repair bill at $5,000,000. Individual towns and cities tackled huge street and bridge repair projects.[51]

On the basis of careful study of the two bitter

petitioned Congress to take immediate action in providing funds for a flood-control program. It also authorized banks to make loans to flood victims on more liberal terms than usual as well as to service loans through the Small Business Administration. For many small businesses, however, it would require years of hard work to pay off their

American Shakespeare Festival Theater at Stratford (opened, 1955).

flood experiences, the Flood Recovery Committee was able to make detailed short- and long-term recommendations to the governor. Some of the larger problems, such as major dams and channel clearance on rivers, would require Federal action. The committee, however, called upon the state to finance flood recovery to the extent of about $35,000,000. Ribicoff called a special Assembly session for November. The legislators voted to spend $15,500,000 for repairs of state highways and bridges, $14,500,000 to restore local roads and bridges, much smaller sums for local redevelopment (Federal funds meeting a part of this cost), transfer of surplus housing to devastated areas, and reimbursement to towns suffering tax losses. To finance the "package," various taxes, including sales, cigarette, and liquor, were increased for a nine-month period. Flood-control commissions were authorized for the Farmington River Valley and the Park River. The Assembly

loans and get back fully on their feet. One of the happier results of the flood has been Federal construction of a large dam at Thomaston, begun in May 1958 and virtually completed by late 1960. It will provide considerable protection to the lower Naugatuck River Valley. Also, Federal projects at Hall Meadow Reservoir, Mad River, and other places will afford additional protection.[52]

The 1956 Republican Sweep, the 1957 Legislature, and a Recession

IN 1956 the rematch of President Eisenhower and Stevenson relegated the state contests to the sidelines. As in 1952, because of the universal use of voting machines, Connecticut's final returns came in first nationally and foretold an even bigger national Eisenhower avalanche. The popular President received 711,837 to 405,079 for Stevenson — the largest plurality ever recorded in any Connecticut political vote. So mammoth was the President's margin that he helped bury Democratic candidates down to the town level. Although Thomas Dodd ran nearly 75,000 votes ahead of Stevenson, he still lost by a huge margin to Senator Bush. All six House seats went Republican, and both Assembly houses were overwhelmingly Re-

$45; raising of the minimum wage from seventy-five cents to one dollar for many workers in retail trades, laundries, and service industries; orders to the Highway Department to make the eastern end of the Connecticut Turnpike into four lanes instead of two; tightened fire-safety codes, in the wake of a disastrous New Haven factory fire in

Scene on the Connecticut Turnpike in Bridgeport

The Charter Oak bridge over the Connecticut River at Hartford.

publican — the House 249 to 30, the Senate, 31 to 5.[53]

With both houses almost solidly Republican, Governor Ribicoff could have little influence on the Assembly's course of action. For the Republican Assembly it meant a great opportunity to write an impressive record, since any gubernatorial veto could be overridden with ease. Many important measures were enacted, such as increased state aid to schools; extension of ten years in the subsidy program for school building; designation of the chief justice as administrative head of the entire state court system; creation of a seven-member State Board of Mental Health; liberalization of farm personal property exemption and limitation on farm real property assessment; a ceiling on the state's debt; compulsory annual filing of financial reports by labor unions; an increase of maximum weekly unemployment compensation to $60 and maximum weekly workmen's compensation to

January; better vacation and other fringe benefits for state employees; a broad prison-reform program, including plans for new security institutions; provision for integration of the state employees' pension system with the Social Security system; establishment of a Civil Service Commission, and expansion of the size and power of the appeal board for state personnel; a small salary increase to all state employees; and a large increase in the State Police force, and other steps for traffic safety.[54]

The most controversial issue was the bill authorizing towns and cities, subject to a local referendum, to provide free bus transportation for pupils in parochial and other private schools. This precipitated an intense fight in the House. Representative Edwin O. Smith of Mansfield, senior member of the Assembly and chairman of the Education Committee, vigorously led opposition to this bill, and his committee recommended rejection. The measure stirred deep feelings and brought direct or indirect statements from church leaders and publications, including Archbishop O'Brien, the *Catholic Transcript*, and the Connecticut Council of Churches (Protestant). Before a jammed House gallery, the legislators debated the bill five and one-half tense hours. Then came the vote — which ended in a 133–133 tie. The Speaker of the House, Nelson C. L. Brown of Groton, dramatically broke the tie by voting "Yes." The governor promptly signed the bill.[55]

Republican leaders felt that on the whole they had compiled an impressive program for the 1958 elections, but Ribicoff chided the Assembly for failure to do anything about court and county government reform, a department for the problem of mental retardation, housing for the elderly, civil rights, and higher education. He also criticized the final budget as excessive. Earlier, he had forcefully vetoed a bill reducing taxes on insurance companies, only to be overridden.[56]

The summer of 1957 brought a record-breaking drought which caused farmers heavy losses. Republican leaders insisted on a special session to help the farmers. When the session met in September, there was a paucity of ideas as to how to provide relief without antagonizing all other taxpaying groups. The "package" finally adopted over Ribicoff's veto provided for a very low-interest loan program to heavily hit farmers, a two-year local tax exemption on farm livestock, and a special tax study commission to examine farm and general tax equalization and report back in 1959. Talk of a direct subsidy to farmers, strongly opposed by Ribicoff, did not produce action. On the other hand, the governor enthusiastically took the side of consumers' and housewives' spokesmen who wanted legalization of milk sales in half-gallon and gallon jugs. Although Republican leaders opposed it, a measure permitting sale in half-gallon jugs finally passed the House; the Senate unanimously confirmed it. Many observers felt that the session had been unproductive and had revealed that legislative leaders really had no adequate program to meet the farmers' problems.[57]

In common with the nation as a whole, Connecticut's economy slumped in the latter half of 1957 and early 1958. Faced by unemployment af-fecting about 90,000 and demands for action by labor leaders, Ribicoff called a special session for March 4, 1958. He requested important changes increasing unemployment benefits, as well as a $410,000,000 highway and public works program. Since Republicans remained overwhelmingly in control, they wrote their own ticket. It involved: *1*] payment of a maximum of thirteen extra weeks of unemployment benefits to jobless persons who had exhausted their regular benefits; *2*] borrowing up to $30,000,000 to keep the highway program at top speed and using available Federal grants; *3*] $15,000,000 in bonds to aid urban renewal and local commercial and industrial development; *4*] $7,500,000 in bonds for public works projects, including housing for the elderly; *5*] addition of $550,000 to the farmers' drought loan fund. Ribicoff signed the antirecession measures but labeled them "not an effective answer to the needs of the state's general economy or of the 94,000 unemployed workers."[58]

The 1958 Democratic Landslide

IN preparation for the fall elections Republicans experienced an exciting race for the gubernatorial nomination, primarily between conservative Fred R. Zeller of Stonington, and liberal John D. Alsop of Avon, with J. Kenneth Bradley of Westport receiving some support. William H. Brennan, Fairfield County leader, succeeded at the critical moment in swinging enough Bradley votes to Zeller to guarantee his nomination. Thus former Governor Lodge's enemies were in firm control. Senator Purtell was renominated for his seat. Zeller set the tone for his campaign by calling Ribicoff's administration wasteful and extravagant.[59]

For Democrats, spirited competition marked the three-cornered race between Dodd, Benton, and Bowles to secure nomination for United States senator. While the governor and the state chairman, John M. Bailey, were officially neutral, the large majority of party regulars seemed to be for Dodd. In the balloting at the state convention, Dodd won on the first ballot. Bowles quickly announced that he would not seek a primary, although he could do so under a state-primary law, passed not long before, permitting a candidate who obtains 20 percent or more of the delegate vote to petition for one. Ribicoff was renamed by acclamation. In his acceptance speech he promised to pursue actively the programs already started and to work for thorough reorganization of the state government, court reform, abolition of county government, better care for aged citizens, an expanded mental health program, and a larger program for attracting new industry to Connecticut. Counted upon as an asset was the strict state highway safety program, which had attracted favorable national attention and had been accompanied by a decline in fatalities on state roads.[60]

As the campaign progressed into mid-October, a *New York Times* survey team reported that Ribicoff was far ahead, with a 75,000 vote margin commonly predicted. They found these factors helping him: personal magnetism, efficient administration, highway safety program, energetic efforts toward rehabilitation after the floods, and emphasis on new industries. Typical of many comments was this feminine one: "I'm a dyed-in-the-wool Republican, but he's done a good job and I'll vote for him." Zeller, an able but quiet man, faced a heavy handicap in not being well known in many sections.[61]

The magnitude of Ribicoff's popularity surprised even the most optimistic Democrats. He polled 607,012 votes to 360,644 for Zeller, carrying even the Republican citadel of Fairfield County — which he had lost by 23,157 in 1954 — by a more than 50,000 plurality! His popularity was great enough to carry the entire state Democratic ticket, all six House seats, county sheriffs, and *both* houses of the Assembly. It was the first time that Democrats had won the House since 1876! Dodd, a proven vote-getter, also won a landslide victory. The overall results constituted an unmistakable and overwhelming personal triumph for Ribicoff. The more obvious factors in his success saga include a very friendly, modest, and appealing personality; a basic conservatism in political philosophy and fiscal policy combined with sincere interest in certain reforms which he considered long overdue; unusual ability to work with legislators of both parties; a high degree of administrative efficiency; a marked ability to dramatize and "sell" issues; and, finally, an unerring instinct for the

right move at the right time in the complicated game of politics.[62]

For Republicans, the story was well told in a headline: "GOP at Lowest Ebb in History." Shorn of state patronage and badly beaten, the G.O.P. faced its greatest rebuilding job. With the Brennan-Zeller wing thoroughly discredited by the debacle, many turned to John Alsop and Edwin H. May, Jr., of Wethersfield, as key figures in the rebuilding. May, who had won the First District Congressional seat in 1956, made an impressive run for re-election in 1958 but was narrowly defeated by the Ribicoff sweep. In December, after May won unanimous election, replacing Clarence F. Baldwin as state chairman, he began an energetic reorganization of the party along more liberal lines.[63]

Almost lost in the 1958 election results were three constitutional changes which received overwhelming popular approval: *1*] establishment of a claims agency by the Assembly; *2*] a ban on dual job-holding; and *3*] permission for legislators to set their own salaries. For years reform groups had sought the first two. The third would permit a more reasonable salary than the $300 yearly maximum set by the constitution many decades earlier. Many have argued for a higher remuneration as one means of attracting a higher caliber of legislator.[64]

The 1959 "Reform" Legislature

ON January 8, 1959, Democrats took over the state government — and even occupied Room 201, which had been G.O.P. headquarters since the capitol was built. There the new Speaker of the House, William J. O'Brien, Majority Leader Samuel S. Googel, and State Chairman John M. Bailey and others discussed politics and patronage under the watchful eyes of forty-one Republican ex-Speakers of the House, whose portraits adorned the walls![65]

In his second inaugural message Ribicoff called for district courts to replace local courts, the end of county government, sweeping reorganization of state government, a department for the problem of mental retardation, new traffic safety measures, continuation of the 1957 school-aid program, revision of the 1957 housing program for the elderly, and an austerity "breather" state budget. The special budget message of February 17 implemented his campaign pledge that no new taxes would be levied. He recommended a broad $346,000,000 four-year highway program — much of which would bring large Federal grants.[66]

The biggest single battle of the session occurred over the proposal to abolish 66 municipal and 102 trial justice courts and replace them by a new state circuit court with 44 full-time judges. The local court system dated back to the first decade of the colony and had developed into a cherished political as well as judicial system. Even though this reform would mean large political patronage losses, Ribicoff and his lieutenants applied very heavy pressure to secure passage. Because of the razor-thin Democratic margin in the House, the outcome of the battle was in great doubt until William H. Brennan, still a major power in the G.O.P., announced his personal support for the Democratic proposal. The Republicans wanted reorganization of the municipal courts only. This proved a turning point, as soon afterward G.O.P. and Democratic leaders worked out a compromise. It retained the basic features but allowed jury trials and a return of one-third of all motor vehicle fines to the towns where arrests occurred. Earlier, Ribicoff had promised to divide the forty-four new positions equally between the parties. Even so, small-town representatives made desperate attempts to save their town courts. Finally, on the evening of March 25, came the climactic vote — 199 to 67 for the administration's bill. The Senate had already passed the measure by 33 to 2. The governor's signature meant that the new Circuit Court would come into existence on January 1, 1961. Thus ended the long battle for court reform proposed over the years by such governors as Cross, Hurley, and Baldwin. Using the momentum gained in earlier successes, the Administration pushed through its bill for abolition of county government, effective October 1, 1960. So another historic institution, dating back to 1666, was deemed no longer necessary under modern conditions. The functions of the county had gradually diminished over many decades to little more than the operation of jails and courthouses.[67]

The Ribicoff budget, with its unorthodox provisions for budget-balancing, involving diversion of motor vehicle fees from the highway fund, the issuance of bonds to finance state school building grants, and a virtual stoppage of building and personnel expansion at state institutions, met vigorous opposition from Republicans. Yet here again Democratic party discipline was highly effective, and the budget squeezed through the House by a 138–136 vote. Education groups throughout the state urgently requested an increase in state aid to towns, even if it meant extra taxes or borrowing. It was pointed out that Connecticut gave much less aid than the average state. Of course, too, the recommendation to continue the 1957 formula meant that the state's relative share of help was declining. Even so, the administration won on this and all major budgetary matters and obtained a budget which was precariously balanced.[68]

The comprehensive plans for reorganization of the state government ran into the expected determined resistance from most of the affected groups. Although some proposals were dropped or defeated, considerable integration and consolidation was achieved, especially through the two new state departments of 1] consumer protection and 2] agriculture, conservation, and natural resources. In general the 1959 session was an unusually productive one.[69]

Undemocratic System of Representation in the General Assembly

AS we look to the future, Connecticut faces many pressing problems. Since space limitations permit attention to only a very few, two problems are presented below.

The basic system of representation in the legislature, drawn up in 1818, has undergone few significant changes since then, although Connecticut's pattern of population distribution has changed sharply. As a result, ninety-nine of the towns, with only 207,091 population (as of the 1950 census), elect 140 of the 279 representatives. This means that approximately *10 percent* of the people elect a *majority* of the representatives — the most undemocratic situation found in any state lower house in the United States! On the other hand, the fourteen most populous cities, having over 1,000,000 population (in 1950), possess only about 10 percent of the House seats![70]

Although the state Senate seems almost fair by comparison, it too has glaring inequalities. Senatorial districts range from about 24,000 population in the lowest district to about 122,000 in the highest, or about a five-to-one ratio. A recent editorial in one of the state's most respected newspapers took as its title: "End the Disgrace of an Unequal Senate." It cites a study by the Connecticut Public Expenditures Council calling for redistricting in 1961, under present constitutional provisions, but it believes that, in the future, redistricting should be without regard to county lines. The council also urges that an amendment to the constitution be passed calling for mandatory redistricting at stated intervals. The 1950 reorganization commission, incidentally, recommended decennial redistricting by a commission of three. The present Senate districting definitely favors the Democrats, while the existing House scheme favors the Republicans even more. Each party has evinced enthusiasm only for reforming the house usually controlled by the other![71]

The 1950 commission bogged down in irreconcilable differences on a reapportionment scheme for the House of Representatives, and suggested as an ad interim plan a House of 169 members, or one per town. Recently this scheme has received serious consideration. Actually it makes the inequality worse by taking away one-half the scanty representation now permitted the fourteen largest cities, leaving them with about 8 rather than 10 percent of the total seats. Granted that there should be gains in efficiency with a smaller House, it seems unfair to heighten the enormous over-representation of small towns. Actually there exists doubt that the Assembly is the proper body to reapportion itself, a procedure tantamount to a man's judging his own case in court. Possibly the Assembly and the people will eventually entrust the decision to a nonpartisan board of reputable citizens — such as members of the State Supreme Court — who would make the reapportionment at stated intervals, perhaps every ten years. Certainly the present system in both houses makes a mockery of the word "democracy."[72]

The Battle for Urban Renewal

MANY of the older cities of the nation have been decaying rapidly in recent decades. Neighborhoods have gradually deteriorated into slums which endanger health and morals and bring little tax revenue. Industry, struggling with antiquated plants, lack of space, and traffic congestion, has often moved to more profitable locations. Meanwhile thousands of families have used their better incomes to escape from the noise, dirt, crowding, crime, and often misgovernment afflicting city life,

Cartoon of 1892 lampooning Connecticut's method of representation in the General Assembly.

moving into the more attractive housing, shopping, and social environment of the suburbs. How to arrest and then reverse this cycle, so ruinous to cities, has engaged some of the best planners in the nation.

In Connecticut, the city of New Haven has pioneered in the planning and implementation of bold, sweeping urban renewal programs, which have attracted nation-wide attention and study. The city's mayor, Richard C. Lee, has forcefully stated the imperative need for decisive action:

American cities can escape blight, decay and decline only through imaginative, comprehensive urban renewal programs.

The continuing task for New Haven and other cities with large-scale programs is to capture the imagination and maintain the enthusiastic approval of the city's residents for the long and arduous renewal process. We must strive constantly to inform the public, describing the evolving nature of projects which require many private decisions and the investment of huge sums of money; describing the sacrifices entailed by the renewal process; and describing the great gains to be made in beauty, convenience, economy and human values.[73]

In common with most cities, New Haven's blight was spreading with ominous speed. In 1954, through a dramatic renewal program, Mayor Lee launched the official drive to reverse the trend.

state, and city grants, plus large infusions of private capital, the Oak Street slum has already been transformed beyond recognition. Nearly nine hundred families have been relocated in decent, sanitary housing. Gone are the noisome slums, replaced by the Connector, a $12,000,000 Southern New England Telephone Company building, the

Artist's drawing of Church Street Redevelopment Project in New Haven.

Associated closely in this governmental effort was the New Haven Citizens Action Commission, a group of influential, public-spirited citizens. Yale's President Griswold early mobilized the university's resources to aid the program. Among the sections urgently requiring rehabilitation was the Oak Street area — forty-two acres of the worst slums in Connecticut — where municipal services cost double the tax revenue received. Downtown New Haven likewise was in a generally dilapidated condition. A major bottleneck was the strangling traffic situation. Here Mayor Lee got his renewal program started by persuading reluctant state officials to build the Oak Street Connector, a $15,000,000 link between the new Connecticut Turnpike and the heart of New Haven.[74]

Once this was approved, other developments followed rapidly. Under a combination of Federal,

new WNHC building, a retail plaza, the College Street Extension, the first of three high-rise apartment buildings and garages, and the South Boulevard Industrial Park. Municipal costs, which were $200,000 yearly for the slums, have declined to about $100,000. Tax revenues are expected to climb from $105,000 in slum days to over $600,000. New Haven's outlay is calculated at $997,000 cash, plus $690,000 in noncash grants-in-aid. Federal, state, and private expenditures, of course, have been far larger.[75]

The revitalization of downtown New Haven has centered about the Church Street Redevelopment Project, covering ninety-six acres. The northern part will include a huge department store, a three-hundred-fifty-room hotel, a large parking garage, an office building, and numerous retail stores. The southern part, stretching from the Oak

Street Connector to the railroad station, is planned as a commercially oriented business area, which is expected to contain a bank building, a medical office building, about twenty acres for commercial development, a junior high school, and apartment developments. This project is to be financed with a Federal loan, a Federal grant, city cash, city

new Interstate Highway 91 will separate the industrial district from the residential one. The three-hundred-fifty-acre Long Wharf Project involves the reclamation of marshland inside the Connecticut Turnpike for industrial use. Sargent & Company, the largest locally owned firm, plans a new plant there, and other companies are ex-

Artist's drawing of Constitution Plaza Redevelopment Project in Hartford.

capital improvements, a Parking Authority program, a state regional market, and, largest of all, private capital. It is anticipated that tax income will increase from $400,000 per year to $980,000 — enough to enable the city to pay off its Parking Authority obligations and all bond issues involved in the project. Hence New Haven should be able to finance the Church Street Project without any tax increase.[76]

Completing the major programs are those at Wooster Square and the Long Wharf. Wooster Square, a dangerously run-down business and residential area, will see private rehabilitation of four hundred salvable properties and replacement of others by a large new school, a central fire station, spot clearance of substandard structures, a middle-income co-operative housing venture, a commercial park, and a large industrial park. The

pected to locate in the area. The new regional market, a marina, a park, and recreational facilities are also planned.[77]

Despite the enormous scope of the four major programs outlined, the city has two more renewal projects in advanced planning stages involving Dixwell and State streets, both areas of encroaching blight. To prevent development of more slums, New Haven has its "Middle Ground" program, for areas susceptible to blight. At present this program involves four neighborhoods — the Hill, Dwight School, Newhallville, and Fair Haven. Intensive work is planned to preserve these well-located and basically sound sections from deterioration.[78]

Finally, New Haven intends to preserve its distinguished neighborhoods, called "Conservation" areas, against commercial infiltration or other un-

399

desirable conversions. This involves very careful and effective zoning. The citizens of the Ronan Street-Edgehill Neighborhood Association recently initiated a revised zoning ordinance aimed at preserving their area from decline. It was accepted by the city planning department and passed by the city's Board of Aldermen in March 1959. Other fine neighborhoods likewise can take the initiative in preserving their high quality as living areas.[79]

Mayor Lee believes that New Haven has the program, the personnel, and the determination to solve major renewal problems. He has distinct reservations, however, about the ability of the American city's present revenue system, based almost entirely upon the property tax, to sustain the efforts required to regenerate our cities. He also sees the need for some kind of governmental consolidation affording a unified metropolitan approach to meeting problems affecting the whole metropolitan New Haven area.[80]

Other Connecticut cities also have embarked upon ambitious urban renewal programs. After lengthy delays, Hartford's comprehensive program is moving forward rapidly. The former blighted Front-Market Street area is being replaced by Constitution Plaza — which will be a national showplace. Recently the seventy-one-acre Windsor Street Project received Federal approval for a grant. A bad slum will disappear in favor of a carefully planned, new business area. In Waterbury, Bristol, Middletown, New Britain, New London, Norwich, and Stamford, renewal programs are planned or under way. Bridgeport's major project will revolutionize a large downtown section. Other Connecticut communities likewise are evincing deep interest in joining the difficult but rewarding battle against urban blight.[81]

Our Past, Present, and Future

AS one looks back over the more than 325 years of Connecticut's recorded history as a colony and state, many dramatic developments come to mind. Courageous Puritan pioneers like Hooker and Davenport brought small bands of dedicated people to a Promised Land, where they created the type of society which they had so long desired. As the colony slowly grew, the self-reliant Connecticut Yankee ran his farm, his village, his church, and his colony with scant consideration for the wishes of the English Government. Long accustomed to a high degree of self-rule, Connecticut found it relatively easy first to protest against British restrictive measures and then to support complete independence in 1776. During the Revolution, the Civil War, and two world wars the state enjoyed the leadership of unusually strong governors and provided generously of its men and munitions. Paradoxically, Connecticut has been "blessed" by a great lack of natural resources, which has forced its people to develop their skills to a very high degree. The shrewd Yankee peddlers, the famous inventors, and the industrial magnates of more recent times all exemplify the Connecticut tradition of hard work and endless experimentation to achieve the goal of a better product.

After the Civil War, "Puritan" Connecticut slowly but surely crumbled under the impact of thousands of immigrants from southern and eastern Europe. As the Industrial Revolution accelerated, Connecticut's expanding factories provided work for most of the newcomers. The population of cities like Bridgeport, Hartford, New Haven, and Waterbury burgeoned, and the Roman Catholic Church became the largest sect. Well into the present century, however, the old-line Yankee families still dominated both politics and business.

The nickname "The Land of Steady Habits" very accurately described Connecticut until the 1920's. Only since then, under the impact of powerful national and local political and economic forces has the state gradually veered away from its deep-seated conservatism. Today in such fields as enlightened labor and welfare legislation, for instance, Connecticut ranks among the more progressive states. The political habits of the state in the past few years suggest that it might better be styled "The Land of Unsteady Habits"! In 1956, Republican Eisenhower won by over 300,000 votes, and two years later Democrat Ribicoff triumphed by over 245,000 votes — the sharpest somersault in Connecticut's modern political history. This suggests that the electorate is becoming more concerned with the candidate and less with the party. The recent voting gyrations should not obscure two basic characteristics of Connecticut's voters: *1*] they prefer moderation to extremes either of radicalism or ultraconservatism (the three most successful governors of the past forty years — Cross, Baldwin, and Ribicoff — have been "moderates" in philosophy and programs); and *2*] they are turning increasingly toward the Democratic party. This trend began about 1930 and continues to run strongly. In July 1960, Democratic registration first surpassed Republican, and further gains were recorded by mid-October. Although the Republican party has lacked decisive leadership much of the time since Boss Roraback's death and has suffered from costly internecine struggles, the Democrats, under John Bailey since 1946, have developed their strongest state organization in history. It is evident that the Republican party under its new chairman, Edwin H. May, Jr. (appointed in December 1958), is veering in a more liberal direction and is energetically seeking to recruit forward-looking "young blood." Whether this drive will succeed in reversing the current Democratic trend remains to be seen.

In national politics the state has played an unusually prominent role recently. On the Republican side, Meade Alcorn of Suffield served as Republican national chairman and was an important figure in the Nixon camp at the 1960 Republican National Convention in Chicago. For the Democrats, Governor Ribicoff was the first Democratic governor to announce all-out support of Kennedy for the Presidency. The governor and John Bailey played vital roles in the preconvention, convention, and campaign periods of Kennedy's drive. Undoubtedly their combined efforts helped Kennedy in carrying Connecticut on November 8, 1960, by over 90,000 votes. In the Kennedy administration an unusual number of key posts are occupied by Connecticut men, including Ribicoff as Secretary of Health, Education, and Welfare; Bowles as Under Secretary of State; and Bailey as Democratic National Chairman. Ribicoff's move to Washington has resulted in the elevation of John N. Dempsey from lieutenant governor to governor.

Connecticut provides living proof that not all of New England is the decaying section vividly described by some pessimists. For the 1950–60 decade the Federal census revealed a population jump from 2,007,280 to 2,535,234 — a lusty 26.3 percent rise. This placed the state *twelfth* nationally in percentage increase and *fifteenth* in absolute numerical growth. In recent years the state

Hammonasset Beach State Park.

has consistently ranked either first or second in per capita income.

A significant recent study of Connecticut's economic prospects for 1959–75, made by the firm of Booz, Allen and Hamilton, clearly indicates that careful planning and energetic action, both in private and public spheres, will be required to prevent Connecticut from declining relatively. It is estimated that by 1975 the state's economy will need to provide an additional 300,000 jobs, including 85,000 in manufacturing. A major deficiency recently has been inadequate capital expenditure for new plants and equipment.

At present citizens of Connecticut may enjoy coastal beaches and sailing, sparkling lakes and rivers, extensive forests, and rolling hills. Few states have such distinctive rural charm so close to large cities. But with the rapid population growth in prospect it will require careful planning to prevent the entire state from being gradually transformed into one large housing development. It seems likely that the state of Connecticut will soon need to acquire additional land from private interests to provide for the future recreational needs of a much larger population.

As Connecticut steps into the 1960's it enters an era fraught with great danger for mankind and simultaneously rich with possibilities of unparalleled advancement. The state possesses immense wealth, an intelligent citizenry, and a body of highly capable leaders in all major fields of human activity. Equipped with these and backed by a great heritage, Connecticut has the potential to forge far beyond all past achievements as it serves its people and nation. Given wise and dedicated leadership at state and local levels there is good reason to believe that Connecticut will become an even finer state in which to grow up, earn a good living, raise a family, worship according to one's creed, and find a high degree of personal and social fulfillment.

Harbor at Essex on Connecticut River reflects great popularity of boating.

The Constitution of Connecticut

Adopted 1818. As amended on June 22, 1953. Effective January 1, 1955.

Amendments to the Constitution of Connecticut "To Incorporate forty-seven Amendments in the Constitution of the State, without Other Revision" and "Concerning the Election and Inauguration of State Officers" were submitted to and approved by the electors of the State at town meetings in the one hundred and sixty-nine towns on June 22, 1953. Governor John Lodge, on July 2, 1953, issued a proclamation declaring the amendments approved and valid.

PREAMBLE

The people of Connecticut acknowledging with gratitude, the good providence of God, in having permitted them to enjoy a free government; do, in order more effectually to define, secure, and perpetuate the liberties, rights and privileges which they have derived from their ancestors; hereby, after a careful consideration and revision, ordain and establish the following constitution and form of civil government.

ARTICLE FIRST.
Declaration of Rights.

That the great and essential principles of liberty and free government may be recognized and established,

WE DECLARE,

Sec. 1. That all men when they form a social compact, are equal in rights; and that no man, or set of men are entitled to exclusive public emoluments or privileges from the community.

Sec. 2. That all political power is inherent in the people, and all free governments are founded on their authority, and instituted for their benefit; and that they have at all times an undeniable and indefeasible right to alter their form of government in such manner as they may think expedient.

Sec. 3. The exercise and enjoyment of religious profession and worship, without discrimination, shall forever be free to all persons in this state; provided, that the right hereby declared and established, shall not be so construed as to excuse acts of licentiousness, or to justify practices inconsistent with the peace and safety of the state.

Sec. 4. No preference shall be given by law to any Christian sect or mode of worship.

Sec. 5. Every citizen may freely speak, write and publish his sentiments on all subjects, being responsible for the abuse of that liberty.

Sec. 6. No law shall ever be passed to curtail or restrain the liberty of speech or of the press.

Sec. 7. In all prosecutions or indictments for

libels, the truth may be given in evidence, and the jury shall have the right to determine the law and the facts, under the direction of the court.

Sec. 8. The people shall be secure in their persons, houses, papers and possessions from unreasonable searches or seizures; and no warrant to search any place, or to seize any person or things, shall issue without describing them as nearly as may be, nor without probable cause supported by oath or affirmation.

Sec. 9. In all criminal prosecutions, the accused shall have a right to be heard by himself and by counsel; to demand the nature and cause of the accusation; to be confronted by the witnesses against him; to have compulsory process to obtain witnesses in his favor; and in all prosecutions by indictment or information, a speedy, public trial by an impartial jury. He shall not be compelled to give evidence against himself, nor be deprived of life, liberty or property, but by due course of law. And no person shall be holden to answer for any crime, the punishment of which may be death or imprisonment for life, unless on a presentment or an indictment of a grand jury; except in the land or naval forces, or in the militia when in actual service in time of war, or public danger.

Sec. 10. No person shall be arrested, detained or punished, except in cases clearly warranted by law.

Sec. 11. The property of no person shall be taken for public use, without just compensation therefor.

Sec. 12. All courts shall be open, and every person, for an injury done to him in his person, property or reputation, shall have remedy by due course of law, and right and justice administered without sale, denial or delay.

Sec. 13. Excessive bail shall not be required, nor excessive fines imposed.

Sec. 14. All prisoners shall, before conviction, be bailable by sufficient sureties, except for capital offenses, where the proof is evident, or the presumption great; and the privileges of the writ of habeas corpus shall not be suspended, unless, when in case of rebellion or invasion, the public safety may require it; nor in any case, but by the legislature.

Sec. 15. No person shall be attainted of treason or felony, by the legislature.

Sec. 16. The citizens have a right, in a peaceable manner, to assemble for their common good, and to apply to those invested with the powers of government, for redress of grievances, or other proper purposes, by petition, address or remonstrance.

Sec. 17. Every citizen has a right to bear arms in defense of himself and the state.

Sec. 18. The military shall, in all cases, and at all times, be in strict subordination to the civil power.

Sec. 19. No soldier shall, in time of peace, be quartered in any house, without the consent of the owner; nor in time of war, but in a manner to be prescribed by law.

Sec. 20. No hereditary emoluments, privileges or honors, shall ever be granted, or conferred in this state.

Sec. 21. The right of trial by jury shall remain inviolate.

ARTICLE SECOND.
Of the Distribution of Powers.

The powers of government shall be divided into three distinct departments, and each of them confided to a separate magistracy, to wit, those which are legislative, to one; those which are executive, to another; and those which are judicial, to another.

ARTICLE THIRD.
Of the Legislative Department.

Sec. 1. The legislative power of this state shall be vested in two distinct houses or branches; the one to be styled the senate, the other the house of representatives, and both together the general assembly. The style of their laws shall be, Be it enacted by the Senate and House of Representatives in General Assembly convened.

Sec. 2. There shall be a regular session of the general assembly to commence on the Wednesday following the first Monday of the January next succeeding the election of its members, and at such other times as the general assembly shall judge necessary; but the person administering the office of governor may, on special emergencies, convene the general assembly at any other time. All regular and special sessions of the general assembly shall be held at Hartford, but the person administering the office of governor may, in case of special emergency, convene said assembly at any other place in this state. The general assembly shall adjourn sine die not later than the first Wednesday after the first Monday in June following its organization.

Sec. 3. The house of representatives shall consist of electors residing in towns from which they are elected. Every town which now contains, or hereafter shall contain a population of five thousand, shall be entitled to send two representatives, and every other one shall be entitled to its present representation in the general assembly. The population of each town shall be determined by the enumeration made under the authority of the census of the United States, next before the election of representatives is held. In case a new town shall hereafter be incorporated, such new town shall not be entitled to a representative in the general assembly unless it has at least twenty-five hundred inhabitants, and unless the town from which the major portion of its territory is taken, has also at least twenty-five hundred inhabitants, but until such towns shall each have at least twenty-five hundred inhabitants such new town shall for the purpose of representation in the general assembly be attached to and be deemed to be a part of the town from which the major portion of its territory is taken, and it shall be an election district of such town for the purpose of representation in the house of representatives.

Sec. 4. The senate shall be composed of not less than twenty-four and not more than thirty-six members, who shall be elected at the electors' meetings held biennially on the Tuesday after the first Monday in November.

Sec. 5. The number of senatorial districts shall not be less than twenty-four nor more than thirty-six, and each district shall elect only one senator. The districts shall always be composed of contiguous territory, and in forming them regard shall be had to population in the several districts, that the same may be as nearly equal as possible under the limitations of this section. Neither the whole or a part of one county shall be joined to the whole or a part of another county to form a district, and no town shall be divided, unless for the purpose of forming more than one district wholly within such town, and each county shall have at least one senator. The districts, as now established by law, shall continue the same until the session of the general assembly next after the completion of the next census of the United States, which general assembly shall have power to alter the same, if found necessary to preserve a proper equality of population in each district, but only in accordance with the principles above recited; after which said districts shall not be altered, nor the number of senators altered, except at a session of the general assembly next after the completion of a census of the United States, and then only in accordance

with the principles hereinbefore provided. The persons voted for senators shall, at the time of such vote, belong to and reside in the respective districts in which they are so voted for.

Sec. 6. The treasurer, secretary, and comptroller, for the time being, shall canvass the votes publicly. The person in each district having the highest number of votes for senator shall be declared to be duly elected for such district; but in the event of an equality of votes between two or more persons so voted for, the house of representatives shall designate by ballot which of such persons shall be declared to be duly elected. The return of votes, and the result of the canvass, shall be submitted to the house of representatives, and also to the senate, on the first day of the session of the general assembly; and each house shall be the final judge of the election returns and qualifications of its own members.

Sec. 7. A general election for members of the general assembly shall be held on the Tuesday after the first Monday of November, biennially, in the even-numbered years. The general assembly shall have power to enact laws regulating and prescribing the order and manner of voting for said members, and also providing for the election of representatives at some time subsequent to the Tuesday after the first Monday of November in all cases when it shall so happen that the electors in any town shall fail on that day to elect the representative or representatives to which such town shall be by law entitled.

Sec. 8. At all elections for members of the general assembly the presiding officers in the several towns shall receive the votes of the electors, and count and declare them in open meeting. The presiding officers shall also make duplicate lists of the persons voted for, and of the number of votes for each, which shall be certified by the presiding officers; one of which lists shall be delivered to the town clerk, and the other within ten days after said meeting, shall be delivered under seal, either to the secretary, or to the sheriff of the county in which said town is situated; which list shall be directed to the secretary, with a superscription expressing the purport of the contents thereof. And each sheriff who shall receive such votes, shall, within fifteen days after said meeting, deliver, or cause them to be delivered to the secretary.

Sec. 9. The members of the general assembly shall hold their offices from the Wednesday following the first Monday of the January next succeeding their election until the Wednesday after the first Monday of the third succeeding January, and until their successors are duly qualified.

Sec. 10. The house of representatives when assembled, shall choose a speaker, clerk and other officers. The senate shall choose its clerk, and other officers, except the president. A majority of each house shall constitute a quorum to do business; but a smaller number may adjourn from day to day, and compel the attendance of absent members in such manner, and under such penalties as each house may prescribe.

Sec. 11. Each house shall determine the rules of its own proceedings, and punish members for disorderly conduct, and, with the consent of two-thirds, expel a member, but not a second time for the same cause; and shall have all other powers necessary for a branch of the legislature of a free and independent state.

Sec. 12. Each house shall keep a journal of its proceedings, and publish the same when required by one-fifth of its members, except such parts as in the judgment of a majority require secrecy. The yeas and nays of the members of either house, shall, at the desire of one-fifth of those present, be entered on the journals.

Sec. 13. The senators and representatives shall, in all cases of civil process, be privileged from arrest, during the session of the general assembly, and for four days before the commencement, and after the termination of any session thereof. And for any speech or debate in either house, they shall not be questioned in any other place.

Sec. 14. The debates of each house shall be public, except on such occasions as in the opinion of the house may require secrecy.

*Sec. 15. The salary of the members of the general assembly shall be six hundred dollars for the term for which they are elected, and in addition to such compensation, the general assembly may provide by law for the transportation of each member by public conveyance by the most convenient route between his home station and the place of meeting during the session or sessions of the general assembly to which he was elected.

ARTICLE FOURTH.
Of the Executive Department.

Sec. 1. A general election for governor, lieutenant-governor, secretary, treasurer and comp-

* Altered by amendment of 1958 (Art. V).

troller shall be held on the Tuesday after the first Monday of November, 1950, and quadrennially thereafter.

Sec. 2. Said officers, shall hold their respective offices from the Wednesday following the first Monday of the January next succeeding their election until the Wednesday following the first Monday of the fifth January succeeding their election and until their successors are duly qualified.

Sec. 3. At the meetings of the electors in the respective towns held quadrennially as herein provided for the election of state officers, the presiding officers shall receive the votes and shall count and declare the same in the presence of the electors. When such votes shall have been so received and counted, duplicate lists of the persons voted for, and of the number of votes given for each, shall be made and certified by the presiding officers, one of which lists shall be deposited in the office of the town clerk, within three days, and the other, within ten days after said election, shall be transmitted to the secretary, or to the sheriff of the county, in which such election shall have been held. The sheriff receiving said votes shall deliver, or cause them to be delivered to the secretary, within fifteen days next after said election. The votes so returned shall be counted, canvassed and declared by the treasurer, secretary, and comptroller, within the month of November. The vote for treasurer shall be counted, canvassed and declared by the secretary and comptroller only; the vote for secretary shall be counted, canvassed and declared by the treasurer and comptroller only; and the vote for comptroller shall be counted, canvassed and declared by the treasurer and secretary only. A fair list of the persons and number of votes given for each, together with the returns of the presiding officers, shall be, by the treasurer, secretary and comptroller, made and laid before the general assembly, then next to be held, on the first day of the session thereof.* In the election for governor, lieutenant-governor, secretary, treasurer, comptroller, and attorney-general, the person found by the general assembly, in the manner herein provided, to have received the greatest number of votes for each of said offices respectively, shall be declared by said assembly to be elected. But if two or more persons shall be found to have an equal and the greatest number of votes for any of said offices, then the general assembly, on the second day of its session, by joint ballot of

* Altered by amendment of 1953 (Art. I).

406

both houses, shall proceed without debate to choose said officer from a list of the names of the persons found to have an equal and greatest number of votes for said office. The general assembly shall have power to enact laws regulating and prescribing the order and manner of voting for said officers. The general assembly shall by law prescribe the manner in which all questions concerning the election of a governor or lieutenant-governor shall be determined.

Sec. 4. The supreme executive power of the state shall be vested in the governor. No person who is not an elector of this state, and who has not arrived at the age of thirty years, shall be eligible.

Sec. 5. The lieutenant-governor shall possess the same qualifications as are herein prescribed for the governor.

Sec. 6. The compensations of the governor and lieutenant-governor shall be established by law, and shall not be varied so as to take effect until after an election, which shall next succeed the passage of the law establishing said compensations.

Sec. 7. The governor shall be captain general of the militia of the state, except when called into the service of the United States.

Sec. 8. He may require information in writing from the officers in the executive department, on any subject relating to the duties of their respective offices.

Sec. 9. The governor, in case of a disagreement between the two houses of the general assembly, respecting the time of adjournment, may adjourn them to such time as he shall think proper, not beyond the day of the next stated session.

Sec. 10. He shall, from time to time, give to the general assembly, information of the state of the government, and recommend to their consideration such measures as he shall deem expedient.

Sec. 11. He shall take care that the laws be faithfully executed.

Sec. 12. The governor shall have power to grant reprieves after conviction, in all cases except those of impeachment, until the end of the next session of the general assembly, and no longer.

Sec. 13. All commissions shall be in the name and by authority of the state of Connecticut; shall be sealed with the state seal, signed by the governor, and attested by the secretary.

Sec. 14. Each bill which shall have passed both houses of the general assembly shall be presented to the governor. If he shall approve, he shall sign and transmit it to the secretary of the state, but if he shall disapprove, he shall transmit it to the secretary with his objections, and the secretary shall thereupon return the bill to the house in which it originated, with the governor's objections, which shall be entered on the journal of the house, which shall proceed to reconsider the bill. If, after such reconsideration, that house shall again pass it, it shall be sent with the objections to the other house, which shall also reconsider it. If approved, it shall be a law and be transmitted to the secretary; but in such case the votes of both houses shall be determined by yeas and nays and the names of the members voting for and against the bill shall be entered on the journal of each house respectively. In case the governor shall not transmit the bill to the secretary, either with his approval or with his objections, within five calendar days, Sundays and legal holidays excepted, after the same shall have been presented to him, it shall be a law at the expiration of that period unless the general assembly shall then have adjourned sine die, in which case the bill shall be a law unless the governor shall, within fifteen calendar days after the same shall have been presented to him, transmit it to the secretary with his objections, in which case it shall not be a law. Bills may be presented to the governor after the adjournment sine die of the general assembly, and the general assembly may by law consistent with this section regulate the time and method of performing all ministerial acts necessary or incidental to the administration of this section.

Sec. 15. The governor shall have power to disapprove of any item or items of any bill making appropriations of money embracing distinct items while at the same time approving the remainder of the bill, and the part or parts of the bill so approved shall become effective and the item or items of appropriation so disapproved shall not take effect unless the same are separately reconsidered and repassed in accordance with the rules and limitations prescribed for the passage of bills over the executive veto. In all cases in which the governor shall exercise the right of disapproval hereby conferred he shall append to the bill at the time of signing it a statement of the item or items disapproved, together with his reasons for such disapproval, and transmit the bill and such appended statement to the secretary. If the general assembly be then in session he shall forthwith cause a copy of such statement to be delivered to the house in which the bill originated for reconsideration of the disapproved items in conformity with the rules prescribed for legislative action in respect to bills which have received executive disapproval.

Sec. 16. The lieutenant-governor shall, by virtue of his office, be president of the senate, and have, when in committee of the whole, a right to debate, and when the senate is equally divided, to give the casting vote.

Sec. 17. In case of the death, resignation, refusal to serve, inability to perform the powers and duties of his office, or removal from office of the governor, or of his impeachment or absence from the state, the lieutenant-governor shall exercise the powers and authority appertaining to the office of governor, until another be chosen at the next periodical election for governor, and be duly qualified; or until the disability be removed, or, until the governor, impeached or absent, shall be acquitted or return.

Sec. 18. When the government shall be administered by the lieutenant-governor, or he shall be unable to attend as president of the senate, the senate shall elect one of their members, as president pro tempore. And if during the vacancy of the office of governor, the lieutenant-governor shall die, resign, refuse to serve, or be removed from office, or if he shall be impeached, or absent from the state, the president of the senate pro tempore, shall, in like manner, administer the government until he be superseded by a governor or lieutenant-governor.

Sec. 19. If the lieutenant-governor shall be required to administer the government, and shall, while in such administration, die or resign during the recess of the general assembly, it shall be the duty of the secretary, for the time being, to convene the senate for the purpose of choosing a president pro tempore.

Sec. 20. If, at the time fixed for the beginning of the term of the governor, the governor-elect shall have died or shall have failed to qualify, the lieutenant-governor-elect may qualify as governor, and, upon so qualifying, shall become governor. The general assembly may by law provide for the case in which neither the governor-elect nor the lieutenant-governor-elect shall have qualified, by declaring who shall, in such event, act as governor or the manner in which the person who

is so to act shall be selected, and such person shall act accordingly until a governor or a lieutenant-governor shall have qualified.

Sec. 21. The treasurer shall receive all monies belonging to the state, and disburse the same only as he may be directed by law. He shall pay no warrant, or order for the disbursement of public money, until the same has been registered in the office of the comptroller.

Sec. 22. The secretary shall have the safe keeping and custody of the public records and documents, and particularly of the acts, resolutions, and orders of the general assembly, and record the same; and perform all such duties as shall be prescribed by law. He shall be the keeper of the seal of the state, which shall not be altered.

Sec. 23. The comptroller shall adjust and settle all public accounts and demands, except grants and orders of the general assembly. He shall prescribe the mode of keeping and rendering all public accounts. He shall, ex officio, be one of the auditors of the accounts of the treasurer. The general assembly may assign to him other duties in relation to his office, and to that of the treasurer, and shall prescribe the manner in which his duties shall be performed.

Sec. 24. Sheriffs shall be elected in the several counties, on the Tuesday after the first Monday of November, 1950, and quadrennially thereafter, for the term of four years, commencing on the first day of June following their election. They shall become bound with sufficient sureties to the treasurer of the state, for the faithful discharge of the duties of their office. They shall be removable by the general assembly. In case the sheriff of any county shall die or resign, or shall be removed from office by the general assembly, the governor may fill the vacancy occasioned thereby, until the same shall be filled by the general assembly.

Sec. 25. A statement of all receipts, payments, funds, and debts of the state, shall be published from time to time, in such manner and at such periods, as shall be prescribed by law.

ARTICLE FIFTH.
Of the Judicial Department.

Sec. 1. The judicial power of the state shall be vested in a supreme court of errors, a superior court, and such inferior courts as the general assembly shall, from time to time, ordain and establish: the powers and jurisdiction of which courts shall be defined by law.

Sec. 2. The justices of the peace, for the several towns in this state, shall be appointed by the electors in such towns; and the time and manner of their election, the number for each town, and the period for which they shall hold their offices, shall be prescribed by law. They shall have such jurisdiction in civil and criminal cases, as the general assembly may prescribe.

Sec. 3. The judges of the supreme court of errors and of the superior court shall, upon nomination of the governor, be appointed by the general assembly in such manner as shall by law be prescribed. They shall hold their offices for the term of eight years, but may be removed by impeachment; and the governor shall also remove them on the address of two-thirds of each house of the general assembly.

Sec. 4. Judges of the courts of common pleas shall, upon nomination of the governor, be appointed by the general assembly in such manner as shall by law be prescribed, for terms of four years. Judges of the district courts shall be appointed by the general assembly for terms of four years.

Sec. 5. Judges of the city courts and police courts shall be appointed for terms of two years. This section shall cease to be effective as a part of this constitution upon the execution by the general assembly of Section 6 of this article by prescribing the term and manner of appointment of judges of minor courts, including town, city, borough and police courts.

Sec. 6. The judges of minor courts, including town, city, borough and police courts, shall, upon nomination by the governor, be appointed by the general assembly for such term and in such manner as shall be by law prescribed.

Sec. 7. Judges of probate shall be elected by the electors residing in their respective districts on the Tuesday after the first Monday of November, 1950, and quadrennially thereafter, and shall hold office for four years from and after the Wednesday after the first Monday of the next succeeding January.

Sec. 8. No judge or justice of the peace shall be capable of holding his office, after he shall arrive at the age of seventy years.

ARTICLE SIXTH.
Of the Qualifications of Electors.

Sec. 1. Every citizen of the United States, who shall have attained the age of twenty-one years, who shall have resided in this state for a term of one year next preceding, and in the town in which he may offer himself to be admitted to the privileges of an elector, at least six months next preceding the time he may so offer himself, and shall be able to read in the English language any article of the constitution or any section of the statutes of this state, and shall sustain a good moral character, shall, on his taking such oath as may be prescribed by law, be an elector.

Sec. 2. The general assembly shall by law prescribe the offenses on conviction of which the privileges of an elector shall be forfeited and the conditions on which and methods by which such rights may be restored.

Sec. 3. Every elector shall be eligible to any office in this state, except in cases provided for in this constitution.

Sec. 4. The selectmen and town clerks or an assistant town clerk of the several towns, shall decide on the qualifications of electors, at such times and in such manner as prescribed by law.

Sec. 5. Laws shall be made to support the privilege of free suffrage, prescribing the manner of regulating and conducting meetings of the electors, and prohibiting, under adequate penalties, all undue influence therein, from power, bribery, tumult, and other improper conduct.

Sec. 6. The general assembly shall have power to provide by law for voting by qualified voters of the state who are absent from the city or town of which they are inhabitants at the time of an election or because of sickness or physical disability are unable to appear at the polling places on the day of election, in the choice of any officer to be elected or upon any question to be voted on at such election.

Sec. 7. In all elections of officers of the state, or members of the general assembly, the votes of the electors shall be by ballot, either written or printed, except that voting machines or other mechanical devices for voting may be used in all elections in this state, under such regulations as may be prescribed by law; provided, however, that the right of secret voting shall be preserved.

Sec. 8. At all elections of officers of the state, or members of the general assembly, the electors shall be privileged from arrest, during their attendance upon, and going to, and returning from the same, on any civil process.

ARTICLE SEVENTH.
Of Religion.

Sec. 1. It being the duty of all men to worship

the Supreme Being, the Great Creator and Preserver of the Universe, and their right to render
that worship, in the mode most consistent with
the dictates of their consciences; no person shall
by law be compelled to join or support, nor be
classed with, or associated to, any congregation,
church or religious association. But every person
now belonging to such congregation, church, or
religious association shall remain a member
thereof until he shall have separated himself
therefrom, in the manner hereinafter provided.
And each and every society or denomination of
Christians in this state, shall have and enjoy the
same and equal powers, rights and privileges; and
shall have power and authority to support and
maintain the ministers or teachers of their respective denominations, and to build and repair houses
for public worship, by a tax on the members of
any such society only to be laid by a major vote
of the legal voters assembled at any society meeting, warned and held according to law, or in any
other manner.

Sec. 2. If any person shall choose to separate
himself from the society or denomination of
Christians to which he may belong, and shall
leave a written notice thereof with the clerk of
such society, he shall thereupon be no longer liable for any future expenses which may be incurred
by said society.

ARTICLE EIGHTH.

Of Education.

Sec. 1. The charter of Yale College, as modified by agreement with the corporation thereof, in
pursuance of an act of the general assembly,
passed in May, 1792, is hereby confirmed.

Sec. 2. The fund, called the SCHOOL FUND,
shall remain a perpetual fund, the interest of
which shall be inviolably appropriated to the support and encouragement of the public, or common
schools throughout the state, and for the equal
benefit of all the people thereof. The value and
amount of said fund shall, as soon as practicable,
be ascertained in such manner as the general assembly may prescribe, published, and recorded in
the comptroller's office; and no law shall ever be
made, authorizing said fund to be diverted to any
other use than the encouragement and support of
public, or common schools, among the several
school societies, as justice and equity shall require.

ARTICLE NINTH.

Of Impeachments.

Sec. 1. The house of representatives shall have
the sole power of impeaching.

Sec. 2. All impeachments shall be tried by the
senate. When sitting for that purpose, they shall
be on oath or affirmation. No person shall be convicted without the concurrence of two-thirds of
the members present. When the governor is impeached, the chief justice shall preside.

Sec. 3. The governor, and all other executive
and judicial officers, shall be liable to impeachment; but judgments in such cases shall not extend
further than to removal from office, and disquali-
cation to hold any office of honor, trust, or profit
under this state. The party convicted, shall, nevertheless, be liable and subject to indictment, trial,
and punishment according to law.

Sec. 4. Treason against the state shall consist
only in levying war against it, or adhering to its
enemies, giving them aid and comfort. No person
shall be convicted of treason, unless on the testimony of two witnesses to the same overt act, or
on confession in open court. No conviction of
treason, or attainder, shall work corruption of
blood, or forfeiture.

ARTICLE TENTH.

General Provisions.

Sec. 1. Members of the general assembly, and
all officers, executive and judicial, shall, before
they enter on the duties of their respective offices,
take the following oath or affirmation, to wit:

You do solemnly swear (or affirm, as the case
may be) that you will support the constitution
of the United States, and the constitution of the
state of Connecticut, so long as you continue a
citizen thereof; and that you will faithfully discharge, according to law, the duties of the office
of _____ to the best of your abilities. So help
you God.

Sec. 2. Each town shall, annually, or biennially, as the electors of the town may determine,
elect selectmen and such officers of local police as
the laws may prescribe.

Sec. 3. No county, city, town, borough, or
other municipality, shall ever subscribe to the
capital stock of any railroad corporation, or become a purchaser of the bonds, or make donation
to, or loan its credit, directly or indirectly, in aid
of any such corporation; but nothing herein con-

tained shall affect the validity of any bonds or debts incurred under existing laws, nor be construed to prohibit the general assembly from authorizing any town or city to protect by additional appropriations of money or credit, any railroad debt contracted prior to October 19, 1877.

Sec. 4. Neither the general assembly nor any county, city, borough, town, or school district, shall have power to pay or grant any extra compensation to any public officer, employee, agent, or servant, or increase the compensation of any public officer or employee, to take effect during the continuance in office of any person whose salary might be increased thereby, or increase the pay or compensation of any public contractor above the amount specified in the contract.

Sec. 5. The rights and duties of all corporations shall remain as if this constitution had not been adopted; with the exception of such regulations and restrictions as are contained in this constitution. All judicial, civil and military officers now in office, shall continue to hold their offices until their terms of office shall expire, or until they shall resign, or be removed from office according to law. All laws not contrary to, or inconsistent with the provisions of this constitution, shall remain in force, until they shall expire by their own limitation, or shall be altered or repealed by the general assembly, in pursuance of this constitution. The validity of all bonds, debts, contracts, as well of individuals as of bodies corporate, or the state, of all suits, actions, or rights of action, both in law and equity, shall continue as if no change had taken place.

Sec. 6. No judge of the superior court, or of the supreme court of errors; no member of congress; no person holding any office under the authority of the United States; no person holding the office of treasurer, secretary, or comptroller; no

* Altered by amendment of 1958 (Art. III).

sheriff, or sheriff's deputy, shall be a member of the general assembly.

ARTICLE ELEVENTH. *
Of Amendments to the Constitution.

Whenever a majority of the house of representatives shall deem it necessary to alter, or amend this constitution, they may propose such alterations and amendments; which proposed amendments shall be continued to the next general assembly, and be published with the laws which may have been passed at the same session; and if two-thirds of each house, at the next session of said assembly, shall approve the amendments proposed, by yeas and nays, said amendments shall, by the secretary, be transmitted to the town clerk in each town in the state; whose duty it shall be to present the same to the inhabitants thereof, for their consideration, at a town meeting, legally warned and held for that purpose; and if it shall appear in a manner to be provided by law, that a majority of the electors present at such meetings, shall have approved such amendments, the same shall be valid, to all intents and purposes, as a part of this constitution.

ARTICLE TWELFTH.

Articles First to Eleventh, inclusive, of the constitution and Articles I to XLVII, inclusive, of the amendments thereto are repealed.

ARTICLE THIRTEENTH.
Of the Effective Date of This Constitution.

This constitution shall be effective as of January 1, 1955, but any amendment to the existing constitution which becomes effective subsequent to September 1, 1951, shall have the same effect as though it were expressly made an amendment to this constitution.

* Altered by amendment of 1955 (Art. 2).

AMENDMENTS TO THE CONSTITUTION OF CONNECTICUT

ARTICLE I *
Of the Executive Department.

Sec. 1. In the election of governor, lieutenant-governor, secretary, treasurer, comptroller and

* This amendment passed prior to the effective date of this constitution. See Article XIII.

attorney general, the person found upon the count by the treasurer, secretary and comptroller as provided in Article Fourth of the Constitution, to be made and announced before December fifteenth of the year of the election, to have received the greatest number of votes for each of said offices, respectively, shall be elected thereto; provided, if the election of any of them shall be contested as provided by statute, and if such a contest shall proceed to final judgment, the person found by the court to have received the greatest number of votes shall be elected. If two or more persons shall be found upon the count of the treasurer, secretary and comptroller to have received an equal and the greatest number of votes for any of said offices, and the election is not contested, the general assembly on the second day of its session shall hold a joint convention of both houses, at which, without debate, a ballot shall be taken to choose such officer from those persons who received such a vote; and the balloting shall continue on that or subsequent days until one of such persons is chosen by a majority vote of those present and voting.

Sec. 2. Article XXX of the amendments to the constitution is repealed. [Reference is to Article XXX of the Constitution prior to its revision effective January 1, 1955. See Article Fourth, Sec. 3.]

ARTICLE II*
Of Amendments to the Constitution.

Sec. 1. Whenever a majority of the house of representatives shall deem it necessary to alter or amend this constitution, they may propose such alterations and amendments, which proposed amendments shall be continued to the next general assembly and be published with the laws, which may have been passed at the same session; and if two-thirds of each house, at the next session of said assembly, shall approve the amendments proposed, by yeas and nays, said amendments shall, by the secretary, be transmitted to the town clerk in each town in this state, whose duty it shall be to present the same to the inhabitants thereof, for their consideration, at a town meeting, legally warned and held for that purpose; and if it shall appear, in a manner to be provided by law, that a

* Adopted August 5, 1955.

majority of the electors present and voting on such amendments at such meetings shall have approved such amendments, the same shall be valid, to all intents and purposes, as a part of this constitution.

Sec. 2. Article Eleventh of the constitution is repealed.

ARTICLE III*
General Provisions.

Sec. 1. No member of the general assembly shall, during the term for which he is elected, hold or accept any appointive position or office in the judicial or executive departments of the state government, or in the courts of the political subdivisions of the state, or in the government of any county. No member of congress, no person holding any office under the authority of the United States and no person holding any office in the judicial or executive department of the state government or in the government of any county shall be a member of the general assembly during his continuance in such office.

Sec. 2. Section 6 of Article Tenth of the constitution is repealed.

ARTICLE IV
General Provisions.

Sec. 1. Article Tenth of the constitution is amended by adding Section 7 as follows: Claims against the state shall be resolved in such manner as may be provided by law.

ARTICLE V
Of Legislative Department.

Sec. 1. Section 15 of Article Third of the constitution is amended to read as follows: The salary of the members of the general assembly and the transportation expenses of its members in the performance of their legislative duties shall be determined by law.

* Articles III, IV, and V adopted November 20, 1958.

Governors of Connecticut

Abbreviations are used for political parties: A, American; AD, American Democrat; AR, American Republican; D, Democrat; F, Federalist; FSA, Free Soil American; O, No Record; R, Republican; U, Union; W, Whig.

Governor	Town & Party	Term of Service	Years of Service
John Haynes	Hartford, O	(1639, '41, '43, '45, '47, '49, '51, '53)	8 yrs.
Edward Hopkins	Hartford, O	(1640, '44, '46, '48, '50, '52, '54)	7 yrs.
George Wyllys	Hartford, O	1642	1 yr.
Thomas Welles	Hartford, O	1655, '58	2 yrs.
John Webster	Hartford, O	1656	1 yr.
John Winthrop	New London, O	1657, '59–76	18 yrs.
William Leete	Guilford, O	1676–83	7 yrs.
Robert Treat[1]	Milford, O	1683–98	15 yrs.
Fitz-John Winthrop	New London, O	1698–1708	9 yrs. 6 m.
Gurdon Saltonstall	New London, O	1708–25	17 yrs. 4 m.
Joseph Talcott	Hartford, O	1725–41	16 yrs. 5 m.
Jonathan Law	Milford, O	1741–50	9 yrs. 1 m.
Roger Wolcott	Windsor, O	1750–54	3 yrs. 6 m.
Thomas Fitch	Norwalk, O	1754–66	12 yrs.
William Pitkin	Hartford, O	1766–69	3 yrs. 5 m.
Jonathan Trumbull	Lebanon, F	1769–84	14 yrs. 7 m.
Matthew Griswold	Lyme, F	1784–86	2 yrs.
Samuel Huntington	Norwich, O	1786–96	9 yrs. 8 m.
Oliver Wolcott	Litchfield, O	1796–97	1 yr. 11 m.
Jonathan Trumbull, Jr.	Lebanon, F	1797–1809	11 yrs. 8 m.
John Treadwell	Farmington, O	1809–11	1 yr. 9 m.
Roger Griswold	Lyme, F	1811–12	1 yr. 5 m.
John Cotton Smith	Sharon, F	1812–17	4 yrs. 7 m.
Oliver Wolcott, Jr.	Litchfield, R	1817–27	10 yrs.
Gideon Tomlinson	Fairfield, W	1827–31	4 yrs.
John S. Peters	Hebron, R	1831–33	2 yrs.
Henry W. Edwards	New Haven, D	1833–34	1 yr.
Samuel A. Foot	Cheshire, R	1834–35	1 yr.
Henry W. Edwards	New Haven, D	1835–38	3 yrs.
Wm. W. Ellsworth	Hartford, W	1838–42	4 yrs.
Chauncey F. Cleveland	Hampton, D	1842–44	2 yrs.
Roger S. Baldwin	New Haven, W	1844–46	2 yrs.
Isaac Toucey	Hartford, D	1846–47	1 yr.
Clark Bissell	Norwalk, W	1847–49	2 yrs.
Joseph Trumbull	Hartford, W	1849–50	1 yr.
Thomas H. Seymour	Hartford, D	1850–53	3 yrs. 1 m.
Charles H. Pond	Milford, D	1853–54	11 m.
Henry Dutton	New Haven, W	1854–55	1 yr.

[1] Gov. Treat's term includes the period when Sir Edmund Andros as royal governor was *de facto* executive.

Governor	Town & Party	Term of Service	Years of Service
William T. Minor	Stamford, A	1855–57	2 yrs.
Alexander H. Holley	Salisbury, AR	1857–58	1 yr.
Wm. A. Buckingham	Norwich, R	1858–66	8 yrs.
Joseph R. Hawley	Hartford, R	1866–67	1 yr.
James E. English	New Haven, D	1867–69	2 yrs.
Marshall Jewell	Hartford, R	1869–70	1 yr.
James E. English	New Haven, D	1870–71	1 yr.
Marshall Jewell	Hartford, R	1871–73	2 yrs.
Charles R. Ingersoll	New Haven, D	1873–77	3 yrs. 9 m.
Richard D. Hubbard	Hartford, D	1877–79	2 yrs.
Charles B. Andrews	Litchfield, R	1879–81	2 yrs.
Hobart B. Bigelow	New Haven, R	1881–83	2 yrs.
Thomas M. Waller	New London, D	1883–85	2 yrs.
Henry B. Harrison	New Haven, R	1885–87	2 yrs.
Phineas C. Lounsbury	Ridgefield, R	1887–89	2 yrs.
Morgan G. Bulkeley	Hartford, R	1889–93	4 yrs.
Luzon B. Morris	New Haven, D	1893–95	2 yrs.
O. Vincent Coffin	Middletown, R	1895–97	2 yrs.
Lorrin A. Cooke	Winsted, R	1897–99	2 yrs.
George E. Lounsbury	Ridgefield, R	1899–1901	2 yrs.
George P. McLean	Simsbury, R	1901–03	2 yrs.
Abiram Chamberlain	Meriden, R	1903–05	2 yrs.
Henry Roberts	Hartford, R	1905–07	2 yrs.
Rollin S. Woodruff	New Haven, R	1907–09	2 yrs.
George L. Lilley	Waterbury, R	1909	3 m. 15 d.
Frank B. Weeks	Middletown, R	1909–11	1 yr. 8 m. 15 d.
Simeon E. Baldwin	New Haven, D	1911–15	4 yrs.
Marcus H. Holcomb	Southington, R	1915–21	6 yrs.
Everett J. Lake	Hartford, R	1921–23	2 yrs.
Chas. A. Templeton	Waterbury, R	1923–25	2 yrs.
Hiram Bingham	New Haven, R	1925	1 d.
John H. Trumbull	Plainville, R	1925–31	6 yrs.
Wilbur L. Cross	New Haven, D	1931–39	8 yrs.
Raymond E. Baldwin	Stratford, R	1939–41	2 yrs.
Robert A. Hurley	Bridgeport, D	1941–43	2 yrs.
Raymond E. Baldwin	Stratford, R	1943–46	3 yrs. 11 m. 21 d.
Wilbert Snow	Middletown, D	1946–47	13 d.
James L. McConaughy	Cornwall, R	1947–48	1 yr. 2 m.
James C. Shannon	Bridgeport, R	1948–49	9 m. 29 d.
Chester Bowles	Essex, D	1949–51	2 yrs.
John Lodge	Westport, R	1951–55	4 yrs.
Abraham Ribicoff	Hartford, D	1955–61	6 yrs.
John N. Dempsey	Putnam, D	1961–	

Selected Important Dates in Connecticut's History

1614 Adriaen Block, representing the Dutch, sailed up the Connecticut River.

1633 The Dutch erected a fort, the House of (Good) Hope, on the future site of Hartford.

1633 John Oldham and others explored and traded along the Connecticut River. Plymouth Colony sent William Holmes to found a trading post at Windsor.

1634 Wethersfield founded by people from Massachusetts.

1635 Fort erected at Saybrook by Lion Gardiner.

1635 Group from Dorchester, Massachusetts, joined Windsor settlement.

1636 Thomas Hooker and company journeyed from Newtown (Cambridge), Massachusetts, to found Hartford.

1637 Pequot War. Captain John Mason led colonists to decisive victory.

1638 New Haven Colony established by Davenport and Eaton.

1639 Fundamental Orders of Connecticut adopted by Hartford, Wethersfield, and Windsor; John Haynes chosen first governor.

1643 Connecticut joined in forming the New England Confederation.

1646 New London founded by John Winthrop, Jr.

1650 Code of laws drawn up by Roger Ludlow and adopted by legislature.

1662 John Winthrop, Jr., obtained a charter for Connecticut.

1665 Union of New Haven and Connecticut colonies completed.

1675– Connecticut participated in King Philip's
76 War, which was fought in Rhode Island and Massachusetts.

1687 Andros assumed rule over Connecticut; Charter Oak episode occurred.

1689 Connecticut resumed government under charter.

1701 Collegiate School authorized by General Assembly.

1708 Saybrook Platform, providing more centralized control of Established (Congregational) Church, approved by General Assembly.

1717 Collegiate School moved to New Haven; called Yale the next year.

1740 Manufacture of tinware begun at Berlin by Edward and William Pattison.

1740's Height of religious "Great Awakening."

1745 Connecticut troops under Roger Wolcott helped capture Louisbourg.

1755 *Connecticut Gazette* of New Haven, the colony's first newspaper, printed by James Parker at New Haven.

1764 *Connecticut Courant*, the oldest American newspaper in continuous existence to the present, launched at Hartford by Thomas Green.

1765 Sharp opposition to Stamp Act.

1766 Governor Thomas Fitch, who supported Stamp Act, defeated by William Pitkin.

1767 Thomas and Samuel Green began publishing *Connecticut Journal and New-Haven Post-Boy*. After numerous changes in management and name the paper continues today as New Haven *Journal-Courier*.

1774 Connecticut officially extended jurisdiction over Susquehannah Company area in northern Pennsylvania.

1774 Silas Deane, Eliphalet Dyer, and Roger Sherman represented Connecticut at First Continental Congress.

1775 Several thousand militia rushed to Massachusetts in "Lexington Alarm."

1775 Connecticut men helped plan and carry out seizure of Fort Ticonderoga.

1776 Samuel Huntington, Roger Sherman, William Williams, and Oliver Wolcott signed the Declaration of Independence; large majority of Connecticut people under Governor Jonathan Trumbull supported the Declaration.

1777 British troops under General Tryon raided Danbury.

1779 British troops under General Tryon raided New Haven, Fairfield, and Norwalk.

1781 Benedict Arnold's attack upon New London and Groton involved massacre at Fort Griswold.

1781 Washington and Rochambeau conferred at Webb House in Wethersfield.

1783 Meeting of ten Anglican clergy at Glebe House, Woodbury, led to consecration of Bishop Samuel Seabury abroad and beginning of Protestant Episcopal Church in United States.

1784 First American law school established at Litchfield by Tapping Reeve.

1784 Earliest Connecticut cities incorporated: Hartford, Middletown, New Haven, New London, and Norwich.

1784 Governor Trumbull retired from governorship.

1784 Connecticut relinquished Westmoreland area to Pennsylvania.

1784 Act passed providing for emancipation of all Negroes at age of twenty-five.

1787 Oliver Ellsworth, William Samuel Johnson, and Roger Sherman served as Connecticut's representatives at Philadelphia Constitutional Convention.

1788 Convention at Hartford approved Federal Constitution by 128-to-40 vote.

1789 Oliver Ellsworth and William Samuel Johnson began service as first United States Senators from Connecticut.

1792 First turnpike road company, New London to Norwich, incorporated.

1792 First banks established at Hartford, New London, and New Haven.

1795 Connecticut Western Reserve lands (now northeastern Ohio) sold for $1,200,000, with proceeds constituting the School Fund.

1795 First insurance company incorporated as the Mutual Assurance Company of the City of Norwich.

1796 *Courier* started at Norwich by Thomas Hubbard. Paper merged in 1860 with the *Morning Bulletin* and continued as Norwich *Bulletin* to present.

1799 Eli Whitney procured his first Federal musket contract; within next decade developed a system of interchangeable parts, applicable to many industries.

1802 Brass industry begun at Waterbury by Abel Porter and associates.

1807 First important English dictionary in United States published by Noah Webster.

1810 Hartford Fire Insurance Company incorporated.

1812– War of 1812 unpopular in Connecticut; new
14 manufactures, especially textiles, boomed.

1812 *Columbian Register* founded at New Haven by Joseph Barber. In 1911 combined with the New Haven *Register* and continued as *Register* to present.

1814 Hartford Convention held in State House.

1815 First steamboat voyage up the Connecticut River to Hartford.

1817 Federalists defeated by reformers in political revolution.

1817 Thomas Gallaudet founded school for the deaf in Hartford.

1817 Hartford *Times* founded.

1818 New constitution adopted by convention in Hartford and approved by voters; ended system of Established Church.

1821 Captain John Davis and Captain Amos Palmer leaders in antarctic exploration.

1823 Washington College (now Trinity) founded in Hartford.

1828 Farmington Canal opened.

1831 Wesleyan University founded in Middletown.

1832 First Connecticut railroad incorporated as the Boston, Norwich, and New London.

1835 Revolver patented by Colt.

1835 Music Vale Seminary, first American music school, founded at Salem by Oramel Whittlesey.

1838 Railroad completed between New Haven and Hartford.

1840's and 1850's Peak of whaling from Connecticut ports and especially from New London.

1842 Wadsworth Atheneum, Hartford, first public art museum, established.

1843 Charles Goodyear developed vulcanizing process for rubber.

1844 Dr. Horace Wells used anesthesia at Hartford.

1847 First American agricultural experiment station, at Yale.

1849 First teachers' college (now Central Connecticut College) founded at New Britain.

1851 Phoenix Mutual Life Insurance Company started (under another name) in Hartford.

1853 Ætna Life Insurance Company started in Hartford.

1860 Lincoln spoke in several Connecticut cities.

1861–65 Approximately 55,000 men served in Union Army; William Buckingham, wartime governor.

1863 Travelers Insurance Company started in Hartford.

1870 United States Coast Guard Academy established at New London.

1875 Hartford made sole capital city.

1877 First telephone exchange in world opened at New Haven.

1879 New capitol building in Hartford completed; Richard Upjohn, architect.

1881 Storrs Agricultural College founded (became University of Connecticut in 1939).

1890 Disputed election caused Morgan Bulkeley to continue two extra years as governor (1891–93).

1897 Manufacture of automobiles begun by Pope Manufacturing Company of Hartford.

1900 First United States Navy submarine constructed by Electric Boat Company.

1901 First American state law regulating automobile speeds.

1911 Connecticut College for Women founded at New London.

1917–18 Approximately 66,000 Connecticut men served in World War I.

1925 St. Joseph College founded in Hartford.

1936 Floods caused enormous damage in Connecticut River Valley.

1938 Hurricane and floods produced heavy loss of life and property.

1938 First section of Merritt Parkway opened.

1941–45 Approximately 210,000 Connecticut men served in World War II.

1950–52 Approximately 52,000 Connecticut men served in Korean War.

1954 *Nautilus,* world's first atomic-powered submarine, launched at Groton.

1955 Serious floods caused heavy damage and loss of life.

1955 Shakespeare Memorial Theater opened at Stratford.

1957 University of Hartford founded.

1957 Ground broken for first building in New Haven's Oak Street redevelopment area.

1958 Connecticut Turnpike opened — 129 miles long.

1959 Assembly voted to abolish county government (effective 1960), also to abolish local justice courts and establish district courts (effective 1961).

1960 Ground broken for first building in Hartford's Front Street redevelopment area.

Brief Statistics on Connecticut

Official designation: "Constitution State" (adopted by 1959 General Assembly)

State motto: "Qui Transtulit Sustinet" (He who transplanted us sustains us)

State emblems:

Seal — provided for in the constitution of 1818

Flag — adopted by legislative act in 1897

Flower — the mountain laurel (adopted 1907)

Bird — the robin (adopted 1943)

Tree — the white oak (adopted 1947)

Capital: Hartford sole capital since 1875 (during most of colonial period New Haven and Hartford were joint capitals)

Population, 1950 — 2,007,280; census return, 1960 — 2,535,234

Area of state: 5,009 square miles

Population density per square mile: 1950 — 401; 1960 — 506

Rank in population, 1960 — twenty-fifth

Rank in size — forty-eighth

Cities with largest population, 1960 final census: 1] Hartford, 162,178; 2] Bridgeport, 156,748; 3] New Haven, 152,048

Towns — 169; *cities* — 22; *boroughs* — 13; *counties* — 8

Birth rate, 1959 — 22.5 *Death Rate,* 1959 — 8.3

Grand list of taxable property, 1958 — $8,155,508,520

Number of houses, 1958 — 545,552 *Average value,* 1958 — $6,538

Length of state's boundary — 371 miles

Highest altitude — 2,380 feet: Mount Frissell in Salisbury (summit of Mount Frissell in Massachusetts)

Number of lakes — over 1,000 *Length of rivers* — about 7,600 miles

State parks — 73, with 21,297 acres

State forests — 27, with 123,356 acres

Rainfall, 1959 — 45.70 inches

Miles in state highway system — 3,395

Miles of divided lane highways — 346

Receipts of state government for year ending June 30, 1960 — $410,559,381.09

Disbursements for the year ending June 30, 1960 — $448,340,580.22

GOVERNMENT AND JUDICIAL

Elective state offices — four-year term beginning January 7, 1959: *Governor,* Abraham Ribicoff; *Lieutenant Governor,* John N. Dempsey; *Secretary of State,* Ella T. Grasso; *Treasurer,* John A. Speziale; *Comptroller,* Raymond S. Thatcher; *Attorney General,* Albert L. Coles. As a result of the resignation of Ribicoff in January 1961, John N. Dempsey became Governor and Anthony Armentano, Lieutenant Governor.

United States Senators: Prescott Bush, 1957–63; Thomas J. Dodd, 1959–65; Representatives — 6

State Senators in General Assembly, for 1961 session — 36

Representatives in General Assembly, for 1961 session — 294

Justices of Supreme Court — 5 *Judges of Superior Court* — 22

Judges of Common Pleas Courts — 12 *Judges of Circuit Court* — 44

State Referees — 11 *Probate Courts* — 124

Referees in Bankruptcy — 2 *Juvenile Court* — 1

Attorneys at Law — about 4,600

Town, City, Borough Courts — 66
Justice Courts — 102 } terminated Dec. 31, 1960
Danbury Traffic Court — 1

MISCELLANEOUS FACTS

Banks of all types, 1959 — 144

National banks — 24

State banks and trust companies — 42

Savings banks — 71

Federal savings and loan associations — 18

Private banks — 2

Industrial banks — 5

Building or savings and loan associations — 25

State credit unions — 163

Federal credit unions — 297

Standard broadcasting stations — 31

Automobile registrations, all classes, July 1, 1959–June 30, 1960 — 1,181,941

AVIATION STATISTICS, MAY 1, 1960

State-owned airports: Bradley Field, Windsor Locks; Trumbull Airport, Groton; Brainard Field, Hartford

Total commercial airports — 32

Private seaplane bases — 11

Commercial heliports — 5

Registered aircraft — 654

Private airports — 31

Private heliports — 11

State heliport — 1

Registered pilots — 2,890

CONNECTICUT AGRICULTURAL FACTS, 1959†

Farms (1959 census): 8,266.

Estimated acreages in 1959: tobacco 9,300; truck crops 12,350; potatoes 6,800; hay, 202,000; corn, 41,000; oats 1,000.

**Total cash farm income from marketing of crops, livestock and livestock products:* $155,151,000.

† Sources for above data: Agricultural Marketing Service, Connecticut Department of Agriculture, United States Census.

* Preliminary

**Cash farm income from marketing of crops:* $55,277,000; tobacco $19,323,000; truck crops $7,047,000; potatoes $2,629,000; apples $2,814,-000; other fruits $1,259,000.‡

Cash farm income from marketing of livestock and livestock products:* $99,874,000; eggs $26,-150,000; broilers $15,803,000; chickens $2,841,-000; turkeys $1,280,000; dairy products $44,560,-000; cattle and calves $6,487,000; hogs $475,000; some other $2,328,000.

**Livestock numbers on farms in 1959:* hens and chickens 4,106,000; turkeys 236,000; milk cows 103,000; all cattle 155,000; sheep 10,000; swine 22,000; horses 4,000.

**Livestock production on farms in 1959:* eggs 721,-000,000; broilers 26,713,000; milk 733,000,000 pounds.

Chicks hatched by commercial hatcheries in 1959: 45,450,000.

‡ Includes blueberries, raspberries, quinces, and other berries.

** Includes ducks, geese, beeswax, honey, horses, rabbits, minks, silver foxes.

VOTE FOR PRESIDENT

COUNTY	1952					1956		1960	
	Eisenhower REP.	Stevenson DEM.	Hoopes SOC.	Hallinan PEOPLE'S	Hass SOC. LABOR	Stevenson DEM.	Eisenhower REP.	Kennedy DEM.	Nixon REP.
Hartford	150,332	146,551	352	370	109	126,923	175,894	195,403	136,459
New Haven	165,917	136,476	622	399	127	112,208	191,215	188,685	136,852
New London	38,148	31,374	75	47	26	27,317	43,453	40,625	38,070
Fairfield	167,278	106,403	1,065	507	240	84,890	199,841	146,442	167,778
Windham	17,979	15,535	29	35	10	13,553	20,029	20,105	15,180
Litchfield	35,735	20,163	54	47	6	17,226	40,029	29,062	34,043
Middlesex	22,157	15,722	26	37	10	13,851	25,496	22,158	22,045
Tolland	13,466	9,425	21	24	7	9,111	15,880	14,575	15,386
	611,012	481,649	2,244	1,466	535	405,079	711,837	657,055	565,813

COUNTY	1954				1958			1958	
	Ribicoff DEM.	Lodge REP.	McLevy SOC.	Kellems IND. REP.	Ribicoff DEM.	Zeller REP.	McLevy SOC.	Dodd DEM.	Purtell REP.
Hartford	145,339	114,998	1,191	305	176,009	92,829	754	162,913	105,458
New Haven	129,732	130,298	2,246	515	169,031	94,449	1,299	156,598	105,006
New London	29,592	28,092	242	273	35,515	24,396	199	33,474	26,039
Fairfield	94,997	118,154	6,891	87	142,514	91,809	4,145	126,121	109,084
Windham	16,466	13,446	123	38	18,548	11,485	65	17,608	12,515
Litchfield	20,890	27,196	236	31	30,157	21,664	180	26,294	25,320
Middlesex	16,525	17,644	144	91	21,768	14,308	108	19,544	16,317
Tolland	10,102	10,700	86	83	13,470	9,704	103	12,289	10,883
	463,643	460,528	11,159	1,423	607,012	360,644	6,853	554,841	410,622

VOTE FOR CONGRESS
First, Second, and Third Districts

	FIRST DISTRICT		SECOND DISTRICT		THIRD DISTRICT	
	1958	1960	1958	1960	1958	1960
D	Daddario 146,115	Daddario 193,330	Bowles 79,672	St. Onge 93,515	Giaimo 101,028	Giaimo 124,547
R	May 122,770	Brennan 137,386	Seely-Brown 69,837	Seely-Brown 93,971	Cretella 78,665	Cretella 102,271

VOTE FOR CONGRESS
Fourth and Fifth Districts and at Large

	FOURTH DISTRICT		FIFTH DISTRICT		AT LARGE	
	1958	1960	1958	1960	1958	1960
D	Irwin 119,766	Irwin 150,205	Monagan 72,604	Monagan 88,310	Kowalski 542,315	Kowalski 657,680
R	Morano 115,505	Sibal 160,654	Patterson 62,353	Patterson 71,964	Sadlak 410,622	Sadlak 560,803
Soc.	—	McLevy 2,350				

420

C.H.S.:	Connecticut Historical Society.
C.H.S.C.:	*Connecticut Historical Society Collections.*
C.R.:	*Public Records of the Colony of Connecticut.*
Col. Univ. Stud. Hist., Econ., and Public Law:	Columbia University Studies in History, Economics, and Public Law.
Conn. Ter. Comm. Pubs.:	Connecticut Tercentenary Commission Publications.
D.A.B.:	*Dictionary of American Biography.*
D.N.B.:	*Dictionary of National Biography.*
M.H.S.:	Massachusetts Historical Society.
M.H.S.C.:	*Massachusetts Historical Society Collections.*
M.R.:	*Records of the Governor and Company of the Massachusetts Bay.*
N.H.C.H.S.:	*New Haven Colony Historical Society.*
N.H.C.R.:	*Records of the Colony or Jurisdiction of New Haven.*
N.L.C.H.S. Recs. & Papers:	*New London County Historical Society Records & Papers.*
N.Y.H.S.C.:	*New York Historical Society Collections.*
R and M:	*Register and Manual.*
S.R.:	*Public Records of the State of Connecticut.*

NOTE 1 Sources are cited in full the first time they appear in each chapter; thereafter shortened titles are used. Exceptions are the abbreviations listed above, which are used throughout.

NOTE 2 In all quotations, both in text and notes, italicized material appears as in the original sources.

NOTE 3 Prior to September 1752 England and its colonies operated under the Julian calendar and began the New Year on March 25. On September 14, 1752, the Gregorian calendar (our current one) went into effect throughout the British Empire. For all dates between January 1 and March 25, through 1752, therefore, the number of the year is given first under the old style Julian calendar, and then in its equivalent, under the new style Gregorian system.

1 Backgrounds in England and Massachusetts Bay

1. Conyers Read, *The Tudors* . . . (New York, 1936), pp. 3–100.
2. Helen M. Cam, *England Before Elizabeth* (London, 1950), pp. 158–159; Read, pp. 67–73.
3. Read, pp. 104–108, 114–116, 119, 151–152.
4. John E. Neale, *Queen Elizabeth* (London, 1934), pp. 283–286; Read, pp. 249–251.
5. Wallace Notestein, *The English People on the Eve of Colonization, 1603–1630,* New Amer. Nation Ser. (New York, 1954), pp. 9–10.
6. Charles M. Andrews, *The Colonial Period of American History* (New Haven, 1954), I, 25–26; Curtis Nettels, *The Roots of American Civilization* . . . (New York, 1938), pp. 50–51, 104–105.

7. Andrews, *Colonial Period*, I, 19–20, 25; William Lunt, *History of England*, rev. ed. (New York, 1938), pp. 346–348; Nettels, pp. 87–89, 101–102.

8. Maurice P. Ashley, *England in the Seventeenth Century*, Pelican Hist. Eng., VI (London, 1952), 12, 15–16; Lunt, pp. 324–326, 360, 487–488; Read, pp. 111–112.

9. George M. Trevelyan, *England Under the Stuarts*, Hist. of Eng. Ser., V (New York, 1930), 45–47.

10. Thomas J. Wertenbaker, *The Puritan Oligarchy . . .* (New York, 1947), pp. 7–9.

11. *Ibid.*, pp. 9–13.

12. Nettels, pp. 90–91, 131.

13. Andrews, *Colonial Period*, I, 85–86; Notestein, pp. 8–10; Louis B. Wright, *The Atlantic Frontier* (New York, 1947), pp. 42–43.

14. Ernest Flagg, *Genealogical Notes on the Founding of New England* (Hartford, 1926), p. 11n; Nettels, p. 130; Notestein, pp. 45, 60, 108–115. From the approximately 5,000 adult males who came to New England between 1620–40, less than 50 belonged to the English upper gentry, and less than 250 to minor landed or mercantile gentry.

15. Lunt, pp. 335–336; Notestein, pp. 147–148.

16. Marshall M. Knappen, *Tudor Puritanism . . .* (Chicago, 1939), pp. 187–216, 341, 488; Notestein, pp. 148–150; Alan Simpson, *Puritanism in Old and New England* (Chicago, 1955), pp. 2, 5–6.

17. Thomas W. Davids, *Annals of Evangelical Nonconformity in the County of Essex . . .* (London, 1863), p. 65; Neale, pp. 308–310.

18. Davids, pp. 1, 88–105; Knappen, p. 269; Neale, pp. 310–312.

19. Knappen, pp. 294–302; Lunt, p. 371; Neale, pp. 315–318.

20. Notestein, pp. 156–157.

21. Wertenbaker, *Puritan Oligarchy*, pp. 30–40.

22. Warren S. Archibald, *Thomas Hooker*, Conn. Ter. Comm. Pubs., No. 4 (New Haven, 1933), p. 1; *Dictionary of American Biography* (New York, 1928–58), IX, 199; *Dictionary of National Biography* (London, 1885–1901), IX, 1189; Edward Hooker, *The Descendants of Rev. Thomas Hooker . . .* (Rochester, 1909), pp. vii, xiv, xv; Frances I. S. Judd, "American Ancestry of Samuel Tompkins and Martha Alphena (Todd) Schureman and Their Descendants," *Detroit Soc. for Genealogical Research Mag.*, V (March 1942), 122–123; Cotton Mather, *Magnalia Christi Americana . . .* (Hartford, 1820), I, 303; George L. Walker, *Thomas Hooker: Preacher, Founder, Democrat* (New York, 1891), pp. 1, 3–5.

23. Walker, *Hooker*, p. 9. There is no documentary proof of his attendance there, but, since he held a Wolstan Dixie fellowship at Cambridge, an award restricted to relatives of the founder or graduates of the Market Bosworth Grammar School, it seems plausible that he attended it.

24. Andrews, *Colonial Period*, I, 503; Notestein, pp. 134–135; Walker, *Hooker*, pp. 18–23.

25. *D.N.B.*, XIII, 374–375; Samuel E. Morison, *The Founding of Harvard College* (Cambridge, Mass., 1935), pp. 92–96; James B. Mullinger, *A History of the University of Cambridge* (London, 1888), pp. 130–133.

26. Thomas Fuller, *The History of the University of Cambridge* (London, 1840), p. 278.

27. Morison, p. 382; Walker, *Hooker*, pp. 21–23.

28. Mather, I, 303–304, 306, 308; Walker, *Hooker*, pp. 28–31.

29. Walker, *Hooker*, p. 34.

30. John K. Floyer, *St. George's Church, Esher* (London, n.d.), pp. 9–11; John Hart, *The Firebrand taken out of the Fire: Or, The Wonderfull History, Care, and Cure of Mis DRAKE, sometimes the wife of Francis Drake of Esher . . .* (London, 1654), pp. 117–120, 129; Walker, *Hooker*, pp. 34–37.

31. Mather, I, 304; Walker, *Hooker*, pp. 38–39. An entry in the Great Baddow, Essex, church register indicates that a daughter, Ann Hooker, was baptized on Jan. 5, 1626. The second parish register of St. Mary's Cathedral, Chelmsford (which the author has viewed), shows that Ann was buried on May 23, 1626. This strongly suggests that the Hooker family had moved to Chelmsford during the period between Jan. 5 and May 23, 1626, so that he could assume his duties there.

32. Walker, *Hooker*, pp. 40–41.

33. Mather, I, 304–306.

34. *Ibid.*, p. 307.

35. *Ibid.*, pp. 304–305, 313.

36. Allen French, *Charles I and the Puritan Upheaval . . .* (Boston, 1955), pp. 276–278; Francis C. Montague, *The History of England from the Accession of James I to the Restoration (1603–1660)* (London, 1907), pp. 170–172.

37. John Bruce, ed. *Calendar of State Papers, Domestic Series . . . 1628–29* (London, 1859), pp. 554, 567; Davids, pp. 150–152.

38. *Cal. of State Papers, 1629–31*, p. 87; Davids, pp. 152–153.

39. Davids, pp. 153–161; Mather, I, 305. In a conversation with the author at Chelmsford on July 15, 1955, the Very Reverend George Eric Gordon, Provost of St. Mary's, expressed the belief that Hooker slipped away quietly and the date of his departure was deliberately left blank to avoid further trouble. The register of St. Mary's shows that Sarah, a daughter of Hooker, was buried Aug. 26, 1629, which indicates that Hooker was still lecturer then.

40. Mather, I, 305, 480–481.

41. Davids, p. 150; Walker, *Hooker*, p. 51.

42. *Cal. of State Papers, 1633–34*, pp. 30–31; Perry Miller, *Orthodoxy in Massachusetts, 1630–1650 . . .* (Cambridge, Mass., 1933), p. 108; Walker, *Hooker*, pp. 55–56.

43. Mather, I, 308; Miller, *Orthodoxy in Mass.*, pp. 111–112.

44. Mather, I, 308–309; Walker, *Hooker*, pp. 59–60; *Winthrop Papers* (Boston, 1929–47), II, 178, 336.

45. William Hubbard, *A General History of New England from the Discovery to MDCLXXX* (Cambridge, Mass., 1815), p. 189; Walker, *Hooker*, pp. 60–61; John Winthrop, *Winthrop's Journal, "History of New England," 1630–1649* (New York, 1908), I, 90.

46. Mather, I, 309.

47. *D.A.B.*, XVIII, 83; *D.N.B.*, LIV, 415; Mather, I, 392–393; George L. Walker, *History of the First Church in Hartford, 1633–1883* (Hartford, 1884), pp. 46–50; Walker, *Hooker*, pp. 61–63.

48. Winthrop, *Journal*, I, 105–106; Alexander Young, *Chronicles of the First Planters of the Colony of Massachusetts Bay, from 1623 to 1636* (Boston, 1846), p. 348.

49. Winthrop, *Journal*, I, 105–106, 111.

50. Mather, I, 242.

51. Young, pp. 439–442.

52. Young, p. 402; William Wood, *Nevv England's Prospect . . .* (London, 1634), p. 41.

53. Winthrop, *Journal*, I, 142.
54. Samuel H. Brockunier, *The Irrepressible Democrat, Roger Williams* (New York, 1940), pp. 58–68; Winthrop, *Journal*, I, 162–163.
55. Winthrop, *Journal*, I, 124, 128.
56. *Ibid.*, pp. 132–134.
57. Andrews, *Colonial Period*, II, 84–87; Colonial Society of Massachusetts, *Publications*, VII, *Transactions, 1900–1902* (Boston, 1905), p. 73; Hubbard, pp. 173, 305. Winthrop asserted that Hooker did not leave Massachusetts because of "any difference between Mr. Cotton and him (soe reporte) for they doe hould a most sweet & brotherly comunion together (thoughe their judgmts doe somewhat differ about the lawfullnesse of the Crosse in the ensigne) but that the people & cattle are so increased as the place will not suffice them."
58. Andrews, *Colonial Period*, II, 82–83; Herbert L. Osgood, *The American Colonies in the Seventeenth Century* (New York, 1930), I, 302–303; James H. Trumbull, ed. *The Public Records of the Colony of Connecticut Prior to the Union with New Haven Colony* (Hartford, 1850–90), I, 582.
59. James Truslow Adams, *The Founding of New England* (Boston, 1922), pp. 189–190; Lucius R. Paige, *History of Cambridge, Massachusetts, 1630–1877* (Boston, 1877), p. 29; Nathaniel B. Shurtleff, ed. *Records of the Governor and Company of the Massachusetts Bay* (Boston, 1853–54), I, 146, 148, 159–160.

2 Settlement of the Connecticut River Valley

1. Alexander C. Flick, ed. *History of the State of New York . . .* (New York, 1933–37), I, 165; Edmund B. O'Callaghan, *History of New Netherland: Or, New York under the Dutch* (New York, 1846–48), I, 73.
2. Charles M. Andrews, *The Colonial Period of American History* (New Haven, 1954), II, 70–71; William Bradford, *Of Plymouth Plantation, 1620–1647*, ed. Samuel E. Morison (New York, 1952), pp. 257–259; Forrest Morgan *et al.*, eds. *Connecticut as a Colony and as a State, or one of the Original Thirteen* (Hartford, 1904), I, 47, 83–84; O'Callaghan, *New Netherland*, I, 149–151; Henry R. Stiles, *The History and Genealogies of Ancient Windsor, Connecticut . . .* (Hartford, 1891), I, 19–20.
3. Andrews, *Colonial Period*, II, 68, 68n, 69.
4. Bradford, p. 259; Stiles, *Windsor*, I, 25–26; John Winthrop, *Winthrop's Journal, "History of New England," 1630–1649* (New York, 1908), I, 109–110.
5. Bradford, p. 259; O'Callaghan, *New Netherland*, I, 154–155; Stiles, *Windsor*, I, 26; Benjamin Trumbull, *A Complete History of Connecticut, Civil and Ecclesiastical . . .* (New London, 1898), I, 16–17.
6. Trumbull, *Connecticut*, I, 16; Winthrop, *Journal*, I, 109.
7. Roger Clap, *Memoirs of Roger Clap, 1630*, Dorchester Antiq. and Hist. Soc. Colls., No. 1 (Boston, 1844), pp. 39–40; Dorchester Antiq. and Hist. Soc., *History of the Town of Dorchester, Massachusetts* (Boston, 1859), pp. iv, 14, 17–19; John Fiske, *The Beginnings of New England . . .* (Boston, 1898), p. 110; Maude P. Kuhns, *The "Mary and John": A Story of the Founding of Dorchester, Massachusetts, 1630* (Rutland, 1943), pp. 1–2.
8. Charles M. Andrews, *The River Towns of Connecticut*, Johns Hopkins Studs. in Hist. and Pol. Sci., 7th Ser., Nos. 7–9 (Baltimore, 1889), pp. 21–23; Trumbull, *Connecticut*, I, 41–42.
9. D.A.H.S., *History of Dorchester*, pp. 35–37.
10. Andrews, *Colonial Period*, II, 72–73; Andrews, *River Towns*, pp. 17–19; Stiles, *Windsor*, I, 28–39.
11. Andrews, *Colonial Period*, II, 70; Andrews, *River Towns*, p. 25; Henry R. Stiles, *The History of Ancient Wethersfield, Connecticut . . .* (New York, 1904), pp. 19–31.
12. Charles M. Andrews, *The Beginnings of Connecticut, 1632–1662*, Conn. Ter. Comm. Pubs., No. 32 (New Haven, 1934), pp. 17–18; Cotton Mather, *Magnalia Christi Americana . . .* (Hartford, 1820), I, 310–311; George L. Walker, *Thomas Hooker: Preacher, Founder, Democrat* (New York, 1891), pp. 92–93.
13. Andrews, *Colonial Period*, II, 74–75.
14. Andrews, *Beginnings of Conn.*, pp. 10–12; Charles J. Hoadly, *The Warwick Patent*, Acorn Club Pubs., No. 7 (Hartford, 1902), pp. 7, 9–17.
15. Andrews, *Beginnings of Conn.*, pp. 12–15; Andrews, *Colonial Period*, II, 80; *C.R.*, I, 1–2; *M.R.*, I, 170–171; Winthrop, *Journal*, I, 173.
16. Andrews, *Colonial Period*, II, 122; *C.R.*, I, 7; *D.A.B.*, VII, 138; Curtiss C. Gardiner, ed. *Lion Gardiner, and His Descendants . . .* (St. Louis, 1890), pp. 49–53; Winthrop, *Journal*, I, 165.
17. Andrews, *Colonial Period*, II, 79, 95–97.
18. Conn. Sec. of State, *Register and Manual, 1955* (Hartford, 1955), p. 623; Conn. State Highway Dept. *et al.*, *Official Map of Connecticut* (Hartford, 1960). All distances are air-line and are based on the *Official Map*. The running mileage of the boundaries, using a straight line in the Sound, is 371.
19. Claude Blanchard, *The Journal of Claude Blanchard . . .*, trans. William Duane, ed. Thomas Balch (Albany, 1876), p. 110; Marquis François Jean de Chastellux, *Travels in North America in the Years 1780, 1781, 1782* (Dublin, 1787), I, 37; Richard F. Flint, *The Glacial Geology of Connecticut*, Conn. Geol. and Natural Hist. Survey Bull., No. 47 (Hartford, 1930), pp. 29, 31; Albert L. Olson, *Agricultural Economy and the Population in Eighteenth-Century Connecticut*, Conn. Ter. Comm. Pubs., No. 40 (New Haven, 1935), pp. 1–2.
20. Thomas A. Cook, *Geology of Connecticut* (Hartford, 1933), pp. 12–13; Olson, pp. 5–7.
21. Trumbull, *Connecticut*, I, 19.
22. *Ibid.*, pp. 20–21.
23. *Ibid.*, p. 21.
24. Wilson S. Dakin, *Geography of Connecticut* (Boston, 1926), pp. 13–27, 111; William N. Rice, *The Physical Geography and Geology of Connecticut*, reprinted from *Conn. Board of Agric. Rept. 1903* (Hartford, 1904), pp. 111–112.
25. Howard I. Chapelle, *The History of American Sailing Ships* (New York, 1935), p. 11; Rice, p. 112.
26. *C.R.*, III, 295–297.
27. Cook, pp. 16, 18–21, 25, 33; Rice, p. 100.
28. Cook, pp. 23, 25, 36; Rice, pp. 106–107.
29. Cook, pp. 23–24, 38–42; Flint, pp. 21, 24–25, 43, 46, 48, 53–55, 59–64; Rice, pp. 108–112; Works Progress Administration, Federal Writers' Project, *Connecticut . . .*, Amer. Guide Ser. (Boston, 1938), pp. 20–21.
30. Conn. Geol. and Natural Hist. Survey, *Preliminary Geological Map of Connecticut, 1956*.

31. George L. Clark, *A History of Connecticut, Its People and Institutions,* rev. ed. (New York, 1914), p. 4; James H. Trumbull, "The Composition of Indian Geographical Names, Illustrated from the Algonkin Languages," *C.H.S.C.,* II (Hartford, 1870), 8.
32. John W. DeForest, *History of the Indians of Connecticut . . .* (Hartford, 1853), pp. 45–48, 59; Trumbull, *Connecticut,* I, 24; Charles C. Willoughby, *Antiquities of the New England Indians . . .* (Cambridge, Mass., 1935), p. 278.
33. Daniel Gookin, "Historical Collections of the Indians in New England," *M.H.S.C.,* 1st Ser., I (Boston, 1806), 149; James Trumbull, *Indian Names of Places, etc., in and on the Borders of Connecticut . . .* (Hartford, 1881), pp. v–vi; Clark Wissler, *Indians of the United States . . .* (New York, 1940), p. 56.
34. DeForest, pp. 5–7.
35. Harold C. Bradshaw, *The Indians of Connecticut . . .* (Deep River, Conn., 1935), p. 13; DeForest, pp. 8–9.
36. Bradshaw, pp. 12–13.
37. Mathias Spiess, *The Indians of Connecticut,* Conn. Ter. Comm. Pubs., No. 19 (New Haven, 1933), pp. 3–4.
38. DeForest, p. 57; Frank G. Speck, *Native Tribes and Dialects of Connecticut,* 43d Annual Report of the Bur. of Amer. Ethnology, 1925–26 (Wash., 1928), pp. 217–218; Spiess, pp. 22–24. The Eastern Nehantics joined the Narragansets and became very powerful there. The Western Nehantics eventually joined the Mohegans.
39. DeForest, p. 55; Winthrop, *Journal,* I, 61.
40. *D.A.B.,* XIX, 108–109; Carroll A. Means, "Mohegan-Pequot Relationships . . . ," *Bull. Arch. Soc. Conn.,* No. 21 (Dec. 1947), pp. 32–33; Froehlich G. Rainey, "A Compilation of Historical Data Contributing to the Ethnography of Connecticut and Southern New England Indians," *Bull. Arch. Soc. Conn.,* No. 3 (April 1936), pp. 5–6; Speck, pp. 207–208; Spiess, pp. 11–13.
41. Spiess, pp. 14–16.
42. DeForest, p. 54; Spiess, pp. 24–26.
43. Spiess, pp. 17–18, 27–28.
44. Spiess, pp. 19–21.
45. DeForest, pp. 48–51; Rollin G. Osterweis, *Three Centuries of New Haven, 1638–1938* (New Haven, 1953), pp. 10–11, 24–25; Rainey, pp. 7–8; Spiess, pp. 26–32.
46. Eva Butler, "The Brush or Stone Memorial Heaps of Southern New England," *Bull. Arch. Soc. Conn.,* No. 19 (April 1946), p. 10; DeForest, p. 51; Spiess, pp. 32–33.
47. Speck, pp. 210–211.
48. Herbert M. Sylvester, *Indian Wars of New England* (Boston, 1910), p. 53.
49. Howard Bradstreet, *The Story of the War with the Pequots, Re-Told,* Conn. Ter. Comm. Pubs., No. 5 (New Haven, 1933), pp. 5–7; William Hubbard, *The History of the Indian Wars in New England . . . ,* rev. Samuel G. Drake (Roxbury, Mass., 1865), II, 7–9; Winthrop, *Journal,* I, 138–140.
50. *D.A.B.,* XIV, 12; Winthrop, *Journal,* I, 183–184.
51. Bradstreet, pp. 8–9; Lion Gardiner, *Relation of the Pequot Warres, Written in 1660 . . . ,* Acorn Club Pubs., No. 4 (Hartford, 1901), p. 9; Winthrop, *Journal,* I, 186–189.
52. Bradstreet, p. 10; Hubbard, II, 13–14.
53. John R. Bartlett, ed. "The Letters of Roger Williams," *Narragansett Club Pubs.,* VI (Providence, 1874), 338; Bradstreet, pp. 9–10; Samuel H. Brockunier, *The Ir-*

54. Stiles, *Wethersfield,* I, 62–64; John Underhill, "Nevves from America; or a New and Experimentall Discoverie of New England . . . ," *M.H.S.C.,* 3d Ser., VI, 12; Winthrop, *Journal,* I, 213.
55. Bradstreet, pp. 10–11.
56. *C.R.,* I, 9–10.
57. Bradstreet, pp. 12–13.
58. Bradstreet, pp. 13–14; Gardiner, *Pequot Warres,* pp. 19–20; Underhill, p. 16.
59. Underhill, pp. 16–17.
60. *Winthrop Papers* (Boston, 1929–47), III, 407–408.
61. John Mason, *Brief History of the Pequot War . . .* (Boston, 1736), pp. 2–3.
62. Bradstreet, p. 18; Mason, pp. 6–7.
63. Mason, pp. 4–5.
64. Mason, pp. 5–7.
65. Bradstreet, p. 20; Mason, p. 7.
66. Mason, pp. 7–8.
67. Mason, pp. 8–10.
68. Bradstreet, p. 22; Mason, p. 10.
69. Mason, pp. 10–12.
70. Mason, pp. 12–13.
71. Bradstreet, p. 24; Mason, p. 14; Underhill, p. 28.
72. *C.R.,* I, 10; Mason, pp. 14–15.
73. Mason, pp. 15–16.
74. Hubbard, II, 35; Mason, p. 16.
75. Bradstreet, pp. 26–27; Mason, p. 17.
76. Mason, pp. 17–21.
77. Andrews, *Beginnings of Conn.,* pp. 28–29; *M.R.,* I, 171.
78. *C.R.,* I, 7; William D. Love, *Colonial History of Hartford . . . ,* 2d ed. (Hartford, 1935), p. 166; Stiles, *Wethersfield,* I, 52–55; Stiles, *Windsor,* I, 66.
79. Andrews, *Beginnings of Conn.,* pp. 29–30; *C.R.,* I, 9.
80. *C.R.,* I, 11–12.
81. *C.R.,* I, 11, 13, 20.
82. *C.R.,* I, 15.
83. Andrews, *Colonial Period,* II, 98; Winthrop, *Journal,* I, 287–290; *Winthrop Papers,* IV, 36–37. According to Ludlow, the General Court met in May 1638 and considered "divers particulers that might or may concerne the generall good of these parts."
84. "Abstracts of Two Sermons by Rev. Thomas Hooker," from the Short-hand Notes of Mr. Henry Wolcott, *C.H.S.C.,* I (Hartford, 1860), 20.
85. Andrews, *Beginnings of Conn.,* pp. 39–40; *D.A.B.,* XI, 493; George M. Dutcher and Albert C. Bates, *The Fundamental Orders of Connecticut,* Conn. Ter. Comm. Pubs., No. 20 (New Haven, 1933), p. 2; John M. Taylor, *Roger Ludlow, the Colonial Lawmaker* (New York, 1900), pp. 91–96; *Tercentenary of the Fundamental Orders of Connecticut,* introd. George M. Dutcher (Hartford [1939]), [pp. 1–6]; Trumbull, *Connecticut,* I, 75; *Winthrop Papers,* IV, 36–37.
86. Andrews, *Beginnings of Conn.,* pp. 40–41; Dutcher and Bates, p. 3.
87. Dutcher and Bates, pp. 3–5.
88. *Ibid.,* p. 7.
89. Andrews, *Beginnings of Conn.,* p. 45; Dutcher and Bates, pp. 5–7.
90. Simeon E. Baldwin, "The Three Constitutions of Connecticut," *N.H.C.H.S. Papers,* V (New Haven, 1894), 180; Fiske, p. 137; Alexander Johnston, *Connecticut: A Study of a Commonwealth Democracy* (Boston, 1900), pp. 73, 79–80; Lewis S. Mills, *The Story of Connecticut* (New York, 1943), p. 124; Morgan,

Connecticut, I, 146–147; Herbert L. Osgood, *The American Colonies in the Seventeenth Century* (New York, 1930), I, 311.

91. Andrews, *Beginnings of Conn.*, pp. 44, 46–47; Andrews, *Colonial Period*, II, 109, 109n; Oliver P. Chitwood, *A History of Colonial America*, 2d ed. (New York, 1948), p. 154; Clark, p. 61; William M. Maltbie in conversation with the author, Feb. 21, 1957; Osgood, *Amer. Colonies in Seventeenth Cent.*, I, 310–311; Jennings B. Sanders, *Early American History . . .* (New York, 1941), pp. 89–90; Maxwell H. Savelle, *The Foundations of American Civilization . . .* (New York, 1942), pp. 160–161; Edwin S. Welles, *The Origin of the Fundamental Orders, 1639* (Hartford, 1936), p. 20.

92. Andrews, *Beginnings of Conn.*, pp. 32–33; *C.R.*, I, 13.
93. *C.R.*, I, 19; *D.A.B.*, xv, 292.
94. Andrews, *Beginnings of Conn.*, pp. 34–35.
95. *C.R.*, I, 42, 133.
96. *C.R.*, I, 35–36, 41, 46; *D.A.B.*, xi, 494; Charles J. Hoadly, ed. *Records of the Colony or Jurisdiction of New Haven* (Hartford, 1858), II, 77–89, 122; Taylor, pp. 111–112, 133, 138–148.
97. Andrews, *Beginnings of Conn.*, pp. 10, 60; *D.A.B.*, vi, 329–330; Trumbull, *Connecticut*, I, 424–425.

98. *C.R.*, I, 30–31, 36.
99. *C.R.*, I, 82, 90n, 99, 103.
100. Andrews, *Beginnings of Conn.*, p. 61; *C.R.*, I, 113, 266–271; "Conn. Archives, Towns and Lands, 1629–1789," 1st Ser., I, 3, Conn. St. Lib., Hartford; *D.A.B.*, vi, 330.
101. *C.R.*, I, 60, 70–71, 164, 218, 570; Frances M. Caulkins, *History of New London, Connecticut . . .* (New London, 1895), pp. 42–44; Florence S. M. Crofut, *Guide to the History and the Historic Sites of Connecticut* (New Haven, 1937), II, 721; *M.R.*, II, 71, 160; Winthrop, *Journal*, II, 275, 287; *Winthrop Papers*, v, 30. On May 22, 1646, the General Court records of the Bay Colony state: "Whereas John Winthrope, Iunior, & oth[e]rs have, by alowance of this Co[u]rte, begun a plantation in ye Pequod country . . ." The tense employed strongly suggests that an actual settlement, perhaps very small, had been started the previous year, 1645. The elder Winthrop here appears to date the start as 1646, but he sometimes inserted under current date events which had happened earlier. A letter from Roger Williams dated June 22, 1645, indicates that Winthrop was at Pequot then.
102. Andrews, *Beginnings of Conn.*, pp. 57–58; *C.R.*, I, 310; Caulkins, *New London*, pp. 67–70.

3 Founding of New Haven and Developments of 1640's in the Connecticut Area

1. Franklin B. Dexter, "Sketch of the Life and Writings of John Davenport," *N.H.C.H.S. Papers*, II (New Haven, 1877), 211.
2. Isabel M. Calder, *The New Haven Colony*, Yale Hist. Pubs., Misc., xxviii (New Haven, 1934), 4; Dexter, pp. 206–210.
3. Dexter, pp. 210–211.
4. Calder, pp. 5–6.
5. Calder, pp. 7–9, 12–17, 30; Dexter, p. 214; Cotton Mather, *Magnalia Christi Americana . . .* (Hartford, 1820), I, 293.
6. *Cal. of State Papers, 1629–1631*, p. 483; Dexter, pp. 218–219; Allen French, *Charles I and the Puritan Upheaval . . .* (Boston, 1955), p. 387.
7. Calder, pp. 19–20; Dexter, pp. 217–220; French, pp. 278–279.
8. Calder, pp. 20–21; Rollin G. Osterweis, *Three Centuries of New Haven, 1638–1938* (New Haven, 1953), p. 7.
9. *Cal. of State Papers, 1633–1634*, p. 324; Calder, pp. 20–23; Perry Miller, *Orthodoxy in Massachusetts, 1630–1650 . . .* (Cambridge, Mass., 1933), pp. 113–114.
10. Calder, pp. 22–29.
11. Calder, pp. 28–29; *D.A.B.*, v, 612; Mather, I, 136–138.
12. Leonard Bacon, "Civil Government in the New Haven Colony," *N.H.C.H.S. Papers*, I (New Haven, 1865), 13; Calder, pp. 30–31; Herbert L. Osgood, *The American Colonies in the Seventeenth Century* (New York, 1930), I, 321–322; Osterweis, p. 6.
13. Calder, pp. 29–31; John Winthrop, *Winthrop's Journal, "History of New England," 1630–1649* (New York, 1908), I, 223.
14. Calder, pp. 32, 44–45.
15. Benjamin Trumbull, *A Complete History of Connecticut, Civil and Ecclesiastical . . .* (New London, 1898), I, 71; John Underhill, "Newes from America; or a New and Experimentall Discoverie of New England . . .," *M.H.S.C.*, 3d Ser., vi, 13; John Winthrop,

The History of New England from 1630 to 1649 . . . (Boston, 1825–26), I, 400–401.
16. Calder, pp. 36–37, 45; Osterweis, p. 8.
17. Calder, pp. 46–49.
18. Edward E. Atwater, *History of the Colony of New Haven to Its Absorption into Connecticut* (New Haven, 1881), pp. 72–73; Calder, p. 83; Osterweis, p. 3. The texts are from Matthew iv.1 and iii.3 respectively.
19. Mather, I, 300; *N.H.C.R.*, I, 1–5; Osterweis, pp. 10–12.
20. Osterweis, p. 12.
21. Bacon, pp. 11–15; Calder, p. 51; Osterweis, pp. 14–15.
22. Calder, p. 84; John Cotton, *The Covenant of Gods free Grace . . .* (London, 1645), pp. 35–40; *N.H.C.R.*, I, 11–17.
23. Calder, p. 106; *N.H.C.R.*, I, 15.
24. *N.H.C.R.*, I, 20–21.
25. *Ibid.*, pp. 22–24.
26–27. *Ibid.*, p. 25.
28. *Ibid.*, pp. 28–29, 35, 42.
29. *Ibid.*, pp. 25–26, 33–34, 40.
30. Atwater, pp. 153–154; *N.H.C.R.*, I, 91–93; Curtis Nettels, *The Roots of American Civilization . . .* (New York, 1938), p. 137.
31. Calder, p. 47; Mather, I, 357.
32. Charles M. Andrews, *The Colonial Period of American History* (New Haven, 1954), II, 158–159, 159n; Calder, p. 57; W.P.A., Federal Writers' Project, *History of Milford, Connecticut, 1639–1939* (Bridgeport, 1939), pp. 1, 3–4.
33. Atwater, pp. 155–158; Calder, p. 57; Henry R. Stiles, *The History of Ancient Wethersfield, Connecticut . . .* (New York, 1904), I, 138–139; W.P.A., *Milford*, pp. 6–7, 18–20.
34. Mather, I, 357–358.
35. *N.H.C.R.*, I, 110–111; W.P.A., *Milford*, p. 17.
36. Calder, p. 55; *D.A.B.*, xx, 133–134; Mather, I, 540–541.

37. Calder, p. 55; Bernard C. Steiner, *A History of the Plantation of Menunkatuck and of the Original Town of Guilford, Connecticut . . .* (Baltimore, 1897), pp. 28–30; Trumbull, *Connecticut*, I, 82.

38. Andrews, *Colonial Period*, II, 161–162; Atwater, p. 169; Calder, pp. 116–117; Mather, I, 541; Osterweis, pp. 24–25.

39. William G. Andrews, "The Henry Whitfield House and the State Historical Museum," *N.H.C.H.S. Papers*, VII (New Haven, 1908), 239; Florence S. M. Crofut, *Guide to the History and the Historic Sites of Connecticut* (New Haven, 1937), II, 546–547. Since 1900 the State of Connecticut has owned the Whitfield House. In 1902 it reproduced the original long, high room supposedly as Whitfield knew it. The building is open to the public.

40. Calder, p. 80; Mather, I, 535; *N.H.C.R.*, I, 40, 199–200; Stiles, *Wethersfield*, I, 156–157.

41. Calder, p. 80; Mather, I, 359–360.

42. Andrews, *Colonial Period*, II, 163; Calder, p. 88; Osterweis, p. 25; *R and M, 1956*, p. 130.

43. Charles M. Andrews, *The Rise and Fall of the New Haven Colony*, Conn. Ter. Comm. Pubs., No. 48 (New Haven, 1936), p. 21; Mather, I, 360; *N.H.C.R.*, I, 45, 45n; Stiles, *Wethersfield*, I, 142–145.

44. Andrews, *New Haven Colony*, p. 22; Calder, pp. 75–76; Osterweis, p. 26.

45. Andrews, *New Haven Colony*, pp. 23–24; Calder, pp. 116–117.

46. *N.H.C.R.*, I, 112–116; Osterweis, p. 27.

47. Charles M. Andrews, *The Beginnings of Connecticut, 1632–1662*, Conn. Ter. Comm. Pubs., No. 32 (New Haven, 1934), pp. 34–35; William Bradford, *Of Plymouth Plantation, 1620–1647*, ed. Samuel E. Morison (New York, 1952), pp. 304–308, 426–430; Albert B. Hart, ed. *Commonwealth History of Massachusetts, Colony, Province and State* (New York, 1927–30), I, 226; David Pulsifer, ed. *Records of the Colony of New Plymouth in New England*, IX, *Acts of the Commissioners of the United Colonies of New England*, I (Boston, 1859), 1–2.

48. Clarence W. Bowen, *The Boundary Disputes of Connecticut* (Boston, 1882), pp. 15–17.

49. Osgood, *Amer. Colonies in Seventeenth Cent.*, I, 397; Winthrop, *Journal*, I, 231–232.

50. Winthrop, *Journal*, I, 287–290.

51. *Ibid.*, pp. 290–291.

52. "Rev. Thomas Hooker's Letter, in Reply to Governor Winthrop," *C.H.S.C.*, I (Hartford, 1860), 3–15.

53. *C.R.*, I, 73; Osgood, *Amer. Colonies in Seventeenth Cent.*, I, 399–400; Winthrop, *Journal*, II, 100.

54. Osgood, *Amer. Colonies in Seventeenth Cent.*, I, 399.

55. Winthrop, *Journal*, II, 100.

56. James Truslow Adams, *The Founding of New England* (Boston, 1922), pp. 226–228; Bradford, pp. 430–437; Calder, pp. 115–116; Osgood, *Amer. Colonies in Seventeenth Cent.*, I, 401; Winthrop, *Journal*, II, 100–105.

57. Adams, *Founding of New England*, pp. 229–230.

58. Adams, *Founding of New England*, pp. 239–241; Andrews, *Colonial Period*, II, 93–94; Hart, *Commonwealth*, I, 231–232; Pulsifer, IX, 11–12; Winthrop, *Journal*, II, 131–136.

59. *C.R.*, I, 254, 275n; Pulsifer, IX, 76–77; X, 59–70. Captain John Underhill, under a Rhode Island commission, had seized the House of Hope in June 1653. The Connecticut Court never recognized this action as legal.

60. Andrews, *Colonial Period*, II, 173–174; Hart, *Commonwealth*, I, 241–245; *N.H.C.R.*, II, 4–14, 36–43;

Osgood, *Amer. Colonies in Seventeenth Cent.*, I, 404–406; Pulsifer, X, 59–65, 72–112; Trumbull, *Connecticut*, I, 164–176.

61. *C.R.*, I, 47.

62. *C.R.*, I, 29, 100, 154.

63. *N.H.C.R.*, I, 46, 393–396.

64. *C.R.*, I, 50–51, 168; *N.H.C.R.*, I, 173.

65. *C.R.*, I, 105, 124.

66. *C.R.*, I, 8; *N.H.C.R.*, I, 47, 70.

67. *C.R.*, I, 47–48, 92, 275, 301, 362, 379. Only four divorce cases are given in *C.R.* for 1636–65.

68. *C.R.*, I, 64.

69. *C.R.*, I, 65–66.

70. *N.H.C.R.*, I, 35–38.

71. *C.R.*, I, 61; *N.H.C.R.*, I, 52–56.

72. *C.R.*, I, 61, 64.

73. *C.R.*, I, 58, 69. The English used the general term "corn" to include what Americans called "wheat."

74. *C.R.*, I, 116–117.

75. Andrews, *Beginnings of Conn.*, pp. 64–66.

76. *C.R.*, I, 91; *N.H.C.R.*, I, 130.

77. Andrews, *Beginnings of Conn.*, pp. 66–67; William D. Love, *Colonial History of Hartford . . .*, 2d ed. (Hartford, 1935), p. 328; Nettels, p. 137.

78. *C.R.*, I, 57, 59–60; *D.A.B.*, IX, 207–208; Love, pp. 260–264; Mather, I, 131–132.

79. *C.R.*, I, 498–502; "Mather Papers," *M.H.S.C.*, 4th Ser., VIII, 544–546; George L. Walker, *Thomas Hooker: Preacher, Founder, Democrat* (New York, 1891), pp. 178–183; Winthrop, *Journal*, II, 326–327. Dr. Ernest Caulfield, who has made significant studies of colonial diseases and epidemics, expressed the opinion, in a conversation with the author Oct. 19, 1955, that Hooker probably died of influenza. Hooker's will, made out on the day of his death, left a substantial estate valued at £1,136 15s.

80. Warren S. Archibald, *Thomas Hooker*, Conn. Ter. Comm. Pubs., No. 4 (New Haven, 1933), pp. 13–14; *Winthrop Papers* (Boston, 1929–47), IV, 418–419. John Haynes wrote about the Westminster Assembly: "the maine busines for which they are cheifly called, already sett in such A way, that they being trew to ther owne principles, may rather become A stumble than otherwis."

81. Mather, I, 316–317; George L. Walker, *History of the First Church in Hartford, 1633–1883* (Hartford, 1884), pp. 151–175.

82. Perry Miller and Thomas H. Johnson, eds. *The Puritans* (New York, 1938), p. 291; Clinton Rossiter, "Thomas Hooker," *New England Quarterly*, XXV (Dec. 1952), 475–476; Walker, *Hooker*, pp. 140–142.

83. Thomas Hooker, *The Application of Redemption . . .* (London, 1659), pp. xiv–xv; Thomas Hooker, *A Survey of the Summe of Church-Discipline . . .* (London, 1648), p. xiv; Walker, *Hooker*, pp. 155–177, 184–195.

84. "Abstracts of Two Sermons by Rev. Thomas Hooker," from the Short-hand Notes of Mr. Henry Wolcott, *C.H.S.C.*, I (Hartford, 1860), 20–21; Hooker, *Survey*, pp. 19, 23–25, 45–54, 69, 187–188; Miller, *Orthodoxy in Mass.*, p. 170; Rossiter, pp. 472–473, 479.

85. Hooker, *Survey*, pp. 191–192.

86. Adams, *Founding of New England*, pp. 193, 258; Perry Miller, "Thomas Hooker and the Democracy of Early Connecticut," *New England Quarterly*, IV (Oct. 1931), 663, 681, 694–698, 708–712; Vernon L. Parrington, *Main Currents in American Thought . . .* (New York, 1927–30), I, 54, 59–60; Rossiter, pp. 473, 482–484, 488; Walker, *Hooker*, pp. 152, 177.

4 From the Code of 1650 to the Charter of 1662 and Absorption of New Haven

1. Samuel Hugh Brockunier, *The Irrepressible Democrat, Roger Williams* (New York, 1940), p. 174; *C.R.*, I, 77–78, 138, 154; William M. Maltbie, "Judicial Administration in Connecticut Colony Before the Charter of 1662," *Conn. Bar Journal*, XXIII (Sept. 1949), 243–244. The "Capitall Lawes" were based on the Old Testament. Except for those on blasphemy and witchcraft, they are not far out of line with contemporary practice.
2. *C.R.*, I, 509.
3. *C.R.*, I, 542–543.
4. *C.R.*, I, 529–533.
5. *C.R.*, I, 520–521, 554–555.
6. *C.R.*, I, 91, 117–118, 521–522, 535–536; Maltbie, p. 242. The grand jury was first set up under a law of July 5, 1643.
7. *C.R.*, I, 103–104, 533–534.
8. *C.R.*, I, 527–528, 547.
9. *C.R.*, I, 524.
10. *C.R.*, I, 523–524.
11. *C.R.*, I, 111–112, 545.
12. Charles M. Andrews, *The Colonial Period of American History* (New Haven, 1954), I, 445–447; *N.H.C.R.*, II, 146, 559–616.
13. Charles M. Andrews, *The Beginnings of Connecticut, 1632–1662*, Conn. Ter. Comm. Pubs., No. 32 (New Haven, 1934), pp. 68–69.
14. Albert Carlos Bates, *The Charter of Connecticut . . .* (Hartford, 1932), p. 11; *C.R.*, I, 361–362, 367–369.
15. *D.A.B.*, XX, 411–413; *D.N.B.*, LXII, 231; Cotton Mather, *Magnalia Christi Americana . . .* (Hartford, 1820), I, 143–144; Samuel E. Morison, *Builders of the Bay Colony* (Boston, 1930), pp. 269–272, 275–281.
16. *C.R.*, I, 218, 297, 346–347; *D.A.B.*, XX, 413; Morison, *Builders*, 281–283.
17. Bates, p. 12. He probably sailed from New Amsterdam rather than Boston since Massachusetts' charter was in abeyance and he could scarcely have gotten away from Boston without being requested to help Massachusetts' cause in London.
18. Andrews, *Beginnings of Conn.*, pp. 72–74.
19. Andrews, *Beginnings of Conn.*, pp. 72–74; Bates, p. 12; Thomas Franklin Waters, *A Sketch of the Life of John Winthrop the Younger . . .*, Ipswich Hist. Soc. Pubs., No. 7 (Cambridge, Mass., 1899), p. 56. Winthrop apparently took a very active part in the Society's program for he read a number of papers on such varied topics as shipbuilding in North America, strange tides, refining of gold and black lead.
20. Andrews, *Beginnings of Conn.*, pp. 72–75; Bates, p. 16.
21. Bates, pp. 21, 25–28. Bates thinks that just two official copies of the charter were issued and received the great seal. He concludes that the remnant, now in possession of the Connecticut Historical Society, was the first one to receive the great seal and to be brought back to Connecticut. By some inexplicable twist of events this copy, around 1817, was partly cut up to form the lining of a lady's bonnet! Approximately two-thirds of the second of the two parchment sheets was saved and the precious remnant can now be seen at the Society. The other charter, complete except for the loss of its seal, is now kept in a special fireproof safe in Memorial Hall of the Connecticut State Library.
22. Herbert L. Osgood, *The American Colonies in the Seventeenth Century* (New York, 1930), I, 328.
23. *The Charter of Connecticut, 1662*, introd. C. M. Andrews and A. C. Bates, Conn. Ter. Comm. Pubs., No. 3 (New Haven, 1933), pp. 9–17.
24. *Ibid.*, pp. 17–21.
25. *Ibid.*, pp. 20–21.
26. Andrews, *Beginnings of Conn.*, pp. 78–79; Mather, I, 144; Osgood, *Amer. Colonies in Seventeenth Cent.*, I, 328; Benjamin Trumbull, *A Complete History of Connecticut, Civil and Ecclesiastical . . .* (New London, 1898), I, 205; Waters, pp. 54–55.
27. Rollin G. Osterweis, *Three Centuries of New Haven, 1638–1938* (New Haven, 1953), pp. 54–55.
28. Edward E. Atwater, *History of the Colony of New Haven to its Absorption into Connecticut* (New Haven, 1881), pp. 421–428, 428n.
29. Atwater, pp. 430–435, 444; Isabel M. Calder, *The New Haven Colony*, Yale Hist. Pubs., Misc., XXVIII (New Haven, 1934), pp. 222–223; Osterweis, p. 56.
30. Atwater, pp. 436–440; *D.A.B.*, V, 331–332; Osterweis, p. 57.
31. Charles M. Andrews, *The Rise and Fall of the New Haven Colony*, Conn. Ter. Comm. Pubs., No. 48 (New Haven, 1936), pp. 46–47; Calder, p. 221; Osterweis, pp. 60–61.
32. Osterweis, p. 61.
33. "Conn. Archives, Misc., 1635–1789," 1st Ser., I, 67–68, Conn. St. Lib., Hartford.
34. *C.R.*, I, 396–397; "Conn. Archives, Misc.," 1st Ser., I, 69–70; *N.H.C.R.*, II, 473–475.
35. Calder, pp. 220–221, 240–249.
36. "Conn. Archives, Misc.," 1st Ser., I, 80–81.
37. Calder, pp. 247–249; "Conn. Archives, Foreign Correspondence with the British Government, 1663–1748," I, 3, Conn. St. Lib., Hartford; *N.H.C.R.*, II, 544–546; "Robert C. Winthrop Collection of Conn. Manuscripts, 1631–1794," III, 308, Conn. St. Lib., Hartford.
38. Calder, pp. 249–250; *C.R.*, I, 437; "Conn. Archives, Misc.," 1st Ser., I, 87; *N.H.C.R.*, II, 544–548, 548n.
39. Calder, pp. 251–252; *C.R.*, II, 15n; *N.H.C.R.*, II, 550–551.
40. Calder, p. 252; *C.R.*, I, 440, 441n; II, 13; *N.H.C.R.*, II, 555–557.
41. Calder, pp. 253–256; Lois K. Mathews Rosenberry, *Migrations from Connecticut Prior to 1800*, Conn. Ter. Comm. Pubs., No. 28 (New Haven, 1934), pp. 3–4.
42. Calder, pp. 256–258; *D.A.B.*, V, 87.
43. Andrews, *New Haven Colony*, pp. 55–56; Osgood, *Amer. Colonies in Seventeenth Cent.*, I, 330.
44. *C.R.*, II, 273; *D.A.B.*, XI, 138; *N.H.C.R.*, II, 402.

5 King Philip's War and Andros' Challenge to the Charter

1. George W. Ellis and John E. Morris, *King Philip's War . . .* (New York, 1906), pp. 32–35, 45–46.
2. *C.R.*, I, 335–336; II, 39; III, 8, 117, 125; Herbert L. Osgood, *The American Colonies in the Seventeenth Century* (New York, 1930), I, 534–536.
3. *C.R.*, II, 157–158; *D.A.B.*, XIV, 587–588; John W. DeForest, *History of the Indians of Connecticut . . .* (Hartford, 1853), pp. 272–276; Daniel Gookin, "Historical Collections of the Indians in New England," *M.H.S.C.*, 1st Ser., I (Boston, 1806), 208–209; Osgood, *Amer. Colonies in Seventeenth Cent.*, I, 537–540.
4. Ellis and Morris, pp. 36–37, 40–43.
5. Ellis and Morris, p. 56; Osgood, *Amer. Colonies in Seventeenth Cent.*, I, 543; Benjamin Trumbull, *A Complete History of Connecticut, Civil and Ecclesiastical . . .* (New London, 1898), I, 294.
6. *C.R.*, II, 217–218; Douglas E. Leach, *Flintlock and Tomahawk . . .* (New York, 1958), pp. 14–19.
7. Ellis and Morris, pp. 69–81, 134–138; William Hubbard, *The History of the Indian Wars in New England . . .*, rev. Samuel G. Drake (Roxbury, Mass., 1865), I, 185–186; Leach, *Flintlock*, pp. 26–38, 57–58, 61.
8. Thomas Church, *The History of the Great Indian War of 1675 and 1676 . . .*, rev. ed. (Hartford, 1851), pp. 108–109.
9. *C.R.*, II, 260–264, 331–333, 338; "Conn. Archives, War, 1675–1775, Colonial," I, 4a, 6, Conn. St. Lib., Hartford; Ellis and Morris, pp. 71–72; Thomas Hutchinson, *The History of the Colony of Massachusets-Bay . . .* (Boston, 1764–1828), I, 288–291, 288n–291n; Leach, *Flintlock*, p. 59.
10. Ellis and Morris, p. 83.
11. Ellis and Morris, pp. 87–95; Leach, *Flintlock*, pp. 66, 81–84; Osgood, *Amer. Colonies in Seventeenth Cent.*, I, 544–545, 551.
12. *C.R.*, II, 345–348.
13. Ellis and Morris, pp. 99–101.
14. *C.R.*, II, 354, 356–361; Ellis and Morris, p. 102; George Sheldon, *A History of Deerfield, Massachusetts . . .* (Deerfield, 1895–96), I, 93.
15. *C.R.*, II, 361–362; Sheldon, I, 100–111; Josiah H. Temple and George Sheldon, *A History of the Town of Northfield, Massachusetts . . .* (Albany, 1875), pp. 73–79.
16. *C.R.*, II, 372–375, 377, 383–384; "Conn. Archives, War, Colonial," I, 24; Osgood, *Amer. Colonies in Seventeenth Cent.*, I, 556–558; Trumbull, *Connecticut*, I, 280–281.
17. Douglas E. Leach, "A New View of the Declaration of War Against the Narragansetts, November, 1675," *Rhode Island History*, XV (April 1956), 33–41; David Pulsifer, ed. *Records of the Colony of New Plymouth in New England*, X, *Acts of the Commissioners of the United Colonies of New England*, II (Boston, 1859), 362–365, 456–460.
18. *C.R.*, II, 383–386.
19. Ellis and Morris, pp. 148–150; Trumbull, *Connecticut*, I, 282–284.
20. Church, p. 61; Ellis and Morris, pp. 150–154; Leach, *Flintlock*, pp. 129–131; Trumbull, *Connecticut*, I, 284–286.
21. *C.R.*, II, 391n; Ellis and Morris, p. 154; Leach, *Flintlock*, p. 137.
22. Ellis and Morris, pp. 157–160; Leach, *Flintlock*, pp. 136–137; Nathaniel Shurtleff, ed. *Court Orders, 1668–1678*, in *Records of the Colony of New Plymouth in New England*, V (Boston, 1856), 184.
23. *C.R.*, II, 395–396.
24. *C.R.*, II, 397–398, 404–405; "Conn. Archives, War, Colonial," I, 36, 40–41, 43, 49; Ellis and Morris, pp. 165–167.
25. Ellis and Morris, pp. 185–186.
26. Ellis and Morris, pp. 170–174, 177–179, 181–184, 187–194; Trumbull, *Connecticut*, I, 287.
27. *D.A.B.*, XX, 411–413; Trumbull, *Connecticut*, I, 290.
28. Ellis and Morris, pp. 201–205; Hubbard, II, 55–60; Leach, *Flintlock*, pp. 171–172.
29. *C.R.*, II, 444, 448–451, 453, 458–459; "Conn. Archives, War, Colonial," I, 85, 97; Ellis and Morris, pp. 214, 238–244, 249–250; Trumbull, *Connecticut*, I, 291.
30. Ellis and Morris, pp. 256–257; Osgood, *Amer. Colonies in Seventeenth Cent.*, I, 571; Trumbull, *Connecticut*, I, 292.
31. Ellis and Morris, pp. 260–272; Hubbard, I, 53, 57–58, 126n, 265, 272; Leach, *Flintlock*, pp. 233–235, 241; Osgood, *Amer. Colonies in Seventeenth Cent.*, I, 571.
32. Ellis and Morris, pp. 282–283; Leach, *Flintlock*, p. 236; Trumbull, *Connecticut*, I, 292–293.
33. *C.R.*, II, 285–286, 297–298, 474–475, 481–482, 488; III, 309–310; Frances M. Caulkins, *History of Norwich, Connecticut . . .* (Hartford, 1874), pp. 113–115; "Conn. Archives, Indians, 1647–1789," I, 33, Conn. St. Lib., Hartford; "Conn. Archives, War, Colonial," I, 80; Ellis and Morris, pp. 286–287.
34. James Truslow Adams, *The Founding of New England* (Boston, 1922), p. 363; *C.R.*, II, 231, 292; Pulsifer, X, 392–393, 402. Plymouth's war expenses were listed as £11,743; Connecticut's as £22,173; Massachusetts' as £46,292.
35. *C.R.*, II, 341–342; "Conn. Archives, Colonial Boundaries, II, New York, 1662–1731," 23–28, Conn. St. Lib., Hartford.
36. *C.R.*, II, 261–262, 333, 342–343; "Conn. Archives, Col. Bounds.," II, 35–36; Trumbull, *Connecticut*, I, 274–276.
37. *C.R.*, II, 263–264, 339–343.
38. Reference for entire section, "Report on Connecticut in 1680" is "Conn. Archives, Foreign Correspondence," I, 14b, 18, 19.
39. Curtis Nettels, *The Roots of American Civilization . . .* (New York, 1938), pp. 296–297.
40. Viola F. Barnes, *The Dominion of New England*, Yale Hist. Pubs., Misc., XI (New Haven, 1923), pp. 14–26, 30–32; Nettels, p. 297.
41. Barnes, pp. 29, 38n. Similar writs were issued against Rhode Island, the Jerseys, Pennsylvania, Maryland, the Carolinas, the Bahamas, and Bermuda.
42. Barnes, pp. 36–37.
43. "Conn. Archives, Foreign Correspondence," I, 16, 36.
44. *C.R.*, III, 347–349.
45. Albert C. Bates, "Expedition of Sir Edmund Andros to Connecticut in 1687," *Amer. Antiq. Soc. Proc.*, XLVIII (Oct. 1939), 3; *C.R.*, III, 352–354; *D.A.B.*, I, 300.
46. *C.R.*, III, 212.
47. Bates, "Expedition of Sir Edmund Andros," p. 4; *C.R.*, III, 376–378, 378n–379n.

48. *C.R.*, III, 237–238; "Conn. Archives, Misc." 1st Ser., I, 21–23, 25–26.

49. Bates, "Expedition of Sir Edmund Andros," pp. 6–12; *C.R.*, III, 388–391; "Conn. Archives, Misc.," 1st Ser., I, 28.

50. Bates, "Expedition of Sir Edmund Andros," pp. 17–18; *C.R.*, V, 507*n*–508*n*; Trumbull, *Connecticut*, I, 313. This, the earliest printed account of the incident, appeared in 1797 in the first edition of Trumbull's history. Trumbull received much help from Secretary George Wyllys (1710–96), grandson of Samuel Wyllys.

51. *C.R.*, V, 507.

52. Bates, "Expedition of Sir Edmund Andros," p. 13; *C.R.*, III, 248.

53. Bates, "Expedition of Sir Edmund Andros," pp. 14–15, 25–26.

54. Trumbull, *Connecticut*, I, 313–314.

55. Adams, *Founding of New England*, p. 422; Charles M. Andrews, *The Colonial Period of American History* (New Haven, 1954), III, 120–121; Trumbull, *Connecticut*, I, 314–316.

56. William Lunt, *History of England*, rev. ed. (New York, 1938), pp. 457–463.

57. Adams, *Founding of New England*, pp. 428–430.

58. *C.R.*, III, 455–457; Trumbull, *Connecticut*, I, 316–317.

59. *C.R.*, III, 250–253, 459.

6 Boundary Disputes and Intercolonial Wars, 1690–1764

1. *Charter of Connecticut, 1662*, introd. C. M. Andrews and A. C. Bates, Conn. Ter. Comm. Pubs., No. 3 (New Haven, 1933), p. 21.

2. Clarence W. Bowen, *The Boundary Disputes of Connecticut* (Boston, 1882), pp. 32–33; "Conn. Archives, Colonial Boundaries," I, 5–6; Roland M. Hooker, *Boundaries of Connecticut*, Conn. Ter. Comm. Pubs., No. 11 (New Haven, 1933), pp. 2–4.

3. Bowen, pp. 32–33; *C.R.*, I, 435; II, 527; "Conn. Archives, Colonial Boundaries," I, 5–6; Hooker, *Boundaries of Conn.*, pp. 3–4.

4. Bowen, p. 36; "Conn. Archives, Colonial Boundaries," I, 13, 20, 31–35, 53–70; Hooker, *Boundaries of Conn.*, pp. 4–7.

5. Bowen, pp. 37–39; "Conn. Archives, Colonial Boundaries," I, 52, 82; Hooker, *Boundaries of Conn.*, pp. 8–9. Connecticut's case was complicated by Winthrop's persistent objections to any violation of the Winthrop–Clarke agreement until the king's pleasure was known.

6. *C.R.*, III, 38*n*, 51*n*; "Conn. Archives, Colonial Boundaries," I, 157–158.

7. "Conn. Archives, Colonial Boundaries," I, 140–152, 157; "Conn. Archives, Foreign Correspondence," I, 29; "Controversies, Before 1682," in "Conn. Archives, Private Controversies," I, 159–163, Conn. St. Lib., Hartford; Hooker, *Boundaries of Conn.*, pp. 9–10.

8. "Bellomont to Lords of Trade and Plantations, Nov. 18, 1699, British Transcripts, P.R.O., C.O. 5," Vol. 1288, 179–180, 183–195, Manuscript Div., Lib. of Cong.; Bowen, pp. 43–44; *C.R.*, IV, 238–239, 243, 259, 271; Hooker, *Boundaries of Conn.*, p. 10. Bellomont himself seems to have leaned toward Connecticut's position, partly because he held a low opinion of Rhode Island's government.

9. Bowen, pp. 45–47; *C.R.*, IV, 399–400; V, 468; Hooker, *Boundaries of Conn.*, pp. 10–13.

10. Charles M. Andrews, *The Colonial Period of American History* (New Haven, 1954), II, 53–54; Bowen, pp. 47–49; *C.R.*, VII, 156–157, 178–180; Hooker, *Boundaries of Conn.*, pp. 13–15; *Report of the Connecticut Commissioners on the Boundary Line between Rhode Island and Connecticut, January, 1888* (Middletown, 1888), pp. 1–41.

11. Hooker, *Boundaries of Conn.*, pp. 15–17.

12. Bowen, pp. 54–57; "Conn. Archives, Colonial Boundaries, III, Massachusetts, 1670–1827," 7, 12, 20–22, 26, 29, 31, 34, 37, Conn. St. Lib., Hartford; Hooker, *Boundaries of Conn.*, pp. 17–19.

13. Bowen, pp. 58–59; *C.R.*, VI, 17–18; "Conn. Archives, Colonial Boundaries," III, 43–51; Hooker, *Boundaries of Conn.*, p. 20.

14. Bowen, pp. 60–61; "Conn. Archives, Colonial Boundaries," III, 60–64, 73–76; Hooker, *Boundaries of Conn.*, pp. 20–21.

15. *C.R.*, IX, 301, 339–340; "Conn. Archives, Colonial Boundaries," III, 75–77, 82; Hooker, *Boundaries of Conn.*, pp. 21–22.

16. Bowen, pp. 62–64; *C.R.*, IX, 431–433, 460; "Conn. Archives, Colonial Boundaries," III, 78–81, 83–84, 86, 94, 97, 100–103, 106, 109, 115–116, 119–126, 145–150; Hooker, *Boundaries of Conn.*, pp. 22–24; Benjamin Trumbull, *A Complete History of Connecticut, Civil and Ecclesiastical . . .* (New London, 1898), II, 248.

17. Bowen, pp. 65–66; "Conn. Archives, Colonial Boundaries," III, 154–180; Hooker, *Boundaries of Conn.*, pp. 25–28.

18. Hooker, *Boundaries of Conn.*, pp. 28–29.

19. *C.R.*, I, 435; "Conn. Archives, Colonial Boundaries," II, 22; Dixon R. Fox, *Yankees and Yorkers* (New York, 1940), pp. 120–122; Hooker, *Boundaries of Conn.*, p. 30. Some of the Long Island towns — such as East Hampton, Southampton, and Southold — were unhappy under New York rule. In 1672 they petitioned the king to be returned to Connecticut, but the Duke of York reacted so strongly against them that they finally submitted.

20. *C.R.*, II, 242; "Conn. Archives, Colonial Boundaries," II, 23, 25–28.

21. *C.R.*, II, 333; III, 330–332; "Conn. Archives, Colonial Boundaries," II, 29–31, 33–36; Hooker, *Boundaries of Conn.*, pp. 31–32; Edmund B. O'Callaghan, ed. *The Documentary History of the State of New York* (Albany, 1849–51), I, 97, 117, 157, 159. In 1617 Governor Dongan strongly urged the British Government to have all of Connecticut annexed to New York.

22. Bowen, pp. 72–73; Fox, pp. 136–137; Hooker, *Boundaries of Conn.*, pp. 33–34.

23. Bowen, pp. 73–74; Fox, pp. 137, 140; Hooker, *Boundaries of Conn.*, pp. 34–35.

24. Andrews, *Colonial Period*, III, 45; Bowen, pp. 78–79; Hooker, *Boundaries of Conn.*, pp. 36–37.

25. Curtis Nettels, *The Roots of American Civilization . . .* (New York, 1938), pp. 361–364.

26. Nettels, p. 364; Herbert L. Osgood, *The American Colonies in the Eighteenth Century* (New York, 1930), I, 69–70, 77–79.

27. *C.R.*, IV, 3–6, 13, 16–18; "Conn. Archives, War, Colonial," II, 22, 54.

28. "Conn. Archives, War, Colonial," II, 57, 119; Edmund O'Callaghan, ed. *Documents Relative to the Colonial History of the State of New York . . .*

(Albany, 1853–87), IV, 195; Osgood, *Amer. Colonies in Eighteenth Cent.*, I, 80–86.

29. "Conn. Archives, War, Colonial," II, 57, 68–69, 78, 81, 86, 93, 102, 107; *D.A.B.*, XX, 414; O'Callaghan, *Documentary Hist. of New York*, II, 253, 265.

30. "Conn. Archives, War, Colonial," II, 115–116, 119; O'Callaghan, *Documents, Colonial Hist. of New York*, IV, 193–196; Osgood, *Amer. Colonies in Eighteenth Cent.*, I, 87.

31. O'Callaghan, *Documents, Colonial Hist. of New York*, IV, 196; Osgood, *Amer. Colonies in Eighteenth Cent.*, I, 88–92; "Winthrop Papers," Part V, *M.H.S.C.*, 6th Ser., III, 13. The abandonment of Winthrop's expedition largely insured the defeat in the fall of 1690 of a Quebec attack led by Phips from the sea. It had been hoped that the force from Albany would join with Phips's to capture Quebec.

32. *C.R.*, IV, 38–39; "Conn. Archives, War, Colonial," II, 121–125.

33. *C.R.*, IV, 77, 77n, 79, 89–90, 102–103; "Conn. Archives, Foreign Correspondence," II, 39–40; "Conn. Archives, War, Colonial," II, 158–160, 165–167, 171; Osgood, *Amer. Colonies in Eighteenth Cent.*, I, 101–103. Apparently there were about 3,000 freemen in the colony, for the October 1692 list of "persons and estates" gave a total of 3,069 persons.

34. "Conn. Archives, War, Colonial," II, 196–202; O'Callaghan, *Documents, Colonial Hist. of New York*, IV, 69–72; "Their Majesties Colony of Connecticut in New-England Vindicated . . .," *C.H.S.C.*, I, 106.

35. *C.H.S.C.*, I, 107; "Conn. Archives, War, Colonial," II, 203; O'Callaghan, *Documents, Colonial Hist. of New York*, IV, 71; Trumbull, *Connecticut*, I, 331–332. Fletcher's own account refers to imminent danger of overt hostilities: ". . . understanding some personall affronts were intended him by the people if he publisht any proclamation then . . . Côl. Fletcher being advised that the people were ready to be in a Cômotion left the colony."

36. Osgood, *Amer. Colonies in Eighteenth Cent.*, I, 105–106; Trumbull, *Connecticut*, I, 467–471. The decision applied also to Rhode Island and East and West Jersey.

37. *C.R.*, IV, 47, 67–68, 149, 159–160, 172, 179–180, 219–220; "Conn. Archives, War, Colonial," II, 223; III, 37–38; Osgood, *Amer. Colonies in Eighteenth Cent.*, I, 102. Governor Phips was furious over Connecticut's failure in 1693 to send reinforcements to the Maine country, which was then under Massachusetts' jurisdiction.

38. *C.R.*, IV, 234, 240; "Conn. Archives, War, Colonial," III, 33–34; William Lunt, *History of England*, rev. ed. (New York, 1938), p. 473; Nettels, p. 365; Osgood, *Amer. Colonies in Eighteenth Cent.*, I, 114–115; "Robert C. Winthrop Coll.," II, 191; Trumbull, *Connecticut*, I, 335–336.

39. Lunt, pp. 473–475; Nettels, pp. 365, 368–369.

40. *C.R.*, IV, 442–443; Osgood, *Amer. Colonies in Eighteenth Cent.*, I, 401–405, 410; "Winthrop Papers," *M.H.S.C.*, 6th Ser., III, 147–148.

41. Samuel A. Drake, *The Border Wars of New England . . .* (New York, 1897), pp. 172–176; Sheldon, I, 292–293.

42. Drake, pp. 177–185; Nettels, p. 370; George Sheldon, *A History of Deerfield, Massachusetts . . .* (Deerfield, 1895–96), I, 293–297; John Williams, *The Redeemed Captive Returning to Zion . . .* (New Haven, 1802), pp. 9–15.

43. *C.R.*, IV, 455–460; "Winthrop Papers," *M.H.S.C.*, 6th Ser., III, 139–141, 145–160.

44. *C.R.*, IV, 462–465; Osgood, *Amer. Colonies in Eighteenth Cent.*, I, 412–413.

45. [Thomas Buckingham], *Roll and Journal of Connecticut Service in Queen Anne's War, 1710–1711*, Acorn Club Pubs., No. 13 ([New Haven], 1916), p. 4; *C.R.*, V, 17–18; Osgood, *Amer. Colonies in Eighteenth Cent.*, I, 424–428.

46. *C.R.*, V, 91–93, 91n–92n, 122–127; "Conn. Archives, War, Colonial," III, 74, 79–85; Drake, pp. 250–254; Osgood, *Amer. Colonies in Eighteenth Cent.*, I, 429–435.

47. Buckingham, p. 13; *C.R.*, V, 163–165, 185; Drake, pp. 259–261; Osgood, *Amer. Colonies in Eighteenth Cent.*, I, 436–439. Connecticut's leaders hoped for profits from the conquest and directed the governor "to inquire into, and look after any profitable interest that shall or may accrue to this Colony, by the conquest of Port Royall."

48. *C.R.*, V, 245–249; O'Callaghan, *Documents, Colonial Hist. of New York*, V, 257.

49. Buckingham, pp. 40–41; *C.R.*, V, 294–295; Osgood, *Amer. Colonies in Eighteenth Cent.*, I, 449–450; Trumbull, *Connecticut*, I, 374–375. Lively recriminations developed over the naval catastrophe. The British blamed the colonial pilots, and vice versa. At a special session in November 1711, the Assembly voted to send John Mayhew of New London, pilot of one ship, to London to explain and defend the New England pilots. The hearings in London produced no important results.

50. Henry Bronson, "A Historical Account of Connecticut Currency . . ." (Read Nov. 30, 1863, and afterward) *N.H.C.H.S. Papers*, I, 29–33; *C.R.*, V, 111, 127, 182, 228, 252; Trumbull, *Connecticut*, I, 381–382.

51. James Truslow Adams, *Revolutionary New England* (Boston, 1923), pp. 164–168; *C.R.*, VIII, 295–296, 324–327, 420; Lunt, p. 517; Forrest Morgan, et al., eds. *Connecticut as a Colony and as a State, or One of the Original Thirteen* (Hartford, 1904), I, 365–367; Trumbull, *Connecticut*, II, 219–222.

52. *C.R.*, IX, 83–89, 93–99; John S. McLennan, *Louisbourg, from its Foundation to its Fall, 1713–1758* (London, 1918), pp. 130–137; George A. Wood, *William Shirley, Governor of Massachusetts, 1741–1756 . . .*, Col. Univ. Stud. in Hist., Econ. and Public Law, XCII, No. 209 (New York, 1920), pp. 220–287. A special Assembly meeting was held in New Haven in February 1744/45 to consider Shirley's proposition. It is of interest that Jonathan Trumbull, future Revolutionary governor of Connecticut, was appointed to go to Boston with Elisha Williams for conferences with leaders of other colonies.

53. *C.R.*, VIII, 361, 411–412; Howard M. Chapin, *Privateering in King George's War, 1739–1748* (Providence, 1928), pp. 96–108; McLennan, pp. 143–144; Nettels, p. 581; Wood, *William Shirley*, p. 283.

54. John B. Brebner, *New England's Outpost, Acadia before the Conquest of Canada*, Col. Univ. Stud. in Hist., Econ. and Public Law, No. 293 (New York, 1927), pp. 114–115; *C.R.*, IX, 158–161, 164; "Conn. Archives, War, Colonial," IV, 289–291, 293–294, 313–315, 321–322, 325–329, 333–334, 380–381, 391–395, 400–472; "Journal of Roger Wolcott at the Siege of Louisbourg, 1745," *C.H.S.C.*, I, 131–161; McLennan, pp. 147–164.

55. Adams, *Revolutionary N.E.*, p. 188; Brebner, p. 119; *C.R.*, IX, 210–216; Nettels, p. 581.

56. Bronson, pp. 46, 50, 52–54, 71, 74n; *C.R.*, VIII, 295, 318–319, 327; IX, 42, 66, 100, 151, 217–218, 235;

"The Law Papers, Correspondence and Documents During Jonathan Law's Governorship of the Colony of Connecticut, 1741–1750," II, *C.H.S.C.*, XIII (Hartford, 1911), 68–82; Glenn Weaver, *Jonathan Trumbull, Connecticut's Merchant Magistrate (1710–1785)* (Hartford, 1956), pp. 34, 39. The Louisbourg expedition involved heavy losses. Nathan Whiting's list of soldiers in the Connecticut regiment indicates that out of 462 men and officers, 152 died. Connecticut's financial policies were inflationary, but far less than those of Rhode Island and Massachusetts.

57. Douglas Southall Freeman, *George Washington, a Biography* (New York, 1948–57), I, 270–411.

58. Adams, *Revolutionary N. E.*, p. 217; *C.R.*, X, 268, 268n, 292–293; "Conn. Archives, War, Colonial," V, 70–71; "The Fitch Papers, Correspondence and Documents During Thomas Fitch's Governorship of the Colony of Connecticut, 1754–1766," I, *C.H.S.C.*, XVII (Hartford, 1918), 34–42; Lawrence H. Gipson, *The British Empire Before the American Revolution*, V, *Zones of International Friction; the Great Lakes Frontier, Canada, the West Indies, India, 1748–1754* (New York, 1942), pp. 149–150; Richard B. Morris, "Benjamin Franklin's Grand Design," *American Heritage*, VII (Feb. 1956), 107–108; Robert C. Newbold, *The Albany Congress and Plan of Union of 1754* (New York, 1955), pp. 22–23, 90–95, 137–140; O'Callaghan, *Documents, Colonial Hist. of New York*, VI, 889–891. For the differing interpretations concerning the origins of the Albany Plan, see: Lawrence H. Gipson, "Thomas Hutchinson and the Framing of the Albany Plan of Union, 1754," *Pa. Mag. of Hist. and Biog.*, LXXIV (Jan. 1950), 5–35; Newbold, pp. 96–114; *Pa. Mag. of Hist. and Biog.*, LXXV (July 1951), 350–362; "Trumbull Papers, M.H.S., Connecticut Colonial Official Papers, 1631–1784, Collected by Governor Jonathan Trumbull under Instruction of the Connecticut General Assembly," I, 93, 94, Conn. St. Lib., Hartford.

59. Brebner, pp. 203–233; *C.R.*, X, 452–453, 461, 615; Frances M. Caulkins, *History of New London, Connecticut . . .* (New London, 1895), pp. 469–470; Frances M. Caulkins, *History of Norwich, Connecticut . . .* (Hartford, 1874), p. 310; "Conn. Archives, War, Colonial," V, 193; VI, 11–13, 331, 370; IX, 249; X, 262–263; Arthur G. Doughty, *The Acadian Exiles . . .*, Chronicles of Canada, IX (Toronto, 1922), 114–117; Lawrence H. Gipson, *The British Empire before the American Revolution*, VI, *The Great War for the Empire: the Years of Defeat, 1754–1757* (New York, 1946), pp. 243–344.

60. *C.R.*, X, 336–337, 344–345, 390; *D.A.B.*, XI, 517; Gipson, *British Empire*, VI, 164–176; Morgan, *Connecticut*, I, 380–382; Francis Parkman, *Montcalm and Wolfe*, 3d ed. (Boston, 1884), I, 306. Altogether Lyman served in eight campaigns during the French and Indian War and earned an excellent reputation as an able general.

61. *C.R.*, X, 459, 554–555, 598–600; XI, 59–60, 108–109; "Diary of Captain Edmund Wells, 1756–1757," Aug. 7–12, 1757, Conn. St. Lib., Hartford; "Fitch Papers," I, *C.H.S.C.*, XVII, 348–349; Gipson, *British Empire*, VI, 157; McLennan, pp. 202–204; Nettels, p. 588; "Rolls of Connecticut Men in the French and Indian War, 1755–1762," I, *C.H.S.C.*, IX (Hartford, 1903), 197–262.

62. *C.R.*, XI, 92–95, 104–107. The colonel also was responsible for "the decent reception and suitable support" of the chaplain.

63. Gipson, *British Empire*, VI, 176–207; Gipson, *British Empire . . .*, VII, *The Great War for the Empire: the Victorious Years, 1758–1760* (New York, 1949), 236–286; McLennan, pp. 236–289; Parkman, II, 127–163.

64. "Fitch Papers," I, *C.H.S.C.*, XVII, 350–351; Gipson, *British Empire*, VII, 221–236; Parkman, II, 94–115; Trumbull, *Connecticut*, II, 330–331.

65. *C.R.*, XI, 221–222, 226, 251–253; "Fitch Papers . . . ," II, *C.H.S.C.*, XVIII (Hartford, 1920), pp. 12–15; Gipson, *British Empire*, VII, 310–313. When the Assembly voted to raise 3,600, it provided that 100 more could volunteer for each of the four regiments. Hence the authorization of the additional 1,000 brought the total to the 5,000 requested.

66. Gipson, *British Empire*, VII, 349–356, 360–427; "Journal of Jonathan Knap of Killingly, Connecticut," p. 6, Conn. St. Lib., Hartford; Parkman, II, 259–316; "Rolls of Connecticut Men in the French and Indian War, 1755–1762," II, *C.H.S.C.*, X (Hartford, 1905), 99–178.

67. *C.R.*, XI, 349–350; *C.H.S.C.*, X, 181–231, 293–359; "Conn. Archives, War, Colonial," X, 1–25; Gipson, *British Empire*, VII, 445–466; William F. Livingston, *Israel Putnam, Pioneer, Ranger and Major-General, 1718–1790* (New York, 1901), pp. 108–112; Morgan, *Connecticut*, I, 391–393; *The Two Putnams, Israel and Rufus, in the Havana Expedition . . .* (Hartford, 1931), pp. 3–5. At the request of the British Government, Connecticut in June 1762 sent 1,000 men (eleven companies of the First Regiment) to Cuba where disease wiped out a large percentage of the men. Maj. Gen. Phineas Lyman was placed in charge of the brigade, which was composed of troops from New York, Massachusetts, and New Jersey also. Lt. Col. Israel Putnam seems to have exercised command of the Connecticut troops. In Israel Putnam's 2d company, 76 of 109 men died. In spite of so many deaths, the Cuban expedition was successful.

68. "Conn. Archives, Finance and Currency, 1677–1789," V, 5, Conn. St. Lib., Hartford; Lawrence H. Gipson, *The Coming of the Revolution, 1763–1775*, New Amer. Nation Ser. (New York, 1954), pp. 128–129; Lawrence H. Gipson, *Connecticut Taxation, 1750–1775*, Conn. Ter. Comm. Pubs., No. 10 (New Haven, 1933), pp. 18n, 20–23, 29–31, 33. The hiatus in taxation was discreetly kept from Great Britain.

7 Social, Economic, and Religious Patterns in the Eighteenth Century

1. James Truslow Adams, *The Founding of New England* (Boston, 1922), pp. 120, 191; *C.R.*, XI, 584; XI, 630; XIV, 483–492; Lawrence H. Gipson, *The Coming of the Revolution, 1763–1775*, New Amer. Nation Ser. (New York, 1954), pp. 10, 128; Evarts B. Greene and Virginia D. Harrington, *American Population Before the Federal Census of 1790* (New York, 1932), pp. 47–50; Benjamin Trumbull, *A Complete History of Connecticut, Civil and Ecclesiastical . . .* (New London, 1898), I, 46. Connecticut's population figures as given in replies to queries of the Board of Trade are unreliable and appear to have been deliberately underestimated.

2. *C.R.*, XIV, 384–385, 485–491; Stella H. Sutherland,

Population Distribution in Colonial America (New York, 1936), opp. p. 62. Middletown's apparent decline was caused by cutting off part of it in 1767 to create the town of Chatham, now East Hampton. The addition of Chatham's 2,397 people would have given Middletown's original area 7,275, an increase of 28 per cent.

3. *C.R.*, xiv, 490; Greene and Harrington, pp. 6–7; Hugh Hastings, ed. *The Public Papers of George Clinton, First Governor of New York, 1777–1795, 1801–1804* (New York, 1899–1914), i, 210; Albert L. Olson, *Agricultural Economy and the Population in Eighteenth-Century Connecticut*, Conn. Ter. Comm. Pubs., No. 40 (New Haven, 1935), p. 18. Population estimates show wide variance.

4. *C.R.*, xiv, 485–490; John W. DeForest, *History of the Indians of Connecticut from the Earliest Known Period to 1850* (Hartford, 1853), pp. 350–351.

5. *C.R.*, xiv, 485–491; Lorenzo J. Greene, *The Negro in Colonial New England, 1620–1776*, Col. Univ. Stud. in Hist., Econ. and Public Law, No. 494 (New York, 1945), pp. 350–351.

6. Charles M. Andrews, "Slavery in Connecticut," *Mag. of Am. Hist.*, xxi (May 1889), 422–423; Frances M. Caulkins, *History of Norwich, Connecticut . . .* (Hartford, 1874), p. 328; Greene, *Negro*, pp. 102–103, 107–108; Sarah K. Knight, *The Journal of Madam Knight . . .* (Boston, 1920), pp. 37–38; Bernard C. Steiner, *History of Slavery in Connecticut*, Johns Hopkins Univ. Stud. in Hist. and Pol. Sci., 11th Ser., Nos. 9–10 (Baltimore, 1893), pp. 11–16; Ralph F. Weld, *Slavery in Connecticut*, Conn. Ter. Comm. Pubs., No. 37 (New Haven, 1935), pp. 6–7.

7. George M. Curtis, *Early Silver of Connecticut and its Makers* (Meriden, 1913), pp. 47–48, 51; Jedidiah Morse, *The American Geography . . .*, 2d ed. (London, 1792), p. 219. The Huguenot silversmiths, René Grignon, active in Norwich, 1708–15, and Timothy Bontecou, in New Haven, 1735–84 are examples. In Salisbury's early development Dutch families played a leading role.

8. *C.R.*, i, 47–48, 77, 105–106, 527; Arthur W. Calhoun, *A Social History of the American Family . . .* (New York, 1945), i, 29–47, 51. A law of 1644 required prompt recording of all marriages and births.

9. *C.R.*, i, 92; Calhoun, i, 55, 129–132.

10. *C.R.*, iv, 136; Calhoun, i, 60–64; Knight, p. 37.

11. Calhoun, i, 62–63; Frances M. Caulkins, *History of New London, Connecticut . . .* (New London, 1895), pp. 216–217.

12. *C.R.*, i, 521; Calhoun, i, 75–76, 112; Alice M. Earle, *Child Life in Colonial Days* (New York, 1899), pp. 191, 227–230.

13. Thomas Brainerd, *The Life of John Brainerd . . .* (Phila., 1865), pp. 45–46; Calhoun, i, 124–127; Earle, pp. 305–308, 314–320.

14. Earle, pp. 344–347, 361–374.

15. "British Transcripts, P.R.O., C.O. 5," Vol. 1285, 271; Calhoun, i, 98; Curtis Nettels, *The Roots of American Civilization . . .* (New York, 1938), p. 441.

16. *C.R.*, i, 275, 301, 362, 379; ii, 129, 292–293, 322, 327–328; iii, 23; iv, 52–53, 59; x, 168–169; Calhoun, i, 146–149.

17. Calhoun, i, 89–92; "Gold Selleck Silliman to Joseph Fish, December 12, 1776." Silliman Family Collection, Yale Univ. Lib.

18. George Lyman Kittredge, *Witchcraft in Old and New England* (Cambridge, Mass., 1929), pp. 3, 366–368, 372–373; Henry C. Lea, *A History of the Inquisition of the Middle Ages* (New York, 1922), iii, 385–386; Wallace Notestein, *A History of Witchcraft in England from 1558 to 1718* (Wash., 1911), pp. 383–419. Kittredge points out that belief in witches was not confined to any one time, race, or religion; but was part of mankind's common heritage and definitely was not a peculiarity of the Puritans, whose record in witch cases may be considered relatively good.

19. *C.R.*, i, 77, 171, 209, 222, 226, 232; *N.H.C.R.*, ii, 576; Montague Summers, *The Geography of Witchcraft* (New York, 1927), p. 257; John Metcalf Taylor, *The Witchcraft Delusion in Colonial Connecticut, 1647–1697* (New York, 1908), pp. 143–157. On May 21, 1650, the Court referred to Mary Johnson's board bill for 24 weeks in a way clearly implying that she still was incarcerated. In New Haven Colony the law stated that "If any person be a Witch, he or she shall be put to death, according to *Exod.* 22.18, *Levit.* 20.27, *Deut.* 18.10, 11."

20. *N.H.C.R.*, ii, 77–89; Taylor, *Witchcraft*, pp. 122–125. A celebrated libel case grew out of Goodwife Knap's death-scene confession to Ludlow that Goodwife Staples was a witch. Ludlow told Davenport, somehow the news leaked out, and Thomas Staples sued Ludlow for defamation of his wife's character. After lengthy testimony, Ludlow was ordered to pay Staples £10 and the court, £5.

21. *C.R.*, iv, 76n–77n; Taylor, *Witchcraft*, pp. 62–78, 150, 154–156. Other Fairfield cases in 1692 were those of Elizabeth Clawson, Mary and Hannah Harvey, Goody Miller, and Mary Staples.

22. Percy W. Bidwell and John I. Falconer, *History of Agriculture in the Northern United States, 1620–1860*, Carnegie Institution of Wash. Pubs., No. 358 (Wash., 1925), pp. 89–91, 93, 98, 101; *C.R.*, iii, 297; Irving G. Davis, *Types of Farming and Type of Farming Areas in Connecticut*, Storrs Agric. Exp. Sta. Bull., 213, 1936, p. 7; Timothy Dwight, *Travels; in New-England and New-York* (New Haven, 1821–22), i, 108–109; ii, 311–312; iii, 519; Norris G. Osborn, ed. *History of Connecticut . . .* (New York, 1925), ii, 307–308, 323.

23. Oscar T. Barck and Hugh T. Lefler, *Colonial America* (New York, 1958), p. 325; *C.R.*, iii, 297; xiv, 499; Morse, *Geography*, p. 215; Olson, p. 2; Osborn, ii, 309; Trumbull, *Connecticut*, i, 19–20.

24. *C.R.*, i, 53; x, 202–203; Adrian F. McDonald, *The History of Tobacco Production in Connecticut*, Conn. Ter. Comm. Pubs., No. 52 (New Haven, 1936), pp. 2–6. As early as June 15, 1640, the legislature ordered a fine of 5s for use of any tobacco except that grown in the River colony.

25. James L. Bishop, *A History of American Manufactures from 1608 to 1860 . . .* (Phila., 1866), i, 360–361; *C.R.*, vii, 494–495; William C. Wyckoff, *Silk Manufacture in the United States* (New York, 1883), p. 32.

26. Bidwell and Falconer, p. 109; *C.R.*, xi, 629–630; xiv, 498; Morse, *Geography*, p. 215; Olson, pp. 4–5.

27. Bidwell and Falconer, pp. 119–120; Osborn, ii, 313, 325; Thomas J. Wertenbaker, *The First Americans, 1607–1690*, Hist. of Amer. Life Ser., ii (New York, 1927), p. 59. Connecticut farming was more intensive than that of the upper South, but definitely *extensive* compared with contemporary European methods.

28. Dwight, i, 108–109. His description applied to methods of the first decade or two in the nineteenth century. Undoubtedly those of 50–100 years earlier were somewhat worse.

29. Jared Eliot, *Essays upon Field Husbandry in New*

England . . . , Col. Univ. Stud. in the Hist. of Amer. Agric., I (New York, 1934), 4, 13–19, 29, 38–39, 158–159; Olson, pp. 15–16.

30. Nettels, pp. 237–239.

31. Bishop, I, 131–132; *C.R.*, I, 246, 262, 393; Lewis W. Hicks, "The First Civil Settlement in Connecticut," *Conn. Mag.*, VII, Nos. 3–4 (1902), 226; Nettels, p. 245.

32. *C.R.*, I, 59–61; III, 196; Arthur H. Cole, *The American Wool Manufacture* (Cambridge, Mass., 1926), I, 11n.

33. *C.R.*, VII, 512–513; Caulkins, *Norwich*, pp. 607–608; Cole, p. 30.

34. Bishop, I, 511–513; *C.R.*, XII, 634–635; "Conn. Archives, Industry, Agriculture, Manufactures, Fisheries, 1708–1789," II, 131–132, Conn. St. Lib., Hartford; Herbert C. Keith and Charles R. Harte, *The Early Iron Industry of Connecticut*, reprinted from Conn. Soc. Civil Engineers, Inc., 51st Annual Report [New Haven, 1935], pp. 7–8, 11, 23; Rollin G. Osterweis, *Three Centuries of New Haven, 1638–1938* (New Haven, 1953), p. 33.

35. Curtis, pp. 83–115; Penrose R. Hoopes, *Early Clockmaking in Connecticut*, Conn. Ter. Comm. Pubs., No. 23 (New Haven, 1934), pp. 1–7; Daniel Howard, *A New History of Old Windsor, Connecticut* (Windsor Locks, 1935), pp. 236–237. Several of the leading silversmiths, including Amos Doolittle, Hezekiah Hotchkiss, and Silas Merriman, all of New Haven, also made clocks. The account book of Daniel Burnap, published by the Connecticut Historical Society, provides an unusual view into the business activities of a clockmaker.

36. J. B. Beers and Co., *History of Middlesex County, Connecticut* . . . (New York, 1884), p. 72; Bishop, I, 50, 90–91; *C.R.*, I, 59; VII, 582–583; X, 625–626; XI, 629; XIV, 498; Caulkins, *Norwich*, pp. 303, 306, 309; Alonzo B. Chapin, *Glastenbury for Two Hundred Years* . . . (Hartford, 1853), p. 126; Charlotte M. Holloway, "Old Whaling Port," *Conn. Quarterly*, III (April–June 1897), 206; "Record of All Ships and Vessels Registered at New Haven, 1762–1795," National Archives; Henry R. Stiles, *The History of Ancient Wethersfield, Connecticut* . . . (New York, 1904), I, 897.

37. Roland M. Hooker, *The Colonial Trade of Connecticut*, Conn. Ter. Comm. Pubs., No. 50 (New Haven, 1936), pp. 35–57; Margaret E. Martin, *Merchants and Trade of the Connecticut River Valley, 1750–1820*, Smith College Stud. in Hist., XXIV (Northampton, 1939), 5–6.

38. Martin, pp. 12–16; Glenn Weaver, "Some Aspects of Early Eighteenth-Century Connecticut Trade," *C.H.S. Bull.*, XXII (Jan. 1957), 23–25, 27.

39. Weaver, "Some Aspects," p. 25. In the *Connecticut Courant* during 1773 these three merchants advertised their specialties from 12 to 26 times apiece. It is possible, of course, that they sold a few other items, but their advertising concentrated on one type of article.

40. *C.R.*, XI, 13–14; XII, 356; XIII, 364–365.

41. Roger Sherman Boardman, *Roger Sherman, Signer and Statesman* (Phila., 1938), pp. 37–38; Willard M. Wallace, *Traitorous Hero, the Life and Fortunes of Benedict Arnold* (New York, 1954), pp. 15–30.

42. William T. Baxter, *The House of Hancock: Business in Boston, 1724–1775*, Harv. Stud. in Bus. Hist., X (Cambridge, Mass., 1945), 189; Carl Bridenbaugh, *Cities in Revolt: Urban Life in America, 1743–1776* (New York, 1955), pp. 47–48, 263; *C.R.*, XI, 629; Samuel E. Morison, "The Commerce of Boston on the Eve of the Revolution," *Am. Antiq. Soc. Proc.*, XXXII (April 1922), 43–44; Weaver, "Some Aspects," p. 25.

43. Robert G. Albion, *The Rise of New York Port, 1815–1860* (New York, 1939), pp. 4–5; Franklin B. Dexter, ed. *Extracts from the Itineraries and Other Miscellanies of Ezra Stiles* . . . (New Haven, 1916), p. 83; Robert A. East, *Business Enterprise in the American Revolutionary Era*, Col. Univ. Stud. in Hist., Econ. and Public Law, No. 439 (New York, 1938), p. 16; Robert Rogers, *A Concise Account of North America* (London, 1765), p. 54; Arthur M. Schlesinger, *The Colonial Merchants and the American Revolution, 1763–1776* (New York, 1939), p. 26; Albert E. Van Dusen, "The Trade of Revolutionary Connecticut," unpub. diss. (Univ. of Penn., 1948), pp. 138–139; Samuel R. Weed, comp. *Norwalk After Two Hundred & Fifty Years* . . . (South Norwalk, [1902]), pp. 244–245. Shipping lists of the 1770's in *New London Gazette* and *Norwich Packet* are very useful for New London entries and clearances; those in *Connecticut Journal* for New Haven.

44. James B. Hedges, *The Browns of Providence Plantations*, Harv. Stud. in Econ. Hist. (Cambridge, Mass., 1952), I, 24, 172–173; Gertrude S. Kimball, *Providence in Colonial Times* (Boston, 1912), p. 275; Ellen D. Larned, *History of Windham County, Connecticut* (Worcester, 1874–1880), II, 88; Glenn Weaver, *Jonathan Trumbull, Connecticut's Merchant Magistrate (1710–1785)* (Hartford, 1956), pp. 16, 69–70, 73.

45. Bidwell and Falconer, pp. 133–136; *C.R.*, XI, 629; XIV, 498; Hooker, *Colonial*, pp. 32–33; Martin, p. 23; Richard Pares, *Yankees and Creoles* . . . (London, 1956), pp. 25–26; Ernest E. Rogers, *Connecticut's Naval Office at New London* . . . , New London County Hist. Soc. Coll., II (New London, 1933), pp. 6–7; "Nathaniel Shaw Papers," New London County Hist. Soc. and Yale; Weaver, *Trumbull*, pp. 97–155.

46. Maria Louise Greene, *The Development of Religious Liberty in Connecticut* (Boston, 1905), pp. 75, 87–97.

47. *C.R.*, I, 302; II, 53–55, 67, 69–70, 84, 109; "Conn. Archives, Ecclesiastical Affairs, 1658–1789," I, 12, 14, Conn. St. Lib., Hartford; Edwin S. Gaustad, *The Great Awakening in New England* (New York, 1957), p. 11; Greene, *Development*, pp. 103–118, 129.

48. *C.R.*, V, 51–52; Congregational Churches in Connecticut. General Association, *Contributions to the Ecclesiastical History of Connecticut* . . . (New Haven, 1861), pp. 32–33; "Conn. Archives, Ecclesiastical Affairs," I, 179; Gaustad, p. 13; Greene, *Development*, pp. 132–136.

49. James Truslow Adams, *Revolutionary New England* (Boston, 1923), pp. 37–38; Leonard Bacon, *Thirteen Historical Discourses on the Completion of Two Hundred Years* (New Haven, 1839), pp. 190–192; *C.R.*, V, 87; Henry M. Dexter, *The Congregationalism of the Last Three Hundred Years* . . . (New York, 1880), pp. 489–490; Greene, *Development*, pp. 136–151; Trumbull, *Connecticut*, I, 481–486.

50. "British Transcripts, P.R.O., C.O. 5," Vol. 1291, 167–171; *C.R.*, I, 283–284, 303, 308, 324; II, 264; IV, 546, 546n; Greene, *Development*, pp. 159–171; *N.H.C.R.*, II, 217, 233n–234n, 238–241, 363. The Rogerenes, a sect closely related both to Baptists and Quakers, suffered much persecution.

51. Greene, *Development*, pp. 222–224, 226–229; Perry Miller, *Jonathan Edwards* (New York, 1949), p. 129; Charles F. Sedgwick, "Historical Discourse . . ." Conn. Towns, Box 379, Sharon Folder, C.H.S.; Joseph Tracy, *The Great Awakening* . . . (Boston,

1842), pp. 101–105; Trumbull, *Connecticut*, II, 119–120; Daniel Wadsworth, *Diary of Rev. Daniel Wadsworth . . .* (Hartford, 1894), pp. 55n–56n, 56; Ola E. Winslow, *Jonathan Edwards, 1703–1758 . . .* (New York, 1940), pp. 162–164.

52. Joshua Hempstead, *Diary of Joshua Hempstead of New London, Connecticut*. New London County Hist. Soc. Coll., I (New London, 1901), p. 377; Mary H. Mitchell, *The Great Awakening and other Revivals in the Religious Life of Connecticut*, Conn. Ter. Comm. Pubs., No. 26 (New Haven, 1934), p. 11; Trumbull, *Connecticut*, II, 121–122.

53. Gaustad, pp. 37–41; Hempstead, pp. 406, 446–447; Mitchell, pp. 13–15; Trumbull, *Connecticut*, II, 126–127.

54. Mitchell, p. 17; Tracy, p. 324.

55. *C.R.*, VIII, 454–457, 500–502; Gaustad, pp. 108–110; Greene, *Development*, pp. 242–244; Isaac Stiles, *The Declaration of the Association of the County of New-Haven in Connecticut . . .* (Boston, 1745), p. 6; Wadsworth, p. 70n.

56. *C.R.*, VIII, 482–484; Gaustad, p. 41; Wadsworth, pp. 83–84, 84n. Pomeroy was discharged without penalty.

57. Eben E. Beardsley, *The History of the Episcopal Church in Connecticut . . .* (New York, 1865–68), I, 128–130, 141–142; Gaustad, pp. 116–117, 120–121; Greene, *Development*, pp. 236–240; Tracy, p. 324.

58. *C.R.*, XIII, 360; Gaustad, pp. 110–112; Greene, *Development*, pp. 327–328, 335–336, 338; Charles J.

Hoadly, ed. *The Public Records of the State of Connecticut . . .* (Hartford, 1894–1953), I, 232–233.

59. Beardsley, I, 20–22, 28–29, 43–47; Origen S. Seymour, *The Beginnings of the Episcopal Church in Connecticut*, Conn. Ter. Comm. Pubs., No. 30 (New Haven, 1934), pp. 1–5.

60. Beardsley, pp. 52, 59, 89–92, 318–319, 330–331; Seymour, pp. 5–7.

61. Beardsley, pp. 99–100, 117–118, 129, 131–133, 138–139, 141–143, 155–156, 173, 190, 211, 237–238, 281; Seymour, pp. 8–12; Oscar Zeichner, *Connecticut's Years of Controversy, 1750–1776* (Chapel Hill, 1949), pp. 91–92, 96–99, 130–131, 229–230, 233.

62. Jarvis M. Morse, *Connecticut Newspapers in the Eighteenth Century*, Conn. Ter. Comm. Pubs., No. 36 (New Haven, 1935), pp. 1–2.

63. Morse, *Newspapers*, pp. 2–3.

64. Albert C. Bates, "Thomas Green," *N.H.C.H.S. Papers*, VIII (New Haven, 1914), 297–298, 307; Morse, *Newspapers*, pp. 5–6; James E. Smith, *One Hundred Years of Hartford's Courant . . .* (New Haven, 1949), pp. 5–9.

65. Morse, *Newspapers*, pp. 6–8.

66. *Courant*, Aug. 21, 1775; Morse, *Newspapers*, pp. 8–12, 16; Smith, *Courant*, pp. 1–11; James H. Trumbull, *The Memorial History of Hartford County, Connecticut, 1633–1884* (Boston, 1886), II, 98. The mill stood along the Hockanum River in present East Hartford.

67. Morse, *Newspapers*, pp. 14, 16–19, 28–29.

8 The Background of the Revolution

1. *Acts and Laws of His Majesty's English Colony of Connecticut in New-England in America* (New London, 1750), p. 240; "Middletown Town Votes, II, 1735–1798," *passim*, Middletown Town Hall; Oscar Zeichner, *Connecticut's Years of Controversy, 1750–1776* (Chapel Hill, 1949), pp. 3–5.

2. *Acts and Laws, 1750*, pp. 28–29; Nelson P. Mead, *Connecticut as a Corporate Colony . . .* (Lancaster, Pa., 1906), pp. 23–24; Zeichner, pp. 4–5.

3. *Acts and Laws, 1750*, pp. 45–46.

4. *Acts & Laws of his Majesties Colony of Connecticut in New England* (Boston, 1702), pp. 40, 58; Charles M. Andrews, *The Colonial Period of American History* (New Haven, 1954), II, 107, 112–113; "Ezra Stiles to Benjamin Gale, October 1, 1766," Ezra Stiles Papers, Yale Univ. Lib.; Zeichner, pp. 6–8.

5. *R and M*, 1959, pp. 51–52, 58.

6. Zeichner, pp. 25–29.

7. Julian Parks Boyd, ed. *The Susquehannah Company Papers . . .* (Wilkes-Barre, Pa., 1930–33), I, xlii–xlv, lxi–lxiv, lxxxi–lxxxiv, 28–39, 50–318; II, 1–196; "British Transcripts, P.R.O., C.O. 5," LXI, 483–491, 493–505; LXIII, 177; *C.R.*, X, 378; *Conn. Gazette*, June 19, 1762; "Trumbull Papers," II, 30; Zeichner, pp. 30–33.

8. Charles M. Andrews, *Connecticut and the British Government*, Conn. Ter. Comm. Pubs., No. 1 (New Haven, 1933), p. 2; Zeichner, pp. 17–18.

9. Andrews, *British Government*, pp. 2–4.

10. Andrews, *British Government*, pp. 3–4; Charles M. Andrews, *The Connecticut Intestacy Law*, Conn. Ter. Comm. Pubs., No. 2 (New Haven, 1933), pp. 8–9; *C.R.*, V, 522–523, 569; Jeremiah Dummer, *A Defence of the New-England Charters* (Boston, 1721), pp. 1–44.

11. Andrews, *British Government*, pp. 6–14; *C.R.*, VII, 580–581; X, 619–626; "Conn. Archives, Foreign Correspondence," I, 18–19, 145, 163–165.

12. Andrews, *Conn. Intestacy*, pp. 4–7; *C.R.*, IV, 306–311.

13. Andrews, *Conn. Intestacy*, pp. 12–28.

14. Andrews, *British Government*, pp. 24–35; Francis Fane, *Reports on the Laws of Connecticut . . .*, ed. Charles M. Andrews, Acorn Club Pubs., No. 12 ([New Haven], 1915), pp. 1–200.

15. "The Fitch Papers, Correspondence and Documents During Thomas Fitch's Governorship of the Colony of Connecticut, 1754–1766," II, *C.H.S.C.*, XVIII (Hartford, 1920), 92, 261–273, 275–279; Zeichner, pp. 45–46.

16. *C.R.*, XII, 357–366; Lawrence H. Gipson, *Jared Ingersoll . . .*, Yale Hist. Pubs., Misc., VIII (New Haven, 1920), pp. 252–255; Glenn Weaver, *Jonathan Trumbull, Connecticut's Merchant Magistrate (1710–1785)* (Hartford, 1956), pp. 97–98; Zeichner, pp. 46–48.

17. *C.R.*, XII, 653–671; Edmund S. Morgan and Helen M. Morgan, *The Stamp Act Crisis, Prologue to Revolution* (Chapel Hill, 1953), pp. 231–232; Zeichner, p. 49.

18. *The Connecticut Courant*, Feb. 3, 1766; Gipson, *Ingersoll*, pp. 144–146, 153–154, 156–158; Morgan and Morgan, pp. 180–181, 186–187, 200; Zeichner, pp. 50–52, 66.

19. *C.R.*, XII, 409–411; *Conn. Gazette*, Sept. 20, 27, 1765; Gipson, *Ingersoll*, pp. 177–189; Morgan and Morgan, pp. 232–234.

20. *C.R.*, XII, 420–425.

21. *Courant*, March 31, 1766; Morgan and Morgan, pp. 202, 235–237; Zeichner, pp. 56–75.

22. *C.R.*, XII, 466–467, 467n; *Courant*, May 26, 1766;

Conn. Gazette, May 24, 1766; *The New-London Gazette*, May 23, 1766; Morgan and Morgan, pp. 264–281.

23. *Courant*, Nov. 13, 1769; Jan. 1, June 18, July 23, 30, 1770; Virginia D. Harrington, *The New York Merchant on the Eve of the Revolution*, Col. Univ. Stud. in Hist., Econ. and Public Law, No. 404 (New York, 1935), pp. 353–355; Curtis Nettels, *The Roots of American Civilization* . . . (New York, 1938), pp. 634–637; *New-London Gazette*, Feb. 9, 1770; Arthur M. Schlesinger, *The Colonial Merchants and the American Revolution, 1763–1776* (New York, 1939), pp. 112, 150–152.

24. Zeichner, pp. 113–117, 121–122.

25. Jonathan Trumbull, *Jonathan Trumbull, Governor of Connecticut, 1769–1784* (Boston, 1919), pp. 88–89.

26. Weaver, *Trumbull*, pp. 124, 131–145; Zeichner, pp. 122–127.

27. *C.R.*, XIV, 161–162; "Correspondence of Silas Deane, Delegate to the First and Second Congress at Philadelphia, 1774–1776," *C.H.S.C.*, II (Hartford, 1870), 131–132; "Trumbull Papers," XX, 72; Zeichner, pp. 143–146.

28. *C.R.*, XIV, 217–219, 219n; Zeichner, pp. 146–148.

29. *The Connecticut Journal, and the New-Haven Post-Boy*, March 18, 1774; *Courant*, March 22, 1774; Zeichner, pp. 149, 151–153.

30. *C.R.*, XIV, 261–262; *Conn. Journal*, April 8, 1774; *Courant*, March 29, April 5, 12, 26, 1774; Benjamin Trumbull, *A Plea, in Vindication of the Connecticut Title to the Contested Lands* . . . (New Haven, 1774), pp. 96–99; "Trumbull Papers," III, 192; Zeichner, pp. 147–148, 150, 153, 158.

31. *The Connecticut Gazette and the Universal Intelligence* (New London), March 18, 1774; Zeichner, pp. 159–162.

32. *C.R.*, XIV, 255; Samuel Lockwood, *Civil Rulers an Ordinance of God, for Good to Mankind* . . . (New London, 1774), pp. 8–39.

33. *Courant*, May 24, 1774; "Norwich Records, Book No. 4, March 1764–June 1784," pp. 115–116, Conn. St. Lib., Hartford; Zeichner, p. 164.

34. *C.R.*, XIV, 324, 347–350; Zeichner, p. 165.

35. *Conn. Gazette* (New London), Sept. 16, 1774; *Courant*, Aug. 23, Sept. 19, 1774; "Huntington Papers: Correspondence of the Brothers Joshua and Jedediah Huntington during the Period of the American Revolution," *C.H.S.C.*, XX (Hartford, 1923), 215–217; Zeichner, pp. 179–180.

36. "Town Meetings 1710–1803. Misc., Town of Mansfield, Conn.," I, 257–258, Mansfield Town Hall.

37. Clarence E. Carter, ed. *The Correspondence of General Thomas Gage* . . . , Yale Hist. Pubs., Manuscripts and Edited Texts, XI–XII (New Haven, 1931–33), I, 366–368, 370, 374, 377; *Courant*, Aug. 23, 1774; "Silas Deane Corr.," *C.H.S.C.*, II, 156, 191; "Manuscripts of Rev. Samuel Peters, 1735–1826," I, 10, New York Hist. Soc.; Zeichner, pp. 172, 176.

38. *C.R.*, XIV, 327–328, 343, 346; "Trumbull Papers," XX, 94.

39. *Conn. Gazette* (New London), Feb. 3, 10, 17, March 3, 1775; *Conn. Journal*, Jan. 4, Feb. 8, March 1, 1775; *Courant*, Jan. 30, 1775; "Extracts from Revolutionary Records, 1774–1784," Branford, p. 1; Derby, p. 1; Guilford, pp. 1–2; Hartford, pp. 2–3; New London, p. 9; Wallingford, p. 1; Windham, p. 9; Woodbury, pp. 22–24, Conn. St. Lib., Hartford; "Norwich Records," Book No. 4, p. 119; Zeichner, pp. 181–182.

40. *C.R.*, XIV, 391–393; *Conn. Gazette* (New London), March 3, 1775; *Conn. Journal*, March 1, 1775; "Trumbull Papers," IV, 63; XX, 101.

9 Connecticut Fights for Independence, 1775–83

1. Peter Force, comp. *American Archives* . . . (Wash., 1837–53), 4th Ser., II, 363–370; Allen French, *The First Year of the American Revolution* (Boston, 1934), pp. 23–24.

2. George Bancroft, *History of the United States* . . . (Boston, 1866–74), VII, 315; French, *First Year*, p. 83; Increase N. Tarbox, *Life of Israel Putnam* . . . (Boston, 1876), pp. 83–85.

3. Edward E. Atwater, ed. *History of the City of New Haven* . . . (New York, 1887), pp. 648–650; *C.R.*, XIV, 404–405; "Conn. Archives, Revolutionary War, 1763–1789," 1st Ser., II, 1–88, Conn. St. Lib., Hartford; Rollin G. Osterweis, *Three Centuries of New Haven, 1638–1938* (New Haven, 1953), pp. 130–131; Willard M. Wallace, *Traitorous Hero; the Life and Fortunes of Benedict Arnold* (New York, 1954), pp. 35–36.

4. "Conn. Archives, Rev. War," 1st Ser., III, 632.

5. "Trumbull Papers," XX, 104.

6. *C.R.*, XIV, 415–431.

7. *C.R.*, XIV, 432–440.

8. *C.R.*, XIV, 415–416.

9. *C.R.*, XIV, 440–441.

10. *C.R.*, XIV, 442–444; Wladimir Hagelin and Ralph A. Brown, eds. "Connecticut Farmers at Bunker Hill: The Diary of Col. Experience Storrs," *New England Quarterly*, XXVIII (March 1955), 87–88; "Governor Joseph Trumbull Collection," IV, 453, Conn. St. Lib.,

Hartford; Oscar Zeichner, *Connecticut's Years of Controversy, 1750–1776* (Chapel Hill, 1949), p. 194.

11. Christopher Ward, *The War of the Revolution*, ed. John R. Alden (New York, 1952), I, 65.

12. "Colonel Samuel H. Parsons to Joseph H. Trumbull, June 2, 1775," *C.H.S.C.*, I, 181–182; John Pell, *Ethan Allen* (Boston, 1929), pp. 75–77; Wallace, *Traitorous Hero*, pp. 37–39.

13. Josiah F. Goodhue, *History of the Town of Shoreham, Vermont* . . . (Middlebury, 1861), p. 14; Stewart H. Holbrook, *Ethan Allen* (New York, 1940), pp. 8–9; Joseph E. A. Smith, *The History of Pittsfield, (Berkshire County,) Massachusetts* . . . (Boston, 1869–76), I, 218–220.

14. "Conn. Archives, Rev. War," 1st Ser., III, 35; Henry Hall, *Ethan Allen, the Robin Hood of Vermont* (New York, 1892), pp. 74–77; Holbrook, pp. 14–19.

15. Ward, I, 69–70.

16. Zeichner, p. 195.

17. Joseph Perry, *Sermon, Preached before the General Assembly of the Colony of Connecticut at Hartford, on the Day May 11, 1775* (Hartford, 1775), pp. 7, 16.

18. *C.R.*, XV, 13–15, 17–31, 51–52, 54.

19. *C.R.*, XV, 39, 315; Jonathan Trumbull, ed. *The Lebanon War Office* . . . (Hartford, 1891), pp. 5–9.

20. Richard Frothingham, *History of the Siege of Boston* . . . (Boston, 1849), pp. 140, 140n; John C. Miller, *Triumph of Freedom, 1775–1783* (Boston, 1948),

pp. 48–53; Willard M. Wallace, *Appeal to Arms . . .* (New York, 1951), pp. 34–47; Ward, I, 73–96.

21. "Amos Wadsworth to his brother, June 14, 1775," Old M.S., J. Gay, D (Inscription on box in which MSS. are kept.), C.H.S.

22. "John Trumbull to David Trumbull, November 8, 1775," Box "Letters of John Trumbull, artist, to his brother David Trumbull," C.H.S. A letter of November 22, 1775, in similar vein, expressed the view that discord seriously threatened the army.

23. *C.R.*, XV, 92–93, 99–102, 105–106.

24. *C.R.*, XV, 107.

25. *C.R.*, XV, 32–33, 123, 145.

26. *C.R.*, XV, 102, 179, 182–183, 482.

27. *C.R.*, XV, 179–180, 252–253, 490–491; Frances M. Caulkins, *History of Norwich, Connecticut . . .* (Hartford, 1874), p. 387.

28. Edmund C. Burnett, ed. *Letters of Members of the Continental Congress*, Carnegie Inst. Wash. Pubs., No. 299 (Wash., 1921–36), II, 362n; *C.R.*, XV, 467–468, 482; Worthington C. Ford, ed. *Journals of the Continental Congress, 1774–1789* (Wash., 1904–37), VII, 291; "Middletown Town Votes," II, 351; *S.R.*, I, 154, 217, 398, 511. In September 1777, £100 was drawn for the expenses of the guard.

29. *C.R.*, XV, 184; Force, *Amer. Archives*, 4th Ser., IV, 180–181.

30. Ward, I, 54, 126–127.

31. *C.R.*, XV, 249–250, 285–286. County Court records list many such cases during the war years. See especially New Haven and Fairfield County Court records.

32. *C.R.*, XV, 291–299.

33. *C.R.*, XV, 398–400.

34. *C.R.*, XV, 411, 416–417.

35. *C.R.*, XV, 414–416; "Conn. Archives, Rev. War," 1st Ser., IV, 338. The original copy indicates that the action passed both houses smoothly with only a minor change in wording.

36. *C.R.*, XV, 450–453.

37. John C. Miller, *Origins of the American Revolution* (Boston, 1943), p. 491.

38. George C. Groce, *William Samuel Johnson: A Maker of the Constitution* (New York, 1937), pp. 92–111.

39. *Courant*, Sept. 19, 1774.

40. "Peters Papers," I, 2–3.

41. Lawrence H. Gipson, *Jared Ingersoll; a Study of American Loyalism in Relation to British Colonial Government*, Yale Hist. Pubs., Miscellany, VIII (New Haven, 1920), pp. 329–331.

42. Frances M. Caulkins, *History of New London, Connecticut . . .* (New London, 1895), p. 503; "Extracts from Revolutionary Records," Colchester, p. 3; "Norwich Records," Book No. 4, p. 119.

43. "Extracts from Revolutionary Records," Ridgefield, pp. 1–3; George L. Rockwell, *The History of Ridgefield, Connecticut* (Ridgefield, 1927), p. 92; Zeichner, pp. 184–185.

44. *Connecticut Journal*, March 1, 8, 1775; Force, *Amer. Archives*, 4th Ser., I, 1215–16, 1258–60, 1270.

45. *C.R.*, XIV, 392–93; "Trumbull Papers," XX, 101.

46. Gipson, *Ingersoll*, pp. 328–331, 344, 356–359, 374–376.

47. "Timothy Hosmer to Amos Wadsworth; Fenn Wadsworth to Amos Wadsworth; July 30, 1775," old M.S., J. Gay, D (inscription on box in which MSS. are kept). The two letters agree closely enough to give authenticity to the episode. Hosmer's is more detailed.

48. "Conn. Archives, Rev. War," 1st Ser., XXIII, 302; Zeichner, pp. 200–201, 338–339, n.20.

49. "Peters Papers," I, 21.

50. "Conn. Archives, Rev. War," 1st Ser., XIII, 232; *Courant*, Dec. 4, 1775; Rockwell, p. 95; Zeichner, p. 206.

51. *C.R.*, XV, 192–195; Zeichner, p. 209.

52. *C.R.*, XV, 411–413; Zeichner, pp. 212–213.

53. *S.R.*, I, 3–5; Zeichner, p. 216.

54. *S.R.*, I, 7–8, 27–28. This session already had given towns the power to confine within certain limits and under guard, if necessary, all inimical persons.

55. *Courant*, April 8, 1776.

56. *Conn. Gazette* (New London), March 14, 1777.

57. *C.R.*, XIV, 491; Zeichner, pp. 232–234.

58. Franklin B. Dexter, ed. *The Literary Diary of Ezra Stiles . . .* (New York, 1901), II, 62; "Gold Selleck Silliman to the Rev. Joseph Fish, March 1, 1777; July 1, 1777," Silliman Family Papers; Zeichner, pp. 233–234.

59. "Conn. Archives, Rev. War," 1st Ser., VIII, 223, 232; "Fairfield County Court Records, 1773–83," Conn. St. Lib., Hartford; "New Haven County Court Records, 1777–82," VIII, 277–280, 315–317, 381–433, 535, Conn. St. Lib., Hartford; *S.R.*, I, 254; II, 279–280, 386–387. A further offer of possible pardon was made in May 1779. Apparently Trumbull failed to issue the proclamation and in August the Council of Safety, angered by Tory co-operation in Tryon's July raid, asked Trumbull not to issue the proclamation until the Assembly could act again.

60. "Fairfield County Court Records, 1773–83." Norwalk led by a wide margin with 93 cases; Stamford had 62; Fairfield, 35; Ridgefield, 33.

61. "Conn. Archives, Rev. War," 1st Ser., XXXIV, 467a; "George Pitkin, Clerk, to the Sheriff, Aug. 29, 1777," Chauncey Family Papers, Loyalists, Yale Univ. Lib.; "Silliman to Rev. and Mrs. Fish, May 27, 1776," Silliman Family Papers.

62. Joseph Anderson, ed. *The Town and City of Waterbury, Connecticut . . .* (New Haven, 1896), I, 434–436; "Papers Relative to the Trial of Moses Dunbar, 1769, 1777," Photostat, Conn. St. Lib., Hartford; Epaphroditus Peck, "Loyal to the Crown," *Conn. Mag.*, VIII, Nos. 1–2 (1903), 129–136, 297–300; *S.R.*, II, 190. Nehemiah Scribner of Norwalk was sentenced to death for high treason, but in January 1779 the Assembly commuted his sentence.

63. "American Loyalists. Transcript of the Commission of Enquiry into the Losses and Services of the American Loyalists . . . 1783–1790," XII, 5–507, 563–701; XXVIII, 5–143, New York Pub. Lib.

64. "Conn. Archives, Rev. War," 1st Ser., XXVI, 247; Charles B. Todd, *The History of Redding, Connecticut . . .* (New York, 1880), p. 42.

65. *C.R.*, XV, 142–143.

66. James M. Bailey, *History of Danbury, Connecticut, 1684–1896 . . .*, comp. Susan B. Hill (New York, 1896), pp. 60–62; Wallace, *Traitorous Hero*, p. 128; Ward, II, 492–493.

67. Bailey, pp. 66–70.

68. Bailey, pp. 72–74; Ward, II, 492.

69. Bailey, pp. 75–77; Ward, II, 494.

70. Benson J. Lossing, *The Pictorial Field-Book of the Revolution* (New York, 1851–52), I, 408, 408n.

71. Lossing, I, 409; Wallace, *Traitorous Hero*, p. 129.

72. Henry B. Dawson, *Battles of the United States, By Sea and Land . . .* (New York, 1858), I, 216; *The Huntington Family in America . . .* (Hartford, 1915), p. 448; Lossing, I, 409–410; Frank Moore, *The Diary*

of the Revolution . . . (Hartford, 1875), pp. 425–426; Wallace, *Traitorous Hero*, p. 129.

73. *S.R.*, II, 41–42.

74. *C.R.*, XV, 290–291, 529; "Conn. Archives, Rev. War," 1st Ser., VII, 356, 363–364, 367; *S.R.*, I, 10, 65, 103.

75. *S.R.*, I, 350–352, 456; II, 397–398, 504; III, 231, 544–545, 551, 553–554.

76. "Extracts from Revolutionary Records, 1774–84," all towns; "Norwich Records," Book No. 4; *S.R.*, I, 475–476.

77. Caulkins, *Norwich*, p. 371; Marquis François Jean de Chastellux, *Travels in North America in the Years 1780, 1781, 1782* (Dublin, 1787), I, 37–39; John C. Fitzpatrick, ed. *The Writings of George Washington . . .* (Wash., [1931–44]), XV, 284–285.

78. *C.R.*, XV, 18, 101, 190–192, 204–205, 213–214, 251, 258, 287–290, 350–351, 357; "Conn. Archives, Rev. War," 1st Ser., V, 330–334, 345; XXXII, 354; *S.R.*, I, 8–9, 133; II, 446–447; Arthur P. Van Gelder and Hugo Schlatter, *History of the Explosives Industry in America* (New York, 1927), p. 52.

79. Richard M. Bayles, ed. *History of Windham County, Connecticut . . .* (New York, 1889), pp. 71, 73; James L. Bishop, *A History of American Manufactures from 1608 to 1860 . . .* (Phila., 1866), I, 516; *C.R.*, XIV, 418; XV, 17–18, 127, 317–318, 323; Caulkins, *Norwich*, pp. 388–389; "Conn. Archives, Rev. War," 1st Ser., XI, 181; Joseph R. Mayer, "Medad Hills, Connecticut Gunsmith," *Antiques*, XLIV (July 1943), 18–19; Louis F. Middlebrook, *History of Maritime Connecticut During the American Revolution, 1775–1783* (Salem, Mass., 1925), I, 201; *S.R.*, I, 244, 246; V, 405, 467–468; Leroy D. Satterlee and Arcadi Gluckman, *American Gun Makers* (Buffalo, 1940), *passim*; William B. Weeden, *Economic and Social History of New England, 1620–1789* (Boston, 1894), II, 793.

80. *C.R.*, XV, 224, 234, 249; Louis F. Middlebrook, *Salisbury Connecticut Cannon, Revolutionary War* (Salem, Mass., 1935), pp. 17–21.

81. *C.R.*, XV, 490, 526; "Trumbull Papers," XXIX, 302. Apparently a few cannon already had been made available to the Continental forces. Trumbull had written Washington in July 1776, telling him that forty cannon, ranging from six-pounders to twelve-pounders, had been cast and were available.

82. "Conn. Archives, Rev. War," 1st Ser., VII, 387–388; *Courant*, April 7, 14, 21, 1778; Middlebrook, *Salisbury*, p. 13; *S.R.*, I, 130–132, 159, 204–205; II, 248, 351, 513; III, 348–349, 460; IV, 102, 111–112.

83. "Conn. Archives, Rev. War," 1st Ser., VII, XIII, XIV, XVI–XVIII, XX.

84. Forrest Morgan *et al.*, eds. *Connecticut as a Colony and as a State, or One of the Original Thirteen* (Hartford, 1904), II, 82; "Rolls and Lists of Connecticut Men in the Revolution, 1775–1783," *C.H.S.C.*, VIII (Hartford, 1901), 132–148.

85. *C.R.*, XV, 225n, 237–238; Force, *Amer. Archives*, 4th Ser., IV, 683–684, 930; Morgan, *Connecticut*, II, 82, 84–85.

86. *C.R.*, XV, 249–250, 417–430, 436–437, 498, 514–515; "Rev. Joseph Fish to Selleck Silliman, Sept. 16, 1776," Silliman Family Papers.

87. John R. Alden, *The American Revolution 1775–1783*, New Amer. Nation Ser. (New York, 1954), pp. 97–99; Morgan, *Connecticut*, II, 86–87; "Silliman to wife, Mar. 29, 1776"; "Silliman to the Rev. Joseph Fish, Apr. 15, 1776," Silliman Family Papers; Wallace, *Appeal to Arms*, p. 114; Ward, I, 227–230.

88. *D.A.B.*, XV, 281–282; Douglas S. Freeman, *George Washington, a Biography* (New York, 1948–57), IV, 367–368.

89. Miller, *Triumph*, p. 127; "Silliman to wife, Oct. 3, 1776," Silliman Family Papers; Ward, I, 239.

90. John Fiske, *The American Revolution* (Boston, 1891), I, 215; Fitzpatrick, VI, 96; Lossing, II, 611; "Silliman to wife, Sept. 10, 1776; Sept. 17, 1776," Silliman Family Papers; Charles H. W. Stocking, *The History and Genealogy of the Knowltons of England and America* (New York, 1897), pp. 90–93; Wallace, *Appeal to Arms*, p. 116; Ward, I, 246–252.

91. Maria Hull Campbell, *Revolutionary Services and Civil Life of General William Hull* (New York, 1848), pp. 33–38; Henry P. Johnston, *Nathan Hale, 1776 . . .*, rev. ed. (New Haven, 1914), pp. 106–107.

92. Campbell, pp. 37–38; Johnston, *Hale*, pp. 111–116, 124–125.

93. Miller, *Triumph*, p. 504; Morgan, *Connecticut*, II, 110–111; Ward, I, 262, 265, 293–294.

94. *S.R.*, I, 181, 240, 425; II, 280, 365; III, 30, 184, 378, 462.

95. "Journal of Oliver Boardman of Middletown in the Burgoyne Campaign, 1777," *C.H.S.C.*, VII (Hartford, 1899), 237.

96. Miller, *Triumph*, pp. 488–491, 505–506; "Silliman to Mary Silliman, Oct. 14, 1776," Silliman Family Papers.

97. "New Haven County Court Records," VIII, 268–276, 283–302, 347–632.

98. "Silliman to Joseph Fish, Dec. 7, 1777; Jan. 19, 1778," Silliman Family Papers; "Fairfield County Court Records, 1779–1783."

99. Middlebrook, *Maritime*, I, 212.

100. Ward, I, 386–388.

101. Isaac N. Arnold, *The Life of Benedict Arnold . . .* (Chicago, 1880), p. 204; Lynn Montross, *Rag, Tag, and Bobtail . . .* (New York, 1952), pp. 223–224; Hoffman Nickerson, *The Turning Point of the Revolution . . .* (Boston, 1928), pp. 362–367; William L. Stone, *The Campaign of Lieut. Gen. John Burgoyne . . .* (Albany, 1877), pp. 63–66, 375; Wallace, *Traitorous Hero*, pp. 155–158; Ward, II, 506, 512, 528–531.

102. "Boardman," *C.H.S.C.*, VII, 231, 235.

103. Morgan, *Connecticut*, II, 111–113, 146.

104. Connecticut, Adjutant General, *Record of Service of Connecticut Men in the War of the Revolution . . .*, ed. Henry P. Johnston (Hartford, 1889), pp. 241–242; Ward, II, 596–603.

105. Ward, II, 623–624.

106. Wallace, *Traitorous Hero*, pp. 193–198, 313–324.

107. Morgan, *Connecticut*, II, 114; Ward, II, 876–877.

108. John C. Fitzpatrick, ed. *The Diaries of George Washington, 1748–1799* (Boston, 1925), II, 216–218; Fitzpatrick, *Writings*, XXII, 105–111.

109. Morgan, *Connecticut*, II, 150–151; "Gov. Trumbull's Diary, 1780–83," C.H.S.; Ward, II, 882, 892–893.

110. Conn. Adjutant General, *Record*, pp. x, xi; "Rolls," *C.H.S.C.*, VIII.

111. *C.R.*, XV, 99–100; Middlebrook, *Maritime*, I, 10.

112. *Courant*, Aug. 26, 1776; Middlebrook, *Maritime*, I, 80–86.

113. Middlebrook, *Maritime*, I, 42–45, 48–54.

114. Middlebrook, *Maritime*, I, 28–29; Morgan, *Connecticut*, II, 123–124.

115. Thomas S. Collier, "The Revolutionary Privateers of Connecticut . . .," *N.L.C.H.S. Recs. & Papers*, I, Pt. 4 (New London, 1893), pp. 46–62. Middlebrook, *Maritime*, I, 204; Morgan, *Connecticut*, II, 121; Charles O. Paullin, *The Navy of the American Revo-*

lution . . . (Cleveland, 1906), pp. 206–207; *S.R.*, I, 567–569. Accounts of the *Trumbull's* armaments vary from 28 to 36 guns.

116. *C.R.*, XV, 474; *S.R.*, II, 136.

117. Middlebrook, *Maritime*, I, 14–15, 214–215.

118. *C.R.*, XV, 233–236; *D.A.B.*, III, 348–349; "Correspondence of Silas Deane, Delegate to the First and Second Congress at Philadelphia, 1774–1776," *C.H.S.C.*, II (Hartford, 1870), 315–318; *S.R.*, I, 212, 580.

119. *C.R.*, XV, 280–281, 318; Ford, *Journals*, III, 372–375; IV, 251–254.

120. George O. Trevelyan, *The American Revolution* . . . (New York, 1899–1913), IV, 345.

121. Collier, pp. 27–31; George F. Emmons, *The Navy of the United States* . . . (Wash., 1853), pp. 127–169; Middlebrook, *Maritime*, I, 10.

122. Middlebrook, *Maritime*, I, ix; Ernest E. Rogers, "Connecticut's Naval Office at New London . . . ," *N.L.C.H.S. Colls.*, II (New London, 1933), 282.

123. Caulkins, *New London*, p. 541; Collier, pp. 22–25; Middlebrook, *Maritime*, II, 51–52.

124. *Courant*, July 20, 1779, e.g. In 1779 and 1780 such notices were very common.

125. Caulkins, *New London*, pp. 536–537; Middlebrook, *Maritime*, II, 258; "Trumbull Papers," XIV, 257.

126. *C.R.*, XV, 15–16, 40; Victor L. Johnson, . . . *The Administration of the American Commissariat During the Revolutionary War* (Phila., 1941), pp. 11, 15, 27.

127. *S.R.*, I, 115–116.

128. *S.R.*, I, 18, 71, 195. Impressment was rarely used, as it was quite costly, time-consuming, and unpleasant.

129. *S.R.*, I, 314, 317–318.

130. *S.R.*, I, 419–420.

131. "Middletown Town Votes," II, 382, 395, 405, 413, e.g.; "Norwich Records," Book No. 4, pp. 145, 152–153.

132. "Connecticut, Misc., 1740–87," Lib. of Cong.; *Courant*, May 10, 1779; "Journal of Joseph Joslin, Jr., of South Killingly, a Teamster in Western Connecticut, 1777–78," *C.H.S.C.*, VII (Hartford, 1899), 299–369.

133. Fitzpatrick, *Writings*, XIV, 221; Johnson, *Administration*, pp. 109, 133–134, 153, 162, 165.

134. Burnett, V, 502; "Conn. Archives, Rev. War," 1st Ser., XIX, 273; Johnson, *Administration*, p. 174; "Trumbull Papers," XI, 240.

135. "Jeremiah Wadsworth, Account Books," Box 146; "Jeremiah Wadsworth, Letter Books, 1778–83," Box 151; "Jeremiah Wadsworth, French Army," Boxes 143–144, C.H.S.

136. Stephen Bonsal, *When the French Were Here* . . . (New York, 1945), pp. 52–53; *S.R.*, III, 187.

137. Johnson, *Administration*, p. 174; *S.R.*, III, 237–238, 559–560, 572, 575–576; Jared Sparks, ed. *Correspondence of the American Revolution* . . . (Boston, 1853), III, 437.

138. George L. Clark, *A History of Connecticut, its People and Institutions*, rev. ed. (New York, 1914), pp. 284–285; Fitzpatrick, *Writings*, X, 423–427. The "Trumbull Papers" alone contain over 200 letters written by Washington to Trumbull in the 1775–82 period. Vol. XXV is especially rich.

139. Fitzpatrick, *Writings*, XVII, 365–367; XVIII, 333, 425–426.

140. Fitzpatrick, *Writings*, XXI, 116–117, 442–443; "The Heath Papers," Part III, *M.H.S.C.*, 7th Ser., V (Boston, 1905), 196–197; Johnson, *Administration*, p. 197; *S.R.*, II, 132–133, 175–176, 521–526, 531, 541; III, 15, 176, 381, 383.

141. Burnett, V, 183–189.

142. "Conn. Archives, Rev. War," 1st Ser., XIII, 48.

143. *S.R.*, II, 455–456; "The Trumbull Papers," II, *M.H.S.C.*, 5th Ser., X (Boston, 1888), 113.

144. *C.R.*, XIV, 432; XV, 14; Ralph V. Harlow, "Aspects of Revolutionary Finance, 1775–1783," *Amer. Hist. Rev.*, XXXV (Oct. 1929), opp. p. 50. In common with other states, Connecticut for years continued to use the British money system in everyday transactions. The use of dollars and cents came in slowly and did not become universal until the mid-1790's.

145. Roger Sherman Boardman, *Roger Sherman, Signer and Statesman* (Phila., 1938), pp. 184–188; *C.R.*, XIII, 300, 516; XIV, 95, 346; *S.R.*, I, 377, 425.

146. Dexter, ed. *Literary Diary, Stiles*, II, 396, 532; *S.R.*, III, 170–171.

147. *Courant*, Dec. 30, 1777; Aug. 4, Oct. 20, 1778.

148. "The Wyllys Papers . . . ," *C.H.S.C.*, XXI (Hartford, 1924), 465–466.

149. *S.R.*, I, 62–63, 97–100, 230–231, 524–528.

150. *C.R.*, XIV, 384–385; *S.R.*, IV, 59–60. Totals are given to the nearest pound.

151. *S.R.*, I, 365–366; II, 13–14.

152. Henry Bronson, "A Historical Account of Connecticut Currency . . . ," Read Nov. 30, 1863 and afterward, *N.H.C.H.S. Papers*, I (New Haven, 1865), 128n, 134; *Courant*, Nov. 6, 13, 20, 1781, e.g.

153. "District of New Haven, List of Coasters Inwards, Sept. 27, 1776–July 2, 1779," National Archives.

154. "Conn. Archives, Rev. War," 1st Ser., XIII, XIX, XXI, XXIV; *S.R.*, II, 324–328. In a sample check of 94 cases in Oct. 1778–Feb. 1783 period, 41 were entirely granted and 8 partially granted.

155. "Nathaniel Shaw Letters," Aug. 9–Dec. 30, 1776, Yale Univ. Lib.

156. "Job and Samuel Taber," Box 1, John Carter Brown Library, Brown University.

157. *S.R.*, I, 160; II, 168; III, 295, 301; IV, 277; V, 105, 193.

158. "Nathaniel Shaw Letters," 1776, Yale Univ. Lib.

159. Robert A. East, *Business Enterprise in the American Revolutionary Era*, Col. Univ. Stud. in Hist., Econ. and Public Law, No. 439 (New York, 1938), p. 97; "James Iredell, Sr., Port of Roanoke, 1771–76," North Carolina Hist. Comm. Archives, Raleigh.

160. *Courant*, June 1, 1779.

161. Middlebrook, *Maritime*, II, 6–9; "New Haven, a List of Foreigners Outwards, Sept. 17, 1762–June 24, 1801," National Archives.

162. Albert E. Van Dusen, "The Trade of Revolutionary Connecticut," unpub. diss. (Univ. of Penn., 1948), pp. 369–379.

163. *Courant*, April 7, 1778; Oct. 23, 30; Nov. 6, 1781, e.g.; "New Haven, Foreigners Outwards."

164. *Conn. Journal*, Oct. 18, 1781.

165. *C.R.*, XIV, 415–416; *S.R.*, I, 12, 71, 123–124.

166. "Conn. Archives, Rev. War," 1st Ser., I, 255; Force, *Amer. Archives*, 5th Ser., III, 1408–09; *S.R.*, II, 450–452; III, 13–14, 39; "Trumbull Papers," XXVI, 108, 111–114.

167. *S.R.*, II, 187; "Trumbull Papers," IX, 16.

168. *S.R.*, II, 188–190.

169. *S.R.*, III, 39; "Trumbull Papers," XXIX, 520.

170. *S.R.*, I, 9.

171. *S.R.*, I, 62–63.

172. *S.R.*, I, 65, 97–100, 230–231, 366, 413–414, 524–530; II, 12–13, 134, 222–223, 266–267, 270, 480, 568, 568n; III, 15–18, 31–32, 34, 233, 384–385; IV, 161–162.

173. *Courant*, April 14, Nov. 25, Dec. 2, 9, 16, 30, 1777.

174. *Conn. Gazette* (New London), Sept. 15, 1780; Fitzpatrick, *Writings*, VII, 402–403.

175. *Conn. Gazette* (New London), Sept. 15, 1780;

NOTES

Frederic G. Mather, *The Refugees of 1776 from Long Island to Connecticut* (Albany, 1913), pp. 202, 209–214.

176. "Conn. Archives, Rev. War," 1st Ser., xv, 272.

177. Lydia Holland and Margaret Leaf, *Greenwich Old & New* . . . (Greenwich, 1935), pp. 77–78.

178. "Conn. Archives, Rev. War," 1st Ser., xx, 207.

179. "Fairfield County Court Records, 1779–83," pp. 467–468; "New Haven County Court Records," viii, 565; *S.R.*, v, 156. After six months at Newgate Prison, Monroe petitioned for release and, upon payment of costs, was ordered released.

180. Oscar T. Barck, *New York City During the War for Independence* . . . , Col. Univ. Stud. in Hist., Econ. and Public Law, No. 357 (New York, 1931), p. 135; "Trumbull Papers," xi, 45.

181. "Conn. Archives, Rev. War," 1st Ser., xviii, 266–268; Morgan, *Connecticut*, ii, 137–138; *S.R.*, ii, 328–329; iii, 50–51.

182. Henry Clinton, *The American Rebellion* . . . , ed. William B. Willcox, Yale Hist. Pubs., Manuscripts and Edited Texts, xxi (New Haven, 1954), p. xxxi.

183. Osterweis, pp. 141–143; Charles H. Townshend, *The British Invasion of New Haven, Connecticut* . . . (New Haven, 1879), pp. 5–7.

184. Chauncey Goodrich, "Invasion of New Haven by the British Troops, July 5, 1779," *N.H.C.H.S. Papers*, ii (New Haven, 1877), 45–46. The original deposition of Daggett, in "Conn. Archives, Rev. War," 1st Ser., xv, 236, employs more restrained language.

185. Goodrich, pp. 51–54; *S.R.*, ii, 545–548, 550–553; Townshend, p. 45.

186. Clinton, p. 412; "Conn. Archives, Rev. War," 1st Ser., xv, 269; *Courant*, July 13, 1779; Osterweis, pp. 145–148.

187. Clinton, pp. 412–413; "Conn. Archives, Rev. War," 1st Ser., xv, 248; Royal R. Hinman, comp. *A Historical Collection, from Official Records, Files, etc., of the Part Sustained by Connecticut, during the War of the Revolution* (Hartford, 1842), p. 609; Lossing, i, 425–426; Morgan, *Connecticut*, ii, 143–144; Elizabeth H. Godfrey Schenck, *The History of Fairfield, Fairfield County, Connecticut* . . . (New York, 1889–1905), ii, 389, 393; Ward, ii, 619. The exact losses given do not seem to agree in any two sources.

188. Morgan, *Connecticut*, ii, 144–146; *S.R.*, iii, 48–49; Ward, ii, 619–620.

189. *Courant*, July 13, 1779.

190. William M. James, *The British Navy in Adversity* . . . (London, 1926), p. 108; Wallace, *Traitorous Hero*, pp. 278–279.

191. Morgan, *Connecticut*, ii, 151–153; Wallace, *Traitorous Hero*, p. 279.

192. Clinton, pp. 565–567; William W. Harris, *The Battle of Groton Heights* . . . , rev. Charles Allyn (New London, 1882), pp. 100–101.

193. Harris, pp. 17–105.

194. Harris, pp. 17–105, 266–270. Doubt still exists as to who murdered Ledyard. William Harris made a careful investigation of the evidence and concluded that a subordinate, rather than Maj. Bromfield or Capt. George Beckwith, committed the heinous act.

195. Caulkins, *New London*, pp. 569–570; Wallace, *Traitorous Hero*, pp. 281–282.

196. Caulkins, *New London*, pp. 569–570; "Conn. Archives, Rev. War," 1st Ser., xxxvi, 294; *S.R.*, vii, 448–449, 466–471; viii, 438–442.

197. Harris, p. 105.

198. Julian P. Boyd, *The Susquehannah Company: Connecticut's Experiment in Expansion*, Conn. Ter. Comm. Pubs., No. 34 (New Haven, 1935), pp. 28–29; *C.R.*, xiv, 217–219, 219n, 490.

199. Carl L. Carmer, *The Susquehanna*, Rivers of Amer. Ser. (New York, 1955), pp. 116–118.

200. *S.R.*, i, 7.

201. Carmer, pp. 123–131; Hinman, pp. 152–154; Morgan, *Connecticut*, ii, 134–135.

202. Morgan, *Connecticut*, ii, 135–136.

203. Morgan, *Connecticut*, ii, 136; Ward, ii, 638–645.

204. Simeon E. Baldwin, "Connecticut in Pennsylvania," *N.H.C.H.S. Papers*, viii (New Haven, 1914), 14–19; Boyd, *Susquehannah*, pp. 43–48; Morgan, *Connecticut*, ii, 222–223; *S.R.*, v, 11.

205. Margaret Burnham Macmillan, *The War Governors in the American Revolution*, Col. Univ. Stud. in Hist., Econ. and Public Law, No. 503 (New York, 1943), pp. 237–239, 244 n31, 252–253. For the period, 1763–76, Zeichner stresses the existence of vigorous internal disputes over political, economic, and religious issues.

206. *C.R.*, xv, 2–5; *S.R.*, v, 107–110. In 1783 thirty-three members from twenty-nine towns still remained in the Lower House out of 134 present in May 1775.

207. *C.R.*, xv, 5, 136; *S.R.*, v, 109–110.

208. Charles Francis Adams, ed. *The Works of John Adams* . . . (Boston, 1850–56), vi, 530; *C.R.*, xv, 39; *S.R.*, v, 120n.

209. Richard J. Purcell, *Connecticut in Transition, 1775–1818* (Wash., 1918), p. 176.

210. Eben E. Beardsley, *The History of the Episcopal Church in Connecticut* . . . (New York, 1865–68), i, 302–305; Franklin B. Dexter, *Biographical Sketches of the Graduates of Yale College* . . . (New York, 1885–1912), ii, 181; Purcell, p. 52; Anson P. Stokes, *Memorials of Eminent Yale Men* . . . (New Haven, 1914), i, 47.

211. Beardsley, i, 318–331, 338–339.

212. "Conn. Archives, Rev. War," 1st Ser., viii, 239; Dexter, ed. *Literary Diary, Stiles*, i, 491; "Peters Papers," i, 3; Purcell, p. 69; Zeichner, pp. 29–30.

213. Dexter, ed. *Literary Diary, Stiles*, iii, 21.

214. Purcell, pp. 94–95.

215. *D.A.B.*, v, 173–174; "The Deane Papers," i, *N.Y.H.S.C.*, xix (New York, 1887–91), x; Miller, *Triumph*, pp. 365–366.

216. "Deane Papers," i, xi–xii; Miller, *Triumph*, pp. 361–375.

217. George L. Clark, *Silas Deane* . . . (New York, 1913), pp. 264–265; Silas Deane, *An Address to the Free and Independent Citizens of the United States of North-America* (Hartford, 1784); "Deane Papers," i, xii–xiv; Miller, *Triumph*, pp. 375–376.

218. *Courant*, March 26, 1782; "Conn. Archives, Rev. War," 1st Ser., xxii, 85–86; "Trumbull Papers," xx, 342.

219. "Conn. Archives, Rev. War," 1st Ser., i, 267b; "Journal of the House of Representatives, 1779–83," May 12, 1780; May 10, 1781; May 9, 1782; May 9, 1783, Conn. St. Lib., Hartford.

220. Jonathan Trumbull, *Jonathan Trumbull, Governor of Connecticut, 1769–1784* (Boston, 1919), pp. 304–312.

221. Macmillan, pp. 135, 212, 274; *S.R.*, v, 218–219.

222. Van Dusen, pp. 382–387.

223. *S.R.*, v, 115–116. The final definitive Peace of Paris of Sept. 3, 1783 appeared in Connecticut newspapers of Dec. 1783 (*Courant*, Dec. 9; *Packet*, Dec. 10, e.g.).

439

10 Federalism Reigns and Is Toppled

1. "Conn. Archives, Rev. War," 2d Ser., LIII, 25–26; *Conn. Journal*, May 1, 1783; *Courant*, May 6, 1783; *S.R.*, IV, 107, 114, 161–162, 281; V, 115.
2. *S.R.*, V, 219, 250–251, 318–319, 374. ·
3. "Record of All Ships and Vessels Registered at New Haven, 1762–1795."
4. *Acts and Laws, 1784*, p. 235; *S.R.*, V, 323–324; IX, 38–39.
5. *S.R.*, V, 257–277, 343–373.
6. *Courant*, March 12, 1787; Merrill Jensen, *The New Nation . . .* (New York, 1950), pp. 181–191, 302–312; Benjamin U. Ratchford, *American State Debts* (Durham, N.C., 1941), p. 45; Charles F. Sedgwick, *General History of the Town of Sharon . . .*, 3d ed. (Amenia, N.Y., 1898), pp. 80–84; *S.R.*, V, viii, 301, 410, 413–415, 454; VI, x, xi, 37–38, 43, 59–60, 103, 174–175, 294–295, 295n; "Uriah Tracy to Oliver Wolcott, May 21, 1787," Conn. Box 1, Folder, "Conn. Shays' Rebellion," New York Pub. Lib.
7. *S.R.*, VI, xiii, 126–127, 126n, 177–178, 195–196, 216, 234–236, 250–251, 407–410, 473–474; Noah Webster, *A Collection of Papers on Political, Literary and Moral Subjects* (New York, 1843), pp. 317–321.
8. *Courant*, May 21, 1787; *S.R.*, VI, 292–293.
9. *D.A.B.*, XVII, 88–91; George C. Groce, *William Samuel Johnson: a Maker of the Constitution* (New York, 1937), p. 145; Bernard C. Steiner, "Connecticut's Ratification of the Federal Constitution," *Amer. Antiq. Soc. Proc.*, XXV (April 1915), 81–83.
10. *D.A.B.*, VI, 111–115; Steiner, "Ratification," pp. 85–91.
11. *D.A.B.*, X, 131–134; Steiner, "Ratification," pp. 84–85.
12. Roger S. Boardman, *Roger Sherman, Signer and Statesman* (Phila., 1938), pp. 242–245, 249–252, 254–258; *Conn. Journal*, Oct. 10, 17, 24, 31, 1787; *Courant*, Oct. 1; Nov. 5, 1787; Max Farrand, *The Framing of the Constitution of the United States* (New Haven, 1913), pp. 33–35, 75, 80–82, 86, 95–98, 104–107, 121–124, 132, 143, 167, 177, 179, 183–187, 190, 200; Groce, pp. 141–150.
13. *Courant*, Nov. 5, 12, 19, 26; Dec. 3, 10, 17, 24, 31, 1787; March 3, 10, 17, 24, 1788; *New Haven Gazette and Connecticut Magazine*, Nov. 15, 22, 29; Dec. 6, 20, 1787.
14. *Collier's (Litchfield) Weekly Moniter*, Jan. 14, 1788; *Courant*, Jan. 7, 14, 1788; Steiner, "Ratification," pp. 106–112.
15. Orin G. Libby, "The Geographical Distribution of the Vote of the Thirteen States on the Federal Constitution, 1787–88," *Univ. of Wisc. Bull., Econ., Pol. Sci., Hist. Ser.*, I, No. 1 (Madison, 1894), 14–17; Steiner, "Ratification," pp. 113–119.
16. *Courant*, Jan. 14, 1788; *S.R.*, VI, 549–571.
17. *Courant*, April 22; June 3, 1799; Eugene Perry Link, *Democratic-Republican Societies, 1790–1800*, Col. Stud. in Amer. Culture, No. 9 (New York, 1942), pp. 14–15; Richard J. Purcell, *Connecticut in Transition, 1775–1818* (Wash., 1918), pp. 229–230, 297n, 298n.
18. *S.R.*, VI, 474–476, 476n, 496–497. Connecticut did not divide the state into Congressional districts until 1835.
19. *S.R.*, VI, 495–496, 496n.
20. Thomas H. LeDuc, *Connecticut and the First Ten Amendments to the Federal Constitution . . .* (Wash., 1937), pp. 2–5; William H. Thomas, "The Federal Bill of Rights," *The Alabama Lawyer*, IV (Oct. 1943), 419–423. Former Connecticut Chief Justice Maltbie referred to the 1939 Connecticut action as "a rather empty gesture."
21. Maria L. Greene, *The Development of Religious Liberty in Connecticut* (Boston, 1905), pp. 386–387, 414; Charles R. Keller, *The Second Great Awakening in Connecticut*, Yale Hist. Pubs., Misc., XL (New Haven, 1942), pp. 72–91; *S.R.*, VII, xii, 488–489.
22. Roland H. Bainton, *Yale and the Ministry . . .* (New York, 1957), pp. 76–77; Greene, *Development*, pp. 413–415; Keller, p. 42; Purcell, pp. 418–419.
23. Greene, *Development*, pp. 372–378; John Leland, *The Rights of Conscience Inalienable . . .* (New London, 1791), pp. 3–29.
24. *American Mercury*, May 17, 1798; *Courant*, May 14, 1798; *D.A.B.*, IX, 418–419; XIX, 17–18; XX, 442–443; Albert E. Van Dusen, "Samuel Huntington, a Leader of Revolutionary Connecticut," *C.H.S. Bull.*, XIX (April 1954), 38–62.
25. *Courant*, July 10, 1797; Sept. 3, 1798; Purcell, p. 194; *S.R.*, IX, ix–xii, 458–467.
26. *American Mercury*, May 15; Sept. 11, 25; Oct. 2, 1800; *Courant*, April 21, 1800; Purcell, pp. 232–252, 235n; Norman L. Stamps, "Political Parties in Connecticut, 1789–1819," unpub. diss. (Yale, 1950), pp. 66–68, 81–82.
27. "At a General Assembly of the State of Connecticut holden at New-Haven on the second Thursday of October, A.D. 1808 . . . Resolutions protesting the Embargo" (n.p., 1808), broadside, Conn. St. Lib., Hartford; "First Draft of Memorial to President Jefferson Augt 1808," Noah Webster Coll., New York Pub. Lib.; Rollin G. Osterweis, *Three Centuries of New Haven, 1638–1938* (New Haven, 1953), pp. 201–202; Purcell, pp. 249–250, 274, 280, 288–292.
28. Purcell, pp. 285–288.
29. James Truslow Adams, *New England in the Republic, 1776–1850* (Boston, 1926), pp. 270–272; *American Mercury*, July 1, 1812; *Courant*, June 16, 23; July 7, 21, 28; Sept. 15, 22, 1812; Julius William Pratt, *Expansionists of 1812* (New York, 1925), pp. 9–14, 48–49, 58–59, 124–125.
30. Conn. Adjutant General, *Record of Service of Connecticut Men in the . . . War of 1812 . . .* (Hartford, 1889), pp. 142–169; *Courant*, Sept. 1, 1812; Forrest Morgan *et al.*, eds. *Connecticut as a Colony and as a State, or One of the Original Thirteen* (Hartford, 1904), III, 63–64; Stamps, pp. 206–208.
31. Frances M. Caulkins, *History of New London, Connecticut . . .* (New London, 1895), pp. 630–631, 635–636; Morgan, *Connecticut*, III, 77–78.
32. Caulkins, *New London*, pp. 632–633; *Courant*, June 29; July 6, 1813; Aug. 23, 1814; Cecil S. Forester, *The Age of Fighting Sail, the Story of the Naval War of 1812* (Garden City, 1956), p. 255; Benson J. Lossing, *The Pictorial Field-Book of the War of 1812 . . .* (New York, 1868), pp. 692–693, 693n; Morgan, *Connecticut*, III, 77.
33. Caulkins, *New London*, p. 636; *Courant*, Aug. 9, 16, 23, 1814.
34. *Courant*, April 12, 19, 1814; Morgan, *Connecticut*, III, 78.

35. Henry R. Palmer, *Stonington by the Sea*, 2d ed. (Stonington, 1957), pp. 28–32, 34; Richard A. Wheeler, *History of the Town of Stonington . . .* (New London, 1900), pp. 61, 68–78.

36. Henry Adams, *The War of 1812*, ed. Harvey A. De-Weerd (Wash., 1944), pp. 13–23; *D.A.B.*, IX, 363–364; Fletcher Pratt, *The Heroic Years; Fourteen Years of the Republic, 1801–1815* (New York, 1934), pp. 225–228; Glenn Tucker, *Poltroons and Patriots: A Popular Account of the War of 1812* (Indianapolis, 1954), I, 147–169.

37. Forester, pp. 61–68, 75, 152–159; Ira N. Hollis, *The Frigate Constitution* (Boston, 1900), pp. 156–173; Morgan, *Connecticut*, III, 73–74; Pratt, pp. 229–232; Tucker, I, 170.

38. H. Adams, *War of 1812*, pp. 209–211; *D.A.B.*, XII, 19–21; Forester, pp. 240–244.

39. *American Mercury*, Feb. 7, 1815; Edgar S. Maclay, *A History of American Privateers* (New York, 1899), p. 506.

40. J. T. Adams, *New England*, pp. 286–291; Simeon E. Baldwin, "The Hartford Convention," *N.H.C.H.S. Papers*, IX (New Haven, 1918), 14; *Courant*, Oct. 25, 1814; Purcell, pp. 290–93. In the fall of 1814 Federalists held a 161–39 edge in the Assembly.

41. Samuel E. Morison, *The Life and Letters of Harrison Gray Otis . . .* (Boston, 1913), II, 130–140; Purcell, pp. 293–294.

42. Baldwin, "Convention," pp. 24, 26–28; *Courant*, Jan. 6, 1815; Theodore Dwight, *History of the Hartford Convention* (New York, 1833), *passim.*; Greene, *Development*, pp. 452–458; Morison, *Otis*, II, 147–159, 167, 171–173; Purcell, pp. 294–296; [George H. Richards], *The Politics of Connecticut . . .* (Hartford, 1817), p. 26; Stamps, pp. 213, 217–219. For a biting satire on the Convention see Hector Benevolus, (pseud.), *The Hartford Convention in an Uproar!* (Windsor, Vt., 1815).

43. Baldwin, "Convention," IX, 28.

44. Percy W. Bidwell, "Rural Economy in New England at the Beginning of the Nineteenth Century," *Conn. Academy of Arts and Sciences Trans.*, XX (April 1916), 319–321, 345; Purcell, pp. 158–160.

45. *Courant*, April 10, 1811; April 8; May 6, 27; June 10, 17; July 8, 22; Sept. 9, 16, 23, 30, 1817; David Humphreys, *A Discourse on the Agriculture of the State of Connecticut . . .* (New Haven, 1816), pp. 5–41; Purcell, pp. 161–166.

46. *D.A.B.*, IX, 373–375; Humphreys, pp. 21–22; Purcell, pp. 167–172; Chester W. Wright, *Wool-Growing and the Tariff . . .*, Harvard Econ. Studies, V (Cambridge, Mass., 1910) pp. 14–16.

47. *D.A.B.*, IX, 374; John C. Pease and John M. Niles, *A Gazetteer of the States of Connecticut and Rhode-Island* (Hartford, 1819), pp. 17, 37, 95, 141, 170, 204, 230, 271, 289; Purcell, pp. 123–125.

48. Ellen D. Larned, *History of Windham County, Connecticut* (Worcester, 1874–1880), II, 402–403, 438; Pease and Niles, pp. 16–17, 213, 217, 219, 224, 226; Purcell, pp. 125–128.

49. *Courant*, May 18, 1813; Purcell, pp. 128–131.

50. Pease and Niles, p. 14; Purcell, pp. 130–131, 138; U. S. Census Office, *Census for 1820* (Wash., 1821), no pagination.

51. Purcell, pp. 131–133.

52. *American Mercury*, Jan. 21, 1817; March 10; Nov. 3, 10, 17; Dec. 1, 1818; James L. Bishop, *A History of American Manufactures from 1608 to 1860 . . .* (Phila., 1866), II, 212–213; *Courant*, Feb. 25, 1817; *The Public Statute Laws of the State of Connecticut, 1817*, Chap. xi, p. 287; Purcell, pp. 133–137.

53. Purcell, pp. 98–108; Patrick H. Woodward, *One Hundred Years of the Hartford Bank . . .* (Hartford, 1892), pp. 12–21.

54. Purcell, pp. 108–111.

55. Charles H. Levermore, *The Town and City Government of New Haven*, Johns Hopkins Univ. Stud. in Hist. and Pol. Sci., 4th Ser., x (Baltimore, 1886), p. 24; Osterweis, p. 201; Thomas R. Trowbridge, "History of the Ancient Maritime Interests of New Haven," *N.H.C.H.S. Papers*, III (New Haven, 1882), 146–163.

56. *Courant*, Dec. 30, 1807; Jan. 6, 13, 20; March 16, 23, 30; April 6, 27; May 4, 11; Aug. 31, 1808; Osterweis, pp. 201–202; Purcell, pp. 115–118, 118n; Trowbridge, 163–169.

57. *American Mercury*, Feb. 27; March 5, 1816; *D.A.B.*, XX, 443–445; Franklin B. Dexter, *Biographical Sketches of the Graduates of Yale College . . .* (New York, 1885–1912), IV, 82–86; Purcell, pp. 332–338; Stamps, pp. 226–227.

58. *American Mercury*, Feb. 20, 1816; Greene, *Development*, pp. 461–463; Purcell, pp. 299–330; Stamps, pp. 155–161. The conservative philosophy of Governor Smith is vividly revealed in his letters which have been published in *C.H.S.C.*, XXV–XXIX (Hartford, 1948–57).

59. *American Mercury*, March 4, 11, 18, 25; April 1, 8, 15, 1817; *Courant*, Nov. 5, 1816; May 13, 1817; Greene, *Development*, pp. 467–472, 467n; *Public Statute Laws, 1816*, Chap. xiii, pp. 279–280; Purcell, pp. 344–346; Stamps, pp. 236–245.

60. Purcell, pp. 371–377; Stamps, pp. 252–254.

61. Purcell, pp. 377–406.

62. Jarvis M. Morse, *A Neglected Period of Connecticut's History, 1818–1850*, Yale Hist. Pubs., Misc., XXV (New Haven, 1933), p. 3; Purcell, pp. 380–407.

63. *American Mercury*, Oct. 13, 1818; *Courant*, Oct. 13, 1818; Purcell, pp. 408–413; Thomas Robbins, *Diary of Thomas Robbins, D.D., 1796–1854*, ed. Increase N. Tarbox (Boston, 1886–87), I, 759; Stamps, pp. 284–287.

64. Purcell, pp. 415–416; Stamps, pp. 300–301, 310.

11 Migrating Yankees

1. Julian P. Boyd, *The Susquehannah Company: Connecticut's Experiment in Expansion*, Conn. Ter. Comm. Pubs., No. 34 (New Haven, 1935), p. 8; *C.R.*, x, 56; XIV, 490–492; Robert C. Gilmore, "Connecticut and the Foundation of Vermont," unpub. diss. (Yale Univ., 1953), pp. 27–28; Evarts B. Greene and Virginia D. Harrington, *American Population Before the Federal Census of 1790* (New York, 1932), pp. 49–50; Albert L. Olson, *Agricultural Economy and the Population in Eighteenth-Century Connecticut*, Conn. Ter. Comm. Pubs., No. 40 (New Haven, 1935), pp. 8, 18–22. Estimates of 1730 population range up to 60,000.

2. Boyd, *Susquehannah*, pp. 1–48; *C.H.S. Bull.*, VII (April 1941), 17–19; Lois K. Mathews Rosenberry, *Migrations from Connecticut Prior to 1800*, Conn.

Ter. Comm. Pubs., No. 28 (New Haven, 1934), pp. 12–15.

3. Clarence W. Alvord, *The Mississippi Valley in British Politics* (Cleveland, Ohio, 1917), II, 172–177; Franklin B. Dexter, *Biographical Sketches of the Graduates of Yale College . . .* (New York, 1885–1912), I, 605–606; Matthew Phelps, *Memoirs and Adventures of Captain Matthew Phelps . . .* (Bennington, Vt., 1802), App., p. 46; *The Two Putnams, Israel and Rufus, in the Havana Expedition . . .* (Hartford, 1931), pp. 9–46, 143–262.

4. Ellis M. Coulter, *A Short History of Georgia* (Chapel Hill, 1933), pp. 90, 112, 114, 120, 148, 156, 267; Dexter, *Yale*, II, 116–117; III, 432–433; *D.A.B.*, I, 530–532; VIII, 139–140; Rosenberry, *Migrations*, pp. 7, 18–19.

5. John B. Brebner, *The Neutral Yankees of Nova Scotia* (New York, 1937), pp. vii, 29, 31, 58–59, 93, 117; Frances M. Caulkins, *History of Norwich, Connecticut . . .* (Hartford, 1874), p. 310.

6. Joseph E. A. Smith, *The History of Pittsfield, (Berkshire County,) Massachusetts . . .* (Boston, 1869–76), I, 55–89. The landed proprietors of Pittsfield were Massachusetts men, but most of the actual settlers came from Connecticut.

7. Smith, *Pittsfield*, I, 102–118.

8. "Cooke Collection, Pittsfield," I, Church Records, 283–285, Berkshire Atheneum, Pittsfield; David D. Field, *A History of the Town of Pittsfield . . .* (Hartford, 1844), pp. 10–11; Smith, *Pittsfield*, I, 92–93, 151–156, 163–165; "William Williams Collection, Pittsfield," III, 331–334, Berkshire Atheneum.

9. Field, *Pittsfield*, p. 11; Lee N. Newcomer, *The Embattled Farmers . . .* (New York, 1953), p. 8; Smith, *Pittsfield*, I, 136; "William Williams Collection," II, 260–261; III, 337, 346.

10. Smith, *Pittsfield*, I, 212–321.

11. Robert R. R. Brooks, ed. *Williamstown, the First Two Hundred Years, 1753–1953* (Williamstown, Mass., 1953), pp. 2–9, 17; David D. Field, *A History of the County of Berkshire, Massachusetts* (Pittsfield, Mass., 1829), pp. 401–407.

12. Brooks, p. 23; Dexter, *Yale*, II, 774–775; III, 677–679; Field, *Hist. of Berkshire County*, p. 167.

13. John Warner Barber, *Massachusetts Historical Collections . . . Relating to History and Antiquities of Every Town in Massachusetts . . .* (Worcester, Mass., 1839), pp. 65–66, 73, 75, 83–85, 88–90, 101–102, 109; "Cooke Collection, Lenox Church Records," pp. 368–371; Field, *Hist. of Berkshire County*, 337–339, 350, 395, 418–419; Charles M. Hyde, *Lee: The Centennial Celebration, and Centennial History of the Town of Lee, Mass.* (Springfield, Mass., 1878), pp. 124–136; Charles J. Palmer, *History of Town of Lanesborough, Massachusetts, 1741–1905* (n.p., [1905]), pp. 11–12; Lois K. Mathews Rosenberry, *The Expansion of New England* (Boston, 1909), pp. 79–80.

14. Barber, *Mass. Hist. Colls.*, pp. 69, 75–77, 83–84, 98–100; Richard D. Birdsall, *Berkshire County, a Cultural History* (New Haven, 1959), pp. 21, 33; Dexter, *Yale*, I, 670–671; III, 306–307; Field, *Hist. of Berkshire County*, p. 454; Rollin G. Osterweis, *Three Centuries of New Haven, 1638–1938* (New Haven, 1953), p. 152; Palmer, *Hist. of Lanesborough*, pp. 12–13; Sarah C. Sedgwick and Christina S. Marquand, *Stockbridge, 1739–1939, A Chronicle* ([Great Barrington], 1939), pp. 110–112; Charles J. Taylor, *History of Great Barrington (Berkshire), Massachusetts . . .* (Great Barrington, 1928), pp. 76–81.

15. "Cooke Collection, Great Barrington"; Joseph Hooper, "The Protestant Episcopal Church in Berkshire," *Berkshire Historical and Scientific Soc., Colls.*, No. 3 (Pittsfield, 1890), pp. 187–212; Taylor, *Great Barrington*, pp. 178–179.

16. "Berkshire Men of Worth," *Berkshire Evening Eagle*, June 2, 1937.

17. Smith, *Pittsfield*, I, 12.

18. Rising L. Morrow, *Connecticut Influences in Western Massachusetts and Vermont*, Conn. Terc. Comm. Pubs., No. 58 (New Haven, 1936), pp. 12–13; Rosenberry, *Expansion of N.E.*, pp. 263–264.

19. Birdsall, pp. 4–9.

20. Gilmore, pp. 38, 42–44; Arthur W. Peach, ed. "John Clarke's Journal (1824–1842)," *Proc. of Vermont Hist. Soc.*, X (Dec. 1942), 188; Lewis D. Stilwell, *Migration from Vermont* (Montpelier, 1948), p. 77.

21. Gilmore, pp. 120–121; William H. Tucker, *The History of Hartford, Vermont* (Burlington, 1889), p. 30.

22. Stilwell, p. 75.

23. John M. Comstock, *The Congregational Churches of Vermont and Their Ministry, 1762–1942* (St. Johnsbury, Vt., 1942), p. 9; Timothy Dwight, *Travels; in New-England and New-York* (New Haven, 1821–22), II, 387–388; Stewart H. Holbrook, *Ethan Allen* (New York, 1940), pp. 225–237; John Pell, *Ethan Allen* (Boston, 1929), pp. 252–254; Nathan Perkins, *A Narrative of a Tour Through the State of Vermont . . .* (Woodstock, Vt., 1930), pp. 24, 26; Stilwell, pp. 75–76.

24. "Hartford Records, Deeds," Vol. A, "1765–1781," microfilm at Montpelier; Tucker, *Hartford*, pp. 1–8, 30–39, 205–209, 242, 278.

25. Walter H. Crockett, *Vermont, the Green Mountain State* (New York, 1921–23), I, 214–218; "Norwich Town and Vital Records," I, "1761–1793," Aug. 26, 1761; March 9, 1779, microfilm at Montpelier.

26. Walter J. Bigelow, *History of Stowe, Vermont . . .* ([Hartford], 1934), pp. 14–16; Austin J. Coolidge and John B. Mansfield, *A History and Description of New England* (Boston, 1859), pp. 405–703, *passim*; Crockett, *Vermont*, I, 214, 217–218, 221–222, 226, 237; Charles A. Downs, *History of Lebanon, N.H., 1761–1887* (Concord, N.H., 1908), pp. 2–8; John Gregory, *Centennial Proceedings and Historical Incidents of the Early Settlers of Northfield, Vt. . . .* (Montpelier, 1878), pp. 58–139, *passim*; Ralph N. Hill, *Contrary Country* (New York, 1950), pp. 39–43; James R. Jackson, *History of Littleton, New Hampshire . . .* (Cambridge, Mass., 1905), I, 166, 173–176; Theodore G. Lewis, ed. *History of Waterbury, Vermont, 1763–1915* (Waterbury, Vt., 1915), pp. 4–8, 12; *The Records of the Town of Hanover, New Hampshire, 1761–1818* (Hanover, N.H., 1905), pp. iii–v, 1–3; *Report of the Celebration of the One Hundred and Fiftieth Anniversary of the Settlement of the Town of Orford, N.H.* (Hanover, N.H., 1915), pp. 19–21; Rosenberry, *Expansion of N.E.*, pp. 112, 115–116, 143; Jeanette R. Thompson, *History of the Town of Stratford, New Hampshire, 1773–1925* (Concord, N.H., 1925), p. 31; Henry H. Vail, *Pomfret, Vermont* (Boston, 1930), I, 1–14, 32, 135; Otis F. R. Waite, *History of the Town of Claremont, New Hampshire* (Manchester, N.H., 1895), pp. 26–27, 41–43.

27. Gilmore, pp. 53–54; Matt B. Jones, *Vermont in the Making, 1750–1777* (Cambridge, Mass., 1939), p. 77; "Middlebury Charter," Town Clerk's office, Middlebury; Samuel Swift, *History of the Town of Middlebury . . .* (Middlebury, Vt., 1859), pp. 142–146.

28. "Middlebury Town Records, Deeds," I, "1788–1820," microfilm at Montpelier; Swift, pp. 147–148, 167, 174, 180–181, 190–222.

29. Rosenberry, *Migrations*, p. 11; George A. Russell, "Historical Sketches Relating to Arlington" (Arlington, Vt., 1943), typed MS. at Vermont Hist. Soc., Montpelier.

30. Morse S. Allen, "A Vermont Sketchbook," *Vermont History*, XXII (Oct. 1954), 273–278; Agnes B. Billings, "Ripton – The Derivation of the Name," *Vermont History*, XXII (Oct. 1954), 305; Abiel M. Caverly, *History of the Town of Pittsford* . . . (Rutland, Vt., 1872), pp. 32–35, 38, 40, 49–50; *Courant*, March 4, 11, 1765; Hiel Hollister, *Pawlet for One Hundred Years* (Albany, N.Y., 1867), pp. 156–267; Zephine Humphrey, *The Story of Dorset* (Rutland, Vt., 1924), pp. 27, 33, 35; Lyman Matthews, *History of the Town of Cornwall, Vermont* (Middlebury, Vt., 1862), pp. 32, 45–113; Morrow, pp. 13–14; Rosenberry, *Expansion of N.E.*, pp. 115–116, 142–143; Rosenberry, *Migrations*, p. 11; H. Perry Smith and William S. Rann, *History of Rutland County Vermont* . . . (Syracuse, 1886), pp. 516–523; Walter Thorpe, *History of Wallingford, Vermont* (Rutland, Vt., [1911]), pp. 17, 23–25, 43; Williston, Vermont, Hist. Comm., *A History of the Town of Williston* (n.p., n.d.), pp. 35–44; Grace E. P. Wood, *A History of the Town of Wells, Vermont* . . . (Wells, 1955), pp. 5–6, 38–82.

31. "Ethan Allen to Oliver Wolcott, Sr., Mar. 1, 1775," Oliver Wolcott MSS., Vol. I, C.H.S.; Holbrook, *Ethan Allen*, pp. 63–74; Jones, *Vermont*, pp. 341–342, 372–374; James B. Wilbur, *Ira Allen* . . . (Boston, 1928), I, 75–98.

32. Jones, *Vermont*, pp. 356–384; Eliakim P. Walton, ed. *Records of the Council of Safety and Governor and Council of the State of Vermont* . . . (Montpelier, 1873), I, 40–41, 54–55.

33. Gilmore, pp. 64–65, 88, 92–93; Jones, *Vermont*, pp. 389–393; Walton, pp. 96–97.

34. *C.R.*, I, 77–78, 515; Walter H. Crockett, ed. *State Papers of Vermont* (Bellows Falls, Vt., 1924), III, Pt. 1, 17; Gilmore, pp. 93, 95–97, 101–103; Benjamin H. Hall, *History of Eastern Vermont* . . . (New York, 1858), pp. 573–574; Jones, *Vermont*, p. 391; William Slade, comp. *Vermont State Papers* . . . (Middlebury, Vt., 1823), pp. 267, 291–294, 298–300, 305–312, 354–355, 375; Walton, I, 83–103.

35. Crockett, *Vermont*, I, 260–261; Gilmore, pp. 128–129, 132–135; Morrow, p. 21.

36. Gilmore, pp. 1, 92n; Morrow, p. 21.

37. Franklin L. Pope, *Western Boundary of Massachusetts*, Berkshire Hist. and Sci. Soc., Colls., No. 1 (Pittsfield, Mass., 1886), p. 71; Rosenberry, *Expansion of N.E.*, pp. 95–96.

38. Stewart H. Holbrook, *The Yankee Exodus* . . . (New York, 1950), pp. 15–16, 299–300; Pomroy Jones, *Annals and Recollections of Oneida County* (Rome, N.Y., 1851), pp. 237–238; Rosenberry, *Expansion of N.E.*, pp. 153–155, 158–160.

39. Dixon R. Fox, *Yankees and Yorkers* (New York, 1940), p. 221; Charles R. Keller, *The Second Great Awakening in Connecticut*, Yale Hist. Pubs., Misc., XL (New Haven, 1942), p. 77.

40. *D.A.B.*, V, 12–14; Holbrook, *Yankee Exodus*, pp. 20–21; Merrill Jensen, *The New Nation* . . . (New York, 1950), pp. 355–356.

41. Cornelius E. Dickinson, *The First Church Organization in the Oldest Settlement in the Northwest Territory*, Ohio Arch. and Hist. Pubs., II (Columbus, 1889), pp. 291–308; Cornelius E. Dickinson, *A History of the First Congregational Church of Marietta, Ohio* (n.p., 1896), pp. 12–13, 17, 25, 118–122, 164; Holbrook, *Yankee Exodus*, pp. 22–24; Rosenberry, *Expansion of N.E.*, pp. 175–176; Thomas J. Summers, *History of Marietta* (Marietta, Ohio, 1903), pp. 43–51.

42. Harlan H. Hatcher, *The Western Reserve* . . . (Indianapolis, 1949), pp. 20–21; *S.R.*, VI, 171–172.

43. Hatcher, pp. 24–25; *S.R.*, VIII, xiii–xvii, 237–239, 237n, 238n.

44. Hatcher, pp. 22–26, 37–39.

45. Hatcher, pp. 52–61; *S.R.*, VII, xi–xii, 448–472; William W. Williams, *History of the Fire Lands, Comprising Huron and Erie Counties, Ohio* . . . (Cleveland, Ohio, 1879), pp. 10–25.

46. Hatcher, pp. 71–73; Holbrook, *Yankee Exodus*, pp. 34–35; Richard J. Purcell, *Connecticut in Transition, 1775–1818* (Wash., 1918), pp. 144–150.

47. Holbrook, *Yankee Exodus*, pp. 34, 37; Purcell, pp. 151–152, 151n, 353–355; *R and M, 1956*, pp. 276–281; Rosenberry, *Expansion of N.E.*, p. 181.

48. *D.A.B.*, IX, 419–420; Holbrook, *Yankee Exodus*, pp. 32–33, 36–37; Rosenberry, *Expansion of N.E.*, pp. 178–180.

49. Rosenberry, *Expansion of N.E.*, pp. 189–190.

50. Hatcher, pp. 13–16.

51. Holbrook, *Yankee Exodus*, pp. 62, 64; Rosenberry, *Migrations*, pp. 201–202.

52. Howard A. Bridgman, *New England in the Life of the World* (Boston, [1920]), pp. 100–103; Holbrook, *Yankee Exodus*, pp. 64–65, 68–70; Rosenberry, *Migrations*, pp. 206–207.

53. Holbrook, *Yankee Exodus*, pp. 87–89, 92; Rosenberry, *Expansion of N.E.*, pp. 227, 231–233.

54. Bridgman, pp. 85–86, 119–120; Holbrook, *Yankee Exodus*, pp. 117, 120, 180; Rosenberry, *Expansion of N.E.*, pp. 238–239, 239n, 244–245.

55. Eugene C. Barker, *The Life of Stephen F. Austin* . . . (Nashville, 1926), pp. 3–31; *D.A.B.*, I, 435–437; Holbrook, *Yankee Exodus*, pp. 279–280.

56. Bridgman, pp. 126, 129, 141–144, 150–155, 159, 172–173; Holbrook, *Yankee Exodus*, pp. 192, 200.

57. *D.A.B.*, III, 131–133; Allan Nevins, *Ordeal of the Union* (New York, 1947), II, 472–476; Oswald G. Villard, *John Brown, 1800–1859* . . . (Boston, 1910), pp. 23–170.

58. Holbrook, *Yankee Exodus*, pp. 212, 221.

59. Bridgman, pp. 192–193; *D.A.B.*, IX, 408–412; Holbrook, *Yankee Exodus*, pp. 152, 155, 158; Fred A. Shannon, *Economic History of the People of the United States* (New York, 1934), p. 427.

60. Charles M. Andrews, "On Some Early Aspects of Connecticut History," *New England Quarterly*, XVII (March 1944), 22–24.

12 Under the New Constitution, 1818–1850

1. Jarvis M. Morse, *A Neglected Period of Connecticut's History, 1818–1850*, Yale Hist. Pubs., Misc., xxv (New Haven, 1933), p. 2.
2. *Ibid.*, pp. 31–32, 37.
3. *Ibid.*, pp. 33–35, 39–42, 48–50.
4. *Ibid.*, pp. 52, 54–59, 64, 71.
5. Morse, *Neglected Period*, pp. 72–74; Thomas Robbins, *Diary of Thomas Robbins, D.D., 1796–1854*, ed. Increase Tarbox (Boston, 1886–87), I, 995.
6. Morse, *Neglected Period*, pp. 75–77.
7. Morse, *Neglected Period*, pp. 77–79; Patrick H. Woodward, *One Hundred Years of the Hartford Bank* . . . (Hartford, 1892), pp. 129–130.
8. *Courant*, May 22, 1826; Morse, *Neglected Period*, pp. 79–80; *Public Statute Laws of the State of Connecticut, 1826*, Chap. xv, p. 101.
9. *Courant*, May 29, June 5, 12, 1826; April 23, 1827; Morse, *Neglected Period*, pp. 80–83.
10. Morse, *Neglected Period*, pp. 85–88.
11. *Courant*, May 7, 21, 28, June 4, 1827; July 8, Sept. 16, Oct. 14, 28, Nov. 25, 1828; Morse, *Neglected Period*, pp. 88–96.
12. *Courant*, Nov. 18, 1828; Nov. 23, 30, 1830; Charles McCarthy, "The Anti-Masonic Party . . . ," *Amer. Hist. Assoc., Annual Report, 1902*, I (Wash., 1903), 554–555; Morse, *Neglected Period*, pp. 96–99, 102–103, 106–108.
13. *Hartford Times*, Feb. 4, 1833; Morse, *Neglected Period*, pp. 115–118.
14. Morse, *Neglected Period*, p. 175.
15. Carl R. Fish, *The Rise of the Common Man*, A Hist. of Amer. Life Ser., VI (New York, 1927), pp. 291–312; Morse, *Neglected Period*, p. 176.
16. [American School for the Deaf], *The American School for the Deaf* ([Hartford, 1947]), pp. [3–24]; *D.A.B.*, VII, 111; *The History of the First School for Deaf Mutes of America* . . . (South Weymouth, Mass., 1883), pp. 5–6, 9–11.
17. *C.R.*, IV, 285–286; VII, 128–129; George L. Clark, *A History of Connecticut, its People and Institutions*, rev. ed. (New York, 1914), pp. 461–463, 467; Norris G. Osborn, ed. *History of Connecticut, in Monographic Form* (New York, 1925), V, 404–408; *S.R.*, VIII, 87–88; IX, 90–91.
18. *D.A.B.*, XVIII, 570–571; Leonard K. Eaton, "Eli Todd and the Hartford Retreat," *New England Quarterly*, XXVI (Dec. 1953), 435–441, 452–453; Morse, *Neglected Period*, p. 178.
19. Conn. Governor, comp. *List of Insane Poor Persons Who Have Received Aid from the State, During the Past Year* (Hartford, 1847), pp. 3, 6–12; Morse, *Neglected Period*, pp. 179–181; *Public Acts, 1866*, Chap. xxxvii, p. 21.
20. Edward W. Capen, *The Historical Development of the Poor Law of Connecticut*, Col. Univ. Stud. in Hist., Econ. and Public Law, XXII (New York, 1905), pp. 231–238; Morse, *Neglected Period*, pp. 181–183.
21. Richard H. Phelps, *Newgate of Connecticut; its Origin and Early History* . . . (Hartford, 1876), pp. 58–60; "Public Records of the State of Connecticut, May, 1826," p. 177, Conn. St. Lib., Hartford.
22. Morse, *Neglected Period*, pp. 185–186.
23. Morse, *Neglected Period*, pp. 190–191; *Statutes of Conn.*, compilation of 1854 (New Haven, 1854), Title VII, Chap. 1, pp. 374–378.

24. Catherine E. Beecher, *Educational Reminiscences and Suggestions* (New York, 1874), pp. 30–50; Charles Beecher, ed. *Autobiography, Correspondence, etc., of Lyman Beecher, D.D.* (New York, 1846–65), I, 507–508, 516; *D.A.B.*, II, 125–126; xx, 231–233; Morse, *Neglected Period*, pp. 186–190.
25. Leonard W. Bacon, *Anti-Slavery Before Garrison*, Conn. Soc. of the Order of the Founders and Patriots of Amer., Pubs., No. 7 (New Haven, 1903), pp. 8–9, 26; Theodore D. Bacon, *Leonard Bacon, a Statesman in the Church*, ed. Benjamin W. Bacon (New Haven, 1931), pp. 182–194; *D.A.B.*, I, 479–481; Franklin B. Dexter, *Biographical Sketches of the Graduates of Yale College* . . . (New York, 1885–1912), II, 656–658; Levi Hart, *Liberty Described and Recommended; in a SERMON, Preached to the Corporation of Freemen in Farmington* . . . (Hartford, 1775), pp. 7–22.
26. Morse, *Neglected Period*, pp. 193–194.
27. *D.A.B.*, IV, 503–504; William Jay, *An Inquiry into the Character and Tendency of the American Colonization, and American Anti-Slavery Societies*, 3d ed. (New York, 1835), pp. 30–31; Edwin W. and Miriam R. Small, "Prudence Crandall, Champion of Negro Education," *New England Quarterly*, XVII (Dec. 1944), 506–510.
28. Jay, pp. 31–32; Small and Small, pp. 511–517.
29. *Courant*, Sept. 2, 9, 1833; Jay, pp. 35–37; *The Liberator*, July 6, 13, 20, Aug. 3, Oct. 26, 1833; *Public Statute Laws, 1833*, Chap. ix, pp. 425–427; Small and Small, pp. 517–523.
30. "Connecticut Superior Court for Windham County. Records, 1798–1883," III, 484–485, Conn. St. Lib., Hartford; Jay, pp. 38–47; *The Liberator*, Sept. 13, 20, 27, 1834; *Report of Cases Argued and Determined in the Supreme Court of Errors of the State of Connecticut* . . . Thomas Day, court reporter, X (Hartford, 1836), 339–372; *Report of the Arguments of Counsel, in the Case of Prudence Crandall, plff. in Error, vs. State of Connecticut, before the Supreme Court of Errors at Brooklyn, July term, 1834*; by a member of the Bar (Boston, 1834), pp. 5–34.
31. Ellen D. Larned, *History of Windham County, Connecticut* (Worcester, 1874–1880), II, 500–502.
32. Small and Small, pp. 527–528; *Special Acts and Resolutions of the State of Connecticut . . . , 1885–1889* (Hartford, 1890), x, 355–356.
33. Simeon E. Baldwin, "The Captives of the Amistad," *N.H.C.H.S. Papers*, IV, 331–365; John Warner Barber, *A History of the Amistad Captives* . . . (New Haven, 1840), pp. 3–24; Fred J. Cook, "The Slave Ship Rebellion," *American Heritage*, VIII (Feb. 1957), 63, 104–106; *Public Acts, 1848*, Chap. lxxix, pp. 70–71.
34. Beecher, *Autobiography*, II, 34–38; *Connecticut Observer*, Jan. 16, 23, 30; Feb. 6, 13, 20, 27; March 6, 13, 20, 27; April 3, 10, 17, 24; May 1, 8, 15, 22, 29; June 5, 12, 19, 26; July 3, 10, 17, 24, 31; Aug. 7, 14, 21, 1826; Joel Hawes, *A Sermon Occasioned by the Death of Calvin Chapin* . . . (Hartford, 1851), p. 33; Morse, *Neglected Period*, pp. 204–209; James H. Trumbull, *The Memorial History of Hartford County, Connecticut, 1633–1884* (Boston, 1886), I, 211.
35. Conn. Temperance Society, Executive Committee, *First Annual Report, May 19, 1830* (Middletown, 1830), pp. 5–12; Duane H. Hurd, ed. *History of New*

London County, Connecticut . . . (Phila., 1882), p. 310; Morse, *Neglected Period*, pp. 208–216; Carroll J. Noonan, *Nativism in Connecticut, 1829–1860* . . . (Wash., 1938), p. 144; *Public Acts, 1854*, Chap. lvii, pp. 54–75.

36. Morse, *Neglected Period*, pp. 286–289.

37. Morse, *Neglected Period*, pp. 266, 289–298; "Governor John S. Peters to L. D. Jacobs, Feb. 22, 1832," John S. Peters Papers; Deeds, Letters, Diaries, Accounts of Travel, etc., 1766–1859, No. 30, Conn. St. Lib., Hartford.

38. Morse, *Neglected Period*, pp. 299–304.

39. *Courant*, May 8, 1841; *D.A.B.*, VI, 115–116; Morse, *Neglected Period*, pp. 304–310.

40. Morse, *Neglected Period*, pp. 310–316.

41. Morse, *Neglected Period*, pp. 317–323; Noonan, pp. 117–118, 127–128, 131; Robbins, II, 757.

42. Forrest Morgan et al., eds. *Connecticut as a Colony and as a State, or One of the Original Thirteen* (Hartford, 1904), III, 188–191; *New Haven Daily Morning Courier*, Dec. 7, 1844; R. H. Potter, Jr., Chief, War Records Dept., Conn. St. Lib., gives as Army figures, 53 officers and 635 enlisted men, and states that no separate state rosters are available for Navy and Marine Corps personnel.

43. *Connecticut Courant*, Nov. 23, 1844; *Hartford Courant*, Nov. 11, 13, 1844; Morse, *Neglected Period*, pp. 324–332; Noonan, pp. 119–121, 130–135; *Public Acts, 1846*, Chap. xx, p. 20; *Public Acts, 1847*, Chap. xxix, p. 28.

44. *D.A.B.*, I, 537; Morse, *Neglected Period*, pp. 332–335.

13   The Civil War Era, 1850–1865

1. Thomas A. Bailey, *The American Pageant* . . . (Boston, 1956), pp. 377–382; Jarlath R. Lane, *A Political History of Connecticut during the Civil War* . . . (Wash., 1941), pp. 1–2, 10–11; Allan Nevins, *Ordeal of the Union* (New York, 1947), I, 380–390; *The Republican*, Jan. 11, 1849.

2. Bailey, *American*, pp. 383–384; *Middletown Sentinel and Witness*, Oct. 29, 1850; *Public Acts, 1854*, Chap. lxv, pp. 80–81; Wilbur H. Siebert, "The Underground Railroad in Massachusetts," *Amer. Antiq. Soc. Proc.*, XLV (April 1935), 25–26; Bernard C. Steiner, *History of Slavery in Connecticut*, Johns Hopkins Univ. Stud. in Hist. and Pol. Sci., 11th Ser., Nos. 9–10 (Baltimore, 1893), pp. 35–37; Horatio T. Strother, "The Underground Railroad in Connecticut from 1830 to 1850," unpub. M.A. thesis (Univ. of Conn., 1957), pp. 15–31, 33–35, App. A.

3. Lane, pp. 3–8.

4. Lane, pp. 14–29; Carroll J. Noonan, *Nativism in Connecticut, 1829–1860* . . . (Wash., 1938), pp. 150–160.

5. Nevins, *Ordeal*, II, 94–100, 144, 316–318, 322–323.

6. Lane, pp. 31–43; Noonan, pp. 181–184; *Public Acts, 1854*, Chap. lvii, pp. 54–75.

7. [American Party. Connecticut], *Constitution of the S[tate] C[ouncil] of the State of Connecticut* (Hartford, 1854), p. 3; Gladys T. Franklin, "The Know Nothing Party in Connecticut," unpub. M.A. thesis (Clark Univ., 1933), pp. 19–24; *Hartford Times*, Feb. 20, 1855; Lane, pp. 45–50; Noonan, pp. 188–209.

8. *Hartford Times*, May 3, 1855; Lane, pp. 50–51; Noonan, pp. 210–220; *Public Acts, 1855*, Chap. lvii, pp. 71–72; *Public Statute Laws, 1854*, Chap. ix, pp. 196–202.

9. *Courant*, March 4, 1856; *Hartford Times*, April 5, 1856; Lane, pp. 52–65; Noonan, pp. 223–246.

10. Lane, pp. 65, 76–78; Noonan, pp. 246–248.

11. *The Connecticut Register* . . . *1857* (Hartford, [1857]), p. 117; Lane, pp. 68–89; Noonan, pp. 279–303.

12. *Conn. Register, 1859*, p. 18; Lane, pp. 91–107; Noonan, pp. 305–321.

13. Lane, p. 117; William J. Niven, Jr., "The Time of the Whirlwind, A Study in the Political, Social and Economic History of Connecticut from 1861 to 1875," unpub. diss. (Col. Univ., 1954), p. 5; James H. Trumbull, *The Memorial History of Hartford County, Connecticut, 1633–1884* (Boston, 1886), I, 131.

14. Lane, pp. 112–116.

15. *Courant*, March 6, 7, 9, 10, 23, 24, 25, 27, 28, 1860; Lane, pp. 117–120.

16. *Courant*, April 23, 1860; *Hartford Times*, April 21, 1860; Lane, pp. 120–122.

17. *Conn. Register, 1861*, p. 127; *Courant*, Nov. 24, 1860; Lane, pp. 135–140; Noonan, pp. 331–334.

18. *Courant*, April 13, 15, 20, 1861; William A. Croffut and John M. Morris, *The Military and Civil History of Connecticut during the War of 1861–65* . . . , rev. ed. (New York, 1868), pp. 39–40; *Hartford Times*, April 15, 1861; Lane, pp. 168–169; Kenneth M. Stampp, *And the War Came* . . . (Baton Rouge, 1950), pp. 291–294; Trumbull, *Hartford County*, I, 89.

19. *Courant*, April 15, 20, 22, 27, May 1, 4, 1861; Lane, pp. 169–170.

20. Croffut and Morris, pp. 57–60; Lane, pp. 170–173.

21. *Courant*, April 20, May 4, 1861; Croffut and Morris, pp. 77–79, 103–104; *Hartford Times*, April 15, 16, June 27, 1861; Lane, pp. 175–176.

22. *Courant*, May 11, 20, 21, 1861; Croffut and Morris, pp. 60–69, 83.

23. Croffut and Morris, pp. 87–100.

24. Croffut and Morris, pp. 104–106; Lane, pp. 177–180.

25. Croffut and Morris, pp. 106–110, 109n; Lane, pp. 180–181; "Official Proclamations of the Governors of Connecticut," V, "1861–1900," 4A, Conn. St. Lib., Hartford.

26. Croffut and Morris, pp. 111–116; *Hartford Daily Post*, July 23, Aug. 14, 15, 1861; Ashbel Woodward, *Life of General Nathaniel Lyon* (Hartford, 1862), pp. 243–320, 342–347.

27. Niven, pp. 81–82.

28. Felicia J. Deyrup, *Arms Makers of the Connecticut Valley* . . . , Smith College Stud. in Hist., XXXIII (Northampton, 1948), p. 182; Charles T. Haven and Frank A. Belden, *A History of the Colt Revolver* . . . (New York, 1940), pp. 86–93, 352–361; Trumbull, *Hartford County*, I, 565–566, 569.

29. Deyrup, p. 183; Harold F. Williamson, *Winchester, the Gun that Won the West* (Wash., 1952), pp. 32–35.

30. *Norwich Courier*, May 9, 1861; Norris G. Osborn, ed. *History of Connecticut, in Monographic Form* (New York, 1925), IV, 178–179; Trumbull, *Hartford County*, I, 210; II, 75, 98, 158, 161.

31. James L. Bishop, *A History of American Manufactures from 1608 to 1860* . . . (Phila., 1866), II, 506;

Victor S. Clark, *History of Manufactures* . . . (New York, 1929), I, 524; II, 17, 20; William T. Davis, ed. *The New England States* . . . (Boston, [1897]), II, 1052–53; *The Great Industries of the United States* . . . (Hartford, 1874), p. 124; Charles R. Harte, *Connecticut's Iron and Copper*, repr. from Conn. Soc. Civil Eng., Inc., Annual Report, No. 60, 1944, pp. 142–143; "Charles Jeremy Hoadly to (recipient unknown)," Oct. 4, 1861," Conn. St. Lib., Hartford; *Norwich Courier*, Sept. 11, 1862; Chard Powers Smith, *The Housatonic, Puritan River* (New York, 1946), p. 364; Trumbull, *Hartford County*, II, 75–76.

32. Clark, *Hist. of Manufactures*, II, 113; Forrest Morgan et al., eds. *Connecticut as a Colony and as a State, or One of the Original Thirteen* (Hartford, 1904), III, 219–225, 231–234; Richard J. Purcell, *Connecticut in Transition, 1775–1818* (Wash., 1918), pp. 125–128; Frank W. Taussig, *The Tariff History of the United States*, 8th ed. (New York, 1931), pp. 197–198; U.S. Census Office. *Manufactures of the United States in 1860; . . . The Eighth Census* . . . (Wash., 1865), pp. xvi–xvii, xxi, xxiii, xxxv, 37–52.

33. *Courant*, May 29, 1863; Niven, pp. 104–108; *Norwich Courier*, June 4, 1861; *Public Acts, 1864*, Chap. xxvi, pp. 40–42.

34. Clark, *Hist. of Manufactures*, II, 29–30; Davis, *New England*, I, 163–165; II, 1008, 1028; Duane H. Hurd, ed. *History of New London County, Connecticut* . . . (Phila., 1882), p. 361; *Manufactures, Eighth Census*, p. xcv; Osborn, IV, 248–253.

35. Clark, *Hist. of Manufactures*, II, 30; Hurd, p. 238; *Manufactures, Eighth Census*, p. xxxiv; Henry J. Raymond, *The Life and Public Services of Abraham Lincoln* . . . (New York, 1865), pp. 523–524; Taussig, p. 198.

36. Conn. General Assembly. House, *Journal . . . May Session, 1861* (Hartford, 1861), pp. 102, 232–234.

37. Carl C. Cutler, *Mystic, The Story of a Small New England Seaport*, Marine Hist. Assoc. Pub., No. 17 (Mystic, 1945), pp. 11, 13–15, 18; Hurd, p. 692.

38. Cutler, pp. 19–23; Thomas A. Stevens and Charles K. Stillman, *George Greenman & Company, Shipbuilders of Mystic, Connecticut* . . . , Marine Hist. Assoc. Pub., No. 13 (Mystic, 1953), pp. 6–18.

39. Cutler, pp. 25–26; Hurd, p. 692; Stevens and Stillman, pp. 19–21.

40. Edward E. Atwater, ed. *History of the City of New Haven* . . . (New York, 1887), p. 71; Pliny L. Harwood, *History of Eastern Connecticut* . . . (Chicago, 1932), II, 472, 483.

41. *Courant*, July 7, 1862; Croffut and Morris, pp. 222–225; Charles D. Page, *History of the Fourteenth Regiment, Connecticut Vol. Infantry* (Meriden, 1906), pp. 13–17.

42. Page, 19–23; *The Soldier's Record and Grand Army Gazette*, Feb. 13, 1869.

43. Page, pp. 24–27.

44. Croffut and Morris, pp. 264–276, 283–285; Michael Kraus, *The United States to 1865* (Ann Arbor, 1959), pp. 497–498; Page, 29–49, 55–57; *Soldier's Record*, Feb. 27, 1869.

45. Croffut and Morris, pp. 288–296; Page, pp. 61, 74–95; James G. Randall, *The Civil War and Reconstruction* (Boston, 1937), pp. 312–315; *Soldier's Record*, March 13, April 3, 1869.

46. Croffut and Morris, pp. 365–377; Page, pp. 116–123; *Soldier's Record*, April 24, 1869.

47. George F. Milton, *Conflict: the American Civil War* (New York, 1941), pp. 261–269; Randall, p. 515.

48. Bruce Catton, *Glory Road* . . . (Garden City, 1952), pp. 335, 337; Page, pp. 143–153, 166; *Soldier's Record*, May 22, 1869.

49. Croffut and Morris, pp. 381–389; Edwin E. Marvin, *The Fifth Regiment, Connecticut Volunteers* . . . (Hartford, 1889), pp. 274–275, 279–283.

50. Croffut and Morris, p. 592; Milton, p. 314; Page, pp. 233–284; Randall, p. 543.

51. Bruce Catton, *A Stillness at Appomattox* (New York, 1958), pp. 44, 68–70, 77–78, 92, 101–106, 112–124; Croffut and Morris, pp. 577–580; *D.A.B.*, XVI, 548–549.

52. Page, pp. 284, 302–311.

53. Page, pp. 312–335.

54. Bernard F. Blakeslee, *History of the Sixteenth Connecticut Volunteers* (Hartford, 1875), pp. 110–114; Charles K. Cadwell, *The Old Sixth Regiment* . . . (New Haven, 1875), p. 119; *Courant*, June 5, 15, 17, 22, 28, 30, 1865; *History of the First Connecticut Artillery* . . . (Hartford, 1893), pp. 166–167, 173; Thomas H. Murray, *History of the Ninth Regiment* . . . (New Haven, 1903), p. 204; Page, pp. 339–342; Winthrop D. Sheldon, *The "Twenty-Seventh"* . . . (New Haven, 1866), pp. 85–87; John W. Storrs, *The "Twentieth Connecticut"* . . . (Ansonia, 1886), p. 171; Theodore F. Vaill, *History of the Second Connecticut Volunteer Heavy Artillery* . . . (Winsted, 1868), pp. 365–366; William C. Walker, *History of the Eighteenth Regiment* . . . (Norwich, 1885), pp. 358–361.

55. Conn. Adjutant General, comp. *Record of Service of Connecticut Men in the Army and Navy of the United States during the War of the Rebellion* . . . (Hartford, 1889), pp. 968–969; Page, pp. 342, 345, 348.

56. Marvin, pp. 149–226, 247–283, 294–365; Murray, *Ninth Regiment*, pp. 70–76, 188–202; *Record of Service, War of the Rebellion*, pp. 223, 259, 291, 327, 361, 394, 431, 471–473, 775, 791, 807–808, 845; Irene H. Mix Root, comp. *Connecticut's Activities in the Wars of this Country* . . . , 72d. Cong., 1st sess., Sen. Doc. No. 14 (Wash., 1932), pp. 47–48; Homer B. Sprague, *History of the 13th Infantry Regiment* . . . (Hartford, 1867), pp. 122–173; Storrs, pp. 147–171.

57. George W. Pierson, *Yale: College and University, 1871–1937*, Vol. I, *Yale College, An Educational History, 1871–1921* (New Haven, 1952), p. 704; Carl F. Price, *Wesleyan's First Century* . . . (Middletown, 1932), p. 113.

58. Croffut and Morris, pp. 64, 120, 131, 304, 611, 686–690; *D.A.B.*, XVIII, 378; *Record of Service, War of the Rebellion*, pp. 18–19, 290, 293; *The War of the Rebellion . . . Official Records, Army*, XLVI, pt. I, 394–400.

59. Blakeslee, pp. 53–62, 107; *Record of Service, War of the Rebellion*, p. 618.

60. *Record of Service, War of the Rebellion*, pp. 51, 58–60, 116–119, 173–175, 968.

61. *D.A.B.*, VI, 499–500; Morgan, *Connecticut*, IV, 89–90; Randall, pp. 279–280, 285, 530–531; *Record of Service, War of the Rebellion*, pp. 919–948.

62. Morgan, *Connecticut*, IV, 90–95.

63. *Record of Service, War of the Rebellion*, pp. 968–969. R. H. Potter, Chief, War Records Dept., Conn. St. Lib., reported a figure of 55,016 Connecticut men in service.

64. *Courant*, Dec. 14, 1861; Jan. 9, 1862; Lane, pp. 181–185.

65. *Courant*, April 10, 28, 1862; Lane, pp. 187–201; *New Haven Register*, March 20, 1862.

66. *Courant*, July 7, Aug. 5, Dec. 10, 1862; Lane, pp. 203–208.
67. Lane, pp. 208–211.
68. *Courant*, March 25, April 11, 30, 1863; *Hartford Times*, April 7, 1863; Lane, pp. 216–238; *New Haven Register*, March 2, 1863.
69. *Courant*, July 13, 1863; David M. Ellis, *et. al.*, *A Short History of New York State* (Ithaca, 1957), p. 337; Lane, pp. 240–249.

70. *Courant*, July 24, Aug. 24, 1863; Croffut and Morris, p. 849; Lane, pp. 248–256; *New Haven Register*, July 23, 1863.
71. *Courant*, April 25, 1864; Lane, pp. 257–270.
72. *Conn. Register*, 1865, p. 123; Lane, pp. 273–290; *New Haven Register*, Sept. 8, 1864.
73. *Conn. Register*, 1866, p. 123; *Courant*, April 4, 29, 1865; Lane, pp. 291–303.

14 Political, Social, and Economic Developments, 1865–1914

1. *Courant*, July 11, 12, 14, Oct. 29, 1862; May 17, 1863; July 7, 1865; *Hartford Times*, July 8, 1865; *Message . . . William A. Buckingham . . . to the Legislature . . . May Session, 1862* (New Haven, 1862), pp. 3–9; *Message, Buckingham, 1863*, pp. 3–10; *Public Acts, 1862*, Chap. lv, pp. 49–54; *1864*, Chap. lxxiv, pp. 99–105; *1865*, Chap. cxvi, pp. 116–120.
2. *Courant*, July 21, 22, 24, 25, Oct. 24, 25, 27, Dec. 1, 1862; Austin C. Dunham, *Reminiscences* (Hartford, n.d.), pp. 79–80; *Hartford Times*, July 11, 12, 14, 17, 19, 21, 1865; *Norwich Courier*, Oct. 30, 1862; *Public Acts, 1865*, Chap. cxvi, pp. 116–120; James G. Randall, *The Civil War and Reconstruction* (Boston, 1937), pp. 444–452.
3. Conn. Bank Commissioners, *Report . . . 1862* (Hartford, 1862), pp. 6–11; *1863*, pp. v–ix; *1864*, pp. 3–10; *1865*, pp. 3–8; *Courant*, July 7, 1865; Randall, pp. 455–458.
4. Phineas T. Barnum, *Life of P. T. Barnum, Written by Himself . . .* (New York, 1885), p. 233; Conn. Bank Commissioners, *Report, 1863*, pp. v–vi; *Courant*, July 7, 1865; *Hartford Times*, July 3, 1865; Edward C. Kirkland, *Men, Cities, and Transportation . . .*, Harvard Stud. Econ. Hist. (Cambridge, Mass., 1948), I, 263–265; II, 73; *Message, Buckingham, 1865*, pp. 7–8.
5. Barnum, pp. 232–233, 247–250; *Courant*, July 13, 14, 1865; *Hartford Times*, July 3, 13, 1865; *Public Acts, 1865*, Chap. xcix, p. 92; Chap. civ, p. 99.
6. Barnum, p. 233; Kirkland, I, 265.
7. William J. Niven, Jr., "The Time of the Whirlwind, a Study in the Political, Social and Economic History of Connecticut from 1861 to 1875," unpub. diss. (Col. Univ., 1954), pp. 233–234.
8. *Courant*, May 5, 18, 19, 20, 24, 25, 26, June 1, Oct. 4, 1865.
9. Kenneth R. Andrews, *Nook Farm, Mark Twain's Hartford Circle* (Cambridge, Mass., 1950), pp. 6–7; *Courant*, Feb. 8, 14, 15, April 18, 19, 1866; *D.A.B.*, VI, 166; VIII, 421; XIX, 462–463; James H. Trumbull, *The Memorial History of Hartford County, Connecticut, 1633–1884* (Boston, 1886), I, 609–611; Gideon Welles, *Diary . . .* (Boston, 1911), II, 425–428.
10. *Courant*, March 3, 14, 20, 27, 29, April 3, 20, 1866; Welles, *Diary*, II, 454–462, 465, 468–469, 474.
11. Edward E. Atwater, ed. *History of the City of New Haven . . .* (New York, 1887), pp. 380–382, 577–580; *Courant*, Jan. 23, 24, 25, April 24, 1867; April 7, 1868; *Hartford Times*, Dec. 1, 1866; Feb. 6, 11, 14, March 14, April 2, 8, 9, 1867; Jan. 21, 1873; *New York Tribune*, Jan. 2, 1873; Frederick C. Norton, *The Governors of Connecticut . . .* (Hartford, 1905), pp. 269–272.
12. *Courant*, July 29, 30, 1868; *Public Acts, 1868*, Chap. lxi, pp. 174–182; Chap. lxii, p. 182.
13. Niven, pp. 181–183.
14. *Courant*, June 20, 23, 1866.

15. *Courant*, May 30, 1868; *Hartford Times*, May 23, 24, 25, 29, 30, 31, June 5, 6, 7, 12, 1867; May 29, June 3, 4, 1868; *Special Acts, 1868*, pp. 327–329.
16. *Courant*, May 8, 14, 1869.
17. *Courant*, July 8, 11, 1870; March 27, 31, April 1, 5, 10, 11, 12, 22, May 4, 5, 6, 9, 10, 11, 12, 1871; *Hartford Times*, April 2, 6, 1870; March 31, April 1, 4, 8, 14, 22, May 4, 11, 12, 13, 1871; Jan. 14, 1874.
18. John D. Hicks and George E. Mowry, *A Short History of American Democracy*, 2d ed. (Boston, 1956), pp. 413–414, 417; Allan Nevins, *The Emergence of Modern America, 1865–1878*, A Hist. of Amer. Life Ser., VIII (New York, 1927), pp. 178–202.
19. *Courant*, June 15, July 15, 19, 20, 28, 1871; May 21, 22, 29, 30, June 23, 30, Oct. 21, 1873; *Documents and Reports Relating to the Connecticut State Capitol Building and Grounds at Hartford* (Hartford, 1922), nos. 1, 6; *Hartford Times*, June 18, 1873; Forrest Morgan *et. al.*, eds. *Connecticut as a Colony and as a State, or One of the Original Thirteen* (Hartford, 1904), IV, 134–136; Norris G. Osborn, ed. *History of Connecticut, in Monographic Form* (New York, 1925), II, 41–45; *R and M, 1947*, pp. 55, 437–438.
20. *Conn. Register, 1873*, pp. 19–25, 118–122, 195–197; *Courant*, June 18, 1873; *Hartford Times*, Jan. 21, Feb. 19, 1873; U.S. Census Office, *Ninth Census, 1870*, Vol. I, *Population and Social Statistics* (Wash., 1872), 93–95.
21. *Courant*, April 7, 28, May 1, June 10, July 16, 17, 24, Nov. 29, 1875; *Hartford Times*, Jan. 22, Feb. 5, 6, April 8, 1873; April 23, May 19, 1874; *New York Tribune*, Jan. 21, 1873.
22. *R and M, 1947*, pp. 55–58. The amendment numbers apply to the Constitution as it existed from the 1870's until recently when new numbers were assigned in a rewriting of 1953, effective January 1, 1955.
23. Earl C. May, *Century of Silver, 1847–1947 . . .* (New York, 1947), pp. 76–78, 99–119; *R and M, 1959*, pp. 312–315; Welles, *Diary*, III, 583.
24. U.S. Census Office, *Ninth Census, 1870*, I, pp. 93–94, 328–329, 336–342.
25. *R and M, 1959*, pp. 312–317; U.S. Census Office, *Ninth Census, 1870*, I, 17.
26. Barnum, pp. 278–280; Trumbull, *Hartford County*, I, 475–484, 489, 512.
27. Andrews, *Nook Farm*, pp. 3, 144–146; *D.A.B.*, VII, 290–291; Vernon L. Parrington, ed. *The Connecticut Wits* (New York, 1926), pp. xxiv–xlviii.
28. Andrews, *Nook Farm*, pp. 3–24, 78–84, 216, 275–276.
29. Samuel Orcutt, *A History of the City of Bridgeport, Connecticut* (New Haven, 1887), pp. 330–331; Osborn, II, 393–397; Rollin G. Osterweis, *Three Centuries of New Haven, 1638–1938* (New Haven, 1953), pp. 279, 331–332, 363, 365–366; Trumbull, *Hartford County*, I, 454–457, 561–562.

30. *Courant*, Dec. 18, 1871; Osterweis, p. 341; Thomas S. Weaver, *Historical Sketch of the Police Service of Hartford . . .* (Hartford, 1901), pp. 58–59.
31. Conn. Bank Commissioners, *Report, 1872*, pp. 5–7; *1873*, pp. 4–11; *1875*, pp. iv–xi, xv; Conn. Bank Commissioners, *Special Report* (Norwich, 1874), pp. 5–8, 40–42, 75, 93, 95, 113, 123, 128, 131, 139, 141, 149, 151, 157, 159, 169, 171, 181, 190–201; *Public Acts, 1874*, Chap. cvi, pp. 252–253, 263.
32. *Conn. Register, 1873*, p. 122; *Courant*, April 19, 20, July 11, 21, Dec. 14, 16, 1871; *General Statutes, 1866*, Title 63, Chap. ii, pp. 692–705; *Public Acts, 1872*, Chap. xcix, pp. 98–101; *1874*, Chap. cxv, pp. 258–261; *Temperance Journal*, Jan. 19, April 27, May 5, 12, 26, June 2, 1871; May 10, 17, 1872.
33. Irving G. Davis, *Types of Farming and Type of Farming Areas in Connecticut*, Storrs Agric. Exp. Sta. Bull. 213, 1936, pp. 7–8.
34. Davis, *Types of Farming*, pp. 8–9.
35. Irving G. Davis and Clarence I. Hendrickson, *A Description of Connecticut Agriculture*, Storrs Agric. Exp. Sta. Bull. 127, 1925, pp. 47–49; Osborn, II, 395–397.
36. Osborn, II, 362–364; Walter Stemmons, *Connecticut Agricultural College — A History* (Storrs, 1931), pp. 19–21, 30, 33, 37, 42.
37. *General Statutes, 1875*, Title III, Chap. 1, Pt. xi, pp. 18–19; Osborn, II, 359–360.
38. William H. Brewer, *A Century of Connecticut Agriculture*, Conn. State Board of Agric., Report of the Secretary, 1894, [Agricultural Pamphlets, I, No. 32] (Hartford, 1894), pp. 17–18; *D.A.B.*, X, 120; XVII, 163; Osborn, II, 365, 373–374.
39. Wilbur O. Atwater, *Calorimeter Respiration Experiments*, [Agricultural Pamphlets, I, No. 23], pp. 4–14; Atwater, *On Commercial Fertilizers at Home and Abroad*, [Agricultural Pamphlets, II, No. 7], pp. 46–47; Atwater, *Report on Farm Experiments with Fertilizers, 1878*, [Agricultural Pamphlets, II, No. 10], pp. 2–66; Conn. General Assembly, House, *Journal, 1875*, pp. 207, 437; *D.A.B.*, I, 417–418; Theodore S. Gold, *Handbook of Connecticut Agriculture*, [Agricultural Pamphlets, I, No. 1], pp. 21–22; Osborn, II, 381.
40. Osborn, II, 377–379; *Public Acts, 1877*, Chap. clviii, pp. 256–258.
41. *Public Acts, 1881*, Chap. lxxiv, p. 40; Stemmons, pp. 23, 28, 31–37.
42. Conn. Agricultural School Comm., *Report . . . 1885* (Hartford, 1886), pp. 3–25; Stemmons, pp. 39–41, 49–55.
43. *General Statutes, 1875*, Title XI, Chap. xiii, pp. 149–151; *Public Acts, 1893*, Chap. lxvii, pp. 238–240; *1899*, Chap. 169, pp. 1086–87; Stemmons, pp. 58–77, 94–96.
44. Gold, pp. 33, 35, 37, 39; Osborn, II, 380–383.
45. Davis and Hendrickson, pp. 51–58.
46. *Ibid.*, pp. 53–55.
47. *Ibid.*, pp. 70–73.
48. John R. Commons *et al.*, *History of Labour in the United States* (New York, 1918–35), II, 15, 86–87; *Hartford Times*, Jan. 25, Feb. 6, March 16, 23, April 2, 1867; *Public Acts, 1855*, Chap. xlv, p. 49; Fred A. Shannon, *Economic History of the People of the United States* (New York, 1934), pp. 597–598.
49. Conn. Bur. of Labor Statistics, *Annual Report . . . 1902* (Hartford, 1902), p. 332; *Public Acts, 1867*, Chap. xxxvii, p. 77; Chap. clii, p. 135.
50. *Hartford Times*, Feb. 17, 24, March 5, 27, April 18, 1872.
51. Conn. Bur. of Labor Statistics, *Annual Report, 1875*, pp. 127–131.
52. Conn. Bur. of Labor Statistics, *Annual Report, 1874*, pp. 9–11, 63–67; *1875*, p. 24; *Conn. Register, 1873*, p. 122; *Public Acts, 1873*, Chap. lxxxii, p. 171.
53. Conn. Bur. of Labor Statistics, *Annual Report, 1902*, pp. 331–332; Conn. State Board of Educ., *Annual Report . . . 1887* (New Haven, 1887), p. 55; *1888*, p. 38; Alba M. Edwards, "The Labor Legislation of Connecticut," *Amer. Econ. Assoc. Pubs.*, 3d Ser., VIII (Aug. 1907), 30–45, 71–73, 319–322; *Public Acts, 1886*, Chap. cxxiv, pp. 624–625; *1895*, Chap. cxviii, p. 504; *1901*, Chap. 109, pp. 1249–51.
54. Conn. Bur. of Labor Statistics, *Annual Report, 1904*, p. 260; Edwards, pp. 76–83; *Public Acts, 1887*, Chap. lxii, pp. 692–693.
55. Conn. Bur. of Labor Statistics, *Annual Report, 1902*, p. 346; Edwards, pp. 311–313.
56. Conn. Bur. of Labor Statistics, *Annual Report, 1902*, pp. 348–349; Edwards, pp. 313–315.
57. Conn. Bur. of Labor Statistics, *Annual Report, 1902*, p. 350; *1904*, pp. 406–409.
58. Gertrude S. Bridge, "The Legislative Deadlock in Connecticut, January 7, 1891 to November 8, 1892," unpub. M.A. thesis (Trinity College, 1943), pp. 1–3, 2n; *R and M*, 1889, p. 418.
59. Bridge, pp. 4–13; *Courant*, Nov. 10, 27, 1890; *Hartford Times*, Nov. 7, 13, 1890; Jan. 26, 1891; *R and M, 1891*, p. 350. The primary sources do not agree on the vote totals.
60. Bridge, pp. 14–32; *Courant*, Jan. 8, 13, 14, 1891; Jan. 19, magazine section, p. 3, 1941; *Hartford Daily Post*, Jan. 28, 1891; *Hartford Times,* Jan. 7, 13, 19, 1891; "Official Proclamation of His Excellency Governor Morgan G. Bulkeley, Jan. 19, 1891," Conn. St. Library, Hartford.
61. Bridge, pp. 32–38, 42–47; *Hartford Times*, Feb. 12, 17, March 21, 23, 1891; Richard Hooker, *Ætna Life Insurance Company . . .* (Hartford, 1956), p. 122.
62. Bridge, pp. 52–64, 68–72; Conn. Board of the World's Fair Managers, *Connecticut at the World's Fair* (Hartford, 1898), *passim*; *Connecticut Reports . . .* (New York, 1892), LXI, 287–378; *Courant*, April 15, July 6, 7, 1891; Jan. 6, Feb. 10, 1892; *Hartford Times*, July 6, 7, 1891; Nov. 9, 1892; Hooker, *Ætna*, pp. 119, 124–127; Morgan, *Connecticut*, IV, 168–176; Osborn, II, 30–33.
63. *Courant*, Oct. 18, 1901; Hooker, *Ætna*, p. 128; *Public Acts, 1901*, Chap. 179, pp. 1380–84.
64. Samuel McSeveney, "Preliminary Report on Political Change, 1890–1896," typed report based on research for University of Iowa doctoral dissertation, pp. 1–2, 4–7, 10; *R and M, 1893*, p. 345; *1895*, p. 365. See *R and M, 1891*, pp. 326–341 for closeness of presidential election results since 1864.
65. Leland D. Baldwin, *The Stream of American History*, 2d ed. (New York, 1957), II, 299–300, 304; Lane W. Lancaster, "Democratic Party in Connecticut," *National Municipal Review*, XVII (Aug. 1928), 453; McSeveney, pp. 7–11; *R and M, 1892*, pp. 340–341; *1893*, p. 328; *1897*, pp. 352, 360, 369; *1899*, p. 394; *1901*, pp. 395, 414.
66. Conn. Adjutant General, *Record of Service of Connecticut Men . . . in the Spanish-American War . . .* (Hartford, 1919), pp. 10–15, 25–27, 98; Conn. National Guard, First Regiment, *Outline History . . . , 1898–1899* (Hartford, 1900), pp. 10–11, 14; Morgan, *Connecticut*, IV, 179–180.
67. Conn. Adjutant General, *Record . . . Spanish-Ameri-*

can War, pp. 27–42, 98, 159, 166, 175, 184–185; Conn. National Guard, First Regiment, pp. 15–77; Morgan, *Connecticut*, IV, 180–184. Statistics on numbers in service from War Records Dept., Conn. St. Lib., Hartford.

68. *Courant*, 1896: Sept. 17, p. 1; 1900: Sept. 22, p. 7; 1901: Jan. 10, p. 7, March 19, p. 10, March 28, pp. 8, 9, March 29, p. 7, April 3, p. 8, June 11, p. 9, June 14, pp. 3, 10, Oct. 3, p. 3, Oct. 4, p. 1, Nov. 6, pp. 1, 2; 1902: May 16, pp. 13, 14; Frederick M. Heath, "Preliminary Report on Connecticut Politics, 1894–1914," typed report based on research for Col. Univ. doctoral diss., pp. 17–19; Morgan, *Connecticut*, IV, 188–190; Osborn, I, 471–490; Frank Putnam, "What's the Matter With New England?" No. 5, "Connecticut: the State Ruled by its Uninhabited Country Towns," *New England Magazine*, XXXVII (Nov. 1907), 267; *R and M*, 1902, pp. 375, 388, 424, 455–456; 1903, pp. 437–438.

69. *Courant*, 1900: June 11, pp. 5, 8, Nov. 9, p. 10; 1902: Sept. 25, p. 1; Heath, pp. 6–8; *R and M*, 1911, pp. 475–476.

70. Heath, pp. 6, 8, 9, 14; *R and M*, 1896, p. 351; 1914, p. 451.

71. *Courant*, 1900: June 11, p. 12, July 2, p. 10, Sept. 6, pp. 1, 7, Nov. 8, p. 8; 1904: Oct. 10, p. 6; 1905: Jan.

13, pp. 1, 8; 1910: Aug. 16, p. 6; 1911: Jan. 11, p. 1; 1912: Aug. 5, p. 2; Heath, pp. 1–3, 5, 14.

72. Heath, p. 1; *R and M*, 1901, p. 414; 1903, p. 428; 1905, p. 433; 1907, p. 448; 1909, pp. 442, 444, 462.

73. Heath, p. 2; Frederick H. Jackson, *Simeon Eben Baldwin, Lawyer, Social Scientist, Statesman* (New York, 1955), pp. 159–163.

74. Jackson, *Baldwin*, pp. 164–165, 170–179; *R and M*, 1911, p. 490.

75. *Courant*, 1912: June 26, p. 7, July 8, p. 1, July 9, pp. 3, 8, July 17, p. 1, July 31, pp. 1, 11; Heath, pp. 10–12; Jackson, *Baldwin*, pp. 188–190; *R and M*, 1913, pp. 456, 459–464, 473–474, 483–511.

76. Jackson, *Baldwin*, pp. 190–194; *Public Acts, 1913*, Chap. 138, pp. 1735–51.

77. *Courant*, 1914: Sept. 9, p. 1, Sept. 11, pp. 1, 3, Sept. 12, p. 1, Sept. 19, pp. 1, 10, Sept. 29, pp. 1, 10, Nov. 4, p. 10; Heath, pp. 12–13; Jackson, *Baldwin*, pp. 196–198; Arthur S. Link, *Woodrow Wilson and the Progressive Era, 1910–1917*, New Amer. Nation Ser. (New York, 1954), p. 78; *New Haven Register*, 1914: Sept. 14, pp. 1, 3, Sept. 15, pp. 1, 2, Nov. 4, p. 1; *R and M*, 1915, pp. 481, 496.

78. U.S. Bur. of the Census, *Thirteenth Census, 1910*, I, 807; II, 247, 250, 254, 256.

79. U.S. Bur. of the Census, *Thirteenth Census, 1910*, I, 32–33, 42, 55, 1106, 1198; II, 237–238, 249.

15 Connecticut During World War I

1. *Public Acts, 1915*, Chap. 2, pp. 1898–1904; Chap. 29, pp. 1919–21; Chap. 255, pp. 2079–80.

2. Arthur S. Link, *Woodrow Wilson and the Progressive Era, 1910–1917*, New Amer. Nation Ser. (New York, 1954), pp. 188–196; *Public Acts, 1916*, Chap. 1, pp. 3–7; Chap. 2, pp. 7–8.

3. Conn. Temporary Comm. to Study the Tax Laws of the State, *Report . . .* (Hartford, 1934), p. 364; *Public Acts, 1911*, Chap. 283, pp. 1596–97; 1913, Chap. 188, pp. 1807–12; 1915, Chap. 292, pp. 2128–40.

4. *Courant*, 1916: Sept. 4, p. 8, Sept. 18, p. 1, Nov. 4, p. 13; *Hartford Times*, 1916: Oct. 27, p. 8, Nov. 2, p. 12; Link, *Wilson*, pp. 145–148. Former Chief Justice William M. Maltbie, once executive secretary to Governor Holcomb, confirmed the governor's genuine indifference to renomination in an interview March 7, 1957.

5. Conn. Democratic Party, *The Year Book of the Democratic Party, 1916*, pp. 45–46; Conn. Republican Party, *Conn. Republican Hand Book, 1916*, pp. 223–224; *Courant*, 1916: Sept. 5, p. 8; *Hartford Times*, 1916: Sept. 6, pp. 1, 10, 11, Sept. 20, p. 1, Oct. 27, p. 8, Nov. 8, p. 1; *R and M*, 1917, pp. 489, 499–505, 514–515.

6. "Connecticut's Military Census," *American Review of Reviews*, LV (May 1917), 533–535; Conn. Special Assistants in the Military Census, *Report to . . . Marcus H. Holcomb*, Public Document, Special (Hartford, 1917), pp. 3–4, 12–13; *Inaugural Message, Marcus Holcomb*, 1919, p. 3; *Public Acts, 1917*, Chap. 4, pp. 2220–21; Chap. 136, pp. 2320; Chap. 145, pp. 2325–26.

7. Corinne M. Barker, "Connecticut's Share in Furnishing Munitions for the World War," unpub. M.A. thesis (Col. Univ., 1925), pp. 86–87.

8. Barker, "Munitions," pp. 5–7; *Courant*, 1919: June

29, Pt. 5, pp. 1, 5, 7; "Germany's Contribution to our War Preparation," *Iron Age*, CI (Jan. 3, 1918), 28–29.

9. Conn. State Council of Defense, *Report, December 1918* (Hartford, 1919), pp. 5, 12–13, 21–24; *Public Acts, 1917*, Chap. 44, p. 2265.

10. Defense Council, *Report*, pp. 36–43.

11. *Ibid.*, pp. 49–54, 110–114; *Public Acts, 1917*, Chap. 292, p. 2425.

12. Defense Council, *Report*, pp. 70–71, 121.

13. *Beware of German Trickery at the Bargain Counter of Europe* (n.p., n.d.), pp. 3–15; *What We Are Fighting For* (n.p., n.d.), pp. 5–15; *Why We Are at War with Germany* (n.p., n.d.), pp. 5–16; *Report*, pp. 71–75, 120–121: all written by Conn. State Council of Defense.

14. Defense Council, *Report*, pp. 82–157.

15. Barker, "Munitions," pp. 9–10, 13, 54–55, 59.

16. Barker, "Munitions," pp. 45–46, 48–49, 51–52, 54; Benedict Crowell and Robert F. Wilson, *The Armies of Industry . . .* (New Haven, 1921), I, 237, 240–243, 247, 253, 293–295.

17. Leonard P. Ayres, *The War with Germany . . .*, 2d ed. (Wash., 1919), p. 72; Barker, "Munitions," pp. 35–38, 41–42; Crowell and Wilson, I, 206–209, 218; *Hartford Times*, 1918: Oct. 26, p. 11.

18. Barker, "Munitions," pp. 33–34; Crowell and Wilson, I, 92–93.

19. Barker, "Munitions," pp. 49–53, 80; Crowell and Wilson, I, 295–296; II, 634; Irene H. Mix Root, comp. *Connecticut's Activities in the Wars of this Country . . .*, 72d Cong., 1st sess., Sen. Doc. No. 14 (Wash., 1932), p. 59; "125 Years of Continuous Operation and Still Going Strong," written by Russell Mfg. Co., Middletown, p. 6.

20. Conn. Adjutant General, *Biennial Report . . . 1916* (Hartford, 1916), pp. 7–9; 1918, pp. 5–6; Root, pp.

54–56; Daniel W. Strickland, *Connecticut Fights, the Story of the 102nd Regiment* (New Haven, 1930), pp. 39–45.

21. Adjutant General, *Report, 1918*, pp. 6–8; Root, pp. 59–61.

22. Adjutant General, *Report, 1918*, pp. 10–11; Root, pp. 60–61.

23. Marcus H. Holcomb, "Connecticut in the Van," *Review of Reviews*, LVII (May 1918), 520; *Public Acts, 1917*, Chap. 32, p. 2257.

24. Harry A. Benwell, *History of the Yankee Division* (Boston, 1919), pp. 12–21; Root, pp. 60–61; Emerson G. Taylor, *New England in France, 1917–1919* . . . (Boston, 1920), pp. 16–18.

25. Benwell, pp. 11–13; Taylor, *New England*, pp. 12n, 16.

26. Strickland, pp. 65–68, 285; Taylor, *New England*, pp. 29–33.

27. Strickland, pp. 76–81, 81n; Taylor, *New England*, pp. 39–41, 58–60.

28. Benwell, pp. 48–49; Strickland, pp. 105–113, 113n; Taylor, *New England*, pp. 65–84.

29. John J. Pershing, *My Experiences in the World War* (New York, 1931), II, 16; Strickland, pp. 133–150; Taylor, *New England*, pp. 96–99, 106, 122–133.

30. Amer. Battle Monuments Comm., *26th Division Summary of Operations in the World War* (Wash., 1944), pp. 9–20; Strickland, pp. 171–214; Taylor, *New England*, p. 202.

31. Pershing, II, 225–227, 389; Strickland, pp. 215–232.

32. Benwell, pp. 204–206; Strickland, pp. 234–294; Taylor, *New England*, pp. 232–277.

33. Ayres, p. 116; Leslie R. Barlow, "World War Daily Diary of the 102d Ambulance Company," pp. 92, 95, typed copy, Conn. St. Lib., Hartford; Benwell, pp. 5–7; Strickland, pp. 182n, 190n, 196n, 220n, 245n–249n, 271n, 273n–276n, 323; Taylor, *New England*, p. 302n; *26th Division Summary*, p. 63; *Welcome Home* (Boston, 1919), pp. [21, 28–33].

34. Laurence L. Driggs, *Heroes of Aviation*, rev. ed. (Boston, 1927), pp. 102, 105, 111–113, 120–121;

Abbott L. Lowell, *New England Aviators, 1914–1918* . . . (Boston, 1919), I, 2–5.

35. Amy Hewes, *Women as Munition Makers* . . . (New York, 1917), pp. 3–68.

36. *Public Acts, 1917*, Chap. 300, pp. 2433–34; "Rushing to Protect Munitions Workers," *Survey*, XXXVII (March 10, 1917), 665–666.

37. Barker, "Munitions," pp. 25–27; Alexander M. Bing, *War-Time Strikes and their Adjustment* (New York, 1921), p. 74n; Conn. Dept. of Labor, *Report on the Conditions of Wage-Earners in the State* . . . (Hartford, 1918), pp. 39, 79–81; Hewes, pp. 79–81, 85–88, 90.

38. Barker, "Munitions," pp. 24–27; Conn. Bur. of Labor Statistics, *Report, 1918*, p. 27; Conn. Dept. of Labor, *Report on Wage-Earners*, pp. 38–39.

39. Barker, "Munitions," pp. 18–21; Edwin S. Blodgett, *How Stamford is Meeting Her War Labor Problems* (Stamford, 1918), pp. 1–18.

40. Barker, "Munitions," pp. 28–32; Bing, pp. 73–80; Conn. Bur. of Labor Statistics, *Report, 1916*, pp. 30, 52; *Courant*, 1918: Sept. 14, p. 10; Hewes, pp. 12–13.

41. Conn. Bur. of Labor Statistics, *Report, 1918*, pp. 29, 39; Holcomb, "Connecticut," p. 521.

42. *Democratic Year Book, 1918*, pp. 5–6; *New Haven Journal-Courier*, 1918: June 26, p. 1, June 27, pp. 4, 8, June 28, pp. 1, 3; *Republican Hand Book, 1918*, pp. 217–219.

43. Leland D. Baldwin, *The Stream of American History*, 2d ed. (New York, 1957), II, 527–528; *Courant*, 1918: Oct. 26, p. 1; *Hartford Times*, 1918: Oct. 25, p. 1; *New Haven Journal-Courier*, 1918: Oct. 28, p. 8; *R and M, 1919*, pp. 463–478, 487–512; *Waterbury Republican*, 1918: Oct. 26, p. 4.

44. *Courant*, 1918: Nov. 8, p. 1, Nov. 11, p. 1, Nov. 12, p. 1; *New Haven Journal-Courier*, 1918: Nov. 12, p. 1; *Waterbury Republican*, 1918: Nov. 12, p. 1.

45. Benwell, pp. 240–245; *Courant*, 1919: May 1, pp. 1, 10; *Hartford Times*, 1919: April 30, pp. 1, 14; Strickland, pp. 302–307.

16 Life in the "Golden Twenties"

1. John M. Clark, *The Costs of the World War to the American People*, Carnegie Endowment for Internatl. Peace, Div. of Econ. and Hist., Econ. and Soc. Hist. of the World War, Amer. Ser. (New Haven, 1931), pp. 264–265; *Courant*, 1919: Jan. 17, p. 10; March 3, p. 9; June 29, Pt. 5; George H. Soule, *Prosperity Decade; From War to Depression: 1917–1929*, The Econ. Hist. of the U.S. Ser., VIII (New York, 1947), pp. 81–87.

2. Frederick Lewis Allen, *Only Yesterday* . . . (New York, 1931), pp. 45–58; Preston W. Slosson, *The Great Crusade and After, 1914–1928*, A Hist. of Amer. Life Ser., XII (New York, 1930), pp. 79–82.

3. *Courant*, 1918: March 11, p. 1; Dec. 30, p. 2; 1919: Jan. 13, pp. 1, 8; Feb. 27, pp. 1, 12.

4. *Courant*, 1919: March 3, pp. 1, 6, March 10, pp. 1, 9, March 13, p. 1.

5. *Courant*, 1919: March 25, p. 1; Nov. 8, pp. 1–2, Nov. 10, pp. 1, 2, Nov. 12, pp. 1, 8, Nov. 13, pp. 1, 11, Nov. 14, pp. 1, 7, Nov. 18, pp. 1, 4; Robert K. Murray, *Red Scare* . . . (Minneapolis, 1955), pp. 196–197; Robert D. Warth, "The Palmer Raids," *The South Atlantic Quarterly*, XLVIII (Jan. 1949), 4–6.

6. *Courant*, 1919: Nov. 19, pp. 1, 2, Nov. 23, Pt. V, pp. 3, 7.

7. *Courant*, 1920: Jan. 3, pp. 1, 9, Jan. 5, pp. 1, 2, Jan. 6, pp. 1, 9, Jan. 9, p. 19; Feb. 27, p. 9; Murray, *Red Scare*, pp. 212–213; U.S. House of Reps., 66th Cong., 2d Sess., *Hearings before the Committee on Rules, Attorney General A. Mitchell Palmer* . . . (Wash., 1920), I, 75–78.

8. *Courant*, 1920: Sept. 9, pp. 1, 10, Sept. 10, pp. 1, 2, Sept. 15, p. 1, Sept. 21, p. 1, Sept. 22, p. 1; *Hartford Times*, 1920: Sept. 10, p. 10, Sept. 11, p. 8; Rowland W. Mitchell, "Social Legislation in Connecticut," (1919–1939), unpub. diss. (Yale, 1954), p. 93; Murray, *Red Scare*, p. 261; *Republican Hand Book, 1920*, pp. 190–192.

9. *Courant*, 1920: Sept. 16, p. 10, Sept. 18, pp. 1, 18; *Democratic Year Book, 1920*, pp. 5–6; *Hartford Times*, 1920: Sept. 16, pp. 1, 2; *New Haven Evening Register*, 1920: Sept. 16, pp. 1, 2.

10. *Courant*, 1920: Oct. 2, pp. 1, 2, 12, Oct. 8, pp. 1, 20, Oct. 14, p. 13, Oct. 15, p. 1, Oct. 16, p. 1; *Hartford Times*, 1920: Sept. 10, p. 1, Sept. 11, p. 8, Sept. 14, p. 10; Oct. 11, p. 10, Oct. 21, p. 10.

11. Allen, *Only Yesterday*, pp. 40–43; Leland D. Baldwin, *The Stream of American History*, 2d ed. (New York, 1957), II, 539–541; *Courant*, 1920: Nov. 4, p. 1; *R and M, 1921*, pp. 466, 476, 478–483, 492; Slosson, pp. 91–92.

12. *Hartford Times*, 1924: July 22, p. 1; 1928: July 31, p. 1; Richard Hofstadter, William Miller, and Daniel Aaron, *The American Republic* (Englewood Cliffs, 1959), II, 436; Edmund A. Moore, *A Catholic Runs for President* . . . (New York, 1956), pp. 23–28, 108–110, 145, 163.

13. *General Statutes, 1918*, Title LIII, Chap. 283, Secs. 5301–03, 5306, pp. 1486–87; Mitchell, "Social Legislation," pp. 179–218; *Public Acts, 1921*, Chap. 188, pp. 3168–69; *1923*, Chap. 6, p. 3479; *1927*, Chap. 144, pp. 4230–31; "Stenographer's Notes of Public Hearings before the Joint Standing Committee on Labor," 1919, pp. 42–110; 1923, pp. 29–69; 1925, pp. 50–65, Conn. St. Lib., Hartford; U.S. Bur. of the Census, *Fourteenth Census* . . . , *1920, Population*, IV, *Occupations*, 57–73; *Fifteenth Census* . . . *1930, Population*, IV, *Occupations*, 256.

14. Joseph A. Hill, *Women in Gainful Occupations, 1870 to 1920* . . . Bur. of the Census, Census Monographs, IX (Wash., 1929), pp. 2, 189, 200–201, 242–243, 284; *R and M, 1929*, pp. 80–91.

15. Allen, *Only Yesterday*, pp. 95–99; Slosson, pp. 270–286.

16. Conn. Commissioner of Motor Vehicles, *Biennial Report* . . . *1920–1922* (Hartford, 1922), p. 4; *1934–36*, p. 27; Lloyd Morris, *Not So Long Ago* (New York, 1949), pp. 379–382; *R and M, 1931*, pp. 759–760.

17. Morris, *Not So Long Ago*, pp. 382–383; *R and M, 1959*, pp. 312–317.

18. Federal Radio Comm., *Annual Report* . . . *1928* (Wash., 1928), pp. 55–61; Morris, *Not So Long Ago*, pp. 447–452, 481–482; Slosson, pp. 191, 388–393; U.S. Bur. of the Census, *Fifteenth Census* . . . *1930, Population*, VI, *Families*, 53.

19. Baldwin, *Stream*, II, 561; *Bridgeport Times-Star*, 1928: Jan. 14, p. 9, Jan. 21, p. 9; Raymond Moley, *Are We Movie Made?* (New York, 1938), pp. 9–64; Morris, *Not So Long Ago*, pp. 117–120, 139–159, 179–183; *New Haven Register*, 1927: Nov. 26, p. 2; 1928: Feb. 4, p. 2; Slosson, pp. 393–397.

20. Allen, *Only Yesterday*, p. 245; *R and M, 1959*, p. 24; Slosson, pp. 107–112.

21. *Public Acts, 1921*, Chap. 291, pp. 3277–79; *R and M, 1920*, pp. 523–524; Slosson, p. 107.

22. *The Connecticut Citizen*, XXV (Feb. 1918), 6–8; XXVI (Nov. 1918), 4; XXVI (Feb. 1919), 4–6; *Courant*, 1918: March 14, p. 14; 1919: Feb. 4, p. 12, Feb. 5, p. 1; *New Haven Journal-Courier*, 1919: Feb. 5, p. 6, Feb. 7, p. 8.

23. *Courant*, 1920: Jan. 16, p. 8, Jan. 17, p. 11; Slosson, p. 121.

24. *Courant*, 1920: Oct. 26, p. 1, Oct. 28, pp. 1, 2; *New Haven Register*, 1927: Nov. 15, p. 1, Nov. 21, pp. 1, 3, Nov. 22, p. 1.

25. *Inaugural Message, Charles A. Templeton, 1923*, pp. 7–8.

26. Conn. State Police Dept., *Report, 1914* (Hartford, 1914), pp. 6–13, 20–27; *1916*, pp. 4–13, 25–33; *1917–18*, pp. 4–13; *1922–24*, pp. 6, 65; *1924–25*, p. 7; *1925–26*, p. 81; *1926–27*, p. 4; *1927–28*, pp. 93–94; *1928–29*, p. 4.

27. Herbert Asbury, *The Great Illusion* . . . (New York, 1950), p. 163; James H. Barnett, "College Seniors and the Liquor Problem," pp. 133, 136, 138; Constantine M. Panunzio, "The Foreign Born and Prohibition," pp. 147–154, both in *Annals of the American Academy of Political and Social Science*, CLXIII (Sept. 1932).

28. Natl. Comm. on Law Observance and Enforcement, *Enforcement of the Prohibition Laws. Official Records* . . . , 71st Cong., 3d Sess., Sen. Doc. No. 307 (Wash., 1931), I, 323–324.

29. *Courant*, 1923: May 5, pp. 1, 2; June 6, p. 10; 1925: May 22, p. 2.

30. Allen, *Only Yesterday*, pp. 251–254; *Courant*, 1924: June 2, p. 1, June 6, p. 1; *New Haven Register*, 1927: Dec. 16, p. 1; Slosson, pp. 114–115.

31. Natl. Comm. on Law Observance and Enforcement, *Enforcement of Prohibition*, IV, 89; *New Haven Register*, 1927: Nov. 15, p. 1; *Public Acts, 1925*, Chap. 207, p. 3997.

32. Allen, *Only Yesterday*, pp. 254–255; Frederick W. Brown, "Prohibition and Mental Hygiene . . . ," *Annals of the American Academy of Political and Social Science*, CLXIII (Sept. 1932), 74; *Courant*, 1926: Sept. 20, p. 12; Slosson, pp. 118–119; *Vital Records of Connecticut, 1916–42, passim*.

33. Martha S. Bensley Bruère, *Does Prohibition Work?* . . . (New York, 1927), pp. 200–208.

34. Natl. Comm. on Law Observance and Enforcement, *Enforcement of Prohibition*, IV, 91, 95–99; V, 117–118.

35. Federal Council of the Churches of Christ in America, Dept. of Research and Educ., *The Prohibition Situation*, Research Bull. No. 5 (New York, 1925), pp. 14–16, 38; Slosson, pp. 126–129.

36. Asbury, pp. 327–330.

37. Raymond E. Baldwin, *Let's Go Into Politics* (New York, 1952), pp. 50–53; *Courant*, 1937: May 20, p. 8; *Hartford Times*, 1924: Sept. 29, p. 10; Frederick M. Heath, "Preliminary Report on Connecticut Politics, 1894–1914" (typed report based on research for Col. Univ. doctoral dissertation), pp. 10–13; Mitchell, "Social Legislation," pp. 79–83.

38. *Courant*, 1927: May 20, p. 8; Lane W. Lancaster, "The Background of a State 'Boss' System," *American Journal of Sociology*, XXXV (March 1930), 783–798; Duane Lockard, *New England State Politics* (Princeton, 1959), pp. 245–249; Mitchell, "Social Legislation," pp. 83–87.

39. Mitchell, "Social Legislation," pp. 88–90; *Special Acts, 1923*, No. 203, pp. 180–181; *1925*, No. 334, pp. 834–837; *1927*, No. 195, pp. 223–225.

40. *Courant*, 1927: May 1, p. 2A; Lancaster, "State 'Boss' System," p. 785; Mitchell, "Social Legislation," pp. 123–127; *New York Times*, 1928: Aug. 8, p. 20.

41. Conn. General Assembly, Senate, *Journal, 1921*, pp. 42–44; *Courant*, 1921: June 8, p. 4.

42. *Courant*, 1922: Aug. 4, pp. 1, 2, Aug. 30, p. 1; Sept. 13, pp. 1, 8, 9, Sept. 14, pp. 1, 2; *Hartford Times*, 1922: Oct. 25, pp. 1, 10; Mitchell, "Social Legislation," p. 94; *Republican Hand Book, 1922*, pp. 205–212.

43. *Courant*, 1922: Aug. 23, p. 1; Sept. 14, p. 1; Nov. 1, p. 14, Nov. 3, p. 1; *Democratic Year Book, 1922*, pp. 5–6; *Hartford Times*, 1922: Sept. 21, pp. 1, 15; Oct. 23, p. 10, Oct. 25, p. 10; *R and M, 1923*, pp. 439–444, 453–454; *Republican Hand Book, 1922*, pp. 205–212.

44. *Courant*, 1923: May 14, pp. 1, 2; *Inaugural Message, Charles A. Templeton, 1923*, pp. 3–5.

45. *Courant*, 1921: May 11, p. 1; 1923: May 8, p. 1, May 16, p. 1; June 5, p. 1, June 6, p. 13; 1925: May 26, p. 1; *Public Acts, 1925*, Chap. 86, pp. 3853–54.

46. Hofstadter, Miller, and Aaron, II, 446–447; Thomas H. Williams, Richard N. Current, and Frank Freidel, *A History of the United States* [since 1865] (New York, 1959), pp. 435–436.

47. *Courant*, 1924: Sept. 9, pp. 1, 2; Oct. 3, pp. 1, 2, Oct. 17, p. 1, Oct. 21, p. 2; *Hartford Times*, 1924: Sept. 10, pp. 1, 18, 19, Sept. 18, pp. 1, 5, 18.

48. *Courant*, 1924: Oct. 15, pp. 1, 22, Oct. 16, pp. 1, 2; *D.A.B.*, II, 598–599; *Hartford Times*, 1924: Oct. 14, pp. 1, 10; Karl Schriftgiesser, *This Was Normalcy . . .* (Boston, 1948), pp. 7, 14.

49. *Courant*, 1924: Oct. 29, p. 14; Nov. 26, pp. 1, 2; *R and M*, 1925, pp. 458, 461–466, 475, 525.

50. Manufacturers' Assoc. of Conn., *Connecticut Industry*, IV (Jan. 1926), 20–21; (Aug. 1926), 12.

51. *Courant*, 1925: May 7, p. 1, May 14, p. 4, May 22, p. 9, May 25, p. 9, May 30, p. 1; June 3, p. 1, June 4, pp. 1, 5, June 19, p. 2; *Inaugural Message, Hiram Bingham, 1925*, pp. 3–32; *Inaugural Message, John H. Trumbull, 1925*, pp. 3–13; *Special Acts, 1925*, No. 299, pp. 807–813.

52. *Courant*, 1926: Oct. 26, p. 1; *Democratic Year Book, 1926*, pp. 5–6; *Hartford Times*, 1926: Sept. 15, p. 1, Sept. 16, pp. 1, 2; *R and M*, 1927, p. 491; *Republican Hand Book, 1926*, pp. 231–234.

53. *Courant*, 1927: May 9, p. 7; *Public Acts, 1927*, Chap. 307, pp. 4397–4404.

54. *Courant*, 1928: June 13, pp. 1, 2, 8, June 14, pp. 1, 2, 4, June 15, pp. 1, 2, 8, June 16, pp. 1, 8, June 19, p. 8, June 27, p. 6, June 29, pp. 1, 4, 8.

55. *Courant*, 1928: Sept. 8, p. 1; *Democratic Year Book, 1928*, pp. 5–8; *Hartford Times*, 1928: Sept. 7, p. 1, Sept. 8, p. 12; *Republican Hand Book, 1928*, pp. 239–243.

56. Moore, *Catholic*, pp. 107–194; *R and M*, 1920, pp. 523–524.

57. *Courant*, 1928: Oct. 11, p. 8, Oct. 19, pp. 1, 2, 8, Oct. 20, p. 1, Oct. 22, p. 1, Oct. 26, pp. 1, 20; Nov. 1, p. 1, Nov. 5, p. 2; *Hartford Times*, 1928: Sept. 14, p. 18, Sept. 25, p. 10, Sept. 26, p. 1.

58. *Courant*, 1928: Oct. 6, p. 6, Oct. 26, pp. 1, 20; *Hartford Times*, 1928: Oct. 26, pp. 1, 10.

59. *Courant*, 1928: Nov. 7, pp. 1, 8; *Hartford Times*, 1928: Nov. 7, pp. 1, 10; Lane W. Lancaster, "Democratic Party in Connecticut," *National Municipal Review*, XVII (Aug. 1928), 453–454; *R and M*, 1929, pp. 490–491, 493, 498, 532.

17   The Depression Decade and Connecticut's "New Deal"

1. *Courant*, 1928: Aug. 12, p. 8B.

2. William E. Leuchtenburg, *The Perils of Prosperity, 1914–32*, The Chicago Hist. of Amer. Civ. Ser. (Chicago, 1958), pp. 241–243; George H. Soule, *Prosperity Decade; From War to Depression: 1917–1929*, The Econ. Hist. of the U.S. Ser., VIII (New York, 1947), pp. 229–231, 275–281.

3. Leuchtenburg, *Perils*, pp. 244–249; Soule, pp. 306–311.

4. Soule, pp. 232, 272–274, 284, 317, 325–327, 332–333.

5. *Courant*, 1929: Oct. 26, pp. 1, 2, Oct. 30, pp. 1, 8, 23; Nov. 27, p. 14; *Hartford Times*, 1929: Oct. 1, p. 10; Nov. 26, p. 1; Dec. 18, pp. 1, 5.

6. *Hartford Times*, 1929: Dec. 18, pp. 1, 5; 1933: Dec. 1, p. 2; Arthur M. Schlesinger, Jr., *The Age of Roosevelt*, Vol. I, *The Crisis of the Old Order, 1919–1933* (Boston, 1957), pp. 167–169.

7. Wilbur L. Cross, *Connecticut Yankee, An Autobiography* (New Haven, 1943), pp. 220–221, 223–226; Eugene A. Davidson, "A Cross for Connecticut," *Outlook and Independent*, CLVII (Jan. 14, 1931), 62–63; *Hartford Times*, 1930: Sept. 11, pp. 1, 2, 21, 23, Sept. 17, p. 11.

8. *Hartford Times*, 1930: Aug. 5, p. 1; Sept. 11, p. 21, Sept. 16, pp. 1, 27, Sept. 17, p. 10; *Republican Hand Book, 1930*, pp. 215–218.

9. Conn. Treasurer, *An Interim Report to the Governor for the Period August 16, 1924–January 5, 1925* (Hartford, 1925), pp. 3–13; *Hartford Times*, 1924: Aug. 13, p. 1, Aug. 16, pp. 1, 8; 1929: Sept. 26, pp. 1, 2; Oct. 18, pp. 1, 10, Oct. 19, pp. 1, 2; Nov. 1, p. 1, Nov. 4, pp. 1, 3; 1930: Oct. 9, p. 1, Oct. 10, p. 1.

10. Cross, pp. 231–232; Davidson, p. 64; *Hartford Times*, 1930: Sept. 27, pp. 1, 2, Sept. 29, pp. 2, 10.

11. Cross, pp. 230, 232–236; *Hartford Times*, 1930: Oct. 7, p. 3, Oct. 9, p. 10, Oct. 11, p. 2, Oct. 15, pp. 1, 2, Oct. 30, p. 14, Oct. 31, p. 10.

12. *Courant*, 1930: Nov. 5, pp. 1, 14, Nov. 6, p. 14; *Hartford Times*, 1930: Nov. 5, pp. 1, 2, Nov. 7, p. 10, Nov. 26, pp. 1, 3, Nov. 28, p. 10; *New London Day*, 1930: Nov. 5, p. 6; *R and M*, 1931, p. 517; *Stamford Advocate*, 1930: Nov. 5, p. 4.

13. *Hartford Times*, 1931: Jan. 7, p. 1.

14. *Courant*, 1931: Jan. 8, p. 14; Cross, pp. 250–251; *Hartford Times*, 1931: Feb. 12, pp. 1, 10.

15. *Courant*, 1931: Feb. 17, p. 14; *Hartford Times*, 1931: Feb. 14, p. 10; March 6, pp. 1, 22.

16. *Courant*, 1931: Jan. 19, p. 10; *Hartford Times*, 1931: Feb. 11, pp. 1, 2, Feb. 12, p. 10, Feb. 24, pp. 1, 35, Feb. 25, p. 10.

17. Cross, pp. 254–257; *General Statutes, 1931*, Chap. 79, pp. 215–217; *Hartford Times*, 1931: March 25, pp. 1, 6, March 26, pp. 1, 9; May 14, pp. 1, 33, May 28, pp. 10, 22, 23.

18. Cross, pp. 258–260; Rowland W. Mitchell, "Social Legislation in Connecticut" (1919–1939), unpub. diss. (Yale, 1954), p. 464.

19. Cross, pp. 265–268; *Hartford Times*, 1932: March 29, pp. 1, 31; May 17, pp. 1, 2; July 2, p. 4.

20. *Hartford Times*, 1932: Feb. 25, pp. 1, 2; April 6, pp. 1, 24; June 18, p. 10; July 26, p. 1; Sept. 7, pp. 1, 19; Sept. 12, p. 10, Sept. 17, pp. 1, 25.

21. *Hartford Times*, 1932: Aug. 31, pp. 1, 2; Sept. 1, pp. 1, 2, Sept. 8, pp. 1, 2, 16, Sept. 9, pp. 1, 20.

22. Cross, pp. 270–273; *Hartford Times*, 1932: Oct. 27, pp. 1, 38; Nov. 2, pp. 1, 2; *New Haven Register*, 1932: Sept. 9, p. 14.

23. *Bridgeport Times-Star*, 1932: Nov. 9, p. 6; *Courant*, 1932: Nov. 9, pp. 1, 14; *Hartford Times*, 1932: Nov. 9, pp. 1, 2, 10, Nov. 10, p. 11; *Meriden Record*, 1932: Nov. 9, p. 6; *New London Day*, 1932: Nov. 9, p. 6; *R and M*, 1933, pp. 423, 426–456.

24. Conn. Bank Commissioner, *Report, 1931*, pp. 13–14, addendum sheet; *1932*, p. 6; *1952*, pp. 121–122; Interview November 1, 1959, with the late Mr. C. Read Richardson of Manchester, Conn., who worked in the Liquidation Department, 1936–1942; Mitchell, "Social Legislation," p. 356.

25. Conn. Bank Commissioner, *Report, 1933*, pp. 5, 6; *Courant*, 1933: March 10, pp. 1, 18, March 11, pp. 1, 16; June 12, p. 5; Cross, pp. 281–282; *Hartford*

Times, 1933: March 4, pp. 1, 12, March 6, pp. 1, 3, March 7, pp. 1, 20, March 8, pp. 1, 19, March 21, p. 1.

26. Conn. Bank Commissioner, *Report, 1952*, pp. xliii, 121; *General Statutes, 1935*, Chap. 205, pp. 602–607.

27. Conn. Unemployment Comm., *Measures to Alleviate Unemployment in Connecticut* (Orange, Conn., 1932), pp. 34–35, 40, 62, 170; U.S. Bur. of the Census, *Fifteenth Census, 1930, Unemployment*, I, 191.

28. Conn. Commissioner of Labor, *Report, 1934*, p. 24; Conn. Unemployment Comm., *Measures*, pp. 42, 45–46, 60–61, 65; *Hartford Times*, 1933: March 22, pp. 1, 22.

29. Cross, pp. 282–283; *General Statutes, 1933*, Chap. 32a, pp. 45–52.

30. Conn. Emergency Relief Comm., *Experience of the Emergency Relief Commission with Relief Administration in Connecticut* . . . (Hartford, 1937), pp. 56–59, 168–171; Otto H. Schroeter, "C.C.C., Connecticut's Youth in the Civilian Conservation Corps," *The Connecticut Circle*, I (May 1935), 26–27, 63–64.

31. Conn. Emergency Relief Comm., *Experience with Relief in Conn.*, pp. 110–111; Cross, pp. 283–284.

32. *Courant*, 1933: Feb. 10, p. 2, Feb. 23, pp. 1, 4, 6, 8; April 18, p. 10, April 29, p. 10; May 31, p. 8; June 9, p. 12, June 12, p. 5; *Hartford Times*, 1933: Jan. 31, pp. 1, 12, Feb. 1, pp. 1, 11, Feb. 6, pp. 1, 19, Feb. 7, pp. 1, 26, Feb. 9, p. 10, Feb. 15, pp. 1, 26, Feb. 18, pp. 1, 9, 10, Feb. 22, pp. 1, 20, Feb. 23, pp. 1, 14; April 5, p. 10, April 29, p. 10; May 4, pp. 1, 32, May 17, p. 1, May 18, p. 10; June 2, pp. 1, 41, June 5, pp. 1, 24.

33. *Courant*, 1933: April 19, pp. 1, 6, 12; Cross, pp. 285–289; *General Statutes, 1933*, Chap. 151, pp. 287–325; *Hartford Times*, 1933: April 8, pp. 1, 2, April 12, pp. 1, 26, April 18, pp. 1, 7, April 19, p. 9, April 20, p. 1; June 21, pp. 1, 16; July 11, pp. 1, 28; *R and M*, 1933, p. 481.

34. Conn. Commissioner of Labor, *Report, 1934*, p. 25; *Courant*, 1933: June 1, pp. 1, 2, June 7, p. 5, June 10, p. 10; *General Statutes, 1933*, Chap. 131, 131a, pp. 261–270; *Inaugural Message, Wilbur L. Cross, 1933*, pp. 15–17; *Hartford Times*, 1933: May 23, pp. 1, 27.

35. Conn. Commissioner of Labor, *Report, 1934*, p. 24; *Courant*, 1934: Jan. 1, p. 14; *Hartford Times*, 1934: Feb. 19, p. 1; May 1, p. 1; July 12, pp. 1, 36.

36. *Courant*, 1933: Aug. 24, p. 10; *Hartford Times*, 1933: Aug. 23, pp. 1, 26, Aug. 25, pp. 1, 2, Aug. 26, p. 10; Sept. 2, pp. 1, 19.

37. *Courant*, 1934: Sept. 4, pp. 1, 2, Sept. 5, pp. 1, 2, Sept. 6, pp. 1, 11, Sept. 7, pp. 1, 2, Sept. 8, pp. 1, 18, Sept. 10, p. 2, Sept. 11, pp. 1, 2, Sept. 12, pp. 1, 2, 8, Sept. 13, pp. 1, 3, 8, Sept. 14, pp. 1, 10, Sept. 15, pp. 1, 5, Sept. 18, pp. 1, 2, Sept. 19, pp. 1, 12, Sept. 24, pp. 1, 9.

38. *Courant*, 1934: Sept. 13, pp. 1, 6; Cross, pp. 305–308; *Hartford Times*, 1934: Sept. 6, pp. 1, 23, 31, Sept. 11, p. 10, Sept. 12, pp. 1, 13, 16, *New Haven Register*, 1934: Sept. 12, p. 14.

39. *Bridgeport Times-Star*, 1934: Oct. 30, p. 6; *Courant*, 1934: Sept. 13, p. 12; Oct. 13, p. 8; *Hartford Times*, 1934: March 24, p. 10; Aug. 27, pp. 1, 25; Sept. 13, p. 10, Sept. 14, p. 10; Oct. 17, pp. 1, 13, Oct. 20, p. 10, Oct. 24, p. 10; Nov. 5, pp. 1, 10, 25.

40. *Hartford Times*, 1934: Oct. 6, p. 8, Oct. 18, p. 1, Oct. 20, p. 10, Oct. 27, p. 8.

41. *Courant*, 1934: Nov. 7, p. 12; *Hartford Times*, 1934: Nov. 7, pp. 1, 10, 16; *New Haven Register*, 1934: Nov. 7, p. 14; *New London Day*, 1934: Nov. 7, p. 4;

R and M, 1935, pp. 50–56, 265–291; *Stamford Advocate*, 1934: Nov. 7, p. 6; *Waterbury Republican*, 1934: Nov. 7, p. 14.

42. *Courant*, 1935: Jan. 10, pp. 1, 8, 12, Jan. 11, pp. 1, 4, 14; Cross, pp. 313–318; *Hartford Times*, 1935: Jan. 7, pp. 1, 11, Jan. 9, pp. 1, 23, Jan. 10, pp. 1, 30, 38, Jan. 11, pp. 1, 3.

43. *General Statutes, 1935*, Chap. 99a, pp. 304–314; Chap. 131, Sec. 909c, p. 373; Chap. 279, Secs. 1598c, 1600c, 1604c, pp. 702–704; *Hartford Times*, 1935: Feb. 14, pp. 1, 35, Feb. 15, p. 10, Feb. 26, pp. 1, 32; March 5, p. 1, March 9, p. 8, March 26, pp. 1, 29; April 17, pp. 1, 33, April 23, pp. 1, 29, April 24, p. 3; May 1, p. 31. To finance the old age pension, a tax of three dollars was imposed on everyone aged 21–60.

44. *Courant*, 1935: May 30, p. 8; *General Statutes, 1935*, Chap. 196, Sec. 1414c, pp. 591–593; Chap. 87, pp. 282–283; *Hartford Times*, 1935: Feb. 4, p. 1, Feb. 5, pp. 1, 19; May 15, p. 4, May 21, p. 6, May 29, pp. 1, 10, May 30, p. 8.

45. *General Statutes, 1935*, Chap. 151, Secs. 1031c–38c, pp. 434–435; *Hartford Times*, 1935: March 19, pp. 1, 29, March 20, p. 10, March 21, pp. 1, 38, March 28, p. 1, March 29, p. 10; April 2, pp. 1, 32; June 1, pp. 1, 2.

46. *Courant*, 1935: May 21, p. 10, May 22, pp. 1, 2, May 23, pp. 1, 4, 22; June 5, pp. 1, 4, June 6, pp. 1, 4, 12, June 10, pp. 6, 7; *Hartford Times*, 1935: March 29, p. 1; April 4, p. 1; May 8, p. 1, May 9, p. 10, May 22, pp. 1, 27, May 23, p. 1, May 25, pp. 1, 21, May 27, pp. 1, 10.

47. *Courant*, 1936: Jan. 1, p. 7; Cross, pp. 329–333; *Hartford Times*, 1935: Oct. 4, p. 28, Oct. 12, pp. 1, 5, 6; *R and M*, 1935, pp. 7–10.

48. Conn. Tercentenary Commission Committee on Historical Publications, *The Tercentenary Pamphlet Series and Its Contributors* (New Haven, 1936), pp. 1–3.

49. *Hartford Times*, 1936: March 12, p. 1, March 13, p. 1, March 14, p. 1; William E. Leuchtenburg, *Flood Control Politics* . . . (Cambridge, Mass., 1953), p. 46.

50. *Courant*, 1936: March 20, p. 1, March 21, pp. 1, 14; April 5, Pt. 6, p. 1; *Hartford Times*, 1936: March 18, p. 1, March 19, pp. 1, 34, 38, March 20, pp. 1, 26, March 28, flood section, p. 17.

51. *Courant*, 1936: March 21, pp. 1, 6, 14, 18, March 23, pp. 1, 16; April 5, Pt. 6, p. 4; *Hartford Times*, 1936: March 21, pp. 1, 6.

52. *Courant*, 1936: March 24, pp. 1, 21, March 25, pp. 1, 10, March 26, p. 13; *Hartford Times*, 1936: March 23, p. 8, March 24, pp. 1, 4, 10.

53. *Courant*, 1936: April 5, Pt. 6, p. 4; Cross, pp. 336–338; *Hartford Times*, 1936: March 23, p. 1, March 24, p. 1, March 25, p. 1, March 26, p. 1, March 27, p. 1.

54. *Courant*, 1936: May 26, pp. 1, 4; July 8, pp. 1, 6, July 9, pp. 1, 6, July 23, pp. 1, 4, July 24, pp. 1, 2; Cross, pp. 351–353. The strike began in Syracuse over reinstatement and pay increase demands. Middletown workers struck in sympathy.

55. *Business Week*, 1940: June 15, p. 41; *Courant*, 1936: Aug. 27, p. 5, Aug. 28, p. 8, Aug. 29, p. 4.

56. *Courant*, 1937: Feb. 24, pp. 1, 7, Feb. 25, pp. 1, 6, 14, Feb. 26, pp. 1, 3; Cross, pp. 354–355.

57. *Courant*, 1936: Sept. 9, pp. 1, 8, Sept. 10, pp. 1, 5; Oct. 9, p. 16, Oct. 14, p. 12, Oct. 22, pp. 1, 8, Oct. 23, pp. 1, 8, 24, Oct. 24, pp. 1, 4, Oct. 30, pp. 1, 9, Oct. 31, pp. 1, 4, 14; Nov. 2, pp. 1, 7.

58. *Courant*, 1936: Nov. 4, pp. 1, 2, 16; Cross, pp. 347–

348; *Hartford Times,* 1936: Nov. 4, pp. 1, 10, 23, Nov. 6, p. 1; *R and M,* 1937, pp. 412–419, 423–466.

59. Conn. Commissioner of Labor, *Report, 1938* (Hartford, 1939), p. 75; *General Statutes, 1936,* Chap. 33c, pp. 75–90; Chap. 38, pp. 90–91; Chap. 280a, pp. 444–468.

60. *Courant,* 1937: Jan. 7, pp. 1, 8.

61. Conn. Comm. Concerning the Reorganization of the State Govt. Depts., *Report* (Hartford, 1937), pp. 1–2, 10–11, 111–115; *Courant,* 1937: June 13, pp. 16A, 17A; Cross, pp. 359–365; *Hartford Times,* 1937: June 10, pp. 1, 2, 12, 28.

62. *Courant,* 1937: June 6, pp. 1, 8, June 10, pp. 1, 8, June 11, p. 16, June 13, p. 16A; *Hartford Times,* 1937: June 8, p. 1, June 9, pp. 1, 28, June 10, pp. 1, 2, June 21, p. 1.

63. *Courant,* 1937: June 10, pp. 1, 18; Cross, p. 366.

64. *Courant,* 1936: Sept. 9, pp. 1, 8, Sept. 10, p. 14; 1937: May 20, pp. 1, 8, 14; Interview with Raymond E. Baldwin, Feb. 18, 1960; Duane Lockard, *New England State Politics* (Princeton, 1959), pp. 247–251, 251n.

65. Cross, pp. 368–371.

66. Charles F. Brooks, "Hurricanes into New England . . . ," *The Smithsonian Institution, Annual Report, 1939* (Wash., 1940), p. 243; Ferry B. Colton, "The Geography of a Hurricane," *National Geographic Magazine,* LXXV (April 1939), 536; Ivan R. Tannehill, "Hurricane of September 16 to 22, 1938," U.S. Weather Bur., *Monthly Weather Review,* LXVI (Sept. 1938), 286–287.

67. *Courant,* 1938: Sept. 21, pp. 1, 8, 9.

68. Leuchtenburg, *Flood,* pp. 110–111.

69. Brooks, "Hurricanes," p. 241; Colton, pp. 536–537, 540.

70. Federal Writers Project, *New England Hurricane . . .* (Boston, 1938), pp. 36–37.

71. [Connecticut Circle], *Photo Record, Hurricane and Flood . . .* (New York, 1938); *Courant,* 1938: Sept. 22, pp. 1, 14, Sept. 23, pp. 1, 6, 12, Sept. 24, p. 1; Leuchtenburg, *Flood,* p. 112.

72. *Courant,* 1938: Sept. 22, pp. 1, 4, 11, 14; "Hurricane Wrecks Chapel Spire, Levels Trees, as 108th Year Opens," *Wesleyan University Alumnus,* XXIII (Oct. 1938), 1–2.

73. *Courant,* 1938: Sept. 23, pp. 1, 28, Sept. 24, p. 1, Sept. 25, p. 1.

74. *Courant,* 1938: Sept. 23, pp. 6, 10, 12, Sept. 24, p. 1; Federal Writers' Project, *New England Hurricane,* pp. 157–158.

75. *Courant,* 1938: Sept. 25, p. 1; U.S. Weather Bur., *Monthly Weather Review,* LXVI (Sept. 1938), 309.

76. Cross, pp. 378–379.

77. Conn. Highway Commissioner, *Biennial Report . . . 1937–38* (Hartford, 1938), p. 15; *Courant,* 1938: April 29, pp. 1, 8, April 30, p. 1; June 30, pp. 1, 2; Cross, pp. 384–388.

78. *Courant,* 1938: May 20, pp. 1, 4, 15; 1939: Aug. 17, pp. 1, 8, Aug. 19, pp. 1, 3, Aug. 22, pp. 1, 4; 1941: March 7, pp. 1, 8, 9, 10, 11. The disposition of the cases of the 27 defendants was as follows: 3 dismissed, 1 judgment suspended, 2 pleaded guilty (Mackenzie); 1 found guilty by Judge Ernest Inglis; 19 found guilty by jury; 1 fled state and never arrested. Of the 14 who appealed, 10 served their sentences and 4 were freed. In the group of 10 were Hayes and Leary, sentenced to 10–15 years apiece.

79. *Courant,* 1938: Sept. 15, pp. 1, 4, 6, Sept. 16, pp. 1, 8, Sept. 17, pp. 1, 4, 6.

80. *Courant,* 1938: Oct. 11, p. 1, Oct. 29, p. 8; Cross, pp. 408–410.

81. Raymond E. Baldwin, *Let's Go Into Politics* (New York, 1952), pp. 89–90; *Courant,* 1938: Sept. 29, p. 2; Nov. 5, pp. 1, 2; Interview with Raymond E. Baldwin, Feb. 18, 1960.

82. *Courant,* 1938: Oct. 12, pp. 1, 9, Oct. 15, pp. 1, 4, Oct. 19, pp. 1, 10, Oct. 21, p. 1, Oct. 22, pp. 1, 4, Oct. 26, p. 1; Nov. 1, pp. 1, 9, Nov. 7, pp. 1, 4, 12; Cross, pp. 412–414.

83. *Courant,* 1938: Oct. 21, p. 1, Oct. 24, pp. 1, 4, Oct. 26, p. 1; Interview with Raymond E. Baldwin, Feb. 18, 1960.

84. *Courant,* 1938: Sept. 22, p. 21, Sept. 24, p. 12; Oct. 12, pp. 1, 9; Nov. 1, p. 10; *Hartford Times,* 1938: Oct. 6, p. 1; Leuchtenburg, *Flood,* pp. 116–119.

85. *Courant,* 1938: Nov. 2, pp. 1, 7, Nov. 5, pp. 1, 2, Nov. 8, pp. 1, 2; Cross, pp. 415–418.

86. *Courant,* 1938: Nov. 9, pp. 1, 2, Nov. 10, pp. 1, 4, 14; *R and M,* 1939, pp. 420–427, 436–438.

87. *Courant,* 1938: Nov. 10, p. 14; Mitchell, "Social Legislation," p. 472.

18   Trade, Transportation, and Industry

1. James Truslow Adams, *New England in the Republic, 1776–1850* (Boston, 1926), pp. 117–119, 187–188; Percy W. Bidwell, "Rural Economy in New England at the Beginning of the Nineteenth Century," *Conn. Academy of Arts and Sciences, Trans.,* XX (April 1916), 294–296, 300; Alan Burns, *History of the British West Indies* (London, 1954), pp. 538, 544–546; John H. Parry and Philip M. Sherlock, *A Short History of the West Indies* (London, 1956), pp. 139–140.

2. Frances M. Caulkins, *History of Norwich, Connecticut . . .* (Hartford, 1874), pp. 475–477.

3. *Ibid.,* pp. 478–479.

4. Adams, *New England in Republic,* pp. 250, 252; Caulkins, *Norwich,* pp. 480–485; Frances M. Caulkins, *History of New London, Connecticut . . .* (New London, 1895), pp. 579–582, 638–641; Rollin G.

Osterweis, *Three Centuries of New Haven, 1638–1938* (New Haven, 1953), p. 243; Richard J. Purcell, *Connecticut in Transition, 1775–1818* (Wash., 1918), pp. 99, 115–117, 119.

5. *C.R.,* I, 154; Caulkins, *New London,* p. 638; Edouard A. Stackpole, *The Sea-Hunters . . .* (Phila., 1953), pp. 18–19; Alexander Starbuck, "History of the American Whale Fishery . . . ," U.S. Comm. of Fish and Fisheries, Part IV, *Report* (Wash., 1878), pp. 9–11.

6. *Conn. Gazette* (New London), March 22, 1771; Stackpole, pp. 27–29, 42; Starbuck, p. 20.

7. Caulkins, *New London,* pp. 639–641; Starbuck, pp. 180–230.

8. Interview with Edouard A. Stackpole, March 28, 1960; Stackpole, pp. 306, 388, 452; Starbuck, pp. 416–419.

9. Elmo P. Hohman, *The American Whaleman* . . . (New York, 1928), pp. 48–73.

10. Hohman, pp. 217–242; Stackpole interview.

11. Hohman, pp. 195–196; Starbuck, pp. 99, 286–287, 328–329, 404–405.

12. Starbuck, pp. 510–511, 520–521, 542–543, 554–555, 572–573.

13. Starbuck, pp. 109–113, 180–658. It is evident that some of these vessels were engaged primarily in sealing rather than whaling. The Charles W. Morgan actually operated out of New Bedford during its notable career.

14. Sidney Withington, *Two Dramatic Episodes of New England Whaling* . . . , Marine Hist. Assoc. Pubs., No. 34 (Mystic, Conn., 1958), pp. 10–17.

15. Withington, *Whaling*, pp. 7, 20–35, 39.

16. Starbuck, pp. 101, 590–591; Withington, *Whaling*, pp. 43–62.

17. Starbuck, pp. 148, 602–603.

18. Hohman, pp. 302–305; Stackpole interview; Starbuck, pp. 103–108, 108n.

19. Frederic J. Wood, *The Turnpikes of New England* . . . (Boston, 1919), pp. 3, 7.

20. S.R., VII, 394–396, 536–537; VIII, xx–xxi, 219–220, 276–277, 286–288, 338–340; IX, 369; Wood, *Turnpikes*, p. 10.

21. Wood, *Turnpikes*, pp. 43, 408–409.

22. Conn. Highway Dept., *Forty Years of Highway Development in Connecticut, 1895–1935*, Conn. Ter. Comm. Pubs., No. 46 (New Haven, 1935), pp. 2–3; Wood, *Turnpikes*, pp. 331, 347–348.

23. Charles R. Harte, *Connecticut's Canals*, reprinted from Conn. Soc. Civil Eng., Inc., *Annual Report*, No. 54 ([New Haven, 1938]), pp. 47–64.

24. Harte, *Canals*, pp. 8–22; Osterweis, pp. 244–247.

25. Harte, *Canals*, pp. 25–35.

26. Harte, *Canals*, pp. 35–45; Osterweis, pp. 247–248.

27. Melancthon W. Jacobus, *The Connecticut River Steamboat Story* (Hartford, 1956), pp. 8–12.

28. *Courant*, May 17, 1815; Jacobus, pp. 34–35; Sidney Withington, "Steamboats Reach New Haven . . . ," *N.H.C.H.S. Papers*, x (New Haven, 1951), 155–159.

29. *Courant*, Sept. 21, 1813; Jacobus, pp. 36–41, 114.

30. Jacobus, pp. 41–52.

31. Jacobus, pp. 52–57; Edward C. Kirkland, *Men, Cities, and Transportation* . . . , Harvard Studies Econ. Hist. (Cambridge, Mass., 1948), II, 209–210.

32. Jacobus, pp. 70–71.

33. Jacobus, pp. 74–75, 89–90.

34. Kirkland, II, 131–132, 137–138; Henry R. Palmer, *Stonington By the Sea*, 2d ed. (Stonington, 1957), pp. 65–69.

35. Oliver O. Jensen, "The Old Fall River Line," *American Heritage*, VI (Dec. 1954), 13–14; Kirkland, II, 132–134, 137–141, 145.

36. Kirkland, I, 231–232.

37. Alvin F. Harlow, *Steelways of New England* (New York, 1946), pp. 170–175; Kirkland, I, 234–236; *Private Laws, 1833*, pp. 1002–05.

38. Harlow, *Steelways*, pp. 179–184; Kirkland, I, 239–241, 284, 284n; *Private Laws, 1844*, pp. 1020–25; Sidney Withington, *The First Twenty Years of Railroads in Connecticut*, Conn. Ter. Comm. Pubs., No. 45 (New Haven, 1935), pp. 14, 17, 20–28.

39. Kirkland, II, 72–78, 81.

40. Conn. General Assembly, *Report of the Special Committee Appointed March 13, 1878, to Investigate the Alleged False Returns of Railroad Companies* (Hartford, 1878), pp. 1–16; Kirkland, II, 79.

41. Kirkland, II, 90–106; *Special Laws, 1889*, pp. 1298–1300; *1893*, p. 32.

42. *Christian Science Monitor*, 1935: Oct. 25, p. 2; *Courant*, 1913: Dec. 11, p. 1; U.S. Senate, *Documents*, 63d Cong., 2d Sess., XIX (Wash., 1914), 692, 923–925; *Time* magazine, 1935: Nov. 4, p. 67.

43. *Christian Science Monitor*, 1935: Oct. 23, pp. 1, 2, Oct. 25, p. 2; Conn. General Assembly, Joint Standing Committee on Railroads, *Report* (Hartford, 1923), pp. 1231–39.

44. *Courant*, 1960: Jan. 6, p. 1; March 3, pp. 1, 2, March 26, p. 1; May 5, pp. 1, 2; June 29, p. 4.

45. William G. Lathrop, *The Brass Industry in the United States* . . . , rev. ed. (Mt. Carmel, Conn., 1926), pp. 38–40; *Brass Roots*, pub. by Scovill Mfg. Co. (Waterbury, 1952), pp. 2–3.

46. Joseph Anderson, ed. *The Town and City of Waterbury, Connecticut* . . . (New Haven, 1896), I, 584; II, 275; Scovill, *Brass Roots*, pp. 5–8.

47. Anderson, II, p. 276; Scovill, *Brass Roots*, pp. 8–12. Many of the documents which illustrate the company's early growth are found in a mimeographed compilation, Kenneth T. Howell, ed. "History of Abel Porter & Company From Which Scovill Manufacturing Company Is The Direct Descendant," (Waterbury, 1952).

48. Lathrop, *Brass, United States*, pp. 102, 111; William G. Lathrop, *The Development of the Brass Industry in Connecticut*, Conn. Terc. Comm. Pubs., No. 49 (New Haven, 1936), p. 7; Scovill, *Brass Roots*, pp. 12–14.

49. Scovill, *Brass Roots*, pp. 15, 18, 21.

50. Anderson, II, 291–292; Scovill, *Brass Roots*, pp. 15–16.

51. Scovill, *Brass Roots*, pp. 21, 23–24.

52. W. Thornton Martin, "The Company War Can't Lick," *Saturday Evening Post*, 1942: Aug. 29, p. 13; Scovill Document Files.

53. Scovill Document Files.

54. Scovill Document Files. An "educational" order was a preparedness measure by which the Federal Government permitted selected companies to accept small orders on new military items, thus giving valuable experience and insuring faster wartime conversion.

55. Scovill Mfg. Co., *Annual Report, 1952*, pp. 7, 14, 15; *1953*, p. 2; *1954*, p. 2; *1955*, p. 1; *1956*, p.3.

56. Conn. Development Comm., *Connecticut Information Letter*, XI (March 1960), 1; Scovill, *Annual Report, 1952*, pp. 14–15; *1956*, p. 1; Scovill Mfg. Co., *Better By the Mile* (Waterbury, 1951), pp. 1–21.

57. Conn. Labor Dept., *Directory of Connecticut Manufacturing and Mechanical Establishments* (Hartford, 1954), *passim.*; *Courant*, 1960: Aug. 27, p. 7; Wayne R. Dickerson, *Rediscovering Connecticut* (Hartford, 1948), p. 14.

58. *D.A.B.*, XX, 157–160; Jeannette Mirsky and Allan Nevins, *The World of Eli Whitney* (New York, 1952), pp. 44, 59–60, 65–81, 92–136.

59. Constance M. Green, *Eli Whitney and the Birth of American Technology*, Library of American Biography Ser. (Boston, 1956), pp. 100–105; Mirsky and Nevins, pp. 136–146, 176.

60. Green, pp. 111–117; Mirsky and Nevins, pp. 192–203.

61. Green, pp. 119–121.

62. Green, pp. 125–132; Mirsky and Nevins, pp. 206–213.

63. Green, pp. 155–170, 175, 194–196; Mirsky and Nev-

ins, pp. 301–302; Joseph W. Roe, *English and American Tool Builders* (New Haven, 1916), pp. 133–137, 162–163.

64. *Directory of New England Manufacturers, 1960*, p. 364; Norris G. Osborn, ed. *History of Connecticut, in Monographic Form* (New York, 1925), IV, 189–192; Harold F. Williamson, *Winchester, the Gun that Won the West* (Wash., 1952), pp. 10–11, 20–22.

65. Simeon N. D. North and Ralph H. North, *Simeon North . . .* (Concord, N.H., 1913), pp. 41–42, 44, 92, 140, 142–190, 205–207; Osborn, IV, 176–185; Roe, *Tool Builders*, pp. 162–163.

66. *Courant*, 1960: Feb. 1, p. 1; *Directory of New England Manufacturers, 1960*, pp. 136, 247, 311, 364.

67. Archibald A. Welch, *A History of Insurance in Connecticut*, Conn. Ter. Comm. Pubs., No. 43 (New Haven, 1935), pp. 2–4; Patrick H. Woodward, *Insurance in Connecticut* (Boston, 1897), p. 2.

68. *S.R.*, VIII, 288–289, 289n; Welch, pp. 4, 14–15; Woodward, *Insurance*, pp. 10–11.

69. Edward E. Atwater, ed. *History of the City of New Haven . . .* (New York, 1887), pp. 338–339; *S.R.*, IX, 92–93, 93n; Welch, p. 5n; Woodward, *Insurance*, pp. 9–10.

70. Conn. Commissioner of Insurance, *Annual Report, 7th*, Pt. 1 (Hartford, 1872), pp. v–vii; *42d*, Pt. 1, 1907, pp. xviii–xix; Welch, pp. 5–12; Woodward, *Insurance*, pp. 12–19, 42.

71. *Ætna Year Book and Schedule of Bonds and Stocks, 1960* (Hartford, 1960), p. 3; Richard Hooker, *Ætna Life Insurance Company . . .* (Hartford, 1956), pp. 18, 80, 94, 142, 214; Welch, pp. 21–22, 24–25; Woodward, *Insurance*, pp. 90–99.

72. Interview with George Malcolm-Smith, April 28, 1960; Welch, pp. 15–16; Woodward, *Insurance*, p. 106.

73. "First Auto Policies" and "Forward Steps Taken by the Travelers," Office of Mr. George Malcolm-Smith, Travelers, Hartford; "The Travelers—and How It Grew," p. 2, Travelers' Library; The Travelers Insurance Companies, *Annual Report, 1959* (Hartford, 1960), pp. 3, 6, 16.

74. Osborn, II, 214; Woodward, *Insurance*, pp. 32–35, 45–48, 82–89.

75. Conn. Comm. of Insurance, *Annual Report, 1959*, pp. iv, 2; *Ranking of 717 Life Companies, Insurance in Force January 1, 1960*, leaflet reprinted from *The National Underwriter*, column 1.

76. Conn. Comm. of Insurance, *Report, 1959*, p. vii; *Courant*, 1960: Jan. 30, pp. 1, 2; Sept. 7, p. 4; Interview with Mr. George Malcolm-Smith, April 28, 1960.

77. George M. Curtis, *Early Silver of Connecticut and its Makers* (Meriden, 1913), pp. 46–47, 82–115.

78. *Directory of New England Manufacturers, 1960*, pp. 262, 495; Earl C. May, *Century of Silver, 1847–1947 . . .* (New York, 1947), pp. 19–21, 48, 68–69, 116–119, 176–196, 370.

79. *D.A.B.*, XVIII, 380–381; Penrose R. Hoopes, *Early Clockmaking in Connecticut*, Conn. Ter. Comm. Pubs., No. 23 (New Haven, 1934), pp. 6–12.

80. Hoopes, pp. 13–18.

81. Hoopes, pp. 19–25.

82. *Directory of New England Manufacturers, 1960*, pp. 212, 216, 261, 300, 351, 430, 484; Hoopes, p. 26; *U.S. Census of Manufactures, 1939*, III, 11, 148; *1947*, III, 124; *1954*, II, Pt. 2, 38–39.

83. *Courant*, 1960: May 8, Sec. F, pp. 2, 4; Joseph W. Roe, *Connecticut Inventors*, Conn. Ter. Comm. Pubs., No. 33 (New Haven, 1934), pp. 2–3, 14–15, 22–27; U.S. Patent Office, *Annual Report, 1946*, pp. 163–165.

84. *U.S. Census of Manufactures, 1954*, III, 106:5 to 106:8.

19   Religion and Education in Modern Connecticut

1. Jarvis M. Morse, *A Neglected Period of Connecticut's History, 1818–1850*, Yale Hist. Pubs., Misc., XXV (New Haven, 1933), pp. 123–125.

2. *Conn. Register, 1850*, p. 140; *D.A.B.*, XIII, 245–246; Morse, *Neglected Period*, pp. 126–127; William W. Sweet, *Religion in the Development of American Culture, 1765–1840* (New York, 1952), pp. 192–195; Conrad Wright, *The Beginnings of Unitarianism in America* (Boston, 1955), pp. 275–280.

3. Morse, *Neglected Period*, pp. 128–130; Sweet, *Religion in Amer. Cult.*, pp. 199–201.

4. Barbara M. Cross, *Horace Bushnell: Minister to a Changing America* (Chicago, 1958), pp. 67–72, 94, 105, 112; Theodore T. Munger, *Horace Bushnell . . .* (Boston, 1899), pp. 67, 75, 77–79, 237–238; Sweet, *Religion in Amer. Cult.*, pp. 201–202.

5. Munger, pp. 342, 350–351, 368–369; Alexander J. W. Myers, *Horace Bushnell and Religious Education* (Boston, 1937), pp. 106–14, 119–121; George Stewart, *A History of Religious Education in Connecticut to the Middle of the Nineteenth Century*, Yale Studies in the History and Theory of Religious Education, I (New Haven, 1924), p. 347; Luther A. Weigle, "The Christian Ideal of Family Life as Expounded in Horace Bushnell's *Christian Nurture*," *Religious Education*, XIX (Feb. 1924), 47–55.

6. Stewart, pp. 316–346.

7. Congregational Churches in Conn., General Association, *Contributions to the Ecclesiastical History of Connecticut . . .* (New Haven, 1861), p. xiii; *The Yearbook of the Congregational and Christian Churches . . . Statistics, 1959* (New York, 1959), p. 49.

8. Eben E. Beardsley, *The History of the Episcopal Church in Connecticut . . .* (New York, 1865–68), I, 346–348, 358–363; Origen S. Seymour, *The Beginnings of the Episcopal Church in Connecticut*, Conn. Ter. Comm. Pubs., No. 30 (New Haven, 1934), pp. 15–16.

9. Beardsley, I, 397, 409–413, 434, 438–439; Seymour, pp. 18–19; William W. Sweet, *The Story of Religions in America* (New York, 1930), p. 380.

10. Beardsley, II, 73, 164–168; Seymour, pp. 18–21.

11. Beardsley, II, 87, 184, 340, 376–380, 439–442.

12. Interview with Bishop Walter H. Gray, November 3, 1960; Seymour, p. 29.

13. Richard J. Purcell, *Connecticut in Transition, 1775–1818* (Wash., 1918), p. 66; William W. Sweet, *Methodism in American History* (New York, 1933), pp. 20–21.

14. Henry S. Burrage, *A History of the Baptists in New England* (Phila., 1894), pp. 235–236; Connecticut Baptist Convention, *Annual Report, 1959* (Hartford, 1959), p. 69; *Conn. Register, 1848*, p. 133; *1860*, p. 135; Philip S. Evans, *History of Connecticut Baptist State Convention, 1823–1907* (Hartford, 1909), pp.

16–65; Morse, *Neglected Period*, pp. 133–134; Purcell, pp. 68–74, 80–81; U.S. Bur. of the Census, *Religious Bodies: 1936*, II, Pt. 1, *Denominations* (Wash., 1941), 93–95, 147; U.S. Census Office, *Report of the Statistics of Churches in the United States at the Eleventh Census: 1890* (Wash., 1894), p. 147.

15. Frances M. Caulkins, *History of New London, Connecticut . . .* (New London, 1895), pp. 595–597; *D.A.B.*, XI, 112–114; Elijah B. Huntington, *History of Stamford, Connecticut . . .* (Stamford, 1868), pp. 331–332; Purcell, pp. 83–89; Thomas Robbins, *Diary of Thomas Robbins, D.D. 1796–1854*, ed. Increase N. Tarbox (Boston, 1886–87), I, 90; Sweet, *Methodism*, pp. 123–124, 126.

16. *Conn. Register, 1848*, p. 137; Purcell, opp. p. 97; Sweet, *Methodism*, pp. 356–396; U.S. Bur. of the Census, *Religious Bodies: 1936*, I, 186; II, Pt. 2, 1091, 1111, 1179, 1189; U.S. Census Office, *Churches, 1890*, p. 502. The 1959 figures are from Rev. Harvey Mousley, Rev. Arthur Tedcastle, and Rev. E. Leslie Wood.

17. *Conn. Register, 1829*, pp. 139–144; *1848*, p. 138; Morse, *Neglected Period*, p. 134; Purcell, p. 89; *R and M, 1960*, p. 650; *The Religious History of New England . . .* (Cambridge, Mass., 1917), pp. 299–306; Sweet, *Story of Religions*, pp. 196–197.

18. See *R and M, 1960*, pp. 630–650, for list of Connecticut clergy. Religious freedom is guaranteed in Article I, Secs. 3, 4, of the state constitution, and in the First Amendment to the Federal Constitution.

19. Thomas S. Duggan, *The Catholic Church in Connecticut* (New York, 1930), pp. 1–2, 7, 10–12; James H. O'Donnell, *History of the Diocese of Hartford* (Boston, 1900), pp. 34–35, 43–48, 58–59.

20. Duggan, pp. 14–15, 17–18, 21, 26–30; Austin F. Munich, *The Beginnings of Roman Catholicism in Connecticut*, Conn. Terc. Comm. Pubs., No. 41 (New Haven, 1935), pp. 6–9.

21. Duggan, pp. 30–35, 37–39; O'Donnell, p. 120.

22. Duggan, pp. 40, 43; O'Donnell, p. 3.

23. Duggan, pp. 56, 63–81.

24. Duggan, pp. 93, 96, 106–111, 124; Munich, p. 29; O'Donnell, p. 3.

25. Conn. State Board of Education, *Annual Report, 1959–60: Statistical, 1958–59*, p. 67; Duggan, pp. 128–131, 136–137, 149.

26. *Official Catholic Directory, 1960*, pp. 101, 323, 557.

27. *Courant, 1957*: Jan. 1, pp. 1, 3, 10, 11.

28. *C.R.*, I, 343; II, 144, 154; Jacob R. Marcus, *Early American Jewry: the Jews of New York, New England, and Canada, 1649–1794* (Phila., 1951), I, 3–4; Morris Silverman, "The History of the Jews in Hartford," *Courant, 1955*: Jan. 2, Sec. 1, pp. 1, 16.

29. Marcus, I, 159–160, 163–166, 171–178.

30. *Public Acts, 1843*, Chap. xxxix, p. 41; Silverman, *Courant, 1955*: Jan. 3, pp. 1, 2.

31. Silverman, *Courant, 1955*: Jan. 4, pp. 1, 3.

32. G. Fox and Co., Public Relations office; Silverman, *Courant, 1955*: Jan. 6, p. 5.

33. Silverman, *Courant, 1955*: Jan. 7, p. 9.

34. *Ibid.*, 1955: Jan. 8, p. 18.

35. Jewish Social Service of Hartford, *Annual Report, 1959*; Silverman, *Courant, 1955*: Jan. 9, p. 18.

36. Israel Goldberg (Rufus Learsi, pseud.), *The Jews in America, a History* (Cleveland, 1954), pp. 283, 320–326; Silverman, *Courant, 1955*: Jan. 10, p. 3; Israel bond figures from the Conn. Israel Bond Office.

37. Interview with Rabbi Morris Silverman, Aug. 9, 1960.

38. Edmund J. James *et al.*, *The Immigrant Jew in America* (New York, 1906), pp. 388–390; Esther Sulman and Leonard J. Goldstein, *A Goodly Heritage: The Story of the Jewish Community in New London, 1860–1955* (New London, 1957), pp. 4, 28–30. Observations on current poultry raising from William A. Aho, Associate Professor of Poultry Science, Univ. of Conn.

39. *American Jewish Year Book, 1960*, pp. 4, 9. Current statistics from Union of American Hebrew Congregations, Union of Orthodox Jewish Congregations of America, and United Synagogue of America.

40. Conn. Baptist Convention, *Annual Report, 1959*, p. 69; U.S. Census Office, *Churches, 1890*, pp. 38–43; U.S. Bur. of the Census, *Religious Bodies: 1936*, I, 387–388; II, Pt. 1, 95, 147–148, 514, 759; II, Pt. 2, 1090, 1111, 1179, 1190, 1481, 1533.

41. *S.R.*, VIII, 237–239; IX, 178–181, 178n, 180n.

42. Henry Barnard, *History of the Legislation of Connecticut Respecting Common Schools Down to 1838* (Hartford, 1853), pp. 160–164; Henry W. Edwards, *Message to the Legislature, 1836*, p. 7.

43. Barnard, pp. 164–166. The school visitors were similar in function to the present-day Board of Education.

44. Barnard, pp. 166–167; *Public Acts, 1838*, Chap. lii, pp. 45–46.

45. Anna L. Blair, *Henry Barnard . . .*, Educational Monograph, No. 1 (Minneapolis, 1938), pp. 274–275; *D.A.B.*, I, 621–625; Orwin B. Griffin, *The Evolution of the Connecticut State School System . . .*, Teachers College, Col. Univ., Contrib. to Educ., No. 293 (New York, 1928), pp. 72–74; Bernard C. Steiner, *The History of Education in Connecticut*, U.S. Bur. of Educ., Circular of Information, No. 2 (Wash., 1893), pp. 43–46; Bernard C. Steiner, *Life of Henry Barnard . . .*, U.S. Bur. of Educ., Bull. 1919, No. 8 (Wash., 1919), pp. 42–43, 84–89.

46. Griffin, pp. 26–27; Steiner, *Education*, pp. 48–49.

47. Griffin, pp. 57–85, 105–107, 117–157; Silas Hertzler, *The Rise of the Public High School in Connecticut*, Univ. Research Monographs, No. 10 (Baltimore, 1930), pp. 13–15, 101–102. Hartford High School was the first fully organized high school in Connecticut.

48. Conn. State Board of Educ., *Annual Report, 1873*, p. 30; *1926–28*, Pt. 3, pp. 115–116; Griffin, pp. 216–217; Hertzler, pp. 139–140, 143–151, 153–156, 174–175, 191–199, 204; *Public Acts, 1856*, Chap. xli, pp. 39–65.

49. William C. Gilman, *The Celebration of the Two Hundred and Fiftieth Anniversary of the Settlement of the Town of Norwich . . .* (Norwich, 1912), pp. 227–228; Steiner, *Education*, pp. 53–55, 55n.

50. *R and M, 1959*, p. 653.

51. Conn. State Board of Educ., *The Board of Education*, VII (March 1950), 1–3; *Public Acts, 1865*, Chap. cxv, pp. 114–116; *R and M, 1960*, p. 452.

52. Conn. State Board of Educ., *Annual Report, 1959–60*, pp. 1, 18.

53. Conn. State Board of Educ., *Annual Report, 1946–47*, p. 15; Conn. Governor's Fact-Finding Comm. on Educ., *Education in Connecticut . . .* (Hartford, 1951), pp. 3–4, 6–12, 18–19.

54. Conn. Governor's Fact-Finding Comm. on Educ., pp. 5, 34–35, 42–46.

55. Conn. State Board of Educ., *Annual Report, 1959–60: Statistical, 1958–59*, p. 93; Conn. State Board of Educ., Div. of Field Service, School Building Sec., *A Brief History from 1945 to Present of Public School Building Aid* (Hartford, 1959), pp. 1, 4.

56. Conn. State Board of Educ., *The Status of Education in Connecticut — 1956 . . .* (Hartford, 1956), pp. 9–10, 17, 19–21. Total expenditures for 1900 and 1925 are for senior high only.

57. *Ibid.*, pp. 41, 43.

58. Conn. State Board of Educ., *Annual Report, 1958–59*, pp. 2, 8, 35–36; *Public Acts, 1959*, No. 408, pp. 747–749.

59. Conn. State Board of Educ., *Annual Report, 1959–60*, pp. 1–2.

60. Conn. State Board of Educ., *Annual Report, 1959–60: Statistical*, pp. 1–2, 66.

61. Hopkins Grammar School, *An Illustrious Heritage* (n.p., n.d.), pp. 2, 4, 9; Steiner, *Education*, pp. 21–23.

62. The Gunnery, Washington, Connecticut, *Catalog, 1959–60*, p. 7; *Miss Porter's School, Farmington, Connecticut, 1959–60*, p. 9; Steiner, *Education*, pp. 59–61, 65–66; *Suffield Academy, Suffield, Connecticut*, p. 3.

63. *The Choate School, Wallingford, Connecticut*, p. 7; The Hotchkiss School, Lakeville, Connecticut, *Catalogue, 1959–60*, p. 7; The Loomis School, Windsor, Conn., *Bulletin, Catalogue, 1960*, pp. 7–8; Mansfield A. Lyon, ed. *Private Independent Schools . . .* , 12th ed. (Wallingford, 1959), pp. 162, 180; Pomfret School, Pomfret, Connecticut, *Catalogue*, 1960, p. 8; *The Taft School, Watertown, Connecticut, 1959–60*, p. 9.

64. *Avon Old Farms, Avon, Connecticut, 1959–60*, p. 1; *Kent School, Kent, Connecticut*, p. 6; Lyon, pp. 104, 165, 184, 188; Porter E. Sargent, *The Handbook of Private Schools . . .* , 40th ed. (Boston, 1959), p. 221.

65. Arthur J. Heffernan, *A History of Catholic Education in Connecticut,* Catholic Univ. of America, Educ. Research Monographs, x, No. 1 (Wash., 1937), pp. 5–8; Stewart, pp. 284–285.

66. Heffernan, pp. 11–14.

67. James A. Burns, *The Growth and Development of the Catholic School System in the United States* (New York, 1912), pp. 13–14; Heffernan, pp. 27–33; Stewart, pp. 289–299.

68. Heffernan, pp. 14–26.

69. Heffernan, pp. 40–44, 49–53.

70. Heffernan, pp. 77–82, 87, 90–95, 97, 99–103.

71. Heffernan, pp. 107–114, 137–138, 155–162, 177–178.

72. *The Catholic Transcript,* 1959: June 4, p. 1; July 9, p. 1, July 30, p. 12; 1960: July 28, pp. 1, 8, 9; Conn. State Board of Educ., *Annual Report, 1959–60: Statistical*, p. 17.

73. Conn. State Board of Educ., *Annual Report, 1959–60: Statistical*, p. 67.

74. *C.R.,* IV, 363–365; Steiner, *Education*, pp. 67–73.

75. Steiner, *Education*, pp. 76–84.

76. *Ibid.*, pp. 86–88, 96–99, 105–107, 112, 114.

77. *Ibid.*, pp. 111–113.

78. *Ibid.*, pp. 115–118, 120–128.

79. *Ibid.*, pp. 137, 141–143, 148–150; Yale Univ., *Bulletin; Catalogue 1959–60*, pp. 127, 385.

80. Steiner, *Education*, pp. 152–153, 170–174; Yale, *Bulletin*, p. 90.

81. John Warner Barber, *History and Antiquities of New Haven, Conn. . . .* , 3d ed. (New Haven, 1870), pp. 159–161; Wilmarth S. Lewis, *The Yale Collections . . .* (New Haven, 1946), pp. 15–16; John Trumbull, *The Autobiography of Colonel John Trumbull, Patriot-Artist, 1756–1834,* ed. Theodore Sizer (New Haven, 1953), pp. 284–290, 322–325.

82. Steiner, *Education*, pp. 186–189; Yale, *Bulletin*, p. 91.

83. Lewis, *Yale,* pp. 28–29; George W. Pierson, *Yale: College and University,* Vol. I, *Yale College, an Educational History, 1871–1921* (New Haven, 1952), p. 52.

84. *Courant,* 1959: March 15, pp. 1, 8; Steiner, *Education*, pp. 163–164, 201.

85. Steiner, *Education*, pp. 164–165, 198, 202, 218.

86. Pierson, I, 53–65, 705.

87. Pierson, I, 66–82, 95–96; Steiner, *Education*, p. 236.

88. Pierson, I, 14–21, 167–232, 248–253, 309–318, 327–341, 542–545.

89. Lewis, *Yale,* p. 4; Yale, *Bulletin*, pp. 92, 126–127.

90. George W. Pierson, *Yale: College and University, 1871–1937,* Vol. II, *Yale: The University College, 1921–1937* (New Haven, 1955), pp. 506–507.

91. *Courant,* 1960: May 12, pp. 1, 2; July 18, p. 2; Yale, *Bulletin*, pp. 92–93.

92. Arthur Adams, *The Founding of Trinity College [Washington College, 1823–1845].* Reprinted with permission from *Historical Magazine of the Protestant Episcopal Church* (n.p., n.d.), pp. [1–13]; Steiner, *Education*, pp. 237–243.

93. Steiner, *Education*, pp. 250–251, 256; Trinity College, *Bulletin, Catalogue,* 1960, pp. 24–26, 128.

94. Carl F. Price, *Wesleyan's First Century . . .* (Middletown, 1932), pp. 16–18, 20–28.

95. Price, pp. 50–51, 61–62, 65–66, 120–121, 145–146, 170–175.

96. Price, pp. 184–188, 207–220.

97. A.A.U.P., *Bulletin,* XLVI (June 1960), 168; *Hartford Times,* 1948: March 8, p. 17; Wesleyan University, *Bulletin, Catalog Number:* 1960–1961, pp. 8–10.

98. Connecticut College, *Bulletin, Catalogue Number, April, 1960*, pp. 22–24, 158.

99. *R and M,* 1960, pp. 610–612.

100. Conn. State College, *Bulletin, Catalog, 1936–37,* pp. 7–9, 150; Conn. State College, *Inauguration of Albert N. Jorgensen as President of Connecticut State College, June 12, 1936* (Hartford, n.d.), pp. 5, 38–39; *Public Acts,* 1939, Chap. 112, Sec. 757e, p. 371; Univ. of Conn., *Bulletin, 1942–43,* pp. 200–206; *1943–44,* pp. 213–225, 232; *1944–45,* pp. 81, 233–243.

101. *Courant,* 1960: Sept. 16, p. 1; Univ. of Conn., *Bulletin, Catalog, 1960–61,* pp. 27–29. Statistics on student earnings from the University Placement Office and on applications and admissions from the Admissions Office.

102. Univ. of Conn., *Bulletin,* 1960–61, pp. 130, 383.

103. Albert N. Jorgensen, "What Should Be the Relationship between the State Government and the Publicly Supported Institutions of Higher Education?" Speech at Annual Conference on Higher Education, Chicago, March 8, 1960, p. 2.

20 Connecticut, an "Arsenal of Democracy," 1939–1945

1. *Courant*, 1939: Jan. 5, pp. 8, 9; Interview with Raymond E. Baldwin, Sept. 13, 1960.
2. Raymond E. Baldwin, *Let's Go Into Politics* (New York, 1952), pp. 115–116; *Courant*, 1939: Jan. 5, pp. 1, 13; May 9, pp. 1, 4, May 10, pp. 1, 6, May 18, p. 2; June 8, p. 10.
3. *Courant*, 1939: May 4, p. 1, May 6, pp. 1, 4, May 12, pp. 1, 6, May 19, pp. 1, 4, May 24, pp. 1, 6, May 26, pp. 1, 4, 30; June 8, pp. 1, 10.
4. *Courant*, 1939: May 5, pp. 1, 8, May 20, p. 1, May 27, pp. 1, 2; June 2, p. 12, June 6, pp. 1, 12, June 8, pp. 1, 2, 10; Interview with Raymond E. Baldwin, Sept. 13, 1960.
5. *Courant*, 1939: June 8, pp. 1, 10.
6. "Acceptance Address of Raymond E. Baldwin . . . Delivered at New Haven, Conn., September 18, 1940"; Governor Baldwin's speeches, Sept. 3, Sept. 6, 1940, on national defense (all speeches cited in this chapter are from Raymond E. Baldwin's personal files); *R and M, 1941*, p. 439.
7. *Courant*, 1940: Nov. 3, pp. 1, 16, Nov. 4, pp. 1, 2, 6, Nov. 6, pp. 1, 2, 16, Nov. 8, p. 14; *Hartford Times*, 1940: Nov. 6, p. 22; Interview with Raymond E. Baldwin, Sept. 13, 1960; *R and M, 1941*, pp. 397, 406, 409–413.
8. *Courant*, 1941: March 26, pp. 1, 4, March 28, p. 6; May 10, pp. 1, 3; *Hartford Times*, 1941: March 25, p. 1; April 22, p. 1.
9. *Courant*, 1941: May 14, pp. 1, 4; June 4, p. 14, June 5, pp. 1, 6, 7, June 6, p. 14; *Hartford Times*, 1941: April 4, p. 22, April 23, p. 1.
10. Interview with Raymond E. Baldwin, Sept. 13, 1960.
11. "Acceptance Speech, Republican State Convention," Sept. 11, 1942; "Address by Raymond E. Baldwin . . . Radio — New Haven, 11:15 p.m.," Nov. 2, 1942; *Courant*, 1942: Oct. 22, pp. 1, 4, Oct. 26, p. 4, Oct. 29, p. 11, Oct. 31, p. 3; Nov. 4, p. 14; *Hartford Times*, 1942: Sept. 11, p. 2, Sept. 16, p. 2; Interview with Raymond E. Baldwin, Sept. 13, 1960; *R and M, 1943*, pp. 439, 444–449, 455–472.
12. *R and M, 1943*, pp. 81–96.
13. *Courant*, 1943: Feb. 5, pp. 1, 7; May 6, p. 2, May 11, pp. 1, 2, May 21, p. 12, May 23, p. 4B; *Hartford Times*, 1943: May 20, pp. 6, 18.
14. *Courant*, 1944: Jan. 27, pp. 1, 3, Jan. 29, pp. 1, 2, 6; *Inaugural Message, Raymond E. Baldwin, Special Session, January 24, 1944*, pp. 1–12.
15. Conn. State Police Dept., *Report . . . to State's Attorney for Hartford County Concerning the Fire in Hartford . . .* ([Hartford, 1945]), p. 17; *Courant*, 1944: July 7, pp. 1, 2; "Radio Address by Governor Raymond E. Baldwin," Oct. 19, 1944.
16. Interview with Raymond E. Baldwin, Sept. 22, 1960; "Radio Address by Governor Raymond E. Baldwin," Oct. 19, 1944; U.S. Treasury Dept., *Annual Report on the State of the Finances . . . 1946* (Wash., 1947), pp. 516, 528–531.
17. "Broadcast to Australia and New Zealand by Raymond E. Baldwin . . . June 12, 1944"; *Courant*, 1944:

May 23, p. 11; "Governor Baldwin Speech, Hartford Advertising Club," Oct. 17, 1944; *Hartford Times*, 1945: July 3, p. 3.
18. War production summary provided by Rockwell Potter, Jr., formerly Chief of War Records Dept., Conn. St. Lib., Hartford.
19. John F. Robinson, "Selective Service in Connecticut, World War II," (n.p., 1946), typed copy at Conn. St. Lib.; U.S. Selective Service System, *Quotas, Calls and Inductions*, Special Monograph No. 12, II, Appendices F–H (Wash., 1948), p. 134; Edward F. Witsell, Maj. Gen., The Adjutant General, to Rockwell H. Potter, Jr., War Records Dept., Conn. St. Lib., June 11, 1946. The service figures were provided by War Records Dept., Conn. St. Lib., Hartford.
20. U.S. Army, 43d Division (National Guard), Veterans Assoc. *First National Convention of the Forty-Third Infantry Division, Veterans Association* (Hartford, 1947), pp. 28–29; U.S. Army Service Forces, Information and Educ. Div., *Combat Divisions of World War II . . .* (Wash., n.d.), p. 35.
21. Carleton B. Clyma, ed. *Connecticut Veterans Commemorative Booklet*, 1, No. 20, Connecticut Men, 43d-Winged Victory-Division (n.p., 1945), pp. 3, 14; Samuel E. Morison, *History of United States Naval Operations in World War II*, VI, *Breaking the Bismarcks Barrier, 22 July, 1942, 1 May, 1944* (Boston, 1950), pp. 144, 148, 155, 177, 198–206; U.S. Army, 43d Division (National Guard), *Winged Victory . . .* (Baton Rouge, 1946), p. 39.
22. Robert R. Smith, *The United States Army in World War II, The War in the Pacific, The Approach to the Philippines* (Wash., 1953), pp. 132–133, 173–174, 189, 202.
23. Clyma, pp. 12–14; Smith, *U.S. Army*, p. 205n; *Winged Victory*, pp. 26–32.
24. See the Commemorative Booklets which Carleton Clyma has edited for each of the divisions.
25. Conn. St. Lib., War Records Dept., *Medal of Honor Files*.
26. *Hartford Times*, 1944: Aug. 5, p. 3, Aug. 8, pp. 1, 3; *R and M, 1945–1946*, pp. 592, 598, 607, 613–618.
27. Raymond E. Baldwin, "Jobs, Not a Dole, For the Veteran," *New York Times*, 1944: May 28, Sec. 6, pp. 13, 39–41; "Broadcast to Australia and New Zealand, Raymond E. Baldwin," June 12, 1944; "Baldwin, Radio Address . . . Reconversion," Sept. 15, 1944; *Courant*, 1944: Oct. 18, p. 10.
28. *Courant*, 1945: Jan. 4, pp. 1, 2, 20; May 9, p. 14; June 8, pp. 2, 12; *Hartford Times*, 1945: May 26, p. 10; Interview with Raymond E. Baldwin, Sept. 22, 1960.
29. *Courant*, 1945: June 7, pp. 1, 6, June 10, p. 10; *Hartford Times*, 1945: June 7, p. 18; 1946: Jan. 1, p. 2.
30. *Courant*, 1945: May 12, p. 1; Sept. 22, p. 1; *Hartford Times*, 1945: Feb. 15, p. 16; May 11, pp. 1, 18, 23, May 30, p. 30.

21 A Brief Survey of Postwar Connecticut

1. *Courant*, 1945: Aug. 5, p. 2A, Aug. 23, p. 2; 1946: March 12, p. 1. Statistics for World War II veterans under the G.I. bill from the Connecticut Veterans Administration office.
2. *Courant*, 1946: May 17, p. 1; *General Statutes, 1947*, Chap. 33C, Secs. 154i–168i, pp. 60–64; *Hartford Times*, 1946: April 18, p. 1; May 7, p. 1, May 15, p. 1, May 18, p. 1, May 20, p. 14.
3. *Courant*, 1946: April 12, p. 1; Oct. 4, p. 1; Nov. 14, p. 4.
4. *Courant*, 1945: June 14, pp. 1, 2; 1946: Jan. 15, p. 7; April 7, p. 5B; Aug. 11, p. 7, Aug. 15, pp. 1, 2; Sept. 10, pp. 1, 6, Sept. 11, pp. 1, 8, Sept. 18, pp. 1, 9.
5. *Courant*, 1946: Sept. 10, pp. 1, 6, Sept. 18, p. 12; Nov. 6, pp. 1, 7, 12; *R and M, 1947*, pp. 490, 499, 504–509.
6. *Courant*, 1946: Dec. 27, p. 1, Dec. 28, pp. 1, 2, Dec. 31, p. 10; *R and M, 1947*, p. 647.
7. *Inaugural Address, James L. McConaughy, 1947*, pp. 3–13.
8. *Courant*, 1947: Feb. 27, p. 1; May 29, pp. 1, 3; June 1, p. 14, June 4, pp. 1, 6, June 8, pp. 13, 14, 15, 16.
9. *Courant*, 1947: June 8, p. 15.
10. *Hartford Times*, 1947: July 17, p. 3; 1948: Feb. 17, pp. 1, 4, Feb. 27, pp. 1, 3; March 8, pp. 1, 17; May 28, p. 14.
11. *Courant*, 1948: Aug. 26, pp. 1, 11; *R and M, 1947*, p. 69.
12. Marilyn J. Abel, "Chester Bowles, Governor of Connecticut, 1949–1951," unpub. M.A. thesis (Col. Univ., 1957), pp. 6–12; *Courant*, 1948: Aug. 14, pp. 1, 14; *R and M, 1959*, p. 81.
13. *Courant*, 1948: Aug. 14, p. 14, Aug. 15, pp. 1, 8; Sept. 20, p. 1, Sept. 26, p. 12, Sept. 28, p. 12.
14. *Courant*, 1948: Sept. 14, pp. 1, 12, Sept. 15, pp. 1, 3, Sept. 19, p. 11.
15. *Courant*, 1948: Sept. 12, p. 7, Sept. 26, p. 7; Oct. 3, p. 1A.
16. *Courant*, 1948: Sept. 9, p. 5, Sept. 13, p. 10, Sept. 23, p. 4, Sept. 30, p. 7; Oct. 8, p. 32, Oct. 14, p. 1, Oct. 15, p. 2, Oct. 21, p. 2, Oct. 24, p. 3A, Oct. 30, p. 2; *New York Times*, 1948: Oct. 22, p. 19.
17. *Courant*, 1948: Sept. 15, pp. 1, 3; Oct. 2, p. 1, Oct. 8, p. 3, Oct. 11, p. 14, Oct. 13, p. 4, Oct. 17, p. 16, Oct. 29, p. 3; Nov. 2, p. 2.
18. *Courant*, 1948: Sept. 26, p. 2; Oct. 1, p. 20, Oct. 3, p. 2, Oct. 14, p. 4, Oct. 19, p. 2, Oct. 21, p. 6, Oct. 24, p. 6, Oct. 28, p. 10, Oct. 29, pp. 1, 2, Oct. 30, pp. 1, 2.
19. Abel, p. 16; *Courant*, 1948: Nov. 4, pp. 1, 2, 10, 14; *R and M, 1949*, pp. 496, 506, 514–521, 537–546.
20. *Courant*, 1948: Nov. 6, pp. 1, 2, Nov. 11, pp. 1, 2, Nov. 27, p. 2; Dec. 3, p. 1, Dec. 5, p. 1, Dec. 7, pp. 1, 2, Dec. 10, pp. 1, 2, Dec. 17, p. 1; 1949: Jan. 6, pp. 1, 6, 13.
21. *Courant*, 1949: April 27, pp. 1, 2, April 28, p. 1; May 1, p. 11A; Interview with Raymond E. Baldwin, Sept. 13, 1960.
22. *Courant*, 1949: March 17, pp. 1, 8; June 2, pp. 1, 10, June 22, pp. 1, 7; July 22, pp. 1, 5.
23. *Courant*, 1949: March 20, p. 15A, March 23, pp. 1, 2, March 27, p. 11; April 27, p. 5; May 1, p. 19, May 5, p. 11, May 25, p. 7, May 27, pp. 1, 2; June 7, p. 1, June 9, pp. 1, 8, June 12, p. 6A, June 14, p. 1.
24. *Courant*, 1949: June 9, pp. 1, 8.
25. *Courant*, 1949: June 15, pp. 1, 2, June 17, pp. 1, 2, June 29, p. 1; July 1, pp. 1, 4, July 7, pp. 1, 6.
26. *Courant*, 1949: June 17, p. 5, June 19, p. 11, June 25, p. 1, June 28, pp. 1, 2, June 30, pp. 1, 2; July 2, pp. 1, 2; Aug. 2, pp. 1, 3, 4.
27. Conn. Dept. of Labor, *Monthly Bulletin*, XIV (July 1949), 10; *Courant*, 1949: Oct. 7, pp. 1, 2; Nov. 22, pp. 1, 2; Dec. 2, pp. 1, 2, Dec. 20, p. 3.
28. Conn. Commission on State Government Organization, *The Report* ([Hartford], 1950), letter of transmittal, pp. 5–6.
29. *Ibid.*, pp. 26–32, 40–44, 49, 51–59, 64–65, 70–77.
30. *Courant*, 1950: March 11, pp. 1, 2, March 22, pp. 1, 5, March 24, p. 18, March 26, Pt. 2, p. 2; April 7, pp. 1, 4, April 13, pp. 1, 2, April 14, pp. 1, 2, April 19, p. 9, April 23, Pt. 1, p. 10, April 26, pp. 1, 2; May 9, pp. 1, 5, May 10, pp. 1, 12, May 24, pp. 1, 5, May 26, pp. 1, 4; *New York Times*, 1950: May 28, Sec. 1, p. 32.
31. *Courant*, 1950: May 27, p. 8, May 28, Pt. 1, p. 9.
32. *Courant*, 1950: June 15, pp. 1, 5; *R and M, 1949*, p. 91; *1951*, p. 69.
33. Conn. Democratic Party, *What We Believe . . . The Platform of the Democratic Party of Connecticut, 1950*; *Hartford Times*, 1950: July 29, p. 1.
34. *Hartford Times*, 1950: Sept. 5, p. 1, Sept. 16, p. 1.
35. *Hartford Times*, 1950: Sept. 16, p. 21, Sept. 22, p. 30, Sept. 27, p. 27; Oct. 5, p. 43, Oct. 17, p. 29, Oct. 25, p. 22.
36. *Hartford Times*, 1950: Sept. 16, p. 21, Sept. 23, p. 21, Sept. 27, p. 27, Sept. 30, p. 3; Oct. 17, p. 29, Oct. 20, p. 26, Oct. 24, p. 21.
37. *Hartford Times*, 1950: Sept. 26, p. 18; Oct. 14, p. 2, Oct. 17, p. 29, Oct. 27, pp. 1, 9.
38. *Hartford Times*, 1950: Oct. 4, p. 1, Oct. 7, p. 15, Oct. 10, pp. 1, 22.
39. *Hartford Times*, 1950: Oct. 11, p. 28, Oct. 18, p. 1, Oct. 19, pp. 8, 14, Oct. 20, p. 1, Oct. 24, p. 21, Oct. 25, pp. 22, 27.
40. Abel, pp. 71–73; *Hartford Times*, 1950: Sept. 16, p. 10, Sept. 23, p. 10, Sept. 30, p. 10; Oct. 5, p. 18, Oct. 13, p. 21, Oct. 25, p. 27, Oct. 28, p. 14; *R and M, 1951*, pp. 357, 367–372, 378–385, 401–411.
41. U.S. Army, 43d Division (National Guard), Veterans Assn., *Seventh Annual Reunion, Sept. 12–13, 1953* (n.p., n.d.), pp. [38–41]; Figures on bonus payments from the State Treasurer's Office, Veterans Bonus Division.
42. Statistics from The War Records Department, Conn. St. Lib., Hartford.
43. *Courant*, 1951: March 8, p. 12; *Hartford Times*, 1951: March 14, p. 18; April 3, p. 1; June 7, p. 4.
44. *Courant*, 1952: May 21, pp. 1, 2, May 24, pp. 1, 2, May 25, pp. 1, 9, May 26, pp. 1, 4, May 28, pp. 1, 5; July 15, p. 14.
45. *Courant*, 1952: Aug. 24, pp. 1, 2; Sept. 6, pp. 1, 3, Sept. 7, pp. 1, 16; *R and M, 1953*, pp. 536, 547–571.
46. *Courant*, 1953: April 25, pp. 1, 2; May 24, p. 26, May 31, Pt. 1, pp. 11, 17, Pt. 2, p. 3; *Public Acts, 1953*, No. 505, pp. 664–667.
47. Conn. Democratic Party, *Connecticut Democratic State Platform, 1954*, pp. 3–7, 10–11; *Courant*, 1954: June 27, pp. 1, 10; July 7, pp. 1, 2, July 10, pp. 1, 2;

Nov. 7, Pt. 1, p. 38; *R and M, 1955*, pp. 459, 465–470, 476–483, 502–509.

48. *Inaugural Message, Abraham Ribicoff, 1955*, pp. 6–12; *Courant*, 1955: June 9, pp. 1, 2, June 12, Pt. 3, pp. 22, 23.

49. *Courant*, 1955: June 23, p. 1, June 24, pp. 1, 4, June 25, p. 1; Duane Lockard, *New England State Politics* (Princeton, 1959), pp. 284–285.

50. Conn. Flood Recovery Committee, *Report to Governor Abraham Ribicoff* ([Hartford], 1955), pp. 1–6, 51; *Courant*, 1955: Aug. 28, p. 1; Sept. 8, p. 1; *Hartford Times*, 1955: Aug. 19, pp. 1, 10, 21, Aug. 20, pp. 1, 3, 5, Aug. 22, pp. 21, 22, Aug. 25, p. 32, Aug. 30, p. 1; Travelers Weather Service, *Tomorrow's Weather Today* (Hartford, n.d.), p. [14].

51. Conn. Flood Recovery Comm., *Report*, pp. 7–8; *Courant*, 1955: Oct. 16, pp. 1, 4, Oct. 17, pp. 1, 2, 22, Oct. 18, pp. 1, 2, Oct. 26, pp. 1, 2; *New York Times*, 1955: Nov. 20, pp. 1, 70.

52. Conn. Flood Recovery Comm., *Report*, pp. 11–43; *Courant*, 1955: Dec. 16, pp. 1, 5; 1960: Oct. 17, p. 19; *Hartford Times*, 1955: Dec. 9, p. 1, Dec. 16, p. 1; *New Haven Register*, 1960: Aug. 26, p. 7.

53. *R and M, 1957*, pp. 481, 484–496, 498–505.

54. *Courant*, 1957: June 6, pp. 2, 3, June 9, p. 4B; *Hartford Times*, 1957: June 6, pp. 4, 7, 33.

55. *Courant*, 1957: June 9, p. 4B; *Hartford Times*, 1957: May 29, pp. 1, 25.

56. *Courant*, 1957: June 6, pp. 1, 2, June 9, p. 4B.

57. *Courant*, 1957: Sept. 29, p. 3B; Oct. 2, pp. 1, 3, 14.

58. *Courant*, 1958: March 4, p. 1; April 16, p. 1, April 19, pp. 1, 2.

59. *Courant*, 1958: June 18, pp. 1, 10.

60. *Courant*, 1958: June 29, pp. 1A, 20A; *New York Times*, 1958: June 29, pp. 1, 35.

61. *New York Times*, 1958: Oct. 16, pp. 1, 30.

62. *Courant*, 1958: Nov. 5, pp. 1, 18, Nov. 6, pp. 1, 2; *R and M, 1959*, pp. 552–575, 596–603.

63. *Courant*, 1958: Nov. 6, pp. 1, 2; Dec. 10, p. 3; 1960: June 8, pp. 1, 6.

64. *Courant*, 1958: Nov. 6, p. 18; *R and M, 1959*, p. 619.

65. *Courant*, 1959: Jan. 8, p. 24.

66. *Courant*, 1959: Jan. 8, p. 24; *Hartford Times*, 1959: Feb. 17, pp. 1, 6.

67. *Courant*, 1959: March 11, pp. 1, 6, March 19, p. 1, March 25, pp. 1, 2, March 26, pp. 1, 2; May 8, pp. 1, 20.

68. *Courant*, 1959: March 27, p. 1; May 12, pp. 1, 2, May 20, pp. 1, 4, May 29, pp. 1, 4.

69. *Courant*, 1959: June 4, pp. 1, 5.

70. *Christian Science Monitor*, 1958: Oct. 2, p. 13; Kendall R. Richardson, "Oligarchy in Twentieth Century Connecticut," unpub. research paper (Univ. of Conn., 1959), pp. 20–25.

71. Conn. Comm. on State Gov't. Org., *Report, 1950*, pp. 51–53; *Courant*, 1960: Oct. 3, p. 12; Richardson, p. 30.

72. Conn., Comm. on State Gov't. Org., *Report, 1950*, pp. 54–55; Richardson, pp. 15–16.

73. Letter from Mayor Richard C. Lee to the author, Sept. 30, 1960.

74. Joe A. Morris, "He Is Saving a 'Dead' City," *Saturday Evening Post*, 1958: April 19, pp. 31–33; Gordon Sweet, "Urban Renewal: What Is It?" *Yale Alumni Mag.*, XXIII (Jan. 1960), 7–9.

75. New Haven Citizens Action Commission, *Annual Report and Development Guide, 1959* (New Haven, [1959]), pp. 30–31; Sweet, "Urban Renewal," p. 10.

76. New Haven Citizens Action Commission, *Annual Report, 1959*, p. 35; New Haven, [Office of the Mayor], *Church Street Redevelopment Project*, brochure.

77. New Haven Citizens Action Commission, *Annual Report, 1959*, pp. 39–44.

78. *Ibid.*, pp. 26, 50–52.

79. *Ibid.*, p. 53.

80. Letter from Mayor Richard C. Lee to the author, Sept. 30, 1960.

81. *Courant*, 1959: Dec. 14, p. 22; 1960: Jan. 30, pp. 1, 2; March 10, pp. 1, 12, 14, 15; July 22, p. 14.

Frontispiece, courtesy of Connecticut Development Commission.

p. *6* Postcard by Photo-Precision, Ltd., St. Albans, U.K. Photo by Clarence Casabella.

p. *13* Copyright *Country Life*. Photo by Clarence Casabella.

p. *14* Connecticut State Library. Photo by Clarence Casabella.

p. *16* Courtesy of Mystic Seaport. Photo by Louis S. Martel.

p. *18* Courtesy of Hartford Electric Light Company. Photo by Dowd, Wyllie and Olson.

p. *21* Connecticut State Library. Photo by Clarence Casabella.

p. *22* Courtesy of The Travelers Insurance Company.

p. *23* From Potter, *Hartford's First Church*. Photo by Clarence Casabella.

p. *24* From Trumbull, *Memorial History of Hartford County*. Photo by Clarence Casabella.

p. *25* From copy in Connecticut State Library. Photo by Clarence Casabella.

p. *27* Yale University Library.

p. *28* Courtesy of Connecticut Development Commission. Photo by Josef Scaylea.

p. *29* From Trumbull, *History of Connecticut, 1, 19*. Photo by Bo and Joan Steffanson.

p. *30* Photo by Ray Mainwaring.

p. *32* Connecticut State Library. Photo by Clarence Casabella.

p. *33* From Willoughby, *Antiquities of New England*. Photo by Clarence Casabella.

p. *34* From Speck, *Decorative Art of Indian Tribes of Connecticut*. Photo by Clarence Casabella.

p. *35* Courtesy of Connecticut Historical Society. Photo by Clarence Casabella.

p. *36* Courtesy of Jared B. Standish. Photo by Clarence Casabella.

p. *39* Courtesy of Ben F. Hubbell, owner.

p. *46* Yale University Library.

p. *49* Courtesy of Yale University Art Gallery.

p. *51* Yale University Library.

p. *53* Courtesy of New Haven Colony Historical Society.

p. *54* Photo by Chapman Studio.

p. *61* Courtesy of Connecticut Historical Society. Photo by Clarence Casabella.

p. *63* From Trumbull, *Memorial History of Hartford County*. Photo by Clarence Casabella.

p. *66* Courtesy of Connecticut Historical Society. Photo by Clarence Casabella.

p. *69* Connecticut State Library. Photo by Clarence Casabella.

p. *71* Connecticut State Library. Photo by Clarence Casabella.

p. *72* Connecticut State Library. Photo by Clarence Casabella.

p. *76* Courtesy of Connecticut Historical Society. From *Governor and Company of Connecticut and Moheagan Indians, Book of Proceedings, 1773*. Photo by Clarence Casabella.

p. *79* Yale University Library.

p. *81* Photo by Ray Mainwaring.

p. *83* Connecticut State Library. Photo by Clarence Casabella.

p. *84* Courtesy of The Society of the Founders of Norwich.

p. *85* Courtesy of The Society of the Founders of Norwich.

p. *86* Courtesy of the Antiquarian and Landmarks Society of Connecticut. Photo by Louis H. Frohman.

p. *88* Connecticut State Library. Photo by Clarence Casabella.

p. *90* Connecticut State Library. Photo by Graphic Arts, Hartford.

p. *92* From Hooker, *Boundaries of Connecticut*. Photo by Clarence Casabella.

p. *93* From Hooker, *Boundaries of Connecticut*. Photo by Clarence Casabella.

p. *95* From Hooker, *Boundaries of Connecticut*. Photo by Clarence Casabella.

p. *99* *Left* and *Right:* Connecticut Historical Society. Photos by Clarence Casabella.

p. *100* Connecticut Historical Society. Photo by Clarence Casabella.

p. *101* Connecticut Historical Society. Photo by Clarence Casabella.

p. *104* Yale University Library.

p. *106* From *New London Gazette*, June 15, 1770. Photo by Clarence Casabella.

p. *107* *Top:* Photo by Ray Mainwaring. *Bottom:* Courtesy of Williams Haynes. Photo by Ezra Stoller.

p. *108* *Top:* Courtesy of Wadsworth Atheneum. *Bottom:* George Dudley Seymour Collection. Courtesy of Connecticut Historical Society. Photo by Clarence Casabella.

p. *109* *Left* and *Right:* Courtesy of Connecticut Historical Society. Photos by Clarence Casabella.

p. *110* Courtesy of Connecticut Historical Society. Photo by Clarence Casabella.

p. *111* From Peters, *General History of Connecticut*. Courtesy of the Connecticut State Library. Photo by Clarence Casabella.

p. *112* Courtesy of Connecticut Historical Society. Photo by Clarence Casabella.

p. *113* *Left:* Owned by and courtesy of Philip Hammerslough. Photo by Meyers Studio. *Right:* Owned by and courtesy of Philip Hammerslough. Photo by E. Irving Blomstrann.

p. *114* Courtesy of Mystic Seaport. Photo by Louis S. Martel.

p. *115* *Left* and *Right:* Courtesy of Connecticut Historical Society.

p. *117* Courtesy of Connecticut State Library. Photo by Clarence Casabella.

p. *119* Photo by Philemon Warzocha.

p. *121* Yale University Library.

p. *125* Courtesy of Yale University Library.

p. *127* Courtesy of Connecticut Historical Society. Photo by Clarence Casabella.

p. *128* Courtesy of Massachusetts Historical Society. Photo by George M. Cushing, Jr.

p. *131* Courtesy of and photo by Richard D. Butterfield.

p. *132* Courtesy of Connecticut Historical Society. Photo by Clarence Casabella.

p. *135* Courtesy of Connecticut State Library. Photo by Clarence Casabella.

p. *141* Courtesy of Yale University Art Gallery.

p. *148* Courtesy of Ben F. Hubbell, owner.

p. *149* *Top:* From the *Connecticut Courant* of April 7, 1778. Photo by Clarence Casabella. *Bottom:* Courtesy of Connecticut Historical Society.

p. *151* Courtesy of Connecticut State Library.

p. *154* Photo by Philemon Warzocha.

p. *155* From Middlebrook, *History of Maritime Connecticut*. Photo by Clarence Casabella.

p. *156* Courtesy of New London County Historical Society.

p. *163* From the *Connecticut Courant*, November 6, 1781. Photo by Clarence Casabella.

p. *166* From the *Connecticut Courant*. Photo by Clarence Casabella.

p. *173* Courtesy of Connecticut Historical Society.

p. *179* Courtesy of Connecticut Historical Society. Photo by Clarence Casabella.

p. *180* Courtesy of Connecticut State Library.

p. *181* Courtesy of Connecticut Historical Society.

p. *183* Courtesy of Connecticut State Library. Photo by Clarence Casabella.

p. *184* Courtesy of Williams Haynes. Photo by Norman J. Driscoll.

p. *204* Courtesy of Connecticut State Library. Photo by Clarence Casabella.

p. *207* Courtesy of Yale University Art Gallery.

p. *208* Courtesy of American School for the Deaf.

p. *209* Courtesy of the Institute for Living. Photo by Clarence Casabella.

p. *211* Courtesy of Connecticut Historical Society.

p. *213* Photo by and courtesy of Williams Haynes.

p. *214* Photo by Philemon Warzocha.

p. *216* Courtesy of Connecticut Historical Society. Photo by Clarence Casabella.

p. *217* Courtesy of Connecticut Historical Society. Photo by Clarence Casabella.

p. *223* Courtesy of Connecticut State Library. Photo by Clarence Casabella.

p. *225* Courtesy of Floyd L. Atkins, owner.

p. *226* Courtesy of Connecticut Historical Society. Photo by Clarence Casabella.

p. *229* Courtesy of Connecticut State Library. Photo by Clarence Casabella.

p. *232* Eaton Collection, Connecticut State Library. Photo by Clarence Casabella.

p. *235* *Top:* Eaton Collection, Connecticut State Library. Photo by Clarence Casabella. *Bottom:* From *Original Photographs Taken on the Battlefield During the Civil War* . . . (Hartford, 1907). Photo by Clarence Casabella.

p. *238* Courtesy of Connecticut State Library. Photo by Clarence Casabella.

p. *242* Courtesy of Connecticut State Library. Photo by Clarence Casabella.

p. *243* Courtesy of Connecticut State Library. Photo by Clarence Casabella.

p. *245* Photo by and courtesy of Ray Kuhn.

p. *246* Courtesy of Mark Twain Memorial.

p. *247* Courtesy of Connecticut Historical Society. Photo by Arrow Photo Service.

p. *248* Courtesy of New Haven Colony Historical Society.

p. *252* Courtesy of Jerauld A. Manter.

p. *253* Courtesy of Connecticut State Library. Photo by Clarence Casabella.

p. *257* *Top:* Courtesy of Connecticut State Library. Photo by Clarence Casabella. *Bottom:* From the Hartford *Times*. Photo by Clarence Casabella.

p. *259* Courtesy of Connecticut Historical Society. Photo by Clarence Casabella.

p. *260* Courtesy of Connecticut State Library. Photo by Clarence Casabella.

p. *271* Courtesy of Connecticut State Library. Photo by Clarence Casabella.

p. *275* Courtesy of Connecticut State Library. Photo by Clarence Casabella.

p. *289* From the Hartford *Times*. Photo by Clarence Casabella.

p. *293* Courtesy of Connecticut State Library. Photo by Clarence Casabella.

p. *295* Photo by Clarence Casabella.

p. *298* Photo by Clarence Casabella.

p. *301* Photo by Clarence Casabella.

p. *304* Courtesy of and photo by the Hartford *Courant*.

p. *305* Courtesy of United States Corps of Engineers.

p. *306* Photo by Clarence Casabella.

p. *309* Courtesy of and photo by the Hartford *Courant*.

p. *310* Courtesy of and photo by the Hartford *Courant*.

p. *314* Photo by Clarence Casabella.

p. *316* Courtesy of Mystic Seaport. Photo by Louis S. Martel.

p. *317* Courtesy of Mystic Seaport. Photo by Louis S. Martel.

p. *322* Courtesy of Mystic Seaport. Photo by Louis S. Martel.

p. *323* Courtesy of Connecticut Historical Society.

p. *327* *Left:* Courtesy of the Scovill Manufacturing Company. Photo by Meyer Studio. *Right:* Courtesy of the Scovill Manufacturing Company.

p. *329* *Top:* Courtesy of and photo by Yale University Art Gallery. *Bottom:* Courtesy of Floyd L. Atkins, owner.

p. *330* Courtesy of Connecticut State Library. Photo by Clarence Casabella.

p. *332* Courtesy of Ætna Life Affiliated Companies.

p. *333* *Top* and *Bottom:* Courtesy of and photos by The Travelers Insurance Company.

p. *334* Courtesy of Connecticut Historical Society.

p. *336* Courtesy of and photo by General Dynamics Corporation, Electric Boat Division.

p. *339* Photo by Philemon Warzocha.

p. *342* From Duggan, *The Catholic Church in Connecticut.* Photo by Clarence Casabella.

p. *344* *Left:* Courtesy of the *Catholic Transcript. Right:* Courtesy of Eggers and Higgins, architects.

p. *346* Courtesy of Temple Beth Israel. Photo by Edward Saxe Studio.

p. *350* Photo by and courtesy of Nichols and Butterfield, architects.

p. *354* *Left* and *Right:* Courtesy of The Hopkins Grammar School. Photos by Earl Colter Studio.

p. *355* *Top:* Courtesy of The Taft School. *Bottom:* Courtesy of the Kent School.

p. *356* Courtesy of the *Catholic Transcript.*

p. *357* Courtesy of the *Catholic Transcript.*

p. *359* Courtesy of Yale University. Photo by Alburtus, Yale News Bureau.

p. *361* Courtesy of Yale University. Photo by Alburtus, Yale News Bureau.

p. *362* Courtesy of Yale University. Photo by Alburtus, Yale News Bureau.

p. *363* Courtesy of Trinity College.

p. *364* Courtesy of Wesleyan University. Photo by The Wiles Studio.

p. *365* Courtesy of University of Hartford. Photo by Edward Saxe Studio.

p. *366* Courtesy of and photo by U.S. Coast Guard Academy.

p. *367* *Top* and *Bottom:* Courtesy of and photos by University of Connecticut Photo Laboratory.

p. *375* From Forty-third Division Veterans' Association, *First National Convention.* Photo by Clarence Casabella.

p. *391* *Left* and *Right:* Courtesy of and photos by the Hartford *Courant.*

p. *392* Courtesy of the Theater.

p. *393* *Left* and *Right:* Courtesy of and photos by Connecticut State Highway Department.

p. *397* From the Hartford *Times*, January 7, 1892. Photo by Clarence Casabella.

p. *398* Courtesy of the City of New Haven.

p. *399* Courtesy of the Hartford Redevelopment Agency.

p. *401* Courtesy of United Aircraft Corporation. Photo by Ray Kuhn.

p. *402* Courtesy of Essex Chamber of Commerce. Photo by Gordon W. Haynes.

ABOUT THE AUTHOR

Albert E. Van Dusen has been Connecticut State Historian since 1952. Associate Professor of History at the University of Connecticut, he is a graduate of Wesleyan University, and received his M.A. and Ph.D. from the University of Pennsylvania. Before coming to the University of Connecticut, he taught at Wesleyan, Duke University, and the University of Pennsylvania, and was a historian for the Department of the Army. A specialist in American colonial and Revolutionary history, he lives in Storrs with his wife.

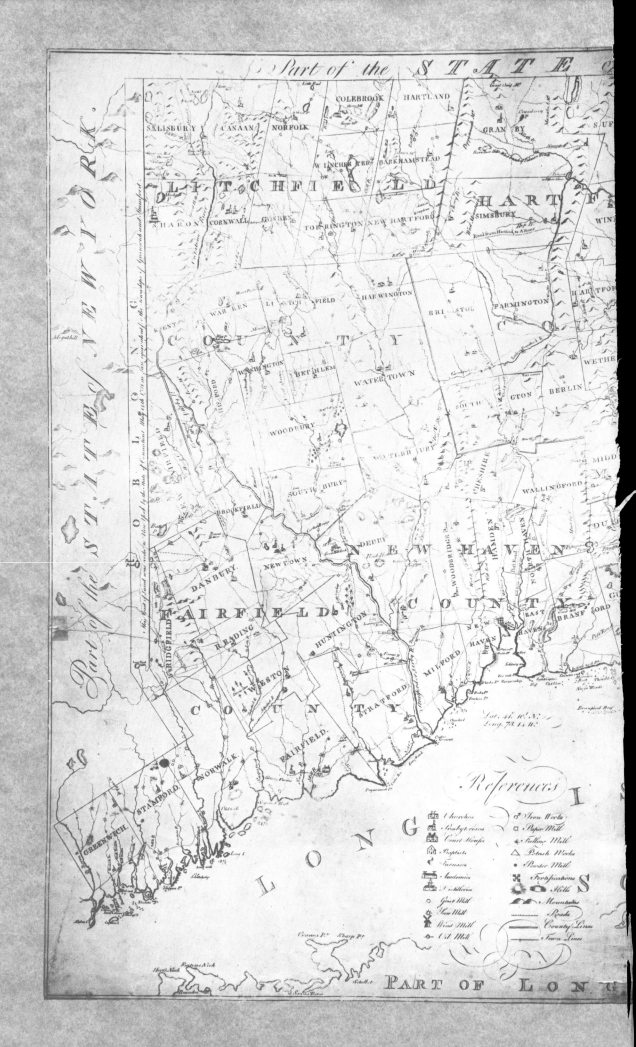